Building Imaging Applications WITH Java™ Technology

Building Imaging Applications WITH Java™ Technology

 Using AWT Imaging, Java 2D™, and Java™ Advanced Imaging (JAI)

LAWRENCE H. RODRIGUES

Addison-Wesley

Boston • San Francisco • New York • Toronto • Montreal
London • Munich • Paris • Madrid
Capetown • Sydney • Tokyo • Singapore • Mexico City

Many of the designations used by manufacturers and sellers to distinguish their products are claimed as trademarks. Where those designations appear in this book, and we were aware of a trademark claim, the designations have been printed in initial capital letters or in all capitals.

Java and all Java-based marks are trademarks or registered trademarks of Sun Microsystems, Inc. in the U.S. and other countries.

The following figures appear courtesy of NASA/JPL/Caltech: Figures 7.15, 11.6, 11.9, 11.10, 12.2, 12.3, 12.4, 12.5, 12.12.

The author and publisher have taken care in the preparation of this book, but make no expressed or implied warranty of any kind and assume no responsibility for errors or omissions. No liability is assumed for incidental or consequential damages in connection with or arising out of the use of the information or programs contained herein.

The publisher offers discounts on this book when ordered in quantity for special sales. For more information, please contact:

Pearson Education Corporate Sales Division
One Lake Street
Upper Saddle River, NJ 07458
(800) 382-3419
corpsales@pearsontechgroup.com

Visit AW on the Web: www.awl.com/cseng/

Library of Congress Cataloging-in-Publication Data

Rodrigues, Lawrence H., 1955–
   Building imaging applications with Java technology : using AWT Imaging, Java 2D, and Java Advanced Imaging (JAI) / Lawrence H. Rodrigues.
      p. cm.
   Includes bibliographical references and index.
   ISBN 0-201-70074-3
   1. Java (Computer program language) 2. Image processing—Digital techniques. I. Title.

QA76.73.J38 R65 2001
006.6'6—dc21

                                        2001022634

ISBN 0-201-70074-3
Text printed on recycled paper
1 2 3 4 5 6 7 8 9 10—WCT—0504030201
First printing, June 2001

Contents

7 Manipulating Images in Java 2D 271

8 Manipulating Image Data in Java 2D 321

9 Building an ROI Application 389

PART III Java Advanced Imaging

10 Introduction to JAI 437

12 Manipulating Images in JAI 533

13 Manipulating Image Data in JAI 573

Preface

The foundation for this book was laid several years ago. I always wanted to write a down-to-earth imaging book for programmers. Many books on image visualization and image processing have been written by academics and are very math oriented. To build real-world applications, programmers don't need to use mathematics that often. This book is written by a programmer for programmers.

My association with imaging goes back many years. Although I have worked in many different areas of electrical engineering and computer science, imaging has always been my first love. Ever since I wrote a simple image-processing program in Pascal back in 1984, I have never stopped being fascinated by imaging. Later, I was fortunate enough to work for one of the biggest medical imaging companies in the world. While working for this company, I realized how important imaging is for health care. Whether the context is diagnosis, surgical planning, or radiation therapy, imaging plays a very important role in many clinical applications.

Because of my long association with medical imaging, many examples in this book are related to medical applications. Besides my experience in the field of medical imaging, I have worked in the areas of satellite imaging, GIS, and recently Internet imaging. The examples in this book reflect my association with these fields. Because the Internet is playing an increasingly important role in all our lives, an entire chapter is devoted to Internet imaging.

When I conceived the idea of writing this book many years ago, my problem was how to write code that readers could run on their own machines. The Java technology came to me as a godsend, with its "write once, run anywhere" concept. I jumped right on the Java bandwagon. Although Java may not be the best language ever written, it embodies many radical concepts, some of which are not very new. These concepts have been implemented in a simple and practical manner in Java.

This book is neither a beginner's book nor a tutorial. Although some sections may look like a tutorial, this is basically a how-to book. Readers are expected to be familiar with Java concepts. An ideal reader will be one who has programmed in Java and has some knowledge of imaging concepts.

Acknowledgments

This book wouldn't have been possible but for the efforts of so many people. First, let me thank my family, who stood by me through this long and winding road. I thank my wife, Cloy, and our children, Joanne and Kenneth, for their support and understanding. My thanks go to my dad, Sylvester, and my sisters, Gracy, Greta, and Cynthia, for their constant support. I wouldn't have written this book but for my late mother, Cecelia Gonsalves-Rodrigues, who, being a schoolteacher, taught me the value of education.

Let me thank Addison-Wesley for giving me the opportunity to write this book. I was fortunate to have a wonderful team from Addison-Wesley to assist me. I would like to thank all the people involved in producing the book. My editor, Julie DiNicola, kept in touch with me throughout the book-writing process. She was extremely helpful, providing me with all the material I needed to write this book. Most importantly, she found me excellent reviewers. The production coordinator for this book, Tyrrell Albaugh, was in touch with me at an early stage of the process and solicited my feedback at different stages of production. My copy editor, Stephanie Hiebert, did a wonderful job correcting my English. She even found bugs in my code! My heartfelt thanks go to everyone at Addison-Wesley who has been involved in this book.

Many thanks, too, to all the reviewers who found obvious and not so obvious mistakes and made valuable suggestions. The reviewers include Marie Luz Ramirez, Antonio Navarro, Fernando Royo, Monica Gille, and many anonymous individuals.

My friend Nihar Shah made many valuable suggestions to improve this book and helped in many different ways. S. Vijayalakshmi looked over the entire manuscript before it went out for formal reviews. She made many excellent suggestions. Mark Williamsen checked the entire manuscript for technical and language errors and suggested many improvements. I am immensely grateful to all of them.

Introduction

THE MAIN PURPOSE OF THIS BOOK is to help software designers and programmers build imaging applications using different Java technologies. Although Java is young compared to many established languages, it has taken the industry by storm. Java has revolutionized many fields, including information technology (IT), e-commerce, and mobile computing. Within a short period of time, server-side computing has already embraced Java. Even though the imaging industry has been slow to react to Java, many industry leaders have realized its merits and are moving to Java. It won't be long before Java plays a key role in the imaging industry.

While Java is new, the imaging industry has been around for many decades. Even if we don't realize it, imaging affects our lives in many different ways. Whether the context is entertainment, health care, or any other industry, many imaging applications are key to its success. With the advent of the World Wide Web, imaging is much closer to home than ever before. When you use the Internet to get directions using a map or to find a car dealer in your area, it is graphical and imaging technology that makes these applications work. Besides forming the backbone of many applications that affect our day-to-day lives, imaging plays a very important role in many high-tech areas, including medical imaging, satellite imaging, and astronomy.

Images are acquired through a variety of means, ranging from cheap digital cameras to expensive medical imaging scanners. Regardless of how an image is acquired, imaging applications typically provide three basic functions for handling images: loading, rendering, and manipulating. This book focuses on these basic functions. We'll discuss how to load, render, and manipulate images using Java, and we'll illustrate these operations through sample applications.

Getting Started with Java

Java is free! You can download the Java Development Kit (JDK) from Sun Microsystems' Web site (http://java.sun.com). But before you download it, you may want to know about the different versions of Java. Java has three versions:

1. **JDK 1.0.x.** This is the early version of Java. The most recent version is JDK 1.0.2. This version cannot be used with Java 2D and JAI.

2. **JDK 1.1.x.** This is the second version of Java. The current release is JDK 1.1.8. This version cannot be used with Java 2D and JAI.

3. **Java 2.** This was JDK 1.2, but Sun later renamed it Java 2. This version of Java has different releases, starting with JDK 1.2. At the time of this writing, the current version is JDK 1.3. Java 2D is part of Java 2. Java Advanced Imaging (JAI), which you must download separately, works only with Java 2. There are three types of Java 2 packages: J2SE (Java 2 Standard Edition), J2ME (Java 2 Micro Edition), J2EE (Java 2 Enterprise Edition).

   To work with Java 2D and JAI, J2SE is what you need. This edition has tools, runtime systems, and application program interfaces (APIs) for developers who are writing, deploying, and running applets and applications in Java. J2SE is compatible with earlier versions of the Java Development Kit. J2ME is for embedded devices, and J2EE is for enterprise applications.

   In addition to its basic language features, J2SE has some other APIs, including

   - **AWT (Abstract Windows Toolkit).** This package consists primarily of APIs to develop graphical user interfaces (GUIs). Java 2D is part of this toolkit, which means you don't need to download Java 2D separately.

   - **Swing.** This package is more sophisticated than the AWT. It was introduced to help develop simple to complex industrial-strength user interfaces. Starting with Java 2, this toolkit became part of the core API. Most of the applications in this book are developed with Swing.

> **Note:** Swing is not part of JDK 1.1, but you can download it separately and put the `swingall.jar` file in the class path.

   - **JavaBeans.** The JavaBeans API implements the basic software component model for Java. Using this API, you can build components for both client- and server-side applications. In this book we use several JavaBeans. Appendix B describes JavaBeans in general, and Appendix C describes some specific JavaBeans in detail.

- **JDBC (Java Database Connection).** You can develop database-related programs using JDBC. This is a generic package that can interact with any type of database.

- **Networking.** The Java core API has several packages that support Internet- and network-related functionality. For example, you can programmatically create a URL to access a Web page, or a socket to read and write data from and to an application running on a remote machine.

- **RMI (Remote Method Invocation) and CORBA (Common Object Request Broker Architecture).** You need to know these APIs if you are developing distributed applications. Chapter 15 deals with RMI and gives a few examples that use RMI for imaging applications.

Once you have downloaded the JDK, install it on your machine. If you already own any of the IDE (integrated development environment) tools, such as JBuilder, VisualAge for Java, or Visual Café, Java is part of it. In that case you don't need to download it from Sun, but make sure that the IDE comes with JDK 1.3 or a higher version. Most of the programs discussed in this book need JDK 1.3.

JAI is not part of the Java core API. It is an extension and part of the Java Media APIs. So when you start reading the JAI chapters (10 through 14), you may want to download the JAI package from Sun's home page.

Types of Java Programs

Depending on your application, you can build four types of Java programs: stand-alone programs, applets, JavaBeans, and servlets. You can mix some of these types. For example, an applet can use JavaBeans and servlets.

Stand-Alone Programs

Building a stand-alone program is the traditional way of developing applications. In this regard, Java is similar to other programming languages, such as C and C++. A stand-alone application needs to have at least one class with an entry point, which is nothing but the `main()` method. To run a java application, all that is needed is a compatible Java Virtual Machine (JVM).

The following code snippet uses a "Hello World" example to show how to build a stand-alone application in Java:

```
public class HelloWorld {
    protected void toConsole(String str){
        System.out.println(str);
    }
```

continued

```
    public static void  main(String[] args){
       HelloWorld helloWorld = new HelloWorld();
       helloWorld.toConsole("Hello World");
    }
}
```

To compile the `HelloWorld` class, type "javac HelloWorld.java" on the command line. If the syntax is correct, the result will be a `HelloWorld.class` file. When a Java program is compiled, a set of bytes called *bytecodes* that conform to the JVM specs is generated. The `HelloWorld.class` file is made up of such bytecodes.

To run this sample program, at the command prompt type "java HelloWorld". The program should print "Hello World" on your console.

Once compiled, the same class can be used on any platform that supports the JVM. For example, let's assume that you compiled the `HelloWorld` program in Windows. Now you can copy or FTP the class file to a UNIX machine and run it there with the same `java` command.

With the Java compiler, you get platform-independent class files. However, some IDEs even provide platform-dependent executables.

Applets

A Java applet is a special Java program in the bytecode form that is capable of running on any Java-enabled Web browser. To execute an applet, the browser needs to have a JVM. When the client clicks on (selects) an applet, the applet classes are downloaded from the selected site to the client site and executed. Because executing an applet means downloading code, applets are typically small.

As most of you are probably aware, the HTML (HyperText Markup Language) used by the World Wide Web consists of markup tags associated with text. The HTML viewer interprets the tags in a document and performs appropriate actions, which may include formatting text and displaying it, displaying images, and playing sound. One of the HTML tags is `APPLET`, which enables loading and execution of Java applets. The following example shows the part of an HTML document with an `APPLET` tag:

```
<APPLET  CODE="ImageViewerApplet.class" WIDTH="256" HEIGHT="256">
<PARAM  NAME="imagesource" VALUE="images">
</APPLET>
```

As this example shows, the `APPLET` block contains several tags. The value of the `CODE` tag provides the Web browser with the address and the name of the applet program. In this example the name of the main bytecode file (class file) to be downloaded is `ImageViewerApplet.class,` and the address is the default directory. The `WIDTH` and `HEIGHT` tags are the implicit parameters that are passed to the `ImageViewerApplet` program. This means that the applet will occupy a 256_256 pixel area on the Web page. Parameters can be passed explicitly with the `PARAM NAME` and

VALUE tags. In the example here, the name is `"imagesource"` and the value is `"images"`. Applets receive both implicit and explicit parameters and use them during execution.

To run applets, Web browsers provide a container. To test applets, however, you don't need a Web browser. The JDK comes with a utility tool called appletviewer, which can launch the applet on your local machine.

Applets follow a life cycle. The life cycle phases include applet creation, initialization, and termination. The container controls an applet's life cycle.

JavaBeans

A JavaBean (or simply *bean*) is a reusable software component that can be visually manipulated in a builder tool. Builder tools help you assemble applications by visually connecting beans. This doesn't mean that you cannot build applications in the conventional way. If you prefer, you can hand-code applications by using beans. When you build applications by visual connection, no coding is involved (though in semivisual tools you may have to write some code).

Builder tools also help you customize beans visually. Once customized, beans can be saved as serialized prototypes (files with the extension *.ser*). When beans are part of an application, they run just like any other objects. They are instantiated differently, though, because saved beans must be resurrected from their serialized prototypes.

The JavaBeans specs define the component model to build, customize, assemble, and deploy general-purpose Java software components. The JavaBeans model describes the structure and behavior of a bean through three basic features: properties, methods, and events.

Properties are a bean's named attributes that can be edited to customize the bean. Methods describe a bean's behavior. Events serve two purposes:

1. **Bean connection.** When a bean is running in a builder tool, events enable visual connection.
2. **Notification.** When a bean is running in an application, events report occurrences and pass data from source to target.

When a bean is inserted in a visual builder tool, its exposed properties, methods, and events are discovered through a twofold process called *introspection:*

1. Discovery from the explicit information, which is provided by the bean provider through a bean-specific class called `BeanInfo.`
2. Automatic discovery of a bean's features by use of the reflection API. To facilitate this, methods in the bean have to adhere to certain naming conventions, as stated in the JavaBeans specs.

To become a JavaBean, a Java class must conform to the JavaBeans specs. At runtime, a bean is just a Java object. Any application can be built using beans. To become a JavaBean, a class must have a constructor with no arguments, and it must be serializable.

Servlets and JSPs

A servlet is to the server what an applet is to the client. A servlet is a program that runs only on the server side and can be invoked from the client (typically a Web browser). Unlike applets, servlet programs cannot have GUI components. Like applets, however, servlets need a container to run them, and they follow a life cycle.

Servlets work on a request-response basis; that is, when a client requests a service, the servlet processes it and responds with a result. Take, for example, the "find a car dealer" application. In this application, the client page consists of a form for inputting your address. When you submit this form with your address, the Web page invokes the servlet with the address fields as the parameters. The servlet then invokes other programs (such as a geo-coding engine) to generate a page that lists the dealers in your area. The servlet response is therefore a Web page, the content of which can be an HTML or XML (eXtensible Markup Language) page, or even an image. To produce such a response, the servlet code needs to be mixed with the Web content. For this reason, when the servlet is complex, the code tends to become highly unreadable and unmaintainable.

The JavaServer Pages (JSP) feature overcomes these problems by helping the programmer separate presentation from content. A JSP is not a Java program as such, but an HTML or XML page that can contain Java code, which is added through special tags. A JSP can be invoked directly from a Web page or from a servlet or another JSP.

The JSP feature has built-in tags that enable you to use any Java class or JavaBean. With this arrangement you can include your presentation logic in the JSP and the application logic in beans. Chapter 16 describes servlets and JSPs in great detail, and it includes examples.

Approaches to Building an Application with Java

In a traditional object-oriented approach, you would build a typical application by developing some classes of your own and borrowing some classes from third-party class libraries. A class library from an application writer's perspective is a set of well-defined interfaces called APIs (application program interfaces) because implementation details of a class library are not typically exposed.

An API is a window to the outside world from a class library. Through this window, applications typically pass data and commands to perform certain tasks. Although implementations of class libraries may change over time, APIs seldom need to change. A change in API would mean modification and recompilation of all applications that use it. With a set of APIs defined, however, there can be several implementations of a class library.

Although this approach has worked well for a long time, it is not the fastest way of building prototypes or applications. First, it involves a lot of coding. Second, it requires skilled programmers. Even if you use third-party class libraries, often you need to extend the functionality. This means that you need expert programmers who can understand the design and semantics of the class libraries.

To hasten application building, application writers now resort to component-based solutions. This approach is fast gaining acceptance because applications can be built with fewer programmers and in a shorter time. In this approach you would use components as building blocks, which can be glued together to build an application. Typically you would buy as many components as possible and develop the rest yourself. Once you have the required components, building the application is easy; you can do it visually or by hand-coding. However, building components requires a lot of skill, so experts in a particular domain typically build components.

Designing software components is a lot different from designing class libraries. Unlike class libraries, software components are built to comply with standard specifications defined by a component model. By meeting these standards, components from different vendors can be glued or connected to compose applications. Many component models support visual building of applications. As mentioned earlier, the general-purpose component model for Java is called *JavaBeans*.

Imaging

As already mentioned, digital images are acquired through a variety of means, such as digital cameras, medical imaging scanners, satellites, radars, and so on. Once an image has been acquired, it is typically rendered onto a computer screen or a printer. Depending on the application, which may range from plain entertainment to scientific visualization, an image is manipulated for a variety of reasons, including better visualization.

In scientific imaging, images are visually inspected and/or automatically processed to extract meaningful information. Visual inspection of images often requires image manipulation operations such as pan, zoom, and brightness/contrast adjustment. A typical visualization application involves image loading, display, and manipulation. In addition, it could involve drawing of graphics and text over images. In this book we'll explore the Java APIs that can be utilized in applications that visualize and process images.

The Evolution of Java Imaging APIs

Imaging APIs were part of Java even in its infancy. Java 1.0 had the `java.awt.image` package, with some basic functionality to render images. The subsequent Java version, JDK 1.1, expanded a few classes in the `java.awt` and `java.awt.image` packages to add some rendering and manipulation functionality. It also added a printing API.

In the early days of Java, the primary targets of Java API design were the Internet and applets. Early versions did not require complex graphical, text, and imaging capabilities because applets were typically small. The limited graphical capabilities that existed in Java were provided by the AWT (Abstract Window Toolkit), which came with the JDK (Java Development Kit). As Java became more mature and robust, it became the main language of many real-world applications.

But some of these applications required complex graphical, text, and imaging features. To address these industry needs, Sun released the Java 2D API, which expanded the graphical capabilities of earlier versions by adding many more graphical features and providing extended font support. It also added very powerful APIs to render and manipulate images by expanding and extending the `java.awt` and `java.awt.image` packages.

Java 2D also improved the graphical capability by adding classes for performing geometric tasks. It added an important class called `AffineTransform` to implement the affine transformation. With this class you can write image manipulation code without much effort. Java 2D also added a new printing model, which is far superior to the AWT imaging model but still did not quite meet industry expectations. As mentioned earlier, Java 2D is part of the Java 2 core API and does not work with JDK 1.1.

The JAI (Java Advanced Imaging) API was developed concurrently with Java 2D, but as a separate package. Whereas Java 2D has both graphical and imaging APIs, JAI is exclusively an imaging platform. It addresses many needs of the imaging industry, including the capability to render large images and support for image processing. JAI comes with a wide variety of commonly used imaging operators that can be used in a wide variety of applications.

As stated earlier, JAI is not part of the Java 2 core API. You must download it from the Java home page and install it separately.

Other Technologies

Besides imaging applications, many other technologies are necessary for building an imaging application. First, you need a toolkit to construct GUIs. The AWT, which was the first GUI package with JDK, has most of the components you may need. However, these components are "heavyweight" because they are derived from the native GUI toolkits. The Swing package is the later addition to the Java core and provides choices of look and feel. You can have a Windows, Motif, Mac, or Java look and feel depending on your application. Although Swing follows the same delegation model as the AWT, it is much more comprehensive and powerful. In this book, we use AWT components in Part I and Swing components everywhere else.

If you're writing distributed-computing applications, you can use the RMI (Remote Method Invocation) package that comes with the JDK. Two or more Java applications residing in different address spaces can communicate among themselves using RMI. But if your Java application needs to communicate with a legacy application or an application written in a different language, you may want to use CORBA. Even though the JDK has the CORBA reference implementation, it may not cover the features you need. Many commercial packages have the Java implementation. With Java and CORBA, you need not discard or rewrite your legacy applications that have withstood the test of time. With the introduction of RMI over IIOP (Internet Inter-ORB Protocol), it is possible for a Java application to communicate with a CORBA application.

If you're writing an Internet-based application, you may want to know about both the Java client- and server-side technologies. Applets, servlets, and JSPs (Java-Server Pages) are the three key Internet technologies that can be used with the imaging APIs. Although applets are part of the core JDK, you may need to separately download implementation that supports servlets and JSPs. This book uses the Apache implementation called Tomcat (see http://jakarta.apache.org/tomcat/index.html). You can use any of the commercial implementations, which typically provide more features and better debugging support than Tomcat does.

How to Use This Book

This book is intended for Java programmers and architects who wish to develop imaging applications. Students and teachers can also use this book to gain insights into practical imaging applications.

To understand the code in this book, you need to know the basic Java language. If you don't, you may want to consult a Java programming book before you start reading the code. The book also assumes that you know some basic imaging and mathematical concepts.

The book is divided into five parts. Parts I through III follow the evolution of Java and the imaging APIs. Examples in this book use Java features such as inner classes and JavaBeans extensively.

Examples in this book make use of object-oriented programming (OOP) principles. Wherever possible, we try to use the model-view-controller (MVC) pattern. If you are new to OOP, you may want to consult an object-oriented programming book before studying the code.

Many examples in this book are built on previous examples. Some of them also reuse classes and interfaces built in preceding chapters or sections.

Part I: AWT Imaging

Part I covers the imaging APIs in the early versions of Java. Some of these APIs are still being used by Java 2D and JAI. If you intend to develop applets and don't want to use Java Plug-in, you may want to read this part in detail. At the time of this writing, Netscape and Microsoft Web browsers don't support Java 2, which means there is no Java 2D support. Even if you don't want to use AWT imaging, you may want to browse the two chapters in Part I to get a historical perspective and to understand how the basic imaging APIs have been transformed into sophisticated imaging platforms.

The main focus of Chapter 2 is image loading. This chapter discusses the difficulties of reading images in the early versions of Java, and it suggests some solutions. This chapter also describes how to load images from JAR files. Chapter 3 describes APIs used for image rendering. The examples in this chapter show how to build applets, as well as stand-alone applications.

Part II: Java 2D

Part II covers Java 2D. Although the focus of this book is imaging, we cover some graphical aspects of Java 2D because knowledge of graphics is essential for building imaging applications. Even if you intend to use JAI, reading about Java 2D is a must. JAI uses many of the underlying concepts in Java 2D and expands Java 2D APIs in many cases.

Chapter 4 covers the basic concepts of Java 2D and the related APIs, including the implementation of shapes and the affine transformation. Chapter 5 is about graphics rendering. This chapter examines the graphics-rendering APIs, including the most important class—`Graphics2D`—knowledge of which is essential for image rendering. What we don't cover in this chapter are the APIs related to text rendering, a topic that has been covered well in other books.

The discussion of imaging in Java 2D starts in Chapter 6, which is about image rendering. This chapter describes the all-important `BufferedImage` class. As the basis of our imaging framework, we discuss some rendering requirements and define the `ImageDisplay` interface, which is the root interface for many imaging components that display images. This chapter also covers the Java 2D printing model.

The next logical step in image rendering is image manipulation. Chapter 7 covers this topic in detail. Before reading this chapter, you may want to revisit Chapter 4 to refresh your memory on the `AffineTransform` class. Chapter 7 discusses image manipulation requirements and develops several interfaces for implementing basic manipulation functions such as pan, zoom, and rotate. We also build sample classes to implement these functions. These classes are reused in subsequent chapters, especially in the JAI chapters (Part III). At the end of Chapter 7 we combine all the manipulation functions and create an image viewer application.

Chapter 8 describes the manipulation of images at the pixel level. It gives an overview of the new API introduced in Java 2D to read, write, and interpret pixels. If you are interested in image processing, this is a must-read chapter. Because some of the APIs are very intuitive and easy to use, we provide several simple examples.

Chapter 9 describes how to build a region of interest (ROI) application using the Java 2D APIs. To build this application, we define the requirements first and build Java interfaces as part of the design. In the implementation, we reuse some JavaBeans and classes already developed in earlier chapters.

Part III: Java Advanced Imaging

JAI is a very powerful imaging package that can be used in a wide variety of imaging applications. JAI's strength comes from its capability to render large images and its extensive collection of commonly used imaging operators. In Part III, chapters are organized in the same logical pattern as in the discussion of Java 2D in Part II.

Chapter 10 is an introduction to JAI. This chapter briefly covers the pull model, basic JAI APIs, and JAI operators. Chapter 11 describes how images are rendered in JAI. It explains both the rendered and renderable image layers and related APIs and includes a description of `PlanarImage,` which is the base class in JAI for representing an image. The chapter also covers the classes that represent the rendered and renderable nodes: `RenderedOp` and `RenderableOp,` respectively. The examples in Chapter 11 show how to render large images.

Following the same logic as in Part II, Chapter 12 explores image manipulation in JAI. This chapter covers the imaging operators that are available in JAI for geometrically manipulating images. In addition to the affine transformation, JAI supports perspective transformations and some nonlinear transformations. The examples in this chapter include an image viewer similar to the one developed in Chapter 7 for Java 2D.

Chapter 13 reviews the APIs and a large number of imaging operators that can be used in image enhancement and analysis. The functionality provided by these operators includes a variety of spatial and frequency domain filters, as well as arithmetic, logical, and relational operations.

Chapter 14, the last chapter in this part, covers image analysis. In JAI 1.0.2, image analysis support is limited to histogram and ROI APIs and related operators. This chapter uses these tools to build an ROI application similar to the one developed in Chapter 9 for Java 2D.

At the time of this writing, the beta version of JAI 1.1 has just been released. We'll cover the important changes wherever applicable.

Part IV: Network Imaging

The main focus of Part IV is how to build applications that can be executed remotely. The client-server and distributed-computing paradigms have been used extensively in enterprise applications. In this part we extend the same philosophy to imaging applications.

There are two chapters in Part IV. Chapter 15 explains the use of RMI to build distributed-computing applications. The chapter develops several examples that use AWT imaging, Java 2D, and JAI on the server side. It also shows how to build stand-alone applications and applets as clients to an RMI server.

Chapter 16 illustrates the use of Internet technologies available in Java with imaging APIs. This chapter covers servlets, JSPs, and applets and gives examples that use them in different combinations. It also discusses architectural issues involved in developing Internet imaging applications.

Part V: Image Reading and Writing

Part V contains two chapters. Chapter 17 describes the three different APIs available for image reading and writing. The first one, the JPEG codec, is a stopgap API that comes with JDK 1.2 and 1.3.

The second API is from JAI, which covers the codec provided by JAI 1.0.2. Using this codec, we have developed image loader and saver programs that are used throughout the JAI chapters. These are designed in such a way that when the image I/O codecs are available, these classes can be replaced without affecting the other code.

The third API is the new Image I/O API that was released after the initial releases of Java 2D and JAI. This is going to be a common image-loading and -saving API that will be used by all the media APIs.

The Image I/O API is also a pluggable framework that allows vendors to plug in their own codecs for reading and writing images in different formats. This API is designed for Java 2 and later versions. Because it uses Java 2D classes such as `BufferedImage,` it cannot be used with JDK 1.1. At the time of this writing, the Image I/O API is in the early release stage. It has a few codecs that support the JPEG, PNG, and GIF formats.

Chapter 18 is a brief summary that compares AWT imaging, Java 2D, and JAI.

Appendixes

Three appendixes cover some of the important Java classes and beans frequently used in the book. Source code is provided wherever appropriate.

The Book's Web Page

The source code developed in this book is available on the book's Web page at http://www.awl.com/cseng/titles/0-201-70074-3/. The readme file on the Web page explains how to compile the code. As stated earlier, you may need to download and install the JDK and other software packages to run this code. Wherever applicable, we have provided the URL of the site for downloading. Also included on the Web page are the Java documents for the entire source code.

On this Web page we will post the errata and bugs in the source code. Because software such as JDK and JAI is upgraded frequently, source code in the book may require modifications to run with new releases. Wherever possible, we'll post the modified code on the Web page.

Conventions Used in the Book

In this book we have used the following primary typographic conventions:

- Monospace type is used for
  - Package names—for example, `java.awt.image`
  - Class and object names—for example, `BufferedImage, Graphics2D`
  - Method names—for example, `displayImage()`
  - Variables—for example, `imageCanvas, CLASSPATH`
  - Directories and file names—for example, `src/util, swingall.jar`
- Italic type is used for
  - Defined terms
  - Strings that explain general command format—for example, *setToXXX(), http://host:port/path?querystring*
  - Messages that appear on the screen
- Boldface type is used for
  - Screen options, buttons, and keyboard keys—for example, **File** menu, **Enter**
  - Key words in lists
- Highlighting identifies the important sections of a listing.
- Underscoring indicates a URL.

Wherever appropriate, we have provided the class hierarchy of the API used in the book. Figure 1.1 shows the conventions used in class hierarchy diagrams.

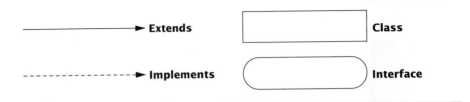

FIGURE 1.1 Conventions used in class hierarchy diagrams

Conclusion

With its powerful APIs for image loading, rendering, and manipulation, Java is well suited for developing image visualization and image-processing applications. The advantages of using Java in such applications are many. For example, software written in Java is platform independent, remotely executable, and selectively downloadable on demand. Numerous areas in engineering are benefiting from the Java revolution. In this book we'll show how the imaging industry can benefit from this revolution.

PART I

AWT Imaging

Loading Images in the AWT 2

IMAGE LOADING IS THE FIRST STEP in a typical imaging application. This chapter covers the image-loading APIs in the Abstract Windows Toolkit.

We'll begin with a short description of the image-loading approaches. Then we'll explain the asynchronous loading approach used by the AWT and the underlying model. Next we'll explain how an image can be loaded in stages.

`MediaTracker` is an important utility class that simplifies asynchronous image loading. It can be used to load a single image or multiple images at a time. We'll explain how to use this class through a couple of examples. We'll then summarize the problems encountered in image loading and develop a multipurpose image-loading class to overcome some of the problems. Using this class, we'll write a simple application to compute pixel statistics.

Images are often archived in a JAR file. We'll describe how to load images from a JAR file through an applet example. Java also has archive APIs. We'll illustrate how to use these APIs to read images directly from the JAR file.

Image-Loading Approaches

There are two basic approaches to loading images:

1. **Synchronous loading.** In this approach an application makes a request to load and waits to start other tasks until the desired image is completely loaded. While the image is loading, the other tasks the application needs to perform are blocked. Blocking of tasks is undesirable, especially in interactive environments.

2. **Asynchronous loading.** In this approach an application makes a request to load and proceeds with other tasks while the image is being loaded. When the image loading is completed, the image-loading program notifies the requesting application. With this approach, unlike the synchronous approach, tasks are not blocked, so asynchronous loading is ideal for applications that take a substantial

amount of time to load images. However, this benefit comes with a price: Image loading is slower in the asynchronous approach than in the synchronous approach. Moreover, a proper synchronization mechanism is needed between the requesting application and the image-loading program. This requirement may necessitate more programming overhead in the application.

Asynchronous Image Loading in the AWT

In the AWT, images are loaded asynchronously. The push model (also called the producer-consumer model) underlies this asynchronous image loading (see Figure 2.1).

Fundamental to this model are the following three objects: image producer, image consumer, and image observer. The image producer generates the image and asynchronously delivers it to an image consumer. While the image is being delivered, an image observer monitors the delivery.

To receive pixel data, an image consumer first registers with the image producer. At a given time, multiple image consumers can be registered with an image producer.

The following three interfaces in the `java.awt.image` package define the push model:

1. **ImageProducer.** This interface specifies methods for creating images.
2. **ImageConsumer.** This interface specifies methods needed for receiving pixels.
3. **ImageObserver.** This interface specifies a method for monitoring the status of image loading and delivery of pixels.

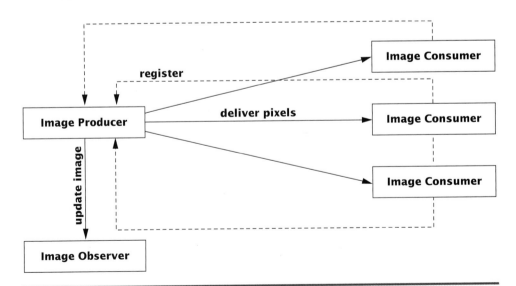

FIGURE 2.1   Producer-consumer architecture

The `ImageProducer` interface has methods for registering with `ImageConsumer` in order to receive images. The `ImageConsumer` interface has two important methods: `setPixels()` and `imageComplete()`. `ImageProducer` calls `setPixels()` to deliver pixels, which are delivered in chunks. The `setPixels()` method can control the starting point and size of the chunk of pixels delivered. Before completing the delivery, `ImageProducer` may call `setPixels()` several times. When `ImageProducer` has completed the delivery of pixels, it calls the `imageComplete()` method.

The `ImageObserver` interface has one method: `imageUpdate()`. This method is called at regular intervals when the image-related asynchronous operations are performed.

If you have used the AWT, you probably have noticed that some methods have the `ImageObserver` object as one of their parameters. These are the methods that are part of the asynchronous operations. The `imageUpdate()` method provides the status of image operations and associated parameters. The asynchronous operations in the AWT are image loading and image rendering.

To become an image producer, a class has to implement the `ImageProducer` interface. Likewise, an image consumer class has to implement the `ImageConsumer` interface, and an image observer class has to implement the `ImageObserver` interface. As already mentioned, `ImageObserver` specifies a method called `image Update()`. Whenever an asynchronous image operation is involved, `imageUpdate()` is invoked at regular intervals to report the status of that image operation. Although the AWT Component class has a built-in `imageUpdate()` method, it is often necessary to override `imageUpdate()` to provide better control over the actions that need to be performed upon image loading.

The `imageUpdate()` method is essentially a callback method that is called by the AWT whenever additional data about the image is available. To receive callbacks, you can create your own `ImageObserver` class by implementing the `ImageObserver` interface—that is, the `imageUpdate()` method. Listing 2.1 shows a typical implementation of the `imageUpdate()` method.

LISTING 2.1 Typical implementation of imageUpdate()

```
public boolean imageUpdate(Image img,
                           int infoflags,
                           int x,
                           int y,
                           int width,
                           int height){

    if((infoflags & ImageObserver.ERROR) != 0){
        // Error-handling code.
        return false;
    }
    if((infoflags & (ImageObserver.WIDTH | ImageObserver.HEIGHT))!= 0){
        // Invoke methods that need width and height.
        ...
    }
```

continued

```
if((infoflags & (ImageObserver.FRAMEBITS | ImageObserver.ALLBITS))!= 0)  {
    // Invoke methods that are waiting for image to be completely loaded.
    ...
    return false;
}
return true;
}
```

As Listing 2.1 shows, the `imageUpdate()` method has six arguments. The `img` parameter represents the `Image` object that is being tracked. The parameters `x`, `y`, `width`, and `height` represent the bounding box of the new pixels that have become available. The `infoflags` parameter provides information about the operations that are being completed. It is an inclusive OR of bit mask flags, which are defined in the `ImageObserver` interface. Table 2.1 gives complete descriptions of these bit masks.

The `imageUpdate()` method returns a `boolean`. If it returns `false`, the AWT won't call it again. In Listing 2.1, for example, if there is an error (i.e., the `ERROR` bit is set), the first `if` block returns `false`. This means that `imageUpdate()` will not be called again.

Image-Loading Stages

Because images are loaded for different purposes, image-loading requirements vary widely. Some applications load images just to display them. Some load them to perform analysis. The complexity of the image-loading operation using the AWT depends on how the loaded images are to be used. If your application involves image animation, for example, there is no need to extract pixels. But if your application involves image analysis, extracting pixels is a must.

Although the steps of the image-loading process vary depending on the application, we can generally group them into the following three stages from the AWT imaging standpoint:

TABLE 2.1   Flags of the imageUpdate() Method

FLAG	MEANING
ERROR	The image operation encountered an error.
ABORT	The image operation aborted before production was complete.
WIDTH/HEIGHT	The image width and height are available.
PROPERTIES	The image properties are available.
ALLBITS	The image operation (loading, drawing) is complete.
FRAMEBITS	Another complete frame of a multiframe image is now available.
SOMEBITS	More pixels that are needed for drawing a scaled variation of the image are available.

1. Obtaining the `Image` object
2. Obtaining the properties of the image
3. Extracting pixel values

Obtaining an Image Object

With JDK 1.1 and 1.2, you can load only JPEG and GIF images. Starting with JDK 1.3, this support has been extended to PNG images. If you need to load other types of images with these Java releases, you may have to use custom-written encoding and decoding programs.

The way in which `Image` objects are obtained differs between applets and applications.

Obtaining Image Objects in Applets

If you're developing an applet, you need to use the `getImage()` method of the `Applet` class to retrieve the `Image` object. There are two flavors of the `getImage()` method in the `Applet` class:

1. **`public Image getImage(URL url)`**

   Here's an example:

   ```
   URL myUrl = new URL("http://www.execpc.com/~larryhr/myimage.jpg");
   Image myImage = getImage (myUrl);
   ```

   You can include this code in a class that is a descendant of `Applet`.

2. **`public Image getImage(URL url, String str)`**

   Here's an example:

   ```
   Image fileImage = getImage("http://www.execpc.com/~larryhr", "myimage.jpg");
   ```

Obtaining Image Objects in Applications

If you're writing an application, you need to use the `getImage()` method from the `java.awt.Toolkit` class to read an image. There are two flavors of this method:

1. **`public abstract Image getImage(String filename)`**
2. **`public abstract Image getImage(URL url)`**

To invoke these methods, you need a `Toolkit` object. Note that both of these methods are abstract, which means that the `Toolkit` class cannot be instantiated. But this is not a problem, because the `Toolkit` class itself has a factory method named `getDefaultToolkit()` that returns a `Toolkit` object. Here's how to call the `getImage()` method in Java applications:

```
Image theImage = Toolkit.getDefaultToolkit().getImage(myUrl);
```

In this case, the parameter `myUrl` can be a URL or a file name.

Note that even though `getImage()` returns the `Image` object immediately, an image is actually loaded only when it is needed. If an image appears blank when it is displayed immediately after a call to `getImage()`, the reason is that the `Image` object contains no pixel data.

Loading of an image doesn't start until a program performs an image-related task such as drawing that image on a canvas. If an application performs the image-drawing operation before the actual image is completely loaded, a blank image is sometimes drawn on the canvas. Therefore, it is desirable to have an asynchronous notification mechanism that triggers redrawing of the image once it is finished being loaded.

In view of this, invocation of `getImage()` can be considered a request to load an image. Pixels are delivered only when the image is needed by a program.

In the case of image rendering, it is necessary to make sure that an image is indeed loaded before it is rendered. We'll see how this can be accomplished later in the chapter.

Obtaining Image Properties

An image can be considered a combination of raw pixel values and information about the image. This information may include geometric parameters, viewing parameters, scanning parameters, ownership, image format, and so on. The properties of an image can be obtained by explicit requests—that is, by using the get methods in the AWT `Image` class.

The `Image` class has three methods for retrieving properties. The `getWidth(ImageObserver)` and `getHeight(ImageObserver)` methods return the width and height of an image, respectively. The other image properties can be obtained by `getProperty(String name, ImageObserver observer)`. This method can be used to retrieve any named property that is specific to an image format.

Although not all the properties are needed to view an image, width and height are musts in many visualization applications.

Obtaining Image Width and Height

In AWT imaging, the operations of getting the width, height, and other properties are asynchronous. Thus the properties requested are immediately obtainable if the image is not loaded. In such cases, these methods return -1.

As in any other asynchronous operation in the AWT, an `ImageObserver` object monitors the status of the image property retrieval operation. `ImageObserver` receives updates about an image operation through the `imageUpdate()` method. When the `WIDTH` bit is set, the width of the image is available. Likewise, when the `HEIGHT` bit is set, the image height is available. If the `imageUpdate()` method returns `false,` further updates for that operation will not be reported, which means that `imageUpdate()` will not be called again. The sample code in Listing 2.2 obtains the width and height of an image.

LISTING 2.2 Obtaining the width and height of an image

```
public Dimension getWidthHeight(Image img) throws TimeOutException {
    long startTime = System.currentTimeMillis();
    long curTime;
    int wid = img.getWidth(this);
    int ht = img.getHeight(this);
    if((wid == -1) || (ht == -1)){
        try{
            while((status & (ImageObserver.WIDTH | ImageObserver.HEIGHT)) ==0) {
                curTime = System.currentTimeMillis();
                wid = curWid; ht = curHt;
                if((curTime - startTime)> TIMEOUT){
                    throw new TimeOutException(1000);
                }
            }
        } catch (TimeOutException e){throw e;}
    }
    Dimension dim = new Dimension(wid, ht);
    return dim;
}

public boolean imageUpdate(Image img,  int infoflags,  int x, int y,  int width,  int
height){
    status = infoflags;
    curWid = width; curHt = height;
}
```

Assume that `curWid` and `curHt` are defined as instance variables. In Listing 2.2, a time-out provision is added to take care of the case in which the `WIDTH` and/or `HEIGHT` bits are never set in the status flag provided to the `imageUpdate()` method.

Extracting Pixel Values

When an image is loaded, pixels are encapsulated in the `Image` object. The `Image` class has no methods for reading or writing pixels directly from an `Image` object. To read pixels, you need to extract them using the `PixelGrabber` class, which implements the `ImageConsumer` interface. A request to extract pixel values also triggers the delivery of pixels. Here's an example that creates a `PixelGrabber` object:

```
PixelGrabber  pg = new PixelGrabber(img, 0,0,width,height, pixMap, 0, width);
```

When the `PixelGrabber` object is created, resources are allocated to enable the pixel grabber operation. Pixels are actually retrieved by the `grabPixels()` method:

```
if(pg.grabPixels() != true){
    System.out.println("pixels not grabbed");
}catch (InterruptedException e){ }
```

With Java 2D, there is no need to use the `PixelGrabber` class; the `BufferedImage` class has methods for extracting pixels directly. We'll describe this class in detail in the chapters on rendering images and manipulating image data (Chapters 6 and 8).

Loading Images Using the MediaTracker Class

From our discussion in the preceding sections, it is clear that image loading in the AWT is somewhat complicated. If your application does some simple operations that don't involve pixels, image loading should be simple and easy. What we need, then, is a utility class to perform the asynchronous image-loading tasks mentioned earlier.

In the AWT, `MediaTracker` is such a class. Its constructor takes `Component` as a parameter, so the `MediaTracker` class is suited for applications that have GUI components. Two important methods in the `MediaTracker` class are `addImage(image, id)` and `waitForID(id)`. Once the images have been added for tracking, `waitForID()` enables tracking. This method returns only when the image is loaded.

The following example illustrates the use of the `MediaTracker` class:

```
MediaTracker imageTracker = new MediaTracker(this);
Image im = getImage(dir,imageName);
imageTracker.addImage(im, 0);
try{
    imageTracker.waitForID(0);
} catch(InterruptedException e){}
```

In this example, `MediaTracker` is used to load only one image. It is possible to use `MediaTracker` to load a set of images, by calling the `addImage()` method with different IDs.

A Simple Image Viewer with MediaTracker

Let's write a simple image viewer application using the `MediaTracker` class as the image loader. To write this application, we must first choose the component to use for drawing images. In the AWT, the choices include `Canvas`, `Panel`, and `Frame`. For this simple application, we'll choose `Frame` because if we choose `Canvas` or `Panel`, we still need a `Frame` object to launch the application. The `SimpleViewer` class shown in Listing 2.3 extends the `Frame` class.

LISTING 2.3 Using `MediaTracker` to load an image

```
import java.awt.*;
import java.awt.image.*;
import java.awt.event.*;
import java.io.*;
public class SimpleViewer extends Frame {
    protected Image awtImage;
```

```java
public void loadAndDisplay(String filename){
    Image img = readImage(filename);
    awtImage = img;
    int width = img.getWidth(this);
    int height = img.getHeight(this);
    displayImage(img, width, height);
}

public void displayImage(Image img, int width, int height) {
    addWindowListener(
        new WindowAdapter() {
            public void windowClosing(WindowEvent e){
                System.exit(0);
            }
        } );
    setTitle("Simple Viewer ");
    pack();
    setSize(new Dimension(width, height));
    show();
    repaint();
}

public Image readImage(String imageName){
    Image image = Toolkit.getDefaultToolkit().getImage(imageName);
    MediaTracker imageTracker = new MediaTracker(this);
    imageTracker.addImage(image, 0);
    try{
      imageTracker.waitForID(0);
    }catch(InterruptedException e){ return null;}
    return image;
}


public void paint(Graphics g){
    Rectangle rect = this.getBounds();
    if(awtImage != null) {
        g.drawImage(awtImage, 0,0,rect.width, rect.height, this);
    }
}

public static void  main(String[] args){
    SimpleViewer ip = new SimpleViewer();
    if(args.length <1) {
        System.out.println("Enter a valid image file name");
        System.exit(0);
    }
    ip.loadAndDisplay(args[0]);
}
}
```

The loadAndDisplay() method calls readImage() and displayImage(). The readImage() method loads an image using the MediaTracker class. The display Image() method launches the Frame object and calls repaint(), which triggers paint().

The image is actually displayed by `paint()`. In this method the loaded image is drawn in a `Graphics` context, which makes the image visible. The `paint()` method is called by the AWT painting threads. Under normal circumstances, it should not be called by an application. Note that `displayImage()` calls `repaint()` at the end. When called, `repaint()` acts as a trigger for invoking the `paint()` method.

As Listing 2.3 shows, `paint()` has an argument of type `Graphics`. Whenever `paint()` is invoked, a `Graphics` object is provided by the AWT. See Chapter 3 for more details on rendering operations.

To run the simple image viewer application, type "java SimpleViewer <image path>" on the command line. Figure 2.2 shows a screen shot of this application.

A Simple Image Viewer without MediaTracker

Now let's write the image viewer application of the preceding section without using the `MediaTracker` class. Listing 2.4 shows this revised version of the application.

LISTING 2.4 The simple viewer without `MediaTracker`

```
public class SimpleViewer1 extends Frame {
    protected Image awtImage;
    protected boolean drawFlag = true;
```

© Zhen Ge China Tourism Press.Peng/The Image Bank

FIGURE 2.2   A simple image viewer

```java
public void loadAndDisplay(String filename){
   awtImage = Toolkit.getDefaultToolkit().getImage(filename);
   int width = awtImage.getWidth(this);
   int height = awtImage.getHeight(this);
   if((width <0 )|| (height <0)) drawFlag = false;
   else displayImage(awtImage, width, height);
}

public void displayImage(Image img, int width, int height) {
   addWindowListener(
      new WindowAdapter() {
         public void windowClosing(WindowEvent e){
            System.exit(0);
         }
      } );
   setTitle("Simple Viewer ");
   pack();
   setSize(new Dimension(width, height));
   show();
   repaint();
}

public boolean imageUpdate(Image img,
                           int infoflags,
                           int x,
                           int y,
                           int width,
                           int height){

   if((infoflags & ImageObserver.ERROR) != 0){
      System.out.println("ERROR in image loading or drawing");
      return false;
   }

   if((infoflags & (ImageObserver.FRAMEBITS | ImageObserver.ALLBITS))!= 0) {
      if(drawFlag == false) {
         displayImage(img,width, height);
         drawFlag = true;
      }
      repaint();
      return false;
   }
   return true;
}


public void paint(Graphics g){
   Rectangle rect = this.getBounds();
   if(awtImage != null) {
      g.drawImage(awtImage, 0,0,rect.width, rect.height, this);
   }
}

public static void  main(String[] args){
   SimpleViewer1 ip = new SimpleViewer1();
   if(args.length <1) {
      System.out.println("Enter a valid image file name");
```

continued

```
        System.exit(0);
    }
    ip.loadAndDisplay(args[0]);
}
}
```

The main difference between Listings 2.3 and 2.4 is that in Listing 2.4 the `SimpleViewer1` class overrides the `imageUpdate()` method. Note that `SimpleViewer1` also has a flag called `drawFlag` to enable drawing.

The `loadAndDisplay()` method first checks whether the width or height of the image is less than zero. This test checks whether the image is loaded. You may recall that if an image is not loaded, `getWidth()` and `getHeight()` return -1. If the returned value is -1, `drawFlag` is set to `false,` and invocation of `displayImage()` is deferred until the image is completely loaded. The `imageUpdate()` method calls `displayImage()` when the image is completely loaded.

Loading Multiple Images

Often multiple pages must be loaded at one time. This can be done with or without the `MediaTracker` class.

To illustrate the loading of multiple images, let's build a somewhat complicated image viewer. This viewer will load a set of images from a local directory and display it in a frame. You can step through the images in the directory by clicking on the image.

In this example, we'll also introduce you to a rendering concept called *double buffering,* which is a technique to eliminate flicker and to make the image display appear smoother. If you display a large image using the code in Listing 2.4, you may see the image slowly unfolding in the frame. The double-buffering technique eliminates this effect.

To implement double buffering, we draw the `Image` object on a `Graphics` context of an off-screen `Image` object. The `paint()` method draws this off-screen `Image` object over the `Graphics` context supplied by the AWT. See Chapter 3 for more details on double buffering.

Again, there are two versions of this image viewer:

1. One that uses `MediaTracker`

2. One that does not use `MediaTracker`

ImageSetViewer with MediaTracker

Listing 2.5 shows the source code for the viewer that uses the `MediaTracker` class.

LISTING 2.5 The ImageSetViewer class

```java
import java.io.*;
import java.awt.*;
import java.awt.event.*;
import java.awt.image.*;
import java.util.*;

public class ImageSetViewer extends Frame {
    static int MAX_IMAGES = 24;
    static int viewerWid = 400;
    static int viewerHt = 300;
    protected String[] fileList;
    protected int numImages=0;
    protected Image currentImage;
    protected int currentIndex =0;
    protected Image[] imageSet;
    protected Image offScrImage;
    protected Graphics offScrGc;

    public ImageSetViewer(){
        setTitle("Image Set Viewer");
        setSize(viewerWid, viewerHt);
        init();
    }

    public void init() {
        enableEvents(AWTEvent.MOUSE_MOTION_EVENT_MASK |
                        AWTEvent.MOUSE_EVENT_MASK);
        addWindowListener(
          new WindowAdapter() {
            public void windowClosing(WindowEvent w) {
                dispose();
                System.exit(0);
            }
          }
        );
    }

    // Creates off-screen image only after peer is created.
    public void addNotify(){
        super.addNotify();
        createOffScreenImage();
    }

    // Creates an off-screen image.
    public void createOffScreenImage(){
        Rectangle rect = getBounds();
        viewerWid = rect.width;
        viewerHt = rect.height;
        offScrImage = this.createImage(rect.width, rect.height);
        offScrGc = offScrImage.getGraphics();
        offScrGc.setColor(Color.black);
        offScrGc.fillRect(0,0,rect.width, rect.height);
    }
```

continued

```java
// Loads images from a given path. First reads the image file names; then
// calls readImages to load images.
public void loadImages(String path, String filter){
    File imgDir= new File(path);
    fileList = readImageFiles(imgDir, filter);
    if(fileList == null) return;
    imageSet = readImages(path, fileList);
    if(imageSet != null) numImages = imageSet.length;
}

public String[] readImageFiles(File dir, String filter){
    ExtensionFilter efilter = new ExtensionFilter(filter);
    String files[] = dir.list(efilter);
    return files;
}

// Loads multiple images at a time.
public Image[] readImages(String path, String[] imList) {
    Vector imv = new Vector();
    for(int i=0;(I<imList.length) && (i< MAX_IMAGES);i++){
        Image image = Toolkit.getDefaultToolkit().getImage(path+ imList[i]);
        MediaTracker imageTracker = new MediaTracker(this);
        imageTracker.addImage(image, i);
        try{
          imageTracker.waitForID(i);
        } catch(InterruptedException e){break;}
        if(image != null) imv.addElement(image);
    }
    int sz = imv.size();
    Image[] imarray= new Image[sz];
    imv.copyInto(imarray);
    return imarray;
}

// Displays images. It first draws the current image on an off-screen image and
// then calls repaint(), which triggers the update() method.
public void displayImage(){
    currentImage = imageSet[currentIndex++ %  numImages];
    if(offScrGc != null) {
        Rectangle rect = getBounds();
        if((viewerWid != rect.width) || (viewerHt != rect.height))
            createOffScreenImage();
        offScrGc.setColor(Color.black);
        offScrGc.fillRect(0,0,rect.width, rect.height);
        offScrGc.drawImage(currentImage, 0,0,rect.width, rect.height, this);
    }
    repaint();
}

public void paint(Graphics gc){
    if(gc == null) return;
    Rectangle rect = getBounds();
    if(offScrImage != null)
        gc.drawImage(offScrImage, 0,0, rect.width, rect.height, this);
}
```

```
public void update(Graphics gc){
   if(gc == null) return;
   Rectangle rect = getBounds();
   if(offScrImage != null)
      gc.drawImage(offScrImage, 0,0, rect.width, rect.height, this);
}

public void quit(){ dispose();}

public void  processMouseEvent(MouseEvent e){
   switch(e.getID()){
      case MouseEvent.MOUSE_PRESSED:
         setCursor(Cursor.getPredefinedCursor(Cursor.HAND_CURSOR));
         displayImage();
         break;
      case MouseEvent.MOUSE_CLICKED:
         break;
      case MouseEvent.MOUSE_RELEASED:
         setCursor(Cursor.getDefaultCursor());
         break;
   }
}
}
```

For an overall picture of how the `ImageSetViewer` class works, let's look at a typical sequence of method calls:

1. A client object instantiates the `ImageSetViewer` object. The constructor calls `init()`.
2. The client object calls `loadImages()`, which in turn calls `readImageFiles()` to load all images and save them in the `imageSet` array.
3. The client object calls `displayImage()`, which displays the first image in `imageSet`.
4. The user clicks on the image, and the mouse event-handling method calls the `displayImage()` method, which displays the next image in `imageSet`.

A detailed explanation of the code follows.

Once `ImageSetViewer` is instantiated, the client object calls the `loadImages()` method, which requires two parameters: `path` and `filter`. The `path` parameter specifies the directory from which the images are to be loaded. The `filter` parameter specifies a string that contains image file extensions separated by commas. For instance, to load GIF and JPEG images, the `filter` string needs to be "gif, jpeg". The `ExtensionFilter` class (see Listing 2.6) filters the file names from the list of files in `path`. The `loadImages()` method calls the `readImageFiles()` method, which returns an array of image file names.

The `readImageFiles()` method lists the image files from the `images` directory and saves the names in the `fileList` array. Once this list has been obtained, the `loadImages()` method calls the `readImages()` method, which uses the `Toolkit` class to get the image objects for the files in `fileList`. The `readImages()` method uses the `MediaTracker` class to load images. The `imageSet` array holds the loaded images.

The client object then calls the `displayImage()` method. Whenever this method is called, the image corresponding to the value of `currentIndex` in the `imageSet` array is drawn on the `offScrImage` object. The `displayImage()` method then increments `currentIndex`.

The image is drawn to fit the size of `Frame`, so the size of `offScrImage` matches the size of `Frame`. If `Frame` is resized, `offScrImage` is constructed again to match the new size. The `displayImage()` method then calls `repaint()`, which triggers `update()`. The `update()` method draws `offScrImage` over the `Graphics` context.

As Listing 2.5 shows, `paint()` has the same code as `update()`. You may ask why. Let's suppose that `ImageSetViewer` has only the `update()` method. If you move another window over the image viewer, you will notice that the image viewer is not repainted. When you add the `paint()` method, the system calls it whenever the visibility status of `Frame` is changed. The `paint()` method redraws `offScrImage`. As we'll see in Chapter 3, if `update()` is not overridden, `paint()` is called. Then why did we add `update()`? If you remove `update()`, you will notice a flicker whenever you click on the image because `paint()` clears the background and `update()` doesn't. By adding `update()`, we eliminate that flicker.

The `ImageSetViewer` class handles mouse events through the `process MouseEvent()` method to capture mouse clicks. Whenever a mouse button is clicked, `displayImage()` is called.

Listing 2.6 shows a generic file extension filter that is used to filter image file extensions such as *.jpeg* and *.gif*. The `ExtensionFilter` class is an inner class of `ImageSetViewer`.

LISTING 2.6 The `ExtensionFilter` class

```
class ExtensionFilter implements FilenameFilter{
    private String extString;
    public ExtensionFilter(String ext){
       extString = ext;
    }
    public boolean accept(File dir, String name){
       StringTokenizer st = new StringTokenizer(extString, ",");
       while(st.hasMoreTokens()){
          if(name.endsWith(st.nextToken())){
             return true;
          }
       }
       return false;
    }
}
```

Running ImageSetViewer

You can create your own class or method for invoking this image viewer. However, the `ImageSetViewer` class has a default `main()` method, which is shown in Listing 2.7.

LISTING 2.7 ImageSetViewer's default `main()` method

```
public static void main(String argv[]){
    ImageSetViewer viewer = new ImageSetViewer();
    viewer.show();
    String path = new String("images/");
    String filterString = ".gif,.jpeg,.jpg";
    viewer.loadImages(path, filterString);
    viewer.displayImage();
}
```

The `main()` method creates the `ImageSetViewer` object first and then calls the `loadImages()` method. You can provide any path in your local machine that has images as the image directory. The `main()` method then calls `displayImage()` to display the image. Once the image is displayed, you can step through the image directory by clicking on the image.

To run `ImageSetViewer`, type "java ImageSetViewer" on the command line.

ImageSetViewer without MediaTracker

In this section we'll build the same image viewer we built in the previous section, but this time without using the `MediaTracker` class. This means that we need to use the `imageUpdate()` method. In this case images are loaded only when they are needed, so we won't save the `Image` objects. Listing 2.8 shows the methods in this application that are different from the `ImageSetViewer` application in preceding section.

LISTING 2.8 Methods from the `ImageSetViewer1` class

```
public void loadImages(String path, String filter){
    if(path == null) return;
    this.path = path;
    File imgDir= new File(path);
    readImageFiles(imgDir, filter);
    if(fileList != null) numImages = fileList.length;
}

public void readImageFiles(File dir, String filter){
    ExtensionFilter jpegFilter = new ExtensionFilter(filter);
    fileList = dir.list(jpegFilter);
    if(fileList != null) numImages = fileList.length;
}

private boolean loadAnImage(int num){
```

continued

```
        if((currentImage =
            Toolkit.getDefaultToolkit().getImage(path+fileList[num]))== null)
            return false;
        else return true;
    }


    public boolean imageUpdate(Image img,
                               int infoflags,
                               int x,
                               int y,
                               int width,
                               int height){
        if((infoflags & ImageObserver.ERROR) != 0){
            System.out.println("ERROR in image load or image draw");
            return false;
        }

        if((infoflags & (ImageObserver.FRAMEBITS | ImageObserver.ALLBITS))!= 0) {
            repaint();
            return false;
        }
        return true;
    }

    public void displayImage(){
        loadAnImage(currentIndex++ % numImages);
        repaint();
    }


    public void update(Graphics gc){
        if(gc == null) return;
        Rectangle rect = getBounds();
        if(currentImage != null)
            gc.drawImage(currentImage, 0,0, rect.width, rect.height, this);
    }


    public static void main(String argv[]){
        ImageSetViewer1 viewer = new ImageSetViewer1();
        viewer.show();
        String path = new String("images/");
        String filterString = ".gif,.jpeg,.jpg";
        viewer.loadImages(path, filterString);
        viewer.displayImage();
    }
```

Note that **ImageSetViewer1** doesn't make use of **imageSet** and **currentIndex**. In addition, the **loadImages()** method doesn't really load images; instead it obtains a list of image files from the **images** directory.

The **loadAnImage()** method uses **getImage()** to obtain an **Image** object and assigns it to the **currentImage** variable. As mentioned earlier, the call to **getImage()** is just a request to load the image. The actual loading happens when there is a need to load the image—in this case when the `paint()` method draws `currentImage` on the `Graphics` context. Once the image loading is initiated, the AWT calls the `imageUpdate()` method at regular intervals until the image is completely loaded.

To verify that `imageUpdate()` is not called, as an experiment you can comment the `gc.drawImage()` statement and run the application.

Image-Loading Problems

Although image loading may not appear to be complex for simple applications, you might encounter some problems when you build complex applications. The primary reason for these problems is the asynchronous nature of image loading. Some of the problems are as follows:

◆ **Image painting.** As mentioned earlier, images are loaded only when they are needed. This could cause problems if the `paint()` method is executed before the image is fully loaded. If double buffering is not implemented, you can see the image slowly unfolding on the screen as it loads. Even with double buffering, if `paint()` or `update()` is executed before the image is drawn on the off-screen `Graphics` context, the screen will be blank.

There are many solutions to the image-painting problem. One solution is to force the image to load in advance. The `java.awt.Component` and `java.awt.Toolkit` classes provide a method called `prepareImage()` to force the images to load in advance. But while this solution might solve the image-painting problem, it would tie up resources for a long time. When a large number of images are involved, forced image loading is certainly not desirable.

As the examples in this chapter have shown, overriding the `imageUpdate()` method is another way to solve the image-painting problem. You can implement this method in such a way that the loaded image is painted only after the image is completely loaded.

◆ **Animation.** Late loading can also result in slow animation as images are being loaded. It may also lead to undesirable flashing. Using the `prepareImage()` method to force images to load in advance solves this problem. As we saw in the preceding sections, you can also use the `java.awt.MediaTracker` class to solve this problem. The `MediaTracker` class also uses `prepareImage()` and `imageUpdate()` to accomplish advance image loading and tracking. One problem with advance loading is that the viewing area in the applet or application remains blank until all the images are loaded. This delay may not be desirable if the loading times are long.

◆ **Loading images for nondisplay applications.** Although the `MediaTracker` class is easy to use, it cannot be used universally. The `MediaTracker` constructor requires a `Component` object as a parameter. Moreover, this `Component` object must be visible on the screen. This is not a problem with multimedia applications because images are always displayed in some subclasses of the `Component` class. In image analysis applications, however, computations are often performed without the image being displayed. In such cases a dummy `Component` object must be made visible in order for the `MediaTracker` class to be used.

◆ **Using `imageUpdate()`.** The `imageUpdate()` method must trigger actions that are appropriate to the image-loading status. So the `imageUpdate()` method becomes the center of control whenever image-related asynchronous operations are involved. Implementation of this method may be accompanied by some programming difficulties in large and complex applications, some of which are described here:

   ◆ Some actions may have to be performed on different objects when certain status information is available. Because of their asynchronous nature, these objects may be in different states. Managing these actions is a difficult task because the state of each object must be known. This requirement means that state variables must be maintained in each object and actions must be triggered on the basis of those states.

   ◆ If several images are to be loaded together, often different tasks must be performed with different images. For example, you may need to display a few images in an image set and then perform image analysis on the entire image set. This requirement means that the `imageUpdate()` method must identify each image object and take appropriate action depending on the object.

   ◆ In a small application, typically a single object handles image loading and drawing. The `ImageObserver` interface is implemented in that object itself. In other words, the same object has the `imageUpdate()` method. In a large application, however, one object may perform loading while another object performs drawing. The status notification may go to different objects, and these objects must be aware of the actions that are to be performed. A solution is to create a separate `ImageObserver` object to which the loading and drawing status for an image is reported.

◆ **Scattered image-loading APIs.** Several different APIs are required to load images. These are scattered over different classes in the `java.awt` and `java.awt.image` packages. Using these different APIs means a longer learning curve to understand image loading, so what we need is a single class that encapsulates the image-loading functionality.

A Multipurpose Image-Loading Class

To solve some of the problems discussed in the previous section, in this section we will build a multipurpose image-loading class called `ImageLoader`. Unlike the `MediaTracker` class, `ImageLoader` does not require a visible AWT component. The

ImageLoader class implements the ImageObserver interface-that is, the imageUpdate() method.

We'll also create a custom event called imageLoaded to notify ImageLoader's registered listeners of the image-loading status. The ImageLoader class is the source for the imageLoaded event. Client objects need to register in advance with ImageLoader to receive the image-loading status. Normally, the imageUpdate() method fires this event at different stages of image loading. Because of this callback, ImageLoader eases the programming difficulty involved with the imageUpdate() method by allowing the clients themselves to perform appropriate actions.

As Listing 2.9 shows, the ImageLoader class has several methods that help load images, obtain properties, and extract pixels. It also has two flavors of the prepareImage() method to enable the applications to load images in advance. The ImageLoader class saves image-related information in an ImageBuffer object. ImageBuffer (see Listing 2.12) holds the image properties, such as width, height, and pixel values (if extracted).

Client applications can monitor the loading progress by checking the loadStatus variable of the ImageLoader class. Listing 2.9 gives the code for ImageLoader.

LISTING 2.9 The ImageLoader class

```java
import java.io.*;
import java.awt.*;
import java.util.*;
import java.net.URL;
import java.awt.image.*;

public class ImageLoader extends Object implements ImageObserver{
   public int loadStatus = ImageLoadedListener.EMPTY;
   private Vector ils = new Vector();
   protected ImageBuffer imageBuffer = new ImageBuffer();

   public ImageLoader(){ loadStatus |= ImageLoadedListener.EMPTY; }

   public ImageBuffer getImageBuffer() { return imageBuffer; }

   public void setWidHt(int wd,  int ht){
      imageBuffer.setWidHt(wd, ht);
      loadStatus |= ImageLoadedListener.HT_WID_KNOWN;
   }

   public void setParams(int rwIm[], int wd, int ht, ColorModel colCm){
      imageBuffer.setParams(rwIm, wd, ht, colCm);
      loadStatus |= (ImageLoadedListener.LOAD_REQUESTED |
                  ImageLoadedListener.HT_WID_KNOWN|
                  ImageLoadedListener.PIXELS_AVAILABLE);
   }

   public void setFileInfo(String path, String name, int id){
      if(path == null || name == null) return;
      imageBuffer.setFileInfo(path, name, id);
   }
```

continued

```java
public  void setUrlInfo(URL ul, String name, int id){
   if(ul == null || name == null) return;
   imageBuffer.setUrlInfo(ul, name, id);
}

public  void load(){
   if(loadStatus == ImageLoadedListener.EMPTY){
      if(!requestImageLoad()) return ;
   }
   fetchWidHt();
}

public  boolean requestImageLoad(){
   URL url = imageBuffer.getURL();
   String fileName = imageBuffer.getFileName();
   if((url == null) && (fileName == null)) return false;
   Image image = null;
   if(url != null) image = Toolkit.getDefaultToolkit().getImage(url);
   if(fileName != null) image = Toolkit.getDefaultToolkit().getImage(fileName);
   imageBuffer.image = image;
   if(image == null) return false;
   loadStatus |= ImageLoadedListener.LOAD_REQUESTED;
   return true;
}

public void jarLoad(String name, int id){
   if(loadStatus == ImageLoadedListener.EMPTY){
      loadFromJarAsStream(name);
      imageBuffer.setImageName(name);
      imageBuffer.setImageId(id);
   }
   fetchWidHt();
}

public  boolean loadFromJar(String name){
   try{
      URL url = this.getClass().getClassLoader().getResource(name);
      Image  img
        =Toolkit.getDefaultToolkit().createImage(((ImageProducer)
        (url.getContent())));
      imageBuffer.image= img;
   }  catch (Exception e){ return false; }
   return true;
}

public  boolean fetchWidHt(){
   if(imageBuffer.image == null) return false;
   int wid = imageBuffer.image.getWidth(this);
   int ht = imageBuffer.image.getHeight(this);
   if((wid == -1) || (ht == -1)) return false;
   setWidHt(wid, ht);
   imageBuffer.setWidHt(wid, ht);
   return true;
}

public boolean fetchPixels(){
   int width = imageBuffer.width;
   int height =  imageBuffer.height;
```

```
   if((width <0) || (height<0)){
      load();
      return false;
   }
   int pixMap[] = new int[width*height];
   PixelGrabber pg =
        new PixelGrabber(imageBuffer.image, 0,0,width,height, pixMap, 0, width);
   try {
          pg.grabPixels();
   } catch (InterruptedException e){return false;}
   if((pg.status()  & ImageObserver.ABORT)!=0){
      loadStatus = ImageLoadedListener.ERRORED;
      fireImageLoadedEvent();
      return false;
   }
   setParams(pixMap, width, height, imageBuffer.cm);
   fireImageLoadedEvent();
   return true;
}


/** Prepares the image to be constructed with its original width and height. */
public boolean prepareImage(){
   return prepareImage(imageBuffer.width, imageBuffer.height);
}


/** Prepares the image to be constructed with a given width and height. */
public boolean prepareImage(int wid, int ht ){
   if(imageBuffer.image == null) return false;
   if(Toolkit.getDefaultToolkit().prepareImage(imageBuffer.image, wid, ht, this)){
      loadStatus |= ImageLoadedListener.IMAGE_READY;
   }
   return true;
}


/** Implements ImageObserver interface. Called at regular intervals when
   * image-related operations are taking place. This method notifies the
   * clients when a certain status becomes available.
   */
public boolean imageUpdate(Image img,
                           int infoflags,
                           int x, int y,
                           int width, int height){
   if((infoflags & ImageObserver.ERROR) != 0){
      loadStatus = ImageLoadedListener.ERRORED;
      return false;
   }
   if((infoflags & (ImageObserver.WIDTH | ImageObserver.HEIGHT))!= 0){
      setWidHt(width, height);
      fireImageLoadedEvent();
   }
   if((infoflags & (ImageObserver.FRAMEBITS | ImageObserver.ALLBITS))!= 0){
      loadStatus |= ImageLoadedListener.IMAGE_READY;
      fireImageLoadedEvent();
      return false;
    }
    return true;
}
```

continued

```
public void addImageLoadedListener(ImageLoadedListener il) {
   ils.addElement(il);
}

public void removeImageLoadedListener(ImageLoadedListener il) {
   ils.removeElement(il);
}

/** Notifies all the registered client objects. */
public void  fireImageLoadedEvent(){
   for(Enumeration e = ils.elements() ; e.hasMoreElements() ;) {
      ImageLoadedEvent ilevent =
            new ImageLoadedEvent(this, imageBuffer.image, loadStatus);
      ((ImageLoadedListener)(e.nextElement())).imageLoaded(ilevent);
   }
 }
}
```

Here's a typical sequence of `ImageLoader` method calls:

1. The client object instantiates the `ImageLoader` object. Initially, the loading status is `EMPTY`.

2. The client object registers with `ImageLoader` to receive the `imageLoaded` events.

3. Once the client object has the URL or the local path of the images, it calls either `setUrlInfo()` or `setFileInfo()`, respectively.

4. The client object calls `load()`. The `load()` method calls `requestImageLoad()` and `fetchWidHt()`. The loading status is set to `LOAD_REQUESTED`.

5. The `requestImageLoad()` method calls the `getImage()` method of the `Toolkit` class.

6. When image loading is initiated, the `ImageProducer` object calls the `imageUpdate()` method at regular intervals:

   ◆ When the height and width are available, `imageUpdate()` calls `setWidHt()`, which sets the loading status to `HT_WID_KNOWN`. This method fires the `imageLoaded` event by calling the `fireImageLoadedEvent()` method.

   ◆ When the entire image is loaded, the `ALLBITS` mask is set. The loading status is set to `IMAGE_READY`. The `imageUpdate()` method then calls `fireImageLoadedEvent()`.

7. If the client requires pixels, it calls `fetchPixels()`. When the pixels are available, this method sets the loading status to `PIXELS_AVAILABLE` and fires `imageLoaded` events to registered listeners.

   The `imageUpdate()` method is called only when there is a need for the image. However, the client objects can use `prepareImage()` to force image loading.

The ImageLoadedEvent Class

The ImageLoadedEvent object is designed in such a way that this event can be used in any application. The ImageLoadedListener interface has just one method—imageLoaded()—which takes ImageLoadedEvent as an argument. When an imageLoaded event is fired, the ImageLoadedEvent object carries either a single image or a set of images. Listing 2.10 shows the ImageLoadedListener interface.

LISTING 2.10 The ImageLoadedListener interface

```java
public interface ImageLoadedListener extends java.util.EventListener{
   static  public final int EMPTY = 0;
   static  public final int ABORTED = 1;
   static  public final int ERRORED = 2;
   static  public final int LOAD_REQUESTED = 4;
   static  public final int HT_WID_KNOWN = 8;
   static  public final int IMAGE_READY = 16;
   static  public final int PIXELS_AVAILABLE = 32;

   public void imageLoaded(ImageLoadedEvent e);
}
```

As Listing 2.10 shows, ImageLoadedListener also defines the loading-status constants. The code for the ImageLoadedEvent class is given in Listing 2.11.

LISTING 2.11 The ImageLoadedEvent class

```java
public class ImageLoadedEvent  extends java.util.EventObject
      implements Serializable{
   Image image;
   Image[] imageset;
   int loadStatus = ImageLoadedListener.EMPTY;

   public ImageLoadedEvent(Object obj, Image img, int status){
      super(obj);
      image = img;
      imageset = new Image[] {img};
      loadStatus = status;
   }
    public int getLoadStatus() {
      return loadStatus;
   }
    public ImageLoadedEvent(Object obj, Image[] img){
      super(obj);
      imageset = img;
      if((img != null) && (img.length >0))image = img[0];
   }
    public Image getImage(){
      return image;
   }
   public Image[] getImages(){
      return imageset;
   }
}
```

Representing an Image

Even though the `Image` class represents an image, it is inadequate in many respects. First, pixels cannot be accessed directly. Second, image properties cannot be obtained easily. The `ImageBuffer` class, in conjunction with the `ImageLoader` class, overcomes some of the difficulties. It saves several image parameters, such as image name, image width and height, and so on. Most importantly, it saves the raw image pixels. Once an `ImageBuffer` object has been created for an image, it is very easy to access pixels. Listing 2.12 shows the code for `ImageBuffer`.

LISTING 2.12 The `ImageBuffer` class

```java
public class  ImageBuffer {
    public Image  image;
    public int width = -1, height = -1;
    public int origPixels[];
    public ColorModel cm;
    public URL url= null;
    public String fileName = null;
    public String dir;
    public String imageName;
    public int imageId;
    public int loadStatus;

    public Image getImage() {
        return image;
    }

    public int getLoadStatus() {
        return loadStatus;
    }

    public void setLoadStatus(int status) {
        loadStatus = status;
    }

    public void setWidHt(int wd,  int ht){
        width = wd; height = ht;
    }

    public void setParams(int rwIm[], int wd, int ht, ColorModel colCm){
        width = wd; height = ht;
        cm = colCm;
        origPixels = rwIm;
    }

    public void setFileInfo(String path, String name, int id){
        if(path == null || name == null) return;
        dir = path;
        imageId = id;
        imageName = name;
        fileName = new String(dir+File.separatorChar+imageName);
```

```
        url = null;
    }

    public  void setUrlInfo(URL ul, String name, int id){
        if(ul == null || name == null) return;
        url = ul;
        imageName = name;
        imageId = id;
        fileName = null;
    }

    public void setImageName(String name){
        imageName = name;
    }

    public String getImageName(){
        return imageName;
    }

    public void setImageId(int id){
        imageId = id;
    }

    public int getImageId(){
        return imageId;
    }

    public void setFileName(String name){
        fileName  = name;
    }

    public String getFileName(){
        return fileName;
    }

    public void setURL(URL url){
        this.url  = url;
    }

    public URL getURL(){
        return url;
    }

}
```

Using the ImageLoader Class

You can also use the ImageLoader class as a bean. Its properties include the
ImageBuffer class. To illustrate how to use the ImageLoader class, let's look at an example that retrieves image pixels and computes simple statistics.

Computing Image Statistics

There is no need to display an image in order to compute its pixel-related statistics. This means that there is no need for a GUI component. In this section we'll develop a class to compute image statistics that can run from the command line. The `ImageStats` class shown in Listing 2.13 computes statistics such as minimum, maximum, and average values from the pixels extracted from an image.

As suggested earlier, using the `MediaTracker` class is not a good solution because it requires a visible `Component` object, so we'll use the `ImageLoader` class developed earlier (see Listing 2.9). Listing 2.13 shows the code for `ImageStats`.

LISTING 2.13 The `ImageStats` class

```java
import java.io.*;
import java.awt.*;
import java.awt.image.*;
import java.util.*;

public class ImageStats implements ImageLoadedListener{
    static final int RED =  1;
    static final int GREEN =  2;
    static final int BLUE = 3;
    static final int ALPHA = 4;

    public static void main(String argv[]){
        if(argv.length == 0) return;
        ImageStats stats = new ImageStats();
        for (int i=0;I<argv.length;i++) {
            stats.loadImage(argv[i]);
        }
        System.exit(0);
    }

    public void loadImage(String image) {
        File img= new File(image);
        ImageLoader im = new ImageLoader();
        im.setFileInfo(".", image, 0);
        im.load();
        loadPixels(im);
    }

    public void loadPixels(ImageLoader il){
        il.addImageLoadedListener(this);
        try{
            Thread.sleep(100);
        } catch(InterruptedException e){}
        il.fetchPixels();
    }


    public void imageLoaded(ImageLoadedEvent e){
        int status = e.getLoadStatus();
        ImageLoader il = (ImageLoader)e.getSource();
        ImageBuffer img = (ImageBuffer)il.getImageBuffer();
```

```java
        if((status & ImageLoadedListener.PIXELS_AVAILABLE) != 0){
            generateAndDisplayStats(img);
            il.removeImageLoadedListener(this);
        }
    }

    private void generateAndDisplayStats(ImageBuffer img){
        int[] stats = computeStats(img.origPixels,RED);
        System.out.println("-----------------");
        System.out.println("Color \tMin \tMax \tAverage");
        System.out.println("-----------------");
        System.out.print("Red");

        System.out.print("\t"+Integer.toString(stats[0]));
        System.out.print("\t"+Integer.toString(stats[1]));
        System.out.println("\t"+Integer.toString(stats[2]));

        stats = computeStats(img.origPixels,GREEN);
        System.out.print("Green");
        System.out.print("\t"+Integer.toString(stats[0]));
        System.out.print("\t"+Integer.toString(stats[1]));
        System.out.println("\t"+Integer.toString(stats[2]));

        stats = computeStats(img.origPixels,BLUE);
        System.out.print("Blue");

        System.out.print("\t"+Integer.toString(stats[0]));
        System.out.print("\t"+Integer.toString(stats[1]));
        System.out.print("\t"+Integer.toString(stats[2]));
        System.out.println();
    }

    public int[] computeStats(int inp[], int clr){
        if(inp == null) return null;
        int pix;
        int stats[] =  new int[3];
        int max = Integer.MIN_VALUE;
        int min = Integer.MAX_VALUE;
        ColorModel cm = ColorModel.getRGBdefault();
        int sum =0;
        for(int i=0; I<inp.length;i++){
            switch(clr){
                case RED:
                    pix = cm.getRed(inp[i]);
                    break;
                case GREEN:
                    pix = cm.getGreen(inp[i]);
                    break;
                case BLUE:
                    pix = cm.getBlue(inp[i]);
                    break;
                case ALPHA:
                    pix = cm.getAlpha(inp[i]);
                    break;
                default:
                    pix =0;
            }
```

continued

```
        if(pix > max) max = pix;
        if(pix < min ) min = pix;
        sum += pix;
    }
    double average = sum/inp.length;
    stats[0] = min; stats[1] = max; stats[2] = (int)average;
    return stats;
  }
}
```

The `loadImage()` method creates an instance of `ImageLoader` and calls the `load()` method to load the image. It then calls the `loadPixels()` method to retrieve pixel values. In the `loadPixels()` method, `ImageStats` registers itself to receive `imageLoaded` events and then calls the `fetchPixels()` method.

Whenever an `imageLoaded` event is received through the `imageLoaded()` method, loading status is checked from the `PIXELS_AVAILABLE` flag. When this flag is set, pixels are retrieved from the `ImageBuffer` object and statistics are computed.

Running ImageStats

To run `ImageStats,` type "java ImageStats <image names>" on the command line. Here's an example:

    java ImageStats im1.jpeg im2.gif im3.jpeg c:\im4.jpeg

You can provide multiple image names on the command line. If the image exists, `ImageStats` will compute statistics and display them on the console.

The following is sample output for the command `java ImageStats T1.gif T2.gif:`

```
Color   Min    Max     Average
-------------------------------
Red     8      248     188
Green   0      248     186
Blue    4      248     186
-------------------------------
Color   Min    Max     Average
-------------------------------
Red     0      248     188
Green   0      248     186
Blue    0      248     186
```

Loading Images from JAR Files

What we've seen so far is how to load images from a local directory or a URL. This section describes how to load images from a JAR (Java Archive) file. It is often convenient to archive an image in a JAR file. In the case of applets, the JAR file may include class files and other resources.

Normally you would use the `getResource()` method (from `java.lang.Class` or `java.lang.ClassLoader`) to load images from a JAR file. If this method is to be used, the JAR file must be in the class path so that the image-loading program knows where it is.

Using the Java Archive API is another way you can load images from JAR files. This API is available in the `java.util.zip` and `java.util.jar` packages. When you load images in this manner, you must specify the location of the JAR file.

In the sections that follow we'll discuss both methods of loading images from JAR files.

Location-Independent Loading

Just like files, images are resources in Java, and they can be bundled in JAR files. Java provides a way to access resources in a location-independent manner. Resources are pointed to by the `CLASSPATH` environment variable, and there is no need to provide the actual path to the resource within a program.

To access resources in a location-independent manner, you can use either of two classes: `ClassLoader` or `Class`. The resource access methods in `Class` call the corresponding methods in `ClassLoader`. First let's describe the naming conventions for representing resources.

Naming Conventions

A resource name is provided as a string. The name can include the complete Java package path or directory; the subpackages or subdirectories are separated by a slash ("/"). At the end of the "/" sequence, the short name of the resource must be provided. The short name may be followed by a file extension. The short name and its extension are separated by a period.

Here's an example: The `MultiImageLoader` bean is in the `com.vistech.imageloader` package. Suppose the images are stored in a directory named `images` in this package. The complete resource name for an image—say, `AnImage.gif`—is defined as

```
/com/vistech/imageloader/images/AnImage.gif
```

The resource name is relative to the `ClassLoader` instance. For the previous example, the resource name `AnImage.gif` in a class in the `com.vistech.imageloader` package is `images/AnImage.gif`. So if a resource name starts with a slash, that resource name is absolute; if it doesn't, the resource name is relative to the `ClassLoader` instance.

Resource Types

Resources are categorized into two groups: system resources and nonsystem resources.

System Resources

A system resource is built into the system or available locally (e.g., a ZIP or JAR file residing in a local directory). You can locate a system resource by searching the directories pointed to by the CLASSPATH environment variable. The `ClassLoader` has two methods for accessing system resources:

1. `public URL getSystemResource(String resourceName)`
2. `public InputStream getSystemResourceAsStream(String resourceName)`

Nonsystem Resources

A nonsystem resource is neither in the system nor available locally. A typical nonsystem resource is retrieved from the network. The `ClassLoader` class also has two methods for retrieving nonsystem resources:

1. `getResource(String resourceName)`
2. `getResourceAsStream(String resourceName)`

The `Class` class has methods by the same names to retrieve resources. When you use these methods, `Class` gets its `ClassLoader` instance and calls the corresponding methods in `ClassLoader`.

Obtaining Resources as URLs

The `getResource(String resourceName)` and `getSystemResource(Stringresource Name)` methods return resources as URLs. Currently, three types of resources are supported: the `Image` object, audio clips, and the `InputStream` object. You can use the `getContent()` method in the URL class to obtain the resource from the returned URL. Listing 2.14 illustrates the use of the `getResource()` method to load an image.

LISTING 2.14 Loading an image from a JAR file

```java
public Image loadAnImageFromJar(String imageName){
    Image img = null;
    String path;
    URL url;
    try{
        url = this.getClass().getResource(imageName);
        img =Toolkit.getDefaultToolkit().createImage(((ImageProducer)
            (url.getContent()))));
    }catch (Exception e){ }
    return img;
}
```

Loading Images from JAR Files in Applets

Images from a JAR file can be loaded in applets by use of the same `getResource()` or `getResourceAsStream()` methods. Unsigned applets have several restrictions regarding access to resources in local machines, as well as in remote sites. However, applets can access files, including JAR files, from the applet directory. Even then there are some restrictions on the performance of certain operations.

To run an applet, you need

- **An HTML driver file.** Applet-related parameters are included within the `APPLET` tag.
- **A class that extends Applet class files and resources.** Applet class files and resources can be in JAR files.

As an example, let's modify the `ImageSetViewer` code (see Listing 2.5) to make it an applet.

> **Note:** The source code and class files for `ImageSetViewerApplet` are available on the book's Web page in the directory `src/chapter2/applet`.

The `ImageSetViewerApplet` class needs to extend the `Applet` class instead of the `Frame` class and override `Applet`'s four life cycle methods: `init()`, `start()`, `run()`, and `dispose()`. As Listing 2.15 shows, these methods are added in place of the constructor and the `main()` method. Because the images are expected to be in a JAR file, the image loading is achieved through the `getResource()` or `getResourceAsStream()` method. If you don't want to use a JAR file for images, you can use the `getImage()` method to load images from an applet's code base.

LISTING 2.15 The `ImageSetViewerApplet` class

```
import java.io.*;
import java.awt.*;
import java.awt.event.*;
import java.awt.image.*;
import java.util.*;
import java.applet.*;
import java.net.*;
public class ImageSetViewerApplet extends Applet implements Runnable{
    static int viewerWid = 400;
    static int viewerHt = 300;
    private String[] fileList;
    private int numImages=0;
    private Image currentImage;
    private int currentIndex =0;
    private Image offScrImage;
```

continued

```java
private Graphics offScrGc;
private Thread mainThread;

public void init() {
    String param = getParameter("IMAGENAMES");
    getFileNamesFromHTML(param);
    param = getParameter("WIDTH");
    if(param != null) viewerWid = Integer.valueOf(param).intValue();
    param = getParameter("HEIGHT");
    if(param != null) viewerHt = Integer.valueOf(param).intValue();
    initApp();
}

public void start(){ mainThread.start(); }

public void run() { displayImage(); }

public void dispose(){
    if(currentImage != null) currentImage.flush();
}

private void getFileNamesFromHTML(String param){
    StringTokenizer st = new StringTokenizer(param, ",");
    int size = st.countTokens();
    if(size <=0) return;
    fileList = new String[size];
    int i=0;
    while(st.hasMoreTokens()){
        fileList[i++] = st.nextToken();
    }
    numImages = fileList.length;
}

public void initApp() {
    this.setSize(viewerWid, viewerHt);
    enableEvents(AWTEvent.MOUSE_MOTION_EVENT_MASK |
                      AWTEvent.MOUSE_EVENT_MASK);
    createOffScreenImage();
    mainThread = new Thread(this);
}
// Creates an off-screen image.
private void createOffScreenImage(){
    Rectangle rect = getBounds();
    viewerWid = rect.width;
    viewerHt = rect.height;
    offScrImage = this.createImage(rect.width, rect.height);
    offScrGc = offScrImage.getGraphics();
    offScrGc.setColor(Color.black);
    offScrGc.fillRect(0,0,rect.width, rect.height);
}

// To overcome the Netscape getResource() bug, use this method to load images
// from JAR files in applets.
public  Image loadAnImage(String name){
    try{
        InputStream is = this.getClass().getResourceAsStream(name);
        ByteArrayOutputStream bout = new ByteArrayOutputStream();
        int aByte;
```

```java
        while((aByte = is.read()) >= 0) bout.write(aByte);
        return Toolkit.getDefaultToolkit().createImage(bout.toByteArray());
    } catch (Exception e){ return null;}
}

public Image loadFromJar(String name){
    try{
        URL url =
            this.getClass().getClassLoader().getResource(name);
        return
         Toolkit.getDefaultToolkit().createImage(((ImageProducer)
         (url.getContent())));
    } catch (Exception e){ return null;}
}

public boolean imageUpdate(Image img,
                           int infoflags,
                           int x,int y,
                           int width,int height){
    if((infoflags & ImageObserver.ERROR) != 0){return false;}
    if((infoflags & (ImageObserver.FRAMEBITS | ImageObserver.ALLBITS))!= 0) {
        repaint();
        return false;
    }
    return true;
}

public void displayImage(){
    currentImage = loadAnImage(fileList[currentIndex++ % numImages]);
    repaint();
}

public void paint(Graphics gc){
    Rectangle rect = getBounds();
    if(currentImage != null)
        gc.drawImage(currentImage, 0,0, rect.width, rect.height, this);
}

public void update(Graphics gc){
    Rectangle rect = getBounds();
    if(currentImage != null)
        gc.drawImage(currentImage, 0,0, rect.width, rect.height, this);
}

public void  processMouseEvent(MouseEvent e){
    switch(e.getID()){
        case MouseEvent.MOUSE_PRESSED:
            setCursor(Cursor.getPredefinedCursor(Cursor.HAND_CURSOR));
            displayImage();
            break;
        case MouseEvent.MOUSE_CLICKED:
            break;
        case MouseEvent.MOUSE_RELEASED:
            setCursor(Cursor.getDefaultCursor());
            break;
    }
}
}
}
```

continued

Here's the sequence of method calls:

1. When the applet is instantiated, `Applet`'s container calls the `init()` method.

2. Once the applet is initialized, `Applet`'s container calls the `start()` method. This method makes the applet thread runnable, which means that the applet thread will run when it gets a chance.

3. When the applet thread gets a chance to run, the `run()` method is invoked. This method calls `displayImage()` to display the first `Image` in the JAR file. The `displayImage()` method calls `loadAnImage()`, which reads the image from the JAR file as a stream and then converts it to an image object.

4. When the user clicks on the image, `displayImage()` is called and the next image from the JAR file is displayed.

Listing 2.16 shows the HTML driver file for the applet. The JAR files are included within the `ARCHIVE` subtag, which can take more than one JAR file.

LISTING 2.16 The HTML driver for `ImageSetViewerApplet`

```
<!DOCTYPE HTML <body>
<center><applet code="ImageSetViewerApplet.class" archive="imagesetviewer.jar,im.jar"
width="350" height="250">
<param name="imagesource" value="im.jar">
<param name="imagenames"
value="T0.jpg,T1.jpg,T2.jpg,T3.jpg,T4.jpg,T5.jpg,T6.jpg,T7.jpg,T8.jpg,T9.jpg,T10.jpg,
T11.jpg,T12.jpg,T13.jpg,T14.jpg,T15.jpg">
</applet></center>
</body></html>
```

The `simpleviewer.jar` file contains class files and the `im.jar` file contains images. The `ARCHIVE` tag contains both of these JAR files. Note that nowhere in the `ImageSetViewerApplet` code is the `im.jar` file referenced, so you can create your own JAR file and the HTML driver file to display images of your choice.

To run this applet, you can use the `appletviewer` utility or any Web browser that supports JDK 1.1. To run the applet using `appletviewer`, type "appletviewer simpleviewer.html" on the command line.

Figure 2.3 shows the applet running in the Netscape browser. To run this applet in the Netscape browser, select **File | Open New Page.** Now you can enter the path for `simpleviewer.html` or use the browser to go to the applet directory and then click on the `simpleviewer.html` file. Upon clicking, the applet will run and you will see an image like the one in Figure 2.3. You can view the images in the JAR file in succession by clicking on each one in turn.

© Andy Williams/FPG International LLC

FIGURE 2.3   ImageSetViewerApplet running in the Netscape browser

Location-Dependent Loading

Java applications and applets can access resources included in a JAR file in a location-dependent manner as well. In this approach the application needs to know where the resource resides. The readImageFromJar() method shown in Listing 2.17 is a way of loading images from a JAR file that need not be in the class path.

LISTING 2.17 Reading an image from a JAR file using the java.util.zip package

```
public static Image readImageFromJar(String jarpath,
                                     String filename){
  Image image = null;
  try {
    ZipFile zipfile = new ZipFile(new File(jarpath));
    Vector imageVect = new Vector();
    ZipEntry zentry = zipfile.getEntry(filename);
    InputStream zstream = zipfile.getInputStream(zentry);
    String flName = zentry.getName();

    byte[] imageBuf = new byte[128];
    ByteArrayOutputStream boutstream = new ByteArrayOutputStream();
    for(;;){
       int bytesread = zstream.read(imageBuf);
       if (bytesread <0) {break;}
       boutstream.write(imageBuf,0,bytesread);
    }
```

continued

```
        byte[] pixmap =boutstream.toByteArray();
        boutstream.flush();
        image = Toolkit.getDefaultToolkit().createImage(pixmap);
        zipfile.close();
    }catch(Exception e){System.out.println(e);}
    return image;
}
```

The `readImageFormJar()` method loads a specified file from a jar file. It reads the image file byte by byte from the file and then creates an image by calling `Toolkit`'s `createImage()` method.

The `readImageFromJar()` method first creates a `ZipInputStream` object for the entry and a `ByteArrayOutputStream` object to save the image as bytes. In the inner `for` loop, bytes are read from `ZipInputStream` and saved in `ByteArrayOutputStream`. Once all the bytes are read and `ByteArrayOutputStream` is thus converted to an array of bytes, a pixel map is created. This pixel map is passed as an argument to the `createImage()` method of the `java.awt.Toolkit` class.

The book's Web page contains two utility classes for using the JAR files under `src/util`: `JarUtil.java` and `ImageUtil.java`. The `JarUtil` class has several static methods for performing JAR file-related tasks, which include the following:

- Listing all JAR entries
- Listing selected JAR entries
- Sorting the listed JAR entries

The `ImageUtil.java` file has many static methods for reading images.

Putting It All Together: The MultiImageLoader Bean

The `MultiImageLoader` bean shown in Figure 2.4 loads images from a local directory or from a JAR or ZIP file. We'll use this bean in many examples in subsequent chapters.

You can manually enter a directory, file name, and filter to display a list of files from either a local directory or a JAR file. You can also launch a file dialog box by clicking on **Launch File Dialog.** Select the images that are to be viewed and click on **Launch Images** to view the images. See Appendix C for a detailed explanation and code listing of this bean.

Conclusion

With the increasing popularity of Internet-based applications, image loading is a topic of considerable interest to many developers. In this chapter we addressed various issues related to image loading in Java.

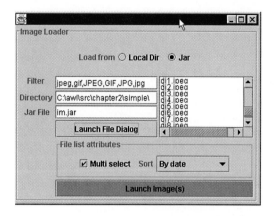

FIGURE 2.4   The `MultiImageLoader` bean

Image loading is usually the first step in any imaging application. As we saw in this chapter, it is not a simple matter. In earlier versions of Java, image loading was based on the push model that supports asynchronous loading. Although asynchronous image loading is well suited for networked and Internet images, it creates a bottleneck in high-performance applications.

Rendering Images in the AWT

3

IN CHAPTER 2 WE INTRODUCED IMAGE RENDERING in an informal manner through some image viewer examples. In this chapter we'll explain the basics of image rendering and expand on the topics already discussed.

In a typical imaging application, you would display an image, manipulate it, and probably print it. Thus the imaging APIs should have the capability of rendering images to a computer monitor as well as to a printer. Although this capability suffices in most cases, some applications require the capability of rendering images onto devices other than a display monitor or printer. In medical imaging, for example, it is a common practice to view images on films, so a medical image visualization application may need to render images to filming cameras, in addition to display monitors and printers. What is desirable, therefore, is a common strategy to render images in a device-independent manner. This goal is not easy to achieve because the characteristics of the devices differ in many respects. The AWT imaging and Java 2D APIs have achieved this goal to a large extent. In this chapter we'll explore various topics related to image rendering in the AWT imaging APIs.

Printing is one of the major weak points of Java. JDK 1.0 did not support printing at all. JDK 1.1 has minimal support. As we'll see in Chapter 6, the printing weakness has been overcome to some extent with the introduction of the Java 2D printing API.

Describing an Image

Before an image can be rendered, an object that represents the image must be created. In Chapter 2 we saw how to create image objects using the image-loading methods—for instance, using the flavors of `getImage()` from the `Applet` and `Toolkit` classes. These are some of the ways of creating `Image` objects.

A *raw* image is an array of pixels. The pixel values encapsulate the attributes of the objects that the image represents. Actual values depend on how an image is acquired. A pixel may represent a single attribute—say, brightness value, as in the case of grayscale images—or it may represent multiple attributes, as in the case of color images. When there are multiple attributes, a pixel may have multiple values or a single value with a set of bits representing an attribute. For instance, each color in an RGB (red-green-blue) image in the AWT is represented by a byte. Because this representation requires 24 bits, it is normally packed in an integer (which is 32 bits in Java). The remaining 8 bits often represent the transparency or alpha values.

The rendering process consists of two logical steps:

1. Extracting pixel information (such as color, transparency, and so on) from the image
2. Converting the extracted pixel information appropriately to suit the destination device in such a way that the image is in a presentable form

This means that an image needs to contain much more information than a mere array of pixels.

Image data typically consists of a variety of information that may include image geometry, viewing parameters, and scanning parameters. Exactly what information is included depends on the type of the image and its use.

Attributes related to image geometry may include

◆ Size of the image
◆ Location and relationship of the image to other images if it is part of an image set

Viewing parameters may include

◆ Brightness and contrast factors (window and level in the case of medical images)
◆ Image orientation
◆ Image manipulation parameters, such as magnification factor, rotation angle, and so on

Scanning parameters depend on the way in which images were acquired. Image-rendering programs obtain appropriate parameters from the image data and render the image in such a way that it accurately reflects the original view in the destination device.

In many instances, even when the image is presented accurately, it may not convey any meaning unless some information is available about the image. Imagine a weather map without the date and time information. Textual information is typically overlaid on the image and is called annotation. In the case of medical images, overlaid information includes patient information, patient orientation, location, and scanning parameters. Medical imaging applications even provide a separate text page for the doctors to view this information in detail.

In addition to textual data, scientific images are often associated with graphical objects such as curves and regions of interest (ROIs). An image representation should be capable of saving these types of objects along with the image data.

In the next section we'll see how images are represented in the AWT imaging APIs.

Image Representation in the AWT

Images in Java are represented in different ways. In the earlier versions of Java (JDK 1.0 and JDK 1.1) , the `java.awt.Image` class encapsulated an image. As Chapter 2 suggested, this representation is inadequate, especially in scientific applications.

One of the major drawbacks is that it doesn't expose pixel data representation. In other words, pixel data from the image is not directly available because the `Image` class has no methods for reading and writing pixel values. Recall from Chapter 2 that we used the `PixelGrabber` class to retrieve pixel data from images. To save this data and other image-related information in cache, we developed the `ImageBuffer` class. In Java 2D the `BufferedImage` class performs this function.

Overview of the AWT Imaging APIs

Image loading and rendering in AWT imaging are based on the push model. In Chapter 2 we covered the basics of this model largely from the image-loading perspective. Now let's look at the APIs in some detail.

The majority of the classes that implement the push model are in the `java.awt.image` package. However, the `Image` class, which represents the image, is in the `java.awt` package. The `java.awt.image` package has three sets of classes:

1. **Image producer classes.** These classes implement the `ImageProducer` interface. The classes are `FilteredImageSource` and `MemoryImageSource`.

2. **Image consumer classes.** These classes implement the `ImageConsumer` interface. The classes are `PixelGrabber`, `Filter`, `CropImageFilter`, and `RGBImageFilter`.

3. **Color-model classes.** These classes encapsulate methods that help translate pixel values into color and transparency components. The `ColorModel` class is the superclass of all the color-model classes. JDK 1.1 has two color-model subclasses: `DirectColorModel`, which uses the existing color map; and `IndexColorModel`, which uses a custom color map. Java 2D has a few more color-model classes. We'll describe color and color models in detail in Chapter 8.

A Closer Look at the Image Class

We introduced the `Image` class in Chapter 2. In this section we'll closely examine this class from an image-rendering point of view.

As mentioned earlier, the `Image` class represents an image in the AWT. Because it is an abstract class, you cannot directly construct `Image` objects. However, the AWT imaging APIs provide many ways of constructing an `Image` object. In Chapter 2 we constructed `Image` objects directly from the source by using the `getImage()` methods.

`Image` objects are constructed in a platform-specific manner. There are two types of `Image` objects:

1. **Images created from an image source.** An `ImageProducer` object is needed to create such an `Image` object.

2. **Images created by an AWT component and used as an off-screen image.**

Let's look at the methods of the `Image` class:

◆ **public ImageProducer getSource()**

This method returns the source of the image as an `ImageProducer` object. As we'll see later in this chapter, this method is used to get the `ImageProducer` object of the original image whenever there is a need to construct a new image object from an existing image object.

> **Note:** The `getSource()` method should not be called when the `Image` object represents an off-screen image, which is not created by an `ImageProducer` object.

◆ **public Object getProperty(String name, ImageObserver observer)**

This method returns the property specified by the input parameter. The method requires an `ImageObserver` object because the property is obtained asynchronously.

◆ **public int getWidth(ImageObserver observer)**
  public int getHeight(ImageObserver observer)

Just like the `getProperty()` method, both of these methods have the `Image Observer` argument to obtain the width and height asynchronously. If the image is yet to be loaded, these methods may return -1. In such cases, actual width and height are obtained from the `imageUpdate()` method. See Chapter 2 for examples.

◆ **public Image getScaledInstance(int width, int height, int hints)**

This method creates a scaled instance of an image. The values of the `width` and `height` parameters depend on the scale factor. The `hints` argument indicates to the image producer how the scaled instance is to be generated. There are four values for this argument: SCALE_DEFAULT, SCALE_FAST, SCALE_SMOOTH, and SCALE_REPLICATE. Depending on the value of `hints`, the image generation program chooses an interpolation method. Hints are just hints. The underlying program need not accept them. The interpolation method used may vary with platforms. See Chapter 7 for an example.

- **public Graphics getGraphics()**

  This method returns the `Graphics` context of an off-screen image. To create an off-screen image, you need to use the `createImage()` method from the `Component` class or its descendants.

> **Note**: The `getGraphics()` method should be called only in off-screen `Image` objects. If this method is invoked in an `Image` object created from an `ImageProducer` object, it will throw an exception.

- **public void flush()**

  This method flushes all resources being used by the `Image` object. When your program no longer needs an `Image` object, call this method to reclaim the memory and other resources used by the image.

Creating an Image Object

You can create an `Image` object by constructing it from a local image file, a URL pointing to an image, or an array of bytes, or by applying a filter to an existing image.

Creating an Image Object from a File or URL Image Source

We covered this topic in Chapter 2 (in the section titled Obtaining an Image Object). Whether you have an applet or an application, you can use the appropriate `getImage()` method to construct an `Image` object. Note that even though the `getImage()` method returns an `Image` object immediately, an image is actually loaded only when that image is needed. If you try to display the image immediately after you get the `Image` object, the image may not appear at all because when an image is displayed, the `Image` object may not contain any pixel data. You can circumvent this problem by using the `MediaTracker` class, which waits until the entire image is loaded.

Creating an Image Object from Memory

The AWT imaging APIs allow you to create images from an array of pixels. You can do so by using the `MemoryImageSource` class. To create an `Image` object from memory, all you need to do is provide image parameters and a color model to the constructor of this class.

The `ColorModel` class has methods for translating pixels into alpha, red, green, and blue components. When painted on the screen, an image pixel is a combination of these four components. In JDK 1.1, you can either use the existing color map by using the `DirectColorModel` class or create your own by using the `IndexColorModel` class.

Here's how you can get a default `ColorModel` object:

```
ColorModel  cm = ColorModel.getRGBDefault();
```

Once you get the `ColorModel` object, you can create an `ImageProducer` object for `MemoryImageSource`.

```
ImagePoducer  ip =  new MemoryImageSource(width, height, cm, pixels, offset,
scansize);
```

The `offset` argument normally has a value of zero, and the value of `scansize` is the same as the width of the image. The pixel array can be an array of bytes or integers. Once you get the `ImageProducer` object, you can create the image as follows:

```
Image img = createImage(ip);
```

Creating an Image Object from FilteredImageSource

Just like `MemoryImageSource`, the `FilteredImageSource` class is an `ImageProducer` object. `FilteredImageSource` creates a new `Image` object from an existing image. Its constructor takes two arguments: the image producer for the existing image, and the image filter. The `ImageFilter` class is the base class for the filter-related classes.

JDK 1.1 has two filter classes: `CropImageFilter` and the `RGBImageFilter`. You can extend these classes to create your own filters. See the section titled Using Image Filters later in this chapter for examples.

Creating an Off-Screen Image

In JDK 1.1 you can create an off-screen image by using the `createImage()` method from `java.awt.Component`. Note that `createImage()` must be called only after the component is visible; otherwise it will throw an exception. To get the `Graphics` context, call the `getGraphics()` method in the off-screen `Image` object. Here's an example:

```
Image offScreenImage  =  createImage(width, height);
Graphics offScrGc = offScreenImage.getGraphics();
```

Once the off-screen image has been created, `Graphics` and `Image` objects can be drawn on the off-screen `Graphics` context. The off-screen image is then painted on the screen at an appropriate time by the `paint()` or `update()` methods, which will be discussed next.

Displaying an Image

An image is displayed only when it is drawn on the `Graphics` context of a visual component. As we'll see in Chapter 5, a `Graphics` context is supplied by the system through paint methods.

The `java.awt.Graphics` class represents a `Graphics` context and has many flavors of `drawImage()` methods for drawing images—for example:

- **`public boolean drawImage(Image theImage, int x, int y, ImageObserver obs)`**

  This method draws the image specified by `theImage` at (x, y) without resizing. If the image does not fit the component, only part of the image will be visible.

- **`public boolean drawImage(Image theImage, int x, int y, Color bg, ImageObserver obs)`**

  This method has an additional parameter, `bg`, to specify the background color.

- **`public boolean drawImage(Image theImage,`**
  `int x, int y,`
  `int width, int height,`
  `ImageObserver obs)`

  This method draws the image within the rectangle whose upper left-hand corner coordinates are x and y and whose dimensions are `width` and `height`. When it is drawn, the image is scaled to fit the rectangle of dimension `width _ height`.

- **`public boolean drawImage(Image theImage,`**
  `int x, int y,`
  `int width, int height,`
  `ImageObserver obs)`

  This method performs scaled drawing with the background color as specified by `bg`.

Note that all the `drawImage()` methods have an `ImageObserver` argument. Just like image loading, drawing an image onto a `Graphics` context is an asynchronous operation. The caller of the `drawImage()` method supplies the `ImageObserver` parameter. In most applications, it is convenient to set the `ImageObserver` argument to `this,` implying that the object that calls the `drawImage()` method is passed as the `ImageObserver` parameter. If the drawing of the image is not completed immediately, the `imageUpdate()` method in the `ImageObserver` object is called. Just as in image loading, `imageUpdate()` provides the status of the image-drawing operations.

As mentioned earlier, drawing images is an asynchronous operation. If `drawImage()` does not return `true` immediately, the `imageUpdate()` method is called at regular intervals until the image is rendered or the `imageUpdate()` method returns `false`. The status bits supplied to `imageUpdate()` provide information on the status of the drawing. By checking for appropriate status bits, you can make sure that an image is completely drawn on a component. The definition of the status bits is given in the `ImageObserver` interface (see Table 2.1). The important status bits to check for are `ERROR, ABORT, WIDTH, HEIGHT,` and `ALLBITS.` For all practical purposes, checking for `ERROR` and `ALLBITS` suffices in an image-drawing operation. For a sample implementation of the `imageUpdate()` method, see Listing 2.1.

As mentioned earlier, images are loaded only when they are needed. If `drawImage()` is not executed, the image will not be loaded at all. Sometimes the late loading of images results in images not being displayed because `drawImage()` is executed before the image is available.

However, it is possible to force the images to load before displaying them. As mentioned in Chapter 2, the AWT provides many options for this purpose—for example:

- Using the `MediaTracker` class, as described in Chapter 2.
- Using the `prepareImage()` and `checkImage()` methods from the **Component** or **Toolkit** class. The `prepareImage()` method forces the image to load, and the `checkImage()` method checks the status of the load and returns the boolean OR of the `ImageObserver` flags. Both of these methods come in two flavors: with and without `width` and `height` arguments. Here's an example:

```
if(!prepareImage(img, this)){
   int status = 0;
   while((status &( ImageObserver.ALLBITS | ImageObserver.ERROR) ==0)
   status =checkImage(img, this);
}
g.drawImage(img, 0,0, this);
```

If the image has already been loaded, `prepareImage()` may not be needed. It is possible to use only `imageUpdate()` to check the status of the image drawing.

Components for Drawing Images

Although you can draw images in any visual component, only a few components are suitable for visualization applications. Your choice of component normally depends on the application. If you're using the AWT, you can draw images on `Canvas`, `Panel`, `Applet`, or `Frame` classes, which are descendants of the abstract `Component` class. The `Canvas` class is an obvious choice for many applications because it is a direct subclass of `Component`, unlike the `Panel`, `Applet`, and `Frame` classes, which are containers. You can easily fit `Canvas` into any layout, especially the gridbag layout. The `Canvas` class overrides just one method: `paint()`. The only difference between the `paint()` method of `Component` and the `paint()` method of `Canvas` is that the latter has a default background color.

You can also use Swing components to draw images. To use Swing with JDK 1.1, all you need to do is to put the `swingall.jar` file in the class path. You can download this JAR file from the Java home site (http://java.sun.com). Swing has no equivalent of the `Canvas` class. Instead, you can use `JComponent` itself as a canvas to draw images. In addition, the container components, such as `JPanel`, `JFrame`, and `JApplet`, can also be used for drawing images.

> **Note:** Whereas Swing is part of Java 2, with JDK 1.1 you need to download it separately.

Double Buffering

We briefly discussed double buffering in Chapter 2. In this section we'll look at this topic in detail. Double buffering is an important concept for rendering images. To understand why we need double buffering, consider the following situations:

- Your application needs to perform an image-drawing operation that takes a significant amount of time. If the image is drawn directly on the `Graphics` context, you will probably see a partially drawn image slowly building to a full image.
- Your application needs to perform multiple drawing operations within a short span of time. If these are performed directly on a component's `Graphics` context, you will see some undesirable flickering effects.

The solution to these problems is double buffering, a technique to make a drawing visible only after it is completely drawn. In this technique, graphical objects are drawn off-screen and displayed on-screen only when they are completely drawn. Earlier in this chapter we discussed how to create an off-screen image.

In the double-buffering technique, there are two things to keep in mind:

1. The off-screen image
2. The off-screen `Graphics` context

The off-screen image is a blank image over which actual images or graphical objects are drawn. The actual drawing operation is performed on the off-screen `Graphics` context. This `Graphics` context is similar to a component's `Graphics` context. The only difference is that the off-screen drawing is not visible. Just like the on-screen `Graphics` context, you can use the same methods of the `Graphics` class to draw the graphical and image objects on the off-screen `Graphics` context.

Here are the steps involved in double buffering:

1. Create an off-screen image and obtain its `Graphics` context—for example:

```
Image offScreenImage = createImage(width, height);
Graphics offScrGc = offScreenImage.getGraphics();
```

2. Draw the original image (or any `Graphics` objects) over the off-screen `Graphics` context. The off-screen image will hold that drawing—for example:

```
private void offScreenDraw(Image theImage){
    offScrGc.drawImage(theImage, 0,0, this);
}
```

3. Once all the drawing operations are complete, draw the off-screen image over the component's `Graphics` context, thereby making the contents of the off-screen image visible:

```
public void paint(Graphics g){
   if(offScrImage != null) {
       g.drawImage(offScrImage, 0,0, this);
   }
}
```

Although the `createImage()` method is available in a `Component,` it returns `null` if the `Component`'s peer has not been created (i.e., is not visible). One way to circumvent this problem is to create the off-screen image on the component that is visible—say, the main `Applet`—and pass it as a parameter to any object that needs to implement double buffering. The other option is to override the `addNotify()` method. This method is called only after the peer component is created. Here's how to do the latter:

```
public void addNotify() {
    super.addNotify();
    createOffScrImage()
}

public void createOffScrImage(){
   offScrImage = createImage(width, height);
   offScrGc = offScrImage.getGraphics();
}
```

In this example you may assume that `offScrImage` and `offScrGc` are instance variables of types `Image` and `Graphics`, respectively.

A Canvas for Displaying Images

Now that we have reviewed the basics of displaying an image, let's put everything we know together and create a class for displaying images. We'll call this class **ImageCanvas**. This class will implement double buffering and will use the classes and interfaces developed in Chapter 2.

The **ImageCanvas** object can be embedded in any GUI. The example in the next section (Using Image Filters) illustrates the use of this class. Listing 3.1 shows the code for **ImageCanvas**.

LISTING 3.1 The ImageCanvas class

```java
import java.io.*;
import java.awt.*;
import java.awt.image.*;
import java.lang.Math;

public class ImageCanvas extends Canvas implements ImageLoadedListener{
    protected int width, height;
    protected Image offScrImage;

    protected Graphics offScrGc;
    protected Image pixImage;
    private ImageBuffer scnImage;

    public  ImageCanvas(int wid, int ht){
        width = wid;
        height = ht;
        setSize(wid, ht);
}

public void setWidHt(int wd, int hgt){
    width  = wd; height = hgt;
}

public  void createOffScrImage(){
    Rectangle r = getBounds();
    if((r.width ==0) || (r.height ==0)) return;
    setWidHt(r.width, r.height);
    // If the component is not visible, offScrImage may be null.
    if((offScrImage = createImage(width, height)) == null){ return;}
    setOffScrGc();
}

public  void setOffScrGc(){
    if(offScrImage == null) return;
    offScrGc = offScrImage.getGraphics();
    // Default attributes
    offScrGc.setColor(Color.cyan);
    Font fnt = new Font("Helvetica", Font.BOLD,9);
    offScrGc.setFont(fnt);
    offScrGc.setColor(Color.black);
    offScrGc.fillRect(0,0, width, height);
}
```

continued

```java
public void setImageBuffer(ImageBuffer ib){
    scnImage = ib;
    pixImage = ib.image;
}

public ImageBuffer getImageBuffer() {
    return scnImage;
}

public void setImage(Image im) {
    pixImage = im;
    imagePaint();
}

public Image getImage() {
    return pixImage;
}

public void imageLoaded(ImageLoadedEvent e){
    ImageLoader il = (ImageLoader)e.getSource();
    int loadStatus = il.getImageBuffer().getLoadStatus();
     if(loadStatus == ImageLoadedListener.IMAGE_READY){
        pixImage = il.getImageBuffer().getImage();
        imagePaint(pixImage);
    }
}

public  boolean imagePaint(Image img){
    if(img == null) return false;
    pixImage = img;
    drawOffScreen(img);
    return true;
}

public  boolean imagePaint(){
    return imagePaint(pixImage);
}

public void paint(Graphics paintGc){
    Rectangle  border = getBounds();
    width = border.width;
    height = border.height;
    paintGc.setColor(Color.cyan);
    if(offScrImage != null)
       paintGc.drawImage(offScrImage,0,0,width,height, this);

}

public  void update(Graphics paintGc){
    Rectangle  border = getBounds();
    width = border.width;
    height = border.height;
    paintGc.setColor(Color.cyan);
    if(offScrImage != null)
       paintGc.drawImage(offScrImage,0,0,width,height, this);

}
```

```
protected void drawOffScreen(Image img){
   if(img == null) return;
   Rectangle r = getBounds();
   if((r.width <=0) ||(r.height <=0)){
      System.out.println("Component not visible. Will draw image later");
      return;
   }
   if((width != r.width) ||(height != r.height))createOffScrImage();
   if(offScrImage == null ) createOffScrImage();
   if(offScrGc == null)setOffScrGc();
   offScrGc.setColor((Color.black));
   offScrGc.setFont(new Font("Helvetica", Font.BOLD, 9));
   offScrGc.fillRect(0,0,width,height);
   if(offScrGc.drawImage(img,0,0,width,height,this)){
      if((scnImage != null) && (scnImage.imageName) !=null){
         offScrGc.setColor(Color.white);
         offScrGc.drawString(scnImage.imageName,12,12);
      }
      repaint();
   }
   else {
      offScrGc.setColor(Color.white);
      if((scnImage != null) && (scnImage.imageName) !=null)
         offScrGc.drawString(scnImage.imageName,12,12);
   }
   repaint();
   }
}
```

The **ImageCanvas** class doesn't load images. Instead, it implements the **ImageLoadedListener** interface to listen to **imageLoaded** events. You may recall from Chapter 2 that the **imageLoaded** event is a custom event that we developed to report the image-loading status (see Listings 2.8 and 2.9). This event also sends the **Image** object to its recipients.

The **imageLoaded()** method is called when the **imageLoaded** event is fired. This method checks the image-loading status, and if the status is **IMAGE_READY,** it extracts the **ImageLoader** object from the **ImageLoadedEvent** object. As you may recall from Chapter 2, **ImageLoader** saves the image in **ImageBuffer.** The **imageLoaded()** method obtains the **Image** object from **ImageBuffer.**

If the image is loaded elsewhere, you can set the **Image** object by calling the **setImageBuffer()** or **setImage()** methods.

As Listing 3.1 shows, there are two flavors of **imagePaint()** methods. The **imagePaint()** method calls **imagePaint(Image).** By calling **drawOffScreen(),** **imagePaint()** performs the tasks that are essential to painting an image off-screen.

The **drawOffScreen()** method performs double buffering. It first creates the **offScrImage** object (i.e., the off-screen image); then it draws the actual image and its name (if one exists) over it. When drawing of the off-screen image has been completed, **drawOffScreen()** calls the **repaint()** method, which in turn prompts the system to execute the paint thread.

When the paint thread gets a chance to run, it calls `update()`, which draws `offScrImage` over the `Graphics` object supplied by the AWT. The image is actually displayed when `paintGc.drawImage()` is executed in `update()`. The `paint()` method is called by the system when a component becomes damaged—for example, as a result of other windows moving over it.

Here's a typical sequence of `ImageCanvas` method calls:

1. A client object creates `ImageCanvas` and adds it to a GUI container.

2. The client object registers `ImageCanvas` to receive the `imageLoaded` events from the image loader.

3. The AWT calls `addNotify()` when the peer component is created.

4. `ImageCanvas`'s `addNotify()` method first calls the `addNotify()` method in the superclass and then calls the `createOffScreenImage()` method.

5. The client loads the image using the `ImageLoader` object, which fires `imageLoaded` events to `ImageCanvas` as image loading progresses.

6. The `imageLoaded()` method receives the `imageLoaded` events. When the image-loading status is `IMAGE_READY`, `imageLoaded()` extracts the loaded image and calls `imagePaint()`. The `imagePaint()` method, in turn, calls `drawOffScreen()` to draw the loaded image over an off-screen image. If the `offScrGc.draw Image()` method returns `true`, `imageLoaded()` calls `repaint()`.

7. The AWT thread calls the `update()` method. When `update()` executes `paintGc.drawImage()`, the off-screen image is drawn on the on-screen `Graphics` context and the image is displayed.

If the image is already loaded, the client object can call `setImage()`, which calls `imagePaint()` directly.

Using Image Filters

An image filter is a function that operates on an existing image to create a different version of it. To produce a filtered image, you need to use the `FilteredImageSource` class. The constructor of this class requires two arguments: `ImageProducer` and `ImageFilter`.

`ImageFilter` is the base class for all image filters. The `ImageFilter` class implements the `ImageConsumer` interface. Accordingly, it has several methods to enable the delivery of pixels from `ImageProducer` to `ImageConsumer`.

JDK 1.1 has the following filter classes: `CropImageFilter`, `RGBImageFilter`, `ReplicateScaleFilter`, and `AreaAverageScaleFilter`. You can extend the `Image Filter` class to create your own filters. Java 2D has one more image filter class: `BufferedImageFilter`.

The RGBImageFilter Class

The abstract `RGBImageFilter` class has the following abstract method:

♦ **`public abstract int filterRGB(int x, int y, int rgb)`**

The subclasses of `RGBImageFilter` need to override this method. The input parameter `rgb` is the input pixel value; `x` and `y` are the pixel locations. The `filterRGB()` method is called for every pixel.

To customize the filter, you need to include the filtering code in the `filterRGB()` method. This code can implement a function that modifies the input `rgb` value and returns the changed value. If the entire pixel data is passed through the `filterRGB()` method, image production will be very slow. The `RGBImageFilter` class has two other filter methods that circumvent this problem: `filterIndexColorModel()` and `filter RGBPixels()`:

♦ **`public IndexColorModel filterIndexColorModel(IndexColorModel icm)`**

This method applies `filterRGB()` to a pixel map in `IndexColorModel` rather than pixels in the image. This method returns a new `IndexColorModel` that represents the filtered colors.

♦ **`public void filterRGBPixels(int x, int y,`**
                            `int w, int h,`
                            `int pixels[], int off,`
                            `int scansize)`

This method is called only for the buffer in the `pixels` array.

Adjusting Brightness Using RGBImageFilter

Adjusting image brightness requires changing the values of individual image pixels. In the case of a grayscale image, pixel values themselves represent the brightness. So to increase the brightness of grayscale images, all you need to do is boost the values of pixels across the image.

For images represented by the RGB model, however, adjusting the brightness is not that easy. Changing the color value of a pixel changes the color of an image. One approach is to convert the RGB values to brightness values, change them appropriately, and convert them back to RGB values. Although not the fastest or the most efficient way to change image brightness, this approach can be easily implemented by use of the `RGBImageFilter` class. Listing 3.2 shows the code that uses `RGBImage Filter`.

LISTING 3.2   The `BrightnessFilter` class

```
public class BrightnessFilter extends RGBImageFilter  {
   float brfactor = (float)1.0;

   public BrightnessFilter(int br) {
      brfactor *= br/(float)50;
   }

   public int  filterRGB (int x, int y, int rgb){
      int a = rgb & 0xff000000;
      int r = rgb & 0xff0000 >>16;
      int g = rgb & 0xff00 >>8;
      int b = rgb & 0xff;

      float[] hsbvalues = {(float)0.0, (float)0.0, (float)0.0};

      float[] hs = Color.RGBtoHSB(r,g,b, hsbvalues);
      float bright = hsbvalues[2];
      bright = bright * (float)brfactor ;
      bright = (bright>1.0) ? (float) 1.0 : bright ;
      int col = Color.HSBtoRGB(hsbvalues[0],hsbvalues[1],bright);
      int rgbx = col & 0xffffff;
      return a|rgbx;
   }
}
```

As Listing 3.2 shows, the `BrightnessFilter` class extends the `RGBImageFilter` class and overrides the `filterRGB()` method.

To create a new filtered image object, you need to pass the `BrightnessFilter` object as a parameter to the `FilteredImageSource` constructor. While the new image is being produced, the `filterRGB()` method is called for every pixel. In this method the **x** and **y** parameters represent the pixel location, and the **rgb** parameter represents the RGB value of the pixel.

The `filterRGB()` method separates red, green, blue, and alpha components of each pixel and converts them to hue-saturation-brightness (HSB) values. This conversion is done by the `RGBtoHSB()` method in the `Color` class. The brightness value is then modified to reflect the current brightness factor, which is a parameter in the `BrightnessFilter` constructor. The `filterRGB()` method converts the HSB value (that includes the changed brightness value) to an alpha-red-green-blue (ARGB) pixel value. The `filterRGB()` method returns this value.

Each time the brightness factor is changed, the `filterRGB()` method is executed on the entire image—a process that is obviously slow and inefficient.

Now that we have developed a `BrightnessFilter` class, let's use it to adjust the image brightness. But first let's create a component class to display images. Although we already developed a similar class called `ImageCanvas` in the preceding section, that class uses the AWT components—that is, heavyweight components. This time we'll use Swing to build such a class. Listing 3.3 shows the code.

> **Note:** As mentioned earlier, if you have JDK 1.1, you need to include
> `swingall.jar` in the class path to compile and run this class. If you have Java 2,
> you don't need to add anything.

LISTING 3.3   The ImagePanel class

```java
import java.awt.*;
import java.awt.event.*;
import java.awt.image.*;
import java.io.*;
import javax.swing.*;
import javax.swing.event.*;

public class ImagePanel extends JComponent {
    protected   Image image,origImage;
    protected   Image offScrImage;
    protected   Graphics offScrGc;
    protected   Image brightImage =null;
    protected   int imWidth = 0, imHeight = 0;
    protected   int viewerWid, viewerHt;
    private int   offsetX = 0, offsetY = 0;
    public ImagePanel(Image img, int wid, int ht){
        origImage = img;
        image = img;
        imWidth = wid;
        imHeight = ht;
        setSize(wid,ht);
    }
    // Creates off-screen image only after peer is created.
    public void addNotify(){
        super.addNotify();
        createOffScreenImage();
    }
    // Creates off-screen image.
    public void createOffScreenImage(){
        Rectangle rect = getBounds();
        viewerWid = rect.width;
        viewerHt = rect.height;
        offScrImage = this.createImage(rect.width, rect.height);
        offScrGc = offScrImage.getGraphics();
        offScrGc.setColor(Color.black);
        offScrGc.fillRect(0,0,rect.width, rect.height);
        if(image != null) offScrGc.drawImage(image, 0,0,this);
    }

    public void setBrightness(int br) {
        BrightnessFilter filter = new BrightnessFilter(br);
        ImageProducer ip = new FilteredImageSource(image.getSource(), filter);
        brightImage = this.createImage(ip);
        prepareImage(brightImage, this);
        repaint();
    }
```

continued

```java
public void setImage(Image image){
    this.image = image;
    createOffScreenImage();
    prepareImage(image, this);
}

public void drawImage(Image image, int x, int y){
    this.image = image;
    Rectangle rect = getBounds();
    viewerWid = rect.width;
    viewerHt = rect.height;
    offScrImage = this.createImage(rect.width, rect.height);
    offScrGc = offScrImage.getGraphics();
    offScrGc.setColor(Color.black);
    offScrGc.fillRect(0,0,rect.width, rect.height);
    offsetX = x; offsetY = y;
    prepareImage(image, this);
}

private void drawOffScreen(Image img, int x, int y) {
    offScrGc.setColor(Color.black);
    offScrGc.fillRect(0,0,viewerWid, viewerHt);
    offScrGc.drawImage(img, x,y, this);
}

public Image getImage(){ return image;}

public Graphics getDisplayedImageGC() { return offScrGc; }
public void paintComponent(Graphics g){
    Rectangle rect = this.getBounds();
    g.setColor(Color.black);
    g.fillRect(0,0,rect.width, rect.height);
    if(offScrImage != null){
    g.drawImage(offScrImage, 0,0, this);
    }
}
public boolean imageUpdate(Image img,
                            int infoflags,
                            int x,
                            int y,
                            int width,
                            int height){

    if((infoflags & ImageObserver.ERROR) != 0){
        System.out.println("ERROR in image load or image draw");
        return false;
    }
    if((infoflags & (ImageObserver.FRAMEBITS | ImageObserver.ALLBITS))!= 0) {
        drawOffScreen(img, offsetX,offsetY);
        repaint();
        image = img;
        return false;
    }
    return true;
}
```

```
    public void resetImage(){
      offsetX =0; offsetY = 0;
      setImage(origImage);
      repaint();
    }
}
```

As mentioned earlier, Swing doesn't have a component similar to the AWT's `Canvas`. So the `ImagePanel` class extends the `JComponent` class to implement the component to draw images.

The constructor of `ImagePanel` expects an `Image` object and its width and height as parameters. So when the `ImagePanel` is constructed, the image must be loaded already because the size of the panel will be set as the size of the image. The input image is drawn on an off-screen `Graphics` context.

Note that the `paintComponent()` method is used instead of `paint()` or `update()` for painting images (see the section titled Painting in Swing Components in Chapter 5). The `paintComponent()` method draws the off-screen image on the `ImagePanel`'s `Graphics` context, thereby displaying the image.

`ImagePanel` also has an `imageUpdate()` method, which is required for images that are set through `setImage()` or `setBrightness()`. These methods are likely to be called by the client objects that created the filtered images.

In the case of the `setBrightness()` method, the client object sets the brightness factor. This method then constructs a `BrightnessFilter` object, which is used along with the source of the original image to construct a `FilteredImageSource` object. Because of the asynchronous push model, `FilteredImageSource` starts producing the image only when there is a need for it. To circumvent this problem, the `setBrightness()` method calls `prepareImage()` to force image production. The `imageUpdate()` method tracks image production. When it is complete, the `imageUpdate()` method calls `drawOffScreen()` to draw the filtered image on the off-screen `Graphics` context. This image is drawn on the on-screen `Graphics` context when `repaint()` triggers the `paintComponent()` method.

The `resetImage()` method restores the original image. The same `ImagePanel` class is used for both the brightness adjustment and the image-cropping examples.

Now let's create a launchable frame in which to display the image. We'll also include the GUI components to adjust the brightness. Listing 3.4 shows the code for the viewer.

LISTING 3.4 The `Viewer` class

```
public class Viewer extends JFrame {
    ImagePanel viewer;
    JSlider brightSlider;
    JTextField brightField;
    float prevbright = (float)1.0;
    int count = 0;
    CropImage crp;
```

continued

```java
public Image loadImage(String filename){
    Image img = Toolkit.getDefaultToolkit().getImage(filename);
    try {
        MediaTracker tracker = new MediaTracker(this);
        tracker.addImage(img, 0);
        tracker.waitForID(0);
    } catch (Exception e) {return null;}
    return img;
}

public void loadAndDisplay(String filename){
    Image img = loadImage(filename);
    displayImage(img);
}

public void displayImage(Image img) {
    int width = img.getWidth(this);
    int height = img.getHeight(this);
    displayImage(img, width, height);
}

public void displayImage(Image img, int width, int height) {
    viewer = new ImagePanel(img, width, height);
    crp = new CropImage(viewer);
    viewer.setPreferredSize(new Dimension(width, height));
    JPanel bp = createBrightnessPanel();

    // Gridbag layout to add brightness panel and image panel.
        ...
    pack();
    setSize(new Dimension(width, height+80));
    show();
    viewer.repaint();
}

public JPanel createBrightnessPanel (){
    int minValue = 10;
    int maxValue =100;
    int brightStartValue = 75;
    brightField = new JTextField(5);
    brightField.setText(Integer.toString(brightStartValue));
    brightSlider = new JSlider(minValue,maxValue, brightStartValue);
    brightField.addActionListener(
        new ActionListener() {
            public void actionPerformed(ActionEvent e){
                try {
                    String str = ((JTextField)e.getSource()).getText();
                    int value = (Integer.valueOf(str)).intValue();
                    brightSlider.setValue((int)value);
                } catch (Exception e1){}
            }
        }
    );

    brightSlider.addChangeListener(
        new ChangeListener(){
            public void stateChanged(ChangeEvent e){
```

```
                    Object obj = e.getSource();
                    if(obj instanceof JSlider) {
                       JSlider jsr = (JSlider)obj;
                       int bright = ((JSlider)(e.getSource())).getValue();
                       brightField.setText(Integer.toString(bright));
                    }
                 }
               }
        );

        JButton apply = new JButton("Apply");
        apply.addActionListener(
           new ActionListener() {
               public void actionPerformed(ActionEvent e){
                  int value = brightSlider.getValue();
                  viewer.setBrightness(value);
               }
           }
        );

        JPanel brightpan = new JPanel();
             // Gridbag layout to add the components.
        return brightpan;
   }

   public static void  main(String[] args){
      Viewer ip = new Viewer();
      if(args.length <1){
         System.out.println("Enter a path name for the image ");
         System.exit(0);
      }
      ip.loadAndDisplay(args[0]);
   }
}
```

Here's a typical sequence of `Viewer` method calls:

1. A client object constructs an instance of `Viewer`. In this case the `main()` method itself performs this task.

2. The client object gets the path of the image file from the command line and calls `loadAndDisplay()`.

3. The `loadAndDisplay()` method first calls `loadImage()` to load an image and then calls `displayImage()` to display the loaded image.

4. The `displayImage()` method creates an `ImagePanel` object for displaying the image and a GUI for brightness adjustment. It also creates a `CropImage` object, which we'll see in the next section. After laying out the components, `displayImage()` launches the `Viewer` frame. `ImagePanel` displays the image.

5. The user adjusts the brightness slider and clicks on **Apply.** The corresponding event-handling method calls `ImagePanel`'s `setBrightness()` method (see Listing 3.4), which creates a new filtered image and displays it on the `ImagePanel` object.

The `createBrightnessPanel()` method creates a panel with a slider for adjusting the brightness values. As Figures 3.1 and 3.2 show, the **Apply** option is included so that the brightness value changes only when this option is selected. This option is needed because the brightness adjustment using the `BrightnessFilter` class is slow and the brightness adjustment cannot be done in real time. Real-time adjustment requires the use of lookup tables. See the section titled Adjusting Window and Level: An Example Using Lookup Tables in Chapter 8.

The `Viewer` class loads the image using the `MediaTracker` class. Unlike the image viewer in the preceding section, the image to be displayed is provided from the command line. To run this viewer, type "java Viewer imagepath" on the command line. Make sure that a JPEG or GIF image exists in the directory.

Figures 3.1 and 3.2 show low-brightness and high-brightness screen shots, respectively, of the viewer with the brightness control GUI.

© GSO Images/The Image Bank

FIGURE 3.1   The image viewer with low brightness setting

© GSO Images/The Image Bank

FIGURE 3.2   The image viewer with high brightness setting

Cropping Images Using CropImageFilter

You may have used the image-cropping feature offered by many image-editing packages. You can implement this feature very easily in Java. With the AWT, one way to implement this feature is to use the `CropImageFilter` class. Using this filter, you can cut an absolute rectangular region from the original image. `CropImageFilter`'s constructor takes dimensions of a rectangle as the input parameters.

Let's create a `CropImage` class to crop the image that is displayed on `ImagePanel`. In order for users to indicate the crop region, this class should be capable of interactively drawing a rectangular region over the image. This means that the `CropImage` class needs to capture the `mouse` and `mouseMotion` events. Listing 3.5 shows the code for `CropImage`.

LISTING 3.5   The CropImage class

```
public class CropImage implements  MouseListener,MouseMotionListener{
    ImagePanel imageCanvas;
    private Point diff = new Point(0,0);
    private Point shapeAnchor  = new Point(0,0);
    boolean mousePressed = false;
```

continued

```java
Rectangle currentShape, prevShape;
boolean cropped = false;
JMenuItem crop;

public CropImage(ImagePanel c){
   imageCanvas = c;
   imageCanvas.addMouseListener(this);
   imageCanvas.addMouseMotionListener(this);
}

public void startDraw(int x, int y) {
   shapeAnchor = new Point(x,y);
   diff = new Point(0,0);
}

public void draw(int x, int y) {
   if(cropped) return;
   diff.x = x - shapeAnchor.x;
   diff.y = y - shapeAnchor.y;
   int wid = diff.x;
   int ht = diff.y;
   Point ulhc = new Point(shapeAnchor);
   if(diff.x <0) {
      wid = -diff.x;
      ulhc.x = x;
   }
   if(diff.y <0){
      ht = -diff.y;
      ulhc.y = y;
   }
   currentShape = new Rectangle(ulhc.x, ulhc.y, wid, ht);
   Graphics g = imageCanvas.getDisplayedImageGC();
   g.setColor(Color.black);
   g.setXORMode(Color.white);
   if(prevShape != null)
      g.drawRect((int)prevShape.getX(), (int)prevShape.getY(),
               (int)prevShape.getWidth(), (int)prevShape.getHeight());
   if(currentShape != null)
      g.drawRect((int)currentShape.getX(), (int)currentShape.getY(),
               (int)currentShape.getWidth(), (int)currentShape.getHeight());
   prevShape = currentShape;
   imageCanvas.repaint();
}

public void mousePressed(MouseEvent e) {
   mousePressed = true;
   if(SwingUtilities.isLeftMouseButton(e)){
      startDraw(e.getX(), e.getY());
   }else {
      popupMenu((JComponent)e.getSource(), e.getX(), e.getY());
   }
}

public void mouseReleased(MouseEvent e) {
   if(!mousePressed) return;
   if(SwingUtilities.isLeftMouseButton(e)){
      System.out.println("released");
      draw(e.getX(), e.getY());
```

```
          prevShape = null;
      }
      mousePressed = false;
  }

  public void mouseClicked(MouseEvent e){}
  public void mouseEntered(MouseEvent e){}
  public void mouseExited(MouseEvent e){}

  public void mouseDragged(MouseEvent e){
     if(cropped) return;
     if(SwingUtilities.isLeftMouseButton(e)){
         draw(e.getX(), e.getY());
     }
  }
  public void mouseMoved(MouseEvent e){}

  protected void popupMenu(JComponent comp,int x, int y){
     JPopupMenu jp = new JPopupMenu("");
     jp.setLightWeightPopupEnabled(true);
     comp.add(jp);
     crop = new JMenuItem("Crop");
     crop.addActionListener(
        new ActionListener(){
          public void actionPerformed(ActionEvent e){
             if(cropped) return;
             CropImageFilter crf = new CropImageFilter((int)currentShape.getX(),
                                              (int)currentShape.getY(),
                                              (int)currentShape.getWidth(),
                                              (int)currentShape.
                                              getHeight());
             FilteredImageSource fis = new
             FilteredImageSource(imageCanvas.getImage().getSource(),crf);
             Image img = Toolkit.getDefaultToolkit().createImage(fis);
             imageCanvas.drawImage(img;
                           (int)currentShape.getX(),
                           (int)currentShape.getY() );
              cropped =true;
              crop.setEnabled(false);
          }
        }
     );
     JMenuItem reset = new JMenuItem("Reset");
     reset.addActionListener(
        new ActionListener(){
          public void actionPerformed(ActionEvent e){
             imageCanvas.resetImage();
             cropped = false;
             crop.setEnabled(true);
          }
        }
     );

     jp.add(crop);
     jp.add(reset);
     jp.show(comp,x,y);
  }
}
```

Here's a typical sequence of `CropImage` method calls:

1. A client object constructs the `CropImage` object. In the example described in the preceding section, `Viewer` is the client object.

2. The client object registers the `CropImage` object for receiving mouse and mouse motion `mouse` and `mouseMotion` events. In the `Viewer` example, the `Viewer` class registers `CropImage` with `ImagePanel` for receiving the `mouse` and `mouseMotion` events from `ImagePanel`.

3. The user left-clicks on the object and drags it. The `mouse` and `mouseMotion` events are received by the `mousePressed()` and `mouseDragged()` methods, respectively. These methods call `draw()` to draw a rectangle interactively.

4. The user right-clicks on the object. The `mousePressed()` method calls `popupMenu()` to launch a pop-up menu.

5. The user selects the **Crop** menu item. Its event-handling method crops the image along the rectangle drawn by the user and creates a new filtered image. The `drawImage()` method is called to draw this image.

6. The user clicks on the **Reset** menu item. Its event-handling method calls `resetImage()` to restore the original image.

Now let's look at the `CropImage` class in detail. When the user clicks on the image and drags it, a rectangle is drawn over the image. To crop the image, first right-click on it to launch the pop-up menu. This menu has two items: **Crop** and **Reset.** If you select **Crop,** the image within the rectangular region is cropped. To get back the original image, click on **Reset.**

To enable users to interactively draw rectangles over the image, the `CropImage` class implements both the `MouseListener` and the `MouseMotionListener` interfaces. The constructor of the `CropImage` class takes `ImagePanel` as the input. In the constructor, the `CropImage` object registers itself with `ImagePanel` to receive both `mouse` and `mouseMotion` events. When the user clicks on or drags the mouse over `ImagePanel`, `CropImage` receives the event through `mousePressed()` or `mouseDragged()`, respectively.

When the left mouse button is pressed, the rectangle begins being drawn. When the mouse is dragged, the `mouseDragged()` method invokes the `draw()` method, which erases the previous rectangle and draws a new one.

Right-clicking on `ImagePanel` launches the pop-up menu, and the `popupMenu()` method creates two menu items: **Crop** and **Reset.** In this method, action events for these menu items are captured. Clicking on the **Crop** menu item invokes the crop-related `actionPerformed()` method in `popUpMenu`'s anonymous inner class. The `actionPerformed()` method creates a `CropImageFilter` object from the currently drawn rectangle on the image. Through this object and the image source, a cropped image is created by use of the `FilteredImageSource` class. This `CropImage` object is

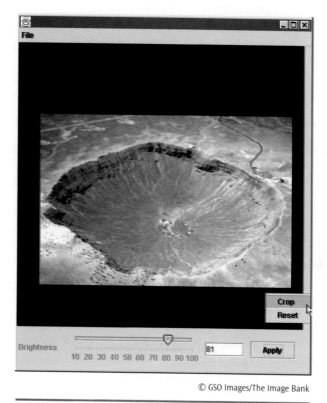

© GSO Images/The Image Bank

FIGURE 3.3 Cropping an image

drawn on `ImagePanel` by invocation of `ImagePanel`'s `drawImage()` method. Note that `drawImage()` takes the upper left-hand corner (UHLC) coordinates as input arguments. This is to enable the cropped image to remain at the same position as in the original image; otherwise it is drawn at the ULHC coordinates of `ImagePanel`.

The `Viewer` class in the preceding section instantiated the `CropImage` object with `ImagePanel` as the input parameter. This viewer uses both the `BrightnessFilter` and the `CropImage` classes, so you can crop an image and adjust its brightness. Figure 3.3 shows the cropped image and the pop-up menu.

Printing

Just like displaying images, printing is also a rendering operation, which is performed on a printer's `Graphics` context. Implementing printing in a platform-independent manner is harder mainly because a large variety of printers have proprietary printing formats. That is one of the primary reasons that JDK 1.0 had no printing capabilities. Even in JDK 1.1, printing support is minimal.

Overview of the Printing API

The `java.awt.PrintJob` class is the main class that controls printing in JDK 1.1. You cannot construct it directly because it is an abstract class. The actual `PrintJob` object is obtained in a platform-dependent manner through a factory method in the `Toolkit` class. Here's the method:

```
public PrintJob getPrintJob(Frame frame, String jobtitle, Properties props)
```

As the signature shows, the `getPrintJob()` method requires a `Frame` object as an input parameter. If your program doesn't have one, you may have to construct a dummy `Frame` object. The `props` parameter contains printing attributes that are sent to the underlying printing mechanism.

These properties are not standardized and are not consistent across implementations. Here are some of the property names and their values:

- `awt.print.destination`: the destination: either "printer" or "file"
- `awt.print.printer`: the name of the printer
- `awt.print.fileName`: the name of the file to print
- `awt.print.numCopies`: the number of copies to be printed
- `awt.print.options`: options such as in UNIX, if allowed
- `awt.print.orientation`: the orientation of the print: either "portrait" or "landscape"
- `awt.print.paperSize`: the size of the paper: "letter," "legal," "executive," or "A4"

The default values of the print properties are as follows:

- `awt.print.destination` = "printer"
- `awt.print.orientation` = "portrait"
- `awt.print.paperSize` = "letter"
- `awt.print.numCopies` = 1

The `PrintJob` class has the following methods:

- **`public Graphics getGraphics()`**
  This method returns a `Graphics` context for the printer. This object implements the `PrintGraphics` interface. To print an image (or any other `Graphics` object), you need to draw it on this `Graphics` context

- **`public Dimension getPageDimension()`**
  This method returns the page dimension in pixels. The value is similar to screen dimension.

- **public int getPageResolution()**

  This method returns the print resolution in pixels per inch.

- **public boolean lastPageFirst()**

  This method returns **true** if the last page is printed first.

- **public abstract void end()**

  This method ends printing. It also cleans up and reclaims resources.

  The **PrintGraphics** interface has one method:

- **public PrintJob getPrintJob()**

Printing a Component

The **Component** class has the **print()** method for printing a component. The code for printing a component is as follows:

```
PrintJob pr =
            Toolkit.getDefaultToolkit().getPrintJob(appFrame, "Print", null);
printComponent(pr, this);
```

The **PrintJob** object is constructed first.

```
public void printComponent( PrintJob prj, Component comp) {
   Graphics printG = prj.getGraphics();
   if(printG == null) return;
   printG.setColor(Color.black);
   comp.print(printG);
   printG.dispose();
   pr.end();
}
```

A print dialog box is launched after the **PrintJob** object has been constructed. Upon clicking **OK** on this dialog box, a **Graphics** object is returned. The component is rendered on that object. When the **dispose()** method is called, the actual printing takes place.

Printing an Image

As we saw in the previous section, the **PrintJob** object is created with a **Graphics** context for the destination printer. To render an image to the printer, all you need to do is to draw the image on this **Graphics** context. You can use the same **drawImage()** methods that are used for rendering images onto a display monitor. If you want the image to be printed in the same way that it is displayed, you can call the paint methods—**paint()**, **update()**, **paintComponent()**, and so on—with the **Graphics** object obtained from **PrintJob**. With this approach, the rendering program doesn't need to know where an image is rendered. The `printImage()` method shown in Listing 3.6 illustrates how to print images displayed on an `ImageCanvas` object (see Listing 3.1).

LISTING 3.6   Printing an image

```
protected void printImage(ImageCanvas  viewer) {
    java.util.Properties pr = new java.util.Properties();
    pr.put("awt.print.orientation", "landscape");
    pr.put("awt.print.numCopies", new Integer(2));
    PrintJob pj = Toolkit.getDefaultToolkit().getPrintJob(this, "Print", pr);
    Graphics printG = pj.getGraphics();
    if(printG==null) return;
    viewer.paint(printG);
    printG.dispose();
    pj.end();
}
```

Putting It All Together: An Image Viewer Applet and Application

The applet described in this section can display multiple images and extract basic statistics from them. This applet has been designed in such a way that it can be run also as an application. When running as an application, it can display images from a named JAR file as well. This applet uses the image-loading classes we developed in Chapter 2.

> **Note:** The complete source code for the image viewer is available on book's Web page in the directory `src/chapter3/viewer`.

Running the Image Viewer as an Applet

To run the image viewer as an applet, type "appletviewer imviewer.html" on the command line. Figure 3.4 shows a screen shot of the applet. You can also run this applet from a Web browser.

Here's the HTML driver file:

```
<center><applet code="ImageViewerApplet.class" archive="viewer.jar,im.jar" width="100"
                    height="100">
<param name="imagesource" value="im.jar">
<param name="imagenames"
value="T1.gif,T2.gif,T3.gif,T4.gif,T5.gif,T6.gif,T7.gif,T8.gif,T9.gif,T10.gif,T11.gif,
     T12.gif,T13.gif,T14.gif,T15.gif">
</applet></center>
```

The images are in the `im.jar` file.

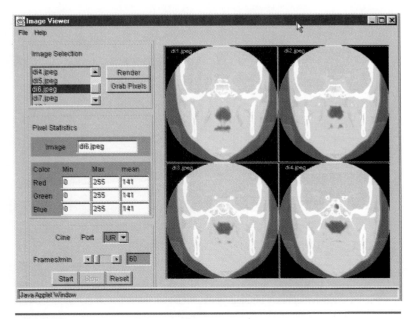

FIGURE 3.4   The image viewer running as an applet

Running the Image Viewer as an Application

To run the image viewer as an application, type "java ImageViewerApplet <image jar file>" on the command line. Before you run this as an application, make sure that the image JAR file is in the class path. In Windows platforms, one way to do this is as follows:

```
set classpath=c:\awl\im.jar;%classpath%
```

To start the application, type "java ImageViewerApplet c:\awl\im.jar". Figure 3.5 shows a screen shot of the application.

Design and Implementation

First let's enumerate the applet requirements. The applet must have the capability to

◆ Load multiple images
◆ Display multiple images
◆ Calculate pixel statistics
◆ Run images in an animation (cine) loop

Let the main applet class be `ImageViewerApplet`. Instead of implementing all the functions in this class, we'll delegate tasks to different classes. The `CommandPanel` class

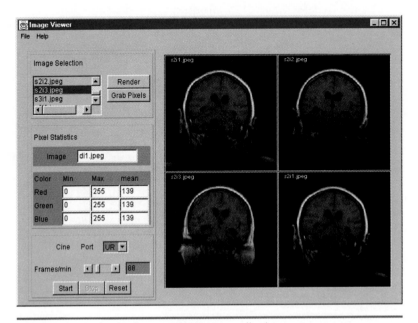

FIGURE 3.5   The image viewer running as an application

will create the GUI. The cine animation loop needs to be performed in a thread. The `Cine` class will perform the cine operation. We'll also reuse the classes we developed in this chapter, as well as the ones we developed in Chapter 2.

The classes used by this applet are as follows:

◆ **ImageViewerApplet.** This is the main applet class. Its inner classes are

   ◆ **Loader,** which loads images using the `ImageLoader` class

   ◆ **ImageStats,** which computes statistics

◆ **CommandPanel.** This class creates the image selection and statistics panel.

◆ **Cine.** This class creates the cine panel and runs a separate thread for the cine loop.

◆ **AppFrame.** This class creates a skeleton application frame.

The applet reuses the following classes developed in this chapter or in Chapter 2:

◆ **ImageCanvas.** This class displays images.

◆ **ImageLoader.** This class loads images.

◆ **ImageBuffer.** This class holds image data in memory.

The applet also uses an interface called `DisplayController`.

The DisplayController Interface

The `DisplayController` interface, which is shown in Listing 3.7, is needed to implement the callback mechanism between the delegate objects and the main applet. The `ImageViewerApplet` class implements this interface. The `CommandPanel` and `Cine` classes have an instance variable of type `DisplayController` and a method called `registerForDisplayCallback()` to set it. When `CommandPanel` and `Cine` are created by the `ImageViewerApplet` class, `ImageViewerApplet` calls `registerForDisplay Callback()` by passing itself as the `DisplayController` object. When an event occurs, the `CommandPanel` and `Cine` objects call an appropriate `DisplayController` method. By creating the `DisplayController` interface, we eliminate the circular dependency. Moreover, because of their nondependence, both `Cine` and `CommandPanel` can be reused elsewhere.

LISTING 3.7   The `DisplayController` interface

```
public interface DisplayController{
    public void displayImage(int id);
    public void loadPixels(int id);
    public void quit();

    public int getCinePortNum();
    public void setCinePort(int num);
    public void cineDispImage();
    public void cineReset();
}
```

Displaying Images

The main purpose of `ImageViewerApplet` is to display images, which it does through the `ImageCanvas` class (see Listing 3.1). It delegates the tasks of image loading and statistics computation to other objects. It uses the `ImageLoader` class to load images and the `ImageBuffer` class to hold them in memory.

The applet GUI is not embedded within the Web. Instead it is a frame that is launched from a Web page. Listing 3.8 shows the code for `ImageViewerApplet.`

LISTING 3.8   The `ImageViewerApplet` class

```
import java.io.*;
import java.awt.*;
import java.awt.image.*;
import java.net.URL;
import java.net.MalformedURLException;
import java.util.*;
import java.applet.*;
import java.util.zip.*;

public class ImageViewerApplet extends Applet implements Runnable,
                    DisplayController {
```

continued

```java
static int MAX_IMAGES = 6,MAX_CINE_IMAGES = 10 ;
static int MAX_LOAD_IMAGES = 4, MAX_IMAGECANVAS = 4;
static final int RED =  1, GREEN =  2, BLUE = 3, ALPHA = 4;
static final int JAR = 1, LOCAL_DIR = 2;
static int vpWid = 400, vpHt = 400;
static int cpWid = 256, cpHt  = vpHt;
static int viewerWid = vpWid+cpWid +30;
static int viewerHt = vpHt+95;

private AppFrame viewerPanel;
private CommandPanel commandPanel;
private Panel canvasPanel = new Panel();

private URL dir = null;
private Thread mainThread;
private ImageLoader  scnImage[] = new ImageLoader[MAX_CINE_IMAGES];
private ImageBuffer curDispImage;
private ImageCanvas Screen[] = new ImageCanvas[MAX_IMAGECANVAS];
private ImageCanvas curScreen;

private int numImages=0;
private Hashtable imageTable = new Hashtable();
private int curVpNum =0, curImageNum =0;
private boolean grabPixelsOn = false;

private ImageCanvas cineVp;
private int cinePortNum = 0, cineIndex =0, numCineImages =0;
private boolean notAllLoaded = false;
private int appWid, appHt;
private String[] fileList;
protected int loadMethod = JAR;
private String path = "images/";
private Loader loader;

public void init() {
    String param = null;
    URL url = null;
    try {
       param = getParameter("IMAGENAMES");
       getFilesFromHTML(param);
       param = getParameter("IMAGESOURCE");
       dir = (param == null) ? getDocumentBase() : new URL(getDocumentBase(),
            param );
       param = getParameter("WIDTH");
       appWid = Integer.valueOf(param).intValue();
       param = getParameter("HEIGHT");
       appHt = Integer.valueOf(param).intValue();
       initApp();
    } catch (MalformedURLException e) {}
}

public void getFilesFromHTML(String param){
    StringTokenizer st = new StringTokenizer(param, ",");
    int size = st.countTokens();
    if(size <=0) return;
    fileList = new String[size];
    int i=0;
```

```
       while(st.hasMoreTokens()) fileList[i++] = st.nextToken();
       numImages = fileList.length;
   }

   private void initApp(){
       createUI();
       initScreen();
       setCinePort(1);
       Loader loader = new Loader();
       numCineImages = (numImages > MAX_CINE_IMAGES) ? MAX_CINE_IMAGES: numImages;
       mainThread = new Thread(this);
   }

   private void initScreen(){
       curVpNum = 0;
       curScreen = Screen[curVpNum];
       commandPanel.registerForDisplayCallback(this);
       curScreen.createOffScrImage();
   }

   public void createUI(){
       viewerPanel = new AppFrame(viewerWid, viewerHt);
       viewerPanel.setTitle("Image Viewer");
       commandPanel = new CommandPanel(cpWid, cpHt, fileList);
       commandPanel.cinePanel.registerForDisplayCallback(this);
       GridBagLayout     gb = new GridBagLayout() ;
       GridBagConstraints c = new GridBagConstraints();
       viewerPanel.setLayout(gb);
       viewerPanel.setBackground(Color.lightGray);
       viewerPanel.setForeground(Color.black);

       createCanvasPanel();
       c.gridheight = 1; c.weighty = 0.0; c.weightx = 0.0;
       c.insets = new Insets(10,10, 0,10);
       c.gridwidth = 1;

       gb.setConstraints(commandPanel,c);
       viewerPanel.add(commandPanel);
       c.gridwidth = GridBagConstraints.REMAINDER;
       c.insets = new Insets(10,5, 10,10);
       c.gridheight = 1; c.weighty = 0.0; c.weightx = 0.0;
       gb.setConstraints(canvasPanel,c);
       viewerPanel.add(canvasPanel);
       viewerPanel.pack();
       viewerPanel.setSize(viewerWid, viewerHt);
       viewerPanel.show();
   }

   public void createCanvasPanel(){
       canvasPanel.setLayout(new GridLayout(2,2));
       canvasPanel.setBackground(Color.lightGray);
       for(int i=0;i<MAX_IMAGECANVAS;i++){
           Screen[i] =  new ImageCanvas(vpWid/2, vpHt/2);
           Screen[i].setBackground(Color.black);
           canvasPanel.add(Screen[i]);
       }
   }
```

continued

```
public void start(){ mainThread.start();}

public void run() { loader.loadImages(); }

public void quit(){ viewerPanel.dispose();}

public void displayImage(int num){
   if(num <0 || num >= numImages) return;
   ImageLoader img = (ImageLoader)imageTable.get(Integer.toString(num));
   if(img == null){
      if(loader.loadAnImage(num)){
         img = (ImageLoader)imageTable.get(Integer.toString(num));
      }
   } else {displayImage(img.getImageBuffer());}
}

public synchronized void displayImage(ImageBuffer img) {
   curDispImage = img;
   curScreen = Screen[(curVpNum++)%MAX_IMAGECANVAS];
   curScreen.setImageBuffer(curDispImage);
   curScreen.imagePaint();
   curImageNum = img.imageId;
}


public int getCinePortNum(){ return cinePortNum;}

public void setCinePort(int portNum){
   cineVp = Screen[portNum];
   cinePortNum = portNum;
}

public void cineDispImage(){
   if(cineVp == null) return;
   if(!notAllLoaded){
      if(scnImage[cineIndex] == null){
         ImageLoader im = new ImageLoader();
         if(loadMethod == LOCAL_DIR){
            URL url = null;
            im.setFileInfo(path, fileList[cineIndex], cineIndex);
            im.load();
         } else {
             im.jarLoad(fileList[cineIndex], cineIndex);
         }
         scnImage[cineIndex] = im;
         scnImage[cineIndex].prepareImage();
         cineIndex++;
         if((cineIndex % numCineImages) ==0) cineIndex =0;
      } else {
         if(loader.checkAllLoaded()) notAllLoaded = true;
         if((cineIndex % numCineImages) ==0) cineIndex =0;
      }
   }else{
      if((scnImage[cineIndex].loadStatus &
         (ImageLoadedListener.ERRORED |ImageLoadedListener.ABORTED)) ==0){
        cineVp.cineDraw(scnImage[cineIndex].getImageBuffer());
      }
```

```
                                            ==0) cineIndex =0;
```

```
                                       resetDisplay();
```

```
                                       geLoader(id);
                                       ;();
```

```
                                     S;i++) loadPixels(i);
```

Here's a typical sequence of **ImageViewerApplet** method calls:

applet link.

system calls the **init()** method, which performs initializa-
the application, including

e names from the **IMAGENAMES** parameter by calling

geometric parameters.

ich is done in conjunction with creation of the
anel, and **Cine** objects. As Figure 3.4 shows, the GUI has
command panel. It registers with the **CommandPanel** and
back.

object.

hread object.

system calls the **start()** method, which calls **mainThread's**

scheduler calls the **run()** method, which in turn calls the
dImages() method. The **loadImage()** method loads a set of
images and the maximum number of images that can be loaded at
one time is determined by the constant **MAX_LOAD_IMAGES**. When an image is
loaded, the **imageLoaded** event is received by the **imageLoaded()** method. The
loaded images are saved in a hash table. The **imageLoaded()** method also calls
displayImage() to display the loaded image.

5. The **displayImage()** method displays the image on a viewport pointed to by the
variable **curVpNum**, which is incremented every time an image is displayed.

When the value of curVpNum reaches 4, it is set to zero again so that the next image is displayed on the first viewport.

6. The user selects an image and clicks on **Render.** The corresponding event-handling method in the CommandPanel object calls the displayImage() method.

7. The user selects an image and clicks on **Grab Pixels.** The corresponding event-handling method in the CommandPanel object calls the loadPixels() method. This method creates a new ImageStats object and calls ImageStats's loadPixels() method, which computes and displays the pixel statistics.

If you add the code shown in Listing 3.9 to the ImageViewerApplet class, the image viewer can be run as an application.

LISTING 3.9   Running the image viewer as an application

```
public static void main(String argv[]){
    ImageViewerApplet viewer = new ImageViewerApplet();
    if(argv.length >=1) {
        viewer.initApplication(argv[0]);
    } else {
        viewer.initApplication();
    }
}

public void initApplication(String jarfile){
    loader = new Loader();
    if(jarfile != null) loader.listFilesInJar(jarfile);
    if(fileList == null) initApplication();
    else {
        initApp();
        loader.loadImages();
    }
}
  public void initApplication(){
    loader = new Loader();
    loadMethod = LOCAL_DIR;
    path = new String("images/");
    File imgDir= new File(path);
    loader.readFiles(imgDir);
    initApp();
    loader.loadImages();
}
```

Loading Images

The Loader class uses the classes and interfaces developed in this chapter and in Chapter 2. It can load images from a JAR file or from a local directory. Listing 3.10 shows how multiple images are loaded. Loader implements the ImageLoadedListener interface.

LISTING 3.10 The Loader class

```java
class Loader implements ImageLoadedListener{

    public void readFiles(File dir){
        if(!dir.exists()) return;
        ExtensionFilter gifFilter = new ExtensionFilter("gif,jpeg,jpg,JPG,JPEG,GIF");
        fileList = dir.list(gifFilter);
        if(fileList == null) return;
        numImages = fileList.length;
    }

    public void loadImages(){
        for(int i=0;i<MAX_LOAD_IMAGES;i++) loadAnImage(i);
        try{
            mainThread.sleep(50);
        }catch(InterruptedException e){}
    }

    private boolean loadAnImage(int num){
        ImageLoader im = new ImageLoader();
        im.addImageLoadedListener(this);
        imageTable.put(Integer.toString(num), im);
        if(loadMethod == JAR) im.jarLoad(fileList[num],num);
        if(loadMethod == LOCAL_DIR) {
            im.setFileInfo(path, fileList[num], num);
            im.load();
        }
        return true;
    }

    public void imageLoaded(ImageLoadedEvent e){
        int status = e.getLoadStatus();
        ImageLoader il = (ImageLoader)e.getSource();

        ImageBuffer img = (ImageBuffer)il.getImageBuffer();
        if((status & ImageLoadedListener.IMAGE_READY) != 0){
            if((img.imageId) >=0 && (img.imageId) < numImages){
                displayImage(img);
                il.removeImageLoadedListener(this);
            }
        }
    }

    public ImageLoader getImageLoader(int id) {
        ImageLoader il = (ImageLoader)imageTable.get(Integer.toString(id));
        if(il != null) return il;
        il = new ImageLoader();
        imageTable.put(Integer.toString(id), il);
        if(loadMethod == LOCAL_DIR){
            il.setFileInfo(path, fileList[id], id);
            il.load();
        } else {
            il.jarLoad(fileList[id],id);
        }
        return il;
    }
```

continued

```java
public boolean checkAllLoaded(){
    int status = ImageLoadedListener.IMAGE_READY;
    for(int i=0;i<numCineImages;i++){
        if((scnImage[i].loadStatus & (ImageLoadedListener.ERRORED
            |ImageLoadedListener.ABORTED)) ==0){
            status &= scnImage[i].loadStatus & ImageLoadedListener.IMAGE_READY;
        }
    }
    if((status & ImageLoadedListener.IMAGE_READY) != 0)return true;
    return false;
}

public void listFilesInJar(URL url){ listFilesInJar(url.getFile());}

public void listFilesInJar(String file){
    try {
    ZipFile zipf = new ZipFile(new File(file));
    String filter[] = {"jpeg", "jpg", "JPEG", "JPG", "gif", "GIF"};
    fileList = listJarEntries(zipf, filter);
    numImages = fileList.length;
    System.out.println(numImages);
    } catch (Exception e) {
      System.out.println(e);
    }
}
public String[] listJarEntries(ZipFile jarfile, String[] filter){
    String fileList[] = null;
    try{
        Vector list = new Vector();
        for(Enumeration e = jarfile.entries(); e.hasMoreElements();){
            String name = ((ZipEntry)e.nextElement()).getName();
            if(filterFileNames(name,filter))
                list.addElement(name);
        }
        fileList = new String[list.size()];
        list.copyInto(fileList);
    } catch (Exception e){
      System.out.println("Jar file reading exception "+ e);}
    return fileList;
}

public boolean filterFileNames(String name, String filter[]){
    if(filter == null) return true;
    for(int i=0; i< filter.length;i++){
        if(name.endsWith(filter[i])) return true;
    }
    return false;
}
}
```

Because the `Loader` class is an inner class of the `ImageViewerApplet` class, it has access to all the methods and variables of `ImageViewerApplet`. When the enclosing object (i.e., `ImageViewerApplet`) calls `loadImages()`, the loading process begins. The `loadImages()` method calls `loadAnImage()` for each of the images in the `fileList` array.

The `loadAnImage()` method creates an `ImageLoader` object for each of the images. `Loader` registers itself with each `ImageLoader` object to receive the `imageLoaded` event. The `ImageLoader` object is then saved in a hash table. If the image is being loaded from a JAR file (i.e., if the value of `loadMethod` is `JAR`), `ImageLoader`'s `jarLoad()` method is called; otherwise `load()` is called.

Whenever the user clicks on an image in the list, the `displayImage(int)` method in `ImageViewerApplet` is called. This method checks the hash table in which the `ImageLoader` objects have been stored to see whether the selected image has already been loaded. If so, the image is displayed; otherwise the selected image is loaded by `loadAnImage()`.

The `readFiles()` and `listFilesInJar()` methods are called by the `init Application()` method.

Running the Cine Loop

You can run the cine (movie) loop in any of the four viewports. You can switch the port by selecting the appropriate port in the cine panel combo box. The `Cine` object is created by `ImageViewerApplet`, which registers itself for callback. The `Cine` object calls the `cineDispImage()` method to display images at regular intervals. This means that images are actually displayed by `ImageViewerApplet` itself. `ImageViewer Applet` calls the `cineReset()` method to start all over again. Listing 3.11 shows the code for `Cine`.

LISTING 3.11   The Cine class

```java
import java.io.*;
import java.awt.*;
import java.awt.event.*;
import java.util.Vector;
import java.util.Hashtable;
import java.lang.Math;
public class Cine extends Panel implements Runnable{
    static int startValue = 60,minCycles = 20,maxCycles = 360;
    protected   int frameDelay;
    private Scrollbar frameSlider;
    private TextField frameValueField;
    private Button startButton,stopButton, resetButton;
    protected boolean startStop = true;
    private Choice cinePort;
    protected int curCinePortNum =1;
    protected DisplayController vpMgr;
    protected int width, height;
    private Thread cineThread;

    public  Cine(int wd, int hgt){
      width = wd; height = hgt;
      createUI();
      setSize(width, height);
```

continued

```java
        initCine();
        cineThread = new Thread(this);
    }

    private  void createUI() {
        GridBagLayout     gb = new GridBagLayout() ;
        GridBagConstraints c = new GridBagConstraints();
        setLayout(gb);
        setBackground(Color.lightGray);

        c.gridheight = 1; c.weighty = 1.0; c.weightx = 1.0;
        c.gridwidth = GridBagConstraints.REMAINDER;
        c.insets = new Insets(5,5, 5,5);
        Panel selPanel = new Panel();
        Label cinePanelLabel = new Label("Cine", Label.LEFT);
        Label cineLabel = new Label("Port", Label.LEFT);
        cinePort = new Choice();
        cinePort.setBackground(Color.gray);
        cinePort.addItem("UL");
        cinePort.addItem("UR");
        cinePort.addItem("BL");
        cinePort.addItem("BR");
        cinePort.addItemListener(
        new ItemListener() {
            public void itemStateChanged(ItemEvent e){
                int portNum = ((Choice)(e.getSource())).getSelectedIndex();
                if(portNum != vpMgr.getCinePortNum()){
                    curCinePortNum = portNum;
                    vpMgr.setCinePort(curCinePortNum);
                }
                else cinePort.select(curCinePortNum);
            }
          }
        );
        selPanel.add(cinePanelLabel);
        selPanel.add(cineLabel);
        cinePort.select(1);

        selPanel.add(cinePort);
        gb.setConstraints(selPanel, c);
        add(selPanel);
        c.gridwidth = 1; c.weightx = 0.0;
        Label frameLabel= new Label("Frames/min", Label.LEFT);
        c.fill = GridBagConstraints.HORIZONTAL;
        gb.setConstraints(frameLabel, c);
        add(frameLabel);

        frameSlider = new Scrollbar(Scrollbar.HORIZONTAL,
                                startValue,1,minCycles,maxCycles);
        frameSlider.addAdjustmentListener(
          new AdjustmentListener(){
            public void adjustmentValueChanged(AdjustmentEvent e){
                int sliderVal = frameSlider.getValue();
                        frameDelay = (int)(100000/(1+(int)(sliderVal*10/6)));
                frameValueField.setText(Integer.toString(sliderVal));
            }
          }
        );
```

```java
c.weightx = 1.0;
gb.setConstraints(frameSlider, c);
add(frameSlider);

frameValueField  = new  TextField(Integer.toString(startValue),3);
frameValueField.setBackground(Color.gray);
c.gridwidth = GridBagConstraints.REMAINDER;
c.weightx = 0.0;
gb.setConstraints(frameValueField, c);
add(frameValueField);
c.fill = GridBagConstraints.NONE;
Panel reportBtns= new Panel();
reportBtns.setLayout(new GridLayout(1,3));
startButton = new Button("Start");
startButton.addActionListener(
   new ActionListener(){
      public void actionPerformed(ActionEvent e){
         if (startStop == false) return;
         startButton.setEnabled(false);
         stopButton.setEnabled(true);
         if(cineThread == null){
            cineThread = new Thread(Cine.this);
         }
         if(cineThread.isAlive() ==true){
            cineThread = new Thread(Cine.this);
         }
         cineThread.start();
         startStop = false;
      }
   }
);
stopButton = new Button("Stop");
stopButton.addActionListener(
  new ActionListener(){
    public void actionPerformed(ActionEvent e){
       if (startStop == true) return;
       startButton.setEnabled(true);
       stopButton.setEnabled(false);
       cineThread.stop();
       cineThread = new Thread(Cine.this);
       startStop = true;
    }
  }
);

resetButton = new Button("Reset");
resetButton.addActionListener(
  new ActionListener(){
    public void actionPerformed(ActionEvent e){
       reset();
       cineThread = new Thread(Cine.this);
    }
  }
);
reportBtns.add(startButton);
reportBtns.add(stopButton);
reportBtns.add(resetButton);
```

continued

```java
        gb.setConstraints(reportBtns, c);
        add(reportBtns);
    }

    private void initCine(){
        frameDelay = (int)(100000/(1+(int)(startValue*10/6)));
        frameSlider.setValue(startValue);
        frameValueField.setText(Integer.toString(startValue));
        stopButton.setEnabled(false);
        startButton.setEnabled(true);
        startStop =true;
    }


    public void run(){
        while(true){
            try{
              vpMgr.cineDispImage();
              if(frameDelay <10) frameDelay =10;
              cineThread.sleep(frameDelay);
            } catch (InterruptedException e){}
        }
    }

    public void registerForDisplayCallback(DisplayController callbackObj){
        vpMgr = callbackObj;
    }

    public void stopCine(){
        if (startStop == true) return;
        stopButton.setEnabled(false);
        startButton.setEnabled(true);
        cineThread.stop();
        cineThread = new Thread(this);
        startStop = true;
    }

    public void reset(){
        if(cineThread != null)
        if(cineThread.isAlive() ==true)cineThread.stop();
        initCine();
        vpMgr.cineReset();
    }
}
```

The Cine class creates the GUI panel for the cine feature. Note that Cine implements the Runnable interface, which makes Cine a thread. A separate thread is necessary to control the rate at which the image is displayed.

The run() method is called when the thread starts running. As Listing 3.11 shows, the thread runs an infinite loop. To control the rate at which the image is displayed, the run() method introduces a delay between two displays. This delay is calculated from the frame rate selected by the user. To display an image, the run() method calls ImageViewerApplet's cineDispImage() method (see Listing 3.8).

The `initCine()` method starts the thread, and the `stopCine()` method stops it. Note that `stopCine()` calls the `cineThread.stop()` method. The `cineThread.stop()` method is a deprecated method in Java 2; it has been determined unsafe because it unlocks all the monitors that a thread has locked. To stop a thread, you can create a flag (such as `stop`) that can be set to `false` in `initCine()` and `true` in `stopCine()`. You can check the status of this flag in the `run()` method's `while` loop. When it becomes `true`, the `run()` method will exit, terminating the thread. Here's an example:

```
public void run(){
    while(!stop){
        try{
            if(vpMgr != null) vpMgr.cineDispImage();
            if(frameDelay <10) frameDelay =10;
            cineThread.sleep(frameDelay);
        } catch (InterruptedException e){}
    }
}
```

Because the `CommandPanel` and `AppFrame` classes have only user interface-related code, their code is not shown.

Conclusion

Although image rendering may appear simple, it often involves complex operations. This is especially true in scientific imaging applications because images used in such applications are often acquired through complex processes.

In this chapter we covered a variety of topics related to image rendering and provided numerous examples written with JDK 1.1. The Java 2D API is a significant improvement over earlier versions of Java. It is based on entirely different imaging models that are well suited for scientific imaging applications such as medical imaging.

PART II

Java 2D

The Basics of Java 2D Graphics

4

WE'LL START THE JAVA 2D part of this book with an introduction to a number of topics on graphics. The main focus of this chapter is the `java.awt.geom` package, which is an entirely new package introduced in Java 2. This package has APIs for describing shapes and performing graphics-related mathematical functions.

We'll begin this chapter with a discussion of coordinate systems. We'll then discuss some basics of graphics involving curves. A description of the shape APIs will follow. Because affine transformations are used in many of the Java 2D and JAI chapters, we'll explain the mathematics behind them and then look at the `AffineTransform` class in detail.

Application Coordinate Systems

It is important to understand the coordinate systems before we describe the rendering model. In graphics and imaging, different types of coordinate systems are in use. For instance, geographic information system (GIS) applications typically use spherical coordinate systems; that is, geography is represented by longitude and latitude (see Figure 4.1). In medical imaging, image geometry is represented by patient coordinate systems (see Figure 4.2):

- **RL:** right to left
- **AP:** anterior to posterior (i.e., front to back of the patient)
- **SI:** superior to inferior (i.e., head to legs)

These coordinate systems can be described in different units, such as degrees, millimeters, and so on. To render images or graphics within a particular device, graphical systems typically normalize the application coordinate system. The Java 2D APIs do not support any application-specific coordinate systems. However, they maintain two types of device coordinate systems: user space and device space.

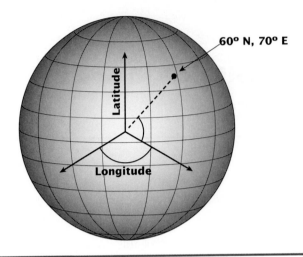

FIGURE 4.1   The GIS coordinate system

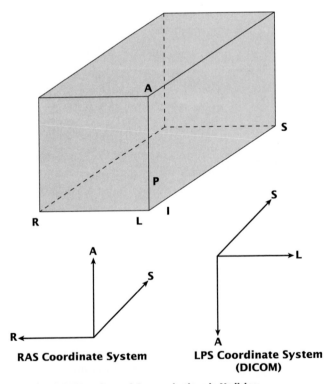

FIGURE 4.2   The patient coordinate system

Device Coordinate Systems

Different devices maintain different coordinate systems. For example, the coordinate system a printer uses may be different from the one a monitor uses. Thus, to render the same geometry to any device without referencing the device in the application, we need an independent coordinate system.

User Space

User space is an independent coordinate system. Geometry in Java 2D is defined in this space. In other words, input parameters that represent geometry are represented in the user space. This coordinate system is device independent. The origin is located at the upper left-hand corner of the viewing space. As shown in Figure 4.3, the x-axis is horizontal and the y-axis vertical to the viewing space. Values increase from left to right on the x-axis, and from top to bottom on the y-axis. When a graphical object is rendered, the user space coordinates are automatically transformed to the corresponding device coordinate system.

Device Space

Often what is needed is platform-specific or machine-specific information. For instance, you may want the size of the screen to set the size of the application frame. To obtain this information, you can use the `java.awt.Toolkit` class, which has the following methods for screen-related information:

- **`public abstract int getScreenResolution()`**

  This method returns the screen resolution in dots per inch.

- **`public abstract Dimension getScreenSize()`**

  This method returns the screen size in pixels.

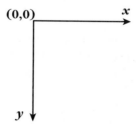

FIGURE 4.3   The user space coordinate system

Here's an example of how to use these methods:

```
Toolkit toolkit = Toolkit.getDefaultToolkit(); //Toolkit Factory
int  dotsPerInch = toolkit.getScreenResolution();
Dimension screenSize = toolkit.getScreenSize();
```

To support device conversion from user space to device space, the following three new classes were introduced in Java 2D:

1. `java.awt.GraphicsEnvironment.` This class represents the graphical environment in which an application is running. It contains the descriptions of graphical devices and the fonts.
2. `java.awt.GraphicsConfiguration.` This class describes the device characteristics, including the color model and the transformation.
3. `java.awt.GraphicsDevice.` This class represents a graphical device. Its attributes include the type of the device and `GraphicsConfiguration.`

You can use these classes from the **java.awt** package to obtain graphical device-, configuration-, and environment-related information. Let's look at the classes in detail.

Representing a Graphical Environment

A graphical environment may consist of several hardware devices, such as monitor, printer, plotter, and so on. It may also include a family of fonts. The `GraphicsEnvironment` class represents such an environment. It contains a collection of objects that represent the rendering devices visible to a Java application. It also holds the names of the fonts in the environment.

The `GraphicsEnvironment` class has the following factory method, which constructs a `GraphicsEnvironment` object:

- **`public static GraphicsEnvironment getLocalGraphicsEnvironment()`**

The methods that return environment attributes are

- **`public abstract String[] getAvailableFontFamilyNames()`**
- **`public abstract String[] getAvailableFontFamilyNames(Locale l)`**
- **`public abstract Font[] getAllFonts()`**

- **`public abstract GraphicsDevice getDefaultScreenDevice()`**
- **`public abstract GraphicsDevice[] getScreenDevices()`**
- **`public abstract Graphics2D createGraphics(BufferedImage img)`**

Representing a Graphical Device

The `GraphicsDevice` class represents a graphical device with the following three constants:

1. `TYPE_RASTER_SCREEN`. This constant represents the raster screen.
2. `TYPE_PRINTER`. This constant represents a printer or a plotter.
3. `TYPE_IMAGE_BUFFER`. This constant represents an image buffer.

You cannot construct a `GraphicsDevice` object directly. To obtain a `Graphics Device` object, you must use methods in the `GraphicsEnvironment` object. The following methods return device attributes:

- **`public abstract int getType()`**
- **`public abstract String getIDstring()`**

  The type returned is any one of the types mentioned above. The ID string is the identification string associated with a graphical device.

More than one graphical configuration may be associated with each device; for example, a video monitor may have multiple screen resolutions. Most of us have configured the screen resolutions to suit our applications. The following methods of the `GraphicsDevice` class return all, default, or the best configurations, respectively:

- **`public abstract GraphicsConfiguration[] getConfigurations()`**
- **`public abstract GraphicsConfiguration getDefaultConfiguration()`**
- **`public GraphicsConfiguration getBestConfiguration(Graphics`**
  `ConfigTemplate gct)`

Representing Graphical Characteristics

The `GraphicsConfiguration` class represents the characteristics of a graphical device. It has the following methods:

- **`public abstract ColorModel getColorModel()`**
- **`public abstract ColorModel getColorModel(int transparency)`**
- **`public abstract AffineTransform getDefaultTransform()`**
- **`public abstract GraphicsDevice getDevice()`**
- **`public abstract BufferedImage createCompatibleImage(int width,`**
  `int height)`
- **`public abstract BufferedImage createCompatibleImage(int width,`**
  `int height,`
  `int transparency)`

We won't explain these methods because they require knowledge of Java 2D.

Obtaining Graphical-Environment Information

The example shown in Listing 4.1 retrieves graphics-related information from a graphical environment. It uses all the classes described in the preceding sections.

LISTING 4.1 A class for obtaining graphical information

```java
import java.awt.*;
import java.awt.event.*;
import java.awt.image.*;
import java.awt.geom.*;
import java.io.*;
import javax.swing.*;
import javax.swing.event.*;
import java.util.*;
public class GraphicsInfo extends JFrame {
    protected GraphicsEnvironment graphicsEnv;
    public static void main(String[] args){
        GraphicsInfo gi = new GraphicsInfo();
    }

    public GraphicsInfo() {
        setTitle(" Graphics Info");
        graphicsEnv = GraphicsEnvironment.getLocalGraphicsEnvironment();
        createUI();
    }

    protected void createUI() {
        String[] deviceNames  =  getGraphicsDevices();
        JList deviceList = new JList(deviceNames);
        deviceList.setBackground(Color.black);
        deviceList.setForeground(Color.green);
        deviceList.setBorder(BorderFactory.createTitledBorder("Screen Devices"));
        String[] fontNames = graphicsEnv.getAvailableFontFamilyNames();
        JTextArea screenInfo = new JTextArea();
        screenInfo.setBackground(Color.black);
        screenInfo.setForeground(Color.green);
        screenInfo.setBorder(BorderFactory.createTitledBorder("Screen Info"));
        screenInfo.setText(getScreenInfo());
        JPanel screenInfoPanel = new JPanel();
        screenInfoPanel.setLayout( new GridLayout(2,1));
        screenInfoPanel.add( deviceList);
        screenInfoPanel.add(screenInfo);
        JList fontList = new JList(fontNames);
        fontList.setBorder(BorderFactory.createTitledBorder("Available Fonts"));
        fontList.setBackground(Color.black);
        fontList.setForeground(Color.green);
        JScrollPane jsp = new JScrollPane(fontList);
        getContentPane().setLayout(new GridLayout(1,2));
        getContentPane().add(screenInfoPanel);
        getContentPane().add(jsp);
        pack();
        setSize(600,400);
        show();
    }
```

```java
public String[] getGraphicsDevices() {
    GraphicsDevice[] gd = graphicsEnv.getScreenDevices();
    int numdevices = gd.length;
    String gdnames[] = new String[numdevices];
    for(int i=0; i<numdevices;i++) {
        int deviceType = gd[i].getType();
        String deviceName = getDeviceTypeAsText(deviceType);
        gdnames[i] = deviceName + gd[i].getIDstring();
    }
    return gdnames;
}

public String getScreenInfo() {
    Toolkit toolkit = Toolkit.getDefaultToolkit();
    Dimension  screenSize = toolkit.getScreenSize();
    int dotsPerInch = toolkit.getScreenResolution();
    String screenInfo = " Screen size "+ "\n"+
                        " width  : " + Integer.toString(screenSize.width) + "\n"+
                        " height : " + Integer.toString(screenSize.height)+ "\n"+
                        "Screen resolution : "+ Integer.toString(dotsPerInch)+ " dots
per inch";
    return screenInfo;
}

public String getDeviceTypeAsText(int deviceType){
    switch (deviceType) {
        case GraphicsDevice.TYPE_PRINTER:
            return "Printer";
        case GraphicsDevice.TYPE_RASTER_SCREEN:
            return "Screen";
        case GraphicsDevice.TYPE_IMAGE_BUFFER:
          return "Image Buffer";
        default:
          return "Unknown";
    }
}
}
```

The constructor of the `GraphicsInfo` class first obtains the `GraphicsEnvironment` object and holds it in an instance variable called `graphicsEnv`. It then calls the `createUI()` method. This method uses `graphicsEnv` to obtain device objects and related information and constructs a GUI to display them. It also shows the names of all the fonts in the environment.

> **Note:** The source code for `GraphicsInfo` is available on the book's Web page in the directory `src/chapter4/devices`.

To run this class, type "java GraphicsInfo" on the command line. When you run this application, you will see an application frame similar to the one in Figure 4.4.

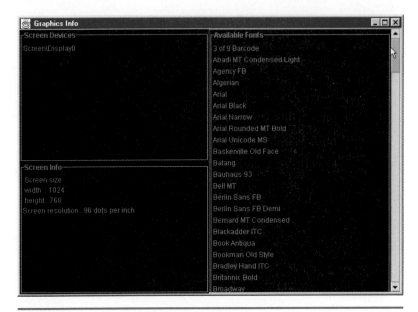

FIGURE 4.4   Displaying graphics-related information

Describing a Shape

In JDK 1.1 there is no generic description of a shape. Instead, the `Graphics` class provides shape-specific methods for drawing simple shapes that include lines, rectangles, arcs, and ovals. In real-world graphical applications, however, you would expect to draw a variety of shapes, including some very complex shapes. So if you needed to draw a complex shape in JDK 1.1, you would probably end up writing a lot of code.

What is desirable, therefore, is a generic description of shape that can be used to implement any type of shape. In other words, we need a method like `draw(Shape shape)` that draws a shape whose type is known only at the last moment at runtime.

There are many approaches for describing such a generic shape. In Chapter 5 we'll describe an approach that is based on shape hierarchy and useful for interactive drawing. In Java 2D, a shape is represented by an outline that can be constructed by straight lines or curves.

Insideness

Graphical programs often need to determine whether a point is inside or outside of a shape. Consider this real-world example: You may have seen the store locator programs in many e-commerce sites. When you type an address or a zip code, the store locator displays stores in the vicinity of the address you typed. The store locator program computes this information by checking whether the *geo-coded* (i.e., longitude-and-latitude-assigned) address lies within the area assigned to a store. This technique is called point-in-polygon in GIS terminology.

The determination of whether a point is inside or outside depends on how a path that represents the shape is described. Here's the definition of *insideness* in Java2D:

A point is considered to lie inside a shape if and only if

♦ It lies completely inside the shape boundary *or*

♦ It lies exactly on the shape boundary and the space immediately adjacent to the point in the increasing x direction is entirely inside the boundary *or*

♦ It lies exactly on a horizontal boundary segment and the space immediately adjacent to the point in the increasing y direction is inside the boundary.

The Shape Interface

The `java.awt.shape` interface specifies a generic geometric shape, which is described by a geometric path with multiple segments. The classes that implement this interface include `Line2D`, `Rectangle2D`, `Polygon`, `QuadCurve2D`, and `CubicCurve2D`.

The `Shape` interface specifies four types of methods, which are described in the subsections that follow.

Obtaining PathIterator Objects

`PathIterator` is an interface (see the next section) that helps to iterate over different segments of a shape's outline. The following methods retrieve `PathIterator` objects from a `Shape` object:

♦ `public PathIterator getPathIterator(AffineTransform transform)`
♦ `public PathIterator getPathIterator(AffineTransform transform,`
`                                      double flatness)`

In these two methods, if the `AffineTransform` argument is non-`null`, the `PathIterator` object returned by the method applies the transformation specified by `transform` to the current path in each iteration. If the `AffineTransform` argument is `null`, no transformation is applied. The amount of subdivision of the curved segments is controlled by the `flatness` parameter, which specifies the maximum distance that any point on the unflattened transformed curve can deviate from the returned flattened path segments.

Checking for Containment

The following methods test whether a point is contained in a shape:

- ◆ **public boolean contains(double x, double y)**

  This method checks whether the point represented by (x, y) is contained in the shape.

- ◆ **public boolean contains(Point2D p)**

  This method checks whether the point represented by Point2D object p is contained in the shape.

- ◆ **public boolean contains(double x, double y, double w, double h)**

  This method checks whether the rectangular area specified by ULHC (upper left-hand corner) coordinates (x, y) and the size specified by w and h lie entirely within the shape.

Checking for Intersection

The following methods test for intersection between a specified rectangular area and the shape:

- ◆ **public boolean intersects(Rectangle2D r)**

  This method checks whether the rectangular area r intersects the shape.

- ◆ **public boolean intersects(double x, double y, double width, double height)**

  This method checks whether the rectangular area whose ULHC is specified by (x, y) and whose size is specified by width and height intersects the shape.

Obtaining Bounds

The following methods obtain the rectangular bounds of a shape:

- ◆ **public Rectangle getBounds()**
- ◆ **public Rectangle2D getBounds2D()**

  Both of these methods return a rectangle that encloses the shape. The second method returns a higher-precision bounding box with float or double coordinates.

The PathIterator Interface

The PathIterator interface helps clients of Shape objects to retrieve the outline of the shape segment by segment.

Iteration

The following methods are needed to perform iteration:

- **`public void next()`**

  This method moves the iterator to the next segment of the path and moves forward along the primary direction of traversal as long as there are more points in that direction.

- **`public boolean isDone()`**

  This method checks whether the iteration is complete. It returns `true` if all the segments have been read; otherwise it returns `false.`

Retrieving Path Segments

Since there are multiple segments in a path, the `PathIterator` interface provides a mechanism to retrieve one segment at a time. The segments of a path could include straight lines, quadratic curves, and cubic curves (see the section on curves later in this chapter).

The `PathIterator` identifies different types of segments through the following constants:

- `SEG_MOVETO`. This constant specifies the starting location for a new subpath and refers to a point.
- `SEG_LINETO`. This constant specifies the end point of a line to be drawn from the most recently specified point.
- `SEG_QUADTO`. This constant represents a quadratic curve segment. Two points are involved in this segment.
- `SEG_CUBICTO`. This constant represents a parametric cubic curve segment. Three points are involved in this segment.
- `SEG_CLOSE`. This constant specifies that the preceding subpath should be closed by appending a line segment to the point corresponding to the most recent `SEG_MOVETO` location.

The following methods return a segment:

- **`public int currentSegment(double[] coords)`**
- **`public int currentSegment(float[] coords)`**

  The return value is one of the segment constants of the preceding list. These methods also return the coordinates through the input argument `coords`, which need to be declared as an array of length six.

Winding Rules

In elementary geometry, identifying the interior region of a standard polygon, such as a triangle, rectangle, or pentagon, is easy because there is no self-intersection; that is, edges intersect only at the vertices. When a shape is complex, however, edges may intersect each other at points other than vertices. In such cases, determining the interior regions of a shape is not easy.

Consider the shape shown in Figure 4.5. It is not very clear which regions are interior and which are exterior. In graphics, two rules are normally used to identify the interior regions of a shape: the even-odd rule and the nonzero winding rule:

- **Even-odd rule.** This rule specifies that *a point lies inside the path if a ray drawn in any direction from that point to infinity is crossed by path segments an odd number of times.* To understand the even-odd rule, draw a line from any position *P* to a distant point *Q* that is outside the bounding box of the shape. Make sure that the line doesn't pass through the vertices. Count the number of times the line crosses the edges. If the number of edges crossed by this line is odd, then *P* is an interior point. Otherwise, it is an exterior point. The line *PQ* in Figure 4.5 crosses the edges three times; therefore, the point *P* lies in the interior region of the polygon. On the other hand, the line *RS* crosses the edges twice. According to the even-odd rule, the point *R* therefore lies in the exterior region of the polygon.

- **Nonzero winding rule.** This rule specifies that *a point lies inside the path if a ray drawn in any direction from that point to infinity is crossed by path segments a different number of times in the counterclockwise direction than the clockwise direction.* For a simple demonstration of this rule, look at Figure 4.6. Trace the outline of the shape in the counterclockwise direction. At each edge, mark an arrow indicating the direction of the trace. Draw a line from the point *P* to the distant point *Q* that lies outside the bounding box of the polygon. If the line *PQ* intersects the right-to-left edge, then add +1. If it intersects the left-to-right edge, add −1. If the resulting count is nonzero, the point *P* lies in the interior region. Otherwise it lies in the exterior region of the polygon.

The even-odd and the nonzero winding rules need not produce the same results. In the two examples given here, observe the region in which the point *U* lies. This region is exterior in Figure 4.5 and interior in Figure 4.6.

The `PathIterator` interface represents the type of winding rule through the following constants:

- `WIND_EVEN_ODD`: the even-odd rule
- `WIND_NON_ZERO`: the nonzero winding rule
- **`public int getWindingRule()`**
  The return value of this method is one of the winding-rule constants.

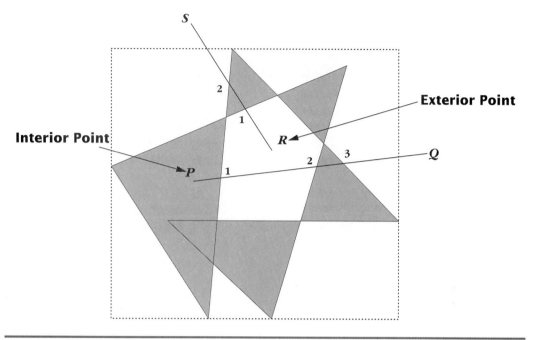

FIGURE 4.5   The even-odd rule

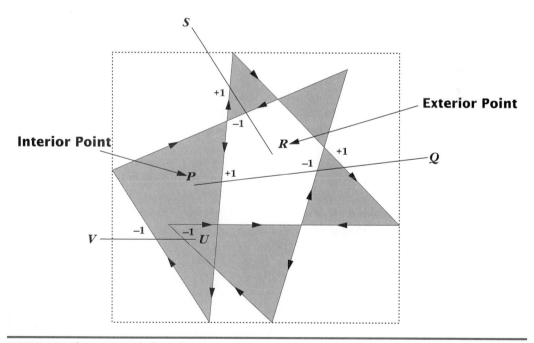

FIGURE 4.6   The nonzero winding rule

Shapes

The `java.awt.geom` package has several classes that implement the `Shape` interface—namely, `Point2D`, `Line2D`, `Rectangle2D`, `RoundRectangle2D`, `Ellipse2D`, and `Arc2D`. In this section we'll briefly look at each class. Most of these `Shape` classes accept `double` coordinates. If you intend to pass the user space coordinates (which are of type `int`), you may have to cast them to `double`.

All of the classes that define the shapes listed here are in the `java.awt.geom` package except the ones that were already there in JDK 1.1.

Point

In the JDK 1.1 `java.awt` package, the `Point` class represents a point. In Java 2D, the `Point` class has been made a subclass of an abstract class named `Point2D`. Besides `Point`, `Point2D` has two concrete subclasses: `Point2D.double` and `Point2D.float`. Both of these classes are inner classes of `Point2D`. To create a `Point` object, you must instantiate one of the three subclasses of `Point2D`. Here's an example:

```
double x = 10.0, y= 20.0
Point2D aPoint  =  new Point2D.double(x, y);
```

In a strict sense, `Point2D` does not represent a shape because it does not implement the `Shape` interface.

Using the `Point2D` class, you can calculate distances and squares of the distances between points. These methods are quite useful in measurements.

Line

A line in Java 2D is represented by the `Line2D` class. Just like `Point2D`, `Line2D` is an abstract class. But unlike `Point2D`, `Line2D` implements the `Shape` interface. It has two concrete subclasses—`Line2D.double` and `Line2D.float`—both of which are inner classes of `Line2D`.

The `Line2D` class has the following three types of methods:

1. Methods for checking for intersection with other lines
2. Methods for computing distances and squares of the distances from a point
3. Methods for computing relative positions of a point with respect to the line: clockwise, counterclockwise, or lying on the line

Rectangle

Java2D supports two types of rectangular shapes with the following two classes: `Rectangle2D` and `RoundRectangle2D`. The difference between the shapes represented by these two classes is that the latter has round corners. Both of the rectangle classes are abstract classes and extend another abstract class—`RectangularShape`—which implements the `Shape` interface.

`Rectangle2D` has three subclasses: `Rectangle`, `Rectangle.double`, and `Rectangle.float`. Just like `Point`, `Rectangle` is in the `java.awt` package for historical reasons. `Rectangle.double` and `Rectangle.float` are the concrete subclasses of `Rectangle2D`.

The `Rectangle2D` classes have two important types of methods:

1. Methods for checking and creating intersections
2. Methods for creating unions

`RoundRectangle2D` has two subclasses: `RoundRectangle.double` and `Round Rectangle.float`.

Ellipse

The `Ellipse2D` class represents an ellipse. Just like `Rectangle2D`, `Ellipse2D` extends `RectangularShape`, because the bounding box of an ellipse is a rectangle.

`Ellipse2D` is an abstract class that has two subclasses: `Ellipse2D.double` and `Ellipse2D.float`.

Arc

An arc is part of an outline that makes an ellipse, so it does not have to be a closed shape. Java 2D supports three types of arcs:

1. **Open.** The arc is not closed.
2. **Chord.** The arc is closed by a line drawn from the starting point to the end point.
3. **Pie.** The arc is closed by lines drawn to the starting point and the end point of the arc from the center of the ellipse that contains the arc.

The `Arc2D` class represents an arc. Just like `Ellipse2D`, `Arc2D` is an abstract class that extends `RectangularShape`.

Curves

Whether the context is data fitting, computer-aided design (CAD), or any other discipline that involves graphics, curves are an important part of any geometric design. The smooth and aesthetically pleasing curvature you see in your car is the result of a design using curves. Curves find applications even in imaging. Marking a region of interest is an example. You might deposit a number of points marking the boundary and ask the application to draw a smooth curve. In dental image scanning, a doctor electronically draws a curve to represent the jaw on a reference image. On this curve, the doctor then graphically prescribes the location at which cross-sectional images of the teeth are to be scanned.

What Is a Curve?

A curve is a function that approximates or interpolates n points, where $n > 2$. When $n = 2$, a curve is a straight line. The surest way of generating a function that describes all n points is by using an $n - 1$ degree polynomial. Imagine that you need a curve to fit more than a hundred points. Computing or solving an equation of that high degree not only is very computation intensive but also may lead to undesirable oscillations. Therefore, constructing a polynomial of degree 100 is entirely impractical.

As with all the other difficult problems, this problem is solved by application of the "divide and conquer" principle. In this solution, the entire set of points is divided into a number of segments, each segment containing a continuous set of points (say, four). Because of the smaller number of points, a smooth curve can be quickly constructed to represent those points. To make the entire curve look continuous, the last point of a segment is made the first point of the next segment. Thus each segment is a piecewise polynomial.

Mathematically speaking, the low-degree polynomial equations $y_i = f(x_i)$, where $i = 0, 1, 2, \ldots, n$, for each segment are joined together in a continuous fashion so that the resulting piecewise polynomial $f(x)$ represents the entire data set.

There are two types of curve fitting: interpolation and approximation.

Interpolating Curves

In interpolation, the resulting curve exactly passes through the entire set of data points. Interpolation is used to create a curve when accuracy is the critical factor—for example, data fitting a plot. In the dental scanning example, a doctor may prescribe points that are on the teeth, and the curve representing the jaw must pass through those points.

Approximating Curves

In approximation, the resultant curve may not pass through the given set of data points. Instead, the curve passes through the points that are an approximation of the given set of data. There are different types of approximation curves, including Hermite, Bezier, and B-spline (see the section titled Why Cubic Curves? later in this chapter).

Curve Definitions and Concepts

In this section we'll look at some definitions of terms and concepts related to curves.

Smoothness

A curve is said to be smooth if it is continuous and has no kinks, wiggles, or corners.

Continuity

There are many ways of defining continuity. One essential condition is that the position at which the two piecewise curve segments meet is continuous. Continuity is also measured by whether the derivative of the curve equation is also continuous. This continuity is mathematically expressed as C^i, where i represents the continuity; that is, the first i derivatives are continuous. For instance, cubic interpolating spline is said to be C^2, which means that for a cubic equation $y = f(t)$, dy/dt and d^2y/dt^2 are continuous. This type of measure is called geometric continuity. The other measures are beyond the scope of this book.

Fairing

The fact that a curve is a best-fitting curve doesn't always guarantee that it is *fair*— that is, smooth, continuous, and with no unwanted abnormalities. The technique of generating fair curves is called curve fairing. A curve is said to be fair if the following conditions are satisfied:

1. The curve has C^2 continuity.
2. There are no undesirable abnormalities (see the next section).
3. The curvature varies in an even manner.

   Condition 1 depends on a local property, which reflects a small neighborhood on the curve. Conditions 2 and 3 reflect the global properties of the curve.

Curve Abnormalities

Figure 4.7 shows the three types of curve abnormalities:

1. **Inflection points.** These are points on the curve at which the curvature is zero. Mathematically, the tangent at the inflection point intersects the curve.
2. **Cusps.** Cusps occur when the first derivative of the curve vanishes.
3. **Loops.** A loop occurs when the curve intersects itself.

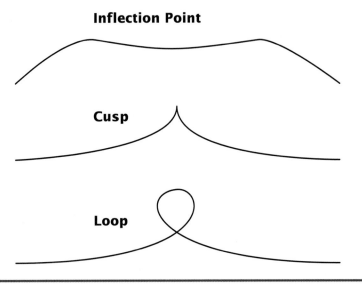

FIGURE 4.7   Curve abnormalities

Parametric Curves

Any function can be described as $y = f(x)$—that is, y as a function of x. But can we plot this function? First, it is hard to find the points that lie on the plot. Second, if the function is multivalued or has infinite slope, the plotting leads to ambiguous situations. This problem is solved by parametric representation of the function. A parametric curve is defined by the following equations:

$$x = f(t)$$

$$y = f(t)$$

where $0 < t < 1$.

With these equations you can plot the points very easily. For a given value of t, you can find both x and y. There are different techniques for making an equation parametric, a process that is referred to as parameterization.

Some Parameterization Techniques

Parametric values should be chosen so that the resulting curve has certain desirable properties, such as

♦ Continuity
♦ No abnormalities like inflection points, cusps, and loops

- No oscillations when data points are not equally spaced or gently curved
- Affine invariance

The ideal parameterization technique is arc length parameterization, in which successive data points are determined by the arc length between the adjacent points. Arc length parameterization is difficult because the shape of the curve cannot be determined in advance.

Let's look at some of the other parameterization techniques.

Uniform Parameterization

In uniform parameterization, the parameter range is divided into equally spaced segments. For n data points, there will be $n - 1$ segments. If the range of t is $0 < t < 1$, then the successive data point is incremented by $1/(n - 1)$. So the parameter values for $P_i = 0, 1, 2, \ldots, n - 1$ are $0, 1/(n - 1), 2/(n - 1), \ldots, (n - 2)/(n - 1)$, respectively.

This scheme is too simplistic and ignores the geometry of points. It produces poor curves, especially when the data points are unevenly spread, because the distances between points are not considered.

Chord Length Parameterization

In this scheme, the Euclidean distance between adjacent points is considered for parameterization by use of the following equations:

$$t_i = \sum_{j=1}^{j=i} d_j$$

where $d_j = \sqrt{(x_j - x_{j-1})^2 + (y_j - y_{j-1})^2}$, and x_j, x_{j-1}, y_j, and y_{j-1} are the coordinates at P_j and P_{j-1}, respectively.

Chord length parameterization is a popular scheme for making an equation parametric. If a curve has small deflections, this method approximates the accuracy of arc length parameterization. Chord length parameterization is not affine invariant and may lead to oscillations if data points are not evenly distributed.

Centripetal Parameterization

Centripetal parameterization is achieved by the equation $t_i = t_{i-1} + \sqrt{d_i}$, where d_i is the Euclidean distance. The principle behind this scheme is that the resulting motion of a point on the curve will have minimum centripetal force acting on it. Centripetal parameterization produces a curve of minimum length.

Why Cubic Curves?

Most of the practical curves are cubic because a lower-order representation doesn't provide the continuity of position and slope at the point where the segments meet. On the other hand, higher-order representations may result in instability because of oscillations.

In the sections that follow, we'll look at some of the most popular cubic curves: Hermite, Bezier, and B-spline.

The Hermite Curve

The positions and tangents at the end point define the Hermite curve (see Figure 4.8).

The Bezier Curve

The Bezier curve is defined by the positions of the end points and two control points, generally not on the curve, that define the tangents at the end points (see Figure 4.9).

The B-Spline Curve

Four control points define the cubic B-spline curve (see Figure 4.10). The curve may not pass through these control points. Moving a control point affects the local area only.

Curves in Java 2D

Java 2D supports two types of curves: quadratic and cubic. A quadratic curve is defined by a second-degree polynomial, a cubic curve by a cubic polynomial. Java 2D implements them both as Bezier curves.

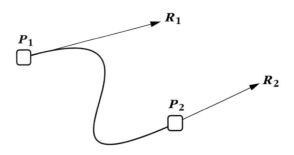

FIGURE 4.8   A Hermite curve

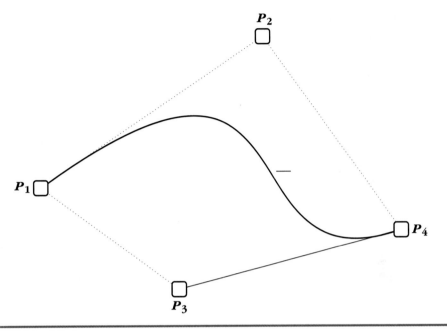

FIGURE 4.9   A Bezier curve

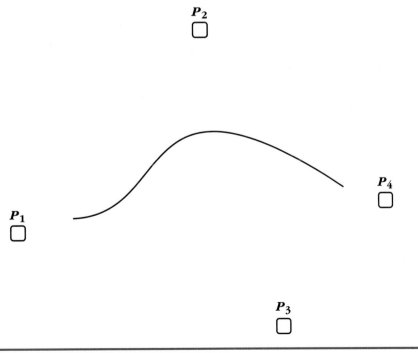

FIGURE 4.10   A cubic B-spline curve

Quadratic Curves

The abstract QuadCurve2D class creates a quadratic curve by implementing the Shape interface. QuadCurve2D has two subclasses: QuadCurve2D.float and QuadCurve2D. double.

Cubic Curves

The abstract CubicCurve2D class creates a cubic curve by implementing the Shape interface. CubicCurve2D has two subclasses: CubicCurve2D.float and CubicCurve2D. double:

```
public void drawCurve(Graphics2D g, int x[], int y[]){
    CubicCurve2D.Float cc = new CubicCurve2D.Float((float)x[0], (float)y[0],
                                       (float)x[1], (float)y[1],
                                       (float)x[2], (float)y[2],
                                       (float)x[3], (float)y[3]);
    g.draw(cc);
}
```

Using the GeneralPath Class

You can draw straight lines and curves using the GeneralPath class. The following example uses GeneralPath to draw a polygon:

```
public void drawPolygon(Graphics2D g, int x[], int y[]){
    int num = x.length;
    path = new GeneralPath(GeneralPath.WIND-EVEN-ODD);
    path.moveTo((float)x[0], (float)y[0]);
    for(int i=1; i<num; i++) {
        path.lineTo((float)x[i], (float)y[i]);
    }
    g.draw(path);
}
```

Introduction to Affine Transformation

This section provides a mathematical introduction to affine transformation, which is essential to understanding the inner workings of the AffineTransform class. To understand this topic, the only mathematical background you need is knowledge of matrix operations. If you're already familiar with affine transformation, you may skip this section. On the other hand, if you wish to learn more, you may want to consult a book on graphics. After this introduction we'll describe the AffineTransform class in detail.

Mathematically, a transformation is a function that maps an object (say, a point or an image) from one point to another. An affine transformation is a transformation that preserves certain properties after the transformation, including

- **Finiteness.** Finite points in an object map to finite points.
- **Parallelism.** The lines of the shape remain parallel after the transformation.

When we deal with geometry or graphics, we come across three basic transformations: translation, scaling, and rotation. When these transformations are applied to an object, the shape of the object is not distorted. The parallelism and internal angles are all preserved after the transformation. In other words, the object is not deformed. Such transformations are called *rigid-body* transformations. Translation, scaling, and rotation belong to this category. In the sections that follow, we'll look at each of these types of transformation in turn.

> **Note:** In these sections, when an equation is represented in vector form, a "+" represents matrix addition and a "·" represents matrix multiplication.

Translation

Translation is an operation that displaces an object by a fixed distance (see Figure 4.11). For the two-dimensional case, the equation is written for each dimension separately. The equations for translating a point at (x, y) by (d_x, d_y) units to (x', y') are as follows:

$$x' = x + d_x \qquad (4.1)$$

$$y' = y + d_y \qquad (4.2)$$

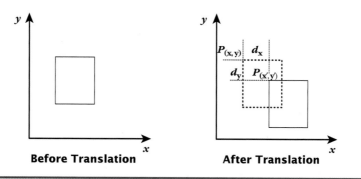

Before Translation   **After Translation**

FIGURE 4.11   Applying translation

These equations can be written in matrix form as follow:

$$P' = \begin{bmatrix} x' \\ y' \end{bmatrix} \qquad P = \begin{bmatrix} x \\ y \end{bmatrix} \qquad T = \begin{bmatrix} d_x \\ d_y \end{bmatrix}$$

Each expression on the right-hand side is a vector, so we can write this as $P' = P + T$. This equation can be used to translate every point in the object.

Scaling

Scaling is an operation that magnifies or shrinks an object (see Figure 4.12). In the two-dimensional case, it is defined by the equations

$$x' = s_x \times x \qquad\qquad\qquad (4.3)$$

$$y' = s_y \times y \qquad\qquad\qquad (4.4)$$

where s_x and s_y are scale factors in the x and the y directions, respectively.
These equations can be written in matrix form as follows:

$$\begin{bmatrix} x' \\ y' \end{bmatrix} = \begin{bmatrix} s_x & 0 \\ 0 & s_y \end{bmatrix} \begin{bmatrix} x \\ y \end{bmatrix}$$

and they can be written in vector form as

$$P' = S \cdot P$$

Scaling can be uniform in all directions—in the two-dimensional case, in both the x and the y directions. In such instances, proportions of the objects don't change, and such an operation is called *uniform scaling*. In uniform scaling, $s_x = s_y$.

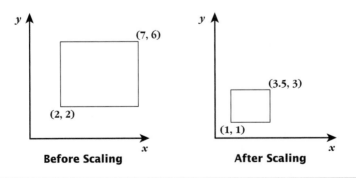

FIGURE 4.12 Applying scaling

Sometimes the proportions of the object must be changed during scaling. Such an operation is called *differential scaling,* in which this case $s_x \neq s_y$.

Rotation

Rotation is an operation that rotates an object through an angle about a fixed point, which is called the center of rotation or pivot. Rotation is a little more complicated than translation or scaling. The rotation center can be the origin of the coordinate system or any other point, as shown in Figure 4.13.

First let's consider rotation about the origin of the axes. In the two-dimensional case, this means that the object is rotated about the z-axis. We can write the equations for rotation about the z-axis as follows:

$$x' = x \times \cos(\theta) - y \times \sin(\theta) \tag{4.5}$$

$$y' = y \times \sin(\theta) + y \times \cos(\theta) \tag{4.6}$$

where θ is the angle of rotation.

These equations can be written in matrix form as follows:

$$\begin{bmatrix} x' \\ y' \end{bmatrix} = \begin{bmatrix} \cos(\theta) & -\sin(\theta) \\ \sin(\theta) & \cos(\theta) \end{bmatrix} \begin{bmatrix} x \\ y \end{bmatrix}$$

and they can be written in vector form as

$$P' = R \cdot P$$

where R is the rotation matrix.

$$\begin{bmatrix} \cos(\theta) & -\sin(\theta) \\ \sin(\theta) & \cos(\theta) \end{bmatrix}$$

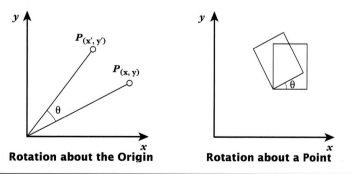

Rotation about the Origin   Rotation about a Point

FIGURE 4.13   Applying rotation

Concatenation

In a real-world application, the need often arises to apply the primitive transformations in a sequence. For example, you might move an image so that part of the image you want to examine is at a convenient position. At that position, you might zoom in on it and then rotate it for closer scrutiny. To achieve this effect, you need to translate the image to the position P and zoom in on it by factor S, and then rotate it by angle θ.

Applying these transformations one by one to an image would require many computation-intensive operations. However, you can achieve the same effect by concatenating all the transformations and then applying the resulting transformation to the image only once, thus saving a lot of CPU time.

You probably noticed that the translation operation is an additive operation and the rest of the transformations are multiplicative operations. This means that a mix of matrix additions and multiplications is involved in concatenation. Representing the Cartesian coordinates in the homogeneous coordinate system, our next topic, eases this problem.

Homogeneous Coordinates

It is certainly convenient to treat all operations in the same way—that is, matrix multiplication. We can do this if we change the coordinate systems to *homogeneous coordinates*. The aim here is to make the translation transformation a multiplicative operation. To accomplish this goal, a third coordinate is added to the Cartesian coordinate system. For example, a point $P_{(x,y)}$ is represented by $P_{(x,y,1)}$ in the homogeneous coordinate system. This means that we use three coordinates to represent a point in two-dimensional space.[1]

Translation

Using the homogeneous coordinate system, we can represent the translation operation as follows:

$$\begin{bmatrix} x' \\ y' \\ 1 \end{bmatrix} = \begin{bmatrix} 1 & 0 & d_x \\ 0 & 1 & d_y \\ 0 & 0 & 1 \end{bmatrix} \begin{bmatrix} x \\ y \\ 1 \end{bmatrix}$$

(4.7)

When you multiply the members of this matrix, you get the equations (4.1) and (4.2), which were given in the section on translation. This means that in the homogeneous coordinate system, the translation operation is multiplicative:

---

1   For a rigorous mathematical treatment of this topic, you may want to refer to a book on graphics.

$$P_1 = T \cdot P \tag{4.8}$$

Next let's suppose you want to perform two successive translation operations as shown.

$$P_1 = T \cdot P \tag{4.9}$$

$$P_2 = T_1 \cdot P_1 \tag{4.10}$$

If we substitute equation (4.9) into equation (4.10), we can show that

$$P_2 = (T_1 + T) \cdot P$$

In other words, the resultant translation matrix is additive.

Next we'll see what happens when successive scaling or rotation operations are performed.

Scaling

Using the homogeneous coordinate system, we can represent the scaling operation as follows:

$$\begin{bmatrix} x' \\ y' \\ 1 \end{bmatrix} = \begin{bmatrix} s_x & 0 & 0 \\ 0 & s_y & 0 \\ 0 & 0 & 1 \end{bmatrix} \begin{bmatrix} x \\ y \\ 1 \end{bmatrix} \tag{4.11}$$

As given earlier, the base equation for scaling is

$$P' = S \cdot P$$

The successive scaling operation is multiplicative; that is, $P_2 = S_1 \cdot S \cdot P$.

Rotation

Using the homogeneous coordinate system, we can represent the rotation operation as follows:

$$\begin{bmatrix} x' \\ y' \\ 1 \end{bmatrix} = \begin{bmatrix} \cos(\theta) & -\sin(\theta) & 0 \\ \sin(\theta) & \cos(\theta) & 0 \\ 0 & 0 & 1 \end{bmatrix} \begin{bmatrix} x \\ y \\ 1 \end{bmatrix} \tag{4.12}$$

As given earlier, the base equation for rotation is

$$P' = R \cdot P$$

Successive rotations are additive; that is, $R(\theta_2) = R(\theta_1 + \theta)$.

Concatenation

When you need to perform a sequence of transformations, you can get the resulting position by applying the transformations one by one. However, you can speed up the process by concatenating the matrices of the transformations and applying the resulting matrix to the image. For example, you can translate, scale, and rotate an image by multiplying the respective transformation matrices as follows:

$$C = T \cdot S \cdot R$$

The composite matrix C is the product of T, S, and R. Note that the order of the operations must be preserved while the matrices are being concatenated because the matrix multiplication operation is not commutative; that is, $A \cdot B$ is not the same as $B \cdot A$. However, matrix multiplication is associative. For example, for any three matrices A, B, and C, the matrix product can be obtained by first multiplying A and B and then multiplying this partial product by C, or by first multiplying B and C and then multiplying the partial product by A.

$$A \cdot B \cdot C = (A \cdot B) \cdot C = A \cdot (B \cdot C)$$

Note that the concatenation of transformations for a two-dimensional image results in a single 3 × 3 matrix.

Other Transformations

Whereas translation, scaling, and rotation are fundamental to manipulation, other types of transformation are also often required. Two prominent additional transformations are reflection and shear.

Reflection

Reflection produces a mirror image of the object. In other words, the reflection operation flips the object. In the two-dimensional case, reflection about the *x*-axis results in a top-to-bottom flip (see Figure 4.14). Here's the transformation matrix for reflection about the *x*-axis:

$$\begin{bmatrix} 1 & 0 & 0 \\ 0 & -1 & 0 \\ 0 & 0 & 1 \end{bmatrix}$$

In this case reflection occurs about the $y = 0$ line.

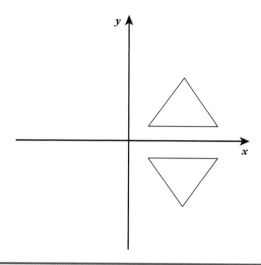

FIGURE 4.14   Applying reflection

Reflection about the y-axis results in a right-to-left flip. Here's the transformation matrix for reflection about the y-axis:

$$\begin{bmatrix} -1 & 0 & 0 \\ 0 & 1 & 0 \\ 0 & 0 & 1 \end{bmatrix}$$

In this case, reflection occurs about the $x = 0$ line.

The reflection operation about both the x- and the y-axes results in right-to-left and top-to-bottom flips. Here's the transformation matrix for reflection about the x- and y-axes:

$$\begin{bmatrix} -1 & 0 & 0 \\ 0 & -1 & 0 \\ 0 & 0 & 1 \end{bmatrix}$$

The matrices shown here are for reflection, which means that they produce a mirror image in a different quadrant. But user space typically covers only one quadrant. In other words, we need the flipped images in the same quadrant and at the same position. We can achieve this result through the translation operation, as already discussed. Figure 4.15 shows different flip operations.

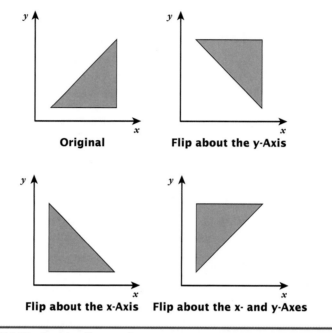

FIGURE 4.15 Applying flip

Shear

Shear is not a well-known operation, but is equally important. Unlike the other operations we discussed before, shear is not a *rigid-body* transformation. Shear distorts the shape of an object in such a way that the shape appears to elongate in the direction shear is applied. See Figure 4.16. The shapes can be sheared in the x and y direction.

In matrix form, shear is represented as follows:

$$Sh_x = \begin{bmatrix} 1 & sh_x & 0 \\ 0 & 1 & 0 \\ 0 & 0 & 0 \end{bmatrix}$$

$$Sh_y = \begin{bmatrix} 1 & 0 & 0 \\ sh_y & 1 & 0 \\ 0 & 0 & 0 \end{bmatrix}$$

where sh_x is the shear factor in the x direction, and sh_y is the shear factor in the y direction.

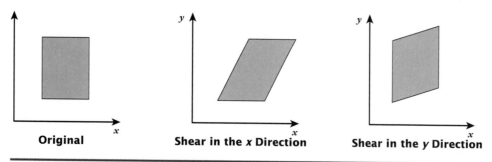

FIGURE 4.16 Applying shear

An important application of shear is in medical imaging. In computed tomography (CT) imaging, for example, the gantry in which the patient is placed is sometimes tilted. Images acquired with a tilted gantry must be transformed to remove the tilt effect. This transformation is accomplished by the shear operation.

The AffineTransform Class

The AffineTransform class is an important class in the Java 2D API. With it, implementing any image manipulation operation is easy. The class is in the java.awt.geom package.

The AffineTransform class represents a two-dimensional affine transformation that is given by the following 3 × 3 matrix:

$$A = \begin{bmatrix} m00 & m01 & m02 \\ m10 & m11 & m12 \\ 0 & 0 & 1 \end{bmatrix}$$

The numerical suffix of each element represents the position of that element in the matrix.

A point $P_{(x,y)}$ will be transformed to $P_{(x',y')}$ through the transformation represented by the equation $X' = A \cdot X$, which is given by

$$\begin{bmatrix} x' \\ y' \\ 1 \end{bmatrix} = \begin{bmatrix} m00 & m01 & m02 \\ m10 & m11 & m12 \\ 0 & 0 & 1 \end{bmatrix}$$

$$
\begin{bmatrix} x \\ y \\ 1 \end{bmatrix} = \begin{bmatrix} m00 \times x + m01 \times y + m02 \\ m10 \times x + m11 \times y + m12 \\ 1 \end{bmatrix}
$$

The `AffineTransform` class has methods for performing basic transformations, concatenation, and inverse transformation. It can transform a point, an array of points, or a shape. To transform an image, you may need to use the `Affine TransformOp` class.

AffineTransform Constructors

The `AffineTransform` class has the following six constructors:

1. **`public AffineTransform()`**

   This constructor creates an identity transformation.

2. **`public AffineTransform(AffineTransform Tx)`**

   This constructor creates an `AffineTransform` object from another `AffineTransform` object specified in the input.

3. **`public AffineTransform(float m00,`**
   `float m10,`
   `float m01,`
   `float m11,`
   `float m02,`
   `float m12)`

4. **`public AffineTransform(double m00,`**
   `double m10,`
   `double m01,`
   `double m11,`
   `double m02,`
   `double m12)`

Constructors 3 and 4 create an `AffineTransform` object from a set of input parameters that represent the variable entries in the following 3×3 transformation matrix:

$$
A = \begin{bmatrix} m00 & m01 & m02 \\ m10 & m11 & m12 \\ 0 & 0 & 1 \end{bmatrix}
$$

These parameters are of type `float` in constructor 3 and of type `double` in constructor 4.

5. `public AffineTransform(float[] flatmatrix)`
6. `public AffineTransform(double[] flatmatrix)`

Constructors 5 and 6 create an `AffineTransform` object from an array of values that represent the entries of the transformation matrix. The array should consist of either four of the nontranslation entries—that is, `{m00 m10 m01 m11}`—or all six variable entries—that is, `{m00 m10 m01 m11 m02 m12}`.

Standard Transformation Methods

The methods of the `AffineTransform` class support all of the following four standard transformation types: translation, scaling, rotation, and shear. There are two types of methods for each of the operations:

1. **Absolute transformation.** The transformation matrix is reset to identity before a specified transformation is performed. The methods of type *setToXXX()* perform absolute transformation.

2. **Relative transformation.** The current transformation matrix is concatenated by a specified transformation. The methods that perform relative transformation are `translate()`, `scale()`, `rotate()`, and `shear()`.

   For instance, if `translate(tx, ty)` is called, the transformation is computed by

   [`this`] = [`this`] · [Tx]

where `this` is the `AffineTransform` object representing the current transformation matrix:

$$
Tx = \begin{bmatrix} 1 & 0 & tx \\ 0 & 1 & ty \\ 0 & 0 & 1 \end{bmatrix}
$$

and Tx is the `AffineTransform` object constructed from input parameters.

Translation

The following methods perform translation:

- `public void setToTranslation(double tx, double ty)`
- `public void translate(double tx, double ty)`

The `tx` and `ty` parameters represent the translations in the x and y directions, respectively.

The translation matrix created by the input parameters is as follows:

$$Tx = \begin{bmatrix} 1 & 0 & tx \\ 0 & 1 & ty \\ 0 & 0 & 1 \end{bmatrix}$$

The get methods for obtaining translation in the x and y directions are

- `public double getTranslateX()`
- `public double getTranslateY()`

Scaling

The following methods perform scaling:

- `public void setToScale(double sx, double sy)`
- `public void scale(double sx, double sy)`

The scaling matrix created by the input parameters is as follows:

$$\begin{bmatrix} sx & 0 & 0 \\ 0 & sy & 0 \\ 0 & 0 & 1 \end{bmatrix}$$

The get methods for obtaining the scale factor in the x and y directions are

- `public double getScaleX()`
- `public double getScaleY()`

Rotation

The following methods rotate an object about the origin by a specified angle:

- `public void setToRotation(double theta)`
- `public void rotate(double theta)`

The transformation matrix created by the input parameters is as follows:

$$\begin{bmatrix} \cos(theta) & -\sin(theta) & 0 \\ \sin(theta) & \cos(theta) & 0 \\ 0 & 0 & 1 \end{bmatrix}$$

Usually we want to rotate an image about its midpoint or another specified point. The following methods perform such rotation:

- **public void setToRotation(double theta, double x, double y)**
- **public void rotate(double theta, double x, double y)**

The transformation matrix created by the input parameters is as follows:

$$
\begin{bmatrix}
\cos(\texttt{theta}) & -\sin(\texttt{theta}) & x - [x \times \cos(\texttt{theta})] + [y \times \sin(\texttt{theta})] \\
\sin(\texttt{theta}) & \cos(\texttt{theta}) & y - [x \times \sin(\texttt{theta})] - [y \times \cos(\texttt{theta})] \\
0 & 0 & 1
\end{bmatrix}
$$

Here **theta** is the rotation angle in radians, and **x** and **y** are the coordinates of the rotation center. The rotation operation with these methods is equivalent to translating the object to the origin, rotating by theta, and then translating the object back to its original position.

Shear

The following methods perform the shear transformation:

- **public void setToShear(double shx, double shy)**
- **public void shear(double shx, double shy)**

The shear transformation matrix created by the input parameters is as follows:

$$
\begin{bmatrix}
1 & \texttt{shx} & 0 \\
\texttt{shy} & 1 & 0 \\
0 & 0 & 1
\end{bmatrix}
$$

The get methods for obtaining the shear factor in the x and y directions are

- **public double getShearX()**
- **public double getShearY()**

Concatenate Methods

The concatenate methods of **AffineTransform** allow you to apply a sequence of transformations and produce a resultant matrix. These methods are needed when the transformation operation is different from the standard operations (i.e., translation, scaling, rotation, and shear). For instance, to flip an image, we need to flip the matrix first. The reflection operation discussed earlier can be used to create a flip effect. The reflection operation creates a mirror image that lies in a different quadrant. So to flip an image, we first create a reflection matrix and then translate it to the position where the image is currently located. Here's the concatenate method:

- ◆ **public void concatenate(AffineTransform Tx)**

The current transformation matrix is concatenated with the input matrix:

[this] = [this] · [Tx]

The example that follows shows how to apply concatenation.

The matrix for reflection about the *x*-axis is

$$Tx = \begin{bmatrix} 1 & 0 & 0 \\ 0 & -1 & 0 \\ 0 & 0 & 1 \end{bmatrix}$$

Here's a code snippet that performs the flip operation:

```
AffineTransform refTx  =  new AffineTransform(new double[] {1.0,0.0,0.0,-1.0});

refTx.translate(0.0, imageHeight);
```

To flip an image that has undergone other manipulation operations, this transformation is concatenated to another **AffineTransform** object as follows:

```
atx.concatenate (refTx);
```

Preconcatenation

As we saw in the preceding section, in a concatenation operation a given transformation matrix is multiplied by the current transformation matrix. In a preconcatenation operation, the opposite is true; that is, the current transformation matrix is multiplied by a given transformation matrix. The method that performs preconcatenation is

- ◆ **public void preConcatenate(AffineTransform Tx)**

The input matrix is concatenated with the current transformation matrix:

[this] = [Tx] · [this]

Because matrix multiplication is not commutative, the preconcatenation operation is not the same as the concatenation operation.

General Transformation Methods

The following method takes an `AffineTransform` object itself as an input parameter:

- ◆ `public void setTransform(AffineTransform Tx)`

  When this method is applied, the current transformation becomes a copy of the input.

The following method takes elements of the top two rows of the transformation matrix as input parameters:

- ◆ `public void setTransform(double m00,`
  `                          double m10,`
  `                          double m01,`
  `                          double m11,`
  `                          double m02,`
  `                          double m12)`

  The values `m00`, `m01`, `m02`, `m10`, `m11`, and `m12` are the six floating point values that compose the 3×3 transformation matrix.

  Note that both of these general transformation methods destroy the existing transformation matrix.

Transforming Points

The following method transforms a single point:

- ◆ `public Point2D transform(Point2D ptSrc, Point2D ptDst)`

Each of the following methods transforms an array of points with a particular combination of source and destination types, as indicated:

- ◆ `int` **to** `int:`
  ```
  public void transform(Point2D[] ptSrc,
                        int srcOff,
                        Point2D[] ptDst,
                        int dstOff,
                        int numPts)
  ```

- ◆ `double` **to** `double:`
  ```
  public void transform(double[] srcPts,
                        int srcOff,
                        double[] dstPts,
                        int dstOff,
                        int numPts)
  ```

- float **to** float:
  ```
  public void transform(float[] srcPts,
                        int srcOff,
                        float[] dstPts,
                        int dstOff,
                        int numPts)
  ```

- double **to** float:
  ```
  public void transform(double[] srcPts,
                        int srcOff,
                        float[] dstPts,
                        int dstOff,
                        int numPts)
  ```

- float **to** double:
  ```
  public void transform(float[] srcPts,
                        int srcOff,
                        double[] dstPts,
                        int dstOff,
                        int numPts)
  ```

Delta Transformation

The following equations transform a relative-distance vector without applying the translation components of the affine transformation matrix:

$$\begin{bmatrix} x' \\ y' \\ (1) \end{bmatrix} = \begin{bmatrix} m00 & m01 & (m02) \\ m10 & m11 & (m12) \\ (0) & (0) & (1) \end{bmatrix}$$

$$\begin{bmatrix} x \\ y \\ (1) \end{bmatrix} = \begin{bmatrix} m00 \times x + m01 \times y \\ m10 \times x + m11 \times y \\ (1) \end{bmatrix}$$

Here are the methods for transforming a single point and an array of points, respectively:

- **public Point2D deltaTransform(Point2D ptSrc,**
  Point2D ptDst)
- **public void deltaTransform(double[] srcPts,**
  int srcOff,
  double[] dstPts,
  int dstOff,
  int numPts)

Transforming a Shape

The following method transforms the input Shape object into a new Shape object:

♦ `public Shape createTransformedShape(Shape pSrc)`

Inverse Transformation

Inverse transformation is often required in image visualization applications. For instance, you may need to compute statistics over a region that you have marked on the transformed image. The application may be required to obtain the actual region on the original image. You can do this easily by computing the inverse of the transformation.

The AffineTransform class has the following three methods for inverse transformation:

1. `public AffineTransform createInverse() throws NoninvertibleTransformException`

   This method creates an inverse of the current transformation matrix. Not all matrices are invertible. For instance, a singular matrix (a matrix whose determinant equals zero) does not have an inverse. In such cases, this method throws an exception: `NoninvertibleTransformException`.

2. `public Point2D inverseTransform(Point2D ptSrc, Point2D ptDst)`
   `                            throws NoninvertibleTransformException`

   This method transforms a point. We'll see some examples in the sections on pan and zoom in Chapter 7.

3. `public void inverseTransform(double[] srcPts,`
   `                        int srcOff,`
   `                        double[] dstPts,`
   `                        int dstOff,`
   `                        int numPts)`
   `                    throws NoninvertibleTransformException`

   This method transforms an array of points.

Utility Methods

The AffineTransform class comes with several utility methods, including

♦ `public void getMatrix(double[] flatmatrix)`
♦ `public double getDeterminant()`

In the second case, the determinant is calculated by the following formula:

$$
\begin{bmatrix}
\text{m00} & \text{m01} & \text{m02} \\
\text{m10} & \text{m11} & \text{m12} \\
0 & 0 & 1
\end{bmatrix}
= \text{m00} \times \text{m11} - \text{m01} \times \text{m10}
$$

◆ `public void setToIdentity()`

This method resets the transform to identity.

◆ `public boolean isIdentity()`

This method retrieves the flag bits describing the conversion properties of the transformation.

◆ `public int getType()`

The type can be any of the following: `TYPE_IDENTITY`, `TYPE_TRANSLATION`, `TYPE_UNIFORM_SCALE`, `TYPE_GENERAL_SCALE`, `TYPE_QUADRANT_ROTATION`, `TYPE_GENERAL_ROTATION`, or `TYPE_GENERAL_TRANSFORM`.

Static Methods

The following methods return an instance of `AffineTransform` that is specific to one of the four basic transformations:

◆ `public static AffineTransform getRotateInstance(double theta,`
`                                                 double x,`
`                                                 double y)`

◆ `public static AffineTransform getRotateInstance(double theta)`

◆ `public static AffineTransform getTranslateInstance(double tx,`
`                                                    double ty)`

◆ `public static AffineTransform getScaleInstance(double sx,`
`                                                double sy)`

◆ `public static AffineTransform getShearInstance(double shx,`
`                                                double shy)`

These methods are self-explanatory.

Applying Inverse Transformation to a Shape

If you review the list of `AffineTransform` methods, you'll see that there are no methods for inverse transformation of a shape. This functionality is needed especially in processing regions of interest (ROIs), as we'll see in Chapter 9. The example in Listing 4.2 illustrates how to perform inverse transformation on a Shape object.

> **Note:** The code in Listing 4.2 is available on the book's Web page in the directory `src/chapter4/at`.

LISTING 4.2   Applying inverse transformation to a shape

```java
package com.vistech.util;
import java.awt.*;
import java.awt.geom.*;
public class AffineTransformUtil {
    public static Shape inverseTransform(Shape sh, AffineTransform atx) {
        try {
            AffineTransform invtx = atx.createInverse();
            GeneralPath path = new GeneralPath();
            PathIterator pi = sh.getPathIterator(new AffineTransform());

            while(!pi.isDone()) {
                double[] curcoord = new double[6];
                int segType = pi.currentSegment(curcoord);
                Point2D destPoint = null;
                double[] destArray = null;
                double[] dest = new double[6];
                switch (segType) {
                    case PathIterator.SEG_MOVETO:
                        destPoint = atx.inverseTransform(new Point2D.Double(curcoord[0],
                                                  curcoord[1]),destPoint);
                        path.moveTo((float)destPoint.getX(), (float)destPoint.getY());
                        break;
                    case PathIterator.SEG_LINETO:
                        destPoint = atx.inverseTransform(new
                                   Point2D.Double(curcoord[0], curcoord[1]),
                                                  destPoint);
                        path.lineTo((float)destPoint.getX(), (float)destPoint.getY());
                        break;
                    case PathIterator.SEG_QUADTO:
                        atx.inverseTransform(curcoord,0, dest, 0,2);
                        path.quadTo((float)dest[0], (float)dest[1],
                                    (float)dest[2], (float)dest[3]);
                        break;
                    case PathIterator.SEG_CUBICTO:
                        atx.inverseTransform(curcoord,0, dest, 0,3);

                        path.curveTo((float)dest[0], (float)dest[1],
                                     (float)dest[2], (float)dest[3],
                                     (float)dest[4], (float)dest[5]);
                        break;
                    case PathIterator.SEG_CLOSE :
                        path.closePath();
                        break;
                }
                pi.next();
            }
            return (Shape)path;
        }catch(Exception e) {
            e.printStackTrace();
```

continued

```
        return null;
    }
  }
}
```

The code shown in Listing 4.2 uses the `PathIterator` interface to traverse the boundary of the shape. At each segment, it applies inverse transformation to the co-ordinates of that segment.

Conclusion

In this chapter we covered several graphics-related topics that are essential for both the Java 2D and the JAI APIs, including the device coordinate system and graphical shapes.

Whether it is an image or a shape, a graphical object eventually is rendered onto a device such as a monitor or a printer. These devices maintain their own coordinate systems. Java 2D maintains two coordinate systems: user space and device space. It maps the coordinate system of the application to the device coordinate system in a manner transparent to the application. In other words, applications do not need to know about the device on which an image or a graphical object is rendered.

We described the Java 2D APIs that represent different types of shapes. Several examples using these classes will be presented in Chapter 5.

Another important topic in this chapter was the `AffineTransform` class. We'll use this class throughout the remainder of the book to implement different types of image manipulation functions.

Rendering Graphics in Java 2D

5

IN THIS CHAPTER WE'LL LOOK AT the key graphical APIs in Java and use them to build interactive graphical applications. Some of the graphical concepts described here will be required in subsequent chapters.

At the heart of graphics rendering in Java 2D is the Graphics2D class. This class extends the Graphics class, which was part of Java even at its inception. Therefore, before we take a closer look at Graphics2D, we'll describe the Graphics class in some detail. This discussion is followed by a detailed discussion of painting graphical objects in AWT and Swing components.

Graphics2D builds on some of the graphical features already available in the Graphics class. It also uses some of the new Java 2D classes, including AffineTransform and Shape, which we described in Chapter 4. In this chapter we'll describe some of the Graphics2D attributes in detail and give some examples.

To illustrate the use of Graphics2D and the related APIs, we'll develop a simple interactive drawing application with three simple shapes: a line, a rectangle, and an ellipse. Real-world applications require many more than these three shapes, so we'll develop a class library that is capable of creating a variety of shapes and performing interactive operations such as draw, fill, erase, move, copy, and paste. Using this class library, we'll then develop an application called JavaPaintShop that will allow users to perform these interactive operations on the shapes supported by our class library.

Rendering Graphical Objects

To understand how graphical objects are rendered onto a device, let's start with a real-world analogy. Drawing shapes or text is analogous to moving a pen filled with ink over a canvas. Before you started drawing on the canvas, you would probably paint the canvas with a certain background color and fill the pen with ink of the desired color. Once you started painting, you would change the drawing color by filling the pen with ink of a different color.

The software world follows a similar model. In the computer model, a virtual pen moves over an electronic canvas to draw shapes and text. But to render the drawing, we need a visual component that acts as an electronic canvas. Graphical user interface (GUI) toolkits typically provide such components.

A GUI component with such a capability is associated or supplied with an environment for performing graphics-related tasks. This environment also holds attributes and instructions that are needed to perform these tasks. Such an environment is generally called the graphical context. Before a graphical operation is performed, instructions and attributes of the graphical context are set programmatically. For example, shape-drawing attributes could include drawing color, background color, fill color, and line width, and text-drawing attributes could include font type, size, and style. An example of a drawing instruction is asking the graphical context to restrict the drawing to a certain region of the component.

Graphics rendering involves performing graphical operations over a graphical context and then mapping that context on to a visual component. The rendered graphics become visible only when the graphical context maps its content to a component. In Java 2D, the graphical context is transparent to the program that renders graphics. In other words, programs that render graphics don't know about the underlying device to which they are rendering.

Real-world graphical applications must support operations that are much more complex than just drawing graphical objects. Once you draw a shape, for instance, you may want to erase, move, copy, paste, or edit it. To accomplish such tasks, graphical toolkits provide a wide variety of built-in features. In this chapter we'll explore the capabilities provided by the AWT and Java 2D packages.

When we say *graphical objects,* we mean shapes, text, and images. Even though images are considered graphical objects, rendering images is somewhat different from rendering shapes and text. We already described rendering images in the AWT in Chapter 3. Chapters 6 and 11 will describe rendering images in Java 2D and JAI, respectively.

Using the Graphics Class

The `java.awt.Graphics` class is an abstract class that encapsulates data and behavior of a graphical context. As already mentioned, a graphical context in Java is constructed in a platform-specific manner. The actual `Graphics` object is constructed from a platform-specific class that extends the `Graphics` class and overrides its abstract methods.

A `Graphics` object is needed for any type of graphical operation in Java. It is constructed by the Java runtime system for a component when the component becomes visible. The `Graphics` class has two types of methods:

1. Methods for setting and retrieving graphical attributes
2. Methods for performing graphical rendering tasks such as draw, fill, clear, and so on

Graphics Attributes

The `Graphics` class supports various attributes that can be set and obtained through set and get methods.

The color Attribute

The `color` attribute determines the current color of a `Graphics` context, which determines the color of the graphical operations. The following are the color attribute's set and get methods:

- **`public void setColor(Color c)`**
- **`public Color getColor()`**

The font Attribute

Here are the set and get methods for the `font` attribute:

- **`public void setFont(Font font)`**
- **`public Font getFont()`**

To render a font, a graphical context requires font measurements such as height, width, ascent, descent, maximum advance and character width. The `java.awt.FontMetrics` class encapsulates these measurements. The `Graphics` class maintains a read-only `fontMetrics` attribute whose get method is as follows:

- **`public FontMetrics getFontMetrics()`**

The following method returns the `FontMetrics` object for a specified font:

- **`public FontMetrics getFontMetrics(Font f)`**

Clip Attributes

The clip attributes define an area described by a shape. When a clip region is set, rendering operations have no effect outside the clip area. In JDK 1.1, a clip area can be only one shape: a rectangle. Here are the methods related to the clip attribute:

- **`public void setClip(int x, int y, int width, int height)`**

    This method sets the current clip area to the rectangle specified by the inputs. It sets the user clip area, which is independent of the clip area associated with device bounds and window visibility.

- **`public Rectangle getClipBounds()`**

    This method returns the bounding rectangle of the current clip area.

- **`public void setClip(Shape clip)`**
- **`public Shape getClip()`**

    The clip area in Java 2D can assume any closed shape. Although these set and get methods are in the `Graphics` class, they are meant to be used in Java 2D. The `Shape` interface is defined in JDK 1.1, but no classes actually implement this interface.

- **`public void clipRect(int x, int y, int width, int height)`**

    This method intersects the current clip area with a rectangle specified in the input. The resulting clip area is the intersection of the current clip area and the specified rectangle. If there is no current clip area, either because the clip area was never set or because it was cleared by `setClip(null)`, the specified rectangle becomes the new clip area. This method can be used only for making the current clip area smaller. To make it larger, use any of the `setClip()` methods.

- **`public boolean hitClip(int x, int y, int width, int height)`**

    This method performs hit testing on the current clip area. It returns `true` if the rectangular area specified in the input intersects the bounding rectangle of the current clip area.

Paint Modes

The `Graphics` class supports two paint modes: normal and XOR (exclusive OR). These modes can be set by the `setPaintMode()` and `setXORMode()` methods, respectively. For the desired effect, these methods must be called before a rendering operation.

Normal Paint Mode

If the color of the `Graphics` context is set and the `setPaintMode()` method is called, any object drawn will be of the current color set on the `Graphics` context. Here's some sample code:

```
g.setColor(Color.green); // Set the drawing color to green.
g.setPaintMode();
g.drawRect(x, y, width, height); // The outline of the rectangle is green.
```

The default drawing mode in the AWT is the normal mode.

XOR Paint Mode

The `setXORMode(Color c)` method performs an exclusive-OR operation on the pixels. The paint mode alternates between the current color of the `Graphics` context and the color specified in the method argument. In other words, when a drawing operation is performed, the pixels that are the current color will be changed to the specified color. The pixels that are not the current color will be unpredictable colors. However, the subsequent drawing at the same location will restore the original pixel colors.

Here's some sample code that shows how to use the XOR mode:

```
g.setColor(Color.black); // Set the current color to black.
g.setXORMode(Color.green); // Color to be XORed with green
g.drawRect(x, y, width, height); // Outline of the rectangle will be a combination of
green and other colors.
g.drawRect(x, y, width, height); // Rectangle disappears.
```

We'll see later in this chapter how the `setXORMode()` method is used to interactively draw and erase shapes.

Rendering Operations

The `Graphics` class has several methods for drawing shapes, text, and images.

Drawing Shapes

The `Graphics` class supports a limited number of shapes. It has shape-specific methods for performing rendering tasks such as draw, fill, clear, and so on. The basic shapes that can be drawn are the line, rectangle, polygon, oval, and arc.

Line

The following methods draw lines:

- ◆ **`public void drawLine(int x1, int y1, int x2, int y2)`**

  This method draws a line between the end points with the coordinates (`x1, y1`) and (`x2, y2`). The color of the line is the current color of the `Graphics` context. With the `Graphics` class you can draw a line that is only 1 pixel wide. To make a line appear thicker, you must draw multiple lines adjacent to each other.

Likewise, if you need to draw a dotted line, you must draw short lines spaced apart along a line.

◆ **public void drawPolyline(int[] xPoints, int[] yPoints, int nPoints)**

This method draws a sequence of connected lines defined by *x* and *y* coordinate arrays. At a specified index *i,* xPoints[i] and yPoints[i] form a pair of (*x, y*) coordinates. Unless the last point is the same as the first point, the shape produced by this method is not closed. Here's an example:

```
int x [] = {10, 20, 30, 40};
int y [] = {40, 50, 60, 70};
g.drawPolyLine(x,y,x.length);
```

In this example the lines drawn extend between the following sets of coordinates: from (10, 40) to (20, 50); from (20, 50) to (30, 60); and from (30, 60) to (40, 70).

Rectangle

The Graphics class supports three types of rectangles: rectangle, three-dimensional rectangle, and round rectangle. You can draw, fill, and erase each type.

The rectangle methods are

◆ **public void drawRect(int x, int y, int width, int height)**
◆ **public void fillRect(int x, int y, int width, int height)**
◆ **public void clearRect(int x, int y, int width, int height)**
◆ **public void clipRect(int x, int y, int width, int height)**

These methods specify a rectangle whose upper left-hand corner (ULHC) coordinates are x and y and whose width and height are width and height.

The three-dimensional rectangle methods are

◆ **public void draw3DRect(int x, int y, int width, int height,**
                          boolean raised)
◆ **public void fill3DRect(int x, int y, int width, int height,**
                          boolean raised)

If the value of raised is true, the rectangle appears to be raised above the surface; otherwise it appears sunk into the surface.

The round rectangle methods are

◆ **public void drawRoundRect(int x, int y, int width, int height,**
                             int arcWidth, int arcHeight)

- ◆ **public void fillRoundRect(int x, int y, int width, int height,**
                                int arcWidth, int arcHeight)

The `arcWidth` and `arcHeight` parameters represent the horizontal and vertical diameters, respectively, of the arc at the four corners of the rectangle.

Polygon

There are two ways of drawing a polygon:

1. Creating a `Polygon` object first and passing it as a parameter to the `drawPolygon()` method. Here are the related methods:

   - ◆ **public void drawPolygon(Polygon p)**
   - ◆ **public void fillPolygon(Polygon p)**

   The `Polygon` object p specifies a polygon.

2. Passing the (*x, y*) coordinate arrays as the points of the polygons. The related methods are

   - ◆ **public void drawPolygon(int[] xPoints, int[] yPoints, int nPoints)**
   - ◆ **public void fillPolygon(int[] xPoints, int[] yPoints, int nPoints)**

   The `xPoints` and `yPoints` parameters are the arrays of *x* and *y* coordinates, respectively. The corresponding elements of `xPoints` and `yPoints` represent a pair of (*x, y*) coordinates.

Oval

You can draw and fill a circle or an ellipse by using the following methods:

- ◆ **public void drawOval(int x, int y, int width, int height)**
- ◆ **public void fillOval(int x, int y, int width, int height)**

  These methods define an oval that is bounded by a rectangle whose ULHC is (x, y) and whose width and height are `width` and `height`.

Arc

You can draw and fill an outline of a circular or elliptical arc using the following methods:

- ◆ **public void drawArc(int x, int y, int width, int height,**
                      int startAngle, int arcAngle)
- ◆ **public void fillArc(int x, int y, int width, int height,**
                      int startAngle, int arcAngle)

These methods define an arc that begins at `startAngle` and extends `arcAngle` degrees. Angles are interpreted such that 0 degrees is at the three-o'clock position. A positive value indicates a counterclockwise rotation, while a negative value indicates a clockwise rotation. The center of the arc is the center of the rectangle whose origin is at (x, y) and whose size is specified by the `width` and `height` arguments.

Drawing Text

The `Graphics` class has the following methods for drawing text:

◆ `public void drawString(String str, int x, int y)`

In this method, `str` specifies the string to be drawn at (x, y).

◆ `public void drawChars(char[] data, int offset, int length, int x,`
`                        int y)`

This method draws the text specified in the `char` array. The baseline of the first character is at position (x, y).

◆ `public void drawBytes(byte[] data, int offset, int length, int x,`
`                        int y)`

This method draws the text specified in the `byte` array.

Drawing Images

We have already covered the image-rendering methods; see Chapter 3.

Next let's explore how AWT and Swing components use the `Graphics` class.

Painting in AWT Components

In the AWT, the `Component` class is the root of all the GUI classes. Although you can use any AWT component to draw images, only `Panel`, `Canvas`, `Frame`, and `Applet` will be of practical use as graphical canvases. As we saw in the preceding section, the `Graphics` class provides a variety of drawing options for drawing text, graphical objects, and images.

The `Component` class has two methods for performing graphical operations over a `Graphics` context object:

◆ `public void paint(Graphics g)`
◆ `public void update(Graphics g)`

Whether you extend `Panel, Canvas,` or any other type of component, you need to override `paint()` and/or `update()` if you wish to control the graphics drawn over the `Graphics` context.

As mentioned earlier, the graphical context is maintained by a `Graphics` object, which is supplied as an argument every time these methods are invoked. Images and graphical objects are drawn on this `Graphics` object only when they become visible. Here's an example:

```
public class  MyCanvas extends Canvas{
   public void  paint(Graphics g) {
      Rectangle bBox = bounds(); // Gets the boundaries of the component.
      g.draw3DRect(0,0, bBox.width, bBox.height, true); // Draws an elevated 3D border.
   }
}
```

The `paint()` method is system triggered, which means that it is invoked by the AWT automatically whenever a component becomes visible or there is a change in its visibility status (such as window move or deiconify, and so on). The `update()` method, on the other hand, is application triggered. The `update()` method is called by the AWT only when the application invokes `repaint()`.

The `repaint()` method automatically triggers a call to `update()`. If the `update()` method does not exist, the background is cleared and the `paint()` method is invoked.

The `Component` class has the following three flavors of `repaint()`:

1. **`public void repaint()`**

   This method triggers a call to `update()`.

2. **`public void repaint(x, y, w, h)`**

   This method triggers a call to `update()` and repaints a rectangle whose ULHC is (`x, y`) and whose width and height are `w` and `h`. If you needed to paint only a small region, from an efficiency standpoint you would be better off calling this method.

3. **`public void repaint(t, x, y, w, h)`**

   This method triggers a call to `update()` within `t` milliseconds and repaints an area whose ULHC is (`x, y`) and whose width and height are `w` and `h`.

Under normal circumstances, there is no need to call `paint()` or `update()` methods directly from an application. Applications can control graphics-rendering operations only by invoking the `repaint()` method.

The `paint()` and `update()` methods are asynchronous and are called by the AWT callback threads. A call to `repaint()` does not guarantee that a paint operation is performed immediately. It means only that a request has been made for painting. A separate thread handles the paint requests. If there are many requests before the painting thread gets a chance to run, the last one is executed. This amounts to collapsing of multiple updates. As a result, some drawing operations may be lost.

However, collapsing multiple repaint updates is often advantageous, especially when the events that result in redundant repaints occur rapidly. Mouse-driven interactive drawing is an example. Mouse events, such as moving the mouse, result in a large number of calls to the event handler. These events may in turn call `repaint()` in rapid succession. Because multiple updates are collapsed, however, fewer paint threads will be executed. As a result, the need to collapse events may not arise in many applications.

The `Graphics` object that maintains the graphical context is constructed automatically upon invocation of the `paint()` and `update()` methods. However, a component's `Graphics` context can also be explicitly constructed by a call to the `getGraphics()` method of the `Component` class. A drawing operation on this graphical context will be immediately visible; that is, the effect will be similar to what happens when `paint()` or `update()` is called. Here's some sample code:

```
Graphics g = getGraphics();
g.drawString("This is a string", x,y);
```

When the `paint()` method executes this code, the message *This is a string* will be visible immediately. Remember that this code must be in a class that extends `Component` or its descendants. Otherwise the `Graphics` object will not be constructed. Once you create the `Graphics` object, you must dispose of it by calling `g.dispose()`.

Under normal circumstances there is no need to construct the `Graphics` context explicitly. It is possible to accomplish any drawing operation through the `repaint()`, `paint()`, and `update()` methods. To draw a `Graphics` object on a component, you need to override the `paint()` or `update()` methods and include code to draw that object.

paint() versus update()

As mentioned earlier, `paint()` is system triggered and `update()` is application triggered. Overriding `paint()` is necessary because the component in which graphics are drawn often changes its visibility state. This can happen when the component is fully or partially covered by other windows, resized, or iconified.

As stated earlier, if `update()` is not overridden, the AWT calls `paint()`. The question then arises, Why override `update()` when `paint()` can do the same job? Although in the majority of cases `paint()` can do the same job, in some instances system-triggered and application-triggered painting may need to be different. In such cases, both `paint()` and `update()` must be overriden. Furthermore, `update()` allows incremental rendering; that is, each call to `update()` can draw a certain region or part of a shape. On the other hand, a call to `paint()` clears the background, so the entire `Graphics` context must be redrawn. Clearing the background may sometimes result in flickering. If there is flickering, override the `update()` method. The example in Listing 2.5 illustrates this point.

Painting in Swing Components

Even though the Swing package is not part of the JDK 1.1 core APIs, it can be used in JDK 1.1–based applications if the `swingall.jar` file is placed in the class path. In JDK 1.2 (and later packages), Swing is part of the core API and the package names start with *javax.swing*.

In Java Foundation Classes (JFC) terminology, the AWT components are called *heavyweight* components. This term means that an AWT component has its own native window that depends on the painting system of the native platform. On the other hand, the majority of the Swing components are *lightweight,* which means that they are written entirely in Java and rely on Java's painting subsystem. However, every lightweight component has one heavyweight ancestor.

The `JComponent` class, which extends `java.awt.Container,` is the root of most Swing components. Thus all the Swing components that are subclasses of `JComponent` are containers.

Painting in Swing components is a little different from painting in AWT components. In Swing, the `update()` method is never invoked with a call to `repaint().` Instead, `paint()` is called by both system-triggered and application-triggered painting. The `paint()` method in Swing does much more than just paint the component. It calls three other methods: `paintComponent()`, `paintBorder()`, and `paintChildren()`. So an application should override just `paintComponent()` rather than `paint()` itself, thereby leaving the `paintBorder()` and `paintChildren()` methods available to the system.

```
public class MyCanvas extends JPanel {
    public void paintComponent(Graphics g){
        super.paintComponent();
        g.drawString("Hello World", x, y);
    }
}
```

A call to the superclass `paintComponent()` method is needed in components that extend Swing components with UI delegates. A UI delegate is an object that implements a component's look and feel. The `ui` property holds the UI delegate object. A call to `paintComponent()` results in invocation of `ui.update()` and `ui.paint()`, which fill in the background and paint the component, respectively. By invoking `paintComponent()` in the superclass, we ensure that its UI delegates are painted.

Enter Java 2D

Graphics rendering in Java 1.1 has a number of shortcomings. The `Graphics` class doesn't support several drawing attributes that are essential for any geometric rendering operations. For example, you cannot set the width of the line or make it dotted, and so on. Another important missing piece is curve drawing. The only curves that are supported are arcs and ovals.

The `Graphics2D` class is designed to overcome some of the Java 1.1 shortcomings. It extends the `Graphics` class. While maintaining the same rendering of the model, the `Graphics2D` class expands the existing rendering functionality substantially. Using this class, you can render lines with different widths, join types, curves, and so on.

Just as in Java 1.1, you must use the `paint()` and `update()` methods of the components to render graphics, text, and images. To use the `Graphics2D` class, cast the `Graphics` context to a `Graphics2D` context. Here's an example:

```
public void paint(Graphics g) {
    Graphics2D g2d = (Graphics2D)g;
    g2d.drawString("Hello World", 10, 20);
}
```

In this example we did not use the new `Graphics2D` features. Even if you're using the Swing `JComponent` or its descendants, you can use the same rendering model. But in all cases you can cast the `Graphics` context to a `Graphics2D` context and use the new features. Unlike Java 2D, however, Swing is a Java standard extension and can be used with Java 1.1. If you use Swing with Java 1.1, you will not be able to use the `Graphics2D` class.

Off-Screen Rendering in Java 2D

In AWT imaging, you can create an off-screen image by calling the `createImage()` method (of `Component` or `Toolkit`). This image is of type `java.awt.Image.` In Java 2D, however, you can use the `BufferedImage` class to represent an off-screen image. `BufferedImage` extends `java.awt.Image` and provides access to image data. As we'll see in Chapter 6, `BufferedImage` is an important class for many features related to image visualization.

An important advantage of the `BufferedImage` class is that a component does not need to be visible in order for an off-screen image to be created. This makes it easier to implement nonvisual imaging and graphical applications. For example, a server-side application can plot a chart on a `BufferedImage` object and send the chart to its clients to display. Drawing a chart in the server-side application is not possible with

Java 1.1 (i.e., by using Image and Graphics classes) without the component being visible.

To create an off-screen Graphics2D context, you must first create a BufferedImage object and then use the createGraphics() method to obtain the Graphics2D context.

We'll look at the BufferedImage class in detail in Chapters 6 and 8. The Graphics2D class has many more flavors of the drawImage() method. The Drawing Canvas class in Listing 5.1 illustrates how to use the BufferedImage class to create an off-screen image.

LISTING 5.1   The DrawingCanvas class

```
public class DrawingCanvas extends JComponent {
    protected BufferedImage bi;
    protected Graphics2D offGc2d;
    public void createOffScreenImage( int wid, int ht) {
        bi  = new BufferedImage ( wid, ht, BufferedImage.INT-RGB);
        offGc2d = bi.createGraphics();
    }

    public void drawRectOffScreen()
        // Now you can draw off-screen.
        offGc2d.drawRect (30,40,100,100,this);
    }

    public void paintComponent(Graphics g) {
        Graphics2D g2d = (Graphics2D)g;
        g2d.drawImage(bi,0,0, this);
    }
}
```

In the DrawingCanvas class, createOffScreenImage() creates a BufferedImage object of a certain width and height and the type INT_RGB. This object can be created even if the DrawingCanvas component is not visible. The drawRectOffScreen() method draws a rectangle on the Graphics2D context obtained from BufferedImage. In the paint() method, the BufferedImage object is drawn on the graphical context of JComponent.

Graphics2D Attributes

The Graphics2D context maintains several attributes, which can be set by set methods and obtained by get methods. In the sections that follow we'll look at each of these attributes.

The stroke Attribute

The `stroke` attribute represents the characteristics of a shape outline such as its thickness, joining and termination style, and so on. The `Graphics2D` class has the following methods for setting and getting the `stroke` attribute:

- `public void setStroke(Stroke s)`
- `public Stroke getStroke()`

The `stroke` attribute is defined by an interface implemented by the `BasicStroke` class. This class defines a set of rendering attributes for the shape outlines. `BasicStroke` has various constructors that accept different types of stroke attributes. These attributes include width, end caps, line joins, and dash patterns. Let's look at each one.

Width

This attribute represents the pen width measured perpendicular to the pen trajectory. You can construct a `BasicStroke` object with a specified stroke width. Here's an example:

```
Graphics2D g2d;
Stroke widthStroke = new BasicStroke(8.0f);
g2d.setStroke(widthStroke);
```

End Caps

This attribute defines the decoration applied to the ends of unclosed subpaths or dash segments. The `BasicStroke` class specifies the following three options for decoration (see Figure 5.1) :

1. **CAP_BUTT.** This option ends unclosed subpaths and dash segments with no added decoration.
2. **CAP_ROUND.** This option ends unclosed subpaths and dash segments with a round decoration that has a radius equal to half the width of the pen.
3. **CAP_SQUARE.** This option ends unclosed subpaths and dash segments with a square projection that extends beyond the end of the segment to a distance equal to half of the line width.

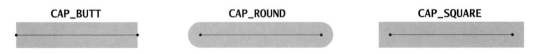

CAP_BUTT   CAP_ROUND   CAP_SQUARE

FIGURE 5.1   End cap styles

Line Joins

This attribute is applied when two path segments are joined. The `BasicStroke` class defines the following three types of line joins (see Figure 5.2):

1. **`JOIN_BEVEL`.** This option joins path segments by connecting the outer corners of their wide outlines with a straight segment.
2. **`JOIN_MITER`.** This option joins path segments by extending the outside edges until they meet.
3. **`JOIN_ROUND`.** This option joins path segments by rounding off the corner at a radius that is half of the line width.

Here's an example:

```
Graphics2D g2d;
Stroke roundStroke = new BasicStroke(8.0f, BasicStroke.CAP_ROUND, JOIN_ROUND);
g2d.setStroke(roundStroke);
```

Dash Patterns

You can define different types of dash patterns using this attribute. The following constructor allows you to construct your favorite pattern:

♦ **`public BasicStroke(float width, int cap, int join, float miterlimit,`**
                       `float[] dash, float dash_phase)`

The arguments `dash` and `dash_phase` define the pattern. The `dash` parameter is an array whose elements represent the dash size and the space size in an alternating fashion. For example, the first element represents the first dash size, the second element represents the first space size, the third element represents the second dash size, and so on. The `dash_phase` parameter is an offset that determines the position at which the dash pattern begins. Here's an example:

FIGURE 5.2   Line join styles

```
Float dashPattern = {4.0f, 2.0f, 4.0f, 2.0f,2.0f, 2.0f, 4.0f}
BasicStroke dashStroke = new BasicStroke( 8.0f,
                                          BasicStroke.CAP_BUTT,
                                          BasicStroke.JOIN_MITER,
                                          dashPattern,
                                          10.0f);

g2d.setStroke(dashStroke);
```

The paint Attribute

The `paint` attribute of `Graphics2D` represents the current painting color or pattern of the `Graphics2D` context. The related `Graphics2D` class methods are

◆ **public void setPaint(Paint paint)**
◆ **public Paint getPaint()**

The `paint` attribute is of type `Paint`, which is an interface in `java.awt` and specifies the following method:

◆ **public PaintContext createContext(ColorModel cm,**
                                   Rectangle deviceBounds,
                                   Rectangle2D userBounds,
                                   AffineTransform xform,
                                   RenderingHints hints)

This method returns an instance of `PaintContext`, which is an interface that defines the painting environment. A class that implements the `Paint` interface must create a `PaintContext` object that will be used by the `Graphics` context while the draw and fill operations are being executed. A `PaintContext` object must maintain the color model and the fill pattern needed for these operations.

The `PaintContext` interface extends the `Transparency` interface, which defines the transparency mode. There are three transparency modes: opaque, transparent, and bit mask.

Currently, the following three classes in `java.awt` implement the `Paint` interface: `Color`, `GradientPaint`, and `TexturePaint`. You can create an object from any one of these classes and pass it as a parameter to the `setPaint()` method. Let's look at the two paint classes.

The GradientPaint Class

`GradientPaint` provides a mechanism to fill a shape with a gradient pattern. This means that the filling color can change gradually across the shape.

`GradientPaint` has four constructors, each of which provides a way to define a color gradient pattern. Basically, you can define two points, P_1 and P_2, with respective colors C_1 and C_2. The colors along the line joining P_1 to P_2 will change from C_1 and

C_2. In other words, if you draw lines parallel to the P_1–P_2 line covering the entire shape, the area contained by these lines will have same color patterns. But what about the colors in the area beyond these lines? The following two rules apply:

1. **Cyclic rule:** The color pattern will alternate between C_1 and C_2.
2. **Acyclic rule:** The color will be constant and will be either C_1 or C_2. The actual color at a point is determined by its proximity to P_1 and P_2. The point will have the C_1 color if it is on the P_1 side of the segment and the C_2 color if it is on the P_2 side of the segment.

To construct a `GradientPaint` object, you can use any of the following constructors:

- ◆ **public GradientPaint(float x1, float y1, Color color1, float x2, float y2, Color color2)**
- ◆ **public GradientPaint(Point2D pt1, Color color1, Point2D pt2, Color color2)**
- ◆ **public GradientPaint(float x1, float y1, Color color1, float x2, float y2, Color color2, boolean cyclic)**
- ◆ **public GradientPaint(Point2D pt1, Color color1, Point2D pt2, Color color2, boolean cyclic)**

Here's a code snippet from DrawGradientPaint.java:

> **Note:** The source code for `DrawGradientPaint.java` is available on the book's Web page in the directory `src/chapter5/paint`.

```
// Cyclic paint example
    int x =20; int y =20;
    int wid = 100; int ht =100;
    GradientPaint gp = new GradientPaint( x+20.0f, y+20.0f, Color.red, x+60.0f,
                                          y+20.0f, Color.green);
    g2d.setPaint(gp);
    g2d.fillRect(x,y, wid,ht);

// Acyclic paint example
    x= 140; y= 20;
    gp = new GradientPaint( x+20.0f, y+20.0f, Color.red, x+60.0f, y+20.0f,
                            Color.green, true);
    g2d.setPaint(gp);
    g2d.fillRect(x,y, wid,ht);
```

Figure 5.3 shows a frame with cyclic and acyclic gradient paints. Implementation of the **DrawGradientPaint** class launched this frame. To run this class, type "java app.DrawGradientPaint" on the command line.

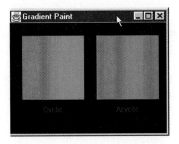

FIGURE 5.3   Cyclic and acyclic filling

The TexturePaint Class

You can use `TexturePaint` to fill a shape with your favorite texture. A shape can be filled with a local pattern that repeats globally. Here's the constructor:

◆ **public TexturePaint(BufferedImage txtr, Rectangle2D anchor)**

To create your own texture, you need to create an off-screen image and draw the desired pattern on it. In Java 2D, the `BufferedImage` class is used for creating off-screen images. Here's a code snippet taken for `DrawTexture.java`.

> **Note:** The source code for `DrawTexture.java` is available on the book's Web page in the directory `src/chapter5/paint`.

```
// First create a local pattern on an off-screen image.
BufferedImage bi = new BufferedImage(10,10, BufferedImage.TYPE_INT_RGB);
Graphics2D offScrGc = bi.createGraphics();
offScrGc.setColor(Color.blue);
offScrGc.fillRect(0,0,10,10);
offScrGc.setColor(Color.red);
offScrGc.fillRect(4,4,3,3);

TexturePaint  texturePaint = new TexturePaint(bi, new Rectangle(0,0,10,10));

g2d.setPaint(texturePaint);
g2d.fillRect(0,0,100,100);
```

Figure 5.4 shows a frame with different patterns of texture. Implementation of the `DrawTexture` class launched this frame. To run this class, type "java app.DrawTexture" on the command line.

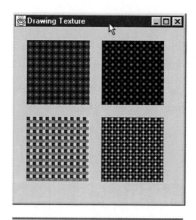

FIGURE 5.4   Drawing texture

The transform Attribute

You can manipulate the Graphics context by setting the transform attribute. The Graphics class has just one transformation method: translate. With the introduction of the AffineTransform class in Java 2D, you can now apply a variety of transformation operations to a Graphics2D context, including translation, scaling, and rotation, among many others.

The set and get methods for the transform attribute are

- **public void setTransform(AffineTransform Tx)**
- **public void transform(AffineTransform Tx)**
- **public AffineTransform getTransform()**

Here are the transform-specific methods:

- Translation:
  - **public void translate(int x, int y)**
  - **public void translate(double tx, double ty)**

- Rotation:
  - **public void rotate(double theta)**
  - **public void rotate(double theta, double x, double y)**

- Scaling:
  - **public void scale(double sx, double sy)**

- Shear:
  - **public void shear(double shx, double shy)**

The composite Attribute

The `composite` attribute is defined by the `Composite` interface that is implemented by the `AlphaComposite` class. Here are the `composite` set and get methods:

- ◆ **public avoid setComposite(Composite comp)**
- ◆ **public Composite getComposite()**

Along with the `CompositeContext` class, the `Composite` interface defines the methods for composing a drawing primitive with the underlying graphical area. After the `composite` attribute is set in the `Graphics2D` context, it combines a shape, text, or an image being rendered with the colors that have already been rendered according to predefined rules. The classes that implement this interface provide the rules and a method for creating the context for a particular operation. `CompositeContext` is an environment used by the compositing operation, which is created by `Graphics2D` before the operation starts. `CompositeContext` contains private information and resources needed for a compositing operation. When the `CompositeContext` object is no longer needed, the `Graphics2D` object disposes of it in order to reclaim resources allocated for the operation.

The renderingHints Attribute

As its name suggests, the `renderingHints` attribute simply contains hints for the renderer. Whether or not a hint is accepted depends on the platform on which an application is running. Here are the `renderingHints`-related methods:

- ◆ **public void setRenderingHints(Map hints)**
- ◆ **public Object getRenderingHint(RenderingHints.Key hintKey)**
- ◆ **public void addRenderingHints(Map hints)**
- ◆ **public RenderingHints getRenderingHints()**
- ◆ **public Object getRenderingHint(RenderingHints.Key hintKey)**

To set a rendering hint, you must provide a key and a value. The keys are fixed and are given by the constants that start with *KEY_* and are defined in the `RenderingHints` class, as are the values. Table 5.1 lists all the keys and their corresponding values.

Here's an example:

```
RenderingHints rh = new RenderingHints( KEY_RENDERING,  VALUE_RENDER_QUALITY);
rh.add(KEY_INTERPOLATION, VALUE_ INTERPOLATION_NEAREST_NEIGHBOR);

offScrGc.setRenderingHints(rh);
```

The `offScrGc` variable is a `Graphics2D` object obtained from `BufferedImage.`

TABLE 5.1   Rendering Hints

KEY	VALUES	COMMENTS
KEY_ALPHA_INTERPOLATION	VALUE_ALPHA_INTERPOLATION_ SPEED VALUE_ALPHA_INTERPOLATION_ QUALITY VALUE_ALPHA_INTERPOLATION_ DEFAULT	This hint suggests the criteria (i.e., speed, quality, or the system default) for choosing an algorithm that computes alpha values.
KEY_ANTIALIASING	VALUE_ANTIALIAS_ON VALUE_ANTIALIAS_OFF VALUE_ANTIALIAS_DEFAULT	This is a general antialiasing hint.
KEY_COLOR_RENDERING	VALUE_COLOR_RENDER_SPEED VALUE_COLOR_RENDER_QUALITY VALUE_COLOR_RENDER_DEFAULT	This hint suggests the criteria (i.e., speed, quality, or the system default) for choosing a method for color mapping.
KEY_DITHERING	VALUE_DITHER_DISABLE VALUE_DITHER_ENABLE VALUE_DITHER_DEFAULT	This hint suggests whether or not dithering needs to be enabled. Programs that render to a lower-resolution device may want to use this hint.
KEY_FRACTIONALMETRICS	VALUE_FRACTIONALMETRICS_ON VALUE_FRACTIONALMETRICS_OFF VALUE_FRACTIONALMETRICS_DEFAULT	Java 2D supports floating-point font metrics. This hint suggests whether or not you want this feature.
KEY_INTERPOLATION	VALUE_INTERPOLATION_BICUBIC VALUE_INTERPOLATION_BILINEAR VALUE_INTERPOLATION_NEAREST_ NEIGHBOR	This hint suggests an interpolation algorithm to be used in reconstructing an image. Programs that geometrically manipulate images may want to use this hint.
KEY_RENDERING	VALUE_RENDER_SPEED VALUE_RENDER_QUALITY VALUE_RENDER_DEFAULT	This hint suggests the criteria (i.e., speed, quality, or the system default) for choosing a rendering algorithm. Programs that render images may want to use this hint.
KEY_TEXT_ANTIALIASING	VALUE_TEXT_ANTIALIAS_ON VALUE_TEXT_ANTIALIAS_OFF VALUE_TEXT_ANTIALIAS_DEFAULT	This is an antialiasing hint for rendering text.

Font Attributes

You must use the superclass's `setFont()` and `getFont()` methods to set and get the fonts of the `Graphics2D` context. However, `Graphics2D` has a method that returns an object that represents a rendering context for fonts:

- **`public FontRenderContext getFontRenderContext()`**

    This rendering context takes into consideration antialiasing and fractional metrics, as well as target device–specific information such as dots per inch.

Clip Attributes

In addition to the clip-related methods inherited from the `Graphics` class (see the discussion of clip in the section titled Using the `Graphics` class earlier in this chapter), the `Graphics2D` class has the following method:

- **`public void clip(Shape s)`**

    This method intersects the current `Clip` with the `Shape` specified in the input. The current instance of `Clip` assumes the shape that is the result of this intersection. Successive clip areas reduce the size of the `Clip` object. To reset, call `setClip()` with a `null` argument. Chapter 7 gives an example that implements clipping, in the section titled Implementing a Lens.

Graphics2D Rendering Operations

Now that we have seen how to set the rendering attributes, it's time for a closer look at the types of rendering operations. The `Graphics2D` class inherits several methods for rendering shapes, text, and images, and in addition it has a few of its own.

Drawing Shapes

The following methods are for drawing shapes:

- **`public void draw(Shape s)`**

    This method draws an outline of a shape using the current settings of the `Graphics2D` context.

- **`public void fill(Shape s)`**

    This method fills the interior of a shape using the current settings of the `Graphics2D` context.

Drawing Text

The following methods are for drawing text:

- ```
  public void drawString(AttributedCharacterIterator iterator,
                          int x,
                          int y)
  ```

- ```
  public void drawString(AttributedCharacterIterator iterator,
                          float x,
                          float y)
  ```

  These methods render the text of the specified iterator.
  `AttributedCharacterIterator` is an interface in the `java.text` package.

- ```
  public void drawGlyphVector(GlyphVector g,
                              float x,
                              float y)
  ```

  A `GlyphVector` object is a collection of glyphs containing geometric information for the placement of each glyph.

Interactive Graphics

Many applications need the capability to perform graphical and text operations interactively; that is, they need to be able to use the mouse to perform operations such as draw, move, and erase. Often these operations are performed over images. Take, for instance, the operation of zooming images. Before zooming, you would interactively draw a rectangle over the image by dragging the mouse. When a desired size was reached, you would release the mouse button. You would then expect to see part of the image within the rectangle zoomed.

A more complicated example is marking a region of interest (ROI) over an image. Drawing an outline surrounding an area of interest marks a region. This is usually done interactively so that a user can manually draw a shape to fit the region. Overlaying graphics and text can also be used as a means of communication. A radiologist, for example, may draw arrows or circles on certain regions and/or write comments over images to communicate her or his findings or draw the attention of other radiologists and doctors.

A Simple Drawing Canvas for Graphics

To implement an interactive drawing application, we need a visual component to draw graphical objects. Such a component must support some basic functionality, such as drawing of shapes and text. To allow interaction through a mouse and a
  ```

keyboard, this component must be capable of firing mouse, mouseMotion, and key events. The SimpleGraphicsCanvas2D class implements a simple graphical canvas (see Listing 5.2).

> **Note:** The source code for SimpleGraphicsCanvas2D is available on the book's Web page in the directory src/chapter5/simpleshapes.

LISTING 5.2   The SimpleGraphicsCanvas2D class

```java
package com.vistech.graphics;
import java.awt.*;
import java.awt.event.*;
import java.awt.image.*;
import java.awt.geom.*;
import javax.swing.*;
public class SimpleGraphicsCanvas2D extends JComponent {
    protected BufferedImage offScrImage;
    protected Graphics2D offScrGc;
    protected int width = 0;
    protected int height = 0;
    protected Color drawingColor = Color.green;

    public void draw(Shape s){
        if(offScrGc != null) offScrGc.draw(s);
        repaint();
    }

    public BufferedImage getDisplayedImage(){
        return offScrImage;
    }

    public Graphics2D getDisplayedImageGC(){
        return offScrGc;
    }

    public void createOffScreenImage(int wid, int ht){
        offScrImage = new BufferedImage(wid, ht,BufferedImage.TYPE_INT_RGB);
        offScrGc = offScrImage.createGraphics();
        offScrGc.setColor(drawingColor);
    }

    public void paintComponent(Graphics g) {
        super.paintComponent(g);
        Graphics2D g2d = (Graphics2D)g;
        Rectangle bounds = getBounds();
        if((width <=0) || (height <=0) ||
           (width != bounds.width) ||
           (height != bounds.height)){
            createOffScreenImage(bounds.width, bounds.height);
            width = bounds.width;
            height = bounds.height;
        }
```

```
        g2d.drawImage(offScrImage, 0,0,bounds.width, bounds.height, this);
    }
}
```

Because `SimpleGraphicsCanvas2D` extends the `JComponent` class, it inherits all of the methods related to the `mouse`, `key`, `propertyChange`, and `vetoableChange` events. Thus we do not need to implement the methods to fire these events.

As Listing 5.2 shows, `SimpleGraphicsCanvas2D` implements only a few methods. The `createOffScreenImage()` method creates a `BufferedImage` object for drawing shapes. The `Graphics` context of this image can hold a variety of attributes, as described earlier. In this simple example, however, we'll set only the `drawingColor` attribute.

To draw a shape, a client object needs to call the `draw()` method with a `Shape` object as the argument. The `draw()` method draws the shape on the `offScrImage` object and calls `repaint()`. As mentioned earlier, `repaint()` triggers the `paintComponent()` method. The `paintComponent()` method first checks the size of the component because the user might have resized the canvas after the last drawing. If that is true, `createOffScreenImage()` is called to create the off-screen image to fit the current component size. The `paintComponent()` method then calls `drawImage()` with `offScrImage` as one of its parameters.

Shapes are drawn over the off-screen image. The shapes are actually painted when `repaint()` is called. The entire off-screen image is painted onto the `Simple GraphicsCanvas2D` component.

Drawing Simple Shapes

Now that we have created a component class for drawing shapes, let's illustrate interactive drawing through a simple example that draws three shapes: a line, a rectangle, and an ellipse. But before we describe this class, let's specify the shape- and text-drawing procedures.

Shape-Drawing Procedure

1. Position the cursor at the desired point over the component. This will become the anchor point of the shape. Hold the mouse button down and drag. As the mouse is being dragged, the size of the shape will vary, reflecting the current position of the cursor.

2. Release the mouse button when the desired size is reached. The shape at that time is the final shape and is drawn permanently over the image.

The `DrawSimpleShapes` class can operate on `SimpleGraphicsCanvas2D` to draw shapes (see Listing 5.3).

> **Note:** The source code for DrawSimpleShapes is available on the book's Web page in the directory **src/chapter5/simpleshapes**.

LISTING 5.3 The `DrawSimpleShapes` class

```
package app;
import java.awt.*;
import java.awt.image.*;
import java.awt.geom.*;
import javax.swing.*;
import java.awt.event.*;
public class DrawSimpleShapes implements MouseListener, MouseMotionListener{
    final static int RECTANGLE = 2;
    final static int ELLIPSE = 4;
    final static int LINE = 1;
    protected int shapeType = LINE;

    protected SimpleGraphicsCanvas2D grCanvas;
    protected Point diff = new Point(0,0);
    protected Point shapeAnchor = new Point(0,0);
    protected boolean scrollOn = true;
    protected boolean mousePressed = false;
    protected Shape currentShape, prevShape;

    public DrawSimpleShapes(SimpleGraphicsCanvas2D c){
        grCanvas = c;
    }

    public void startDraw(int x, int y) {
        shapeAnchor = new Point(x,y);
        diff = new Point(0,0);
    }

    public void draw(int x, int y) {
        switch(shapeType) {
          case LINE:
            currentShape =
            new Line2D.Float((Point2D)shapeAnchor, (Point2D)new Point(x,y));
            break;
          case RECTANGLE:
          case ELLIPSE:
            diff.x = x - shapeAnchor.x;
            diff.y = y - shapeAnchor.y;
            int wid = diff.x;
            int ht = diff.y;
            Point ulhc = new Point(shapeAnchor);
            if(diff.x <0) {
                wid = -diff.x;
                ulhc.x = x;
            }
            if(diff.y <0){
                ht = -diff.y;
                ulhc.y = y;
            }
```

```
              if(shapeType == RECTANGLE)
                 currentShape = new Rectangle(ulhc.x, ulhc.y, wid, ht);
              else currentShape = new Ellipse2D.Double(ulhc.x, ulhc.y, wid, ht);

              break;
       }
       Graphics2D g = grCanvas.getDisplayedImageGC();
       g.setColor(Color.black);
       g.setXORMode(Color.blue);
       if(prevShape != null) grCanvas.draw(prevShape);
       grCanvas.draw(currentShape);
       prevShape = currentShape;
   }

   public void mousePressed(MouseEvent e) {
      if(!scrollOn) return;
      if(mousePressed) return;
      mousePressed = true;

      if(SwingUtilities.isLeftMouseButton(e)){
         startDraw(e.getX(), e.getY());

      }else {
         popupMenu((JComponent)e.getSource(), e.getX(), e.getY());
       }
   }

   public void mouseReleased(MouseEvent e) {
      if(SwingUtilities.isLeftMouseButton(e)){
         Graphics2D g = grCanvas.getDisplayedImageGC();
         draw(e.getX(), e.getY());
         prevShape = null;
      }
      mousePressed = false;
   }


   public void mouseClicked(MouseEvent e){}
   public void mouseEntered(MouseEvent e){}
   public void mouseExited(MouseEvent e){}

   public void mouseDragged(MouseEvent e){
      if(SwingUtilities.isLeftMouseButton(e)){
         draw(e.getX(), e.getY());
      }
   }
   public void mouseMoved(MouseEvent e){}
   protected void popupMenu(JComponent comp,int x, int y){
      JPopupMenu jp = new JPopupMenu("");
      jp.setLightWeightPopupEnabled(true);
      comp.add(jp);
      JMenuItem line = new JMenuItem("Line");
      line.addActionListener(
        new ActionListener(){
          public void actionPerformed(ActionEvent e){
            shapeType = LINE;
          }
```

continued

```java
                }
            );
            JMenuItem rect= new JMenuItem("Rectangle");
            rect.addActionListener(
                new ActionListener(){
                  public void actionPerformed(ActionEvent e){
                      shapeType = RECTANGLE;
                  }
                }
            );

            JMenuItem eli = new JMenuItem("Ellipse");
            eli.addActionListener(
                new ActionListener(){
                  public void actionPerformed(ActionEvent e){
                      shapeType = ELLIPSE;
                  }
                }
            );

            jp.add(line);
            jp.add(rect);
            jp.add(eli);
            jp.show(comp,x,y);
        }

        public static void  main(String[] args){
            SimpleGraphicsCanvas2D gc = new SimpleGraphicsCanvas2D();

            DrawSimpleShapes dss = new DrawSimpleShapes(gc);

            gc.addMouseListener(dss);
            gc.addMouseMotionListener(dss);

            gc.setSize(600,400);
            JFrame fr = new JFrame();
            fr.addWindowListener(
              new WindowAdapter(){
                public void windowClosing(WindowEvent e){
                    System.exit(0);
                }
              }
            );
            fr.setTitle("Graphics Canvas");
            fr.getContentPane().add((Component)gc);
            fr.pack();
            fr.setSize(400,300);
            fr.show();
            fr.repaint();
        }
    }
```

Let's start with the main() method. This method first creates the SimpleGraphicsCanvas2D and DrawSimpleShapes objects. Then it registers Draw SimpleShapes with SimpleGraphicsCanvas2D to receive mouse and mouseMotion events. So when a user clicks the mouse, `DrawSimpleShapes` receives the `mouse` event through the `mousePressed()` method. When the user drags the mouse, `Draw SimpleShapes` receives `mouseMotion` events through the `mouseDragged()` method.

Next let's describe the `DrawSimpleShapes` methods by reviewing the shape-drawing scenario. This class supports only three shapes: line, rectangle, and ellipse. To select a shape, first right-click on the drawing canvas represented by `Simple GraphicsCanvas2D.` to launch a pop-up menu with three items: **Line, Rectangle, and Ellipse.** Then choose the desired shape. The pop-up menu is launched by the `mousePressed()` method, which is invoked when the right mouse button is pressed.

When you left-click on one of the shape options, the shape-drawing procedure begins. The `mousePressed()` method in this case calls the `startDraw()` method. As already described, the shape-drawing procedure requires that the position at which the mouse is clicked be saved. Let's define this position as the anchor point of the shape. The `startDraw()` method assigns the anchor point to the `shapeAnchor` variable. The arguments for this method are the (x, y) coordinates of the point at which the mouse was clicked.

As you drag the mouse, the `mouseMotion` events are received through `mouse Dragged()`, which in turn calls `draw()` to draw the other end of the shape at the current position pointed to by the mouse. The `draw()` method constructs the selected shape. As you drag the mouse, you will see the shape drawn at the new position with the anchor point fixed. The `draw()` method does this by erasing the previously drawn shape. As mentioned earlier, the erasing effect can be achieved through exclusive-OR operations. In XOR mode, if you draw a shape at the same position twice, the previous shape is erased. That's what the `draw()` method does. It first constructs a shape and then draws it in the previous position, thereby erasing the previous shape. The `draw()` method then constructs the new shape in the new position.

Finally, when you release the mouse, `mouseReleased()` is called. As Listing 5.3 shows, this method also calls `draw()`, to ensure that the other end of the shape is drawn at the position where the mouse was released. The shape drawn when the mouse is released remains permanently on the canvas.

Implementing DrawSimpleShapes

To run the simple interactive shape-drawing program shown in Listing 5.3, type "java app.DrawSimpleShapes". As a result, the frame shown in Figure 5.5 will be launched. To select a shape, right-click on it. You will see a pop-up menu with three menu items: **Line, Rectangle, and Ellipse.** Choose any shape and drag the mouse to draw that shape.

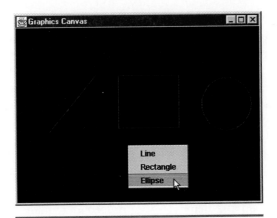

FIGURE 5.5 Drawing simple shapes interactively

Building Interactive Drawing Applications

The `SimpleGraphicsCanvas2D` and `DrawSimpleShapes` classes discussed in the previous example are too simple for any real-world applications. Our aim in this section is to design practical classes capable of creating different shapes and performing interactive operations such as fill, erase, move, copy, and paste. To accomplish this goal, we'll develop first a component class that renders shapes and then a class library of shapes.

Designing a Component Class for Interactive Drawing

A component class should be capable of drawing any shape without being aware of its type. Before we develop such a class, let's specify its behavior in terms of methods in an interface. There are many advantages to having an interface. First, it provides a clean separation between client classes and the class that implements the interface. This means that the component class and its client classes can be compiled separately.

Second, it can simulate multiple inheritance. For example, suppose we have an `ImageCanvas` class (that extends `JComponent`) that can display images, and a `GraphicsCanvas` class that can paint graphics. Now suppose also that we need a class that overlays graphics on images. The new class cannot extend both `ImageCanvas` and `GraphicsCanvas` because Java doesn't support multiple inheritance. One option is to cut and paste the entire `GraphicsCanvas` code into the `ImageCanvas` class. This is certainly not a good option because then `ImageCanvas` cannot be passed as an argument to the methods that take `GraphicsCanvas` as an argument.

Another option, then, is to create an interface—say, `GraphicsDisplay`—to define the methods required to set the attributes and to draw graphics. Now `GraphicsCanvas` can implement the `GraphicsDisplay` interface. The new composite class can extend the `ImageCanvas` class and implement the `GraphicsDisplay` interface. This new class is also of `GraphicsDisplay` type, so it can be passed as a parameter to the methods that take `GraphicsDisplay` as an argument. Listing 5.4 shows the code for `Graphics Display`.

LISTING 5.4   The `GraphicsDisplay` interface

```
public interface GraphicsDisplay {
    public void setFont(Font font);
    public Font getFont();

    public void setFontSize(int size);
    public int getFontSize();

    public void setFontType(int size);
    public int getFontType();

    public void setFontStyle(int style);
    public int getFontStyle();

    public void setDrawingColor(Color drawingColor);
    public Color getDrawingColor();

    public void setFillColor(Color fillColor);
    public Color getFillColor();

    public void setTextColor(Color textColor);
    public Color getTextColor();

    public void setComposite(Composite composite);
    public Composite getComposite();

    public void setPaint(Paint paint);
    public Paint getPaint();

    public void setTransform(AffineTransform transform);
    public AffineTransform getTransform();

    public void setCapStyle(int capStyle);
    public int getCapStyle();

    public void setStrokeWidth(int wid);
    public int getStrokeWidth();

    public void setStroke(Stroke stroke);
    public Stroke getStroke();
```

continued

```
public void setClip(Shape clipshape);
public Shape getClip();

public void setRenderingHints(RenderingHints renderingHints);
public RenderingHints getRenderingHints();


public void setGraphicsParams(GraphicsParams params);
public GraphicsParams getGraphicsParams();
public void reset();

public void addKeyListener(KeyListener kl);
public void removeKeyListener(KeyListener kl);

public void addMouseListener(MouseListener ml);
public void addMouseMotionListener(MouseMotionListener e);

public void removeMouseListener(MouseListener ml);
public void removeMouseMotionListener(MouseMotionListener ml);

public void addPropertyChangeListener(PropertyChangeListener pc);
public void removePropertyChangeListener(PropertyChangeListener pc);

public void addVetoableChangeListener(VetoableChangeListener vl);
public void removeVetoableChangeListener(VetoableChangeListener vl);


public BufferedImage getDisplayedImage();
public Graphics2D getDisplayedImageGC();

public void setCursor(Cursor cursor);

public void draw(Shape shape);
public void repaint();
}
```

The GraphicsDisplay interface has several set and get methods for graphics-related properties. In addition, it has methods for adding and removing mouse and keyboard events, as well as methods for supporting bound and constrained properties.

Listing 5.5 shows the code for the GraphicsCanvas2D class, which implements the GraphicsDisplay interface and follows the same basic principle as the Simple GraphicsCanvas2D class.

> **Note:** The source code for GraphicsCanvas2D is available on the book's Web page in the directory src/chapter5/gracanvas.

LISTING 5.5 The GraphicsCanvas2D class

```java
package com.vistech.graphics;
import java.awt.*;
import java.awt.event.*;
import java.awt.image.*;
import java.awt.geom.*;
import javax.swing.*;

public class GraphicsCanvas2D extends JComponent implements GraphicsDisplay {
    protected BufferedImage offScrImage;
    protected Graphics2D offScrGc;
    protected Shape clipShape;
    protected int width = 0, height = 0;
    protected Color drawingColor = Color.green;
    protected Color fillColor = Color.blue, textColor = Color.green;
    protected Paint paint = null;
    protected Shape clip = null;
    protected AffineTransform xform = null;
    protected Stroke basicStroke = null;
    protected RenderingHints renderingHints = null;
    protected Composite composite = null;
    protected Font font = null;

    protected float strokeWidth = 1.0f;
    protected int capStyle = BasicStroke.CAP_SQUARE;
    protected int joinStyle = BasicStroke.JOIN_MITER;
    protected int fontStyle, fontSize =10,fontType = 5;
    static String[] allfonts =
        GraphicsEnvironment.getLocalGraphicsEnvironment().getAvailableFontFamilyNames();

    public GraphicsCanvas2D() {}

    public void setFontType(int type){
        fontType = type;
        Font fnt = new Font(allfonts[fontType], fontStyle, fontSize);
        setFont(fnt);
    }
    public int getFontType(){return fontType;}

    public void setFontSize(int sz){
        fontSize = sz;
        Font fnt = new Font(allfonts[fontType], fontStyle, fontSize);
        setFont(fnt);
    }
    public int getFontSize(){return fontSize;}

    public void setFontStyle(int style){
        fontStyle = style;
        Font fnt = new Font(allfonts[fontType], fontStyle, fontSize);
    }
    public int getFontStyle(){return fontStyle;}

    public void setFont(Font font) {this.font = font;}
    public Font getFont() {return font;}
```

continued

```java
public void setDrawingColor(Color drawingColor) {this.drawingColor = drawingColor;}
public Color getDrawingColor() { return drawingColor;}

public void setFillColor(Color fillColor) { this.fillColor = fillColor;}
public Color getFillColor() { return fillColor;}

public void setTextColor(Color textColor) { this.textColor = textColor;}
public Color getTextColor() { return textColor;}

public void setComposite(Composite composite) {
    this.composite = composite;
}
public Composite getComposite() { return composite;}

public void setPaint(Paint paint) { this.paint = paint;}
public Paint getPaint() { return paint; }

public void setTransform(AffineTransform transform) { this.xform = transform;}
public AffineTransform getTransform() { return xform; }

public void setCapStyle(int capStyle){
    this.capStyle = capStyle;
    basicStroke = new BasicStroke(strokeWidth, capStyle, joinStyle);
    offScrGc.setStroke(basicStroke);
}
public int getCapStyle(){ return capStyle;}

public void setStrokeWidth(int enum){
    strokeWidth = 0.5f + 0.5f*enum;
    basicStroke = new BasicStroke(strokeWidth, capStyle, joinStyle);
    offScrGc.setStroke(basicStroke);
}
public int getStrokeWidth(){ return (int)strokeWidth;}

public void setJoinStyle(int style) {
    joinStyle = style;
    basicStroke = new BasicStroke(strokeWidth, capStyle, joinStyle);
    offScrGc.setStroke(basicStroke);
}
public int getJoinStyle() { return joinStyle; }

public void setStroke(Stroke stroke) { this.basicStroke = stroke; }
public Stroke getStroke() { return basicStroke; }

public void setRenderingHints(RenderingHints renderingHints) {
    this.renderingHints = renderingHints;
}
public RenderingHints getRenderingHints() { return renderingHints;}

public void draw(Shape s){
    if(offScrGc != null) offScrGc.draw(s);
    repaint();
}

public void setClip(Shape clipShape){
    this.clipShape = clipShape;
}
```

```
public Shape getClip(){ return clipShape;}

public BufferedImage getDisplayedImage(){ return offScrImage; }

public Graphics2D getDisplayedImageGC(){ return offScrGc;}

public void createOffScreenImage(int wid, int ht){
    offScrImage = new BufferedImage(wid, ht,BufferedImage.TYPE_INT_RGB);
    offScrGc = offScrImage.createGraphics();
    offScrGc.setColor(drawingColor);
}

public void paintComponent(Graphics g) {
    super.paintComponent(g);
    Graphics2D g2d = (Graphics2D)g;
    Rectangle bounds = getBounds();
    if((width <=0) || (height <=0) ||
       (width != bounds.width) ||
       (height != bounds.height)){
       createOffScreenImage(bounds.width, bounds.height);
       width = bounds.width;
       height = bounds.height;
    }
    g2d.drawImage(offScrImage, 0,0,bounds.width, bounds.height, this);
}

public void reset(){
    Rectangle bounds = getBounds();
    createOffScreenImage(bounds.width, bounds.height);
    width = bounds.width;
    height = bounds.height;
    strokeWidth = 1.0f;
    repaint();
  }
}
```

You can use GraphicsCanvas2D as a canvas for drawing both graphics and text. To draw graphics, a client object first needs to obtain the off-screen graphical context (offScrGc) from GraphicsCanvas2D. The client object can use any of the drawing methods from the Graphics2D class to draw graphics and text.

Designing a Library of Shapes for Interactive Drawing

In this section we'll design a library of classes that are capable of interactively drawing several commonly used shapes on a GraphicsDisplay component. Henceforth we'll call this library the *shapes* class library. In order for a client application to use this class library, we need to provide a set of interfaces for the outside world. So before we implement the classes that represent shapes, we need to design the interfaces to these classes. First, however, let's specify the procedures to be performed on these shapes and text.

Drawing Shapes

The operations for drawing shapes are draw, move, erase, fill, and copy/paste.

Draw

1. Select the **Draw** operation.
2. Position the cursor at the desired point over the component. This will become the anchor point of the shape. Hold the mouse button down and drag. As the mouse is being dragged, the size of the shape will vary, reflecting the current position of the cursor.
3. Release the mouse button when the desired size is reached. The shape at that time is the final shape and is drawn permanently over the image.

Move

1. Select the **Move** operation.
2. Position the cursor over the desired shape and click the left mouse button. If the shape is selected, it becomes active; that is, the shape is surrounded by small squares.
3. Holding the left mouse button down, drag the shape until you reach the desired position.

Erase

1. Select the **Erase** operation.
2. Position the cursor over the desired shape and click the left mouse button. If the shape is selected, it is erased.

Fill

1. Select the **Fill** operation.
2. Position the cursor over the desired shape and click the left mouse button. If the shape is selected, it is filled with the color chosen in the **Filling Color** combo box. Note that some shapes cannot be filled.

Copy/Paste

1. Select the **Copy/Paste** operation.
2. Position the cursor over the desired shape and click the left mouse button. If the shape is selected, the shape is copied.
3. Position the cursor at a desired position on the canvas shape and click the left mouse button. The copied shape is pasted at that position.

Drawing Text

Drawing text is similar to drawing shapes. Set the text parameters before you start typing the text string. The operations for drawing text are draw, move, and erase.

Draw

1. Select the **Draw** operation.
2. Position the cursor at the desired position on the viewport and click the left mouse button.
3. Type the characters. If you hit **Backspace** or **Delete,** the latest character is deleted and the cursor moves back by one character.
4. To type another set of characters, move the cursor to a new position and repeat steps 1 and 2.

Move

1. Select the **Move** operation.
2. Move the cursor over the desired text and click the left mouse button.
3. Holding the left mouse button down, drag the text string to a new position.
4. When you release the button, the text string is written permanently. You can move it again any number of times.

Erase

1. Select the **Erase** operation.
2. Position the cursor on the desired text and click the left mouse button. If the text is selected, it is erased.

Designing an Interface for Interactive Drawing

Application classes or beans are expected clients of the shapes class library. In order for client objects to interact with the class library, we need to design well-defined APIs. This means that we need to design the interfaces first.

The Drawable Interface

To specify methods, let's look at a typical shape-drawing scenario. To start drawing a shape, the user first clicks the mouse at a desired position. In the preceding section we defined this position as the anchor point, and we need to save this point to draw the entire shape. Let's specify a method named `init()` that can save the anchor point and initialize other attributes. The arguments for this method can be the (x, y) coordinates of the point at which the mouse was clicked.

As the user drags the mouse, the other end of the shape must be drawn at the current position pointed to by the mouse. To set this point, let's specify a method named `setCurrentPoint(int x, int y)`. The parameters `x` and `y` are the current mouse coordinates.

We need to distinguish between interactive drawing and permanent drawing. When you draw a shape interactively, the previously drawn shape is erased before a new one is drawn. On the other hand, permanent drawing draws the shape at the current position. Let's specify `drawInteractive()` as the interactive drawing method and `draw()` as the permanent drawing method. When the user drags the mouse, the client object should call the `drawInteractive()` method, and when the user releases the mouse, it should call `draw()`. Both of these methods should have a `Graphics2D` object as an argument because a graphical context is required for drawing.

Once a shape is drawn, the user might want to move or erase it. Accordingly, let's specify move and erase methods. These methods should have the `Graphics2D` class as one of their input parameters. In the case of `move()`, we need to provide the destination position. Because move can also be interactive—that is, the shape can be dragged with the mouse—we can specify the displacement rather than the absolute coordinates of the destination.

Listing 5.6 summarizes the definition of the interface we have designed here, which we'll call `Drawable.` Note that it also defines several constants to specify the types of graphical objects.

LISTING 5.6   The `Drawable` interface

```
package com.vistech.shapes;
import java.awt.*;

public interface Drawable{
    public static final int NONE=0;
    public static final int BOX=1;
    public static final int ELLIPSE=2;
    public static final int LINE =3;
    public static final int ARROW= 4;
    public static final int DOUBLE_HEADED_ARROW= 5;
    public static final int CURVE = 7;
    public static final int CUBIC_CURVE = 8;
    public static final int POLYGON = 9;
    public static final int ANNOTEXT=6;

    public abstract void init(int x, int y);
    public abstract void setCurrentPosition(Point cp);
    public abstract void drawInteractive(Graphics2D g);
    public abstract void draw(Graphics2D g);
    public abstract void move(Graphics2D g, int dispX, int dispY);
    public abstract void erase(Graphics2D g);
}
```

The Fillable Interface

The Drawable interface assumes any type of shape, closed or open. Closed shapes can be filled. Let's define an interface for closed shapes called Fillable. To fill a closed shape, we'll specify the method fill(), as shown in Listing 5.7. A shape that is of Fillable type needs all the Drawable methods, so Fillable extends Drawable.

LISTING 5.7 The Fillable interface

```
package com.vistech.shapes;
import java.awt.*;

public interface  Fillable extends Drawable{
    public abstract void fill(Graphics2D g, Color cl);
}
```

The Typable Interface

Even though text is not strictly a shape, we can include it in the shapes hierarchy by adding one more interface, called Typable. A text shape consists of characters. To set the characters of a text, let's specify the method setCurChar(int key). As the user types a character, the client object calls this method to send that character. Listing 5.8 shows the code for Typable.

LISTING 5.8 The Typable interface

```
package com.vistech.shapes;

public interface Typable extends Drawable{
    public abstract void setCurChar(int key);
}
```

The ShapeFactory Class

To use the object that represents a shape, a client object must construct it or obtain it by calling a factory method. But all the client has is the interface to the shapes class library. There are two choices here:

1. The class library exposes the classes that represent shapes.
2. The class library provides a factory class that returns objects that represent shapes. The client must send only the shape type.

Here we'll choose the latter option, which provides the ShapeFactory class. Listing 5.9 shows the code for ShapeFactory.

LISTING 5.9   The ShapeFactory class

```java
package com.vistech.shapes;

public class ShapeFactory {

    static public Shapes createShapes(int shapeType){
        switch(shapeType){
            case Drawable.BOX: return( new Box());
            case Drawable.ELLIPSE: return(new Ellipse());
            case Drawable.ARROW: return(new Arrow());
            case Drawable.DOUBLE_HEADED_ARROW:
                Arrow arrow = new Arrow();
                arrow.setDoubleHeaded(true);
                return arrow;
            case Drawable.LINE:return(new Line());
            case Drawable.ANNOTEXT: return(new AnnoText());
            case Drawable.CURVE: return(new Curve());
            default: return null;
        }
    }

    static public Shapes copyShape(Shapes shape){
        Shapes sh = null;
        if(shape instanceof Box){ sh = new Box(); }
        if(shape instanceof Ellipse) { sh = new Ellipse();}
        if(shape instanceof Arrow) { sh = new Arrow();}
        if(shape instanceof AnnoText) {
            sh = new AnnoText();
            AnnoText newShape = ((AnnoText)sh);
            AnnoText oldShape = ((AnnoText)shape);
            newShape.curStr =  new StringBuffer(oldShape.curStr.toString());
            newShape.backSpaceOn = oldShape.backSpaceOn;
            newShape.curChar = oldShape.curChar;
            newShape.totWid = oldShape.totWid;
            newShape.lastChar = oldShape.lastChar;
        }
        if(shape instanceof Curve){ sh = new Curve();}
        if(shape instanceof Line){sh = new Line();}

        if(sh == null) return null;
        sh.init(shape.getStartPosition().x,shape.getStartPosition().y );
        sh.setCurrentPosition(new java.awt.Point(shape.cur.x,shape.cur.y));
        sh.setDrawingColor(shape.getDrawingColor());
        sh.setStroke(shape.getStroke());
        sh.setFont(shape.getFont());
        sh.setFillColor(shape.getFillColor());
        sh.setFillOn(shape.getFillOn());
        sh.setGeneralPath(shape.getGeneralPath());
        sh.setSmallRectsOn(shape.getSmallRectsOn());
        return sh;
    }

    static public String getTypeAsString(int shapeType){
        switch(shapeType){
            case Drawable.BOX: return("Box");
            case Drawable.ELLIPSE:return("Ellipse");
```

```
                 case Drawable.ARROW: return("Arrow");
                 case Drawable.DOUBLE_HEADED_ARROW:return "Double Headed Arrow";
                 case Drawable.LINE:return( "Line");
                 case Drawable.ANNOTEXT:return( "Text");
                 case Drawable.CURVE:return("Curve");
                 default:return null;
         }
     }
}
```

Having a factory class like the one shown in Listing 5.9 gives more flexibility to a class library implementer, who can change the class names and even the design without affecting the interfaces.

The `createShapes()` method instantiates a specified **Shapes** object and returns it to the caller (the **Shapes** class is defined in Listing 5.10). The `copyShape()` method copies a shape to create a new **Shapes** object. This is a deep copy; that is, the entire **Shapes** object is copied. The `getTypeAsString()` method is a utility method useful for displaying the shape types in the GUI.

Implementing the Shapes Class Library

Client applications or beans will interface with the shapes class library through the interfaces specified in the preceding section. We are free to choose our object-oriented design as long as we implement the interfaces. In a generic graphical application, one can expect shapes such as box, ellipse, line, arrow, and so on.

The Shapes Class

In the implementation we present here, the shapes class library has an abstract class called **Shapes**. We can implement the classes that represent shapes by extending the **Shapes** class and implementing the appropriate interfaces defined in the preceding section. Figure 5.6 shows the **Shapes** class hierarchy, and Listing 5.10 shows the relevant code.

> **Note:** The source code for the **Shapes** class is available on the book's Web page in the directory **src/chapter5/shapes**.

LISTING 5.10   The Shapes class

```
package com.vistech.shapes;
import java.awt.*;
import java.awt.geom.*;
```

continued

```
abstract public class Shapes implements java.io.Serializable, Cloneable{
    public Point st = new Point(0,0);
    public Point cur = new Point(0,0);
    public Color drawingColor =  Color.green.brighter();
    public Color fillColor = Color.blue;
    public Font font =  new Font("Helvetica", Font.BOLD,10);
    public Stroke basicStroke;
    public int shapeCount =0;
    public boolean fillOn = false;
    public boolean smallRectsOn = false;

    public GeneralPath path = new GeneralPath(GeneralPath.WIND_EVEN_ODD);

    public void setDrawingColor(Color col) { drawingColor = col;}
    public Color getDrawingColor() { return drawingColor;}

    public void setFillColor(Color col) { fillColor = col;}
    public Color getFillColor() { return fillColor;}

    public void setStartPosition(Point stp){
        st = stp; cur = stp;
    }
    public Point getStartPosition(){ return st;}

    public void setCurrentPosition(Point cp){ cur = cp;}
    public Point getCurrentPosition(){ return cur;}

    public void setFont(Font fnt) { font = fnt;}
    public Font getFont() { return font;}
```

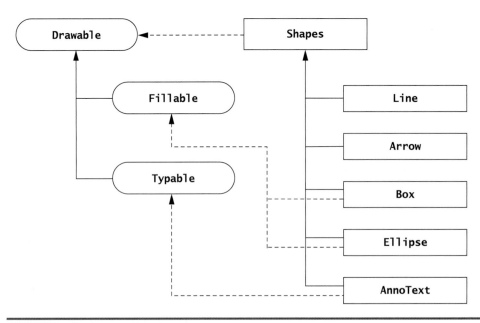

FIGURE 5.6   The Shapes class hierarchy

```
public void setStroke(Stroke stk){ basicStroke = stk;}
public Stroke getStroke(){ return basicStroke;}

public void setShapeCount(int count){shapeCount = count;}
public int getShapeCount(){ return shapeCount;}

public void setGeneralPath(GeneralPath pt){path=pt;}
public GeneralPath getGeneralPath(){return path;}

public void setSmallRectsOn(boolean onOrOff) {smallRectsOn = onOrOff;}
public boolean getSmallRectsOn() { return smallRectsOn;}

public void setFillOn(boolean onOrOff){ fillOn = onOrOff;}
public boolean getFillOn() { return fillOn;}

public boolean contains(int x, int y){
   return path.contains((double)x, (double)y);
}

public Object copy() throws CloneNotSupportedException{
   return clone();
}

abstract public void init(int x, int y);
abstract public boolean contains(Graphics2D g, int x, int y);
abstract public void drawSmallRects(Graphics2D g);
}
```

The **Shapes** class has several attributes that are needed for shape-rendering operations. Table 5.2 lists these attributes.

TABLE 5.2   Shapes Attributes

ATTRIBUTE	TYPE	DESCRIPTION
basicStroke	Stroke	Stroke of the lines that constitute a shape.
cur	Point	Current position of the shape. This is the position of the cursor.
drawingColor	Color	Color of the shape outline.
fillColor	Color	Color inside the shape.
fillOn	boolean	Fill mode. If true, the shape is filled while being drawn.
font	Font	Text font.
path	GeneralPath	Path traversed by the shape.
shapeCount	int	Number of shapes drawn so far.
smallRectsOn	boolean	Shape-active mode. When a user clicks on shape, the shape becomes "active"; that is, small rectangles are attached to it. An active shape can be moved, filled, copied, and erased.
st	Point	Starting position of the shape. This is the anchor point in interactive drawing.

The `Shapes` class has three abstract methods: `init()`, `contains()`, and `draw SmallRects()`. The `init()` method initializes the shape. The `contains()` method performs the hit testing. The `drawSmallRects()` method draws small rectangles at the shape vertices to indicate that a shape has been selected.

The Box Class

As a sample implementation of a shape, let's look at the `Box` class code, which is shown in Listing 5.11. The `Box` class has methods for performing interactive operations on a rectangle.

LISTING 5.11 The Box class

```
package com.vistech.shapes;
import java.awt.*;
import java.lang.Math;
import java.awt.geom.*;

public class Box extends Shapes implements Fillable{
    protected int xp[] = new int[5];
    protected int yp[] = new int[5];
    protected boolean filled = false;

    public void init(int x , int y){
       st.x = x; st.y = y;
       cur.x =x; cur.y =y;
       setPolygonVertices();
    }

    public void drawInteractive(Graphics2D g ){
       basicStroke = g.getStroke();
       g.setColor(Color.black);
       g.setXORMode(drawingColor);
       drawPolygon(g, xp,yp);
       setPolygonVertices();
       drawPolygon(g, xp,yp);
    }


    public void move(Graphics2D g, int diffx, int diffy){
       Stroke savedStroke = g.getStroke();
       if(basicStroke != null) g.setStroke(basicStroke);
       g.setColor(Color.black);
       g.setXORMode(drawingColor);
       drawPolygon(g, xp,yp);
       if(smallRectsOn) drawSmallRects(g);
       if(fillOn) {
          g.setXORMode(fillColor);
          fillPolygon(g, xp,yp);
       }
       st.x += diffx; st.y += diffy;
       cur.x += diffx; cur.y += diffy;
       setPolygonVertices();
```

```
         g.setXORMode(drawingColor);
         drawPolygon(g, xp,yp);
         drawSmallRects(g);
         if(fillOn) {
            g.setXORMode(fillColor);
            fillPolygon(g, xp,yp);
         }
         g.setStroke(savedStroke);
      }

      public void erase(Graphics2D g){
         Stroke savedStroke = g.getStroke();
         if(basicStroke != null) g.setStroke(basicStroke);

         g.setColor(Color.black);
         g.setXORMode(drawingColor);
         setPolygonVertices();
         drawPolygon(g, xp,yp);
         if(smallRectsOn) drawSmallRects(g);
         if(fillOn) {
            g.setXORMode(fillColor);
            fillPolygon(g, xp,yp);
         }
         g.setStroke(savedStroke);
      }

      public void fill(Graphics2D g, Color color){
         if(filled) return;
         filled = true;
         fillOn = true;
         fillColor = color;
         g.setXORMode(color);
         fillPolygon(g, xp,yp);
      }

      private final void setPolygonVertices(){
         xp[0] = st.x; yp[0] = st.y;
         xp[1] = st.x; yp[1] = cur.y;
         xp[2] = cur.x; yp[2] = cur.y;
         xp[3] = cur.x; yp[3] = st.y;
         xp[4] = st.x; yp[4] = st.y;
      }

      public boolean contains(Graphics2D g, int x, int y) {
         if(!path.contains((double)x, (double)y)) return false;
         drawSmallRects(g);
         return true;
      }

      public void drawSmallRects(Graphics2D g) {
         smallRectsOn = !smallRectsOn;
         g.setColor(Color.black);
         g.setXORMode(drawingColor);
         for (int i=0; i< xp.length-1;i++) {
             int x, y;
             if(xp[i] > xp[(i+2)%4]) x = xp[i]+1;
             else x = xp[i]-6;
```

continued

```
            if(yp[i] > yp[(i+2)%4]) y = yp[i]+1;
            else y = yp[i]-6;
            g.drawRect(x, y, 5,5);
        }
    }
    public void drawPolygon(Graphics2D g, int x[], int y[]){
        if((x == null) || (y==null))return;
        int num = x.length;
        path = new GeneralPath(GeneralPath.WIND_EVEN_ODD);
        path.moveTo((float)x[0], (float)y[0]);
        for(int i=1; i<num;i++) {
            path.lineTo((float)x[i], (float)y[i]);
        }
        g.draw(path);
    }

    public void fillPolygon(Graphics2D g, int x[], int y[]){
        if((x == null) || (y==null))return;
        int num = x.length;
        path = new GeneralPath(GeneralPath.WIND_EVEN_ODD);
        path.moveTo((float)x[0], (float)y[0]);
        for(int i=1; i<num;i++) {
            path.lineTo((float)x[i], (float)y[i]);
        }
        g.fill(path);
    }
}
```

The **Box** class extends the **Shapes** class and implements **Fillable.** Thus it inherits its attributes from the **Shapes** class. To understand how the **Box** class works, let's look at a typical sequence of method calls.

Interactive Drawing

1. The user selects the box shape. The client object constructs a **Box** object.

2. The user clicks the mouse at a desired position. The client object calls the `init()` method with the mouse position as the input. This mouse position is the anchor point for drawing a box.

3. The user drags the mouse. The client object calls the `setCurrentPosition()` method with the current mouse position as the input. Observe that the **Box** class inherits `setCurrentPosition()` from the superclass—that is, **Shapes.** The client object then calls the `drawInteractive()` method with a **Graphics** object as the input. This method erases the previously drawn rectangle and then draws a new rectangle with the anchor point and the current position of the mouse as opposite corners.

4. The user releases the mouse. The rectangle drawn at the last position remains as the final rectangle.

Interactive Moving

1. The user selects the **Move** command and clicks inside the box. The client object calls `drawSmallRects()` to draw small rectangles at the corners of the box.
2. The user drags the mouse. The client object calls `move()` with x and y displacement parameters. This method is similar to the `drawInteractive()` method. The difference is that while a shape is being moved, the anchor point changes. So each time `move()` is called, both the anchor point and the current point are computed.
3. The user releases the mouse. The client object calls `drawSmallRects()` to erase the small rectangles. The rectangle drawn at the last position remains as the final rectangle.

The fill and erase operations are straightforward. Whenever an operation is selected, the client object calls the corresponding method. The `erase()` method just erases the shape drawn at the current position. The `fill()` method fills the polygon with the color specified in the argument.

Now let's look at some of **Box**'s methods in more detail.

The init() Method

The `init()` method initializes the **Box** object. Even though the **Box** object is a rectangle, it is treated as a polygon with five vertices. The last and the first vertices are the same. The `init()` method establishes the anchor point.

The drawInteractive() Method

There is no direct way to erase a drawn shape in Java. One way to accomplish erasing is to use `setXORMode()`, which sets the paint mode of the **Graphics** context to XOR (exclusive OR). With XOR paint mode, if a shape is drawn twice at the same location, it is erased, leaving the current color of the background intact. When we need to draw a shape permanently, the normal paint mode can be set by `setPaintMode()`.

In the `drawInteractive()` method, the paint mode of the **Graphics** object is set to XOR, which means that the existing color value of a pixel on which a drawing operation is performed is exclusive ORed with the color value set by `setXORMode()`. With this mechanism, if the same pixel is drawn twice, a pixel gets back its original color. The first time a drawing is performed, however, the pixels of the current color (black in this case) are changed to the color specified by the input parameter of `setXORMode()`. As the mouse is dragged, the outline of the shape will be a mixture of colors. This color scheme works well for grayscale images. The black pixels will turn green, and pixels with other colors will have unpredictable color values. You need to adopt a proper color scheme depending on the image that is being drawn.

The `drawInteractive()` method calls `setXORMode()` first to set the mode to XOR paint mode. It then constructs the shape at the previous position and draws it there. This action erases the previous shape. Once the previous shape has been erased, `drawInteractive()` updates the polygon vertices by calling the `setPolygon Vertices()` method. Now the polygon vertices reflect the current position set by `set CurrentPosition()`. The `drawInteractive()` method calls `drawPolygon()` to draw the polygon at the new position.

Other Methods

The `setPolygonVertices()` method populates the polygon vertices array. Note again that there are five vertices; the last and the first are the same. The `contains()` method overrides the method in the `Shapes` superclass. It checks whether a point specified in the argument is inside the `Box` object. If it is, `contains()` draws small rectangles surrounding the shape. The `drawPolygon()` and `fillPolygon()` methods use the `GeneralPath` class to draw the polygon.

Other shapes have similar methods, so each shape has the capability to draw, fill, move, and erase itself.

Writing a Shapes Class Library Client

Let's write a class that uses the shapes class library to create a shape and to run several interactive commands on that shape. We'll call this class `DrawShapes`. This class needs to construct different types of shapes and draw them on a graphical canvas. We already developed an interface for a graphical canvas class named `GraphicsDisplay` (see Listing 5.4). `DrawShapes` will take this interface as a constructor parameter and invoke its methods to draw shapes.

To draw shapes interactively, the `DrawShapes` class needs to handle `mouse`, `mouseMotion`, and `key` events. The `GraphicsDisplay` object is the source of these events, which must be received by the `DrawShapes` class.

Separating GUIs from the Application Logic

To perform an operation, `DrawShapes` requires two types of information: shape type and a command. Commands are nothing but the names of the tasks to be performed, including draw, move, fill, erase, copy, and paste. Let's enumerate the commands in an interface called `DrawShapesController` (see Listing 5.12).

To allow users to select shape types and commands, we need to create graphical user interfaces. But so that we have the freedom to choose any GUI, these GUIs should not be part of the `DrawShapes` class. To achieve a clean separation of GUIs from the `DrawShapes` class, let's specify the set and get methods for shape type and command attributes in the `DrawShapesController` interface. Listing 5.12 shows the code for `DrawShapesController` with these methods.

LISTING 5.12   The DrawShapesController interface

```
package com.vistech.graphics;
import java.awt.*;
import java.awt.event.*;
import java.awt.image.*;
import java.awt.geom.*;

public interface DrawShapesController {
    public final static int DRAW  =  0;
    public final static int MOVE  =  1;
    public final static int ERASE = 2;
    public final static int FILL = 4;
    public final static int COPY = 8;
    public final static int PASTE = 16;
    public final static int ERASE_ALL = 32;
    public final static int LOAD = 64;
    public final static int SAVE = 128;

    public void setCommand(int command);
    public int getCommand();

    public void setShapeType(int shapeType);
    public int getShapeType();
}
```

The DrawShapes class will implement the DrawShapesController interface. By using an interface like this, you can change DrawShapes without changing the GUI classes.

Completing an Operation

When an operation has been completed, the DrawShapes class may need to notify its clients. For this purpose let's create a custom event called shapesEvent. A custom event has two parts: an event listener and an event state object. Listing 5.13 shows the listener for shapesEvent.

LISTING 5.13   The ShapesEventListener interface

```
package com.vistech.graphics;
import java.io.*;

public interface ShapesEventListener extends java.util.EventListener{
    public void shapeDrawn(ShapesEvent e);
}
```

The ShapesEvent class (as shown in Listing 5.14) encapsulates shapes event–related data.

LISTING 5.14 The ShapesEvent class

```
package com.vistech.graphics;
import java.awt.*
import com.vistech.shapes.*;

public class ShapesEvent extends java.util.EventObject implements java.io.Serializable{
    protected Shapes shape;
    protected int command;
    public ShapesEvent(Object src,Shapes sh){
        super(src);
    }

    public Shapes getShapes(){
        return shape;
    }

    public void setCommand(int command){
        this.command = command;
    }

    public int getCommand(){
        return command;
    }
}
```

The `ShapesEvent` class has methods for extracting data from the `ShapesEvent` object. This class holds two types of data: the `Shapes` object and the command. A list of commands is defined in the `DrawShapesController` interface, which is shown in Listing 5.12.

The DrawShapes Class

Now that we have defined all the interfaces and classes needed for `DrawShapes`, let's develop this class. `DrawShapes` must perform the tasks listed in the `DrawShapes Controller` interface (see Listing 5.12). Each of them can be implemented in a method.

Listing 5.15 shows the code for `DrawShapes`. Because this is a large class, we'll divide our description into many parts.

> **Note:** The entire source code for `DrawShapes` is available on the book's Web page in the directory `src/chapter5/grcanvas`.

LISTING 5.15 The DrawShapes class

```
package com.vistech.graphics;
import java.awt.*;
import java.awt.image.*;
```

```java
import java.awt.geom.*;
import javax.swing.*;
import java.awt.event.*;
import com.vistech.shapes.*;
import java.util.*;
import java.beans.*;

public class DrawShapes implements DrawShapesController,
        MouseListener,MouseMotionListener, KeyListener{
   protected int shapeType = Drawable.BOX;
   protected int savedShapeType = Drawable.BOX;
   protected GraphicsDisplay grCanvas;
   private Point oldPoint, currentPoint;
   private Point diff = new Point(0,0);
   private Point anchor = new Point(0,0);
   private boolean mousePressed = false;
   private Shapes currentShape, prevShape;
   private Drawable shape;
   private Vector shapesList = new Vector();
   private Vector savedShapesList = new Vector();
   private Graphics2D destGc;
   private int currentCommand = DrawShapesController.DRAW;
   private int shapeCount = 0;
   private Vector shapesEventListeners = new Vector();

   private boolean graphicsOn = true, shapesOn = true, textOn = false,dragOn = false;

   private boolean shapeNumberingOn = true;
   private boolean defaultFillOn = false;
   private boolean firstTime = true;
   private Shapes copiedShape, prevCopiedShape;
   private String commandString ="Draw";
   private PropertyChangeSupport pcs;

   public DrawShapes(GraphicsDisplay c){
      grCanvas = c;
      destGc = grCanvas.getDisplayedImageGC();
      shape = (Drawable)ShapeFactory.createShapes(Drawable.BOX);
      pcs = new PropertyChangeSupport(this);
   }

   public synchronized void setTextOn(boolean onOrOff){ textOn = onOrOff; }
   public synchronized void setShapesOn(boolean onOrOff){ shapesOn = onOrOff; }

   public synchronized void setShapeType(int shapeType){
      int oldType = this.shapeType;
      this.shapeType = shapeType;
      if(shapeType  == Drawable.ANNOTEXT){
         setTextOn(true);
         setShapesOn(false);
      } else{
         setTextOn(false);
         setShapesOn(true);
      }
      pcs.firePropertyChange("shapeType", oldType, shapeType);
   }
   public int getShapeType(){ return shapeType; }
```

continued

```
public synchronized void setCommandAsString(String command){
    String oldCommand =this.commandString;
    this.commandString = command;
    pcs.firePropertyChange("commandString", oldCommand, commandString);
}
public String getCommandAsString(){ return commandString; }

public synchronized void setCommand(int command){
    pcs.firePropertyChange("command", currentCommand, command);
    setCommandAsString(getCommandAsText(command));
    currentCommand = command;
    switch (currentCommand) {
        case DrawShapesController.ERASE_ALL:eraseShapes(); break;
        case DrawShapesController.LOAD:loadShapes();break;
        case DrawShapesController.SAVE:saveShapes();break;
        default: return;
    }
}
public int getCommand(){ return currentCommand; }
```

Listing 5.15 also shows the set and get methods for the **shapeType** and **command** attributes. Recall that these are the **DrawShapesController** interface methods. There is also a convenient attribute called **commandAsString,** which is used for displaying the names of the commands. All of the set methods fire **propertyChange** events.

Handling mousePressed Events

The **DrawShapes** class handles both **mouse** and **mouseMotion** events. When the left button is pressed, the shape is constructed and initialized. When the mouse is released, the shape is drawn permanently on the canvas. When the right button is pressed, a pop-up menu with shape-drawing commands is launched.

```
public void mousePressed(MouseEvent e) {
    if(SwingUtilities.isLeftMouseButton(e)){
        initGraphics(e.getX(), e.getY());
    }
}
```

Whenever the user selects a new shape, the **DrawShapes** object constructs a **Shape** object corresponding to that selection. To construct an appropriate **Shape** object, the **DrawShapes** class provides the **createAndDrawShape()** method. This method is called by **initGraphics()**, which is an entry point method for new command and shape selections.

```
protected void initGraphics(int x, int y) {
    destGc = grCanvas.getDisplayedImageGC();
    if(shape != null) {
        if(((Shapes)shape).getSmallRectsOn()){
            ((Shapes)shape).drawSmallRects(destGc);
        }
    }
    if(prevCopiedShape != null) {
        if(((Shapes)prevCopiedShape).getSmallRectsOn()){
```

```
                ((Shapes)prevCopiedShape).drawSmallRects(destGc);
            }
        }
        switch (currentCommand) {
            case InteractiveGraphics.DRAW:
                createAndDrawShape(x,y);
                return;
            case  InteractiveGraphics.PASTE:
                pasteShape(x,y);
                return;
            case InteractiveGraphics.MOVE:
            case InteractiveGraphics.COPY:
            case InteractiveGraphics.FILL:
            case InteractiveGraphics.ERASE:
                hitTest(x,y,currentCommand);
                return;
        }
    }
```

The `initGraphics()` method is called by `mousePressed()`. It first erases the small rectangle drawn over the previous shape. To indicate that the selected shape is active, these rectangles are drawn whenever a shape is selected for copying or moving.

The `initGraphics()` method then checks for the shape operation selected. If the operation is `DRAW`, `initGraphics()` creates a new shape and draws it at the anchor point. If the operation is `PASTE` and the `COPY` command has already been executed, `initGraphics()` pastes the copied shape.

For all other commands, the point at which the mouse is clicked is tested for containment. If the point is within or near the shape, the selected command is executed. For example, if the selected command is `ERASE`, the shape is erased.

The `createAndDrawShape()` method is called when the command is `DRAW:`

```
protected void createAndDrawShape(int x, int y) {
    destGc = grCanvas.getDisplayedImageGC();
    if(shapesOn){
        oldPoint = new Point(x, y);
        currentPoint = new Point(x, y);
        anchor = new Point(x, y);
        shape = (Drawable)ShapeFactory.createShapes(shapeType);
        ((Shapes)shape).drawingColor = grCanvas.getDrawingColor();
    }else {
        shape = (Drawable)ShapeFactory.createShapes(shapeType);
        Color textColor = grCanvas.getTextColor();
        destGc.setFont(grCanvas.getFont());
        ((Shapes)shape).setDrawingColor(textColor);
        ((JComponent)grCanvas).requestFocus();
    }
    if(shape != null){
        shapesList.addElement(shape);
        shape.init(x, y);
        grCanvas.repaint();
    }
}
```

This method creates a graphical or text shape depending on whether the value of shapesOn is true or false. The type of shape is set by the setShapeType() method. Any client object of the DrawShapes class can set this method. The ShapeFactory class (see Listing 5.9) creates the selected shape. Once the shape has been created, it is added to the shapesList array.

The pasteShape() method is called when PASTE is selected:

```
protected void pasteShape(int x, int y) {
    if(copiedShape != null){
        ((Drawable) copiedShape).move(destGc, x-oldPoint.x, y-oldPoint.y);
        shapesList.addElement(copiedShape);
        oldPoint = new Point(x, y);
        currentPoint = new Point(x, y);
        prevCopiedShape = copiedShape;
        copiedShape = ShapeFactory.copyShape( (Shapes)copiedShape);
        grCanvas.repaint();
    }
}
```

If the value of copiedShape variable is not null, it is assumed that the COPY command has already been executed. The paste operation is nothing more than moving the copied shape to the current position. Once the shape has been pasted, one more copy of it is created to enable another paste.

Commands other than DRAW or PASTE require hit testing—that is, testing to see whether a shape is near the point where the mouse was clicked. So for these commands, the hitTest() method is called:

```
protected void hitTest(int x, int y, int command){
    for(Enumeration e = shapesList.elements() ; e.hasMoreElements() ;) {
        Shapes sh = (Shapes)(e.nextElement());
        if(sh.contains(destGc,x,y)){
            oldPoint = new Point(x, y);
            currentPoint = new Point(x, y);
            shape = (Drawable)sh;
            switch (command) {
                case InteractiveGraphics.MOVE :
                    grCanvas.repaint();
                    break;
                case InteractiveGraphics.FILL :
                    if(shape instanceof Fillable) {
                        ((Fillable)shape).fill(destGc, grCanvas.getFillColor());
                        grCanvas.repaint();
                    }
                    break;
                case InteractiveGraphics.ERASE :
                    shape.erase(grCanvas.getDisplayedImageGC());
                    shapesList.removeElement(sh);
                    grCanvas.repaint();
                    break;
                case InteractiveGraphics.COPY:
                    copiedShape = ShapeFactory.copyShape( (Shapes)shape);
                    grCanvas.repaint();
                    break;
            }
        }
```

```
            break;
        } else shape = null;
    }
}
```

The `shapesList` attribute contains the list of all the shapes drawn on the canvas. Recall that the `Shapes` class has the abstract `contains()` method for this purpose. Each shape has its own way of performing the hit test. If a shape passes the hit test, the appropriate command is executed on that shape. In the case of `MOVE`, there is no action other than repaint because the shape is moved when the mouse is dragged.

The `hitTest()` method is called when the mouse is pressed. If the command is `FILL`, the selected shape is filled by a call to the `fill()` method of the `Fillable` shape with the current fill color set on the `GraphicsCanvas2D` class. Note that only closed shape objects like `Box` and `Ellipse` implement the `Fillable` interface. For this reason, the `shape` variable is first checked to see whether it is an instance of `Fillable`.

If the command is `ERASE`, the shape is erased by a call to the `shape.erase()` method. When erased, the shape is removed from the `shapesList` parameter. If the command is `COPY`, a copy of the shape is created by the `ShapeFactory` class. This copy is saved in the `copiedShape` variable. Whenever `PASTE` is selected, this copied shape is pasted by the `pasteShape()` method.

Handling mouseMotion Events

When the mouse is dragged, the `mouseDragged()` method is called, as the following example shows. The mouse-dragging method is used for drawing only graphical shapes. Text shapes are drawn by key events.

```
public void mouseDragged(MouseEvent e){
    if(SwingUtilities.isRightMouseButton(e)) return;
    dragOn = true;
    int x = e.getX();
    int y = e.getY();
    drawGraphics(x,y);
}
public void mouseMoved(MouseEvent e){}


    protected void drawGraphics(int x, int y) {
        switch (currentCommand) {
            case InteractiveGraphics.DRAW :
                if((shapesOn) &&(shape == null)) {
                    shape.setCurPoint(x,y);
                    shape.drawInteractive(grCanvas.getDisplayedImageGC());
                    grCanvas.repaint();
                }
                break;
            case InteractiveGraphics.MOVE:
                moveShape(x, y);
                break;
        }
    }
```

The `mouseDragged()` method calls `drawGraphics()`. The `DRAW` and `MOVE` commands require dragging of the mouse. If `DRAW` is selected, the `drawInteractive()` method is called. If `MOVE` is selected, `moveShape()` is called, as the following example shows:

```
protected void moveShape(int x, int y) {
    if(shape == null) return;
    destGc = grCanvas.getDisplayedImageGC();
    shape.move(destGc, x-oldPoint.x, y-oldPoint.y);
    oldPoint = new Point(x, y);
    currentPoint = new Point(x, y);
    grCanvas.repaint();
}
```

Handling mouseReleased Events

When the mouse is released, the `mouseReleased()` method is called. If the mouse is released after dragging, the `releaseDrag()` method is called. This method fires the shapes event to the registered listeners:

```
public void mouseReleased(MouseEvent e) {
    if(SwingUtilities.isRightMouseButton(e)) return;
    int x = e.getX();
    int y = e.getY();
    drawGraphics(x,y);
    if(dragOn) {
        dragOn = false;
        if((shapesOn) && (shape != null)) releaseDrag(x,y);
        fireShapesEvent();
    }
    mousePressed = false;
}
```

If the command is `MOVE`, `releaseDrag()` erases the small rectangles surrounding the shape. If the command is `DRAW`, the `shapeCount` is incremented:

```
protected void releaseDrag(int x, int y){
    switch (currentCommand) {
        case InteractiveGraphics.MOVE:
            ((Shapes)shape).drawSmallRects(grCanvas.getDisplayedImageGC());
            break;
        case InteractiveGraphics.DRAW:
            if(shapeNumberingOn)
                shapeCount++;
            break;
    }
}
```

Handling key Events

The key events are received when characters are typed:

```
public void keyTyped(KeyEvent k) {
    if(!textOn) return;
```

```
   if((currentCommand == InteractiveGraphics.DRAW) && (shape instanceof Typable)){
      destGc = grCanvas.getDisplayedImageGC();
      destGc.setColor(Color.green);
      ((Typable)shape).setCurChar(k.getKeyChar());
     shape.drawInteractive(destGc);
     grCanvas.repaint();
   }
 }
```

Note that the `setCurChar()` method is called instead of `setCurPoint()`. There is no need to send the current position in the case of text. The `AnnoText` object receives a typed character and draws it on the `Graphics` context.

Registering and Firing Shapes Events

When a drawing operation is completed, the `DrawShapes` object fires shapes event instances to the registered listeners. The following methods allow client objects to register and unregister for the shapes event:

```
public void addShapesEventListener(ShapesEventListener s){
   shapesEventListeners.addElement(s);
}

public void removeShapesEventListener(ShapesEventListener s){
   shapesEventListeners.removeElement(s);
}
```

The `fireShapesEvent()` method constructs the `ShapesEvent` object with the currently drawn shape and invokes the `shapeDrawn()` method in all the registered listeners:

```
protected void fireShapesEvent() {
    ShapesEvent ise = new ShapesEvent(this,currentShape);
    for(Enumeration e = shapesEventListeners.elements(); e.hasMoreElements();){
        ShapesEventListener ist = (ShapesEventListener)(e.nextElement());
        ist.shapeDrawn(ise);
    }
}
```

Putting It All Together: The JavaPaintShop Application

Now that we have developed a graphical canvas class, a shapes class library, and a client class to use this library, it's time to build an application that uses all these classes. The purpose of this application is to enable users to draw a shape over a graphical canvas and to perform operations such as fill, move, copy, paste, and erase on that shape.

First let's formulate the requirements. The JavaPaintShop application shall provide the following capabilities:

- The ability to perform interactive operations
- The ability to choose shapes
- The ability to set shape parameters
- The ability to choose commands
- The ability to save drawn shapes
- The ability to load saved shapes

To implement these requirements, let's reuse two important classes we have already developed: `GraphicsCanvas2D` and `DrawShapes`. We'll use the `Graphics Canvas2D` class as a canvas for drawing shapes and the `DrawShapes` class to perform drawing-related operations over the `Graphics2D` context of `GraphicsCanvas2D`. Recall that `DrawShapes` uses the shapes class library to create shapes.

We need to write a few more classes to create the graphical user interfaces. The `JavaPaintShop` class will be the main class that will launch the application. This class will bring up a frame with a menu bar and a `GraphicsCanvas2D` component. This class will also instantiate objects required for the application.

To allow users to choose a shape, let's create a class called `ShapeSelection Panel,` which will implement a menu component with names of the shapes. The `Java PaintShop` class will attach this menu to its menu bar.

To allow users to select a drawing command, let's create a class called `CommandSelectionPanel` that will implement a pop-up menu component that can be launched from `GraphicsCanvas2D`.

To allow users to set the shape parameters, let's create a class called `ParamsSelectionPanel` that will implement a panel that can be launched from the JavaPaintShop menu bar. This class will create a panel with combo boxes for selecting drawing color, filling color, stroke width, line width, and shape style. Figure 5.7 shows how objects communicate in the JavaPaintShop application.

Before we delve into the source code, let's look at how to run the JavaPaintShop application.

Running JavaPaintShop

To run JavaPaintShop, type "java app.JavaPaintShop" on the command line. This command will launch the frame shown in Figure 5.8. Before running JavaPaintShop, you may want to make sure that the shapes class library and other related classes are in the class path. The main JavaPaintShop window has three menus: **File, Params,** and **Shapes.** The **Params** menu launches a **Params** panel in which you can set different graphics- and text-related parameters. When you set a parameter, the `Graphics Canvas2D` object receives the value and sets its property. The **Shapes** menu has sev-

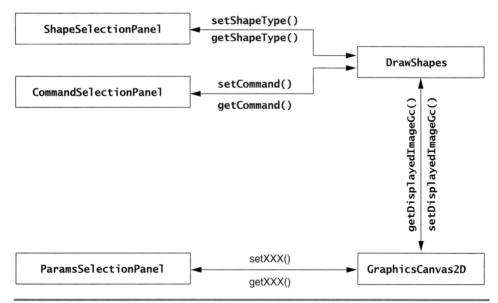

FIGURE 5.7   Communication between objects in the JavaPaintShop application

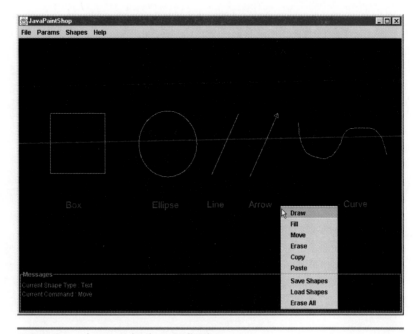

FIGURE 5.8   The JavaPaintShop application

eral menu items representing shapes, which include **Box, Ellipse, Line,** and **Curve** (see Figure 5.9).

Select a command by right-clicking on it. Figure 5.8 shows the resulting pop-up menu launched over the JavaPaintShop application. To draw a shape, first select a shape from the **Shapes** menu (see Figure 5.9). Then right-click on a command to select it. Always remember to set the correct parameters before starting an operation. The message bar at the bottom of the window tells you the shape type and current operation you chose.

To move a shape, first select the **Move** command and then click inside (or near) the shape to be moved. When the small rectangle is displayed, drag it to the desired position. To fill the shape, select the **Fill** command and click inside the shape to be filled.

To copy and paste a shape, first select **Copy** and then click inside the shape. To paste, select **Paste** and position the mouse at a desirable position and click. Even if the shape is not pasted at the right position, you can use the move operation to move it to the right place. Once copied, you can paste a shape as many times as desirable.

The command **Save Shapes** will save the shapes on the canvas. **Load Shapes** will display them again. **Erase All** will erase the canvas completely. Before erasing, you can click on **Save Shapes** to save shapes you have drawn on the drawing canvas. After selecting **Erase All,** choose **Load Shapes** to restore shapes saved by **Saved**

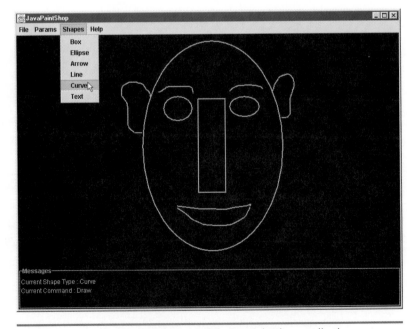

FIGURE 5.9   The shape selection menu of the JavaPaintShop application

Shapes. These commands are useful for drawing a shape incrementally. For example, you can draw part of the shape, save it, and then draw more. If you don't like what you drew last, restore the saved shape and start drawing again from that point. By taking this approach, you don't need to erase unwanted shapes one by one.

Implementing JavaPaintShop

First let's look at the JavaPaintShop class, which is shown in Listing 5.16. This class creates a frame with a menu bar. The frame contains two components: GraphicsCanvas2D and MessageBar. The DrawShapes object operates on the Graphics Canvas2D object.

> **Note:** The code for the JavaPaintShop class is available on the book's Web page in the directory src/chapter5/grcanvas.

LISTING 5.16   The JavaPaintShop class

```
package app;
import java.io.*;
import java.awt.*;
import java.awt.event.*;
import java.util.*;
import javax.swing.*;
import javax.swing.event.*;
import java.beans.*;

import java.awt.print.*;
import com.vistech.shapes.*;
import com.vistech.graphics.*;
import com.vistech.util.*;

public class JavaPaintShop extends
    com.vistech.util.ApplicationFrame implements PropertyChangeListener{
   protected GraphicsCanvas2D grCanvas;
   protected JTextArea messageBar;
   protected DrawShapes drawShapes;
   protected CommandSelectionPanel commandSelectionPanel;
   protected ShapeSelectionPanel shapeSelectionPanel;
   protected ParamsSelectionPanel paramPanel;

   protected JFrame paramFrame;

   public static void  main(String[] args){
      JavaPaintShop iv = new JavaPaintShop();
   }
   public JavaPaintShop() {
      addWindowListener(
        new WindowAdapter() {
           public void windowClosing(WindowEvent w){
```

continued

```
                JavaPaintShop.this.dispose();
                System.exit(0);
            }
        });
    }

    public void quit(){ this.dispose();}

    protected void createGUI(){
        grCanvas = new GraphicsCanvas2D();
        drawShapes = new DrawShapes(grCanvas);
        // To update message bar
        drawShapes.addPropertyChangeListener(this);

        grCanvas.addMouseListener(drawShapes);
        grCanvas.addMouseMotionListener(drawShapes);
        grCanvas.addKeyListener(drawShapes);

        commandSelectionPanel = new CommandSelectionPanel(drawShapes);
        grCanvas.addMouseListener(commandSelectionPanel);
        shapeSelectionPanel = new ShapeSelectionPanel(drawShapes);

        ViewerMenuBar viewerMenuBar = new ViewerMenuBar();
        setJMenuBar((JMenuBar)viewerMenuBar);
        Dimension ssize= Toolkit.getDefaultToolkit().getScreenSize();
        int vwid = (int)(ssize.width*3/4.0);
        int vht = (int)(ssize.height*3/4.0);
        this.setLocation((ssize.width/4),
                        (ssize.height/4));
        this.setSize((int)(ssize.width*3/4.0), (int)(ssize.height*3/4.0));
        messageBar = new JTextArea();
        messageBar.setBorder(BorderFactory.createTitledBorder("Messages"));
        messageBar.setBackground(Color.black);
        messageBar.setForeground(Color.green);
        this.updateMessageBar();

        GridBagLayout gb = new GridBagLayout() ;
        GridBagConstraints c = new GridBagConstraints();
        this.getContentPane().setLayout(gb);
        c.fill = GridBagConstraints.BOTH;
        c.weighty = 1.0; c.weightx = 1.0;
        c.gridheight =1;
        c.gridwidth = 1;
        c.gridwidth = GridBagConstraints.REMAINDER;

        gb.setConstraints(grCanvas, c);
        this.getContentPane().add(grCanvas);
        c.fill = GridBagConstraints.BOTH;
        c.weighty = 0.05; c.weightx = 1.0;
        gb.setConstraints(messageBar, c);
        this.getContentPane().add(messageBar);

        this.show();
        this.repaint();
    }
```

```java
    public void propertyChange(PropertyChangeEvent p){
        updateMessageBar();
    }

    public void updateMessageBar(){
        if(grCanvas == null)return;
        messageBar.setBackground(Color.black);
        messageBar.setText("Current Shape Type : "+
        ShapeFactory.getTypeAsString(drawShapes.getShapeType())+ "\n"+
                        "Current Command : " + drawShapes.getCommandAsString());
        messageBar.repaint();
        repaint();
    }


    public class ViewerMenuBar extends com.vistech.util.ApplicationFrame.AppMenuBar {
        public ViewerMenuBar(){
            add(createGraphicsParamsMenu());

            add(shapeSelectionPanel.createShapeTypesMenu());
            createHelpMenu();
        }

        public JMenu createGraphicsParamsMenu(){
            JMenu selMenu = new JMenu("Params");
            JMenuItem ls = new JMenuItem(" Launch Params Panel");
            ls.addActionListener(
                new ActionListener() {
                    public void actionPerformed(ActionEvent e){
                        if(paramFrame != null) paramFrame.dispose();
                        paramFrame = new JFrame();
                        paramPanel = new ParamsSelectionPanel(grCanvas);
                        paramFrame.getContentPane().add(paramPanel);
                        paramFrame.pack();
                        paramFrame.show();

                    }
                }
            );
            selMenu.add(ls);
            return selMenu;
        }
    }
}
```

The JavaPaintShop class extends the ApplicationFrame class (see Appendix A), which represents a skeleton frame that can contain components and a menu bar. The createGUI() method creates and adds GraphicsCanvas2D, as well as an instance of JTextArea as a message bar. The message bar is updated by the updateMessageBar() method. This method is called whenever JavaPaintShop receives a propertyChange event.

In the createGUI() method, JavaPaintShop first constructs the DrawShapes object and then registers itself to receive propertyChange events. The JavaPaintShop class implements the propertyChange event through the propertyChange() method. So whenever the `setCommand()` method in the DrawShapes object is called, a `property Change` event is fired (see Listing 5.15). The `createGUI()` method then registers the DrawShapes object with GraphicsCanvas2D to receive `mouse`, `mouseMotion`, and `key` events.

Next the `createGUI()` method constructs the `ShapeSelectionPanel` and `CommandSelectionPanel` objects with DrawShapes as the input parameter. Recall that the `DrawShapes` class implements the `DrawShapesController` interface. The `create GUI()` method registers the `ShapeSelectionPanel` object with GraphicsCanvas2D to receive `mouse` events. This step is necessary so that the pop-up menu will be launched when the user clicks the right mouse button.

`ViewerMenuBar` is an inner class of JavaPaintShop and constructs the menu bar for the application frame. Its constructor calls the `createGraphicsMenuBar()` method to create the **Params** menu. It then calls the `createShapeTypesMenu()` method of `ShapeSelectionPanel` to create the shape type menu. Because `createGraphics MenuBar()` and `createShapeTypesMenu()` have code only for constructing and laying out GUI components, we don't include them in Listing 5.16.

The `createGraphicsMenuBar()` method constructs the `ParamsSelectionPanel` object with `GraphicsCanvas2D` as an input. Then `createGraphicsMenuBar()` adds that object to a frame, which is launched whenever the **Launch Params Panel** command is selected.

Selecting Shapes

The `ShapeSelectionPanel` class creates a menu that is attached to JavaPaintShop's menu bar (see Figure 5.9). Listing 5.17 shows the code for `ShapeSelectionPanel`.

LISTING 5.17   The `ShapeSelectionPanel` class

```
package com.vistech.graphics;
import java.io.*;
import java.awt.*;
import java.awt.event.*;
import java.util.*;
import javax.swing.*;
import javax.swing.event.*;
import java.beans.*;
import com.vistech.shapes.*;

public class ShapeSelectionPanel {
    protected DrawShapesController drawShapes;
    public ShapeSelectionPanel(DrawShapesController drawShapes){
        this.drawShapes = drawShapes;
    }
    public JMenu createShapeTypesMenu(){
        JMenu shapesMenu = new JMenu("Shapes");
        JMenuItem box = new JMenuItem("Box");
        JMenuItem el = new JMenuItem("Ellipse");
        JMenuItem ar = new JMenuItem("Arrow");
```

```java
        JMenuItem line = new JMenuItem("Line");
        JMenuItem text = new JMenuItem("Text");
        JMenuItem curve = new JMenuItem("Curve");
        shapesMenu.add(box);
        shapesMenu.add(el);
        shapesMenu.add(ar);
        shapesMenu.add(line);
        shapesMenu.add(curve);
        shapesMenu.add(text);

        box.addActionListener(new ShapesAdapter(Drawable.BOX));
        el.addActionListener(new ShapesAdapter(Drawable.ELLIPSE));
        ar.addActionListener(new ShapesAdapter(Drawable.ARROW));
        line.addActionListener(new ShapesAdapter(Drawable.LINE));
        text.addActionListener(new ShapesAdapter(Drawable.ANNOTEXT));
        curve.addActionListener(new ShapesAdapter(Drawable.CURVE));
        return shapesMenu;
    }

    class ShapesAdapter implements ActionListener{
        int shapeType;
        public ShapesAdapter(int sh){
            shapeType = sh;
        }
        public void actionPerformed(ActionEvent e){
            drawShapes.setShapeType(shapeType);
            drawShapes.setCommand(DrawShapesController.DRAW);
        }
    }
}
```

Each of the **Shapes** menu items receives a `ShapesAdapter` object for handling action events. For each of the menu items, a `ShapesAdapter` object is constructed. Whenever a shape item is selected, the `actionPerformed()` method in the `ShapesAdapter` class is called. This method in turn calls `setShapeType()` in the `DrawShapes` object. It also sets the shape operation to `DRAW.`

Selecting an Operation

The `CommandSelectionPanel` class launches a pop-up menu when the user clicks the right mouse button over the graphical canvas. Listing 5.18 shows the code for `CommandSelectionPanel`.

LISTING 5.18 The `CommandSelectionPanel` class

```java
package com.vistech.graphics;
import java.awt.*;
import java.awt.image.*;
import java.awt.geom.*;
import javax.swing.*;
import java.awt.event.*;
import java.util.*;
import java.beans.*;
```

continued

```java
public class CommandSelectionPanel extends MouseAdapter{
    protected DrawShapesController drawShapes;
    public CommandSelectionPanel(DrawShapesController drawShapes){
        this.drawShapes = drawShapes;
    }

    public void mousePressed(MouseEvent e) {
        if(SwingUtilities.isRightMouseButton(e)){
            popupMenu((JComponent)e.getSource(), e.getX(), e.getY());
        }
    }
    protected void popupMenu(JComponent comp,int x, int y){
        JPopupMenu jp = new JPopupMenu("");
        jp.setLightWeightPopupEnabled(true);
        comp.add(jp);
        JMenuItem draw = new JMenuItem("Draw");
        draw.addActionListener(
          new ActionListener(){
            public void actionPerformed(ActionEvent e){
                drawShapes.setCommand(DrawShapesController.DRAW);
            }
          });

        JMenuItem fill = new JMenuItem("Fill");
        fill.addActionListener(
          new ActionListener(){
            public void actionPerformed(ActionEvent e){
                drawShapes.setCommand(DrawShapesController.FILL);
            }
          });

        JMenuItem move = new JMenuItem("Move");
        move.addActionListener(
          new ActionListener(){
            public void actionPerformed(ActionEvent e){
                drawShapes.setCommand(DrawShapesController.MOVE);
            }
          });

        JMenuItem erase = new JMenuItem("Erase");
        erase.addActionListener(
          new ActionListener(){
            public void actionPerformed(ActionEvent e){
                drawShapes.setCommand(DrawShapesController.ERASE);
            }
          });

        JMenuItem copy = new JMenuItem("Copy");
        copy.addActionListener(
          new ActionListener(){
            public void actionPerformed(ActionEvent e){
                drawShapes.setCommand(DrawShapesController.COPY);
            }
          });
        JMenuItem paste = new JMenuItem("Paste");
        paste.addActionListener(
          new ActionListener(){
```

```
            public void actionPerformed(ActionEvent e){
                drawShapes.setCommand(DrawShapesController.PASTE);
            }
        });

        JMenuItem eraseall = new JMenuItem("Erase All");
        eraseall.addActionListener(
          new ActionListener(){
            public void actionPerformed(ActionEvent e){
                drawShapes.setCommand(DrawShapesController.ERASE_ALL);
                drawShapes.setCommand(DrawShapesController.DRAW);
            }
        });

        JMenuItem save = new JMenuItem("Save Shapes");
        save.addActionListener(
          new ActionListener(){
            public void actionPerformed(ActionEvent e){
                drawShapes.setCommand(DrawShapesController.SAVE);
                drawShapes.setCommand(DrawShapesController.DRAW);
            }
        });

        JMenuItem load = new JMenuItem("Load Shapes");
        load.addActionListener(
          new ActionListener(){
            public void actionPerformed(ActionEvent e){
                drawShapes.setCommand(DrawShapesController.LOAD);
                drawShapes.setCommand(DrawShapesController.DRAW);
            }
        });
        jp.add(draw);
        jp.add(fill);
        jp.add(move);
        jp.add(erase);
        jp.add(copy);
        jp.add(paste);
        jp.addSeparator();
        jp.add(save);
        jp.add(load);
        jp.add(eraseall);
        jp.show(comp,x,y);
    }
}
```

Remember from the `JavaPaintShop` code (see Listing 5.16) that `Command SelectionPanel` is registered to receive `mouse` events from the `GraphicsCanvas2D` object. The `CommandSelectionPanel` class extends the `java.awt.MouseAdapter` class, which is a utility class that implements all the `MouseListener` interface methods. `CommandSelectionPanel` overrides only the `mousePressed()` method. When the user clicks on the drawing canvas represented by `GraphicsCanvas2D`, this method is called. As Listing 5.18 shows, `mousePressed()` checks for right clicks. When the right-hand button of the mouse is clicked, `mousePressed()` calls the `popupMenu()` method, which launches a pop-up menu (see Figure 5.8).

The pop-up menu contains several items, including **Draw, Move, Fill, Erase, Copy, Paste,** and **Erase All.** When the user selects a menu item, the corresponding menu component fires an action event, which is received by the corresponding action event–handling method in the anonymous inner classes defined in the `popupMenu()` method. The methods that handle action events call the `setCommand()` method of `DrawShapesController` with the selected command as a parameter.

Setting Shape Parameters

Listing 5.19 shows the code for the `ParamsSelectionPanel` class, which creates the panel shown in Figure 5.10.

LISTING 5.19   The `ParamsSelectionPanel` class

```
package com.vistech.graphics;
import java.io.*;
import java.awt.*;
import java.awt.event.*;
import java.util.*;
import javax.swing.*;
import java.beans.*;
import javax.swing.event.*;
import javax.swing.border.*;

public class ParamsSelectionPanel extends JPanel {
    protected GraphicsDisplay target;
    public ParamsSelectionPanel(GraphicsDisplay gd){
        target = gd;
        createUI();
    }

    private void createUI(){
        JTabbedPane tab = new JTabbedPane();
        JPanel shpan = createShapesPanel();
```

FIGURE 5.10   The **Parameter Selection Panel** for setting graphical and text parameters

```java
    JPanel textpan = createTextPanel();
    tab.add(shpan, "Shapes");
    tab.add(textpan, "Text");
    tab.setBorder(BorderFactory.createTitledBorder(new EtchedBorder(),
                "Shape Selection"));
    add(tab);
}

public void setTarget(GraphicsDisplay tar){
    target = tar;
}

protected JPanel createTextPanel(){
    String fonttags[] =
        GraphicsEnvironment.getLocalGraphicsEnvironment().getAvailableFontFamily
        Names();
    int[] fontvalues = new int[fonttags.length];
    for(int i=0;i<fonttags.length;i++) {
        fontvalues[i] = i;
    }
    JComboBox fontnames = AttributeSetterUtil.createChoice(target,"FontType",
                                    fonttags,fontvalues);
    int minFontSize = 4;
    int maxFontSize = 48;
    int numOfSizes = (maxFontSize - minFontSize)/2;
            String fontsizetags[] = new String[numOfSizes];
    int fontsizevalues[] = new int[numOfSizes];
    for(int i=0; i<numOfSizes; i++) {
        fontsizetags[i] = (new Integer(2*i+minFontSize)).toString();
        fontsizevalues[i] = (2*i)+minFontSize;
    }
    JComboBox fontsizes = AttributeSetterUtil.createChoice(target, "FontSize",
                                    fontsizetags, fontsizevalues);

    String fontstyletags[] = {"PLAIN", "BOLD", "ITALIC"};
    int fontstylevalues[] ={Font.PLAIN, Font.BOLD, Font.ITALIC};
    JComboBox fontstyles = AttributeSetterUtil.createChoice(target, "FontStyle",
                                    fontstyletags, fontstylevalues);

    JComboBox txtcolor = AttributeSetterUtil.createColorChoice(target, "TextColor");
    Component com[] = {new JLabel("Text Color"),new JLabel("Fonts"),
                    new JLabel("Font Size"), new JLabel("Font Style"),
                    txtcolor,fontnames, fontsizes, fontstyles};
    JPanel fontpan = AttributeSetterUtil.doGridbagLayout(com, 4);
    return fontpan;
}


protected JPanel createShapesPanel() {
    JLabel drawcolorlab = new JLabel("Drawing Color");
    JComboBox drawcolor = AttributeSetterUtil.createColorChoice(target,
                                                "DrawingColor");

    JLabel fillcolorlab = new JLabel("Filling Color");
    JComboBox fillcolor = AttributeSetterUtil.createColorChoice(target, "FillColor");
```

continued

```
JPanel paramspan = new JPanel();
Component comp[] = {drawcolorlab,drawcolor, fillcolorlab,fillcolor};
JPanel pan1 = AttributeSetterUtil.doGridbagLayout(comp,4);

JLabel strokelab = new JLabel("Basic Stroke");
String widthtags[] = {"0.5", "1.0", "1.5", "2.0", "2.5",
                      "3.0", "3.5", "4.0", "4.5", "5.0",
                      "5.5", "6.0", "6.5", "7.0", "7.5"};
int[] widthvalues = new int[widthtags.length];
for(int i=0;i<widthtags.length;i++) {
    widthvalues[i] = i;
}

JComboBox strokewidth = AttributeSetterUtil.createChoice(target,"StrokeWidth",
                                   widthtags,widthvalues);
String captags[] = {"CAP_BUTT", "CAP_ROUND","CAP_SQUARE"};

int[] capvalues = {BasicStroke.CAP_BUTT,
                   BasicStroke.CAP_ROUND,
                   BasicStroke.CAP_SQUARE};
JComboBox  capstyle = AttributeSetterUtil.createChoice(target,"CapStyle",
                                   captags,capvalues);

String jointags[] = {"JOIN_MITER", "JOIN_ROUND","JOIN_BEVEL"};
int[] joinvalues = {BasicStroke.JOIN_MITER,
                    BasicStroke.JOIN_ROUND,
                    BasicStroke.JOIN_BEVEL};

JComboBox joinstyle = AttributeSetterUtil.createChoice(target,"JoinStyle",
                                   jointags, joinvalues);

Component comp1[] = {new JLabel("Stroke Width"),
                     new JLabel("Cap Style"),
                     new JLabel("Join Style"),
                     strokewidth, capstyle, joinstyle};

        // Gridbag layout code not shown

    return paramspan;
  }
}
```

The `ParamsSelectionPanel` constructor takes the `GraphicsDisplay` object as the input parameter. Whenever a parameter is set, the corresponding *setXXX()* method is called to set it.

The `createUI()` method creates a panel with two tabbed panes: **Shapes** and **Text.** The `createShapesPanel()` method creates the **Shapes** panel, and the `create TextPanel()` method creates the **Text** panel. Both of these methods use the static methods of the `AttributeSetterUtil` class to create combo boxes. Listing 5.20 shows the code for `AttributeSetterUtil`.

LISTING 5.20   The `AttributeSetterUtil` class

```
package com.vistech.graphics;
import java.io.*;
import java.awt.*;
import java.awt.event.*;
import java.util.*;
import javax.swing.*;
import javax.swing.event.*;
import java.beans.*;
import java.lang.reflect.*;

public class AttributeSetterUtil {

    public static JComboBox createChoice(Object obj,
                                    String prName,
                                    String[] tag,
                                    int[] value){
        final String propName = prName;
        final int[] values = value;
        final String[] tags = tag;
        final Object bean = obj;
        final Class cl = bean.getClass();
        String str = "get"+propName;
        JComboBox  cb = new JComboBox();
        for(int i=0;i <tags.length;i++){
            cb.addItem(tags[i]);
        }
        try{
            Method getM = cl.getMethod(str, null);
            Object args[] = { };
            Object val = getM.invoke(bean, args);
            int index =0;
            int  intval = ((Integer)val).intValue();
            for(int i=0;i <tags.length;i++){
              if(intval == values[i]){
                 index=i;
                 break;
              }
            }
            cb.setSelectedIndex(index);
        }catch(Exception e){
            e.printStackTrace();
            return cb;
        }
        cb.addItemListener(
            new ItemListener(){
                public void itemStateChanged(ItemEvent e){
                    try{
                        int ind =((JComboBox)(e.getSource())).getSelectedIndex();
                        Class[] cla = {int.class};
                        Method setM = cl.getMethod("set"+propName, cla);
                        Integer[] args ={new Integer(values[ind])};
                        setM.invoke(bean, args);
                    }catch(Exception x){System.out.println("choice exception"); }
                }
            }
```

continued

```
    );
    return cb;
}
public static JComboBox createColorChoice(Object obj, String prName){
    final String propName = prName;
    final Object bean = obj;
    final Class cl = bean.getClass();
    JComboBox  cb = new JComboBox();
    for(int i=0;i <colors.length;i++){
        cb.addItem(colorNames[i]);
    }
    try{
        String str = "get"+propName;
        Method getM = cl.getMethod(str, null);
        Object args[] = { };
        Object clr =  getM.invoke(bean, args);
        int index =0;
        for(int i=0;i <colors.length;i++){
          if(clr == colors[i]){
              index=i;
              break;
          }
        }
        cb.setSelectedIndex(index);
    }catch(Exception e){
        System.out.println("Reflection exception");
        return cb;
    }
    cb.addItemListener(
        new ItemListener(){
            public void itemStateChanged(ItemEvent e){
                try{
                    int ind =((JComboBox)(e.getSource())).getSelectedIndex();
                    Class[] cla = {Color.class};
                    Method setM = cl.getMethod("set"+propName, cla);
                    Color[] args ={colors[ind]};
                    setM.invoke(bean, args);
                }catch(Exception x){   System.out.println("choice exception"); }
            }
        }
    );
    return cb;
}
static Color[] colors = {Color.black, Color.blue, Color.red, Color.green,
                Color.yellow, Color.cyan, Color.magenta, Color.white};
static String[] colorNames = {"black", "blue", "red", "green",
                "yellow", "cyan", "magenta", "white"};
}
```

The static methods in the AttributeSetterUtil class are generic methods that can be used on any JavaBean or on any class that conforms to JavaBeans-style property set and get methods (see Appendix B). The createChoice() method creates a JComboBox component, with the drop-down items specified in the input parameter tag. The createColorChoice() method creates a color-specific JComboBox, with the drop-down items given in a static array called colors.

Both `createChoice()` and `createColorChoice()` use Java's reflection feature (`java.lang.reflect`) to set and get an attribute value in a generic manner. By using reflection, we eliminate the need to hard-code the attribute names. The `itemState Changed()` methods defined in the anonymous event-handling classes use the `java. lang.reflect.Class` and `java.lang.reflect.Method` classes to invoke a method whose name is created dynamically. The method invoked in this block is a set method whose name is constructed according to the JavaBeans design patterns (see Appendix B).

Conclusion

In this chapter we covered numerous graphics-related topics in JDK 1.1, as well as Java 2D. Java2D has very powerful graphical APIs. With these APIs you can easily create any shape and render it to a visual component. In this chapter we used many graphical APIs to implement a shapes class library and an interactive drawing application called JavaPaintShop.

Rendering Images in Java 2D

6

IN THIS CHAPTER WE'LL COVER some of the image-rendering topics we covered in the AWT imaging-rendering chapter (Chapter 3) with Java 2D in mind. Although the mechanism for rendering an image to a device remains the same, the way in which an image is represented and stored is different in Java 2D.

Java 2D has different rendering models: immediate mode and pull. The focus of this chapter is the immediate-mode model. Although the pull model–related interfaces are defined in Java 2D, the actual implementation is in Java Advanced Imaging. So, we'll cover the pull model in Part III.

This chapter will begin with a brief introduction to the immediate mode, followed by a detailed description of the `BufferedImage` class, which is at the center of Java 2D rendering. We'll then look at a few simple examples involving loading and displaying images. To develop real-world applications, we'll formulate some requirements for designing a canvas to render images. We'll translate these requirements into a Java interface and implement it in a class called `ImageCanvas.` Later we'll use this class to build a simple image viewer.

Printing is crucial to many imaging applications. Java 2D has an entirely new printing model. We'll describe this model and the printing APIs. A discussion of formulating requirements for printing images will follow, and we'll illustrate printing through a couple of examples.

The chapter will end with a sample application that is capable of loading, displaying, and printing images. This application will use all the classes and concepts developed in this chapter. The same application will be further developed in Chapter 7 to incorporate image manipulation features.

The Immediate-Mode Model

The Java 2D API addresses some of the weaknesses of the push model that was introduced in Chapter 2. Whereas asynchronous imaging operations may work well with networked applications, they are slow in stand-alone applications. The immediate mode is specially designed to improve rendering performance. In this mode the entire image is preloaded in memory. Various operations are performed directly on this memory image.

The immediate-mode model is not about image loading or saving, which is handled by the Image I/O framework. It is about the quick accessibility of image data once an image has been loaded. The immediate-mode model overcomes some of the drawbacks of the push model by caching the entire image in memory.

The immediate-mode model revolves around one class: `BufferedImage.` With this class, the pixel data cached in memory can be easily accessed, manipulated, and modified. Because the entire image resides in the cache, rendering operations are fast. So this model works well in stand-alone applications that use images that fit well within primary memory.

The BufferedImage Class

The `BufferedImage` class, which extends `Image,` represents an image in detail. Although the `Image` class also represents an image, it has very limited access to image data.

`BufferedImage` is a multifaceted class. As we saw in Chapter 5, this class is used to create off-screen images. You may recall that `BufferedImage` eliminates the need for a visible GUI component in order to create an off-screen image, which is the case with `Image.` From the image-rendering perspective, `BufferedImage` allows synchronous image rendering. From the image data manipulation perspective, it allows direct access to image pixels, thereby eliminating the need to use the `PixelGrabber` class.

The `BufferedImage` class extends `Image` and implements the `RenderedImage` and `WritableRenderedImage` interfaces, which are part of the pull model API. So in a way `BufferedImage` is a bridge between the push model and the pull model. However, other Java 2D APIs don't utilize `BufferedImage`'s support for the pull model.

The `BufferedImage` class, along with the `Graphics2D` class, enables image rendering. In this chapter we'll look at only the image-rendering aspect of `BufferedImage.` In Chapter 8 we'll examine the data access aspect of it.

`BufferedImage` overrides most of the `Image` class methods. But the majority of its methods are devoted to implementation of the `RenderedImage` and `WritableRendered Image` interfaces. We'll describe these methods in Chapter 10. Here we'll explain the methods that are specific to image rendering.

Constructing a BufferedImage Object

The `BufferedImage` class has three constructors, two of which are shown here:

1. `public BufferedImage(int width, int height, int imageType)`

2. `public BufferedImage(int width, int height, int imageType,`
   `IndexColorModel cm)`

Both of these constructors require `imageType` parameters, the values for which are defined in the `BufferedImage` class itself and are listed in Table 6.1. The second constructor requires an `IndexColorModel` parameter, and the `imageType` parameter in this case can be only `TYPE_BYTE_BINARY` or `TYPE_BYTE_INDEXED`. We'll describe the third constructor in Chapter 8.

Rendering-Related Methods

Let's look at some of the rendering-related methods:

- `public int getWidth(ImageObserver observer)`
- `public int getHeight(ImageObserver observer)`

TABLE 6.1 BufferedImage Types

TYPE	DESCRIPTION
TYPE_3BYTE_BGR	Each pixel is 3 bytes wide, representing BGR color components.
TYPE_4BYTE_ABGR	Each pixel is 4 bytes wide, representing alpha and BGR color components.
TYPE_4BYTE_ABGR_PRE	Same as TYPE_4BYTE_ABGR, but data is premultiplied with alpha.
TYPE_BYTE_BINARY	Each pixel is a byte representing a binary value that represents an indexed color model.
TYPE_BYTE_GRAY	Each pixel is a byte representing grayscale.
TYPE_BYTE_INDEXED	Each pixel is a byte representing an index that points to an indexed color model.
TYPE_CUSTOM	Not a recognized type.
TYPE_INT_ARGB	Each pixel is an integer representing 8-bit RGB color and alpha components.
TYPE_INT_ARGB_PRE	Same as TYPE_INT_ARGB, but data in this image is premultiplied with alpha.
TYPE_INT_BGR	This is also an integer RGB image, but it conforms to a Windows- or Solaris-style BGR color model.
TYPE_INT_RGB	Each pixel is an integer representing 8-bit RGB color components.
TYPE_USHORT_555_RGB	Each pixel is an unsigned short with 5 bits for red, 5 bits for green, and 5 bits for blue.
TYPE_USHORT_565_RGB	Each pixel is an unsigned short with 5 bits for red, 6 bits for green, and 5 bits for blue.
TYPE_USHORT_GRAY	Each pixel is a short representing grayscale.

These two methods return the size of the actual image drawn on the `BufferedImage`. If the size is not known, the value returned is –1. These methods override the corresponding superclass methods.

- **`public int getWidth()`**
- **`public int getHeight()`**

These two methods return the size of `BufferedImage`. Notice that there is no `ImageObserver` argument in this case.

- **`public Object getProperty(String name, ImageObserver observer)`**

This method overrides the corresponding superclass method.

- **`public Object getProperty(String name)`**

This method gets a property specified by the `name` parameter.

- **`public String[] getPropertyNames()`**

This method returns all the recognizable property names as an array of `String`.

- **`public Graphics2D createGraphics()`**

This method creates a `Graphics2D` object that can be used for drawing images.

- **`public BufferedImage getSubimage(int x, int y, int w, int h)`**

This method returns a rectangular region of the original image. It can be used for cropping an image.

- **`public ImageProducer getSource()`**

This method returns the source of the image as an `ImageProducer` object.

Rendering an Image onto a Device

Rendering images in Java 2D can be performed with the `Graphics2D` class. It has two flavors of `drawImage()` methods, either one of which can be used:

- **`public boolean drawImage(Image img,`**
  `                          AffineTransform xform,`
  `                          ImageObserver obs)`

Notice that this method does require an `ImageObserver` argument. However, it is perfectly valid to pass `null` as a value of `ImageObserver`.

- **`public void drawImage(BufferedImage img,`**
  `                       BufferedImageOp op,`
  `                       int x,`
  `                       int y)`

This method draws the `BufferedImage` directly. Note that this method has no `ImageObserver` argument. It also takes the `BufferedImageOp` argument. We'll describe this interface next.

The BufferedImageOp Interface

The `BufferedImageOp` interface specifies methods for performing single-input/single-output operations on `BufferedImage` objects. Implementing this interface in the Java 2D API are the following classes: `LookupOp`, `ConvolveOp`, `AffineTransformOp`, `ColorConvertOp`, and `RescaleOp`.

In this chapter we'll discuss only the `LookupOp` class, which performs lookup table operations on `BufferedImage`. Lookup tables are used in features such as brightness or contrast adjustments, inverse videos, window and level adjustments, and so on. We'll use the other `BufferedImageOp` classes in Chapter 8.

At the heart of the `BufferedImageOp` interface is the following method:

- **`public BufferedImage filter (BufferedImage src, BufferedImage dest)`**

  This method performs a single-input/single-output operation on a `Buffered Image` object. The implementation of this method defines the operation to be performed. In the case of the `LookupOp` class, the operation constructs a destination image by retrieving pixel values from a lookup table whose index corresponds to a value of a pixel in the source image.

  If the color model for the source and the destination do not match, the color model for the destination is converted to match the color model for the source. If the destination image is `null`, the filter method creates a `BufferedImage` object with the proper `ColorModel` class. The `filter()` method throws an exception—`IllegalArgumentException`—if the source and destination images are incompatible.

  The other methods in this interface are as follows:

- **`public BufferedImage createCompatibleDestImage(BufferedImage src, ColorModel destCM)`**

  As its name suggests, this method creates a destination image that is compatible with the source. It is preferable to obtain the destination `BufferedImage` object using this method.

- **`public Rectangle2D getBounds2D(BufferedImage src)`**
- **`public Point2D getPoint2D(Point2D srcPt, Point2D dstPt)`**

  For a specified point in the source image, this method returns the corresponding point in the destination image.

- **`public RenderingHints getRenderingHints()`**

  This method returns the rendering hints associated with the `BufferedImageOp` class. If no rendering hints are set, it returns `null`.

Bridging the Immediate-Mode and Push Models

The immediate-mode model can be made compatible with the push model. The `java.awt.BufferedImageFilter` class is designed for this purpose. This is a subclass of `ImageFilter,` and its constructor takes a `BufferedImageOp` object as input:

♦ **public BufferedImageFilter(BufferedImageOp op)**

Recall from Chapters 2 and 3 that an `ImageFilter` object is an `ImageConsumer` object. This means that the `BufferedImageFilter` class can act as a bridge between the immediate-mode model and the push model.

To use the immediate-mode and push models interchangeably, we need to convert a `BufferedImage` object to an AWT `Image` object and vice versa.

Converting BufferedImage to AWT Image

As we learned in the previous section, `BufferedImage` is a subclass of `Image.` So you can use a `BufferedImage` object directly as an `Image` object or perform the downcasting operation wherever appropriate. Note that downcasting doesn't change an object. The following example shows how downcasting is done:

```
Image anAWTImage = (Image) aBufferedImage;
```

Converting in this way is not always desirable because `BufferedImage` objects are much larger than `Image` objects. Furthermore, applications that receive the `Image` object may be running with Java 1.1, which, you may recall, does not understand `BufferedImage.` So we need to find other ways of converting `BufferedImage` to `Image.`

Here's another way to create an `Image` object from an instance of `BufferedImage`:

```
Image img = Toolkit.getDefaultToolkit().createImage(aBufferedImage.getSource());
```

You may recall from the AWI imaging chapters that the **createImage()** method requires an `ImageProducer` parameter. In this example, this parameter is obtained from the `BufferedImage` object by a call to the **getSource()** method, which is defined in `BufferedImage`'s superclass (i.e., `Image`) .

A much more elaborate and flexible way to convert a `BufferedImage` object to an `Image` object is by using the `BufferedImageFilter` class. To create a `BufferedImageFilter` object, we must first create a `BufferedImageOp` object. One way to do this is to use the `AffineTransformOp` class, which implements the `BufferedImageOp` interface.

As we saw in Chapters 2 and 3, it is easy to create an `Image` from an `ImageFilter` object. All you need to do is create a `FilteredImageSource` object to act as an `ImageProducer` object.

The `FilteredImageSource` constructor requires an `ImageProducer` parameter. To obtain an `ImageProducer` object, call the `getSource()` method in the `BufferedImage` object itself. Once you have created a `FilteredImageSource` object, use the `create Image()` method of the `Toolkit` class to create the `Image` object from `FilteredImage Source`. Listing 6.1 shows a method that uses the `BufferedImageFilter` class to convert a `BufferedImage` object to an `Image` object.

LISTING 6.1   Converting a `BufferedImage` object to an AWT `Image` object

```
public static Image convertToAWTImage(BufferedImage bufImage) {
    AffineTransformOp aop = new AffineTransformOp(new AffineTransform(),
                                            AffineTransformOp.TYPE_BILINEAR);
    BufferedImageFilter bif = new BufferedImageFilter(aop);
    FilteredImageSource fsource = new FilteredImageSource(bufImage.getSource(), bif);
    Image img = Toolkit.getDefaultToolkit().createImage(fsource);
    return img;
}
```

The `AffineTransformOp` and `BufferedImageFilter` classes make this conversion very flexible: You can apply any geometric transformation on the image before conversion.

To apply a desired geometric transformation on the image, you must use the `AffineTransform` class (which is an input to the `AffineTransformOp` constructor). This means that you can perform operations such as translation, scaling, and rotation on the input `BufferedImage` object before converting it to an `Image` object. In Chapter 7 we'll see how to use the `AffineTransform` and `AffineTransformOp` classes to perform geometric transformations.

Converting AWT Image to BufferedImage

Java 2D applications often require the image to be encapsulated in a `BufferedImage` object. If an application loads an image into an `Image` object, it must be converted to a `BufferedImage` object. One approach to conversion is to draw the `Image` object on a `BufferedImage` object. The static method shown in Listing 6.2 does exactly that.

LISTING 6.2   Converting an AWT `Image` object to a `BufferedImage` object

```
public static BufferedImage convertToBufferedImage(Image img,
                            int wid, int ht, int type){
    BufferedImage bi = new BufferedImage(wid, ht, type);
    Graphics2D g2d = bi.createGraphics();
    g2d.drawImage(img, 0,0,wid, ht, null);
    return bi;
}
```

A more accurate way to achieve this conversion is to use the `BufferedImage` constructor that takes raster data as input. To use this constructor, you must first extract the pixel data using the `PixelGrabber` class. In Chapter 8 we'll see how to construct the `BufferedImage` object directly from the data.

Now that we've established the relationship between the immediate-mode model and the push model, let's develop a simple image-viewing example using `Buffered Image`.

JPEG Viewer: A Simple Image-Rendering Example

To be displayed, an image must first be loaded. As mentioned earlier, the AWT image-loading mechanism loads an image as an `Image` object. If we use the AWT image-loading API, we may lose many of the benefits of Java 2D (e.g., flexible data and color representation).

What we really need is a loading mechanism that reads an image as a `BufferedImage` object. The new Image I/O API has this capability. It is also capable of saving an AWT `Image` object or a `BufferedImage` object in any format for which a coder/decoder (codec) plug-in is available.

At the time of writing, the Image I/O implementation is in the beta stage. As a stopgap measure, Sun provided a JPEG codec package (`com.sun.image.codec.jpeg`) with the JDK 1.2 distribution. This codec is explained in detail in Chapter 17. The JPEG codec is adequate for simple load and save operations. However, if you are looking for a sophisticated JPEG codec, you may want to use a commercially available package.

Using the JPEG Codec

Listing 6.3 shows the code for a JPEG image viewer that loads a JPEG image from a local directory and displays it in a panel. This viewer uses the JPEG-decoding API to load an image as a `BufferedImage` object, which is then painted by the `drawImage()` method of the `Graphics2D` class.

LISTING 6.3   A JPEG image viewer

```
import java.awt.*;
import java.awt.event.*;
import java.awt.image.*;
import java.io.*;
import javax.swing.*;

import com.sun.image.codec.jpeg.*;

public class JPEGViewer extends JPanel {
    ImagePanel viewer;

    public static BufferedImage readAsBufferedImage(String filename) {
        try {
```

```java
            FileInputStream fis = new FileInputStream(filename);
            JPEGImageDecoder decoder = JPEGCodec.createJPEGDecoder(fis);
            BufferedImage bi = decoder.decodeAsBufferedImage();
            return bi;
        } catch(Exception e) {
            System.out.println(e);
            return null;
        }
    }

    public void loadAndDisplay(String filename){
        BufferedImage img = loadImage(filename);
        displayImage(img);
    }

    public BufferedImage loadImage(String filename){
        return readAsBufferedImage(filename);
    }

    public void displayImage(BufferedImage img) {
        int width = img.getWidth();
        int height = img.getHeight();
        displayImage(img, width, height);
    }

    public void displayImage(BufferedImage img, int width, int height) {
        JFrame fr = new JFrame();
        fr.addWindowListener(
            new WindowAdapter() {
                public void windowClosing(WindowEvent e){
                    System.exit(0);
                }
            } );
        fr.setTitle("JPEG Viewer");
        viewer = new ImagePanel(img);
        viewer.setPreferredSize(new Dimension(width, height));
        Container cp = fr.getContentPane();
        fr.getContentPane().setLayout(new GridLayout(1,1));
        cp.add(viewer);
        fr.pack();
        fr.setSize(new Dimension(width, height));
        fr.show();
        viewer.repaint();
    }


class ImagePanel extends JComponent {
    BufferedImage image;
    public ImagePanel(BufferedImage img){
        image = img;
    }

    public void paintComponent(Graphics g){
        Rectangle rect = this.getBounds();
        if(image != null) {
            g.drawImage(image, 0,0,rect.width, rect.height, this);
        }
    }
}
```

continued

```
    }

    public static void  main(String[] args){
        JPEGViewer ip = new JPEGViewer();
        if(args.length <1) {
            System.out.println("Enter a valid JPEG file name");
            System.exit(0);
        }
        ip.loadAndDisplay(args[0]);
    }
}
```

When the JPEG viewer is launched, the `main()` method gets the image file names from the command-line parameters and calls the `loadAndDisplay()` method. This method in turn calls `readAsJPEGImage()` and `displayImage()`. The `readAsJPEG Image()` method loads a JPEG image, and the `displayImage()` method creates an `ImagePanel` object to display the loaded image. The size of this object is set to be the same as the size of the image. The `paintComponent()` method then displays the image when `repaint()` is called.

To learn how the `readAsBufferedImage()` method works, you may want to read the section on the JPEG codec in Chapter 17.

To launch the JPEG viewer, type "java JPEGViewer <JPEG file>" on the command line. Figure 6.1 shows a screen shot of the JPEG viewer.

© Richard Passmore/Stone

FIGURE 6.1   The JPEG viewer

Using the Image I/O API

The Image I/O API allows you to install custom-written plug-ins for reading and writing any type of image format. So you can run the example shown in Listing 6.4 with any type of image supported by your Image I/O codec.

LISTING 6.4   The image viewer using the Image I/O API

```java
import java.awt.*;
import java.awt.event.*;
import java.awt.image.*;
import java.io.*;
import javax.swing.*;
import javax.swing.event.*;
import javax.imageio.*;

public class ImageIOViewer extends JPEGViewer {
    ImagePanel viewer;

    public static BufferedImage readAsBufferedImage(String filename) {
        try {
         BufferedImage img = ImageIO.read(new File(filename));
         return img;
        }catch (Exception e) {
         e.printStackTrace();
         return null;
        }
    }
    public BufferedImage loadImage(String filename){
        return ImageIOViewer.readAsBufferedImage(filename);
    }
    public static void  main(String[] args){
        ImageIOViewer ip = new ImageIOViewer();
        if(args.length <1) {
           System.out.println("Enter a valid image file name");
           System.exit(0);
        }
        ip.loadAndDisplay(args[0]);
    }
}
```

To run the example in Listing 6.4, install the `imageio.jar` file in your class path or in the `<JDK_HOME>/lib/ext` directory.

> **Note:** The example in Listing 6.4 was tested with the early-release version of the Image I/O reference implementation, which was based on the 0.5 version of the spec. If the API has changed, you may want to modify the code to suit the current release.

Image Browser: An Example of Aggregating Multiple Images

The image browser example described in this section loads multiple images using the `MultiImageLoader` bean (see Chapter 2 and Appendix B) and then displays them in an image panel. You can save all the images on this image panel as a single JPEG image. `MultiImageLoader` can also act as a GIF-to-JPEG converter. Using the image browser, you can load a GIF image and save it as a JPEG image.

When you run the Java image browser, it launches the `MultiImageLoader` bean. Using this bean, select one or more images and click on **Launch Image Browser** to launch an image panel (see Figures 6.2 and 6.3). To run the image browser, type "java ImageBrowser".

You can save the `MultiImageLoader` GUI by selecting the image browser's **Save** menu. To save the images in the image panel, click on its **Save** menu. Both of these **Save** menus have two options: **Save** and **Save As.** The **Save** option saves the image with a default file name. The **Save As** option launches a file dialog box for entering the image file name. After you enter the file to be saved, you can use the same image browser to check whether the image or component has been saved.

Listing 6.5 shows the code for the image browser.

LISTING 6.5   The `ImageBrowser` class

```java
import java.io.*;
import java.awt.*;
import java.awt.event.*;
import javax.swing.*;
import java.util.*;
import com.vistech.util.*;
import com.vistech.events.*;
import com.vistech.imageloader.*;

public class ImageBrowser extends com.vistech.util.ApplicationFrame{
    protected MultiImageLoader il;
    protected ViewerPanel viewer;
    public ImageBrowser() {
        createUI();
    }

    protected void setAboutStrings() {
        setAboutString(" Java Image Browser \n Version 1.0 \n"+
                        "Author: Lawrence Rodrigues\n");
        setAboutTitle(" Java Image Browser");
    }

    private void createUI() {
        setAboutStrings();
        il = new MultiImageLoader();
        il.setLoadButtonLabel("Launch Image Browser");
        il.addImageLoadedListener(
            new ImageLoadedListener() {
                public void imageLoaded(ImageLoadedEvent e) {
```

continued

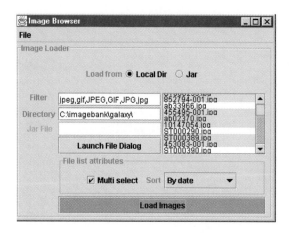

FIGURE 6.2   Launching the image browser

© Jack Zehrt/FPG International LLC; © World Perspectives/FPG International LLC; © Paul & Lindamarie
Ambrose/FPG International LLC; © StockTrek/PhotoDisc; © Jim Ballard/Stone ; © World Perspectives/Stone ;
© John Lund/Stone ; © Derek Berwin/The Image Bank ; © Dr. Robert Muntefering/The Image Bank

FIGURE 6.3   The image browser frame with multiple images

```
                    Image[] imset = e.getImages();
                    displayImage(imset);
                    il.setLoadButtonLabel("Load Images");
                }
            });
        this.getContentPane().add(il);
        this.setSize(il.getPreferredSize().width+30, il.getPreferredSize().height+50);
    }

    public void displayImage(Image[] imset) {
        if(viewer == null) {
            viewer = new ViewerPanel();
            viewer.setTitle("Image Browser");
            viewer.addWindowListener(
              new WindowAdapter() {
               public void windowClosing(WindowEvent e){
                  System.exit(0);
               }
            });
        }
        viewer.setImageSet(imset);
        viewer.show();
        viewer.repaint();
    }

    public static void  main(String[] args){
        ImageBrowser ib = new ImageBrowser();
        ib.setTitle("Java Image Browser");
        ib.show();
    }
}
```

The `createUI()` method adds the `MultiImageLoader` bean to the `ImageBrowser` object. The `imageLoaded()` method (defined in the anonymous inner class of `createUI()`) calls the `displayImage()` method, which launches the `ImageBrowser` frame. The `displayImage()` method constructs the `ImageBrowser` frame using the `ViewerPanel` class. The source code for `ViewerPanel` is shown in Listing 6.6.

LISTING 6.6   The `ViewerPanel` class

```
import java.io.*;
import java.awt.*;
import java.awt.image.*;
import java.awt.event.*;
import java.util.*;
import javax.swing.*;
import com.vistech.util.*;
import com.sun.image.codec.jpeg.*;

public class ViewerPanel extends com.vistech.util.ApplicationFrame {
    protected int curIndex =0;
    protected int numImages= 0;
    protected Image[] imageset;
    protected int cellWidth = 100;
    protected int cellHeight = 80;
```

```
protected int rows =1;
protected int cols =1;
protected int maxWidth = 600, minWidth =340;
protected int maxHeight= 400, minHeight =220;
transient protected ImagePanel vp[] = null;
protected JPanel vpGrid;
protected String defaultFileName = "defaultimage";

public ViewerPanel() { init(); }
public void init(){
   createUI();
}

public void setImageSet(Image images[]){
   imageset = images;
   createNewPanel();
}

private void createUI (){
   vpGrid = createViewportGrid();
   getContentPane().setLayout(new GridLayout(1,1));
   getContentPane().add(vpGrid);
   pack();
   setSize(maxWidth, maxHeight);
}

protected JPanel createViewportGrid() {
   JPanel vpGrid = new JPanel();
   vpGrid.setBackground(Color.black);
   vpGrid.setSize(maxWidth, maxHeight);
   if(imageset == null) return vpGrid;
   numImages = imageset.length;
   if(numImages ==0) return vpGrid;
   int numvp = (int)(Math.ceil( Math.sqrt((double)numImages)));
   vp = new ImagePanel[numvp*numvp];
   cols = numvp;
   rows = (int)(Math.ceil(numImages/(double)numvp));
   vpGrid.setLayout(new GridLayout(rows, cols));
   cellWidth = maxWidth/cols;
   cellHeight= maxHeight/rows;
   for(int i=0;i<rows;i++){
       for(int j=0;j<cols;j++){
           if(vp[(i*cols)+j] == null){
               try{
                 if(((i*cols)+j) < imageset.length){
                    vp[(i*cols)+j] = new ImagePanel(imageset[(i*cols)+j]);
                    vp[(i*cols)+j].repaint();
                 } else vp[(i*cols)+j] = new ImagePanel();
               } catch(Exception e){}
           }
           vp[(i*cols)+j].setSize(new Dimension(cellWidth,cellHeight));
           vpGrid.add(vp[(i*cols)+j]);
       }
   }
   vpGrid.setSize(maxWidth, maxHeight);
   return vpGrid;
}
```

continued

```java
public Dimension getPreferredSize(){
    return new Dimension(maxHeight, maxWidth);
}

private void createNewPanel() {
    remove(vpGrid);
    invalidate();
    vpGrid = createViewportGrid();
    getContentPane().add(vpGrid);
    validate();
    paintImages();
}

public ImagePanel[] getViewports(){
    return vp;
}

public void paintImages(){
    for(int i=0;i<numImages;i++){
        if(imageset[i] == null) continue;
        vp[i].setImage(imageset[i]);
        vp[i].repaint();
        curIndex++;
        curIndex %= numImages;
    }
}

public void display(int imageIndex){
    if((imageIndex <0) ||
       (vp == null) ||
       (imageset[imageIndex] == null)) return;
    vp[curIndex].setImage(imageset[imageIndex]);
    vp[curIndex++].repaint();
    curIndex %= numImages;
}

public Dimension getCellSize(){
    if(vp[0] != null){
        return vp[0].getSize();
    }
    else return (new Dimension(cellWidth, cellHeight));
}

public BufferedImage createBufferedImage() {
    Dimension dim = getCellSize();
    int imWid = cols*dim.width;
    int imHt =  rows*dim.height;
    BufferedImage bi = new BufferedImage((int)imWid,
                                         (int)(imHt),
                                         BufferedImage.TYPE-INT-RGB);

    Graphics2D g2d = bi.createGraphics();
    int x = 0; int y=0;
    for(int i=0; i< rows; i++) {
        for(int j=0;j<cols; j++) {
            if(i*cols+j >= imageset.length) break;
            Image img = imageset[i*cols+j];
            if(img != null)
```

```
            g2d.drawImage(img, x+1,y+1, dim.width-2, dim.height-2,this);
         x += dim.width;
      }
      x =0;
      y += dim.height;
   }
   return bi;
}

protected void saveAs(){
   JpegUtil.saveImageAsJPEG(createBufferedImage(), .9f);
}

protected void save(){
   JpegUtil.saveImageAsJPEG(createBufferedImage(), .9f, defaultFileName);
}
}
```

The `ViewerPanel` class has many methods that are not directly related to image rendering. We won't discuss these methods.

When you select a set of images and click on **Load Images,** the `ImageBrowser` class sends the selected images to the `ViewerPanel` object by calling `setImageset()`. `ViewerPanel` creates several `ImagePanel` objects and lays them in a grid fashion.

When you select the **Save** or **Save As** option, either the `save()` or the `saveAs()` method is called. These methods first call the `createBufferedImage()` method that creates a single `BufferedImage` object for all the images displayed in the image panel. The `save()` and `saveAs()` methods then call the appropriate flavors of `JpegUtil.` `saveImageAsJPEG()` to save the image grid as a single JPEG image. See Chapter 17 for a detailed explanation of `saveImageAsJPEG()` methods.

Note: The source code for the `JpegUtil.java` class is available on the book's Web page in the directory `src/util`.

The `ImagePanel` class shown in Listing 6.7 is an inner class of `ViewerPanel`. Each of the images in the browser is displayed in an instance of `ImagePanel`.

LISTING 6.7   The `ImagePanel` class

```
class ImagePanel extends JComponent {
   protected Image image;
   public ImagePanel(){}
   public ImagePanel(Image img){ image = img;}

   public void setImage(Image img){ image = img; }

   public void paintComponent(Graphics g){
      Rectangle rect = this.getBounds();
      if(image != null) {
```

continued

```
        g.drawImage(image, 0,0,rect.width, rect.height, this);
      }
    }
  }
```

Designing a Component Class for Displaying Images

Now that we've seen a few examples, it's time to develop classes to build real-world applications. First let's develop a general-purpose component class to display images. To accomplish this we need to look at the requirements.

In many image-viewing applications, the component that displays images must do a lot more than just displaying images. Images are displayed for a variety of purposes, which may include animation, visual inspection, and quantitative analysis. Here are some common issues in image-viewing applications:

◆ **Image orientation.** Users often want to change the image orientation so that they don't need to mentally reconstruct different orientations. In a map-viewing application, for instance, a user might want to rotate the map to an orientation to which she or he is accustomed. In medical imaging, images are acquired with different patient orientations, such as head first, feet first, face up, face down, and so on. Sometimes images are taken at an angle to the normal patient plane. But when radiologists or doctors view these images, they like to see them in an orientation to which they are accustomed. This means that the image-viewing software should have the capability to flip and rotate images.

◆ **Image quality.** Visual inspection plays a very important role in gathering information from images. Because devices that display an image are different from devices that acquired it, it is often necessary to adjust the brightness and contrast of the images. The range of pixels that a computer monitor can distinguish is frequently narrower than the range of pixels in an image. This is especially true of scientific images. A typical computer monitor can differentiate a range of 256 values, but image acquisition devices often used in the scientific arena can have larger depths. For instance, computed tomography (CT) images are typically 12 bits, which means that pixel values can range from 0 to 4,028. If such images are displayed on an 8-bit display monitor, the image may appear dim. In addition, doctors may fail to notice certain important features in the image because the pixel values for a feature—say, bone—tend to be concentrated in a certain narrow range compared to the entire pixel range. Moreover, when we view images, our eyes limit the range of pixels we can actually differentiate. This is another reason why our eyes may not be able to notice or differentiate certain important features in an image. What we need, therefore, is a mechanism to brighten images and a way to accentuate a range of pixel values so that an area is contrasted with respect to the rest of the image.

- **Panning and zooming images.** Consider the map-viewing example again. If you are looking for a region or an address in a map, you might scroll the map until you see the desirable region in the viewing area. To obtain more information, you might zoom the viewing area and scroll it further. Such applications require panning and zooming to be performed together. In Chapter 7 we'll describe how to implement commonly used features such as pan and zoom.

- **Adding text and graphics to an image.** Once an image is displayed, users often want to draw text and graphics over that image. This capability is a requirement in many types of applications. You might have seen weather forecasters on TV drawing arrows or circles on weather images. In Internet GIS applications, you probably have seen regions marked on a map to indicate, for example, the area of primary responsibility of a dealership. In scientific imaging, regions are marked for calculating statistics. In view of all these applications, the component that displays images should have the capability to lay text and graphics over images. In addition, it must be capable of firing mouse and keyboard events so that the user can interactively draw shapes and text.

Let's first define specifications to write classes or components that can be used as a canvas to render images. By doing so, we can build other classes or components to operate on this canvas to perform different operations, such as flip, rotate, pan, zoom, and so on. Since specifications in Java can be converted into methods of an interface, let's define an interface called `ImageDisplay` along the same lines as `Graphics Display`, which we developed in Chapter 5.

The ImageDisplay Interface

The basic idea here is that the class that implements the `ImageDisplay` interface should act as a canvas to draw images. It will provide methods for setting the attributes of the canvas and for displaying the image. You can write different types of operator classes to operate on `ImageDisplay.` These operator classes can be used on any class that implements the `ImageDisplay` interface.

Typically the operator interfaces will have GUI components to manipulate the `ImageDisplay` component. For example, a pan and zoom operator class may use mouse events to pan and zoom the displayed image. A brightness/contrast operator may require sliders to vary brightness and contrast.

In the `ImageDisplay` interface discussed here, we'll specify bare minimum methods. In the next two chapters we'll specify more methods to include image manipulation functions. These methods will be in an interface that is a subclass of `ImageDisplay.` If the interfaces are divided in this way, a simple application need not be burdened with a large number of unnecessary methods.

In the `ImageDisplay` interface, we need to define the methods to satisfy the following basic required functions:

- ◆ Setting the image
- ◆ Setting the image size and orientation
- ◆ Rendering the image

We'll develop this interface in such a way that the naming conventions are JavaBeans compliant. The ImageCanvas class implements the ImageDisplay interface.

Note: The source code for ImageDisplay is available on the book's Web page in the directory src/chapter6/ImageDisplay.

Next we'll define the ImageDisplay methods. Along with these methods, we'll provide their implementation in the ImageCanvas class:

```
public class ImageCanvas extends JComponent
                         implements ImageDisplay, ImagePrint{

    ...

}
```

As you can see, this class extends JComponent and implements the ImageDisplay and ImagePrint interfaces. We'll talk about the ImagePrint interface later in this chapter. The ImageCanvas class does not implement any of the event-related methods because it inherits them from JComponent.

Setting the Image

Let's make the image attribute a property. Because there are two different image classes—Image and BufferedImage—we need to create two separate attributes: awtImage and bufferedImage. As a convenience, we'll also define the following two constants:

```
public static final int TYPE_AWT_IMAGE = 1;
public static final int TYPE_BUFFERED_IMAGE = 2;
```

The awtImage attribute holds the Image object, and the bufferedImage attribute holds the BufferedImage object.

Let's specify the JavaBeans-compliant (see Appendix B) set and get methods for setting and retrieving these image attributes:

- ◆ **public void setAWTImage(Image image);**
- ◆ **public Image getAWTImage();**

- ◆ **public void setBufferedImage(BufferedImage image);**
- ◆ **public Image getBufferedImage();**

A client object can use either of the set methods to set the image. For example, a client program that uses the AWT image-loading program will call the `setAWTImage()` method, whereas the program that uses the Java 2D JPEG codec or the Image I/O codec will call the `setBufferedImage()` method. In either case, the component that implements the `ImageDisplay` interface needs to convert the image appropriately.

We'll specify both `awtImage` and `bufferedImage` as bound properties. Registered listeners to either property will receive the `propertyChange` event notification whenever the `awtImage` or `bufferedImage` property is changed. Listing 6.8 shows a sample implementation of the `setAWTImage()` method.

LISTING 6.8   Setting the `awtImage` attribute

```
public void setAWTImage(Image image){
    reset();
    Image oldImage = this.awtImage;
    this.awtImage = image;
    originalImageType = ImageDisplay.TYPE_AWT_IMAGE;

    imageWidth = this.awtImage.getWidth(this);
    imageHeight = this.awtImage.getHeight(this);
    if((imageWidth <=0)||(imageHeight<=0)) paintFlag = true;
    else {
      firePropertyChange("awtImage",this.awtImage,oldImage);

      bufferedImage =
          convertToBufferedImage(image, imageWidth, imageHeight, imageType);

      paintImage();
      repaint();
    }
}
```

The `setAWTImage()` method assigns the input image to the `awtImage` property. Assume that the class that implements this method has an instance variable called `awtImage.` The `setAWTImage()` method then computes the image height and width.

The `getWidth()` and `getHeight()` methods may not return the width and height immediately. If these methods do return the width and height, the `setAWTImage()` method fires the `propertyChange` event for the `awtImage` property. In Listing 6.8 we assumed that the class that implements the `ImageDisplay` interface is a subclass of `JComponent`, which has the `firePropertyChange()` method. This method fires a `propertyChange` event to all the listeners that registered for `propertyChange` events. If this class is not a subclass of `JComponent`, you can use the `java.beans.PropertyChangeSupport` class to delegate this task (see Appendix B for more details).

The `setAWTImage()` method then calls the `paintImage()` method that paints the current image. As we'll see shortly (in the section titled Displaying an Image) `paintImage()` also applies the current display modes and flip modes. Observe that the `setAWTImage()` method also converts the input AWT `Image` object to an equivalent `BufferedImage` object. This action is to ensure that the `ImageDisplay` objects are compatible with both the immediate-mode model and the push model. (See Listing 6.2 for the `convertToBufferedImage()` method.)

If the `getWidth()` and `getHeight()` methods return a value of –1 each, the `setAWTImage()` method sets `paintFlag` to `false`. Image painting is deferred until this flag is set to `true`.

Recall from Chapters 2 and 3 that an AWT `Image` object is created when the `getImage()` method in the `Applet` or `java.awt.Toolkit` class is invoked. The fact that an `Image` object is created doesn't mean that the image has been loaded. The image does not start loading until it is needed—that is, until it is set for drawing or pixel grabbing. To cater to such situations, the `ImageDisplay` interface should extend the `ImageObserver` interface. This means that a class that implements the `ImageDisplay` interface should have the `imageUpdate()` method. If the `getWidth()` or `getHeight()` method returns –1, the actual width and height will be obtained by the `imageUpdate()` method, as shown in Listing 6.9.

LISTING 6.9   The `imageUpdate()` method

```
public boolean imageUpdate(Image img, int infoflags, int x, int y, int wid, int ht){
    if((infoflags & ImageObserver.ERROR) != 0){ return false; }
    if((infoflags & (ImageObserver.WIDTH | ImageObserver.HEIGHT))!= 0){
        this.imageWidth = wid;
        this.imageHeight = ht;
    }
    if((infoflags & (ImageObserver.FRAMEBITS | ImageObserver.ALLBITS))!= 0){
        if(paintFlag) {
            paintFlag = false;
            this.imageWidth = wid;
            this.imageHeight = ht;
            Image oldImage = this.awtImage;
            this.awtImage = img;

            firePropertyChange("awtImage",this.awtImage,oldImage);
            bufferedImage = convertToBufferedImage(awtImage, wid, ht, imageType);
            paintImage();
            repaint();
        }
        return false;
    }
    return true;
}
```

When the image has been completely loaded—that is, `ALLBITS = 1`—the `imageUpdate()` method does what the `setAWTImage()` method does; that is, it fires the `propertyChange` event and then calls the `paintImage()` method, which paints the image.

If an image is loaded as a `BufferedImage` setting, the image attribute is straightforward. Listing 6.10 shows the code for the `setBufferedImage()` method.

LISTING 6.10   Setting the bufferedImage attribute

```
public void setBufferedImage(BufferedImage bimage){
    reset();
    BufferedImage oldImage = this.bufferedImage;
    this.bufferedImage = bimage;
    originalImageType = ImageDisplay.TYPE_BUFFERED_IMAGE;

    imageWidth = bufferedImage.getWidth();
    imageHeight = bufferedImage.getHeight();

    firePropertyChange("bufferedImage",this.bufferedImage,oldImage);

    this.awtImage = convertToAWTImage(bimage);
    paintImage();
    repaint();
}
```

The `setBufferedImage()` method assigns the input `BufferedImage` object to the `bufferedImage` property. It then obtains the image width and height and fires the `propertyChange` event for the `bufferedImage` property to the registered listeners. Before painting the image, `setBufferedImage()` converts the `BufferedImage` object to an AWT `Image` object and assigns it to the `awtImage` property (see Listing 6.1). By this conversion, an `ImageDisplay` object is guaranteed to have both the AWT `Image` and the `BufferedImage` versions of an input image.

Setting the Image Type

As mentioned earlier, the `BufferedImage` class defines several different image types (see Table 6.1). Let's specify the set and get methods for the `imageType` property.

◆ **public void setImageType(int imageType);**
◆ **public int getImageType();**

The implementing class should use the `imageType` property while creating the `BufferedImage` objects for double buffering.

Displaying an Image

An image is displayed by being drawn on a component's graphical context. The AWT and Swing components have methods like `paint()`, `update()`, and `paint Component()` for drawing images over the graphical context. These methods are not directly invoked in the application but are triggered by the system or the application. So let's define a method called `paintImage()` to invoke the actual paint method:

◆ **public void paintImage();**

As we said earlier, in the section titled Setting the Image, `awtImage` and `bufferedImage` are properties. The `paintImage()` method will draw the image held by one of these properties. The implementer of the `ImageDisplay` interface may choose to implement double buffering, so the `paint()` methods may draw the double-buffered image. Listing 6.11 shows the implementation of `paintImage()` from the `ImageCanvas` class.

LISTING 6.11 The `paintImage()` method

```
public boolean paintImage() {
   if((awtImage != null) || (bufferedImage != null))
      return doDisplayModeAndFlip(imageWidth, imageHeight);
   else return false;
}
```

See the section titled Setting the Display Mode a little later in this chapter for an implementation of the `doDisplayModeAndFlip()` method, which applies the current display and flip modes. Depending on the original image type, this method chooses the image to paint: either `awtImage` or `bufferedImage.`

In Swing components, the `paintComponent()` method actually draws the image. This method is called by the painting threads when `repaint()` is called. Listing 6.12 shows the code for the `paintComponent()` method implemented in the `ImageCanvas` class.

LISTING 6.12 The `paintComponent()` method

```
public void paintComponent(Graphics gc){
   super.paintComponent(gc);
   Graphics2D g = (Graphics2D)gc;
   Rectangle d = getBounds();
   if((d.width != width)|| (d.height != height)){
       width = d.width;
       height = d.height;
       redraw();
   }
   if(displayImage!= null){
      g.drawImage(displayImage,0,0,this);
   }else createDisplayImage();
}

protected void redraw() {
    createDisplayImage();
    paintImage();
    repaint();
}
```

The original image is not drawn on the graphical context directly, for reasons we have already explained. Instead, it is drawn on a buffered image called `display Image.` Listing 6.13 shows how `displayImage` is created.

The `paintComponent()` method first checks the canvas size because users might have resized the canvas after the last call to `paint().` If the size is different, a new instance of `displayImage` is created and the original image is redrawn.

Double Buffering

The `createDisplayImage()` method shown in Listing 6.13 constructs a buffered image with the same size as the canvas. The `setOffScrGc()` method creates a `Graphics` object from `displayImage` and sets some default drawing parameters.

LISTING 6.13   The `createDisplayImage()` method

```
protected void createDisplayImage(){
    displayImage = new BufferedImage(width,height,BufferedImage.TYPE_INT_RGB);
    setOffScrGc();
}

protected void setOffScrGc(){
    if(displayImage!= null){
        dispGc = displayImage.createGraphics();
        dispGc.setFont(font);
        dispGc.setColor(getBackground());
        dispGc.fillRect(0,0, width, height);
        dispGc.setColor(getForeground());
        dispGc.setRenderingHint(RenderingHints.KEY_RENDERING,
                            RenderingHints.VALUE_RENDER_QUALITY);
    }
}
```

The `displayImage` object acts as an off-screen image. In Java 2D imaging, unlike AWT imaging, there is no need to use the `createImage()` method to construct an off-screen image. You can directly construct the `BufferedImage` object and use it as an off-screen image. To get the `Graphics2D` context from a `BufferedImage` object, call the `createGraphics()` method. Note the difference: In AWT imaging, you would call the `getGraphics()` method.

Inverting an Image

Applications are often required to generate an inverse video of the image. Inverse video sometimes provides better contrast, especially with grayscale images. In vascular imaging, for instance, inverse video of a grayscale image sometimes provides better visualization of arteries. Even in other types of imaging, inverse video may enhance the contrast.

In Java 2D, image inversion can be easily accomplished through lookup tables. In an inverted image, black pixels become white and vice versa.

Let's specify a `boolean` property to keep track of the current state of the inversion mode—that is, inverted or noninverted. The set and get methods for this property are

- `public void setInvert(boolean onOrOff);`
- `public boolean getInvert();`

In addition, we'll specify a method that performs the inversion. If the inversion mode is set to `true`, this method should invert the image. If it is set to `false`, the method should revert to the original image if it is inverted. Here's the method signature:

◆ **public void invert(boolean on);**

Listing 6.14 is a sample implementation of the `invert()` method.

LISTING 6.14 The `invert()` method

```
public void invert(boolean on){
    if(offScrImage == null) return;
    BufferedImage bi = null;
    if(on) {
        byte lut[] = new byte[256];
        for (int j = 0; j < 256 ; j++) lut[j] = (byte) (256-j);
        LookupOp lookupop = new LookupOp(new ByteLookupTable(0,lut), null);
        bi = lookupop.filter(offScrImage, bi);
    } else bi =  offScrImage;
    createDisplayImage();
    dispGc.drawImage(bi, 0,0, this);
    repaint();
}
```

In the implementation shown in Listing 6.14, the `invert()` method uses the `java.awt.image.ByteLookupTable` class to create a lookup table. `ByteLookupTable` is used for creating a `LookupOp` object, which acts like an image filter. The source for `LookupOp` is the off-screen image, and the destination is a buffered image. When the `filter()` method is called, it creates the destination pixels by "looking them up" on the `ByteLookupTable` object. The destination image is then drawn on the graphical context of the `displayImage` object.

Setting the Display Mode

When an image is displayed on a canvas, the original image size may not match the canvas size. There are many ways of viewing such an image. You can expand the image in such a way that the image fits the viewport exactly. Although this approach may be aesthetically pleasing, the displayed image may not accurately represent the original image. The reason is that the aspect ratio of the displayed image may not match the aspect ratio of the original image. So you may want to display the image in such a way that the image aspect ratio doesn't change. This means that the image may fit the viewport along either the vertical or the horizontal direction, but not necessarily both. This is acceptable in many scientific applications in which accuracy means more than aesthetics.

The three display mode types are

1. Original size
2. To fit
3. Scaled

Let's create an interface to define these enumerated types. Listing 6.15 shows this interface.

LISTING 6.15 The `DisplayMode` interface

```
public interface DisplayMode {
    public static final int TO_FIT = 0;
    public static final int SCALED = 1;
    public static final int ORIG_SIZE = 2;
}
```

We'll make the display mode a property in the `ImageDisplay` interface. The `displayMode` property can assume any of the following three values:

1. **ORIG_SIZE.** The displayed image is displayed as is.
2. **TO_FIT.** The displayed image is scaled to fit exactly within the canvas. In this case the original aspect ratio of the image is not maintained.
3. **SCALED.** The displayed image is scaled to fit the canvas. The aspect ratio of the image is maintained in this case. If the aspect ratio of the canvas is different from that of the image, the image will fill the canvas in only one direction.

We'll specify the following methods for the `displayMode` property:

- `public void setDisplayMode(int dispMode);`
- `public int getDisplayMode();`

When `setDisplayMode()` is called, the `displayMode` property must be set to the specified value, and the image displayed on the screen must be updated to reflect the changed mode. We'll also specify `displayMode` to be a bound property. Listing 6.16 is a sample implementation of the `setDisplayMode()` method of the `ImageCanvas` class.

LISTING 6.16 Setting the display mode

```
public synchronized void setDisplayMode(int mode){
    if(mode == displayMode) return;
    int oldmode = displayMode;
    displayMode = mode;
    firePropertyChange("displayMode", oldmode, mode);
    reset();
    paintImage();
    repaint();
}
```

After setting the display mode and firing the `propertyChange` event, the `setDisplayMode()` method calls the `paintImage()` method, which paints the currently displayed image with the new display mode. See the section titled Displaying an Image earlier in the chapter, as well as Listing 6.11. Recall from this section that the `paintImage()` method calls the `doDisplayModeAndFlip()` method, which implements the three types of display modes we discussed before. Listing 6.17 shows the code for this method.

LISTING 6.17   The doDisplayModeAndFlip() method

```
protected synchronized boolean doDisplayModeAndFlip(int imWid, int imHt){
    width = this.getBounds().width;
    height = this.getBounds().height;
    // To_fit case
    int dx1 = 0;
    int dy1 = 0;
    int dx2 = width;
    int dy2 = height;
    int sx1=0;
    int sy1=0;
    int sx2=imageWidth;
    int sy2=imageHeight;

    switch(displayMode){
     case DisplayMode.ORIG_SIZE:
        dx2 = imageWidth;
        dy2 = imageHeight;
        break;
     case DisplayMode.SCALED:
        Dimension d = drawingDim();
        dx2 = d.width;
        dy2 = d.height;
        break;
     case DisplayMode.TO_FIT:
        default:
        break;
    }

    int bufferWid = dx2-dx1;
    int bufferHt = dy2-dy1;
    offScrImage = new BufferedImage(bufferWid, bufferHt,imageType);
    offScrGc = offScrImage.createGraphics();
    offScrGc.setColor(Color.black);
    offScrGc.fillRect(0,0,imageWidth,imageHeight);

    if(originalImageType == ImageDisplay.TYPE_AWT_IMAGE)
        doFlip(awtImage, offScrGc, flipMode,
                dx1, dy1, dx2, dy2, sx1,sy1, sx2, sy2);
    else doFlip(bufferedImage,offScrGc,flipMode,
                dx1, dy1, dx2, dy2, sx1,sy1, sx2, sy2);

    dispGc.setColor(Color.black);
    dispGc.fillRect(0,0,width,height);
    invert(invertOn);
    return true;
}
```

In the doDisplayModeAndFlip() method, imageWidth and imageHeight are the image width and height of the original image. These values are obtained when the image property is set. The width and height variables are the dimensions of the canvas, which are computed whenever the image is painted.

The doDisplayModeAndFlip() method uses drawImage(image, dx1, dy1, dx2, dy2, sx1, sy1, sx2, sy2, ImageObserver) of the Graphics class to paint the original image over an off-screen image. In this `drawImage()` method, the corner coordinates for the source image and the destination image must be provided. The parameters `dx1`, `dy1`, `dx2`, and `dy2` specify the opposite corner coordinates of the destination image. Likewise, `sx1`, `sy1`, `sx2`, and `sy2` specify the opposite corner coordinates of the source image.

The source image dimensions remain the same for all three display modes. The destination image dimensions change. When the display mode is `TO_FIT`, the destination image dimensions are 0, 0, `width`, `height`; that is, the destination image is as big as the canvas. In the case of `ORIG_SIZE`, the source and destination image dimensions are the same. The `SCALED` case requires some computation. The `drawingDim()` method returns the destination image coordinates (see Listing 6.18).

LISTING 6.18   The `drawingDim()` method

```
public Dimension drawingDim(){
    Rectangle d = this.getBounds();
    width = d.width;
    height = d.height;
    double magX= (double)imageWidth/(double)width;
    double magY = (double)imageHeight/(double)height;
    int dwidth, dheight;
    if(magY >  magX){
        Double db = new Double(imageWidth/magY);
        dwidth = db.intValue();
        dheight = height;
    }
    else{
        Double db = new Double(imageHeight/magX);
        dheight = db.intValue();
        dwidth = width;
    }
    return new Dimension(dwidth, dheight);
}
```

Once the destination image coordinates have been computed, `doDisplayMode AndFlip()` creates a destination image with these coordinates. In this case, the destination image is a `BufferedImage` object, but if you're using JDK 1.1, you can use the `createImage()` method to construct an off-screen image. Before the off-screen image is drawn on the `displayImage` object, it is run through the `doFlip()` method (see Listing 6.20). The off-screen image is then drawn on the `displayImage` object to display the image on a call to `repaint()`.

You may ask why there is a need for a separate `displayImage` object when the off-screen image itself could have been drawn on the graphical context. The primary reason is that you can save the off-screen image with the display modes applied. In image manipulation applications, transformations are applied to this image, as illustrated in Figure 6.4.

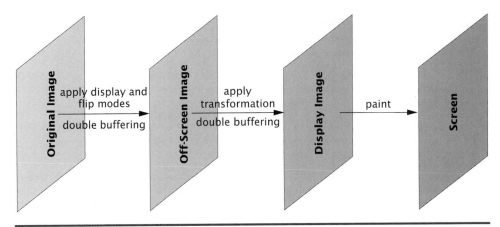

FIGURE 6.4 Steps to paint an image on the canvas

The `drawingDim()` method computes the destination image dimensions by retaining the same aspect ratio as for the original image. It first computes the amount of scaling to be applied to fit the canvas size. The direction—*x* or *y*—that has the greater magnification factor determines the magnification factor applied to both directions.

Setting the Image Orientation

Often the orientation of an image must be exact. This is especially true with medical images that are acquired with patients in different positions, such as face up, face down, feet first, head first, and so on. Even with proper annotation, it is hard to mentally reconstruct the image if the scanning mode is other than what is normally expected. In such cases, images can be flipped or rotated so that they are suitable for normal viewing.

We'll specify the `flipMode` property, which can assume any one of the following values: `NORMAL`, `LEFT_RIGHT`, `TOP_BOTTOM`, and `TOP_BOTTOM_LEFT_RIGHT`. Listing 6.19 shows the `FlipMode` interface.

LISTING 6.19 The `FlipMode` interface

```
public interface FlipMode {
    public static final int NORMAL = 0;
    public static final int LEFT_RIGHT = 1;
    public static final int TOP_BOTTOM = 2;
    public static final int TOP_BOTTOM_LEFT_RIGHT = 4;
}
```

In the `ImageDisplay` interface we can specify the following methods for setting and getting the `flipMode` property:

- ◆ `public void setFlipMode(int flipMode);`
- ◆ `public int getFlipMode();`

To flip an image, just reverse the appropriate source coordinates in the `drawImage()` method. Listing 6.20 gives a sample implementation.

LISTING 6.20 The doFlip() method

```
public static boolean doFlip(Image img, Graphics gc,int flipMode,
                        int dx1, int dy1, int dx2, int dy2,
                        int sx1, int sy1, int sx2, int sy2){
   switch(flipMode){
      case FlipMode.NORMAL:
        // Nothing is reversed.
        return gc.drawImage(img,dx1, dy1, dx2, dy2, sx1,sy1, sx2, sy2,null);
      case FlipMode.TOP_BOTTOM:
        // Y coordinates of the source image are reversed.
        return gc.drawImage(img,dx1, dy1, dx2, dy2, sx1,sy2, sx2, sy1,null);
      case FlipMode.LEFT_RIGHT:
        // X coordinates of the source image are reversed.
        return gc.drawImage(img,dx1, dy1, dx2, dy2, sx2,sy1, sx1, sy2,null);
      case FlipMode.TOP_BOTTOM_LEFT_RIGHT:
        // Both X and Y coordinates of the source image are reversed.
        return gc.drawImage(img,dx1, dy1, dx2, dy2, sx2,sy2, sx1, sy1,null);
      default:
        return false;
   }
}
```

The `doFlip()` method takes the AWT `Image` object as an input. There is a similar method for `BufferedImage`.

Overlaying Graphics

Whether the context is animation or interactive drawing, it is often necessary to draw graphics over images. To satisfy this requirement, let's specify a method that draws a shape on the displayed image:

- ◆ `public void draw(Shape shape);`

Sometimes the need arises to limit the rendering to a smaller region—for example, for faster rendering or animation. Let's define a method that clips the displayed image by a specified shape:

- ◆ `public void setClip(Shape clipshape);`

Setting the Cursor

Let's make the cursor a property of the `ImageDisplay` component. Here are the set and get methods for this property:

- ◆ `public void setCursor(Cursor cursor);`
- ◆ `public Cursor getCursor();`

Firing Events

A component that displays images may have to fire different types of events. These events can be tied to actions of a GUI or to its internal operations. In the sections that follow, we'll specify methods to make this component a source for mouse and keyboard events.

Mouse and Keyboard Events

A component that displays images must fire mouse and keyboard events for many reasons, including

- ◆ To enable users to interactively draw graphics and text over the image
- ◆ To control image manipulation—for instance, panning and zooming images

Clients of an `ImageDisplay` object can capture these events and control the image display and manipulation.

The `mouse`, `mouseMotion`, and `key` events are standard events in the AWT. Here are the methods for adding and removing these events:

- ◆ `public void addMouseListener(MouseListener e);`
- ◆ `public void removeMouseListener(MouseListener e);`
- ◆ `public void addMouseMotionListener(MouseMotionListener e);`
- ◆ `public void removeMouseMotionListener(MouseMotionListener e);`
- ◆ `public void addKeyListener(KeyListener e);`
- ◆ `public void removeKeyListener(KeyListener e);`

Property Change and Vetoable Change Events

Our intention is to make the `ImageDisplay` component conform to JavaBeans specs. We have already defined a few properties that are bound, meaning that the `ImageDisplay` component must be a source for `propertyChange` events. The following methods conform to JavaBeans specs:

- ◆ `public void addPropertyChangeListener(PropertyChangeListener pc);`
- ◆ `public void removePropertyChangeListener(PropertyChangeListener pc);`
- ◆ `public void firePropertyChange(String propertyName,`
                                `boolean oldValue,`
                                `boolean newValue)`

Although we didn't define any constrained properties, in some instances a constrained property is included in the `ImageDisplay` component. The following methods are needed for registering and firing `vetoableChange` events:

- `public void addVetoableChangeListener(VetoableChangeListener vl);`
- `public void removeVetoableChangeListener(VetoableChangeListener vl);`
- `protected void fireVetoableChange(String propertyName,`
                                    `Object oldValue,`
                                    `Object newValue)`
              `throws PropertyVetoException`

All these event methods are defined in the `JComponent` class, so if the component class extends `JComponent,` there is no need to implement these methods.

Printing in Java 2D

Java 2D has a new printing model, which is a vast improvement over printing in AWT imaging. This is a callback model in which the application's printing program is called whenever there is a need to print.

At the center of the printing API is the interface called `Printable.` This interface must be implemented by the objects that have printing programs. The `Printable` interface has one method, called `print(),` which is called by the system's printing program to render the page. If the printer buffer is small, the system might need to print a page in chunks. The Java 2D printing model achieves this by calling the `print()` method a number of times to print an entire page.

Whether the context is an image or a document, the need often arises for printing multiple pages. To do this in AWT imaging, you must write your own page-formatting code. For example, printing a table that had 3,000 rows would run into many pages. In addition, the table might not fit the paper size exactly. To print this table in AWT imaging, you would get the dimensions of a page and draw the table in such a way that it fit the paper. To achieve multiple-page printing, your program would first determine how many rows fit on a page. Your program then would divide the table into multiple pages, each with a fixed number of rows. For each page, the `paint()` method would be called to print it.

Writing such a program is tedious and time-consuming. This weakness has been addressed in Java 2D, which introduced the concepts of *book* and *paper*. A book has multiple pages, each of which may have a different page format. The `Book` class represents the book, and the `Paper` class represents the paper on which a page is drawn. The `PageFormat` class sets the format of the page. For printing multiple pages, all you need to do is create a book with pages and then format the pages using the `PageFormat` class.

The new printing API is implemented in a separate package named `java.awt.print`. Let's take a look at this package.

Overview of the Printing API

We can divide the printing API into two categories: print control and page control. The print control API enables printing, and the page control API enables setting up and formatting of pages.

The Print Control API

The `Printable` and `PrintGraphics` interfaces and `PrinterJob` class control printing.

The PrinterJob Class

The `PrinterJob` class is similar to the `PrintJob` class in AWT imaging. Just like `PrintJob`, `PrinterJob` is an abstract class. Unlike `PrintJob`, however, the `Printer Job` object is obtained through a factory method in the `PrinterJob` class itself.

To get a `PrinterJob` object, call the `getPrinterJob()` method as shown here:

```
PrinterJob pj = PrinterJob.getPrinterJob();
```

The `PrinterJob` object is constructed in a platform-dependent manner for a specific printer. You can get a graphical context for the printer from this object in the form of a `Graphics` object. This `Graphics` object implements the `PrinterGraphics` interface, which is similar to the `PrintGraphics` interface. The similarity, however, ends with the name. Note that the `getPrinterJob()` method has no input parameters. This means that there is no need for a `Frame` object. Instead of the printing-properties parameter, the `PrinterJob` class has several methods for setting the printing attributes. Listing 6.21 shows a simple example.

LISTING 6.21 The `simplePrint()` method

```
public void simplePrint(Printable painterObj) {
    PrinterJob pj = PrinterJob.getPrinterJob();
    PageFormat pf = pj.defaultPage();
    pj.setPrintable(painterObj);
    try{
      pj.print();
    } catch(Exception e){}
}
```

Once the `PrinterJob` object has been obtained, `simplePrint()` sets the page format. It then registers for the callbacks by passing the `painterObj` parameter through the `setPrintable()` method. The `painterObj` parameter implements the `Printable` interface. To initiate printing, `simplePrint()` calls the `print()` method, at which point the system calls `painterObj`'s `print()` method to execute printing.

Recall from Chapter 3 that printing is initiated when the `dispose()` method of the `Graphics` object is called. This means that the printing program requires the `Graphics` object. In Java 2D printing, however, there is no need to obtain the `Graphics` context because the system itself passes the `Graphics` context to `painterObj`'s `print()` method.

The Printable Interface

As mentioned earlier, an object that needs to print something must implement the `Printable` interface that specifies just one method. Here's the signature of this method:

- ◆ `public int print(Graphics graphics,`
  `PageFormat pageFormat,`
  `int pageIndex) throws PrinterException`

This method is called by the system when the `PrinterJob` object initiates printing. The `Graphics` context supplied by the system is the graphical context of the printer. Your code in this method should draw images or other graphical objects on this `Graphics` context.

The `pageFormat` parameter specifies how the printing page is to be formatted. The system gets this object from the `PrinterJob` object and passes it to the `print()` method. The `pageIndex` parameter indicates the index (page number) of the page being printed. When only one page is being printed, the value of `pageIndex` is zero.

The `print()` method should return one of the two values `PAGE_EXISTS` and `NO_SUCH_PAGE`, which are defined in the `Printable` interface. When the printing is still going on, this method should return the former value, and when it is finished it should return the latter. For instance, if your program is printing just one page, the `print()` method should return `NO_SUCH_PAGE` if the value of `pageIndex` is greater than zero.

In the Java 2D printing model, printing is performed asynchronously; that is, the `print()` method may be called many times before a page is printed. The `print()` method is usually called by the system, and it is similar to the `paint()` method.

The Pageable Interface

The `Pageable` interface specifies methods that are required for printing multiple pages. Each page painter object must implement the `Printable` interface and can have a different page format. As we'll see later in this section, the `PageFormat` class represents the page format. Here are the `Pageable` interface methods:

- ◆ `public Printable getPrintable(int pageIndex) throws`
  `IndexOutOfBoundsException`
- ◆ `public PageFormat getPageFormat(int pageIndex) throws`
  `IndexOutOfBoundsException`
- ◆ `public int getNumberOfPages()`

The `Pageable` interface is implemented by the `Book` class, which represents multiple pages.

The PrinterGraphics Interface

The `PrinterGraphics` interface is similar to the `PrintGraphics` interface of JDK 1.1. It has just one method—`getPrinterJob()`—which retrieves the `PrinterJob` object. Normally you don't need to use this interface at all.

The Page Control API

The three classes `PageFormat`, `Paper`, and `Book` determine how a printed page looks. As the name suggests, the `Paper` class represents the paper.

The Paper Class

`Paper` is a convenient class that holds several attributes (see Figure 6.5). Here are the get methods for retrieving these attributes:

- `public double getHeight()`
- `public double getWidth()`
- `public double getImageableX()`
- `public double getImageableY()`
- `public double getImageableWidth()`
- `public double getImageableHeight()`

The unit of measure for each of the values returned by the get methods is ½ inch.
Here are the set methods:

- `public void setImageableArea(double x, double y, double width,`
  `                             double height)`
- `public void setSize(double width, double height)`

The PageFormat Class

The `PageFormat` class has methods for setting the page format. It has all the attributes of the `Paper` class, and it has methods for setting the page orientations.
The methods for setting page dimensions are

- `public double getWidth()`
- `public double getHeight()`
- `public double getImageableWidth()`
- `public double getImageableHeight()`
- `public double getImageableX()`
- `public double getImageableY()`

Just as with the `Paper` class, the unit of measure of the returned values is ½ inch.

(ImageableX, ImageableY)

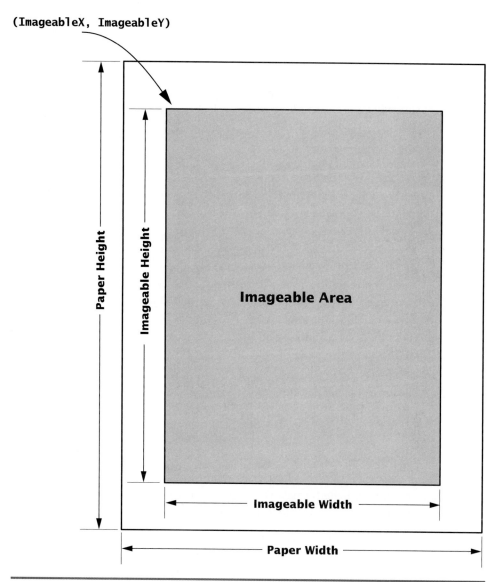

FIGURE 6.5   Attributes of paper

The PageFormat class defines three page orientation modes:

1. **PORTRAIT.** In this mode the origin is at the top left-hand corner of the paper, with x running to the right and y running down the paper.

2. **LANDSCAPE.** In this mode the origin is at the bottom left-hand corner of the paper, with x running bottom to top and y running left to right. This mode is considered landscape in Windows and PostScript.

3. **REVERSE_LANDSCAPE.** In this mode the origin is at the top right-hand corner of the paper, with x running top to bottom and y running right to left. This is considered landscape mode in Macintosh.

You can set and get the orientation of the printed page with the following methods:

- **`public int getOrientation()`**
- **`public void setOrientation(int orientation) throws IllegalArgumentException`**

Other methods of the `PageFormat` class include the following:

- **`public double[] getMatrix()`**

  This method returns a transformation matrix that transforms the user space to the requested page orientation. The returned value is an array that corresponds to {m00, m10, m01, m11, m02, m12} values of the `AffineTransform` constructor (see Chapter 4 for more details).

- **`public void setPaper(Paper paper)`**
- **`public Paper getPaper()`**

  These are the set and get methods for the `paper` attribute. If the `paper` parameter passed to the `setPaper()` method is `null`, `setPaper()` throws an exception: `NullPointerException`.

The Book Class

As its name suggests, the `Book` class represents a book. Each page in the book can have a different page format. The following three methods can be used to obtain the page-related information from a `Book` object:

- **`public Printable getPrintable(int pageIndex)`**
  `                    throws IndexOutOfBoundsException`
- **`public PageFormat getPageFormat(int pageIndex)`**
  `                    throws IndexOutOfBoundsException`
- **`public int getNumberOfPages()`**

  You can print an arbitrary page of a book by obtaining the `Printable` and `PageFormat` objects for that page. The `getPrintable()` and `getPageFormat()` methods, respectively, return these objects for a page specified by the **`pageIndex`** parameter. Make sure that the value of **`pageIndex`** passed to these methods does not exceed the total number of pages, which can be obtained by a call to `getNumberOfPages()`.

◆ `public void setPage(int pageIndex, Printable painter, PageFormat page)`
    `throws IndexOutOfBoundsException`

This method sets the page parameters (i.e., `Printable` and `PageFormat`) of a page specified by `pageIndex`.

◆ `public void append(Printable painter, PageFormat page)`
◆ `public void append(Printable painter, PageFormat page, int numPages)`

The first method adds a page to the end of the book. The second method adds the number of pages specified by `numPages` to the end of the book.

Image-Printing Requirements

Let's define image-printing requirements in the same way that we did image display requirements. We'll call the interface that captures this interface `ImagePrint`. `ImagePrint` has fewer requirements than `ImageDisplay`.

Setting Print Location and Image Size

Although generally you can manage with just the `Printable` interface, sometimes you may need to set the size of the printed image or location. For example, you may want to print multiple images on a single page. The `print()` method then needs the locations of the images to paint them at different positions on the graphical context. So the object that prints images should have set and get methods for the print location property.

Likewise, the displayed image may be too large or too small for the page so we need a print size property to set the size of the printed image.

Painting an Image on a Page

Even though the `print()` method of the `Printable` interface does just that—print—a method that is similar to `paint(Graphics g)` is also needed. Let's name this method `printImage(Graphics2D g)`. Listing 6.22 shows the `ImagePrint` interface.

LISTING 6.22   The `ImagePrint` interface

```
public interface ImagePrint extends Printable {
    public void setPrintLocation(Point d);
    public Point getPrintLocation();
    public void setPrintSize(Dimension d);
    public Dimension getPrintSize();
    public void printImage(Graphics2D g);
}
```

Any object can implement the `ImagePrint` interface. In the example we have been developing in this chapter, the `ImageCanvas` class can implement it. Note that

ImagePrint extends Printable, which means that ImageCanvas must implement the print() method.

Implementing ImagePrint

Listing 6.23 shows the implementation of ImagePrint in the ImageCanvas class.

LISTING 6.23   ImagePrint methods in the ImageCanvas class

```
public void setPrintLocation(Point d) {
    printLoc = d;
}

public Point getPrintLocation() {
    return printLoc;
}

public void setPrintSize(Dimension d){
    printSize = d;
}

public Dimension getPrintSize(){
    if(printSize == null) {
        Rectangle r = this.getBounds();
        printSize = new Dimension(r.width, r.height);
    }
    return printSize;
}


public int print(Graphics g, PageFormat f, int pageIndex){
    if(pageIndex >= 1) return Printable.NO_SUCH_PAGE;
    Graphics2D g2d = (Graphics2D) g;
    g2d.translate(f.getImageableX(), f.getImageableY());
    if(displayImage != null){
        printImage(g2d);
        return Printable.PAGE_EXISTS;
    } else  return Printable.NO_SUCH_PAGE;
}


public void printImage(Graphics2D g2d){
    if((displayImage != null)|| (g2d == null)) return;
    if(printLoc == null) printLoc = new Point(0,0);
    if(printSize == null) printSize = new Dimension(imageWidth, imageHeight);
    int x = printLoc.x;
    int y = printLoc.y;
    int wid = printSize.width;
    int ht = printSize.height;
    g2d.drawImage(displayImage, x, y, wid, ht, this);
}
```

The print() method translates the origin of the Graphics context to the upper left-hand corner of the *imageable* area. The user coordinates are translated to this origin. As we saw in Chapter 5, the `Graphics2D` object can be scaled, rotated, and sheared. If you need better resolution, you can perform the scale operation on the `Graphics` context.

The `ApplicationFrame` class (see Appendix 1) has a `printContents()` method that can be overridden by the `printContents()` method shown in Listing 6.24. `ApplicationFrame`'s `printContents()` method is called by the action event–handling method whenever the user clicks on the Print menu item on the menu bar.

LISTING 6.24   The `printContents()` method of the `ApplicationFrame` class

```
protected void printContents() {
    if(printerObj == null) return;
    PrinterJob pj = PrinterJob.getPrinterJob();
    pj.setPrintable(printerObj);
    pj.printDialog();
    try{
        pj.print();
    }catch(Exception e){System.out.println(e);}
}
```

The `printerObj` parameter is set by the `setPrinterObj()` method. In this case, it can be the `ImageCanvas` object. The `createGUI()` method calls `setPrinterObj()` to set the `printerObj` object.

Printing Multiple Images on the Same Page

To illustrate how multiple images can be printed on the same page, let's modify the image browser example we developed earlier. We'll add printing capability to this application. Now that we have developed a class for displaying components (i.e., `ImageCanvas`), we can replace the `ImagePanel` class with it. So all we need to do is add the printing code to the `ViewerPanel` class.

> **Note:** The modified code for the image browser is available on the book's Web page in the directory `src/chapter6/ImageBrowser2`.

The `ViewerPanel` object holds a grid of `ImageCanvas` objects, each of which displays images. Because we want all the images on the page, we'll make the `ViewerPanel` object itself the page painter object; that is, the `ViewerPanel` class will implement the `Printable` interface. This means that `ViewerPanel` must implement the `print()` method in addition to overriding the `printContents()` method. Listings 6.25 and 6.26 show the `printContents()` and `print()` methods, respectively, defined in `ViewerPanel`.

LISTING 6.25 The `printContents()` method defined in the `ViewerPanel` class

```
protected void printContents() {
    PrinterJob pj = PrinterJob.getPrinterJob();
    pj.setPrintable(this);
    pj.printDialog();
    try{
       pj.print();
    }catch(Exception e){System.out.println(e);}
}
```

The printing process is initiated when the `pj.print()` method is executed. The AWT's printing program calls the `print()` method shown in Listing 6.26.

LISTING 6.26 The `print()` method defined in the `ViewerPanel` class

```
public int print(Graphics g, PageFormat f, int pageIndex){
    if(pageIndex >= 1) return   Printable.NO_SUCH_PAGE;
    Graphics2D g2d = (Graphics2D) g;
    g2d.translate(f.getImageableX(), f.getImageableY());
    ImagePrint cmp[] = (ImagePrint)getViewports();
    if(cmp == null) return   Printable.NO_SUCH_PAGE;
    for(int i=0;i<cmp.length;i++){
       cmp[i].setPrintLocation(((Component)cmp[I]).getLocation());
       cmp[i].setPrintSize((((Component)cmp[i]).getSize()));
       cmp[i].printImage(g2d);
    }
    return Printable.PAGE-EXISTS;
}
```

The `print()` method first checks whether the value of `pageIndex` exceeds zero. If it does, `print()` returns `NO_SUCH_PAGE` to indicate that it is done printing. Otherwise it goes ahead with the printing.

The `print()` method translates the origin of the `Graphics` context of the page to the origin of the *imageable* area. This translation needs to be done only once per page. The `print()` method then places all the canvases in the `ViewerPanel` and prints them one by one. To get the location and size, `print()` calls the `getLocation()` and `getSize()` methods of the `Component` class itself.

Note that the `print()` method calls the `printImage()` method rather than the `print()` method of the `ImageCanvas` class. The reason is that the `print()` method will translate the `Graphics` context each time it is called on different `ImageCanvas` objects.

As an alternative, `ViewerPanel` can print the aggregated `BufferedImage` object it creates to save it as a JPEG image. In that case there is no need to call the `printImage()` method on each of the `ImageCanvas` objects.

Putting It All Together: A Java 2D Image Viewer

Let's build an image viewer using the interface and classes we have developed so far. Apart from displaying images, this image viewer should provide the user the ability to choose both display and flip modes. To load images, we'll reuse the `MultiImage Loader` bean developed in Chapter 2.

Let's make use of the `ApplicationFrame` class (see Appendix 1) to create an application frame with a menu bar. The menu bar will have the following menus: **File, Load,** and **View.** The **File** menu will be inherited from the `ApplicationFrame` class. This menu will have three menu items: **Save, Print,** and **Exit.** The **Save** option will save the image displayed in the canvas as a JPEG image. To save images, this application uses the JPEG codec, which is described in Chapter 17. The **Print** option will print the image (see the section titled Printing in Java 2D earlier in this chapter).

The **Load** menu will have one item—**List Select**—which will launch the `MultiImageLoader` bean.

The **View** menu will have two menu items: **Display Modes** and **Flip Modes.** These menu items will have subitems corresponding to the cases described earlier in this chapter, in the sections titled Setting the Display Mode and Setting the Image Orientation, respectively. By choosing any subitem in the **View** menu, you should be able to change the display mode or image orientation. A message bar at the bottom of the frame will display status messages. Normally, the messages will indicate the state of the current display and flip modes. If there is an error, the error message will be shown there as well.

Figure 6.6 shows a screen shot of the image viewer, and Listing 6.27 presents the corresponding code.

LISTING 6.27 The `ImageViewer2D` class

```
public class ImageViewer2D extends ApplicationFrame{
   protected ImageCanvas viewerPane;
   protected int dispMode = DisplayMode.SCALED;
   protected int flipMode = FlipMode.NORMAL;
   protected JTextArea messageBar;
   protected String filterString;
   protected MultiImageLoader imageLoader;
   protected JFrame ilFrame;

   public static void  main(String[] args){
      ImageViewer2D iv = new ImageViewer2D();
   }
   public ImageViewer2D() {}


   protected void createGUI(){
      setAboutStrings();
      createImageLoader();
      ViewerMenuBar viewerMenuBar = new ViewerMenuBar();
```

continued

```
        setJMenuBar((JMenuBar)viewerMenuBar);
        Dimension ssize= Toolkit.getDefaultToolkit().getScreenSize();
        int vwid = (int)(ssize.width*3/4.0);
        int vht = (int)(ssize.height*3/4.0);
        this.setLocation((ssize.width/4),
                         (ssize.height/4));
        this.setSize((int)(ssize.width*3/4.0), (int)(ssize.height*3/4.0));
        viewerPane = new ImageCanvas();
        messageBar = new JTextArea();
        messageBar.setBorder(BorderFactory.createTitledBorder("Messages"));
        messageBar.setBackground(Color.black);
        messageBar.setForeground(Color.green);
        this.updateMessageBar();
    }

    public void createImageLoader(){
        imageLoader = new MultiImageLoader();
        imageLoader.setLoadButtonLabel("Launch Image(s)");
        imageLoader.addImageLoadedListener(
        new ImageLoadedListener() {
          public void imageLoaded(ImageLoadedEvent e) {
            Image[] imset = e.getImages();
            viewerPane.setAWTImage(imset[0]);
```

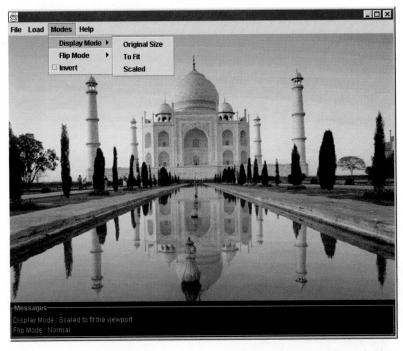

© Doug Corrance/FPG International LLC

FIGURE 6.6   The image viewer

```
        }
      });
      ilFrame = new JFrame();
      ilFrame.getContentPane().add(imageLoader);
      ilFrame.addWindowListener(
      new WindowAdapter() {
        public void windowClosing(WindowEvent e){
          hideImageLoader();
        }
      });
      ilFrame.setSize(imageLoader.getPreferredSize());
      ilFrame.pack();
  }

  public void showImageLoader() {
    ilFrame.show();
  }

  public void hideImageLoader() {
    ilFrame.hide();
  }

  protected void save() {
      if(saveFileName == null) saveAs();
      BufferedImage bi = viewerPane.getDisplayedImage();
      if(bi != null) JpegUtil.saveImageAsJPEG(bi, saveFileName);
  }

  protected void saveAs() {
      String filename = JpegUtil.launchFileDialog();
      if(filename != null){
        saveFileName = filename;
        save();
      }
  }

  protected void printContents() {
      if(printerObj == null) return;
      PrinterJob pj = PrinterJob.getPrinterJob();
      pj.setPrintable(printerObj);
      pj.printDialog();
      try{
        pj.print();
      }catch(Exception e){System.out.println(e);}
  }

  public void updateMessageBar(){
    if(viewerPane == null)return;
      messageBar.setBackground(Color.black);
      messageBar.setText("Display Mode : "+
                    getDisplayModeString(viewerPane.getDisplayMode())+"\n"+
                    "Flip Mode : " +
                    getFlipModeString(viewerPane.getFlipMode()));
      messageBar.repaint();
      repaint();
  }
```

continued

```
    public String getFlipModeString(int mode) {
       switch (mode) {
          case FlipMode.NORMAL: return "Normal";
          case FlipMode.LEFT_RIGHT: return "Left to right";
          case FlipMode.TOP_BOTTOM: return "Top to bottom";
          case FlipMode.TOP_BOTTOM_LEFT_RIGHT: return "Top to bottom and left to right";
          default: return null;
       }
    }

    public String getDisplayModeString(int mode) {
       switch (mode) {
          case DisplayMode.ORIG_SIZE: return "Original size";
          case DisplayMode.TO_FIT: return "Fit the viewport";
          case DisplayMode.SCALED: return "Scaled to fit the viewport";
          default: return null;
       }
    }
}
```

ImageViewer2D is the class that has the main() method. Upon instantiation, main() will create the ImageCanvas and JTextArea objects. The JTextArea object is used as a message bar. The main() method will also create an image loader object. ImageViewer2D uses the MultiImageLoader bean discussed in Chapter 2 to create the image loader. This bean is embedded in a JFrame object, which can be hidden when not needed. You can make it visible again by selecting the **Load Images** option on the **Load** menu.

Here's a typical sequence of method calls:

1. The main() method constructs the ImageViewer2D object. The superclass of ImageViewer2D calls the createGUI() method.

2. The createGUI() method calls createImageLoader() to instantiate a MultiImageLoader bean and embed it in a frame. It then creates an ImageCanvas object for displaying images and a JTextArea object for displaying messages. The createGUI() method also constructs a menu bar from ImageViewer2D's inner class ViewerMenuBar and attaches it to the menu bar. It then adds the GUI components to the ContentPane object of the JFrame component.

3. The user selects **Load | List Select.** The event-handling method for the **List Select** item launches the MultiImageLoader bean.

4. The user selects or enters the name of a JAR file or local directory that contains images. The user then selects an image and clicks on the **Load Images** option in the MultiImageLoader bean. This action prompts the bean to fire the imageLoaded event. This event is received by the imageLoaded() method in the anonymous inner class passed as a parameter to the addImageLoadedListener() method. See the createImageLoader() method of the ImageViewer2D class (Listing 6.27).

5. The `imageLoaded()` method extracts an image from the `imageLoaded` event and calls `ImageCanvas`'s `setImage()` method, which displays the image.

6. The user selects **Modes | Display Modes** and a desired display mode (see the screen shot in Figure 6.6). The event-handling method for this option calls the `setDisplayMode()` method in the `ImageCanvas` object. (See the `DisplayAdapter` class in Listing 6.28.)

7. The user selects **Modes | Flip Modes** and a desired flip mode. The event-handling method for this item calls the `setFlipMode()` method in the `ImageCanvas` object. (See the `FlipAdapter` class in Listing 6.28.)

8. The user selects **Modes** and checks the **Invert** box (see Figure 6.7). The event-handling method for this option calls the `setInvert()` method in the `ImageCanvas` object, which inverts the displayed image.

The `ViewerMenuBar` class is an inner class of `ImageViewer2D`, and it extends the `AppMenuBar` inner class of the `ApplicationFrame` class. Listing 6.28 shows the code for `ViewerMenuBar`.

LISTING 6.28   The `ViewerMenuBar` class

```
public class ViewerMenuBar extends ApplicationFrame.AppMenuBar {
    public ViewerMenuBar(){
        createImageSelectionMenu();
        createViewModeMenu();
        createHelpMenu();
    }

    public JMenu createImageSelectionMenu(){
        JMenu selMenu = new JMenu("Load");
        JMenuItem ls = new JMenuItem("List/Select");
```

continued

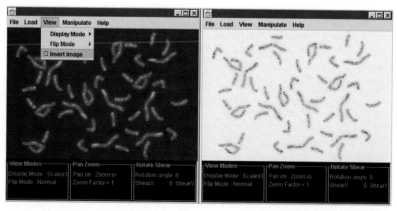

© Rob Atkins/The Image Bank

FIGURE 6.7   Inverting an image

```java
        ls.addActionListener(
            new ActionListener() {
                public void actionPerformed(ActionEvent e){
                    showImageLoader();
                }
            }
        );
        selMenu.add(ls);
        add(selMenu);
        return selMenu;
    }

    public JMenu createViewModeMenu(){
        JMenu viewModeMenu = new JMenu("Modes");
        JMenu dispMode = new JMenu("Display Mode");
        JMenu flipMode = new JMenu("Flip Mode");
        viewModeMenu.add(dispMode);
        viewModeMenu.add(flipMode);
        JMenuItem orig = new JMenuItem("Original Size");
        JMenuItem tofit = new JMenuItem("To Fit");
        JMenuItem scaled= new JMenuItem("Scaled");
        orig.addActionListener(new DisplayAdapter(DisplayMode.ORIG_SIZE));
        tofit.addActionListener(new DisplayAdapter(DisplayMode.TO_FIT));
        scaled.addActionListener(new DisplayAdapter(DisplayMode.SCALED));

        dispMode.add(orig);
        dispMode.add(tofit);
        dispMode.add(scaled);

        JMenuItem normal = new JMenuItem("Normal");
        JMenuItem leftright = new JMenuItem("Left to Right");
        JMenuItem topbottom = new JMenuItem("Top to Bottom");
        JMenuItem topbotlefrig = new JMenuItem("Top to Bottom and left to right");

        flipMode.add(normal);
        flipMode.add(leftright);
        flipMode.add(topbottom);
        flipMode.add(topbotlefrig);
        normal.addActionListener(new FlipAdapter(FlipMode.NORMAL));
        leftright.addActionListener(new FlipAdapter(FlipMode.LEFT_RIGHT));
        topbottom.addActionListener(new FlipAdapter(FlipMode.TOP_BOTTOM));
        topbotlefrig.addActionListener(new
                    FlipAdapter(FlipMode.TOP_BOTTOM_LEFT_RIGHT));

        JCheckBoxMenuItem invertOn = new JCheckBoxMenuItem("Invert");
        invertOn.addChangeListener(
            new ChangeListener() {
                public void stateChanged(ChangeEvent e){
                    JCheckBoxMenuItem jce = (JCheckBoxMenuItem)e.getSource();
                    if(viewerPane != null) viewerPane.setInvert(jce.getState());
                }
            }
        );
        viewModeMenu.add(invertOn);
        add(viewModeMenu);
        return viewModeMenu;
    }
```

```
class DisplayAdapter implements ActionListener{
    int dispMode;
    public DisplayAdapter(int mode){
        dispMode = mode;
    }
    public void actionPerformed(ActionEvent e){
        if(viewerPane != null) viewerPane.setDisplayMode(dispMode);
    }
}

class FlipAdapter implements ActionListener{
    int flipmode;
    public FlipAdapter(int mode){
        flipmode = mode;
    }
    public void actionPerformed(ActionEvent e){
        if(viewerPane != null) viewerPane.setFlipMode(flipmode);
    }
}
}
```

ViewerMenuBar creates two menus: **Load** and **Modes.** The **Load** menu has one option: **Load Images.** The **Modes** menu has three options: **Display Mode, Flip Mode,** and **Invert.** The action event handler for **Load Images** calls showImage Loader(). The createViewModeMenu() method creates both the display mode and the flip mode menu items and their corresponding subitems. The inner class DisplayAdapter provides the event-handling code for the **Display Mode** menu item. Depending on the subitem selected, appropriate parameters are passed to DisplayAdapter's constructor. The actionPerformed() method in turn passes these parameters to ImageViewer2D's setDisplayMode() method. The FlipAdapter inner class works in a similar fashion.

Conclusion

In this chapter we covered a variety of topics related to image rendering and provided numerous examples written with the Java 2D API. The Java 2D API is a significant improvement over AWT imaging. It is based on an entirely different imaging model that is well suited for both multimedia and scientific imaging applications.

Any commercial application requires reliable and flexible printing support. The earlier versions of Java lacked this support. The printing API in Java 2D meets industry needs, though problems persist in implementation of this API at the time of this writing.

In many applications, images are large, and sometimes they do not even fit the primary memory of your computer. Although displaying large images is a topic that pertains to image rendering, we'll cover it in Part III because it requires an introduction to Java Advanced Imaging.

Manipulating Images in Java 2D

7

AFTER YOU DISPLAY AN IMAGE, the next logical step is to manipulate it. Although image manipulation may mean different things to different people, it generally means handling an image in such a way that its geometry is changed. Operations such as panning, zooming, and rotation can be considered image manipulations.

AWT imaging offers only minimal support for image manipulation. In JDK 1.1, usually images are manipulated through clever use of the `drawImage()` methods of the `Graphics` class. If you need to perform complex manipulation operations such as rotation, you must write your own transformation functions. With the introduction of the `AffineTransform` class in Java 2D, you can now implement any complex manipulation operation.

Many applications need the ability to apply image manipulations in a random order. With a map, for instance, you might want to pan it and then zoom it to look for a place of interest. Then you might want to rotate the map so that it is oriented in a direction to which you are accustomed. To inspect the map closely, you might zoom it again. To see nearby locations, you might pan it. This scenario illustrates that an application must be capable of performing manipulations in a random order in such a way that at every step operations are concatenated. Such capability would be difficult to implement without affine transformations. Because this chapter requires a thorough knowledge of affine transformations, you may want to read Chapter 4 first.

The quality of the rendered image is an important consideration in many image manipulation applications. The quality of the image often depends on the type of interpolation chosen. But quality comes with a price: The higher the quality, the more time it takes to generate the image.

This chapter will begin with an introduction to interpolation. After the basics of interpolation have been presented, we'll discuss image manipulation requirements. As we did in Chapter 6 for image rendering, we'll specify requirements for performing manipulation functions. On the basis of these specifications, we'll build a class for an image manipulation canvas. We'll then build several operator classes to operate on this canvas. Just as in Chapter 6, we'll also build an image viewer to illustrate all the concepts presented here. All the operator classes are part of this image viewer, which is an extension of the image viewer of Chapter 6.

> **Note:** The source code and classes for this image viewer are available on the book's Web page in the directory `src/chapter7/manip`. To understand this chapter better, you may want to run the image viewer and perform the relevant transformations as you read.

What Is Interpolation?

As you may know already, pixels of an image occupy integer coordinates. When images are rendered or manipulated, the destination pixels may lie between the integer coordinates. So in order to create an image from these pixels, destination pixels are interpolated at the integer coordinates.

Interpolation is a process of generating a value of a pixel based on its neighbors. Neighboring pixels contribute a certain weight to the value of the pixel being interpolated. This weight is often inversely proportional to the distance at which the neighbor is located. Interpolation can be performed in one-dimensional, two-dimensional, or three-dimensional space. Image manipulation such as zooming and rotation is performed by interpolation of pixels in two-dimensional space. Volume imaging operations perform interpolation in three-dimensional space.

Java 2D supports some widely used interpolation techniques. You can choose them through the `RENDERING_HINTS` constant. The choice will depend on what is more important for your application: speed or accuracy.

Next we'll discuss different types of interpolation. Although you may not need to implement any interpolation code, knowledge of the different types of interpolation is helpful in understanding image rendering and manipulation.

Nearest-Neighbor Interpolation

In this simple scheme, the interpolating pixel is assigned the value of the nearest neighbor. This technique is fast, but it may not produce accurate images.

Linear Interpolation

In linear interpolation, immediate neighbors of the pixel to be interpolated are used to determine the value of the pixel. The distance-to-weight relationship is linear; that is, the relationship is of the form $y = ax + b$. In linear interpolation, left and right neighbors of the pixel are used to compute the pixel value (see Figure 7.1).

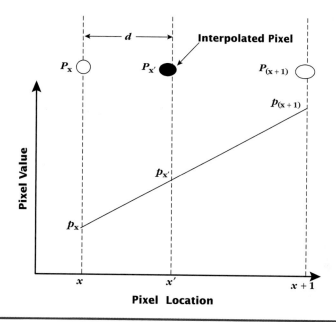

FIGURE 7.1   Linear interpolation

Let $P_{x'}$ be the pixel that lies between P_x and P_{x+1}, the respective pixel values of which are p_x and p_{x+1}. Let d be the distance between $P_{x'}$ and the left neighbor, P_x. The value of the pixel $P_{x'}$ is given by

$$P_{x'} = p_x + [(p_{x+1} - p_x) \times d]$$
$$= p_x(1 - d) + (p_{x+1} \times d)$$

There are two types of linear interpolation: bilinear and trilinear.

Bilinear Interpolation

Bilinear interpolation is the method used for two-dimensional operations—for instance, magnifying an image. The interpolation is performed in a 2×2 neighborhood (see Figure 7.2).

Linear interpolation is performed in one direction, and the result is applied to the linear interpolation in the other direction. For example, if $P_{(x',y')}$ is the pixel at d_x and d_y from the upper left-hand neighbor, its value is computed by

$$p_u = [p_{(x,y)} - (1 \times d_x)] + (p_{(x+1,y)} \times d_x) \qquad \textbf{(7.1)}$$

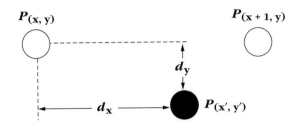

FIGURE 7.2   Bilinear interpolation

which represents the contribution to the upper row, and by

$$p_l = [p_{(x,y+1)} \times (1 - d_x)] + (p_{(x+1,y+1)} - d_x) \tag{7.2}$$

which represents the contribution to the lower row.

From equations (7.1) and (7.2), we get $P_{(x',y')} = [p_u \times (1 - d_y)] + (p_l \times d_y)$.

Trilinear Interpolation

Trilinear interpolation is computed in a 3 × 3 neighborhood (see Figure 7.3). To compute trilinear interpolation, bilinear interpolation is first performed in the *xyz* plane. Then the linear interpolation is applied to the resulting value in the *z* direction.

Cubic Interpolation

Cubic interpolation is performed in a neighborhood of four pixels (see Figure 7.4). The cubic equation is of the form $P_x = ax^3 + bx^2 + cx + d$.

Just as bilinear interpolation is performed in a 2 × 2 neighborhood, bicubic interpolation is performed in a 4 × 4 neighborhood.

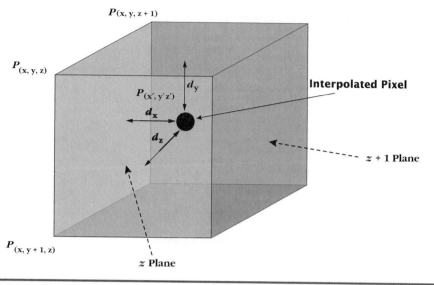

FIGURE 7.3   Trilinear interpolation

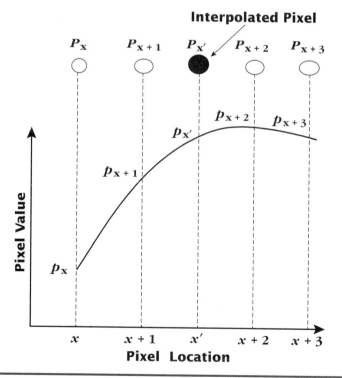

FIGURE 7.4   Cubic interpolation

Applying Affine Transformation to Images

In Chapter 4 you may have noticed that the `AffineTransform` class does not explicitly provide a way to apply the affine transformation to an image. However, we can do this by using the `Graphics2D` class or the `AffineTransformOp` class, as described in the sections that follow.

Using the Graphics2D Class

The `Graphics2D` class has a flavor of the `drawImage()` method that takes an `AffineTransform` object as an input parameter. This method applies the transformation to the image before rendering. Listing 7.1 gives an example.

LISTING 7.1 The `applyTransform()` method

```
protected BufferedImage applyTransform(BufferedImage bi,
                                      AffineTransform atx,
                                      int interpolationType){
    Dimension d = getSize();
    BufferedImage displayImage =
               new BufferedImage(d.width, d.height, interpolationType);
    Graphics2D dispGc = displayImage.createGraphics();
    dispGc.drawImage(bi, atx, this);
    return displayImage;
}
```

The `drawImage()` method used in Listing 7.1 applies the transformation parameter `atx` to the `BufferedImage` object before it draws onto the `dispGc` graphical context that belongs to `displayImage`. So in effect, one buffered image is transformed and drawn onto another buffered image. If `displayImage` is drawn on a context obtained through `paint()` or `paintComponent()`, you can see the transformed image.

As mentioned in Chapter 5, the `Graphics2D` object maintains a `transform` attribute. This attribute is applied after the transformation from the input parameter is applied.

Using the AffineTransformOp Class

Here's a quick introduction to the `AffineTransformOp` class. The class has two constructors:

- `public AffineTransformOp(AffineTransform xform, int interpolationType)`
- `public AffineTransformOp(AffineTransform xform, RenderingHints hints)`

The `interpolationType` parameter in the first constructor should be one of `TYPE_BILINEAR` and `TYPE_NEAREST_NEIGHBOR`, which are defined in the Affine

TransformOp class itself. If you use the second constructor, you may have more choices of interpolation techniques, depending on your platform.

The `AffineTransformOp` class implements two interfaces: `BufferedImageOp` and `RasterOp`. It applies the affine transformation to the source image and creates a transformed destination image. While transforming the image, `AffineTransformOp` applies the interpolation technique provided through its constructor. It has two filter methods:

- ```
  public final BufferedImage filter(BufferedImage src,
                                    BufferedImage dst)
  ```
- ```
  public final WritableRaster filter(Raster src, WritableRaster dst)
  ```

In this chapter only the first filter method is of interest. We'll explore the second one in Chapter 8.

Listing 7.2 shows a sample implementation of the `applyTransform()` method using the `AffineTransformOp` class.

LISTING 7.2   The `applyTransform()` method using `AffineTransformOp`

```
protected BufferedImage applyTransform(BufferedImage bi,
                                       AffineTransform atx,
                                       int interpolationType){
    Dimension d = getSize();
    BufferedImage displayImage = new BufferedImage(d.width,
                                                   d.height,
                                                   interpolationType);
    Graphics2D dispGc = displayImage.createGraphics();
    AffineTransformOp atop = new AffineTransformOp(atx, interpolationType);
    return atop.filter(bi, displayImage);
}
```

In Listing 7.2 an `AffineTransformOp` object is created with `AffineTransform` and `interpolationType` parameters. The `filter()` method in the `AffineTransformOp` class is invoked next. This method takes two arguments: source and destination `BufferedImage` object. It applies the transformation to the source buffered image and puts the resulting image in the destination buffered image.

With both `Graphics2D` and `AffineTransformOp,` the transformation is applied to a `BufferedImage` object. The resulting `BufferedImage` object is then rendered to a `Graphics2D` context in the paint methods.

Although we didn't mention it explicitly in Chapter 6, there was some image manipulation in the `ImageCanvas` class, which was achieved through the `drawImage()` methods. For instance, setting up display modes and flip modes involved some image manipulation. These operations can now be performed with the `AffineTransform` class.

Image Manipulation Requirements

In Chapter 6 we enumerated various display requirements and designed an interface based on these requirements. Let's continue the discussion and extend it to incorporate the image manipulation requirements. These requirements will be the basis for designing interfaces to specify image manipulation methods.

Although image manipulation may mean different things to different people, certain common operations are performed by many imaging applications, including pan, zoom, rotate, and flip. In this chapter we'll consider each of these in turn. First, however, we need a canvas that can display manipulated images. To develop such a canvas, let's consider the following two approaches:

1. **Using the `ImageCanvas` class.** In this case image manipulation must be performed in separate class(es), and the resulting image is displayed on `ImageCanvas.` This approach is simple and works well for noninteractive operations. In interactive operations, however, the current transformation and other information must be retained. So a separate class is needed to manage such things.

2. **Creating a new class by extending the `ImageCanvas` class and implementing all the manipulation functions in it.** This is not a good solution because not all manipulation functions are required in an application. Even if they are needed, they may not be needed at a given time.

What is desirable is a flexible design that helps build only the desired manipulation functions at runtime. To achieve this, we'll adopt an approach that is a hybrid of the two approaches just presented. In this hybrid approach we'll build a controller class for each manipulation function. This controller class will operate on the image that is to be manipulated in the canvas. With this approach, an application needs to construct only required controller objects at any time.

Another important point to consider is the GUI required for generating manipulation parameters. The GUI and the controller classes must be clearly separate. The reason for this requirement is obvious: An application must be able to choose its own GUI for generating manipulation parameters.

The design pattern here is that the manipulation GUI feeds the data to the controller object, which in turn operates on the image canvas to manipulate the image. Often the manipulation GUI may need to capture some events from the image canvas. For example, `mouse` events are often needed to get the cursor position.

We'll design our interfaces from a user's point of view. First, let's design the `ImageManipulator` interface, which will be implemented by a component class to support image manipulation functionality. Such functionality includes pan, zoom, rotate, shear, and flip. For each of the manipulation types, we can define a property, the value of which can be set and retrieved by the clients of `ImageManipulator` objects.

In addition, we'll allow the client objects to choose an interpolation mechanism through a property called `interpolationType`. Currently, the `AffineTransformOp` class supports only two types of interpolation techniques: nearest-neighbor and bilinear. The `interpolationType` property can assume either of two values: `AffineTransformOp.TYPE_BILINEAR` and `AffineTransformOp.TYPE_NEAREST_NEIGHBOR`.

Because images are manipulated through the affine transformation, we need to specify the current transformation of the canvas as a property. The current transformation can be concatenated outside the canvas. The controller objects need to get and set this property. For example, a client program can allow the user to set the rotation angle in an external GUI. This program can send the rotation angle to the rotation controller object, which will generate a transformation matrix for the rotation angle selected by the user. The rotation controller will concatenate this transformation with the current transformation obtained from the image canvas. It will then set the resulting transformation to be the current transformation of the image canvas. Table 7.1 summarizes the image manipulation properties.

Besides the set and get methods for the properties shown in Table 7.1, the `ImageManipulator` canvas requires two more methods:

1. A method for applying the transformation
2. A method for resetting manipulation

Current Transformation

Client objects require the current transformation (i.e., `AffineTransform` object) for several purposes. Applying the manipulation externally is one. All the manipulation features discussed in this chapter check out the current transformation, concatenate it, and put it back. Ideally, the current transformation should be locked so that only one program updates it at a given time.

TABLE 7.1   Image Manipulation Properties

PROPERTY	TYPE	DESCRIPTION
interpolationType	int	Interpolation type; one of `AffineTransformOp.TYPE_NEAREST_NEIGHBOR` or `AffineTransformOp.TYPE_BILINEAR`
magFactor	double	Magnification factor
panOffset	Point	Translation
rotationAngle	double	Rotation
shearFactor	double	Shear
transform	AffineTransform	Current transformation

The current transformation is required for other purposes as well. For example, in region of interest (ROI) computations, the current transformation matrix is needed to convert the region (marked by the user) from user space to image space. So let's specify the current transformation as a property. The set and get methods for this property are

- ◆ **public AffineTransform getTransform()**
- ◆ **public void setTransform(AffineTransform atx)**

Resetting Manipulation

After you manipulate an image, normally you will start over again. So the client objects need a method for resetting the manipulation to a default value. Let's specify the following method for this purpose:

- ◆ **public void resetManipulation();**

Listing 7.3 shows the code for the ImageManipulator interface.

LISTING 7.3   The ImageManipulator interface

```
public interface ImageManipulator extends ImageDisplay {

    public void setPanOffset(Point panOffset);
    public Point getPanOffset();

    public void setMagFactor(double magFactor);
    public double getMagFactor();

    public void setRotationAngle(double theta);
    public double getRotationAngle();

    public void setShearFactor(double shear);
    public double getShearFactor();

    public AffineTransform getTransform();
    public void setTransform(AffineTransform at);

    public void applyTransform(AffineTransform atx);

    public void setInterpolationType(int interType);
    public int getInterpolationType();

    public void resetManipulation();
}
```

Any image-drawing component can implement ImageManipulator. Keep in mind that the components that implement this interface don't manipulate the image. The manipulation is actually performed by an external program. This canvas only holds the properties, applies the transformation, and paints the image.

Not all types of manipulations are required by an application. By separating the actual manipulation from the component, the image manipulation canvas does not have to carry the code to perform different types of manipulation. Instead, the manipulation code is in separate classes or beans.

Implementing a Canvas for Image Manipulation

Our goal is to build an image-viewing application that allows users to interactively manipulate images. The image manipulation functions we intend to implement are pan, zoom, rotate, flip, and shear. Clearly we need a component class or bean that renders images and provides manipulation functionality.

In Chapter 6 we implemented an image-rendering component called `ImageCanvas`. The image manipulator class, which we'll name `ImageCanvas2D`, will extend the `ImageCanvas` class. To implement the requirements described in the preceding section, `ImageCanvas2D` will implement the `ImageManipulator` interface (see Figure 7.5).

Besides all the set and get methods for the properties listed in Table 7.1, `Image Canvas2D` must implement two important methods: `paintImage()` and `apply Transform()`. Listing 7.4 shows the implementation.

LISTING 7.4   The `ImageCanvas2D` class

```
package com.vistech.imageviewer;
import java.io.*;
import java.awt.*;
import java.awt.event.*;
import java.awt.image.*;

import java.util.*;
import java.beans.*;
import javax.swing.*;
import java.awt.geom.*;
import com.vistech.events.*;
```

continued

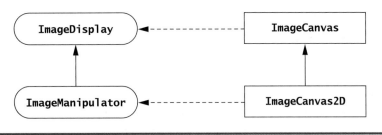

FIGURE 7.5   The `ImageCanvas2D` class hierarchy

```java
public class ImageCanvas2D extends ImageCanvas implements
                    ImageManipulator{

  protected AffineTransform atx = new AffineTransform();
  protected AffineTransform dispModeAtx = new AffineTransform();
  protected AffineTransform flipAtx = new AffineTransform();

  // Pan variables
  protected Point panOffset = new Point(0,0);
  // Zoom variables
  protected boolean magOn = true;
  protected double magFactor = 1.0;
  protected int magCenterX = 0;
  protected int magCenterY =0;
  protected Point zoomOffset = new Point(0,0);
  // Rotation variables
  protected double rotationAngle = 0.0;
  protected boolean rotateOn = true;
  protected int rotationCenterX = 0;
  protected int rotationCenterY = 0;
  // Shear variables
  protected boolean shearOn = true;
  protected double shearFactor = 0.0;
  protected double shearX =0.0, shearY=0.0;
  // Off-screen image width and height
  private int bufImageWidth = -1;
  private int bufImageHeight = -1;
  protected int interpolationType = AffineTransformOp.TYPE_NEAREST_NEIGHBOR;

  public ImageCanvas2D(){ init();}

  protected void init(){
     setDoubleBuffered(false);
     setBackground(Color.black);
     setForeground(Color.white);
     this.setSize(200,150);
  }

  public void setMagFactor(double magFactor){
     firePropertyChange("MagFactor",
                        new Double(this.magFactor),
                        new Double(magFactor));
     this.magFactor = magFactor;
  }
  public double getMagFactor(){ return magFactor;}
  public void setShearFactor(double shearFactor){
     firePropertyChange("ShearFactor",
                        new Double(this.shearFactor),
                        new Double(shearFactor));
     this.shearFactor = shearFactor;
  }

  public double getShearFactor(){ return shearFactor; }
  public double getShearFactorX(){ return shearX;}
  public double getShearFactorY(){ return shearY;}

  public void setRotationAngle(double rotationAngle){
     firePropertyChange("RotationAngle",
```

```
                        new Double(this.rotationAngle),
                        new Double(rotationAngle));
   this.rotationAngle = rotationAngle;
}
public double getRotationAngle(){ return rotationAngle; }

public void setPanOffset(Point panOffset){
   firePropertyChange("PanOffset",
                        this.panOffset,
                        panOffset);
   this.panOffset = panOffset;
}

public Point getPanOffset(){ return panOffset; }

public void setInterpolationType(int interType) {interpolationType = interType;}
public int getInterpolationType() { return interpolationType;}

public AffineTransform getTransform(){ return atx; }
public void setTransform(AffineTransform at){ atx = at; }

public  void setMagOn(boolean onOff){ magOn = onOff;}
public  boolean getMagOn(){ return magOn;}

public synchronized boolean doDisplayModeAndFlip(int imageWidth, int imageHeight){
   width = this.getBounds().width;
   height = this.getBounds().height;
   double magX= (double)width/(double)imageWidth;
   double magY = (double)height/(double)imageHeight;
   int bufferWid = width, bufferHt=height;
   dispModeAtx = new AffineTransform();
   switch(displayMode){
     case DisplayMode.ORIG_SIZE:
       bufferWid = imageWidth;
       bufferHt = imageHeight;
       break;
     case DisplayMode.SCALED:
       double mag= (magY > magX)? magX:magY;
       dispModeAtx.setToScale(mag, mag);
       bufferWid = (int)(imageWidth*mag);
       bufferHt = (int)(imageHeight*mag);
       break;
    case DisplayMode.TO_FIT:
       dispModeAtx.setToScale(magX, magY);
       bufferWid = width;
       bufferHt = height;
       default:
       break;
   }
   BufferedImage bi = new BufferedImage(bufferWid, bufferHt,imageType);
   Graphics2D bigc = bi.createGraphics();
   if(originalImageType == TYPE_AWT_IMAGE)
      bigc.drawImage(awtImage, dispModeAtx, this);
   else bigc.drawImage(bufferedImage, dispModeAtx, this);

   flipAtx = createFlipTransform(flipMode, bufferWid, bufferHt);
```

continued

```
        AffineTransformOp atop = new AffineTransformOp(flipAtx, interpolationType);
        offScrImage =  atop.filter(bi, null);
        offScrGc = offScrImage.createGraphics();
        applyTransform(offScrImage, atx);
        repaint();
        return true;
    }

    protected void applyTransform(BufferedImage bi, AffineTransform atx){
        if(offScrImage == null) return;
        if(displayImage == null) createDisplayImage();
        AffineTransformOp atop = new AffineTransformOp(atx, interpolationType);
        dispGc.setColor(Color.black);
        dispGc.fillRect(0,0,displayImage.getWidth(), displayImage.getHeight());
        dispGc.setClip(clipShape);
        if(clipShape == null) atop.filter(bi, displayImage);
        else dispGc.drawImage(bi,atx,this);
    }

    public void applyTransform(AffineTransform atx){
        applyTransform(offScrImage, atx);
        this.atx = atx;
        repaint();
    }

    public void reset(){
        panOffset = new Point(0,0);
        magCenterX = 0; magCenterY =0;
        magFactor = 1.0;
        rotationAngle = 0.0;
        shearX = 0.0; shearY = 0.0;
        atx = new AffineTransform();
        paintImage();
    }

    public void resetManipulation(){
        panOffset = new Point(0,0);
        magCenterX = 0; magCenterY =0;
        magFactor = 1.0;
        shearX = 0.0; shearY = 0.0;
        rotationAngle = 0.0;
        atx = new AffineTransform();
        paintImage();
        repaint();
    }

}
```

The `ImageCanvas2D` class holds the current value of the transform property in `atx`, which is concatenated whenever the current image is manipulated.

Recall from Chapter 6 how images are painted (see Figure 6.4). When the `setAWTImage()` or `setBufferedImage()` method is called, the original image is loaded. When the `setDisplayMode()` or `setFlipMode()` method is called, an `offScreenImage` object is created by application of the current `displayMode` and `flipMode` properties. The `offScrImage` variable holds this image.

Any manipulation function will either concatenate `atx` or create a new instance of `atx` and apply it to `offScrImage`. The `applyTransform()` method discussed earlier (see Listings 7.1 and 7.2) does this. The `applyTransform()` method creates another `BufferedImage` object, which is saved in the `displayImage` variable. You may recall that `offScrImage` and `displayImage` are defined in the superclass `ImageCanvas`. Having two copies of the same image may seem wasteful, but they are needed for performance.

Using the Affine Transformation to Set Display and Flip Modes

The `doDisplayModeAndFlip()` method overrides the `doDisplayModeAndFlip()` method in the `ImageCanvas` class. As far as the display mode is concerned, we need to apply just one type of transformation: scaling. On the basis of the requirements listed in Chapter 6, when the display modes are set, the viewport is reset. This means that we need to reset the underlying `AffineTransform` object.

The `doDisplayModeAndFlip()` method in Listing 7.4 first creates an `Affine Transform` object—`dispModeAtx`—and then checks for display mode type, which can be any one of `ORIG_SIZE`, `SCALED`, or `TO_FIT`. In the case of `ORIG_SIZE`, the affine transformation is the identity transformation itself because there is no scaling. In the case of `SCALED`, the scale factor is calculated in both the x and the y directions, and the larger factor is chosen. The `doDisplayModeAndFlip()` method then calls the `setToScale()` method to create a transformation with a specified scale factor. In this case the scale factor is the same in both the x and the y directions because of the need to preserve the aspect ratio of the image. In the `TO_FIT` case, the scale factors in both directions are taken into consideration, and an `AffineTransform` object is created.

Next the `doDisplayModeAndFlip()` method creates a `BufferedImage` instance that is as big as the image to be rendered. The original image is drawn on this `BufferedImage` object by the `drawImage()` method. The `dispModeAtx` object is passed as a parameter to `drawImage()`, thus applying the desired display mode to the original image. The image thus created may need to be flipped, depending on the flip mode selected.

The `doDisplayModeAndFlip()` method then creates a flip transformation. It uses the `filter()` method of the `AffineTransformOp` class to apply the flip transformation to the current image and creates another `BufferedImage` object. Although this image is ready for rendering, the `doDisplayModeAndFlip()` method performs one more transformation because we may use this image for image manipulation purposes. The `BufferedImage` object obtained after the flip mode operation is called `offScrImage`, and we'll make this image the base for all other image manipulation operations.

The `doDisplayModeAndFlip()` method transforms the image through the `applyTransform()` method, which we described earlier. The resulting image—`displayImage`—is the one that is rendered (see Figure 6.4). So there are two instance variables: `atx` and `displayImage.` The variable `atx` will be concatenated when an image is manipulated, and it will be reset when the display or flip modes are set.

Flipping

The `AffineTransform` class does not have direct methods for creating a transformation matrix for flip. We'll use the reflection transformation to create a flip matrix (see Chapter 4). You may recall that the reflection transformation creates a mirror image rather than a flipped image. To create a flip transformation, all we need to do is to translate the reflection matrix to the same quadrant as the image. Listing 7.5 shows how to do this.

LISTING 7.5   Creating a flip transformation

```
static public AffineTransform createFlipTransform(int mode,
                                                  int imageWid,
                                                  int imageHt){
    AffineTransform at = new AffineTransform();
    switch(mode){
        case FlipMode.NORMAL:
          break;
        case FlipMode.TOP_BOTTOM:
          at =  new AffineTransform(new double[] {1.0,0.0,0.0,-1.0});
          at.translate(0.0, -imageHt);
          break;
        case FlipMode.LEFT_RIGHT :
          at = new AffineTransform(new double[] {-1.0,0.0,0.0,1.0});
          at.translate(-imageWid, 0.0);
          break;
        case FlipMode.TOP_BOTTOM_LEFT_RIGHT:
          at = new AffineTransform(new double[] {-1.0,0.0,0.0,-1.0});
          at.translate(-imageWid, -imageHt);
          break;
        default:
    }
    return at;
}
```

As Listing 7.5 shows, the `createFlipTransform()` method constructs an `AffineTransform` object for reflection by passing a flat matrix array. This array contains the elements of a top left-hand 2 × 2 matrix, which is different for each of the flip mode cases. Once the reflection transformation has been constructed, it is translated to the original image location itself.

In the sections that follow we'll look at the different types of manipulation, starting with pan.

Pan

When an image is bigger than the viewport, we tend to scroll the image to see parts that are not visible. To pan or scroll images in a viewport, applications provide different types of user interfaces—for example, scroll bars. Some applications provide mouse-based scrolling. With mouse-based schemes, you normally hold the mouse down and drag the image so that you can view the desired portion of the image. In our design, however, we'll separate the GUI from the controller. The controller will have the logic to scroll on an image canvas, and it will accept input from any type of user interface.

Let's discuss the requirements and design an interface named `ScrollController`. Figure 7.6 shows how images are panned, or scrolled. The position at which you click the mouse is the anchor point, and as you drag, the current mouse position is the current position of the image. The pan offset is the displacement between the current position and the anchor point. The current image is drawn with this offset from the previous position.

To hold this displacement, let's specify a property named `panOffset.` The set and get methods for this property are

- `public void setPanOffset(Point panOffset);`
- `public Point getPanOffset();`

We need a method that initiates the scrolling. This method should set the anchor point. Let's call this method `startScroll()`:

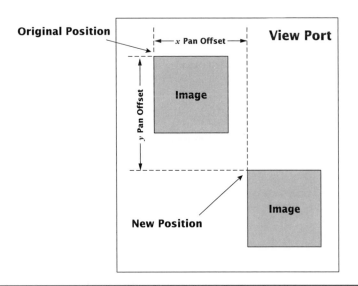

FIGURE 7.6 Panning an image

◆ **`public void startScroll(int x, int y)`**

We also need a method that stops the scrolling:

◆ **`public void stopScroll()`**

When the image is scrolled, it is painted at a new position. The `paintImage()` method we defined in the `ImageDisplay` interface will not suffice to accomplish this task. So let's specify a method for this purpose, with the displacement in the x and y directions as its inputs:

◆ **`public void scroll(int xOffset, int yOffset);`**

This method paints the current image at an offset of `xOffset` and `yOffset` from the previous position in the x and y directions, respectively.

The `ScrollController` interface, shown in Listing 7.6, contains all the methods defined here.

LISTING 7.6 The `ScrollController` interface

```
public interface ScrollController {
    public void setPanOffset(Point panOffset);


    public Point getPanOffset();
    public void startScroll(int x, int y);
    public void scroll(int x, int y);
    public void stopScroll();
}
```

Implementing Pan

Now that we have designed an interface to implement scrolling (panning), let's implement a mouse-driven scroll feature. It will have two classes:

1. **Scroll.** This class will control scrolling by implementing the `ScrollController` interface. `Scroll` will operate on an image canvas, so it needs to hold a reference to an object that implements the `ImageManipulator` interface.

2. **ScrollGUI.** This class will accept user input and pass it on to `Scroll Controller`. In the case of mouse-driven scrolling, `ScrollGUI` must receive `mouse` and `mouseMotion` events from `ImageManipulator`.

Figure 7.7 shows a design similar to model-view-controller (MVC) architecture[1] for scrolling. The `ScrollGUI` object receives the mouse positions through `mouse` and

---

1 If you are not familiar with MVC architecture, you may want to consult an object-oriented programming book. *Design Patterns: Elements of Reusable Object-Oriented Software* (1995), by Gamma, Helm, Johnson, and Vlissides, is a good source.

`mouseMotion` events. It passes the mouse positions as pan offset to the `ScrollController` interface, which modifies the current transformation to take the translation into account.

We'll follow the same design pattern for all the other manipulation functions. This pattern clearly separates the GUI and the application logic, so you are free to replace `ScrollGUI` with another class for a different type of GUI.

Two schemes are popular for scrolling images in a viewport:

1. Using scroll bars
2. Using mouse-driven interfaces

Because we use the mouse-driven interface in this book, let's look at how a mouse-driven client object must interact with a `Scroll` object.

The `Scroll` object must remember two positions: the anchor point and the current position of the image. When the mouse is pressed, the `mousePressed()` method of a client object must call `startScroll(int x, int y)` and pass the current coordinates of the mouse as the input parameters. The `startScroll()` method must save this position as the anchor point. Whenever the mouse is dragged, the `mouseDragged()` method of the client object must call `scroll(int x, int y)` and pass the current position of the mouse as input parameters. The `scroll()` method must compute the displacement between the current position of the mouse and the anchor position. It must then pass this displacement to the `ImageManipulator` object so that it can paint the image at the current mouse position. When the mouse button is released, the `mouseReleased()` method of the client object must call `stopScroll()`.

Listing 7.7 shows the code for `Scroll`.

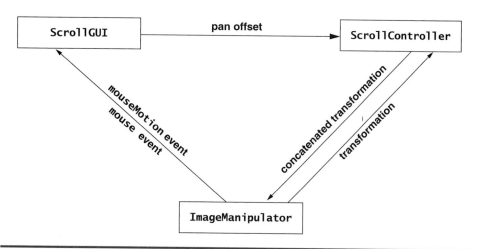

FIGURE 7.7   The data flow for scrolling

LISTING 7.7 The Scroll class

```java
package com.vistech.imageviewer;
import java.io.*;
import java.awt.*;
import java.awt.image.*;
import java.util.*;
import java.awt.geom.*;

public class Scroll implements ScrollController  {
   protected AffineTransform atx = new AffineTransform();
   protected Point panOffset = new Point(0,0);
   private Point diff = new Point(0,0);
   private Point scrollAnchor  = new Point(0,0);
   protected ImageManipulator imageCanvas;

   public Scroll() {}

   public Scroll(ImageManipulator imageCanvas) {
      this.imageCanvas = imageCanvas;
   }
   public void setImageManipulator(ImageManipulator imageCanvas){
      this.imageCanvas = imageCanvas;
   }

   public void setPanOffset(Point panOffset){
      this.panOffset = panOffset;
      imageCanvas.setPanOffset(panOffset);
   }

   public Point getPanOffset(){return panOffset; }

   public void translateIncr(double incrx, double incry) {
      atx.translate(incrx, incry);
      imageCanvas.applyTransform(atx);
   }

   public void translate(double diffx, double diffy) {
      double dx = diffx -panOffset.x;
      double dy = diffy -panOffset.y;
      panOffset.x = (int)diffx;
      panOffset.y = (int)diffy;
      translateIncr(dx,dy);
   }

   public void resetAndTranslate(int dx, int dy) {
      atx.setToTranslation((double)dx, (double)dy);
      imageCanvas.applyTransform(atx);
   }

   public void scroll(int x, int y){
      if((x <0 )|| (y<0)) return;
      try {
         Point2D xy = null;
         xy = atx.inverseTransform((Point2D)(new Point(x,y)), xy);
         double ix  = (xy.getX()-scrollAnchor.x);
         double iy =  (xy.getY()-scrollAnchor.y);
```

```
            translateIncr(ix,iy);
        }catch(Exception e) {System.out.println(e);}
    }

    public void startScroll(int x, int y){
        atx = imageCanvas.getTransform();
        // Create a new anchor point so that every time mouse button is clicked,
        // the image does not move, but instead the anchor point moves.
        try {
            Point2D xy = null;
            xy = atx.inverseTransform((Point2D)(new Point(x,y)), xy);
            scrollAnchor = new Point((int)(xy.getX()),(int)(xy.getY()));
            imageCanvas.setCursor(Cursor.getPredefinedCursor(Cursor.HAND_CURSOR));
        }catch(Exception e) {System.out.println(e);}
    }

    public void stopScroll(){ imageCanvas.setCursor(Cursor.getDefaultCursor());}

    public void reset() {
        scrollAnchor = new Point(0,0);
        diff = new Point(0,0);
    }
}
```

The `Scroll` class implements the `ScrollController` interface. Note that `Scroll`'s constructor takes the `ImageManipulator` object as an input. This means you can pass any component class that implements the `ImageManipulator` interface as a parameter to this constructor.

The `Scroll` object gets the current transformation from the canvas, concatenates it with the transformation generated for the translation, and sets this concatenated transformation as the current transformation of the canvas. Let's look at `Scroll`'s methods.

Scrolling

The `startScroll()` method first computes the anchor position and assigns it to the variable `scrollAnchor`. The position passed as an input parameter to `startScroll()` is in the user coordinate space. These coordinates need to be converted to the image space because the displayed image might have already undergone some transformations. User space is converted to image space through the inverse transformation.

What would happen if this transformation were not done? You would get different results, depending on the transformation(s) already applied to the image. If the image were flipped right to left, it would move in the opposite direction along the *x*-axis; that is, if you tried to pan the image left to right, it would move right to left. If the image were rotated, it would move in the direction of the rotation when you tried to pan along the *x*- or *y*-axis. Inverse transformation solves this problem. The `startScroll()` method also launches a new cursor to indicate that the image is being panned.

The `scroll()` method converts the input coordinates to the image space and computes the displacement from the anchor point. This displacement is passed to the `translateIncr()` method, which performs the actual translation of the image. The `stopScroll()` method is called when the mouse is released, and it returns the original cursor.

Next we'll look at the translation-related methods in more detail.

Translation

Applying translation makes the image move. The `translateIncr()` method takes translation increments as input parameters. For instance, if an image is moved to position $P_{(x',y')}$ from $P_{(x,y)}$, the translation parameters are the displacements from $P_{(x,y)}$ to $P_{(x',y')}$. The reason is that the current transformation, which is contained in the `atx` variable, has already taken into account the translation to $P_{(x,y)}$ from the original position.

As stated earlier, if the translation parameters are the coordinates from the user space (i.e., viewport), the inverse transformation needs to be applied to these coordinates so that they are in `atx` space.

The `translate()` method does the same thing as the `translateIncr()` method, but it takes the absolute translation from the anchor point. This method resets `atx` and sets the translation to the parameters specified in the inputs. It calls the `setToTranslation()` method of the `AffineTransform` class to reset `atx` and then translates the images to (d_x, d_y). Note that the input arguments are of type `int`. The reason is that the coordinates in the user space are integer types, and these coordinates are expected to be passed directly to this method.

User Interface for Scrolling

As stated earlier, panning in our implementation is performed through `mouse` and `mouseMotion` events. The `ScrollGUI` class must capture these events, which means it needs to implement the `MouseListener` and `MouseMotionListener` interfaces. Listing 7.8 shows the implementation.

LISTING 7.8   The `ScrollGUI` class

```
package com.vistech.imageviewer;
import java.io.*;
import java.awt.*;
import java.awt.event.*;
import javax.swing.*;

public class ScrollGUI implements  MouseListener,MouseMotionListener{
    protected ScrollController scrollController;
    protected boolean scrollOn = true;
    protected boolean mousePressed = false;
```

```
public ScrollGUI(ScrollController c){scrollController = c;}
public  void setScrollOn(boolean onOff){ scrollOn = onOff;}
public void init() { setScrollOn(true);}

public  boolean getScrollOn(){ return scrollOn; }
public void startScroll(){ scrollOn = true;}

public void reset(){
   if(scrollController != null)scrollController.stopScroll();
   setScrollOn(false);
}

public void mousePressed(MouseEvent e) {
   if(!scrollOn) return;
   if(mousePressed) return;
   mousePressed = true;
   if(SwingUtilities.isLeftMouseButton(e)){
      scrollController.startScroll(e.getX(), e.getY());
   }
}

public void mouseReleased(MouseEvent e) {
   scrollController.stopScroll();
   mousePressed = false;
}
public void mouseClicked(MouseEvent e){}
public void mouseEntered(MouseEvent e){}
public void mouseExited(MouseEvent e){}

public void mouseDragged(MouseEvent e){
   if(SwingUtilities.isLeftMouseButton(e)){
      if(scrollOn) scrollController.scroll(e.getX(), e.getY());
   }
}
public void mouseMoved(MouseEvent e){}
}
```

Note that the ScrollGUI constructor takes ScrollController as the input. It communicates with the ImageManipulator object through Scroll (see Figure 7.7).

In order for ScrollGUI to receive mouse and mouseMotion events, a separate object must register ImageManipulator with ScrollGUI. The reason is that both the ImageManipulator and the ScrollController objects are unaware of the ScrollGUI object. This registration needs to be done when ScrollGUI is constructed by an application, as shown here:

```
ImageManipulator imageCanvas = new ImageCanvas2D();

ScrollController scroll = new Scroll(imageCanvas);
ScrollGUI scrollUI = new ScrollGUI(scroll);

imageCanvas.addMouseListener(scrollUI);
```

To refresh your memory, `Scroll` implements the `ScrollController` interface, and `ImageCanvas2D` implements the `ImageManipulator` interface. These objects can be used as `ScrollController` and `ImageManipulator` objects, respectively.

Let's construct a typical sequence of method calls with `ScrollGUI`, `Scroll Controller`, and `ImageManipulator` objects:

1. The application that needs the scroll feature registers `ScrollGUI` to receive `mouse` and `mouseMotion` events with the `ImageManipulator` object.

2. The user presses the left mouse button. The `ImageManipulator` object, which is the mouse event source, fires the `mousePressed` event to the `ScrollGUI` object. The `mousePressed()` method is invoked when any mouse button is clicked. Because the `Scroll` class uses only the left mouse button, the `isLeftMouse Button()` method of the `SwingUtilities` class checks for this condition; that is, it returns `true` only when the left mouse button is pressed.

3. The `mousePressed()` method calls the `startScroll()` method in the `ScrollController` object, which saves the position at which the mouse was pressed as the anchor point (in the variable called `anchorPoint`).

4. The user drags the mouse while holding the left mouse down. The `ImageManipulator` object fires the `mouseDragged` event, which is received by the `mouseDragged()` method in `ScrollGUI`. The `mouseDragged()` method is called repeatedly as the user drags the mouse.

5. The `mouseDragged()` method calls the `scroll()` method in the `Scroll Controller` object and passes the current mouse coordinates as its parameters.

6. The `ImageManipulator` object paints the current image (i.e., `displayImage`) at the new position.

7. The user releases the mouse button, prompting the `ImageManipulator` object to fire a `mouseReleased` event. This event is received by the `mouseReleased()` method.

8. The `mouseReleased()` method calls `stopScroll()` to halt scrolling.

Zoom

As with pan, different applications provide different types of user interfaces for zooming images. Some applications allow you to zoom in or zoom out by clicking on the image. When the image is magnified or reduced, the point on the image where you clicked remains at the same position on the viewport. In some applications you are asked to mark a rectangular region over the image. The image within this rectangular region is then zoomed onto the viewport.

As we did with `ScrollController` to implement the pan operation, let's create an interface called `ZoomController` for implementing GUI-independent zoom logic and then build a GUI-specific class for a zoom feature. The `ZoomController` interface will have a property called `magFactor` whose set and get methods are

- **`public void setMagFactor(double magFactor);`**
- **`public double getMagFactor();`**

We'll design two types of magnification methods:

1. A method for magnifying the original image by a specified factor
2. A method for magnifying a displayed image by a specified factor and then setting the magnified image as the new displayed image

Both types of methods are required in practice.

Magnifying the Original Image

Let's specify the following method for magnifying the original image:

- **`public boolean magnify(int magCenterX, int magCenterY, double mag);`**
  This method will reset any other transformation that has been performed on the image, except when the image is transformed to set the `displayMode` and `flipMode` properties. It magnifies the image with (`magCenterX`, `magCenterY`) as the coordinates of the center of magnification. This means that if you click at position $P_{(magCenterX, magCenterY)}$ on the viewport, the corresponding point on the magnified image will be located at the same position (see Figure 7.8).

Let's define one more flavor of the `magnify()` method for implementing the zoom feature:

- **`public boolean magnify(int  magCenterX, int magCenterY);`**
  This method is same as the preceding `magnify()` method, except that it gets the magnification factor from the `magFactor` property.

Magnifying the Displayed Image

It may be convenient in some cases to magnify the displayed image itself. To meet this requirement, let's define one more `paintImage()` method:

- **`public void paintImage(int magCenterX, int magCenterY, double mag);`**
  When this method is executed, the magnified image becomes the new `displayImage` object.

The `ZoomController` interface, shown in Listing 7.9, contains all the methods defined here.

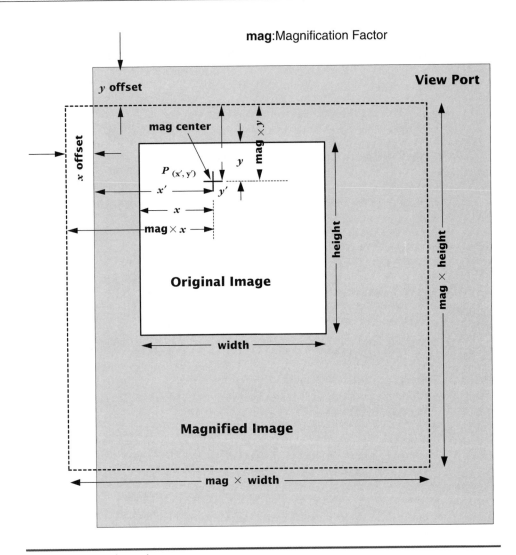

FIGURE 7.8 Zooming an image

LISTING 7.9 The ZoomController interface

```
public interface ZoomController {
    public void setMagFactor(double magFactor);
    public double getMagFactor();
    public void magnify(int magCenterX, int magCenterY, double mag);
    public void magnify(int magCenterX, int magCenterY);
    public void paintImage(int magCenterX, int magCenterY, double mag);
}
```

Implementing Zoom

The `ZoomController` interface specifies several methods for magnification as well. The design of the zoom feature is similar to the scroll feature. We'll define two classes: one for controlling zoom, and the other for the GUI:

1. **Zoom.** This class will control zoom by implementing the `ZoomController` interface.

2. **ZoomGUI.** This class will implement the zoom feature. It will contain the mouse user interface.

The zoom feature follows the same design pattern as scroll (see Figure 7.9). Listing 7.10 shows the code for the `Zoom` class.

LISTING 7.10   The Zoom class

```
package com.vistech.imageviewer;
import java.io.*;
import java.awt.*;
import java.awt.image.*;
import java.awt.geom.*;
public class Zoom implements ZoomController  {
    protected AffineTransform atx = new AffineTransform();
    protected boolean magOn = true;
    protected double magFactor = 1.0;
    protected int magCenterX = 0;
    protected int magCenterY =0;
    protected Point zoomOffset = new Point(0,0);
    protected ImageManipulator imageCanvas;

    public Zoom(){}
    public Zoom(ImageManipulator imageCanvas){ this.imageCanvas = imageCanvas;}
```

continued

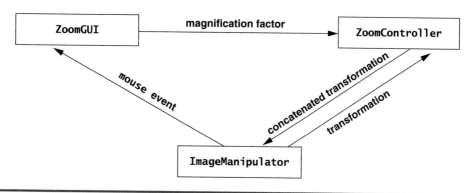

FIGURE 7.9   The data flow for zoom

```java
public void setImageManipulator(ImageManipulator imageCanvas){
   this.imageCanvas = imageCanvas;
}

public void setMagOn(boolean onOff){ magOn = onOff;}
public boolean getMagOn(){ return magOn; }

public void setMagFactor(double magFactor){
   this.magFactor = magFactor;
   imageCanvas.setMagFactor(magFactor);
}

public double getMagFactor(){ return magFactor;}

public void magnify(int magCenterX, int magCenterY){
    magnify(magCenterX, magCenterY, magFactor);
}

public void magnify(int magCenterX, int magCenterY, double magFac){
   setMagFactor(magFac);
   this.magCenterX = magCenterX;
   this.magCenterY = magCenterY;
   Point panOffset = imageCanvas.getPanOffset();
   int x = (int)((magCenterX-panOffset.x)*magFactor)-magCenterX;
   int y = (int)((magCenterY-panOffset.y)*magFactor)-magCenterY;
   atx = imageCanvas.getTransform();
   atx.setToTranslation(-x, -y);
   atx.scale(magFactor, magFactor);
   applyTransform(atx);
}

public void paintImage(int magCenterX, int magCenterY, double mag){
   setMagFactor(this.magFactor *mag);
   int dx = this.magCenterX -magCenterX;
   int dy = this.magCenterY-magCenterY;
   this.magCenterX = magCenterX;
   this.magCenterY = magCenterY;
   try {
     Point2D mgp = null;
     atx = imageCanvas.getTransform();
     mgp =
     atx.inverseTransform((Point2D)(new Point(magCenterX, magCenterY)),
                                              (Point2D)mgp);
     double x = (mgp.getX()*mag)-mgp.getX();
     double y = (mgp.getY()*mag)-mgp.getY();
     scale(-x,-y, mag);
   }catch (Exception e) {System.out.println(e); }
}

public void scale(double magOffsetX, double magOffsetY, double mag){
   atx.translate(magOffsetX,magOffsetY);
   atx.scale(mag,mag);
   applyTransform(atx);
}
```

```
public void resetAndScale(double magOffsetX, double magOffsetY, double mag){
    atx.setToTranslation(magOffsetX,magOffsetY);
    atx.scale(mag,mag);
    applyTransform(atx);
}

public void applyTransform(AffineTransform atx) {
    imageCanvas.applyTransform(atx);
}

public void reset() {
    magCenterX = 0;
    magCenterY = 0;
    magFactor = 1.0;
}
}
```

The `paintImage()` method is the key method for implementation of the zoom feature. The `mag` input parameter holds the zoom increment or decrement value. Just as with the `scroll()` method in the scroll feature, `paintImage()` converts the point at which the mouse is clicked to the image space by using the inverse transformation. Once that point has been obtained, `paintImage()` computes the amount of translation that needs to be applied. As Figure 7.8 shows, translations in the x and y directions are calculated as follows:

$$T_x = (\text{mag} \times x) - x$$

$$T_y = (\text{mag} \times y) - y$$

The `scale()` method takes these translations and the `mag` increment value as inputs.

Scaling

The `scale()` method of the `Zoom` class does the uniform scaling. The scaling is performed at a reference point (the magnification center) whose coordinates are specified by `magCenterX` and `magCenterY`. The `scale()` method of the `AffineTransform` class performs scaling with the origin as the reference point. In most applications, however, the reference point is somewhere in the viewport. This can be a point where the mouse is clicked, or it can be the center of a rectangle that was drawn over the image. To achieve scaling at a reference point, the image is translated by a certain amount. So the `scale()` method of the `Zoom` class first translates the image to the reference point specified by (`magOffsetX`, `magOffsetY`) and then scales it by `mag`.

The `resetAndScale()` method performs absolute scaling. It resets `atx` and translates the images to (`magOffsetX`, `magOffsetY`) and then applies scaling.

User Interface for Zoom

Let's design a GUI interface that zooms an image in or out at a position where the mouse is clicked. The zoom operator has two modes: zoom in and zoom out. If the zoom-in mode is selected, the magnification of the image increases every time the user clicks the mouse. If the zoom-out mode is selected, the opposite happens.

The `ZoomGUI` class implements the `MouseListener` interface. That means it captures only `mouse` events, and not `mouseMotion` events. Listing 7.11 shows the code for `ZoomGUI`.

LISTING 7.11 The ZoomGUI class

```
package com.vistech.imageviewer;
import java.io.*;
import java.awt.*;
import javax.swing.*;

public class ZoomGUI implements MouseListener{
    protected ZoomController zoomController;
    protected final static double baseZoomFactor = 1.0;
    protected boolean zoomOn = false;
    protected double zoomFactor = 1.0;
    protected double increment = 0.1;
    protected boolean zoomOut = false;
    protected boolean mousePressed = false;

    public ZoomGUI(ZoomController c){ zoomController = c;}

    public  void setZoomOn(boolean onOff){zoomOn = onOff;}
    public  boolean getZoomOn(){ return zoomOn;}
    public  void setZoomOut(boolean outIn){zoomOut = outIn;}
    public  boolean getZoomOut(){ return zoomOut; }
    public void setZoomfactor(double mag){ zoomFactor = mag; }
    public double getZoomFactor(){ return zoomFactor; }
    public void setZoomIncrement(double incr){ increment = incr; }
    public double getZoomIncrement(){ return increment;}

    public void zoom(int x, int y, double zoomfact){
       if(zoomOut) {
          zoomController.paintImage(x,y,baseZoomFactor-increment);
          zoomFactor *= baseZoomFactor-increment;
       }
       else {
          zoomController.paintImage(x,y,baseZoomFactor+increment);
          zoomFactor *= baseZoomFactor+increment;
       }
    }
    public void reset() {
       setZoomOn(false);
       zoomFactor = 1.0;
    }
    public void mousePressed(MouseEvent e) {
       if(mousePressed) return;
       mousePressed = true;
       if(!zoomOn) return;
```

```
         if(SwingUtilities.isLeftMouseButton(e)){
            zoom(e.getX(), e.getY(), zoomFactor);
         }
      }
   public void mouseReleased(MouseEvent e){ mousePressed = false;}
   public void mouseClicked(MouseEvent e){}
   public void mouseEntered(MouseEvent e){}
   public void mouseExited(MouseEvent e){}
}
```

The properties of the zoom operator include zoomOn, zoomOut, zoomFactor, and zoomIncrement. When you reset the zoom feature, the zoomFactor property starts with 1.0—that is, no magnification. When the mouse is clicked, the mousePressed() method calls zoom(), which increments or decrements zoomFactor depending on the current zoom mode. The zoom() method then calls the paintImage() method of ZoomController and passes the current position of the mouse and magFactor.

The following code fragment shows how to use the zoom-related classes:

```
ImageManipulator  imageCanvas = new  ImageCanvas2D();

ZoomController zoom = new Zoom(imageCanvas);
ZoomGUI  zoomUI = new ZoomGUI(zoom);

imageCanvas.addMouseListener(zoomUI);
```

Implementing Pan and Zoom Together

Now let's use both the scroll (pan) and the zoom features to implement a combined pan-zoom operator and use it in the image viewer described in Chapter 6. The Scroll and Zoom operator classes provide no GUIs. But we need a GUI interface that indicates to Scroll and Zoom objects when to zoom and when to pan. So let's provide a pop-up menu that is launched by right-clicking on the image. This pop-up menu will have the following three menu items:

1. **Zoom in**
2. **Zoom out**
3. **Pan**

You can choose any of these options at any time.

The PanZoom class (see Listing 7.12) combines the pan and zoom features.

LISTING 7.12   The PanZoom class

```
package com.vistech.imageviewer;
import java.io.*;
import java.awt.*;
import java.awt.event.*;
import javax.swing.*;
```

continued

```java
public class PanZoom extends MouseAdapter{
    protected ImageManipulator imageCanvas;
    protected ScrollGUI pan;
    protected Scroll scroll;
    protected ZoomGUI zoomGUI;
    protected Zoom zoom;
    protected boolean panOn,zoomOn, zoomOut, panZoomOn = true;

    public PanZoom(ImageManipulator manip) {
        imageCanvas = manip;
        scroll = new Scroll(imageCanvas);
        pan = new ScrollGUI(scroll);

        zoom = new Zoom(imageCanvas);
        zoomGUI = new ZoomGUI(zoom);
        init();
    }
    protected void init() {
        if(imageCanvas == null) return;
        imageCanvas.addMouseListener(pan);
        imageCanvas.addMouseListener(zoomGUI);
        imageCanvas.addMouseListener(this);
        imageCanvas.addMouseMotionListener(pan);
        panOn = true;
        zoomOn = false;
        zoomOut = false;
    }

    protected void setStates() {
        pan.setScrollOn(panOn);
        zoomGUI.setZoomOn(zoomOn);
        zoomGUI.setZoomOut(zoomOut);
    }
    public void setPanZoomOn(boolean onOrOff){
        if(panZoomOn == onOrOff) return;
        panZoomOn = onOrOff;
        if(panZoomOn){
            imageCanvas.addMouseListener(pan);
            imageCanvas.addMouseListener(zoomGUI);
            imageCanvas.addMouseListener(this);
            imageCanvas.addMouseMotionListener(pan);
        }else {
            imageCanvas.removeMouseListener(pan);
            imageCanvas.removeMouseListener(zoomGUI);
            imageCanvas.removeMouseListener(this);
            imageCanvas.removeMouseMotionListener(pan);
        }
    }
    public boolean getZoomOut(){ return zoomOut; }
    public boolean getZoomOn(){ return zoomOn; }
    public double getZoomFactor(){
        return zoomGUI.getZoomFactor();
    }

    public boolean getPanOn(){ return panOn; }
    public void reset(){
        zoomGUI.reset();
```

```
      pan.reset();
   }
   protected void popupMenu(JComponent comp,int x, int y){
      JPopupMenu jp = new JPopupMenu("");
      jp.setLightWeightPopupEnabled(true);
      comp.add(jp);
      JMenuItem zout = new JMenuItem("Zoom out");
      zout.addActionListener(
         new ActionListener(){
            public void actionPerformed(ActionEvent e){
               zoomOut = true; zoomOn = true; panOn = false;
               setStates();
            }
         }
      );
      JMenuItem zin = new JMenuItem("Zoom in");
      zin.addActionListener(
         new ActionListener(){
            public void actionPerformed(ActionEvent e){
               zoomOut = false; zoomOn = true; panOn = false;
               setStates();
            }
         }
      );

      JMenuItem pn = new JMenuItem("Pan");
      pn.addActionListener(
         new ActionListener(){
            public void actionPerformed(ActionEvent e){
               zoomOn = false; panOn = true;
               setStates();
            }
         }
      );
      jp.add(zin);
      jp.add(zout);
      jp.add(pn);
      jp.show(comp,x,y);
   }

   public void mousePressed(MouseEvent e) {
      if(!SwingUtilities.isLeftMouseButton(e)){
         popupMenu((JComponent)e.getSource(), e.getX(), e.getY());
      }
   }
}
```

The PanZoom class extends the java.awt.events.MouseAdapter class, which implements the MouseListener interface. This interface is required to launch the pop-up menu. The constructor for the PanZoom class takes the ImageManipulator interface as input. It creates Pan and Zoom objects by passing the ImageManipulator parameter to their constructor and calls the init() method. The init() method registers the Pan object to receive mouse and mouseMotion events.

When pan mode is selected, the position where the mouse is pressed is the anchor for pan. While the mouse is being dragged, the difference in distance from the current position to the anchor is computed and passed to the `ImageManipulator` object to paint the image at the new position. The `init()` method registers the `Zoom` object to receive `mouse` events and then sets the default values for the three state variables: `panOn`, `zoomOn`, and `zoomOut`.

The `popupMenu()` method takes x and y coordinates of the position at which the mouse is clicked as the input parameters and uses them to show the pop-up menu at that location. This method creates three menu items—**Pan, Zoom out,** and **Zoom in**—each of which has an anonymous inner class to handle action events. These `actionPerformed()` methods set the member variables `panOn`, `zoomOn`, and `zoomOut` and call the appropriate `setStates()` methods in the `Pan` and `Zoom` objects, depending on the menu item selected.

The screen shot in Figure 7.10 shows an image viewer that implements the combined pan-zoom feature. In this image viewer, you can right-click on the image to select the operation you want to perform by choosing the appropriate item from the

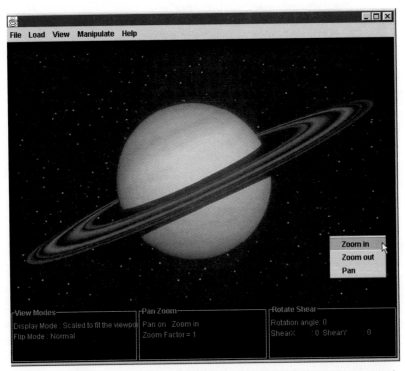

© Antonio M. Rosario/The Image Bank

FIGURE 7.10   An image viewer with the pan-zoom feature

pop-up menu. This image viewer is an extension of the one in Chapter 6. As the figure shows, the status bar displays the image manipulation status messages. Regarding pan-zoom, the status bar tells you which feature is currently active and the current zoom factor.

Now let's implement a special feature called Lens using the zoom API.

Implementing a Lens

A moving lens over an image is quite a useful feature in many applications where visual inspection is an important factor in analyzing images. In addition to the AffineTransform class, the lens feature, which is implemented by the Lens class, uses many aspects of the Graphics2D class. Listing 7.13 shows the code for Lens.

LISTING 7.13   The Lens class

```
package com.vistech.imageviewer;
import java.io.*;
import java.awt.*;
import java.awt.event.*;
import javax.swing.*;

public class Lens implements MouseListener, MouseMotionListener{
    protected ImageManipulator imageCanvas;
    protected Dimension lensSize = new Dimension(60,80);
    protected Point prevPoint = new Point(0,0);
    protected boolean lensOn = false;
    protected int sizeIncrement = 10;
    protected double magIncrement = 0.5;
    protected double lensMag = 2.0;
    protected Zoom zoom;

    public Lens(ImageManipulator c){
       imageCanvas = c;
       zoom = new Zoom(imageCanvas);
    }
    public void init() { setLensOn(true);}

    public void setLensSize(Dimension d){ lensSize = d; }

    public Dimension getLensSize(){ return lensSize; }

    public void setLensMag(double mag){ lensMag = mag; }

    public double getLensMag(){ return lensMag; }

    public void setLensMagIncrement(int incr){ magIncrement = incr; }

    public double getLensMagIncrement(){ return magIncrement; }

    public void setLensSizeIncrement(int incr){ sizeIncrement = incr; }
```

continued

```java
public int getLensSizeIncrement(){ return sizeIncrement; }

public  void setLensOn(boolean onOff){ lensOn = onOff; }

public  boolean getLensOn(){ return lensOn; }

public void drawLens(int x, int y){
   int wid = lensSize.width; int ht = lensSize.height;
   Shape lens = new Ellipse2D.Float(prevPoint.x-wid,prevPoint.y-ht, wid,ht);
   imageCanvas.setClip(lens);
   zoom.magnify(0,0, 1);
   Shape ch = new Ellipse2D.Float(x-wid,y-ht, wid,ht);
   imageCanvas.setClip(ch);
   zoom.magnify((x-wid/2), (y-ht/2), lensMag);

   imageCanvas.draw(ch);
   prevPoint = new Point(x,y);
}

public void incrementLensSize(){
   lensSize.width += sizeIncrement;
   lensSize.height += sizeIncrement;
}
public void decrementLensSize(){
   lensSize.width -= sizeIncrement;
   lensSize.height -= sizeIncrement;
}

public void incrementLensMag(){
   lensMag += magIncrement;
}

public void decrementLensMag(){
    lensMag -= magIncrement;
}

public void reset() { setLensOn(false); }

public void mousePressed(MouseEvent e) {
   if(!lensOn) return;
   if(SwingUtilities.isLeftMouseButton(e)){
       drawLens(e.getX(), e.getY());
   }
}
public void mouseClicked(MouseEvent e){}
public void mouseEntered(MouseEvent e){}
public void mouseExited(MouseEvent e){}

public void mouseReleased(MouseEvent e) {
   if(!lensOn) return;
   imageCanvas.setClip(null);
   zoom.magnify(0,0,1);
}

public void mouseDragged(MouseEvent e){
   if(SwingUtilities.isLeftMouseButton(e)){
       if(lensOn) drawLens(e.getX(), e.getY());
   }
```

```
  }
  public void mouseMoved(MouseEvent e){}
}
```

The `Lens` class constructor takes `ImageManipulator` as an input parameter. This means that we can pass the `ImageCanvas2D` object, which implements the `ImageManipulator` interface, as this parameter.

The `Lens` class implements both the `mouse` and the `mouseMotion` event–handling methods. A third-party object registers `Lens` with `ImageManipulator` to receive these events. Both of these events are needed for dragging the lens over the image.

When the mouse is pressed, a `Lens` object is created at the mouse position, and when the mouse is released the object is destroyed. When the mouse is dragged, the lens is moved. Figure 7.11 shows a screen shot of a lens overlaid on an image.

The principle of drawing the lens is simple. The shape of the lens is oval, so we use the `Ellipse2D` class for drawing it. Before the lens is drawn, the graphical context is clipped over a region covering the lens. For this reason, the same shape that is

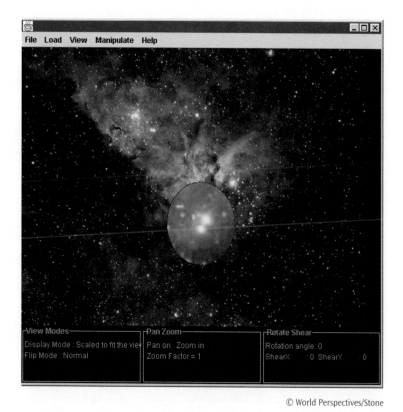

© World Perspectives/Stone

FIGURE 7.11   An interactive lens over an image

used for creating the lens is also used for clipping the graphical context. The image is then magnified and is drawn over the entire viewport. Because the graphical context is clipped, the image is drawn only over the region where the clipping is in effect.

When you drag the mouse, the lens is drawn at the previous position to erase that image. Recall from Chapter 5 that the XOR paint mode erases the graphical object if it is drawn twice. Drawing the original image at the previous clip area does exactly this. When the mouse is released, the clip region is reset, by the passing of `null` to the `setClip()` method.

The `Lens` class has several properties, including lens size and magnification factor. These properties allow the user to set the desirable lens and magnification attributes. Figure 7.12 shows a screen shot of a simple panel we created to add to our image viewer. When the `Lens` feature is invoked, this panel is launched. Listing 7.14 shows the code for the `LensPanel` class.

LISTING 7.14   The `LensPanel` class

```
public class LensPanel extends JPanel {
    protected ImageManipulator imageCanvas;
    protected Lens lens;
    protected boolean lensOn = false;
    public LensPanel(ImageManipulator manip) {
        imageCanvas = manip;
        if(manip != null) {
            manip.resetManipulation();
            lens = new Lens(manip);
            createUI();
        }
    }

    public void setLensOn(boolean onOrOff){
        if(lensOn ==  onOrOff) return;
        lensOn = onOrOff;
        if(lensOn) {
            imageCanvas.addMouseListener(lens);
            imageCanvas.addMouseMotionListener(lens);
        } else {
            imageCanvas.removeMouseListener(lens);
            imageCanvas.removeMouseMotionListener(lens);
        }
        lens.setLensOn(lensOn);
    }
```

FIGURE 7.12   The **Lens** panel

```
private void createUI() {
    // Code that creates lens panel
}

}
```

In our image viewer we added a new menu called **Manipulate** for selecting manipulation-related features. To invoke the lens feature, select this menu and click on **Lens.** The panel shown in Figure 7.12 will appear. Invoking `Lens` will reset all the manipulation operations but will preserve the display mode and flip mode settings.

Other Zooming Techniques

If your application requires a simple zoom feature, you can try other ways of zooming. We already mentioned one technique in Chapter 6: manipulating `drawImage()` parameters.

Using the Image Class

You need to use the following method to create a scaled instance of an image:

- ◆ `public Image getScaledInstance(int width, int height, int hints)`

Set the `width` and `height` parameters to suit the scale factor. If S_x is the desired scale factor in the x direction (magnified image width divided by original image width), then magnified width = $S_x \times$ image width. Likewise, if S_y is the desired scale factor in the y direction, then magnified height = $S_y \times$ image height.

The `hints` parameter is similar to the `renderingHints` attribute we saw in Chapter 5. This parameter can take any one of the following values:

- ◆ **SCALE_DEFAULT.** With this option the default scaling algorithm is used.
- ◆ **SCALE_FAST.** This option produces the image fast rather than smoothly. In this case scaling might use the nearest-neighbor algorithm.
- ◆ **SCALE_SMOOTH.** This option produces a smoother scaled image. Here the choice is image quality rather than speed. In this case the scaling algorithm used could be bilinear or bicubic, depending on the availability of the implementation in a given platform.
- ◆ **SCALE_REPLICATE.** With this option the scaling algorithm provided in the `ReplicateScaleFilter` class is used.
- ◆ **SCALE_AREA_AVERAGING.** With this option the area-averaging scaling algorithm provided in the `AreaAverageScaleFilter` class is used.

Using Filters

Two filter classes are available for scaling: `ReplicateScaleFilter` and `AreaAverage ScaleFilter`. Listing 7.15 shows an example using the latter:

LISTING 7.15 Scaling using filters

```
public Image scale(Image image, double magfactor) {
    int imageWidth = image.getWidth(imObs);
    int imageHeight = image.getHeight(imObs);
    AreaAverageScaleFilter scalefilter =
        new AreaAverageScaleFilter(imageWidth*magfactor,
                                    imageHeight*magfactor);
    ImageProducer ip =
        new FilteredImageSource(image.getSource(), scalefilter);
    return Toolkit.getDefaultToolkit().createImage(ip);
}
```

If you want to obtain the width and height of the original image, the input for the method shown in Listing 7.15 should pertain to an already loaded image.

Rotation, Flip, and Shear

Now that we have described the pan and zoom features in detail, it's time to look at other manipulation functions, which include rotate, flip, and shear. For the sake of convenience, instead of building individual interfaces for each of these functions, we'll build a common interface called `GeomManipController` for all of them. Again, we'll use the same design pattern we used for scroll and zoom. As mentioned earlier, with this design pattern the GUI is separated from control logic. Let's look at the manipulation operations one by one.

Rotation

Rotation may not be used as frequently as pan and zoom. Nevertheless, it is important to have it in your image viewer. Typically, rotation is performed around the midpoint of the image, but our interface can provide a method that specifies the rotation center. First, let's specify the get and set methods for the rotation angle property:

- `public double getRotationAngle();`
- `public void setRotationAngle(double theta);`

Here are the methods that perform rotation:

- `public void rotate(double theta);`
- `public void rotate(double theta, int rotCenterX, int rotCenterY);`

The first method rotates the image around the midpoint of the image. The second one rotates the image around a point specified by the input parameters.

Flip

We discussed the fundamentals of flip in Chapter 4. The method for flipping an image at any position or at any state is

◆ `public void flip(int flipMode)`

The `flipMode` parameter can be any one of the four values defined in the `FlipMode` class (see Chapter 6).

Shear

Just as we specified the `magFactor` property for the scaling operation, for shear we'll specify the `shearFactor` property. The get and set methods for this property are

◆ `public double getShearFactor();`
◆ `public void setShearFactor(double shear);`

The method for shearing an image at any stage of the manipulation is

◆ `public void shear(double shx, double shy);`

The `shx` and `shy` parameters are the shear factors in the x and y directions, respectively.

Implementing Rotation, Flip, and Shear

Let's develop the `GeomManip` class in a manner similar to what we did for pan and zoom. We'll build the controller class first and then the GUI class. Here are the two classes:

1. **`GeomManip`.** This class implements the `GeomManipController` interface.
2. **`ManipUI`.** This class implements the slider interfaces for adjusting the rotate and shear values.

Figure 7.13 shows the model-view-controller architecture for the rotation and shear features, which resembles the design for scroll and for zoom. Listing 7.16 shows the code for `GeomManip`.

LISTING 7.16 The GeomManip class

```
package com.vistech.imageviewer;
import java.io.*;
import java.awt.*;
```

continued

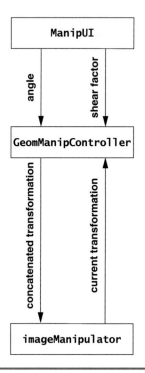

FIGURE 7.13   The data flow for rotation and shear

```java
import java.awt.event.*;
import java.awt.image.*;
import java.awt.geom.*;

public class GeomManip  implements GeomManipController  {
    protected AffineTransform atx = new AffineTransform();
    // Rotation variables
    protected double rotationAngle = 0.0;
    protected boolean rotateOn = true;
    protected int rotationCenterX = 0;
    protected int rotationCenterY = 0;
    // Shear variables
    protected boolean shearOn = true;
    protected double shearFactor = 0.0;
    protected double shearX =0.0, shearY=0.0;
    protected ImageManipulator imageCanvas;
    protected int flipMode = 0;

    public GeomManip(){}
    public GeomManip(ImageManipulator imageCanvas){ this.imageCanvas = imageCanvas;}

    public void setImageManipulator(ImageManipulator imageCanvas){
        this.imageCanvas = imageCanvas;
    }
}
```

```
public synchronized void setFlipMode(int mode){
   if(mode == flipMode) return;
   int oldmode = flipMode;
   flipMode = mode;
}

public int getFlipMode(){ return flipMode;}

public void setShearFactor(double shearFactor){
   this.shearFactor = shearFactor;
   imageCanvas.setShearFactor(shearFactor);
}
public double getShearFactor(){ return shearFactor;}

public double getShearFactorX(){ return shearX;}
public double getShearFactorY(){return shearY;}

public void setRotationAngle(double rotationAngle){
   this.rotationAngle = rotationAngle;
   imageCanvas.setRotationAngle(rotationAngle);
}

public double getRotationAngle(){ return rotationAngle;}

public void rotate(double theta){
   double ang = this.rotationAngle -theta;
   Dimension dim = imageCanvas.getImageSize();
   int wid = dim.width;
   int ht  = dim.height;
   setRotationAngle(theta);
   atx = imageCanvas.getTransform();
   atx.rotate(ang, wid/2, ht/2);
   imageCanvas.applyTransform(atx);
}

public void rotate(double theta, int rotCenterX, int rotCenterY){
   double ang = this.rotationAngle -theta;
   setRotationAngle(theta);
   atx = imageCanvas.getTransform();
   atx.rotate(ang, rotCenterX, rotCenterY);
   imageCanvas.applyTransform(atx);
}

public void resetAndRotate(double theta) {
   BufferedImage image = imageCanvas.getOffScreenImage();
   int wid = image.getWidth();
   int ht  = image.getHeight();
   setRotationAngle(theta);
   atx.setToRotation(theta, wid/2, ht/2);
   imageCanvas.applyTransform(atx);
}

public void shear(double shx, double shy){
   double shxIncr = shearX -shx;
   double shyIncr = shearY -shy;
   setShearFactor(shx);
```

continued

```java
      this.shearX = shx;
      this.shearY = shy;
      atx = imageCanvas.getTransform();
      atx.shear(shxIncr, shyIncr);
      imageCanvas.applyTransform(atx);
   }

   public void shearIncr(double shxIncr, double shyIncr){
      shearX += shxIncr;
      shearY += shyIncr;
      setShearFactor(shearX);
      atx.shear(shxIncr, shyIncr);
      imageCanvas.applyTransform(atx);
   }

   public void resetAndShear(double shx, double shy){
      shearX =shx; shearY = shy;
      atx.setToShear(shx,shy);
      setShearFactor(shearX);
      imageCanvas.applyTransform(atx);
   }

   public static AffineTransform createFlipTransform(int mode,
                                           int imageWid,
                                           int imageHt){
      AffineTransform at = new AffineTransform();
      switch(mode){
          case FlipMode.NORMAL:
            break;
          case FlipMode.TOP_BOTTOM:
            at =  new AffineTransform(new double[] {1.0,0.0,0.0,-1.0});
            at.translate(0.0, -imageHt);
            break;
          case FlipMode.LEFT_RIGHT :
            at = new AffineTransform(new double[] {-1.0,0.0,0.0,1.0});
            at.translate(-imageWid, 0.0);
            break;
          case FlipMode.TOP_BOTTOM_LEFT_RIGHT:
            at = new AffineTransform(new double[] {-1.0,0.0,0.0,-1.0});
            at.translate(-imageWid, -imageHt);
            break;
          default:
      }
      return at;
   }

   public void flip(int mode){
      Dimension dim = imageCanvas.getImageSize();
      int wid = dim.width;
      int ht  = dim.height;
      AffineTransform flipTx = createFlipTransform(mode,wid,ht);
      atx = imageCanvas.getTransform();
      atx.concatenate(flipTx);
      imageCanvas.applyTransform(atx);
   }

   public void resetAndFlip(int mode){
      atx = new AffineTransform();
```

```
        flip(mode);
    }

    public void resetManipulation(){
        shearX = 0.0; shearY = 0.0;
        rotationAngle = 0.0;
        atx = new AffineTransform();
    }
}
```

Typically, images are rotated about their midpoint. In some situations, however, an image can be rotated around any arbitrary point. The `rotate()` methods in the `GeomManip` class meet both of these requirements.

The `rotate(theta)` method rotates the image about its midpoint, irrespective of where the image is positioned in the viewport. The input parameter `theta` is the angle of rotation from the original position of the image. When this method is called, the image might have been rotated already. This method therefore computes the difference between current rotation angle and the input. Then it gets the midpoint of the current image on the canvas. It then calls the `rotate()` method of the `AffineTransform` class with the difference in angles and the center point of the image as its inputs.

The `rotate(theta, rotCenterX, rotCenterY)` method rotates the image about any arbitrary point. The `resetAndRotate()` method implements absolute rotation about the midpoint. The `setToRotation()` method resets `atx` and rotates it by a fixed amount.

The shear methods are similar to the scale and rotate methods.

The `AffineTransform` class doesn't have an explicit flip transformation. We discussed how to implement flip in the preceding section and defined a method called `createFlipTransform()`. The `flip()` method uses `createFlipTransform()` to flip the image at any stage of image manipulation. Note that here we use the `concatenate()` method to concatenate the flip transformation to the current transformation `atx`. The `resetAndFlip()` method resets the current transformation and flips the image in the direction specified in the input.

User Interface for Rotation and Shear

Implementing rotation and shear is straightforward. We can directly use the transformation methods for rotation and shear in the `GeomManip` class. But first we need a GUI to operate on the `GeomManip` class. Figure 7.14 shows a screen shot of a panel that has two tabs: **Rotate** and **Shear.** To launch this panel, select the **Rotate/Shear** option in the **Manipulate** menu. You can either use the slider or enter a value in the text field. Notice that in the **Rotate** tab, the angles vary from −360 to +360, thereby enabling rotation in the clockwise or counterclockwise direction. When you move the slider, the text field reflects the slider's current value.

FIGURE 7.14   The **Rotate** and **Shear** panel

We'll provide only some code snippets because implementing the GUI involves a large chunk of code. Listing 7.17 shows the code for `ManipUI`.

LISTING 7.17   The `ManipUI` class

```java
public class ManipUI extends JPanel{
    protected JTabbedPane jtp;
    protected  int startValue = 0;
    protected  int minValue = -360, maxValue = 360;
    protected  JTextField rotateValueField;
    protected  double rotateValue = 0.0;
    protected  int rotateStartValue = 0;
    protected  JSlider rotateSlider;

    protected int shearMinValue = -200;
    protected int shearMaxValue = 200;
    protected JTextField shearValueField;
    protected int shearValue = 0;
    protected int shearStartValue = 0;
    protected JSlider shearSlider;
    protected GeomManipController imageViewer;

    public ManipUI(GeomManipController manip) {
        imageViewer = manip;
        createUI();
    }

    private void createUI() {
        JPanel rpanel = createRotatePanel();
        JPanel spanel = createShearPanel();
        jtp = new JTabbedPane();
        jtp.addTab("Rotate", rpanel);
        jtp.addTab("Shear", spanel);
        add(jtp);
    }

    protected JPanel createRotatePanel() {
        JButton resetButton = new JButton("Reset Rotate");
        resetButton.addActionListener(
            new ActionListener() {
                public void actionPerformed(ActionEvent e){
                    rotateSlider.setValue(rotateStartValue);
                    rotateValueField.setText((new Double(rotateStartValue)).toString());
                    imageViewer.rotate(0.0);
```

```java
                }
            }
        );

        rotateValueField = new JTextField(5);
        rotateValueField.addActionListener(
            new ActionListener() {
                public void actionPerformed(ActionEvent e){
                    try {
                        String str = ((JTextField)e.getSource()).getText();
                        rotateValue = (Double.valueOf(str)).doubleValue();

                        rotateSlider.setValue((int)rotateValue);
                        imageViewer.rotate(rotateValue*(Math.PI/180.0));
                    } catch (Exception e1){}
                }
            }
        );

        rotateValueField.setText(Integer.toString(rotateStartValue));
        JLabel rotateLabel = new JLabel("Rotate");

        rotateSlider = new JSlider(minValue,maxValue,startValue);
        rotateSlider.setMajorTickSpacing(120);
        rotateSlider.setMinorTickSpacing(12);
        rotateSlider.setExtent(12);
        rotateSlider.setPaintTicks(true);
        rotateSlider.setPaintLabels(true);

        rotateSlider.addChangeListener(
            new ChangeListener() {
                public void stateChanged(ChangeEvent e){
                    double rotateValueOld = rotateValue;
                    rotateValue = ((JSlider)(e.getSource())).getValue();
                    imageViewer.rotate(rotateValue*(Math.PI/180.0));
                    rotateValueField.setText(Integer.toString((int)rotateValue));
                }
            }
        );

        JPanel rotatepan = new JPanel();
       // Grid layout
      return rotatepan;
    }

    protected JPanel createShearPanel() {

        // Code similar to createRotatePanel
    }

    public void resetManipulation(){
        shearSlider.setValue((int)(shearStartValue*100));
        shearValueField.setText(Double.toString(shearStartValue));
        rotateValueField.setText(Integer.toString((int)rotateStartValue));
        rotateSlider.setValue((int)rotateStartValue);
    }
}
```

Most of the code in Listing 7.17 is self-explanatory. The `rotateSlider` event–handling method calls the `rotate()` method with the current `rotateSlider` value. Likewise, the `shearSlider` event–handling method calls the `shear()` method with the current `shearSlider` value.

The code snippets that follow, which are from the `ImageManip2D` application, show how to use the `GeomManip` and `ManipUI` classes in an application:

```
ImageManipulator  viewer = new ImageCanvas2D();
GeomManipController manip = new GeomManip(viewer);
```

```
rot.addActionListener(
    new ActionListener() {
      public void actionPerformed(ActionEvent e){
          if(manipFrame == null) {
              manipFrame = new JFrame();
              ManipUI manipui = new ManipUI(manip);
              manipFrame.getContentPane().add(manipui);
              manipFrame.pack();
          }
          manipFrame.show();
      }
    }
);
```

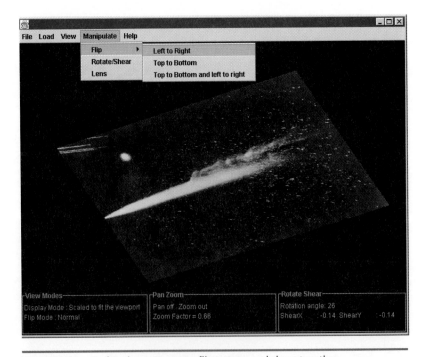

FIGURE 7.15 Performing pan, zoom, flip, rotate, and shear together

The `rot` parameter represents the **Rotate/Shear** option on the **Manipulate** menu. The code snippet is the event handler that launches the frame shown in Figure 7.14.

The screen shot in Figure 7.15 shows the image viewer when pan, zoom, rotate, and shear have all been performed. Besides the **Lens** and **Rotate/Shear** options, the **Manipulate** menu also has the option **Flip.**

Running the Image Viewer

To run the `ImageManip2D` application, type "java app.ImageManip2D" on the command line. When the application frame comes up, select **Load | List Select** to launch the `MultiImageLoader` bean. When this bean is launched, you can either enter the desired directory or click on the **Browse** option. Once you have selected an image, click on **Load Image** to display it.

To pan and zoom the displayed image, right-click on the viewport to launch a pop-up menu with three items: **Pan, Zoom in,** and **Zoom out** (see Figure 7.10). If you select **Pan,** drag the mouse to pan the image. If you select **Zoom in** or **Zoom out,** position the cursor at a desired position and click. If **Zoom in** is selected, the displayed image will be magnified with the position of the mouse as the center of the image. Likewise, **Zoom out** will shrink the displayed image whenever you click on the image.

To rotate and shear the image, select the **Manipulate** menu, which has three menu items: **Flip, Rotate/Shear,** and **Lens** (see Figure 7.15). If you select **Lens,** the image viewer application will launch a **Lens** panel as shown in Figure 7.12. Note that the lens feature resets all manipulations. To use the lens feature, drag the mouse over the image. You can change the size of the lens with the options in the **Lens** panel.

If you select **Rotate/Shear,** the panel shown in Figure 7.14 will be launched. To rotate the image, select the **Rotate** tab and adjust the slider. You can see the image rotating at its midpoint. Likewise, to shear the image, adjust the **Shear** slider.

The **Flip** menu item has three subitems: **Left to Right, Top to Bottom,** and **Top to Bottom and left to right** (see Figure 7.15). Select any one of these options to flip the image in the desired direction.

To reset manipulation, select **View | Display Mode** and click on the desired display mode. This action will move the image to the default position with the selected display mode.

Conclusion

In this chapter we discussed how to implement different types of image manipulation operations. Implementation of manipulation functions is much easier with the

`AffineTransform` class, which allows the functions to be combined in any order without much coding.

The image viewer application that we built in this chapter incorporates different types of image manipulations. While running these operations, you may have noticed that performance is not at all a problem.

With the design described in this chapter, the manipulation operations are built like building blocks. Applications need to construct only the functions they require at a given time. In addition, the manipulation logic is separated from the GUI, allowing application developers to choose any GUI they like for generating image manipulation parameters. As we'll see in Part III (the JAI chapters), the manipulation classes described in this chapter are reused in other applications.

Manipulating Image Data in Java 2D

8

IN THE PRECEDING CHAPTERS we used the `BufferedImage` object as an off-screen image; that is, we created data content in the `BufferedImage` object indirectly by drawing over its graphical context. In this chapter we'll look at the `BufferedImage` class from a different perspective: how to use it to read and write underlying pixel data.

Reading and writing pixels in Java 2D require the knowledge of two basic concepts: color model and sample model. To read image data, we need to know how pixels are stored. The `SampleModel` class associated with `BufferedImage` describes that. To manipulate image data, we need to know how to interpret the pixel values. The `ColorModel` class associated with `BufferedImage` describes that. In this chapter we'll look at both `ColorModel` and `SampleModel` class hierarchies. We'll use these classes to create different types of `BufferedImage` objects directly from data. These classes can also be used for extracting pixels, as we will show through some examples.

Java 2D also has classes that can manipulate the image without explicitly reading pixels. There are six filter operator classes that can perform several different operations. We'll provide some examples showing how to use these operators. One example is about adjusting window and level, which are common operations in medical image visualization.

Another Look at the BufferedImage Class

The `BufferedImage` class can directly represent an image. As we saw in Chapter 6, both the JPEG and the Image I/O codecs read an image as a `BufferedImage` object. This is similar to how the `getImage()` method in AWT imaging loads image data into the `Image` object (see Chapter 2). Unlike the `Image` class, however, the `Buffered Image` class has the capability to read and write pixel data. So if you load your image

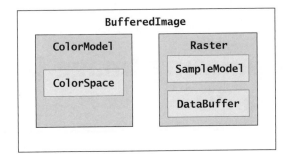

FIGURE 8.1   The `BufferedImage` structure

as a `BufferedImage` object, there is no need to use the `PixelGrabber` class to read pixels or the `MemoryImageSource` class to write pixels.

To use the `BufferedImage` class for reading and writing pixels requires the knowledge of many other classes and concepts. Let's look inside the `BufferedImage` object. As shown in Figure 8.1, it contains two objects: `ColorModel` and `Raster`. The `ColorModel` object interprets how a pixel is represented in terms of color. The `Raster` object describes how the image data is to be stored and accessed. We'll discuss these classes in great detail later in this chapter.

As Figure 8.1 shows, a `Raster` object is made up of two objects: `SampleModel` and `DataBuffer`. A pixel may have one more components called *samples*. A sample can represent anything. For example, it may represent color-related information such as the color value, an index to a color, or an alpha value. In a nonvisual type of image, it may not represent color at all. For instance, an image in the frequency domain may represent some frequency values.

The `SampleModel` class provides a description of how samples are organized into a pixel. The `DataBuffer` object contains the actual image data stored in a manner specified by `SampleModel`. Thus you need both `ColorModel` and `SampleModel` to describe an image. `ColorModel` interprets the components of a pixel, and `SampleModel` describes how the pixels and its components are organized to make up the image data.

First let's look at the general concepts and the related APIs.

Color Management

Color is a visual sensation experienced by our eyes. The perceived color of an object depends on many factors, including the light source that illuminates it and the color of the surrounding area. The physics of light therefore plays an important role in color representation.

Light is electromagnetic energy (its wavelength varies from 350 to 780 nanometers [nm]) that produces visual sensation by stimulating the retina of the eye. The retina has two types of photoreceptors:

1. **Rods.** These receptors provide scotopic vision, which means they respond to lower magnitudes of illumination, such as darkness. They are long, thin, and numerous (on the order of 100 million per eye).

2. **Cones.** These receptors provide photopic vision, which means they respond to a higher order of magnitude of illumination, such as bright sunlight. Cones are shorter, thicker, and fewer in number compared to rods. Cones are also responsible for color vision.

Colored Light

According to Thomas Young, the nineteenth-century scientist who presented the classical theory of color, any color can be reproduced by the appropriate mixing of three primary colors. Our eyes have three different types of cones, whose responses peak at three different wavelengths of the visible electromagnetic spectrum. These peaks occur at 630 nm (red), 530 nm (green), and 450 nm (blue). This is the basis for displaying color on video monitors, which use the three primary colors red, green, and blue.

Before we proceed further, let's describe the difference between luminance and brightness. *Luminance* is the intensity of an object. It doesn't depend on the luminance of the surrounding objects. *Brightness,* on the other hand, is the *perceived* luminance of an object, and it does depend on the luminance of surrounding objects. This means that two objects with the same luminance can have different brightness if the surroundings are different.

The human eye has the ability to discriminate thousands of colors. Our eyes distinguish colors through perceptual attributes such as shade, tint, and tone. On the basis of our perception, models have been developed to represent colors. The three types of attributes used to describe a color based on our intuition are

1. **Hue.** This attribute represents the "colorness," the attribute that determines why we name a color in a particular way—say, red, yellow, or blue.

2. **Saturation.** This attribute tells how much white is added to monochromatic light. For instance, red is highly saturated, whereas pink is relatively unsaturated.

3. **Brightness.** This attribute describes how bright a color appears.

In this discussion we have indirectly described two ways of representing a color:

1. Using a combination of red, green, or blue primaries
2. Using a combination of hue, saturation, and brightness

These are some of the most popular schemes, but there are many other ways of representing colors. Let's look at some of them.

Color Space

Specifying and measuring colors is a huge challenge. The perceived color depends on many factors, including the human observer's judgment, lighting, and surrounding color. What is needed, therefore, is a quantitative way of measuring colors.

Colorimetry is the science of specifying and measuring colors. The parameters that are used for measuring colors are dominant wavelength, excitation purity, and luminance. They correspond approximately to hue, saturation, and brightness.

Color space is a coordinate system that represents a color numerically. A typical color coordinate system has three or more coordinate axes. In other words, color space is a color representation scheme.

An ideal color representation system should be able to do the following:

◆ Describe a color.
◆ Represent all visible colors. The range of colors represented by a color coordinate system is called the *gamut*.
◆ Represent a color so that it appears the same regardless of the devices used to capture it. For instance, if you print an image, it should appear the same as on the monitor. This means that we need a device-independent system of color specification. Developing such a specification is not an easy task. Over the years, there have been many attempts to achieve such a specification. The pioneering work in this area was done by the International Commission on Illumination (usually referred to as CIE, an abbreviation that comes from its French name) in 1931. This space, called XYZ, will be discussed later in this section.

Recently, Hewlett-Packard and Microsoft proposed a device-independent color space called standard RGB (sRGB). This specification is gaining ground, especially in the Internet imaging area.

Not all color spaces have all the capabilities mentioned here. Some, for example, are device dependent. Let's look at device-dependent color coordinate systems first, followed by device-independent systems.

The RGB System

We can represent the RGB color system as a unit cube with three primary colors—red (*R*), green (*G*), and blue (*B*)—as the axes (see Figure 8.2). Each point within the cube is represented as a color, which can be generated as a linear combination of red, blue, and green values. So a color (*C*) is given by the following equation:

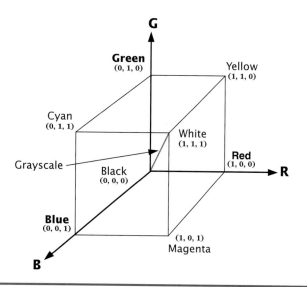

FIGURE 8.2   The RGB color coordinate system

$$C = R\boldsymbol{i} + G\boldsymbol{j} + B\boldsymbol{k}$$

where $\boldsymbol{i}, \boldsymbol{j}$, and $\boldsymbol{k}$ represent vectors in a three-dimensional RGB color space.

With the RGB scheme, the origin of the cube (0, 0, 0) is black, and the opposite vertex of the origin (1, 1, 1) is white. The shades of gray are therefore represented along the main diagonal. In other words, each point along this diagonal has equal contributions from the primary colors.

The RGB system is an additive system; that is, the primary colors are added together to produce another color. This scheme works well for video monitors, which produce a color by combining light from the screen phosphors. However, the RGB system is device dependent. The color space is determined by the amount of signal applied to the hardware that generates red, green, and blue signals. In the case of CRT monitors, this hardware consists of three electron guns.

The CMYK System

Whereas the RGB system is widely used in video monitors, hard-copy devices such as printers and plotters use a different color system, called CMY. In this system the primary colors are cyan (*C*), magenta (*M*), and yellow (*Y*) (see Figure 8.3). This is a subtractive system; that is, the components of the incident light are subtracted to produce different colors.

The unit cube shown in Figure 8.3 is the inverse of the cube in Figure 8.2: The origin is white, and its opposite vertex is black. This model is often called the CMYK

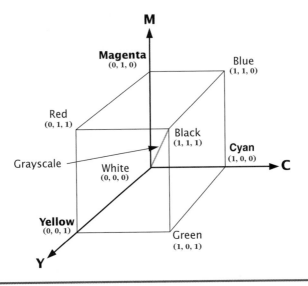

FIGURE 8.3   The CMY color coordinate system

system because the printing process uses a collection of four ink dots—one each for the primary colors and black. Black is needed because a combination of cyan, magenta, and yellow produces dark gray instead of black.

The HSV (HSB) System

The HSV (hue, saturation, value) system is also called the HSB (hue, saturation, and brightness) system, which we discussed earlier. Whereas the RGB and CMY systems were developed with hardware systems in mind, the HSB system is user oriented. It is a cylindrical coordinate system with hue, saturation, and brightness as the axes (see Figure 8.4). As mentioned earlier, this system somewhat maps to the artist's tint, shade, and tone.

In reference to Figure 8.4,

1. **Hue** (H) is presented as an angle about the vertical axis. Its 360-degree range is divided into intervals of 60 to form a hexagon. Each vertex of this hexagon represents a color.

2. The **saturation** (S) value is a ratio that ranges from 0 at the center line to 1 at the triangular sides of the hexacone.

3. **Brightness** (or value, V) is represented along the vertical axis. At the bottom point of the hexacone, $V = 0$; at the top, $V = 1$.

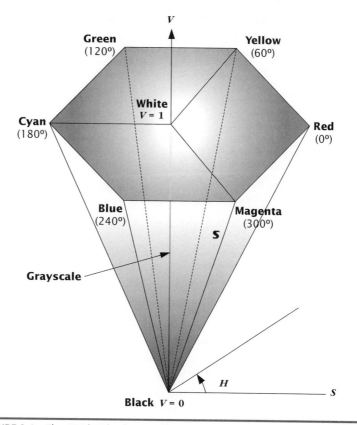

FIGURE 8.4   The HSV (HSB) color coordinate system

A point within the unit hexacone shown in Figure 8.4 represents a color. When $S = 0$ and $V = 1$, the color is white. The intermediate values of V when $S = 0$ represent shades of gray. (Note that when $S = 0$, H is irrelevant.)

The CIEXYZ System

CIE defined a color system with three primary colors, called X, Y, and Z. These are not real colors; rather they defined mathematically with positive color-matching functions, which specify the amount of each color needed to describe any color.

The CIEXYZ system is a standard that is recognized internationally for defining all colors. A color in this system is given by the equation $C = X\mathbf{X} + Y\mathbf{Y} + Z\mathbf{Z}$, where X, Y, and Z are the amount of weight applied to match a color C. X, Y, and Z replace the red, green, and blue of the RGB system.

To specify a color, CIE defines *chromaticity* values, which are given by the following equations:

$$x = \frac{X}{(X + Y + Z)}$$

$$y = \frac{Y}{(X + Y + Z)}$$

$$z = \frac{Z}{(X + Y + Z)}$$

and $x + y + z = 1$. Chromaticity values are normally specified by only x and y because these values depend on the dominant wavelength and saturation, and not on luminance.

The Standard RGB System

The standard RGB color space (also known as sRGB) is the result of a recent attempt at developing a device-independent color space. It was originally proposed by Microsoft and Hewlett-Packard with the Internet as its primary target. As its name suggests, it is based on the RGB color space.

In a device-dependent RGB color space, a color depends on the hardware. In a CRT terminal for instance, different colors are generated by variation in the voltages applied to the three electron guns (red, green, and blue) in the cathode ray tube. This process amounts to mapping the color space of a monitor to the voltages. The same is true with the CMYK color space. In an ink-jet printer, for example, cyan, magenta, yellow, and black are sprayed onto the paper. Again the color depends on the amount of signal applied to the ink-jet heads.

Although the primary colors of the sRGB space are red, green, and blue, the color space does not depend on voltages. Instead, it is determined by colorimetry. The sRGB color space is defined by the following:

- **Viewing-environment parameters.** The specs define many parameters. Some examples are luminance level, illuminant white, image surround, and viewing flare.
- **Standard device space colorimetric definitions and transformations.** The color encoding is based on the CIE colorimetry. The CIE colorimetric values depend on the viewing environment and the spectral sensitivities of the device.

Red, green, and blue were chosen as primary colors mainly because of their wide use in devices such as computer monitors, scanners, and digital cameras. Moreover, the conversion of RGB space to sRGB space is straightforward.

The sRGB space is now gaining wider acceptance. As we'll see later in the chapter, sRGB is the default color space of the `Color` class in Java. To view the proposal, visit http://www.w3.org/Graphics/sRGB.html. The second part of the sRGB proposal defines both the viewing-environment parameters and the transformations that are to be used to encode a color.

The ICC Color Profile

The International Color Consortium (ICC) has developed its own standard to map colors correctly from one device to another. The basic idea here is to build a profile for each type of device based on the specification developed by the ICC. When an image or a document is read in another device, the profile from the device that captured the image is used for decoding the color.

An ICC profile consists of a table of contents that is followed by tagged data. The ICC profile specs define several types of profiles:

◆ Input device
◆ Display device
◆ Output device
◆ Color space conversion
◆ Device linking
◆ Abstract profile

Each profile type has some mandatory tags.

Vendors use the viewing-environment parameters and CIE-based colorimetry to generate a profile for a device. For instance, to create a profile for an output device such as a printer, a reference image is printed and the printed colors are measured according to the CIE-based colorimetry. This data is compared with the reference data to build a profile. The reference image contains the CIE colors, which are distributed as evenly as possible. A reverse process is employed for building a profile for input devices such as scanners.

The ICC profile specs also describe how to embed profiles in encapsulated PostScript, PICT, and TIFF files.

Vendors distribute the device profiles. These profiles can be part of the operating system or Web browser. The schematic in Figure 8.5 illustrates how the profiles are used for correctly mapping colors.

Overview of the Color API in Java 2D

Now that we have described the basics of color, it's time to discuss the support for color in Java. In AWT imaging, the support for color is limited. AWT imaging has just

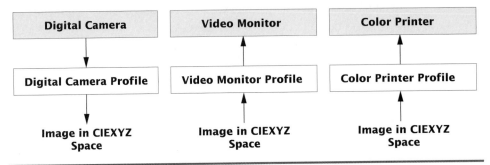

FIGURE 8.5   Sample color conversion from a digital camera to a video monitor and a color printer

a few classes to represent and manage color. The `Color` class represents the color, and the two color-model classes—`DirectColorModel` and `IndexColorModel`—indirectly represent color spaces. Java 2D has extensive support for color, with APIs defined to explicitly represent color spaces and ICC profiles. Even the basic `Color` class was modified to fit the new architecture.

Starting with JDK 1.2, the core Java API has a new package, called `java.awt.color`, to support color management. For historic reasons, the `Color` class and the two color-model classes remain in the `java.awt` package itself. The `java.awt.color` package has the following classes:

- `ColorSpace`
- `ICC_ColorSpace`
- `ICC_Profile`
- `ICC_ProfileGray`
- `ICC_ProfileRGB`

The relationships among these classes are illustrated in Figure 8.6.

Using the ColorSpace Class

The `ColorSpace` class is a convenient abstract class that has methods and constants for representing color coordinates. An RGB color space, for instance, is the color within the unit cube in Figure 8.2. This color space, however, is not device independent. Every device represents its own RGB color space, so a color in one device may appear to be different in another device. The same is true with the CMYK system.

The CIEXYZ system, however, as mentioned earlier, does not depend on any devices. Here the color definition is absolute. This system is used for converting one color system to another. The sRGB system is also device independent, and it is the default color space in Java.

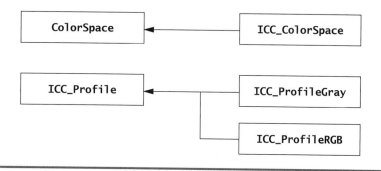

FIGURE 8.6   Classes in the `java.awt.color` package

The `ColorSpace` class defines constants for different color coordinate systems. There are two types of constants. Table 8.1 shows the color space types that can be instantiated as `ColorSpace` objects by the `getInstance()` method. Table 8.2 shows the `ColorSpace` family types, which are needed by the other APIs in Java 2D.

Creating a ColorSpace Instance

The `ColorSpace` class has the following factory method, which can create one of the color spaces given in Table 8.1:

♦ **`public static ColorSpace getInstance(int colorspace)`**

Here's an example:

```
ColorSpace crgbSpace = ColorSpace.getInstance(ColorSpace.CS_sRGB);
```

TABLE 8.1   `ColorSpace` Types

TYPE	DESCRIPTION
CS_sRGB	The standard RGB space.
CS_LINEAR_RGB	A color space based on the same RGB primaries as CS_sRGB, but with a linear tone reproduction curve.
CS_CIEXYZ	The CIEXYZ conversion color space.
CS_GRAY	The built-in linear grayscale color space.
CS_PYCC	The photo YCC conversion color space. Photo YCC is a color-encoding scheme developed by Kodak. Images in Photo CD are stored using this scheme. YCC represents a luminance channel (Y) and two chrominance channels (CC).

TABLE 8.2   ColorSpace Family Types

TYPE	DESCRIPTION
TYPE_GRAY	Any of the family of gray color spaces.
TYPE_HSV	Any of the family of HSV (HSB) color spaces.
TYPE_HLS	Any of the family of HLS (hue, lightness, saturation) color spaces. This system is similar to the HSV model, except that it is represented by a double hexacone.
TYPE_CMYK	Any of the family of CMYK color spaces.
TYPE_CMY	Any of the family of CMY color spaces.
TYPE_2CLR	Generic 2-component color spaces.
TYPE_3CLR	Generic 3-component color spaces.
TYPE_4CLR	Generic 4-component color spaces.
TYPE_5CLR	Generic 5-component color spaces.
TYPE_6CLR	Generic 6-component color spaces.
TYPE_7CLR	Generic 7-component color spaces.
TYPE_8CLR	Generic 8-component color spaces.
TYPE_9CLR	Generic 9-component color spaces.
TYPE_ACLR	Generic 10-component color spaces.
TYPE_BCLR	Generic 11-component color spaces.
TYPE_CCLR	Generic 12-component color spaces.
TYPE_DCLR	Generic 13-component color spaces.
TYPE_ECLR	Generic 14-component color spaces.
TYPE_FCLR	Generic 15-component color spaces.

The input parameter should be one of the constants that starts with *CS_*. The ColorSpace class constants that start with the substring *TYPE_* (see Table 8.2) should not be used with the getInstance() method.

The ColorSpace class has a subclass called ICC_ColorSpace, the constructor of which takes an ICC_Profile object as input, which we'll discuss shortly.

Color Conversion

The ColorSpace class has methods that convert a value from CIEXYZ or sRGB space to the color space represented by the ColorSpace object:

- **public abstract float[] fromCIEXYZ(float[] colorvalue)**
- **public abstract float[] fromRGB(float[] rgbvalue)**

The input parameter of these methods is an array that represents the color component values and is of length three. For the first method, the array should contain the X, Y, and Z values; for the second, the R, G, and B values.

These are abstract methods that are implemented to represent an actual color space. For example, to convert a color value that is in CIEXYZ space to sRGB space, you would do something like this:

```
float[] someValue = { 100, 25, 86};
ColorSpace crgbSpace = ColorSpace.getInstance(ColorSpace.CS_sRGB);
crgbSpace.fromCIEXYZ(someValue);
```

The following methods convert the color values in the color space represented by `ColorSpace` to CIEXYZ or sRGB space, respectively:

- **`public abstract float[] toCIEXYZ(float[] colorvalue)`**
- **`public abstract float[] toRGB(float[] colorvalue)`**

Other Utility Methods

The following methods obtain the color space information with regard to type, number of components, and name, respectively:

- **`public int getType()`**
- **`public int getNumComponents()`**
- **`public String getName(int idx)`**

And this utility method checks whether the `ColorSpace` object is of sRGB type:

- **`public boolean isC_sRGB()`**

Using the ICC_Profile Class

As its name suggests, the `ICC_Profile` class represents the ICC profile. It is an abstract class with two concrete subclasses: `ICC_ProfileGray` and `ICC_ProfileRGB`.

The `ICC_Profile` class has a large number of fields representing the tags of the ICC profile, and it has methods for reading and writing to an `ICC_Profile` file.

Constructing an ICC_Profile Object

To construct an `ICC_Profile` object, you can use the following factory methods:

- **`public static ICC_Profile getInstance(byte[] data)`**
- **`public static ICC_Profile getInstance(String fileName)`**
  `throws IOException`
- **`public static ICC_Profile getInstance(InputStream s)`**
  `throws IOException`

An `ICC_Profile` object can be created directly from data in a file, an `InputStream` object, or an array of bytes. Here's an example:

```
try {
    ICC_Profile  prof = ICC_Profile("SomeProfile.icm");
}catch(IOException e) { }
```

If a color space is represented by one of the constants in Table 8.1, the `ICC_Profile` can be directly generated from the following method:

- ◆ **public static ICC_Profile getInstance(int cspace)**

Obtaining the Profile Type Information

The following method returns the color space type of the profile connection space (PCS):

- ◆ **public int getPCSType()**

The returned value is one of the constants defined in the **ColorSpace** class that starts with *TYPE_* (see Table 8.2). This is the output color space of the profile. In Figure 8.5 the output color space of the digital camera profile is represented by the constant `CIE_XYZ`.

As mentioned earlier, `ICC_Profile` is defined for many types of devices. For input, display, or output types of profiles, this method returns either `TYPE_XYZ` or `TYPE_LAB`. For a device link profile, the return value can be any of the color space type constants.

The following method returns the input color space of the profile:

- ◆ **public int getColorSpaceType()**

In Figure 8.5 the input color space is represented by the constant `CIE_XYZ`. The return value is one of the *TYPE_* constants in the **ColorSpace** class (see Table 8.2).

The following methods obtain other information about the profile:

- ◆ **public int getProfileClass()**
- ◆ **public int getMinorVersion()**
- ◆ **public int getMajorVersion()**

Reading and Writing to the Profile File

The following methods get the profile data, set it, and write it to an **OutputStream** object or a file.

- ◆ **public byte[] getData()**
- ◆ **public byte[] getData(int tagSignature)**
- ◆ **public void setData(int tagSignature, byte[] tagData)**

- ◆ `public void write(OutputStream s) throws IOException`
- ◆ `public void write(String fileName) throws IOException`

Constructing an ICC_ColorSpace Object

The `ICC_ColorSpace` class is a concrete subclass of `ColorSpace`. It can be directly instantiated by its constructor:

- ◆ `public ICC_ColorSpace(ICC_Profile profile)`

If you have the profile file for a color space, you can create a `ColorSpace` object by using this method, as illlustrated here:

```
ICC_Profile myCSProfile = new ICC_Profile("myprofilefile");
ColorSpace myColorSpace = new ICC_ColorSpace(myCSProfile);
```

Using the ColorModel Classes

The `ColorModel` class hierarchy is shown in Figure 8.7. This class represents the organization of a pixel in terms of its color and alpha components. The alpha component refers to the transparency of the pixel.

The `ColorModel` class supports two representations of pixels:

1. As a single `byte` or `int` type
2. As an array of Java primitive types

The first type of representation was introduced in JDK 1.0 for AWT imaging. Java 2D and JAI, however, require more flexibility in pixel representation. The second type of representation was introduced in Java 2D.

The `DirectColorModel` and `IndexColorModel` classes were introduced in JDK 1.0. To maintain compatibility with that version, these classes retain their old methods.

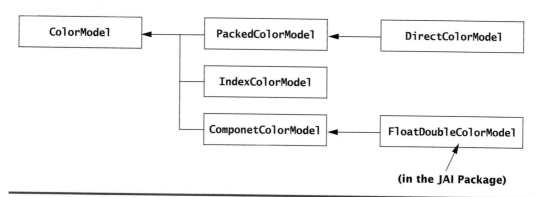

FIGURE 8.7   The `ColorModel` class hierarchy

However, a new abstract class, called `PackedColorModel`, was interposed between the `ColorModel` and `DirectColorModel` classes in the class hierarchy.

The `ColorModel` class also describes how the alpha component is stored in the pixel. It implements the `Transparency` interface, which has only the following method:

- `public int getTransparency()`

The return type can be any one of the following: `Transparency.BITMASK`, `Transparency.TRANSLUCENT`, or `Transparency.OPAQUE`.

What Is Premultiplied Alpha?

A term that is frequently used in Java 2D documentation is *premultiplied alpha*. This term means that each of the color components is multiplied by the alpha component and stored as that color component. This is done to improve the rendering performance. When an image is drawn on a graphical context or composited with another image, each of the color components is multiplied by the alpha value. To eliminate this computation, the color component values are premultiplied by alpha values.

DirectColorModel

This color model exists mostly to support the legacy AWT imaging code. It is similar to an X11 TrueColor visual and represents a default RGB model. All the components of a pixel are packed into a `byte`, `int`, or `short` element, including the alpha component. Here are the constructors:

- `public DirectColorModel(int bits, int rmask, int gmask, int bmask)`
- `public DirectColorModel(int bits, int rmask, int gmask, int bmask,`
                `int amask)`
- `public DirectColorModel(ColorSpace colorSpace, int bits,`
                `int rmask, int gmask, int bmask, int amask,`
                `boolean isAlphaPremultiplied, int transferType)`

The first two constructors are carried over from AWT imaging. The value of the `colorSpace` argument for these constructors is `sRGB`. The `amask`, `rmask`, `gmask`, and `bmask` parameters represent the positions of the alpha, red, green, and blue components in the pixel element, respectively. If the `amask` parameter is not present, the default transparency value will be `Transparency.OPAQUE`. The transfer type will be the smallest of `DataBuffer.TYPE_BYTE`, `DataBuffer.TYPE_USHORT`, or `DataBuffer.TYPE_INT` that can hold a single pixel. The third constructor supports the Java 2D color architecture. The `colorSpace` argument can be any of the constants in Table 8.1 that belongs to the RGB family. Table 8.3 shows the default set of arguments for these constructors.

TABLE 8.3   Default Arguments for `DirectColorModel`'s Constructors

ARGUMENT	VALUE
Number of bits	32
Red mask (`rmask`)	0x00ff0000
Green mask (`gmask`)	0x0000ff00
Blue mask (`bmask`)	0x000000ff
Alpha mask (`amask`)	0xff000000
Color space (`colorSpace`)	sRGB
`isAlphaPremultiplied`	false
Transparency	Transparency.TRANSLUCENT
`transferType`	DataBuffer.TYPE_INT

IndexColorModel

This `ColorModel` represents pixels that are indices to a table containing the actual color values. This model corresponds to the X11 pseudo color visual. Here are the constructors for this class:

- ```
  public IndexColorModel(int bits, int size, byte[] r, byte[] g,
                         byte[] b)
  ```
- ```
  public IndexColorModel(int bits, int size, byte[] r, byte[] g,
                         byte[] b, int transparencyIndex)
  ```
- ```
  public IndexColorModel(int bits, int size, byte[] r, byte[] g,
                         byte[] b, byte[] a)
  ```
- ```
  public IndexColorModel(int bits, int size, byte[] cmap, int start,
                         boolean hasAlpha)
  ```
- ```
  public IndexColorModel(int bits, int size, byte[] cmap, int start,
                         boolean hasAlpha, int transparencyIndex)
  ```
- ```
  public IndexColorModel(int bits, int size, int[] cmap, int start,
                         boolean hasAlpha, int transparencyIndex,
                         int transferType)
  ```

The arguments for these constructors are as follows:

- `bits`. This argument contains the number of bits each pixel occupies.
- `size`. This argument contains the size of the color component arrays.
- `cmap`. This argument is an array of color components.
- `start`. This argument contains the starting offset of the first color component.
- `hasAlpha`. This argument indicates whether alpha values are contained in the `cmap` array.

◆ transparencyIndex. This argument contains the index of the fully transparent pixel. If hasAlpha is true, the transparency value is Transparency. TRANSLUCENT. If hasAlpha is false, the transparency value is Transparency.BITMASK or Transparency.OPAQUE, depending on whether or not transparencyIndex is a valid index in the color map.

◆ transferType. This argument contains the data type (see the section titled The DataBuffer Class a little later in this chapter).

The table of color components is of byte type. If the transparencyIndex argument is not provided in a constructor, Transparency.TRANSLUCENT is taken as its default value. If the transferType argument is not provided, its default value is the smallest of DataBuffer.TYPE_BYTE, DataBuffer.TYPE_USHORT, or DataBuffer. TYPE_INT that can hold a single pixel.

ComponentColorModel

The ComponentColorModel class represents the new color model that was introduced in Java 2D. In this model, each color component (including the alpha component) is stored as a separate element of an array. The constructor for this class is as follows:

```
◆ public ComponentColorModel(ColorSpace colorSpace,
                             int[] bits,
                             boolean hasAlpha,
                             boolean isAlphaPremultiplied,
                             int transparency,
                             int transferType)
```

This constructor takes the following arguments:

◆ colorSpace. This argument contains the color space associated with this color model.

◆ bits. This argument contains the number of significant bits per component.

◆ hasAlpha. If the value of this argument is true, this color model supports alpha.

◆ isAlphaPremultiplied. If the value of this argument is true, alpha is premultiplied.

◆ transparency. This argument specifies what alpha values can be represented by this color model.

◆ transferType. This argument specifies the type of primitive array used to represent pixel values.

Here's an example that creates a grayscale color model:

```
int imageDepth = 8;
ComponentColorModel ccm = new ComponentColorModel(
```

```
ColorSpace.getInstance(ColorSpace.CS_GRAY),
new int[] {imageDepth},
false, // hasAlpha
false,  // Alpha premultiplied
Transparency.OPAQUE,
DataBuffer.TYPE_BYTE);
```

Using the Color Class

The `java.awt.Color` class has been around since JDK 1.0. It is commonly used by graphical and GUI programmers to set the color of a component, graphical context, and the like. This class has the following constants of type `Color` to represent the basic colors: `Color.black`, `Color.white`, `Color.red`, `Color.green`, `Color.blue`, `Color.magenta`, `Color.cyan`, `Color.pink`, `Color.orange`, `Color.yellow`, `Color.gray`, `Color.darkGray`, and `Color.lightGray`. You can use these constants directly to set a color. Here's an example:

```
g2d.setColor(Color.green);
```

The colors represented by these constants are in the sRGB color space, which is the default color space for the `Color` class. You can explicitly construct colors in other spaces by using the `Color` class constructors:

- **public Color(ColorSpace cspace, float[] components, float alpha)**
- **public Color(float r, float g, float b, float a)**
- **public Color(float r, float g, float b)**
- **public Color(int rgba, boolean hasAlpha)**
- **public Color(int rgb)**
- **public Color(int r, int g, int b, int a)**
- **public Color(int r, int g, int b)**

The first constructor allows the creation of the `Color` object in any color space. This object can also contain the `alpha` value. The rest of the constructors are meant for RGB space. The parameters r, g, and b refer to red, green, and blue, respectively.

Most of the `Color` class methods are get methods that retrieve color components in different forms. Apart from these methods, the `Color` class has a few utility methods:

- **public static float[] RGBtoHSB(int r, int g, int b, float[] hsbvals)**
- **public static int HSBtoRGB(float hue, float, float brightness)**

These two methods can be used for converting a color from RGB color space to HSB color space and vice versa.

The `Color` class in Java 2 also implements the `PaintContext` interface, through its `createPaintContext()` method.

Managing Image Data Storage

Now that we've described the color-related APIs in Java 2D, our next topic will be image data storage in Java 2D. In AWT imaging, image data storage is not directly exposed through APIs. The two classes that allow access to pixels are the `PixelGrabber` class to get pixels and the `MemoryImageSource` class to create an image from an array of bytes. In addition, only two color-model classes are available: `DirectColorModel` and `IndexColorModel`. So there is not much flexibility in AWT image storage.

Java 2D changed the scene entirely. With Java 2D, you can control not only how pixels are represented, but also how they are stored. As mentioned earlier, in the section on color-model classes, each of the color components can be a separate element in an array. And we can even specify the data type of this element. The price you pay for this flexibility is complexity. The Java 2D data storage API is somewhat complicated and confusing to a beginner.

What Is a Digital Image?

For the sake of the discussion in this chapter, let's reexamine the notion of an image. A digital image is nothing but a rectangular grid of pixels.[1] Pixels in a row make up a *scanline* (see Figure 8.8). The image data organized in this manner is called *raster*.

A pixel at any location represents the physical attributes at the corresponding location of the actual scene. A pixel, therefore, is associated with a value, a location, and a size. For example, a pixel in a grayscale image represents gray values or brightness values of the objects in a scene.

A pixel value may have one or more components, each representing an attribute. In an RGB image, a pixel has three components: red, green, and blue. In Java 2D terms, each component of a pixel is called a *sample*. Samples that are of the same type are called a *band*. For example, in an RGB image, the R band consists of all the red values. A multispectral image is a collection of such bands.

> **Note:** Satellite images are typically multispectral. The Landsat 7 satellite[2] images have eight bands. The input for each is obtained through different sensors operating at different wavelengths. In other words, each band in the Landsat image represents a frequency range that covers from visual to nonvisual data of Earth.

---

1 *Pixel* is a short form for *picture element.*

2 This satellite monitors Earth resources.

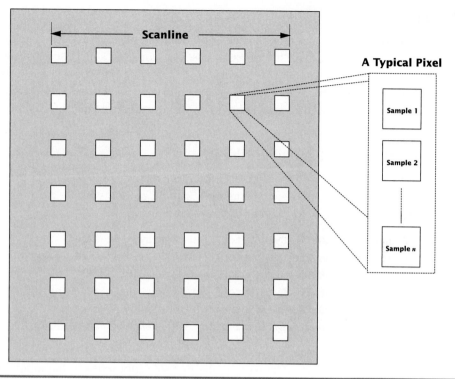

FIGURE 8.8 Pixel layout in an image

You may think storing pixels is easy because an image is nothing but a rectangular grid of pixels. But, as mentioned earlier, pixels are represented in many different ways, and most images have bands. To represent diverse images, a higher-level data abstraction is needed. Java 2D provides such an abstraction through several classes that manage the storage and extraction of pixels.

The Raster Class

The `Raster` class encapsulates raster image data as a rectangular grid of pixels. Because pixels are represented in a variety of ways, a `Raster` object contains two objects to manage the pixel storage: `DataBuffer` and `SampleModel.` Both of these are abstract classes that have several concrete subclasses each.

The `DataBuffer` object stores the image data. The `SampleModel` describes how the image data is stored. We'll revisit the `Raster` class after we discuss the `DataBuffer` and `SampleModel` classes.

The DataBuffer Class

The DataBuffer class stores image data in one or more arrays. Each array is referred to as a bank. The DataBuffer class has four concrete subclasses: DataBufferByte, DataBufferInt, DataBufferShort, and DataBufferUShort. You can create a DataBuffer object for specific types of data using these classes. The DataBuffer class also has several set and get methods for setting and retrieving the data elements.

Constructing a DataBuffer Object

DataBuffer is an abstract class. A DataBuffer object stores pixel data in one or more arrays referred to as *banks*. Bands of a sample model typically map to banks. Here are the constructors for the DataBufferByte class:

- public DataBufferByte(byte[][] dataArray, int size)
- public DataBufferByte(byte[][] dataArray, int size, int[] offsets)
- public DataBufferByte(byte[] dataArray, int size)
- public DataBufferByte(byte[] dataArray, int size, int offset)
- public DataBufferByte(int size)
- public DataBufferByte(int size, int numBanks)

You can construct the DataBuffer class with one- or two-dimensional arrays. When the array is two-dimensional, the first subscript refers to the index of the bank, and the second subscript refers to the index of the data element. So the value of dataArray.length equals the number of banks. The size parameter refers to the size of a bank. The offset parameter specifies the starting index of a data array. When the input data array is two-dimensional, you need to specify these offsets in an array whose length equals the number of bands.

You must use the appropriate DataBuffer constructor, depending on the SampleModel object. For example, to create a band-interleaved sample model, which will be described shortly, you need to use the constructor that takes the two-dimensional data array.

Transfer Type

The transfer type is the data type of the array containing the pixel values. The Java 2D API supports four transfer types: byte, integer, short, and unsigned short. These types are represented by the constants in the DataBuffer class: TYPE_BYTE, TYPE_INT, TYPE_SHORT, and TYPE_USHORT. JAI supports the float and double transfer types.

Both the ColorModel and the SampleModel classes use the TransferType object to indicate the data type of the pixel.

The SampleModel Class

As mentioned earlier, the `SampleModel` class describes how pixels are stored in a `Data Buffer` object. A pixel may consist of a single sample, as in the case of a grayscale image, or it may consist of multiple samples, as in the case of an RGB image. The `SampleModel` class also controls the image data type. It allows unsigned data to be stored in signed Java data types such as `byte`, `short`, and `int`.

There are two types of sample models, depending on how samples are stored:

1. **Packed models.** Each component occupies certain bit positions *in a single element.*
2. **Component models.** Each component is an element *in an array.*

Packed Models

In packed models, samples are packed in a single array element. There are two packed models: single-pixel and multiple-pixel.

Single-Pixel Packed Sample Model

In this model, each pixel becomes an array element. The samples are stuffed into this element as bits (see Figure 8.9). For instance, an ARGB image can be stored as an array of `int` values. In each `int` element, 8 bits each are allocated to alpha, red, green, and blue samples. This model is compatible with the packed color model.

Multiple-Pixel Packed Sample Model

In this storage scheme, multiple pixels are stored in a single array element. As Figure 8.10 shows, each array element is packed with samples from multiple pixels.

Component Models

In this type of sample model, the components (or samples) that make up a pixel are the elements of an array. First let's review some definitions that are frequently used in the Java 2D documentation:

Array Element 0 **Pixel 0**			Array Element 1 **Pixel 1**					Array Element *n–1* **Pixel *n–1***		
Sample 0	Sample 1	Sample 2	Sample 0	Sample 1	Sample 2			Sample 0	Sample 1	Sample 2

FIGURE 8.9   The single-pixel packed sample model

Array Element 0		Array Element 1		Array Element 2	
Pixel 0	**Pixel 1**	**Pixel 2**	**Pixel 3**	**Pixel 4**	**Pixel 5**

FIGURE 8.10   The multiple-pixel packed sample model

- **Scanline stride.** This is the number of array elements between corresponding samples in the same column of consecutive rows. In other words, it is the number of elements of an array that constitute a row. For instance, if a pixel is at the location (x, y), the scanline stride is the number of array elements between (x, y) and $(x, y + 1)$.

    Scanline stride depends on how pixels are stored. If a pixel has just one component, the scanline stride is the width of the image.

- **Pixel stride.** This is the number of array elements between the corresponding samples of two consecutive pixels.

- **Band offset.** This is the index that points to the position of a band. For instance, in an RGB pixel, the index of red is 0, the index of green is 1, and the index of blue is 2.

In Java 2D, arrays for storing pixel components can be formed by band interleaving or pixel interleaving.

Band Interleaving

In this scheme, samples belonging to a band are stored contiguously in an array (see Figure 8.11). For example, all red samples in an RGB image are stored in a single array. If there are k bands, the number of arrays or banks in the DataBuffer object for band interleaving will be equal to k.

The scanline stride in this case is the number of elements per row. The pixel stride is always equal to 1 with band interleaving.

Pixel Interleaving

In this scheme, samples belonging to a pixel are stored contiguously (see Figure 8.12). For instance, pixels of an RGB image are stored as RGBRGB . . .

The DataBuffer object in this case has one large array. Each sample or component is an array element. The scanline stride n in this case is equal to the number of array elements per row, multiplied by the number of bands. The pixel stride equals the number of bands.

The ComponentSampleModel class represents this model.

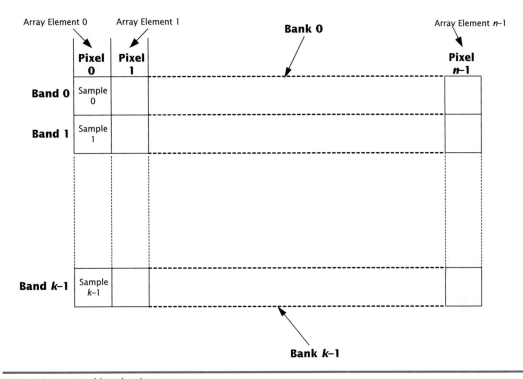

FIGURE 8.11 Band interleaving

Using the SampleModel Classes

The `SampleModel` class is an abstract class with the class hierarchy shown in Figure 8.13. The most important thing to know about a sample model is how to construct it. Each of the concrete subclasses of `SampleModel` has its own constructors. We'll look at them one by one.

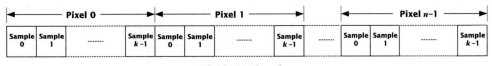

FIGURE 8.12 Pixel interleaving

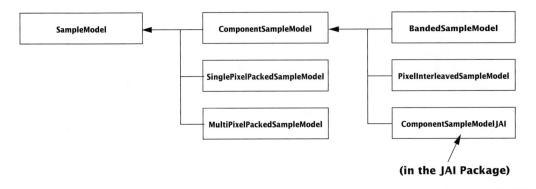

FIGURE 8.13 The SampleModel class hierarchy

Constructing Sample Models

Let's look at the constructors of all the SampleModel classes. This detailed examination is important because a SampleModel object is needed to construct a BufferedImage object from data.

The SinglePixelPackedSampleModel Constructors

- ◆ `public SinglePixelPackedSampleModel(int dataType, int width, int height, int[] bitMasks)`
- ◆ `public SinglePixelPackedSampleModel(int dataType, int width, int height, int scanlineStride, int[] bitMasks)`

The MultiPixelPackedSampleModel Constructors

- ◆ `public MultiPixelPackedSampleModel(int dataType, int width, int height, int numberOfBits)`
- ◆ `public MultiPixelPackedSampleModel(int dataType, int width, int height, int numberOfBits, int scanlineStride, int dataBitOffset)`

The ComponentSampleModel Constructors

- ◆ `public ComponentSampleModel(int dataType, int width, int height, int scanlineStride, int[] bandOffsets)`

◆ `public ComponentSampleModel(int dataType, int width, int height,`
                          `int pixelStride, int scanlineStride,`
                          `int[] bankIndices, int[] bandOffsets)`

The first constructor here constructs a `SampleModel` object with pixel-interleaved storage and the second constructs one with band-interleaved storage.

Note that the elements of a `bandOffsets` array refer to the positions or order of the bands. So the length of the `bandOffsets` array equals the number of bands. If there are *k* bands, the values of the elements vary from 0 to *k* − 1.

The `bankIndices` array is needed only for the band-interleaved sample model. Its elements point to a band index, which refers to the banks of the `DataBuffer` object. In other words, this array tells how the band is mapped to the bank. For example, a `bankIndices` array {0,3,2,1} indicates that the first bank has the first band, the second bank has the fourth band, the third bank has the third band, and the last bank has the second band.

As shown in Figure 8.13, `ComponentSampleModel` has two subclasses. You can also construct the `bandOffsets` and `bankIndices` arrays directly from the subclasses. The parameters have the same meaning.

The PixelInterleavedSampleModel Constructor

◆ `public PixelInterleavedSampleModel(int dataType, int width,`
                              `int height, int pixelStride,`
                              `int scanlineStride,`
                              `int[] bandOffsets)`

The BandedSampleModel Constructors

◆ `public BandedSampleModel(int dataType, int width, int height,`
                       `int numBands)`
◆ `public BandedSampleModel(int dataType, int width, int height,`
                       `int scanlineStride, int[] bankIndices,`
                       `int[] bandOffsets)`

We'll see examples of all these constructors later in this chapter.

Constructing a Raster Object

As mentioned earlier, the `Raster` class is a higher-level abstraction for representing pixel data. It has only protected constructors. To construct a `Raster` object, you must use the factory methods in the `Raster` class. The `Raster` class has one subclass, called `WritableRaster`, which allows you to write pixels. Most of the factory methods return a `WritableRaster` object.

To create a `Raster` object, you need at least two objects: `SampleModel` and `DataBuffer`. The `Raster` class has `SampleModel`-specific as well as general factory methods.

SampleModel-Specific Methods

♦ **public static Raster createRaster(SampleModel sm, DataBuffer db,**
                                                                    Point location)
♦ **public static WritableRaster createWritableRaster(SampleModel sm,**
                                                                    Point location)
♦ **public static WritableRaster createWritableRaster(SampleModel sm,**
                                                                    DataBuffer db,
                                                                    Point location)

A `Raster` object need not start at pixel location (0, 0). The `location` argument provides an offset to the ULHC (upper left-hand corner).

General Methods

The following are the types of `Raster` factory methods.

Packed Raster

♦ **public static WritableRaster createPackedRaster(DataBuffer dataBuffer,**
                                                                    int h, int scanlineStride,
                                                                    int[] bandMasks,
                                                                    Point location)
♦ **public static WritableRaster createPackedRaster(DataBuffer dataBuffer,**
                                                                    int width, int height,
                                                                    int bitsPerPixel,
                                                                    Point location)
♦ **public static WritableRaster createPackedRaster(int dataType,**
                                                                    int width, int height,
                                                                    int[] bandMasks,
                                                                    Point location)
♦ **public static WritableRaster createPackedRaster(int dataType,**
                                                                    int width, int height,
                                                                    int bands,
                                                                    int bitsPerBand,
                                                                    Point location)

Banded Raster

- `public static WritableRaster createBandedRaster(int dataType,`
  `int width, int height,`
  `int bands,`
  `Point location)`
- `public static WritableRaster createBandedRaster(int dataType,`
  `int width, int height,`
  `int scanlineStride,`
  `int[] bankIndices,`
  `int[] bandOffsets,`
  `Point location)`
- `public static WritableRaster createPackedRaster(DataBuffer dataBuffer,`
  `int width, int height,`
  `int scanlineStride,`
  `int[] bandMasks,`
  `Point location)`
- `public static WritableRaster createBandedRaster(DataBuffer dataBuffer,`
  `int width, int height,`
  `int scanlineStride,`
  `int[] bankIndices,`
  `int[] bandOffsets,`
  `Point location)`

Interleaved Raster

- `public static WritableRaster createInterleavedRaster(int dataType,`
  `int width,`
  `int height, int bands,`
  `Point location)`
- `public static WritableRaster createInterleavedRaster(DataBuffer`
  `dataBuffer,`
  `int width,`
  `int height,`
  `int`
  `scanlineStride,`
  `int pixelStride,`
  `int[]`
  `bandOffsets,`
  `Point location)`

Constructing a BufferedImage Object from Data

The need often arises to construct images directly from an array of Java primitive types. The data may come from another image, or it may be synthetically generated. The BufferedImage class allows you to construct images using the following constructor:

- ◆ **public BufferedImage(ColorModel cm,**
  WritableRaster raster,
  boolean isRasterPremultiplied,
  Hashtable properties)

This constructor requires ColorModel and Raster objects as parameters. To create a BufferedImage object from an array of data, you need to first create a DataBuffer object with the input data and then a compatible SampleModel object. You can then use these objects to create a WritableRaster object by using the factory methods in the Raster class. You can use the properties parameter in the BufferedImage constructor to pass your own property, or the value can be null.

Next let's create different types of buffered images from a byte array using the ComponentColorModel class and different types of sample models.

Note that there are a lot of constraints on the parameters of the ColorModel, SampleModel, and DataBuffer constructors. If these parameters are not compatible, you'll see runtime errors. In the case of mismatched data, you'll see errors while painting or accessing pixels. Here are some tips:

- ◆ The ColorModel and SampleModel parameters passed to the BufferedImage constructor must be compatible with each other. For example, to create a BufferedImage object with ComponentSampleModel, the color model must be of type ComponentColorModel or its descendants.
- ◆ Some of the ColorModel and SampleModel constructor parameters must be compatible. For example, the TransferType parameter must be the same in the ColorModel and the SampleModel objects.
- ◆ If ColorModel's hasAlpha parameter is true, the DataBuffer object should have an extra bank to include the alpha values. For example, if the CS_sRGB color space has an alpha value, the DataBuffer object should contain four banks; otherwise it should contain three.
- ◆ If you wish to use BandedSampleModel, observe the following:
  - ◆ The bankIndices array cannot have elements that are not in the bandOffsets array.
  - ◆ The value of scanlineStride should be equal to the image width.

- Because the band-interleaved sample model has multiple banks, the data passed to the `DataBuffer` constructor must be two-dimensional. The number of banks should be equal to the number of bands.
- The size of the `DataBuffer` bank must be equal to or greater than the image width.

- In the case of `PixelInterleavedSampleModel`,
  - The scanline stride parameter cannot exceed the image width multiplied by the pixel stride.
  - Because the pixel-interleaved sample model has a single piece of data passed to the `DataBuffer`, the constructor must be one-dimensional.
  - The size of the `DataBuffer` bank must be equal to or greater than the image width multiplied by the number of bands.

- In the case of the `ComponentColorModel` class, if `hasAlpha` is `true`, the `transparency` parameter may not be `Transparency.OPAQUE`, which could result in runtime errors.

> **Note:** The methods in Listings 8.1 through 8.7 are contained in the `ImageFactory.java` class, which is available on the book's Web page in the directory `src/util`.

Creating a Grayscale Image

Although advances in technology have made color monitors and image acquisition devices such as digital cameras less expensive, grayscale images are still being used in some areas, especially medical imaging. The primary reason is that many doctors and radiologists are trained to examine the grayscale image. In addition, color does not add much value in certain types of medical images, and often it can be a distraction. However, color plays a very important role in functional medical images.

With Java 2D's support for grayscale color space and the component color model, it is now easy to create grayscale images directly from the data. The method shown in Listing 8.1 illustrates how to create grayscale images from an array of unsigned shorts.

LISTING 8.1   Creating a grayscale image

```
public static BufferedImage createGrayscaleImage(int imageWidth,
                             int imageHeight,
                             int imageDepth,
                             short data[]){
    ComponentColorModel ccm = new ComponentColorModel(
                ColorSpace.getInstance(ColorSpace.CS_GRAY),
                new int[] {imageDepth},
                false, // hasAlpha
```

continued

```
                    false, // Alpha premultiplied
                    Transparency.OPAQUE,
                    DataBuffer.TYPE_USHORT);

    ComponentSampleModel csm = new ComponentSampleModel(
                        DataBuffer.TYPE_USHORT,
                        imageWidth, imageHeight,1,imageWidth, new int[] {0});

    DataBuffer dataBuf = new DataBufferUShort((short[])data, imageWidth);

    WritableRaster wr = Raster.createWritableRaster(csm, dataBuf, new Point(0,0));
    Hashtable ht = new Hashtable();
    ht.put("owner", "Lawrence Rodrigues");
    return  new BufferedImage(ccm, wr, true, ht);
}
```

The `createGrayscaleImage()` method uses the CS_GRAY color space. You can create grayscale images of different depths. This method uses the unsigned short as the transfer type, so the depth cannot exceed 16 bits. In Listing 8.2 this method is used to create a grayscale bar that is used in medical-imaging visualization screens.

LISTING 8.2   Creating a grayscale bar

```
public static BufferedImage createGrayscaleBar(int wid, int ht, int maxvalue){
    if((wid <0) || (ht <0)) return null;
    int bits = 8;
    if( maxvalue > 255) bits = 16;
    short data[] = new short[wid*ht];
    int ratio = (int)(maxvalue/ht);
    for(int i=0; i<ht; i++){
        for(int j=0; j<wid; j++){
            data[i*wid+j] = (short)(i*ratio);
        }
    }
    return createGrayscaleImage(wid,ht,bits,data);
}
```

The image created in Listing 8.2 will show shades of gray varying from 0 to a maximum value. All the pixels in a scanline have the same value. This value is incremented by the same amount as the scanline is moved from the top of the image to the bottom.

Creating a Pixel-Interleaved RGB Image

Now let's create the more popular RGB image. Java 2D has two built-in RGB color spaces: CS_sRGB and CS_LINEAR_RGB. The `createInterleavedRGBImage()` method, shown in Listing 8.3, creates an sRGB image.

LISTING 8.3   Creating a pixel-inlerleaved sRGB image

```
public static BufferedImage createInterleavedRGBImage(int imageWidth,
                                        int imageHeight,
```

```
                                              int imageDepth,
                                              short data[],
                                              boolean hasAlpha){
    int pixelStride,transparency;
    if(hasAlpha) {
       pixelStride = 4;
       transparency = Transparency.TRANSLUCENT;
    }
    else {
       pixelStride = 3;
       transparency = Transparency.OPAQUE;
    }
    int[] numBits = new int[pixelStride];
    int[] bandoffsets = new int[pixelStride];

    for(int i=0;i<pixelStride;i++){
        numBits[i] = imageDepth;
        bandoffsets[i] =i;
    }

    ComponentColorModel ccm = new ComponentColorModel(
                    ColorSpace.getInstance(ColorSpace.CS_sRGB),
                    numBits,
                    hasAlpha,
                    false, // Alpha premultiplied
                    transparency,
                    DataBuffer.TYPE_USHORT);

    PixelInterleavedSampleModel csm = new PixelInterleavedSampleModel(
                    DataBuffer.TYPE_USHORT,
                    imageWidth, imageHeight,
                    pixelStride, // Pixel stride
                    imageWidth*pixelStride, // Scanline stride
                    bandoffsets);

    DataBuffer dataBuf = new DataBufferUShort(data,
                        imageWidth*imageHeight*pixelStride);

    WritableRaster wr = Raster.createWritableRaster(csm, dataBuf, new Point(0,0));
    Hashtable ht = new Hashtable();
    ht.put("owner", "Lawrence Rodrigues");
    return  new BufferedImage(ccm, wr, false, ht);
}
```

The `createInterleavedRGBImage()` method can create an sRGB image with or without the **alpha** parameter. Either way, when you call this method, make sure that the data array is constructed appropriately. If the image is to be constructed with just the RGB bands, the `SampleModel` object will have three bands. Therefore, the value of `pixelStride` should be 3. If the image is to be constructed with alpha, the `SampleModel` object will have four bands and the value of `pixelStride` should be 4.

The `createRandomInterleavedImage()` method (shown in Listing 8.4) calls the `createInterleavedRGBImage()` method (see Listing 8.3) to create an sRGB image with random pixel values.

LISTING 8.4   Creating a random sRGB image

```
public static BufferedImage createRandomInterleavedImage(int wid, int ht,
                                             boolean hasAlpha){
     int numBands =3;
     if(hasAlpha) numBands = 4;
     short data1[]= new short[wid*ht*numBands];
     for(int i=0; i<ht; i++){
         for(int j=0; j<wid; j++){
             for(int k=0;k<numBands;k++) {
                 if(k==0 && hasAlpha) data1[((i*wid+j)*numBands)+k] = (short)(255);
                 else data1[((i*wid+j)*numBands)+k] =
                     (short)(255* Math.abs(Math.random()));
             }
         }
     }
     return ImageFactory.createInterleavedRGBImage(wid, ht, 8, data1, hasAlpha);
}
```

Converting a Packed-Model Image to a Pixel-Interleaved Image

When the JPEG codec is used to load an image, the image is typically constructed with the RGB color space (`DirectColorModel`) and `SinglePixelPackedSampleModel`. But often you'll want the image to be in a different color space. And sometimes you may also want to use a different data storage mechanism. The `convertPacked ToInterleaved()` method, shown in Listing 8.5, converts such an RGB image obtained from the JPEG codec to an sRGB image with pixel-interleaved data storage.

LISTING 8.5   Converting a `DirectColorModel` image to a `ComponentColorModel` image with pixel-interleaved storage

```
public static BufferedImage convertPackedToInterleaved(BufferedImage img) {
     ColorModel cm = img.getColorModel();
     if(! (cm instanceof DirectColorModel)) return null;
     int wid = img.getWidth(), ht = img.getHeight();
     short data1[] = new short[wid*ht*3];
     SampleModel sm = img.getSampleModel();
     WritableRaster wr = img.getRaster();
     DataBuffer db = wr.getDataBuffer();
     int numbands = wr.getNumBands();
     int sample[] = new int[numbands];
     for(int i=0; i<ht; i++){
         for(int j=0; j<wid; j++){
             int pix[] = null;
             sample = (sm.getPixel(j,i, pix, db));
             for(int l =0 ; l<numbands;l++)
                 data1[i*wid*3+(j*3)+l] =  (short)sample[l];
         }
     }
     return ImageFactory.createInterleavedRGBImage(wid, ht, 8, data1, false);
}
```

Creating a Band-Interleaved Image

The `createBandedRGBImage()` method, shown in Listing 8.6, is similar to `create InterleavedRGBImage()` (see Listing 8.3), but it differs in the construction of the `SampleModel` object.

LISTING 8.6   Creating a band-interleaved sRGB image

```
public static BufferedImage createBandedRGBImage(int imageWidth,
                                   int imageHeight,
                                   int imageDepth,
                                   short data[][],
                                   boolean hasAlpha){
     int numbits,transparency ;
     if(hasAlpha) {
        numbits = 4;
        transparency = Transparency.TRANSLUCENT;
     } else {
        numbits = 3;
        transparency = Transparency.OPAQUE;
     }
     int[] bits = new int[numbits];
     int[] bandoffsets = new int[numbits];

     for(int i=0;i<numbits;i++){
         bits[i] = imageDepth;
         bandoffsets[i] =i;
     }

     ComponentColorModel ccm = new ComponentColorModel(
                     ColorSpace.getInstance(ColorSpace.CS_sRGB),
                     bits,
                     hasAlpha,
                     false,
                     Transparency.OPAQUE,
                     DataBuffer.TYPE_USHORT);

     BandedSampleModel csm = new BandedSampleModel(
                     DataBuffer.TYPE_USHORT,
                     imageWidth, imageHeight, imageWidth,
                     new int[] {0,1,2}, //Bank indices
                     new int[] {0,1,2} );//Band offsets

     DataBuffer dataBuf = new DataBufferUShort(data, imageWidth*imageHeight);

     WritableRaster wr = Raster.createWritableRaster(csm, dataBuf, new Point(0,0));

     return  new BufferedImage(ccm, wr, false, null);
  }
```

Notice that there is no pixel stride argument in the `BandedSampleModel` constructor. The reason is that the pixel stride is always equal to 1 with band-interleaved storage. However, this constructor does have the **bankIndices** argument, whose elements map the bank index to the band index. For example, if the second element is 1, the second bank belongs to bank number 1.

Notice also that the `size` argument of the `DataBuffer` constructor refers to the size of an individual bank.

The `createRandomBandedImage()` method, shown in Listing 8.7, calls `create BandedRGBImage()` (see Listing 8.6) to create a random sRGB image with band-interleaved storage.

LISTING 8.7   Creating a random band-interleaved sRGB image

```
public static BufferedImage createRandomBandedImage(int wid, int ht){
    short data1[][] = new short[3][wid*ht];
    for(int k=0;k<3;k++) {
    for(int i=0; i<ht; i++){
        for(int j=0; j<wid; j++){
            data1[k][i*wid+j] = (short)(j*k);
        }
    }
    }
    return createBandedRGBImage(64, 64, 8, data1, false);
}
```

Notice that the `data` array is two-dimensional. The first subscript contains the bank index and the second, data elements.

Working with the Raster, SampleModel, and DataBuffer Classes

We used the `ColorModel`, `Raster`, `SampleModel`, and `DataBuffer` classes to construct a `BufferedImage` object directly from the data. These classes can also be used to read and write pixels, among many other things. Before we explore the methods for these classes, let's look at the attributes in the `Raster` class.

Raster Attributes

The attributes of `Raster` include `rectangle` (the bounding box), `SampleModel`, `DataBuffer`, and `parent`.

Bounding Box

The bounding box can be obtained by the following method:

♦ **`public Rectangle getBounds()`**

Although you can obtain the ULHC, width, and height from this bounding box, the `Raster` class has methods to obtain them explicitly:

- **public final int getMinX()**
- **public final int getMinY()**
- **public final int getWidth()**
- **public final int getHeight()**

Notice that these are final methods. You can override them if you create a subclass for `Raster`.

SampleModel

You can obtain a `Raster` object's `SampleModel` parameter by the following method:

- **public SampleModel getSampleModel()**

    The number of bands can be obtained by

- **public final int getNumBands()**

Although a `Raster` object's ULHC (i.e., its `minX` and `minY` parameters) can be any value, the ULHC of its `SampleModel` is always (0, 0). The `SampleModel` class has methods for reading and writing pixels. This means that a coordinate within the `Raster` object must be translated appropriately before these methods can be used.

The `sampleModelTranslateX` and `sampleModelTranslateY` attributes represent the translation in the x and y directions, respectively, of a `SampleModel` object from `Raster`'s coordinate space. Here are the respective get methods:

- **public final int getSampleModelTranslateX()**
- **public final int getSampleModelTranslateY()**

DataBuffer

The get method for obtaining `DataBuffer` is

- **public DataBuffer getDataBuffer()**

    You can get the data type of the data using the following method:

- **public final int getTransferType()**

Parent

You can create a child `Raster` from any `Raster` object by using the following method:

- **public Raster createChild(int parentX, int parentY,**
                        int width, int height,
                        int childMinX, int childMinY,
                        int[] bandList)

The bounding box for the child `Raster` should be contained within the parent `Raster`. The child `Raster` will share the `DataBuffer` parameter with the parent. It holds the reference to the parent through an attribute called **parent,** which can be obtained by the following method:

- **public Raster getParent()**

A `Raster` object that has no parent will return `null`.

Reading Pixels

Once you have created a `Raster` object, you can read the pixels or samples using the methods in the `SampleModel` or `DataBuffer` subclasses of `Raster`. Although using `DataBuffer` is the fastest way to read or write pixels, it requires knowledge of `ColorModel` to interpret the pixels or samples. In addition, the code may not be very readable. If performance is not an issue, use the `Raster` or `SampleModel` classes to read and write pixels.

Both the `Raster` and the `SampleModel` classes have parallel methods for reading pixels. You can use either class, but keep in mind that the `SampleModel` ULHC is always (0, 0), whereas the `Raster` ULHC need not be (0, 0). All the `SampleModel` methods require a `DataBuffer` parameter.

The methods that follow read pixels from a point or a rectangular region.

Raster Methods

- **public float[] getPixel(int x, int y, float[] fArray)**
- **public double[] getPixel(int x, int y, double[] dArray)**
- **public int[] getPixel(int x, int y, int[] iArray)**

- **public int[] getPixels(int x, int y,**
                          int width, int height,
                          int[] iArray)

- **public float[] getPixels(int x, int y,**
                            int width, int height,
                            float[] fArray)

- **public double[] getPixels(int x, int y,**
                             int width, int height,
                             double[] dArray)

SampleModel Methods

These methods are similar to those of the Raster class, but they require the DataBuffer parameter.

- ◆ `public float[] getPixel(int x,  int y, float[] fArray, DataBuffer`
                                                          `data)`
- ◆ `public double[] getPixel(int x, int y, double[] dArray, DataBuffer`
                                                          `data)`
- ◆ `public int[] getPixel(int x, int y, int[] iArray, DataBuffer data)`
- ◆ `public int[] getPixels(int x, int y,`
                  `int width, int height,`
                  `int[] iArray, DataBuffer data)`
- ◆ `public float[] getPixels(int x, int y,`
                    `int width, int height,`
                    `float[] fArray,`
                    `DataBuffer data)`
- ◆ `public double[] getPixels(int x, int y,`
                      `int width, int height,`
                      `double[] dArray,`
                      `DataBuffer data)`

Reading Samples

Just like reading pixels, you can read a sample at a given location or a rectangular area. The methods are similar to those for reading pixels, with an additional argument to specify the band.

Raster Methods

- ◆ `public int getSample(int x, int y, int b)`
- ◆ `public float getSampleFloat(int x, int y, int b)`
- ◆ `public double getSampleDouble(int x, int y, int b)`

- ◆ `public int[] getSamples(int x, int y, int w, int h, int b,`
                    `int[] iArray)`
- ◆ `public float[] getSamples(int x, int y, int w, int h, int b,`
                      `float[] fArray)`
- ◆ `public double[] getSamples(int x, int y, int w, int h,`
                        `int double[] dArray)`

SampleModel Methods

- ◆ `public abstract int getSample(int x, int y, int b, DataBuffer data)`
- ◆ `public float getSampleFloat(int x, int y, int b, DataBuffer data)`
- ◆ `public double getSampleDouble(int x, int y, int b, DataBuffer data)`
- ◆ `public int[] getSamples(int x, int y, int w, int h,`
  `int b, int[] iArray, DataBuffer data)`
- ◆ `public float[] getSamples(int x, int y, int w, int h,`
  `int b, float[] fArray, DataBuffer data)`
- ◆ `public double[] getSamples(int x, int y, int w, int h,`
  `int double[] dArray, DataBuffer data)`

- ◆ `public abstract int[] getSampleSize()`
- ◆ `public abstract int getSampleSize(int band)`

Listings 8.8 and 8.9 show two flavors of a method that extracts pixels—one from `BufferedImage` and the other from `Raster`.

LISTING 8.8   Retrieving pixel samples from a `BufferedImage` object

```
public static int[][] getPixelSamples(BufferedImage img) {
    WritableRaster wr = img.getRaster();
    Dimension size = new Dimension(img.getWidth(), img.getHeight());
    return getPixelSamples(wr, size);
}
```

The `getPixelSamples(BufferedImage)` method gets the `WritableRaster` object first and then calls the `getPixelSamples(Raster)` method (see Listing 8.9) to get the pixel samples as a two-dimensional array, the first dimension representing the band and the second the data elements.

LISTING 8.9   Retrieving pixel samples from a `Raster` object

```
public static int[][] getPixelSamples(Raster raster, Dimension imageSize){
    if((raster == null) || (imageSize ==null)) return null;
    SampleModel sm = raster.getSampleModel();
    DataBuffer db = raster.getDataBuffer();
    int imageWidth = imageSize.width;
    int imageHeight = imageSize.height;
    int totalPix = imageHeight*imageWidth;
    int sample[][] = new int[totalPix][];
    for(int i=0;i<imageHeight;i++){
        for(int j=0; j<imageWidth;j++) {
            int pix[] = null;
            sample[i*imageWidth+j] =  sm.getPixel(j,i, pix, db);
        }
    }
    int pixel[][] = new int[sample[0].length][ totalPix];
    for(int i=0; i<pixel.length;i++){
        for(int j=0; j<totalPix;j++) {
```

```
            pixel[i][j] = sample[j][i];
        }
    }
    return pixel;
}
```

The getPixelSamples() method shown in Listing 8.9 first gets the SampleModel and DataBuffer objects from the Raster object. It then uses the getPixel() method in the SampleModel class to get the individual pixels. The getPixel() method uses the DataBuffer object extracted from Raster.

Reading Data Elements

Here are the methods in the Raster and SampleModel classes that read data elements:

- ◆ `public Object getDataElements(int x, int y, Object outData)`
- ◆ `public Object getDataElements(int x, int y, int w, int h,`
                                `Object outData)`

- ◆ `public abstract Object getDataElements(int x, int y, Object obj,`
                                        `DataBuffer data)`
- ◆ `public Object getDataElements(int x, int y, int w, int h, Object obj,`
                                `DataBuffer data)`

The getDataElements() method is more efficient than the getPixels() method.

Writing Pixels

To write pixels, you need to create a WritableRaster object. The WritableRaster class has methods for writing pixels at a single location, as well as on a rectangular region. Just as with reading pixels, you can use the SampleModel class methods to write pixels.

WritableRaster Methods

- ◆ `public void setPixel(int x, int y, int[] iArray)`
- ◆ `public void setPixel(int x, int y, float[] fArray)`
- ◆ `public void setPixel(int x, int y, double[] dArray)`

- ◆ `public void setPixels(int x, int y, int w, int h, int[] iArray)`
- ◆ `public void setPixels(int x, int y, int w, int h, float[] fArray)`
- ◆ `public void setPixels(int x, int y, int w, int h, double[] dArray)`

- ◆ `public void setRect(int dx, int dy, Raster srcRaster)`
- ◆ `public void setRect(Raster srcRaster)`

- ◆ `public void setDataElements(int x, int Object inData)`
- ◆ `public void setDataElements(int x, int y, Raster inRaster)`
- ◆ `public void setDataElements(int x, int y, int w, int h, Object inData)`

SampleModel Methods

- ◆ `public void setPixel(int x, int y, double[] dArray, DataBuffer data)`
- ◆ `public void setPixel(int x, int y, float[] fArray, DataBuffer data)`
- ◆ `public void setPixel(int x, int y, int[] iArray, DataBuffer data)`
- ◆ `public void setPixels(int x, int y, int w, int h, double[] dArray,`
                    `DataBuffer data)`
- ◆ `public void setPixels(int x, int y, int w, int h, float[] fArray,`
                    `DataBuffer data)`
- ◆ `public void setPixels(int x, int y, int w, int h, int[] iArray,`
                    `DataBuffer data)`

Creating a Subregion of Raster

With `WritableRaster`, you can create a writable child:

- ◆ `public WritableRaster createWritableChild(int parentX, int parentY,`
                                `int width, int height,`
                                `int childMinX,`
                                `int childMinY,`
                                `int[] bandList)`

The `createWritableChild()` method returns a `WritableRaster` object. Just like the similar method in `Raster`, the child created by this `Raster` object shares the `DataBuffer` parameter with its parent. Creating a `WritableRaster` object is very useful in ROI (region of interest) processing. You can mask pixels within an ROI by creating a child `WritableRaster` and then write the masked pixels to the child `DataBuffer`. See the section titled Thresholding in Chapter 14 for an example.

The reference to `Raster`'s parent can be obtained by the following method:

- ◆ `public WritableRaster getWritableParent()`

Next let's build some simple examples using some of the classes described in the previous sections.

Calculating Image Statistics

You may recall that we developed an application that computes image statistics (`ImageStats`) in Chapter 2 using the `ImageLoader` class. This application works well with the AWT Image object. Let's write a similar application for computing statistics from buffered images. To do this, we need to get the SampleModel object and the related DataBuffer object for the image. Using these objects, you can retrieve the pixels one by one and compute the desired statistics.

The getImageStats() method, shown in Listing 8.10, extracts pixels from the DataBuffer object and computes minimum, maximum, and average values of the pixels.

LISTING 8.10 Computing image statistics

```
public static int[][] getImageStats(SampleModel sm,
                                     DataBuffer db,
                                     Dimension imageSize){
    int imageWidth = imageSize.width;
    int imageHeight = imageSize.height;
    int pixel[][] = new int[imageHeight*imageWidth][];
    for(int i=0;i<imageHeight;i++){
        for(int j=0; j<imageWidth;j++) {
            int pix[] = null;
            pixel[i*imageWidth+j] =  sm.getPixel(j,i, pix, db);
        }
    }

    int len = pixel[0].length;
    int sum[] = new int[len];
    int max[] = new int[len];
    int min[] = new int[len];
    int[][] imageStats = new int[len][3];
    for(int j=0;j<len;j++) {
        sum[j] =0;
        max[j] = Integer.MIN_VALUE;
        min[j] = Integer.MAX_VALUE;
        for(int i=0;i<pixel.length;i++) {
            int pix = pixel[i][j];
            if(pix > max[j]) max[j] = pix;
            if(pix < min[j] ) min[j] = pix;
            sum[j] += pix;
        }
        imageStats[j][0] = min[j];
        imageStats[j][1] = max[j];
        imageStats[j][2] = sum[j]/(imageHeight*imageWidth);
    }
    return imageStats;
}
```

Obtaining Image Information

Let's develop a simple application that displays information about an image that includes some of its attributes. To obtain a variety of information about an image, we must first obtain the ColorModel, SampleModel, and DataBuffer objects from

Buffered Image. Using the get methods, we can then retrieve related information. For example, the ColorModel-related information would include the name of the color model and the color space. The SampleModel-related information would include the type of sample model, the number of bands, the pixel stride, and the scanline stride.

Listing 8.11 shows the getImageInfo() method, which returns the image information as a table—that is, a two-dimensional array of String objects. We can use the array to display the information on a JTable object.

> **Note:** The methods in Listings 8.11 and 8.12 are contained in the ImageInfoUtil.java class, which is available on the book's Web page in the directory src/chapter8/readdata.

LISTING 8.11   Retrieving image information

```java
public static String[][] getImageInfo(BufferedImage img) {
    SampleModel sm = img.getSampleModel();
    WritableRaster wr = img.getRaster();
    DataBuffer db = wr.getDataBuffer();
    ColorModel cm = img.getColorModel();
    String str = getColorModelAsText(getColorModelType(cm));
    ColorSpace cs = cm.getColorSpace();
    String[][] rowData = new String[10][2];
    int i =0;
    rowData[i][0] = "Color Model";
    rowData[i++][1] =  str;
    rowData[i][0] = "Color space";
    rowData[i++][1] = getColorSpaceAsText(cs.getType());

    rowData[i][0] = "Sample Model";
    rowData[i++][1] = getSampleModelAsText(getSampleModelType(sm));
    rowData[i][0] = "Data type";
    rowData[i++][1] = getDataTypeAsText(db.getDataType());
    int numbands = sm.getNumBands();
    rowData[i][0] = "Number of Bands";
    rowData[i++][1] = Integer.toString(numbands);
    int numbanks = db.getNumBanks();
    rowData[i][0] = "Number of Banks";
    rowData[i++][1] = Integer.toString(numbanks);

    rowData[i][0] = "Width";

    rowData[i++][1] = Integer.toString(img.getWidth());
    rowData[i][0] = "Height";
    rowData[i++][1] = Integer.toString(img.getHeight());
    int scanlineStride=0;
    if(sm instanceof ComponentSampleModel) {
        ComponentSampleModel csm = (ComponentSampleModel)sm;
        scanlineStride = csm.getScanlineStride();
        rowData[i][0] = "Scanline stride";
```

```
            rowData[i++][1] = Integer.toString(scanlineStride);
            int pixelStride = csm.getPixelStride();
            rowData[i][0] = "Pixel stride";
            rowData[i++][1] = Integer.toString(pixelStride);
        } else {
            if( sm  instanceof SinglePixelPackedSampleModel){
                SinglePixelPackedSampleModel ssm = (SinglePixelPackedSampleModel)sm;
                scanlineStride = ssm.getScanlineStride();
                rowData[i][0] = "Scanline stride";
                rowData[i++][1] = Integer.toString(scanlineStride);
                rowData[i][0] = "Pixel stride";
                rowData[i++][1] = "N/A";
            } else if ( sm  instanceof MultiPixelPackedSampleModel){
                MultiPixelPackedSampleModel msm = (MultiPixelPackedSampleModel)sm;
                scanlineStride = msm.getScanlineStride();
                rowData[i][0] = "Scanline stride";
                rowData[i++][1] = Integer.toString(scanlineStride);
                int pixelBitStride = msm.getPixelBitStride();
                rowData[i][0] = "Pixel bit stride";
                rowData[i++][1] = Integer.toString(pixelBitStride);;
            }
        }
    }
    return rowData;
}
```

The `getImageInfo()` method extracts a variety of information from the `Buffered Image` object, returning the information in a two-dimensional array so that the calling program can display it in a table.

The `ImageInfoUtil` class has several methods that convert the enumerated types to text strings. For example, `getColorSpaceAsText()` returns the name of the color space, and `getSampleModelAsText()` returns the name of the sample model (see Listing 8.12).

LISTING 8.12 Retrieving color space and sample-model names

```
public static String getColorSpaceAsText(int cs){
    switch(cs) {
        case ColorSpace.CS_GRAY:
          return " Gray";
        case ColorSpace.CS_PYCC:
          return " Photo YCC";
        case ColorSpace.CS_sRGB:
          return " sRGB ";
        case ColorSpace.CS_LINEAR_RGB:
          return " Linear RGB";
        case ColorSpace.CS_CIEXYZ:
          return " CIEXYZ ";
         default:
          return " Unknown";
    }
}

public static String getSampleModelAsText(int smtype){
```

continued

```
switch(smtype) {
    case PIXEL_INTERLEAVED:
        return " Pixel interleaved";
    case BANDED:
        return " Banded";
    case SINGLE_PIXEL_PACKED:
        return "Single pixel packed";
    case MULTI_PIXEL_PACKED:
        return "Multi pixel packed";
    case COMPONENT_SAMPLE:
        return " Component ";
    default:
        return " Unknown";
    }
}
```

The constants in Listing 8.12 are defined in the `ImageInfoUtil.java` class itself.

Histograms

Histograms are a statistical technique commonly used in image analysis. Histograms indicate the frequency of occurrence of pixel values. They are often represented as bar charts. Listing 8.13 shows a method that computes a histogram from an array of data, whose type can be **short**, **int**, **long**, **float**, or **double**. This method also takes the number of bins as an argument. It returns a structure with several parameters, as shown in Listing 8.14.

LISTING 8.13 Computing histogram values from data

```
static public HistoData computeHistogram(Object dataObj, int maxbars){

    if((dataObj == null) || (maxbars <=0)) {
        System.out.println("data = null");
        return null;
    }
    int yMinmax[] = new int[2];
    int binCount[] = new int[maxbars];
    int bin;
    Object binMinmax = getMinMax(dataObj);
    if(binMinmax == null) {
        System.out.println("bin minmax= null");
        return null;
    }
    int max =0, min= Integer.MAX_VALUE;
    HistoData histoData = new HistoData();
    if(dataObj instanceof int[]){
        int[] xMinmax1 = new int[2];
        xMinmax1[0] = ((int[])binMinmax)[0];
        xMinmax1[1] = ((int[])binMinmax)[1];
        int fullRange = xMinmax1[1] - xMinmax1[0]+1;
        int[] data = (int[])dataObj;
        for(int i=0;i<data.length;i++){
```

```
        bin =(int)(((double)(data[i] -xMinmax1[0])/fullRange)*maxbars);
        binCount[bin]++;
    }
    min = data.length;
    histoData.setBinMinmax(xMinmax1);
}

if(dataObj instanceof double[]){
    double[] xMinmax2 = new double[2];
    xMinmax2[0] = ((double[])binMinmax)[0];
    xMinmax2[1] = ((double[])binMinmax)[1];
    double fullRange = xMinmax2[1] - xMinmax2[0]+1;
    double[] data = (double[])dataObj;
    for(int i=0;i<data.length;i++){
        bin =(int)(((double)(data[i] -xMinmax2[0])/fullRange)*maxbars);
        binCount[bin]++;
    }
    min = data.length;
    histoData.setBinMinmax(xMinmax2);
}
        // Similarly other types


for(int i=0;i<maxbars;i++){
    if(binCount[i] > max) max = binCount[i];
    if(binCount[i] < min) min = binCount[i];
}
yMinmax[0] = min;
yMinmax[1] = max;

histoData.setFrequency(binCount);
histoData.setFreqMinmax(yMinmax);

return histoData;
}
```

The `computeHistogram()` method initially divides the entire range of data into a number of bins that is equal to the number of bars. Each bin covers a range of data values. The size of this range is the same for all bins. A bin is identified by its starting value, and the starting value of the first bin is the minimum value of the data. The bin size is recursively added to the starting value of subsequent bins.

To compute the histogram, we perform an iteration over input data, each time checking the input data values to determine the bin to which they belong. When a data value is within the range of a bin, the frequency count for that bin is incremented. At the end of this iteration, a bin contains the frequencies of occurrence for its range of values.

To plot a histogram, we need certain data about each bin. The `HistoData` class encapsulates such histogram-related data, which includes the array of frequency counts, the minimum and maximum values of the frequency counts, and the starting values of the bins. The `computeHistogram()` method constructs a `HistoData` object from the calculated values and returns it to the calling method. Listing 8.14 shows the code for `HistoData`.

LISTING 8.14 The HistoData class

```
public class HistoData implements Serializable{
    public int[] frequency;
    public Object data;
    public int[] freqMinmax;
    public Object binMinmax;
    public void setData(Object da){
        data = da;
    }

    public Object getData(){
        return data;
    }


    public void setBinMinmax(Object minmax){
        binMinmax = minmax;
    }

    public Object getBinMinmax(){
        return binMinmax;
    }

    public void setFrequency(int[] fr){
        frequency = fr;
    }

    public int[] getFrequency(){
        return frequency;
    }

    public void setFreqMinmax(int[] minmax){
        freqMinmax = minmax;
    }

    public int[] getFreqMinmax(){
        return freqMinmax;
    }
}
```

To compute histogram values and to display them as a bar chart (see Figure 8.14), the Histogram bean uses several classes, including MultiHistogram, Histogram Data, and Util.

> **Note:** The Histogram bean, along with other plotter beans, is available on the book's Web page in the directory src/beans/plotter/histogram.

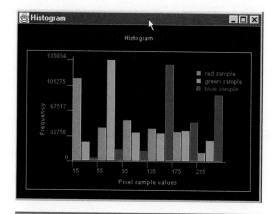

FIGURE 8.14   The Histogram bean displaying a histogram of different color bands in an image

Putting It All Together: An Image Data Viewer

Let's use the classes and beans we have discussed so far to build an application that displays information about an image. This application will display an image on a canvas and associated information as a table. We have already developed methods to extract two types of information: image statistics and attribute information. Let's create two JTable objects to display both types of information. We'll also add the capability to show the histogram of image data in both graph form and bar chart form.

We will not show the code related to displaying the image because we have already discussed this. Listings 8.15 and 8.16 show the code for two related methods in the ImageDataViewer class: displayImageInfo() and displayStats(). The display ImageInfo() method (Listing 8.15) displays the image information in a table.

LISTING 8.15   Displaying image information

```
public void displayImageInfo(BufferedImage img){
    SampleModel sm = img.getSampleModel();
    WritableRaster wr = img.getRaster();
    DataBuffer db = wr.getDataBuffer();
    ColorModel cm = img.getColorModel();

    String str = ImageInfoUtil.getColorModelAsText(ImageInfoUtil.getColorModelType(cm));
    String rowdata[][] = ImageInfoUtil.getImageInfo(img);
    if(rowdata == null) return;
    String colnames[] = {"Properties ", "value"};
    imageInfoTable = new JTable(rowdata, colnames);
    displayStats(cm,sm,db);
}
```

The `displayImageInfo()` method calls the `getImageInfo()` method (see Listing 8.11) to retrieve information about the attributes of the displayed image. The `displayImageInfo()` method displays these attributes in a `JTable` object called `image InfoTable`, which is an instance variable in the `ImageDataViewer` class. To compute and display statistics, `displayImageInfo()` calls the `displayStats()` method (see Listing 8.16).

LISTING 8.16   Displaying image statistics

```
public void displayStats(ColorModel cm, SampleModel sm, DataBuffer db){
    ColorSpace cs = cm.getColorSpace();
    int numComponents = cs.getNumComponents();
    String name[] = new String[numComponents];
    for(int i=0;i<numComponents;i++){
        name[i] = cs.getName(i);
    }

    int[][] imstats = ImageInfoUtil.getImageStats(sm, db,
                          new Dimension(imageWidth, imageHeight));
    String[] colnames = new String[] {"Sample", "Min", "Max", "Mean"};
    String rowdata[][] = new String[imstats.length][colnames.length];

    for(int i=0; i<imstats.length;i++){
        rowdata[i][0] = name[i];
        // Columns
        for(int j=0;j<imstats[0].length;j++){
            rowdata[i][j+1] = Integer.toString(imstats[i][j]);
        }
    }
    imageStatsTable = new JTable(rowdata, colnames);
}
```

The `displayStats()` method calls `getImageStats()` (see Listing 8.10) and displays the results in a `JTable` object called `imageStatsTable`.

Listing 8.17 shows how to use the `Histogram` bean. The `displayHistogram()` method instantiates the bean and launches a frame to display it (see Figure 8.14).

LISTING 8.17   Displaying the histogram

```
public void displayHistogram(BufferedImage img) {
    try {
        int[][] pix = ImageInfoUtil.getPixelSamples(img);

        ClassLoader cl = (MultiHistogram.class).getClassLoader();
        MultiHistogram histo = (MultiHistogram)Beans.instantiate(cl,
                          "vis.beans.plotter.MultiHistogram");
        histo.setSize(400,300);
        histoFrame = new JFrame();
        histoFrame.addWindowListener(
        new WindowAdapter() {
            public void windowClosing(WindowEvent e){
                histoFrame.hide();
            }
```

```
    } );
    histoFrame.setTitle("Histogram");
    Container cp = histoFrame.getContentPane();
    histoFrame.getContentPane().setLayout(new GridLayout(1,1));
    cp.add(histo);
    histoFrame.pack();
    histoFrame.setSize(new Dimension(400, 300));
    histoFrame.show();
    String[] colstr = {"red sample", "green sample", "blue sample", "yellow"};
    Color[]  col = {Color.red, Color.green, Color.blue, Color.yellow};
    histo.setLegendOn(true);
    for (int i=0; i<pix.length;i++) {
        histo.addGraph(null, pix[i]);
        histo.addLegend(col[i], colstr[i]);
    }
    histo.setNumBars(6);
    histo.setTitleString("Histogram ");
    histo.setXLabelString("Pixel sample values");
    histo.setYLabelString("Frequency");
    histo.repaint();
    }catch (Exception e) {
        System.out.println(e);
    }
}
```

The `displayHistogram()` method uses the `ImageInfoUtil` class to obtain the pixel samples and passes it to the `Histogram` bean to compute the histogram. You can launch the `Histogram` bean by clicking on the image.

Running the Image Data Viewer Application

To run this application, type "java app.ImageDataViewer <imagename>" on the command line. The image name must refer to a valid image on the local machine.

This application lets you view the histogram of the pixels as a graph or a bar chart. To display a histogram, you need to launch the pop-up menu by right-clicking on it. The pop-up menu has two options: **Histogram** and **XY Plot.** When you choose one of these options, a frame is launched to display the appropriate plot, as shown in Figure 8.14. Both plots use beans to draw graphs.

Figure 8.15 shows a screen shot of the image data viewer application. On the right-hand side are the tables that display image statistics and a variety of other information.

Using Filters to Manipulate Image Data

Now that you know how to read pixel data, let's explore how to enhance an image by manipulating its pixels. The Java 2D API has various interfaces and classes for this purpose. You may recall that we used the `AffineTransformOp` class to generate a transformed `BufferedImage` object. Six such operator classes can perform different

Image Statistics

Sample	Min	Max	Mean
Unnam...	0	239	84
Unnam...	0	245	86
Unnam...	0	241	64

Image Info

Properties	value
Color Model	Component
Color space	RGB
Sample Model	Pixel interleaved
Data type	Unsigned short
Number of Bands	3
Number of Banks	1
Width	320
Height	480
Scanline stride	960
Pixel stride	3

© Guido Alberto Rossi/The Image Bank

FIGURE 8.15   The image data viewer application

types of filtering or enhancement operations on images. Figure 8.16 shows all the operator classes in the Java 2D API:

- **AffineTransformOp.** As we saw in Chapter 7, this class creates a destination image by geometrically transforming the source image using the affine transformation.

- **ConvolveOp.** This class implements the convolution operation, which is nothing but obtaining a pixel value in the destination image by computing a weighted sum of neighborhood pixels. See the next section for more details.

- **LookupOp.** This class implements the lookup operation.

- **RescaleOp.** This class creates a destination image by performing pixel-by-pixel scaling of the source image pixel values. This operator can be used for adjusting the brightness of an image.

- **ColorConvertOp.** This class creates a destination image by performing pixel-by-pixel color conversion of the source image.

- **BandCombineOp.** This class creates a destination image by linearly combining bands in a **Raster** object. For example, you can create a grayscale image by combining the red, green, and blue bands in an RGB image.

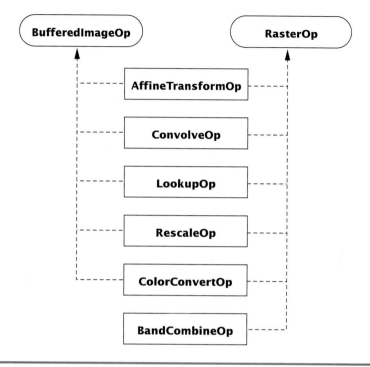

FIGURE 8.16   Operator classes for filtering

Except for BandCombineOp, all of these classes implement the BufferedImageOp and RasterOp interfaces.

Both BufferedImageOp and RasterOp do the same thing: perform filter operations on image data. In the case of the former, image data is presented as the BufferedImage input; in the latter case, image data is presented through Raster (see Figure 8.17).

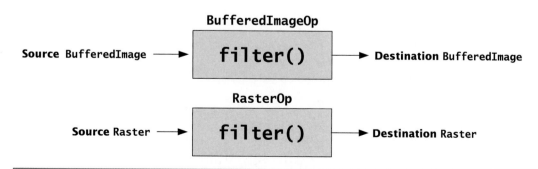

FIGURE 8.17   The structure of filter operations

`BufferedImageOp` and `RasterOp` have five methods each, two of which are common to both interfaces. The common methods are

- `public Point2D getPoint2D(Point2D srcPt, Point2D dstPt)`
- `public RenderingHints getRenderingHints()`

The methods that are different are as follows:

- For `BufferedImageOp`:
  - `public final BufferedImage filter(BufferedImage src,`
    `                                   BufferedImage dst)`
  - `public BufferedImage createCompatibleDestImage(BufferedImage src,`
    `                                                ColorModel destCM)`
  - `public Rectangle2D getBounds2D(BufferedImage src)`

- For `RasterOp`:
  - `public final WritableRaster filter(Raster src, WritableRaster dst)`
  - `public BufferedImage createCompatibleDestImage(BufferedImage src,`
    `                                                ColorModel destCM)`
  - `public Rectangle2D getBounds2D(Raster src)`

Convolution

The `ConvolveOp` class supports the convolution operation, a technique that is used extensively in image processing. In this technique, each pixel in the destination image is obtained by computation of the weighted sum of the corresponding neighborhood pixels in the source image. We perform this computation by moving a small window called a *kernel* over the image pixel by pixel, each time computing the weighted sum. The kernel is nothing but a matrix of coefficients, as shown here:

$$
K = \begin{bmatrix} k_{11} & k_{12} & k_{13} \\ k_{21} & k_{22} & k_{23} \\ k_{31} & k_{32} & k_{33} \end{bmatrix}
$$

Figure 8.18 shows a 3×3 neighborhood of pixels in which the kernel is positioned on pixel $P_{(x,y)}$.

The pixel value $D_{(x,y)}$ is computed by:

$$
\begin{aligned}
D_{(x,y)} = {} & (P_{(x-1,y-1)} \cdot k_{11}) + (P_{(x,y-1)} \cdot k_{12}) + (P_{(x+1,y-1)} \cdot k_{13}) \\
& + (P_{(x-1,y)} \cdot k_{21}) + (P_{(x,y)} \cdot k_{22}) + (P_{(x+1,y)} \cdot k_{23}) \\
& + (P_{(x-1,y+1)} \cdot k_{31}) + (P_{(x,y+1)} \cdot k_{32}) + (P_{(x+1,y+1)} \cdot k_{33})
\end{aligned}
$$

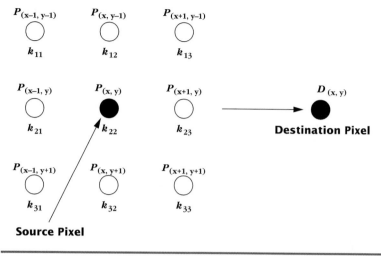

FIGURE 8.18   Convolution

By creating appropriate kernels, you can perform a variety of convolution opera-tions, such as sharpening, blurring, edge detection, and so on. Java 2D has a class called `Kernel` to construct a kernel that can be used as a parameter to construct a `ConvolveOp` object.

Constructing a Kernel

The `Kernel` class has just the following constructor:

- **`public Kernel(int width, int height, float[] data)`**

The `width` and `height` parameters specify the number of rows and columns, respec-tively, of the kernel matrix. The `data` parameter specifies an array of type `float` con-taining the elements of the kernel matrix. The length of the data array should be width × height. If it is less than that, the constructor will throw an exception: `IllegalArgumentException`. Here's an example of constructing a `Kernel` object:

```
float sharpMatrix[] = {-1.0f, -1.0f, 1.0f,
                       -1.0f, -9.0f, 1.0f,
                       -1.0f, -1.0f, 1.0f};
Kernel sharpKernel = new Kernel (3,3, sharpMatrix);
```

The kernel matrix typically has odd numbers of rows and columns. The position of the pixel under consideration is called the origin and is defined with respect to the kernel's upper left-hand corner position. So the x and y origins of a kernel are de-fined by (width − 1)/2 and (height − 1)/2, respectively. The `Kernel` class has methods for obtaining the kernel's origin, as well as its width and height and the data.

Next let's see how we can use the `Kernel` object for convolution. As stated earlier, the `ConvolveOp` class helps perform convolution.

Constructing a ConvolveOp Object

The `ConvolveOp` class has two constructors:

- **`public ConvolveOp(Kernel kernel)`**
- **`public ConvolveOp(Kernel kernel,`**
  `int edgeCondition,`
  `RenderingHints hints)`

As you probably have noticed, when the kernel is positioned at the edges, you cannot perform the weighted sum operation on all the neighboring pixels because they don't exist. The `ConvolveOp` class provides two options for obtaining the edge pixels in the destination image:

1. `EDGE_ZERO_FILL`. With this option, pixels at the edge of the destination image are set to zero. This is the default option. If you use the first constructor, you will get this option.

2. `EDGE_NO_OP`. With this option, pixels at the edge of the destination images are copied from the corresponding locations in the source image.

In the case of 3 × 3 kernels, the edge consists of one row and column at the border of the image. In the case of a 5 × 5 kernel or a kernel with larger dimensions, the `edgeCondition` parameter applies to two rows and two columns at the border of the image. You may want to keep this in mind while deciding which `edgeCondition` option to choose.

Here's an example of constructing a `ConvolveOp` object:

```
public static ConvolveOp getConvolveOp(Kernel kernel) {
    RenderingHints hints =
                new RenderingHints(RenderingHints.KEY_RENDERING,
                                   RenderingHints.VALUE_RENDER_QUALITY);
    ConvolveOp op = new ConvolveOp( kernel,
                                    ConvolveOp.EDGE_NO_OP,
                                    hints);
    return op;
}
```

Note: The methods in this section are available on the book's Web page in the directory `src/chapter8/imenhance`.

To construct a destination image, all you need to do is call the `filter()` method in the `ConvolveOp` object with appropriate source and destination parameters. Here's an example:

```
public static BufferedImage createDestImage(BufferedImage srcImage, ConvolveOp op){
    BufferedImage destImage = op.createCompatibleDestImage(srcImage,
                                        srcImage.getColorModel());
    destImage = op.filter(srcImage, destImage);
    return destImage;
}
```

The `ConvolveOpFactory` class has several methods that create different types of convolution operators. Figure 8.19 shows a screen shot of an application that uses the methods in this class to sharpen and blur images.

> **Note:** The code for `ConvolveOpFactory` is available on the book's Web page in the directory `src/chapter8/imenhance`.

Color Conversion

You can easily convert an image from one color space to another using the `ColorConvertOp` class. This class comes in handy when you're converting images that are loaded with the `getImage()` method. Even if an image is in grayscale, this method

FIGURE 8.19   Image enhancement using `ConvolveOp`

creates images with the `DirectColorModel` class. You can use the `ColorConvertOp` class to restore the original color space.

Constructing a ColorConvertOp Object

The `ColorConvertOp` class has four constructors:

1. `public ColorConvertOp(ColorSpace srcCspace, ColorSpace dstCspace,`
      `RenderingHints hints)`
2. `public ColorConvertOp(ColorSpace cspace, RenderingHints hints)`
3. `public ColorConvertOp(ICC_Profile[] profiles, RenderingHints hints)`
4. `public ColorConvertOp(RenderingHints hints)`

The destination color space can be one of the color spaces in the `ColorSpace` class (see Table 8.1) or an array of `ICC_Profile` objects. Here's an example:

```
protected void grayColorConvert() {
    ColorSpace graySpace = ColorSpace.getInstance(ColorSpace.CS_GRAY);
    ColorConvertOp ccOp = new ColorConvertOp(graySpace, null);
    displayDestImage(ccOp);
}
```

The `renderingHints` parameter can be `null`. Figure 8.20 shows a screen shot of an application that uses the `grayColorConvert()` method to convert an RGB image to a grayscale image.

Using the BandCombineOp Class

With multibanded images, it is often necessary to combine bands linearly and create a new image. A simple example would be to create a grayscale image from an RGB image. The grayscale pixel value is obtained by linear combination of the red, green, and blue sample values. The `BandCombineOp` class can accomplish this job elegantly. It has one constructor that requires an input matrix:

◆ `public BandCombineOp(float[][] matrix, RenderingHints hints)`

The important thing here is to design the band combine matrix. For example, if there are three bands, the input matrix should be at least 3×3.

$$\begin{bmatrix} C_{11} & C_{12} & C_{13} \\ C_{21} & C_{22} & C_{23} \\ C_{31} & C_{32} & C_{33} \end{bmatrix} \cdot \begin{bmatrix} B_1 \\ B_2 \\ B_3 \end{bmatrix}$$

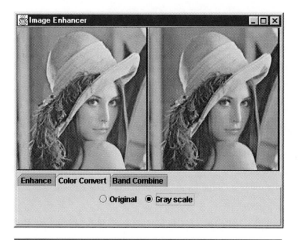

FIGURE 8.20   Converting an RGB image to grayscale
using `ColorConvertOp`

B_1 to B_3 are the band sample values in the source image. The elements C_{11} to C_{33} are
the band combine matrix elements that are provided as an input array. These are multiplied with the band sample values pixel by pixel to create a new image.

In the grayscale example, the grayscale value (G) is given by the following
equation:

$$G = (r \times 0.212671) + (g \times 0.715160) + (b \times 0.071169)$$

where r, g, and b are the red, green, and blue sample values, respectively.

The band combine matrix for the grayscale destination image is implemented as
follows:

```
float[][] grayBandCombine =  {{0.212671f,   0.715160f,   0.071169f}};
```

In the grayscale example, there is only one destination band. In many situations,
however, there are more than one destination band. So to create a band combine matrix, here are the rules:

- The number of rows in the band combine matrix should equal the number of
  bands in the destination image.
- The number of columns in the band combine matrix should equal the number
  of bands in the source image.

Lookup Operations

Lookup operations can be used for image enhancement, among other things. For instance, brightness and contrast adjustments can easily be implemented by a lookup operation.

Constructing a Lookup Table

In addition to the methods that implement the `BufferedImageOp` and `RasterOp` interfaces, the `LookupOp` class has one more method—`getTable()`—which returns a `LookupTable` object. The Java 2D API has two lookup table classes: `ByteLookupTable` and `ShortLookupTable.`

The lookup operation can be carried out on a `Raster` object or a `BufferedImage` object. In the case of `Raster` objects, the lookup operates on bands. The number of lookup arrays may be one, in which case the same array is applied to all bands, or a number equal to the number of source `Raster` bands. In the case of `BufferedImage` objects, the lookup operates on color and alpha components.

Adjusting Window and Level: An Example Using Lookup Tables

Adjusting window width and level is an operation that is commonly performed on medical images. The underlying concept is similar to adjusting brightness and contrast. Whether the context is CT, MRI, nuclear imaging, or any other modality, medical images are reconstructed from projections. The range of pixel values of medical images varies widely. In the case of CT, pixel values are measured in Hounsfield units. These values vary from –1,000 (air) to 3,000 (bone). The application requires 12 bits to represent the entire range, so CT images are typically 12 bits. However, this doesn't mean that CT images contain the entire range of pixels. For instance, the range of a CT brain image may be 0 to 200 Hounsfield units, and the range of a chest image may be 0 to 2,000. If we map the entire range and display the image on a screen of 8-bit depth, the brain image may not be bright and may have poor contrast. The *window* and *level* operations overcome this problem.

The window operation assigns a range of pixel values to the window width, and the level operation assigns a value to the center of the window (see Figure 8.21). Varying window width is similar to adjusting contrast and varying level is similar to adjusting brightness.

The pixel values in the window are mapped onto the screen values by a particular function, which can be linear or nonlinear. If P_r is the pixel value at $P_{(x,y)}$, then its window value (P_w) is given by

$$P_w = P_r - (level + window/2)$$

where the values of *level* and *window* are provided by the user.

If f is a function that maps window values to screen values, the screen value (P_s) corresponds to the pixel at $P_{(x,y)}$ given by

$$P_s = f(P_w)$$

Using Lookup Tables to Adjust Window and Level

The function f can be linear or nonlinear. Applying a window-mapping function to each pixel in the image is a computation-intensive operation. So it may not be possible to perform window and level operations in real time on low-performance machines. With lookup tables (LUTs), however, window or level operation can be substantially sped up. When a LUT is used, the window mapper converts the image pixel values to screen pixel values by directly reading from a LUT. Another advantage of using LUTs is that an application can maintain several LUTs, which can be switched to suit the user's needs.

We'll use the `LookupTable` and `LookupOp` classes for performing lookup operations. We already saw a sample use of lookup tables in Chapter 6 for inverting images.

Linear Window Mapping

As shown in Figure 8.21, the window-mapping function is a ramp. The higher the slope of this ramp, the better the contrast is. Linear window mapping is fast and mostly adequate for anatomical images. This is why it is popular for CT and MRI images.

Listing 8.18 shows a class that implements the linear window-mapping function.

LISTING 8.18   The `WindowLevel` class

```
public class WindowLevel{
    int minValue =0;
    int maxValue =255;
    int MIN_SCREEN_VALUE = 0;
    int MAX_SCREEN_VALUE = 255;
    int LUT_SIZE = 256;
    int lutSize = LUT_SIZE;
    BufferedImage wlImage;
    int window, level;

    ImageDisplay imageCanvas;
    public WindowLevel(ImageDisplay imageCanvas) {
        this.imageCanvas = imageCanvas;
    }
```

continued

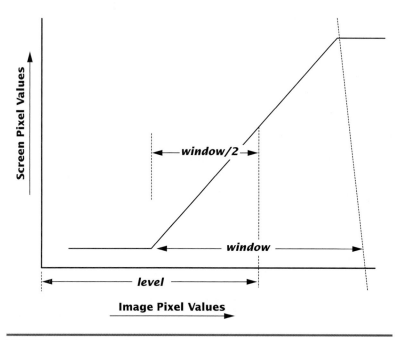

FIGURE 8.21 Linear window mapping

```java
public void setLUTSize(int size) {
   if(size <=0) return;
   lutSize = size;
}

public int getLUTSize(){
   return lutSize;
}

public void setWindow(int win) {
   window = win;
}

public void setLevel(int lev) {
   level = lev;
}

public void setWindowLevel(int win, int lev) {
   ByteLookupTable blut = createByteLookupTable(win, lev);
   LookupOp lkop = new LookupOp(blut, null);
   wlImage = lkop.filter(imageCanvas.getOffScreenImage() , null);
   imageCanvas.setDisplayImage(wlImage);
}
```

```
public ByteLookupTable createByteLookupTable(int win, int lev) {
    int windowStart = lev-win/2;
    int windowEnd = lev+win/2;
    if(windowStart <=0) windowStart =0;
    if(windowEnd > lutSize) windowEnd = lutSize;
    byte lut[] = new byte[lutSize];
    double windowMappingRatio = (MAX_SCREEN_VALUE-MIN_SCREEN_VALUE)/(double)(win);
    for(int i=0;i<windowStart;i++) {
        lut[i] = (byte)MIN_SCREEN_VALUE;
    }
    for(int i = windowStart; i< windowEnd; i++) {
        lut[i] = (byte)((i-windowStart)* windowMappingRatio);
    }
    for(int i = windowEnd; i< lutSize; i++) {
        lut[i] = (byte)MAX_SCREEN_VALUE;
    }
    return new ByteLookupTable(0, lut);
}
}
```

The `createByteLookupTable()` method creates a lookup table of bytes for given `window` and `level` values. The code in Listing 8.18 creates a lookup table for linear window mapping. You can override this method to create lookup tables for any other functions.

The `for` loops in `createByteLookupTable()` implement the three segments of the window and level functions. The initial segment of the LUT, which goes from 0 to the value of `windowStart,` will have a constant value given by `MIN_SCREEN_VALUE.` The middle segment creates the ramp, the slope of which is the screen pixel range divided by `window`. Each value in the middle segment is multiplied by the slope. The last segment will have a constant value of `MAX_SCREEN_VALUE` starting from `windowEnd` and ending at `lutSize`.

The `setWindowLevel()` method creates a `BufferedImage` object with specified `window` and `level` values. It first creates a LUT by calling `createByteLookupTable()`. The `LookupOp` class is used for creating a lookup table operator. As mentioned earlier, this class implements `BufferedImageOp`. `BufferedImage`'s `filter()` method performs the filter operation by applying the lookup table operation—that is, reading in a screen pixel value from the table for each of the image pixel values. The source image for this operation is `offScreenImage,` and the destination image is the `displayImage` object. When the lookup table is used for filtering, only the image that is painted onto the screen is changed to reflect the new `window` and `level` values.

Note that image type determines the LUT size. The size of the LUT for viewing CT images, which are typically 12 bits, will be 4,096. For MRI images, which are typically 16 bits, LUT size can be as high as 64,000. But if we know the pixel range of an image, the LUT size can be trimmed.

The `setWindow()` or `setLevel()` method can be called from any GUI. The GUI may be a scroll bar, or it may even be mouse or keystroke driven. Each mouse click or keystroke increments or decrements the `window` and `level` values by a fixed amount.

In our case, we implemented the GUI with sliders. The `WindowLevelGUI` class (see Listing 8.19) creates two sliders: **Window** and **Level** (see Figure 8.22). By adjusting the sliders, you can vary the window width and level.

LISTING 8.19   The `WindowLevelGUI` class

```
public class WindowLevelGUI extends JPanel {
    JSlider windowSlider;
    JSlider levelSlider;
    JTextField windowField;
    JTextField levelField;
    int minValue =0;
    int maxValue =255;
    int window, level;
    WindowLevel wl;

    public WindowLevelGUI(WindowLevel wl){
        this.wl = wl;
        init();
    }
```

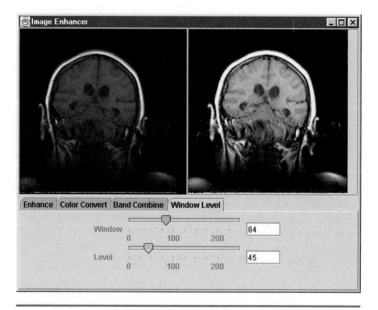

FIGURE 8.22   Adjusting the window and level

```java
void init(){ add(createWindowLevelPanel());}

public JPanel createWindowLevelPanel (){
    int brightStartValue = 50;
    windowField = new JTextField(5);
    levelField = new JTextField(5);

    windowField.setText(Integer.toString(brightStartValue));
    windowSlider = new JSlider(minValue,maxValue, brightStartValue);
    levelSlider = new JSlider(minValue,maxValue, brightStartValue);

    int majorTickSpacing = 100;
    int minorTickSpacing = 25;
    windowSlider.setMajorTickSpacing(majorTickSpacing);
    windowSlider.setMinorTickSpacing(minorTickSpacing);
    windowSlider.setExtent(minorTickSpacing);
    windowSlider.setPaintTicks(true);
    windowSlider.setPaintLabels(true);

    levelSlider.setMajorTickSpacing(majorTickSpacing);
    levelSlider.setMinorTickSpacing(minorTickSpacing);
    levelSlider.setExtent(minorTickSpacing);
    levelSlider.setPaintTicks(true);
    levelSlider.setPaintLabels(true);


    windowField.addActionListener(
        new ActionListener() {
            public void actionPerformed(ActionEvent e){
                try {
                  String str = ((JTextField)e.getSource()).getText();
                  int value = (Integer.valueOf(str)).intValue();
                  windowSlider.setValue((int)value);
                  wl.setWindowLevel(window,level);

                } catch (Exception e1){}
            }
        }
    );


    levelField.addActionListener(
        new ActionListener() {
            public void actionPerformed(ActionEvent e){
                try {
                  String str = ((JTextField)e.getSource()).getText();
                  int value = (Integer.valueOf(str)).intValue();
                  levelSlider.setValue((int)value);
                  wl.setWindowLevel(window,level);
                } catch (Exception e1){}
            }
        }
    );
```

continued

```
        windowSlider.addChangeListener(
            new ChangeListener(){
                public void stateChanged(ChangeEvent e){
                    Object obj = e.getSource();
                    if(obj instanceof JSlider) {
                        JSlider jsr = (JSlider)obj;
                        window = ((JSlider)(e.getSource())).getValue();
                        wl.setWindowLevel(window, level);
                        windowField.setText(Integer.toString(window));
                    }
                }
            }
        );

        levelSlider.addChangeListener(
            new ChangeListener(){
                public void stateChanged(ChangeEvent e){
                    Object obj = e.getSource();
                    if(obj instanceof JSlider) {
                        JSlider jsr = (JSlider)obj;
                        level = ((JSlider)(e.getSource())).getValue();
                        wl.setWindowLevel(window, level);
                        levelField.setText(Integer.toString(level));
                    }
                }
            }
        );


        JPanel brightpan = new JPanel();
        // Gridbag layout
        return brightpan;
    }

    public void initSliders(int[] minmax){
        int min = minmax[0];
        int max = minmax[1];
        minValue = (int)min; maxValue=(int) max;
        windowSlider.setMinimum(minValue);
        windowSlider.setMaximum(maxValue);
        levelSlider.setMinimum(minValue);
        levelSlider.setMaximum(maxValue);
    }
}
```

Before creating the sliders, WindowLevelGUI calls the initSliders() method to determine the minimum and maximum pixel values in the image. These values are used as the slider initial values. The slider event-handling methods call the setWindowLevel() method of the WindowLevel class whenever the sliders are adjusted.

Figure 8.22 shows a screen shot of the window and level operations. Because of the lookup table, we get a real-time response. The JAI versions of the classes that implement window and level functionality are described in Chapter 13.

Conclusion

In this chapter we introduced some new concepts related to reading, writing, and manipulating image data. These concepts are encapsulated in the `SampleModel` and `ColorModel` classes at the lower level, and in the operator classes at the higher level. These APIs are higher-level abstractions for storing, interpreting, and manipulating pixels.

Because of these new APIs, Java 2D can now support wide-ranging color spaces and image data types. This support has made Java 2D quite useful for building real-world scientific imaging applications. However, this capability has come at a price. The Java 2D APIs for reading, writing, and interpreting pixels are more complicated and may require more programming effort than the AWT imaging APIs do.

JAI expands the classes described in this chapter to provide much richer functionality. JAI has a broad spectrum of image data manipulation operators, which are very easy to implement (see Chapter 13).

Building an ROI Application   9

NOW THAT WE'VE LOOKED AT DIFFERENT ASPECTS of the Java 2D API, it's time to utilize them in a real-world application. Not many applications are better suited for this purpose than an application that performs ROI (region of interest) analysis, because such analysis requires both graphical and imaging APIs.

The ability to analyze ROIs is a common feature of imaging applications. In medical imaging, for instance, many practical applications use ROI techniques for diagnosis.

In this chapter we'll build an ROI-based quantitative analysis application that will compute the statistics of a region and display them as charts and tables. It will also perform some image-processing functions. We'll look at the requirements, design, and implementation of this application in an informal manner. Although our examples will show medical images, this application can be used in other areas of imaging as well.

> **Note:** The source code developed in this chapter is available on the book's Web page in the directory `src/chapter9/simpleroi`.

A Medical Imaging Scenario

To understand the requirements, let's look at a simple medical imaging scenario. Suppose that you are required to develop a cardiac application that performs quantitative analysis on cardiac images. Cardiac images are acquired at different time intervals but at the same position of the heart. A doctor may draw a region of interest on a cardiac image and may want to compute certain statistics of the underlying area on the image. The doctor will then map the same ROI on all the cardiac images taken at the same position and have the statistics computed. This information will enable the doctor to compare the state of the heart at different cardiac cycles.

Besides cardiac analysis, ROI techniques are used in a variety of diagnostic applications that involve medical images—for example,

- Bone mineral densitometry (BMD)
- Blood flow measurements using phase-contrast images

Steps in Building an ROI Application

Applications that perform quantitative analysis on images typically use ROI processing. Building such an application involves implementing the following tasks:

- Marking a shape
- Obtaining pixels contained within the shape from the original image
- Calculating pixel statistics
- Detecting edges automatically
- Thresholding

Marking ROI Shapes

There are many approaches to marking a region of interest. Typically, users draw ROI shapes interactively over the image. However, ROI shapes can be generated automatically. One way to do this is to use edge detection software to detect the edges and then draw a boundary. In the case of vascular images, for instance, the edges can be the boundary of an artery. In the case of satellite images of Earth, the edges can represent the boundaries of a specific geographic area.

With cardiac images, it is possible to automatically detect edges of different regions of the heart. Sometimes this approach is more accurate than manual drawing, which differs from user to user. On the other hand, edge detection algorithms may not find very accurate edges. To overcome this problem, a compromise approach is normally adopted—that is, marking a shape by using a combination of automatic edge detection and interactive drawing techniques. In this approach, first an ROI shape is generated with an edge detection algorithm. A human operator then accepts the automatically generated shape as is or uses interactive drawing techniques to edit it.

Interactive Drawing

The outline of an ROI can take any shape. It can be a regular shape like a rectangle, ellipse, or circle. Or it can be an irregular shape that can be generated by freehand drawing or by curve fitting. When you mark a region the first time, it may not be very accurate. So you may need to edit it a few times before you arrive at a desired shape.

Depending on how accurately you want the ROI shape to reflect the underlying boundary, you may choose different approaches for marking and editing shapes, as described in the sections that follow.

Regular Shapes

Drawing and editing regular shapes such as rectangles and ellipses is easy. A major disadvantage of this approach, however, is that you may not be able to fit the region accurately because ROIs in general are not well-defined shapes.

If your application requires accurate computation of statistics, you may not want to use regular shapes. However, regular shapes can be a starting point for drawing irregularly shaped boundaries. Consider the vascular images again. If the edge detection algorithm is applied to the entire image, besides being a very computation-intensive operation, it may detect edges all over the image. To reduce the search space, first a regularly shaped ROI is drawn covering the desired region.

Irregular Shapes

You can choose any of the following approaches for producing irregular shapes, depending on the accuracy desired.

Freehand Drawing

An easy way to draw an irregular shape is freehand drawing. Move the mouse (or any other pointing device, such as a trackball) over the image to draw a desired shape. The shape generated in this way may depend on the steadiness of your hand.

Polygons

You can create a closed shape by drawing straight lines. ROIs generated in this way are more accurate than regular shapes.

Curves

We discussed the basics of curves in Chapter 4. For a given number of points, there are two approaches to generating a curve to fit those points:

1. **Interpolating.** You can mark the salient points on the desired boundary and ask the spline-fitting software to draw a smooth curve to mark the boundary. In this case, editing the curve is not easy. Changing a point requires the entire curve to be regenerated, and there is no guarantee that the original shape will be retained in other segments.

2. **Approximating.** The curve outline in this case is generated by approximation of the deposited points. Such approximation can be achieved by B-spline or Bezier curve fitting. You may recall from Chapter 4 that the generated shape is

localized; that is, the shape depends on the $n + 1$ control points, where n is the degree of the B-spline. So in the case of cubic B-spline, the current shape depends on the last four control points.

Curve drawing by approximating splines is like the freehand approach, but more accurate. In this approach you move the cursor, and the spline-fitting software makes use of the most recent points to generate an approximating curve (such as B-spline or Bezier). You can edit the boundary by editing a segment.

Graphical Overlay

To draw ROIs interactively, we need a canvas that paints images and allows graphics to be drawn over it. In Chapter 5 we developed a drawing canvas that allows you to draw graphics interactively, and in Chapters 6 and 7 we developed image canvases that can display images. What we need is a combination of the two.

To develop such a canvas, one approach is to extend the `ImageCanvas2D` class that we developed in Chapter 7. Recall that this class allows image manipulation. To allow interactive graphics, we can implement the `GraphicsDisplay` interface that we developed in Chapter 5. However, this is overkill for the ROI application we are going to develop in this chapter, so let's define a simpler interface called `Drawing Canvas` with a subset of methods defined in the `GraphicsDisplay` interface. The basic methods we need here include methods for getting the off-screen graphical context and the current transformation from the canvas. Listing 9.1 shows the code for this interface.

LISTING 9.1 The `DrawingCanvas` interface

```
package com.vistech.imageviewer;
import java.awt.*;
import java.awt.event.*;
import java.awt.geom.*;

public interface DrawingCanvas {
    public Graphics2D getDisplayedImageGC();
    public AffineTransform getTransform();
    public void setTransform(AffineTransform atx);
    public void eraseShapes();
    public void repaint();
    public void reset();
    public void addMouseListener(MouseListener ml);
    public void removeMouseListener(MouseListener ml);
    public void addMouseMotionListener(MouseMotionListener ml);
    public void removeMouseMotionListener(MouseMotionListener ml);
}
```

A client object can obtain the off-screen graphical context and draw a shape or text over it. When the image canvas calls the `paintComponent()` method, the off-screen image is drawn over its graphical context.

Listing 9.2 shows the code for the `CompositeCanvas2D` class, which implements the `DrawingCanvas` interface.

LISTING 9.2   The `CompositeCanvas2D` class

```
package com.vistech.imageviewer;
import java.awt.*;
import java.awt.event.*;
import java.awt.image.*;
import java.awt.geom.*;
import java.io.*;
import javax.swing.*;
import javax.swing.event.*;
import java.util.*;

public class CompositeCanvas2D extends ImageCanvas2D implements DrawingCanvas{
   protected BufferedImage bufferedImage;
   protected int imageWidth = 0, imageHeight = 0;
   protected int viewerWid =400, viewerHt =300;
   protected int  offsetX = 0, offsetY = 0;
   protected Shape currentShape = null;
   protected Point roiPoints[];

   public CompositeCanvas2D(){}

   public CompositeCanvas2D(BufferedImage img, int wid, int ht){
      image = img;
      viewerWid = wid;
      viewerHt = ht;
      setSize(wid,ht);
      setImage(img);
   }
   public void setImage(BufferedImage img){
      if(img == null) return;
      bufferedImage = img;
      paintImage(img);
      repaint();
   }

   public boolean paintImage(){
      return paintImage(bufferedImage);
   }

   protected void redraw(){
      if(bufferedImage != null) redraw(bufferedImage);
      repaint();
   }

   protected void redraw(BufferedImage img) {
      createDisplayImage();
      paintImage(img);
      repaint();
```

continued

```
       }

       public synchronized boolean paintImage(BufferedImage img){
          width = this.getBounds().width;
          height = this.getBounds().height;
          imageWidth = img.getWidth();
          imageHeight = img.getHeight();
          if(imageWidth <0 ) {
            System.out.println("width  <0");
          }
          double magX= (double)width/(double)imageWidth;
          double magY = (double)height/(double)imageHeight;
          int bufferWid = width, bufferHt = height;
          dispModeAtx = new AffineTransform();
          switch(displayMode){
          case DisplayMode.ORIG-SIZE:
            bufferWid = imageWidth;
            bufferHt = imageHeight;
            break;
          case DisplayMode.SCALED:
            double mag = (magY > magX)? magX:magY;
            dispModeAtx.setToScale(mag, mag);
            bufferWid = (int)(imageWidth*mag);
            bufferHt = (int)(imageHeight*mag);
            break;
          case DisplayMode.TO-FIT:
            dispModeAtx.setToScale(magX, magY);
            bufferWid = width;
            bufferHt = height;
            default:
            break;
          }
          BufferedImage bi = new BufferedImage(bufferWid, bufferHt, imageType);
          Graphics2D bigc = bi.createGraphics();
          bigc.drawImage(img, dispModeAtx, this);

          flipAtx = createFlipTransform(flipMode, bufferWid, bufferHt);
          AffineTransformOp atop = new AffineTransformOp(flipAtx, interpolationType);
          offScrImage = atop.filter(bi, null);
          offScrGc = offScrImage.createGraphics();
          applyTransform(offScrImage, atx);
          repaint();
          return true;
       }

       public AffineTransform getAllAtx(){
          AffineTransform atx1 = new AffineTransform(dispModeAtx);
          atx1.concatenate(atx);
          return atx1;
       }
       public AffineTransform getDispModeAtx(){
          return dispModeAtx;
       }

       public void drawShape(Shape s){
          currentShape = s;
          dispGc = displayImage.createGraphics();
```

```
        dispGc.setColor(Color.red);
        dispGc.draw(s);
        repaint();
    }

    public void fillShape(Shape s) {
        dispGc = displayImage.createGraphics();
        dispGc.setColor(Color.red);
        dispGc.fill(s);
        repaint();
    }

    public void eraseShapes() { reset();}

    public void setBufferedImage(BufferedImage bi) {
        bufferedImage = bi;
    }

    public BufferedImage getBufferedImage() {return bufferedImage;}

    public Graphics2D getDisplayedImageGC() {
        return displayImage.createGraphics();
    }

    public BufferedImage getDisplayedImage() {return displayImage;}
    public void reset() {repaint();}
}
```

We'll use the `CompositeCanvas2D` class in the ROI application to display images and draw ROI shapes over them.

ROI Measurements

ROIs are typically deposited over a displayed image, which is in the user space. When you deposit an ROI, the displayed image might have undergone some geometric manipulations, so a shape drawn over such an image must be converted to image space. As we saw in Chapter 4, this conversion is accomplished through application of the inverse affine transformation to the ROI shape and mapping of the transformed shape on the original image (see Figure 9.1).

If a shape S is a shape in user space, then the corresponding shape in image space is given by $S' = [T]^{-1} \cdot S$, where T is the current transformation matrix of the displayed image. By transforming the shape to the original image space, we ensure that the statistics measured are accurate.

The quantitative analysis is performed on the pixels within the ROI shape. Some measurements that are common in scientific imaging fields are area, mean, standard deviation, and minimum and maximum pixel values. The area of an ROI is measured in terms of the number of pixels.

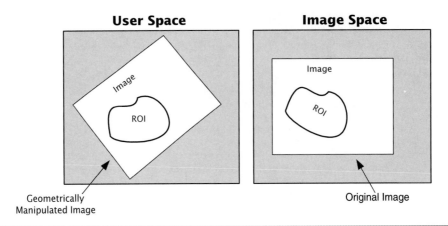

FIGURE 9.1   Transforming an ROI from user space to image space

Next let's design and develop some classes that can be used for developing ROI applications.

Designing APIs for ROI Analysis

As part of an API for ROI analysis, we must develop a class that represents an ROI. To do so, we need the description of an ROI with its attributes.

An ROI is an area marked over an image, and its attributes are the shape of its outline and the image data covered by that shape. Pixels that lie under the outline are not normally considered ROI pixels. The class that represents the ROI need not hold the actual pixel data because if the bounding box is known, pixel data can always be retrieved.

Because multiple ROIs can be deposited on a single image, an ROI object must belong to a context, which is like a logical container. A context is set for an image over which the ROI is marked. In other words, all the ROIs marked over an image belong to the same context.

The same ROI shapes can be used with different images. Take, for example, temporal images (images taken at the same location but at different times). Once marked, the same ROI shapes can be used for computing statistics of all the images in the temporal set. In this case, even though we use the same shapes, the ROIs belong to different contexts.

Let's design two classes—`ROI2D` and `ROIContext`—to represent an ROI and its context, respectively. Let's make the `ROI2D` class a bean with two important properties: `roiContext` and `shape`.

Let's start with the `ROIContext` class.

The ROIContext Class

An image can have more than one ROI deposited over it. These ROIs use the same DataBuffer object to obtain pixels. This means that all the ROIs deposited over an image have the same context. The ROIContext class captures this concept. ROIContext will hold the original image, as well as the image with ROIs. Whenever an application adds an ROI, it adds it to this image. Listing 9.3 shows the code for ROIContext.

LISTING 9.3   The ROIContext class

```
package com.vistech.roi;
import java.awt.*;
import java.awt.event.*;
import java.awt.image.*;
import java.awt.geom.*;
import java.io.*;
import javax.swing.*;
import java.awt.color.*;
import java.util.*;

public class ROIContext {
    protected BufferedImage originalImage;
    protected BufferedImage displayImage;
    private AffineTransform atx = new AffineTransform();
    public ROIContext (BufferedImage img) {
        originalImage = img;
        createDisplayImage();
    }

    public BufferedImage getOriginalImage(){
        return originalImage;
    }

    public BufferedImage getDisplayImage(){
        return displayImage;
    }

    protected void createDisplayImage(){
        AffineTransformOp atop =
            new AffineTransformOp(atx, AffineTransformOp.TYPE_NEAREST_NEIGHBOR);
        displayImage = atop.createCompatibleDestImage(originalImage,
                                            originalImage.getColorModel());
        displayImage = atop.filter(originalImage, displayImage);
    }

    public WritableRaster getOriginalRaster() {
        if(originalImage != null) return originalImage.getRaster();
        else return null;
    }

    public WritableRaster getDisplayRaster() {
        if(displayImage!= null) return displayImage.getRaster();
        else return null;
```

continued

```
   }

   public String[] getComponentNames() {
       if(originalImage == null) return null;
       ColorModel cm = originalImage.getColorModel();
       ColorSpace cs = cm.getColorSpace();
       int numComponents = cs.getNumComponents();
       String[] componentName = new String[numComponents];
       for(int i=0;i<numComponents;i++){
            componentName[i] = cs.getName(i);
       }
       return componentName;
   }
   public void reset(){
       displayImage.flush();
       displayImage = null;
       createDisplayImage();
   }
}
```

All the ROI objects deposited over an image share the same context. The `ROIContext` class is instantiated with a `BufferedImage` object. The `ROIContext` class has two properties: `originalImage` and `displayImage`. To start with, `displayImage` is a copy of `originalImage`. As users keep marking ROI shapes, `displayImage` is updated with the data for the deposited ROIs.

ROI objects that share a context use the same instance of `originalImage` to obtain the image data. Because pixels within an ROI shape are typically masked, ROI objects use the same instance of `displayImage` to write the pixel data within an ROI shape. When the image is displayed, it will show all the deposited ROIs with masked pixels.

As we learned in Chapter 8, a pixel is made up of one or more components called samples. Each sample is identified by a name. For instance, in the case of an RGB pixel, the component names are *red, green,* and *blue.* The `getComponent Names()` method is a utility method that gets the sample names from the `ColorSpace` class.

Representing an ROI

Now that we've defined the context class for ROIs, let's design a base class—ROI2D— to represent an ROI. This class will have minimal properties and functionality. You can extend this class to add more functionality depending on your application.

The `ROI2D` class must operate on the original image data to calculate pixel-related statistics from the pixels within the shape deposited by the user. Two objects are required for computing these statistics:

1. **Image.** The image must be in the form of a `BufferedImage` object. As already stated, an ROI object can obtain this instance of `BufferedImage` from `ROIContext`.

2. **ROI shape.** The ROI shape can be in the form of a **Shape** object. The **shape** property should hold the inverse-transformed shape deposited over the image.

This means that we need to add two properties: **roiContext** and **shape**. In addition, let's add a property to hold the ROI statistics called **roiStats**.

Because an image can have multiple ROIs, it is often necessary to identify the ROI with a number. To do so, let's add a property called **ID**. The **ID** property holds a number that identifies the ROI. The client program can use this ID while listing the statistics.

Besides computing statistics, an ROI object must perform certain other tasks, such as thresholding. Let's create a property named **threshold** for holding the threshold values and add methods to perform thresholding.

Listing 9.4 shows the code for **ROI2D**.

LISTING 9.4 The ROI2D class

```
package com.vistech.roi;
import java.awt.*;
import java.awt.event.*;
import java.awt.image.*;
import java.io.*;
import java.awt.color.*;

public class ROI2D implements java.io.Serializable{
    protected Shape currentShape = null;
    protected transient ROIContext roiContext = null;
    protected String[] roiColNames =
            new String[] {"Num", "Sample", "Min", "Max", "Mean", "Std Dev", "Area"};
    protected int stats[][] = new int[roiColNames.length][];
    protected String[][] roiData = null;
    protected int roiNumber = 0;
    protected ROIStatistics roiStats[];
    protected int threshold;
    protected int maskValue = 255;
    protected transient BufferedImage origImage, displayImage;
    protected Point[] curPoints;

    protected Color drawingColor = Color.white, fillColor = Color.white;

    public ROI2D (){ }

    public void setROIContext(ROIContext roiContext){
        this.roiContext = roiContext;
        origImage = roiContext.getOriginalImage();
        displayImage = roiContext.getDisplayImage();
    }

    public ROIContext getROIContext(){
        return roiContext;
    }

    public void setShape(Shape sh){
```

continued

```
        currentShape = sh;
        computeStats();
        double mean = roiStats[0].getMean();
        setThreshold((int)mean);
    }

    public void drawShape(Shape shape, Color color){
        displayImage = roiContext.getDisplayImage();
        if(displayImage == null) return;
        Graphics2D g2d = displayImage.createGraphics();
        g2d.setColor(color);
        g2d.draw(shape);
    }

    public Shape getShape(){return currentShape;}

    public void setID(int number){roiNumber = number;}
    public int getID(){ return roiNumber; }

    public void setMaskValue(int number){maskValue = number;}
    public int getMaskValue(){ return maskValue; }


    public void setFillColor(Color color){fillColor = color;}
    public Color getFillColor(){ return fillColor; }

    public void setDrawingColor(Color color){drawingColor = color;}
    public Color getDrawingColor(){ return drawingColor; }

    public String[] getColumnNames() {return roiColNames;}

    public String[][] getStatsAsString() {
        computeStats();
        return roiData;
    }

    public ROIStatistics[] getStats() {
        computeStats();
        return roiStats;
    }

    public int getThreshold(){ return threshold; }

    public void setThreshold(int thresh){
        threshold = thresh;
        Point[] thPoints = ROIUtil.getThresholdPoints(origImage, currentShape, thresh);
        if(thPoints == null) return;
        setMask(thPoints, maskValue);
    }

    public void setMask(Point[] points, int maskValue){
        if(points == null) return;
        clearMask();
        displayImage = roiContext.getDisplayImage();
        WritableRaster ra = displayImage.getRaster();
        int num =  ra.getNumBands();
        int mask[] = new int[num];
```

```
                for(int i=0;i<num;i++) mask[i] = maskValue;
                for(int i=0; i<points.length;i++){
                    ra.setPixel(points[i].x, points[i].y,mask);
                }
                curPoints = points;
                drawShape(currentShape,drawingColor);
        }

        public void clearMask(){
            WritableRaster origRaster = origImage.getRaster();
            WritableRaster displayRaster = displayImage.getRaster();
            int num = displayRaster.getNumBands();
            if(curPoints == null) return;
            for(int i=0; i<curPoints.length;i++) {
                int pix1[] = new int[num];
                int[] pix = origRaster.getPixel(curPoints[i].x, curPoints[i].y, pix1);
                displayRaster.setPixel(curPoints[i].x, curPoints[i].y,pix);
            }
        }


        private void computeStats(){
            SampleModel sampleModel = origImage.getSampleModel();
            DataBuffer dataBuffer = origImage.getRaster().getDataBuffer();
            if((sampleModel == null)|| (dataBuffer == null) || (currentShape == null))
                                                            return;
            double[][] roist = ROIUtil.getROIStats(sampleModel, dataBuffer,currentShape);
            int numSamples = roist.length;
            roiStats = new ROIStatistics[numSamples];
            for(int i=0;i<numSamples;i++) {
                roiStats[i] = new ROIStatistics(roist[i][0],
                                                roist[i][1],
                                                roist[i][2],
                                                roist[i][3],
                                                roist[i][4]);
            }
            statsToString(roist);
        }
        private void statsToString( double roistats[][]){
            roiData = new String[roistats.length][roiColNames.length];
            String roinum =  Integer.toString(getID());
            String componentName[] = roiContext.getComponentNames();
            for(int i=0; i<roistats.length;i++){
                roiData[i][0] =  roinum;
                if((componentName != null) && (componentName[i] != null))
                    roiData[i][1]= componentName[i];
                else roiData[i][1] = "Unknown";
                for(int j=0;j<roistats[0].length;j++){
                    roiData[i][j+2] = Double.toString(roistats[i][j]);
                }
            }
        }
    }
}
```

Let's look at the code for **ROI2D** in a little more depth.

Setting the Context

As Listing 9.4 shows, `roiContext` is one of the properties of the `ROI2D` class. The client object instantiates the `ROI2D` object and sets the `roiContext` property. The `ROI2D` class makes use of this property to obtain the original and display images while calculating pixel statistics.

Masking Pixels

Pixels that are above a certain threshold are masked. For simplicity, we will assume that all the bands have the same threshold values.

Three methods accomplish this functionality: `setThreshold()`, `getThreshold Points()`, and `setMask()`. The `setThreshold()` method sets the threshold property and calls the `getThresholdPoints()` method from the `ROIUtil` class (see Listing 9.6) to obtain the pixels that are above the threshold value. With the points so obtained, `setThreshold()` then calls `setMask()` to mask the pixels at those positions. Because the current ROI may overlap with other ROIs, the `setMask()` method first calls the `clearMask()` method to set the values of the already masked pixel values to the original value.

The `setMask()` method then gets the `WritableRaster` object from the `displayImage` property and calls the `setPixel()` method to write the masked values.

Computing Statistics

The `computeStats()` method computes statistics. The `setShape()` method calls `compute Stats()` whenever a new shape is assigned. The `computeStats()` method calls the `ROIUtil.getROIStats()` method (see Listing 9.7) to obtain statistics as an array of `double` values.

The statistics computed are minimum, maximum, average, area of the ROI, and standard deviation of the pixel values. The `ROI2D` class saves the ROI statistics in two different ways:

1. **As an `ROIStatistics` object** (see Listing 9.5).
2. **As an array of `String` values whose elements represent statistics as text.** This representation is convenient for displaying statistics on a `JTable` object. The `computeStats()` method calls `statsToString()` to convert the array of `double` values to an array of `String` values. The `getROIStatsAsText()` method returns this value.

The `columnNames` property is a convenient property that holds the column names of the table in which the statistics can be displayed. The `ROI2D` class has default column names. When you create your own class, you can override the set and get methods for this property.

ROIStatistics is a convenient class that represents some basic statistics. Listing 9.5 shows the code for ROIStatistics.

LISTING 9.5 The ROIStatistics class

```java
public class ROIStatistics implements java.io.Serializable {
    double min, max, mean, area, stdDev;

    public ROIStatistics(double min, double max, double mean, double area,
                         double stdDev){
        setStats(min, max, mean, area, stdDev);
    }

    public void setStats(double min, double max, double mean,
                         double area, double stdDev) {
        this.min = min;
        this.max = max;
        this.mean = mean;
        this.area = area;
        this.stdDev = stdDev;
    }

    public double getMin() {
        return min;
    }

    public double getMax() {
        return max;
    }

    public double getMean() {
        return mean;
    }

    public double getArea() {
        return area;
    }

    public double getStdDev() {
        return stdDev;
    }
}
```

Extracting Pixel Samples within an ROI

The ROIUtil class has several static methods to help calculate ROI-related statistics. The getROIPixelSamples() method, for example, returns the sample values of the pixels within an ROI. The return value is a two-dimensional array. The first subscript represents the band; the second, the sample value. Listing 9.6 shows two flavors of getROIPixelSamples(). Both are used in computing statistics.

LISTING 9.6 The static methods of the ROIUtil class

```java
public static int[][] getROIPixelSamples(BufferedImage img, Shape shape){
    if(img == null) return null;
    SampleModel sm = img.getSampleModel();
    WritableRaster wr = img.getRaster();
    DataBuffer db = wr.getDataBuffer();
    ColorModel cm = img.getColorModel();
    return getROIPixelSamples(sm, db, shape);
}

public static int[][] getROIPixelSamples(SampleModel sm,
                                         DataBuffer db,
                                         Shape shape) {
    Rectangle2D rect = shape.getBounds();
    int x = (int) rect.getX();
    int y = (int) rect.getY();

    int wid = (int)rect.getWidth();
    int ht = (int)rect.getHeight();
    int k=0;
    int totalPixels = wid*ht;
    int sample[][] = new int[totalPixels][];
    for(int i=0; i<wid;i++){
        for(int j=0;j<ht;j++){
            if(shape.contains((double)(x+j),(double)(y+i))){
                int pix[] = null;
                sample[k++] = (sm.getPixel(x+j, y+i, pix, db));
            }
        }
    }
    int len = sample[0].length;
    int roiPixels[][] = new int[len][k];
    for(int l=0;l<len;l++) {
        for(int j=0; j<k;j++) {
            roiPixels[l][j] = sample[j][l];
        }
    }
    return roiPixels;
}
```

The getROIPixelSamples() method computes the bounding box by using the getBounds() method of the Shape interface. This narrows the search space. The Shape interface has a method called contains(), which checks whether a point lies inside the shape. The getROIPixelSamples() method uses contains() to extract the pixels inside a shape. Once the contains() check has succeeded, getROIPixel Samples() extracts the sample values by using the getPixel() method, which returns sample values in an array.

Computing ROI Statistics

The `getROIStats()` method returns the statistics of ROI pixels as a two-dimensional array of **double** values. The first subscript represents the band number; the second, the type of statistics. Here are the types of statistics computed:

- Maximum sample value
- Minimum sample value
- Average sample value
- Standard deviation
- Area of the ROI

Listing 9.7 shows two methods involved in computing ROI statistics: `getROIStats()` and `computeStats()`.

LISTING 9.7 Computing ROI statistics

```java
public static double[][] getROIStats(SampleModel sm, DataBuffer db, Shape shape) {
    int data[][] = getROIPixelSamples(sm, db, shape);
    return computeStats(data);
}

public static double[][] computeStats(int[][] pixel) {
    if((pixel == null)||(pixel[0] == null)) return null;
    int len = pixel.length;
    int totalPixels =  pixel[0].length;
    int sum[] = new int[len];
    int max[] = new int[len];
    int min[] = new int[len];
    double[][] roiStats = new double[len][5];

    for(int j=0;j<len;j++) {
        sum[j] =0;
        max[j] = Integer.MIN_VALUE;
        min[j] = Integer.MAX_VALUE;
        for(int i=0;i<pixel[j].length;i++) {
            int pix = pixel[j][i];
            if(pix > max[j]) max[j] = pix;
            if(pix < min[j] ) min[j] = pix;
            sum[j] += pix;
        }

        roiStats[j][0] = (double)min[j];
        roiStats[j][1] = (double)max[j];
        roiStats[j][2] = sum[j]/(double)totalPixels;
        roiStats[j][3] = totalPixels;
        roiStats[j][4] = computeStdDev(pixel[j], roiStats[j][2]);
    }
    return roiStats;
}
```

As Listing 9.7 shows, getROIStats() calls computeStats(), which is a common method used in computing image statistics. To compute the standard deviation, computeStats() calls computeStdDev(), which is shown in Listing 9.8.

Computing Standard Deviation

Standard deviation is calculated as follows:

$$\sqrt{\frac{1}{(n-1)} \sum_{i=1}^{n} x_i^2 - \mu^2(n)}$$

where n is the total number of pixels and μ is the mean value.

Standard deviation is a measure that indicates the data spread. The computeStdDev() method has two arguments: **data** and **mean** (see Listing 9.8). Although it is possible to compute the mean from the data itself, the **mean** argument is provided to improve performance because it is typically available in most computations.

LISTING 9.8   Computing standard deviation

```
public static double computeStdDev(int[] data, double mean){
    if(data == null) return 0;
    int n = data.length;
    if (n == 1) return 1;
    double sumOfSquares = 0.0;
    for(int i=0; i<data.length;i++){
        sumOfSquares += data[i]*data[i];
    }
    double stdDev = Math.sqrt((sumOfSquares/(n-1)) - mean*mean*(n/(double)(n-1)));
    return stdDev;
}
```

Obtaining Pixel Positions within an ROI

To perform any operation within an ROI, applications must get the pixel position within an ROI. The getROIPoints() method does exactly that. This method returns the pixel positions from the original image, and it does not include the boundary pixels.

All Pixels

The getROIPoints() method (see Listing 9.9) gets all the pixel positions within the ROI.

LISTING 9.9 The getROIPoints() method

```
public static Point[] getROIPoints(BufferedImage img, Shape shape){
   if((img == null) || (shape == null)) return null;
   Rectangle rect = shape.getBounds();
   int x = rect.x;
   int y = rect.y;
   int wid = rect.width;
   int ht = rect.height;
   Raster ra =  img.getRaster();
   int k=0;
   Vector spoints = new Vector();
   for(int j=y; j< y+ht; j++ ){
      for(int i=x; i< x+wid; i++ ){
         if(shape.contains((double)(i),(double)(j))){
            spoints.addElement(new Point(i,j));
            }
         }
      }
   int size = spoints.size();
   Point srcPoint[] = new Point[size];
   spoints.copyInto(srcPoint);
   return srcPoint;
}
```

The **getROIPoints()** method first gets the bounding-box shape and checks whether a point is within the shape by calling the **contains()** method. These points are returned as an array of **Point** values.

Thresholded Pixels

The **getThresholdPoints()** method (see Listing 9.10) is similar to **getROIPoints()**, except that it gets the pixels within the ROI and checks whether they are above the specified threshold.

LISTING 9.10 The getThresholdPoints() method

```
public static Point[] getThresholdPoints(BufferedImage img,
                                  Shape shape,
                                  int threshold){
   Rectangle rect = shape.getBounds();
   int x = rect.x;
   int y = rect.y;
   int wid = rect.width;
   int ht = rect.height;
   Raster ra = img.getRaster();
   Vector spoints = new Vector();
   for(int j=y; j< y+ht; j++ ){
      for(int i=x; i< x+wid; i++ ){
         if(shape.contains((double)(i),(double)(j))){
```

continued

```
            int[] pixels = ra.getPixel(i, j, pix);
            if(pixels[0] > threshold) {
                spoints.addElement(new Point(i,j));
            }
        }
    }
}
int size = spoints.size();
Point srcPoint[] = new Point[size];
spoints.copyInto(srcPoint);
return srcPoint;
}
```

The `getThresholdPoints()` method is called if the pixels within the ROI need to be masked. You can create similar methods for any other operation that needs to be performed.

Building a Quantitative Analysis Application

Now that we have developed the foundation classes for performing ROI-related tasks, let's build a simple quantitative analysis application that can generate a report on the ROIs marked over an image. In other words, this application will let users mark ROIs over an image, compute a variety of statistics from ROI pixels, and display the statistics in table and graph form. Building such an application requires both graphical and imaging APIs. First we'll specify the requirements.

Requirements

An ROI application must have the capability to do the following:

◆ **Provide a viewport to display an image.** This viewport must have the capability to allow users to draw multiple ROI shapes interactively. The capability should also exist to allow users to geometrically manipulate the displayed image. By doing so, users can mark the shape accurately. For example, the ROI shape may be small compared to the displayed image. In such cases, users can pan and zoom the image before depositing an ROI.

◆ **Provide a separate viewport to display the marked ROIs on the original image.** This allows the user to verify what the shape is and where it is located in the image space.

◆ **Mask the pixels that are greater than a certain threshold within an ROI.** This requirement means that the application must provide a GUI to allow users to adjust the threshold interactively.

- **Provide a report panel to display the following:**
  - A histogram of the current ROI
  - Pixel statistics of all the deposited ROIs

Design

To satisfy requirements 1 and 2, we need a canvas that is capable of displaying and manipulating images and also allows the drawing of shapes. The `CompositeCanvas2D` class that we developed earlier (see Listing 9.2) meets this requirement. We need two image canvases: one to display the original image and mark ROI shapes, and another to display the ROIs deposited on the original image. We'll reuse the same `Composite Canvas2D` class for both panels.

A real-world ROI application would require the user to draw many different shapes. To meet this requirement, we can use the `DrawShapes` class developed in Chapter 5. To keep matters simple, however, we'll build a simpler class called `Shape Marker` that can draw three types of shapes: freehand, rectangle, and ellipse.

As stated earlier, to determine the position and shape of the ROI in the image space, we need to invert the shape drawn on the displayed image. The next step is to extract the pixels from the original image that are within that shape. To implement the threshold feature, we need to check whether these pixel values are above a certain threshold. In the previous section we developed static methods for handling both of these tasks.

To plot the histogram, we'll use the `Histogram` bean that we introduced in Chapter 8 (see Appendix C) and show the statistics. We'll use the `JTable` class as we did in the image data viewer example in Chapter 8. As we have seen, the `ROI2D` class generates the required statistics.

On the basis of our design, we implemented the simple application shown in Figure 9.2.

Running the Application

To launch the ROI application, type "java app.QuantAnalyzer <image path>" on the command line. If the image path is valid, the application frame in Figure 9.2 will appear on the screen.

There are two image viewports: the source canvas and the destination canvas. The source canvas shows the original image. Before you draw a shape, you can pan and zoom this image. To perform pan/zoom, select the **Pan/Zoom** radio button and right-click on the source canvas. The **Pan/Zoom** menu pops up. To start drawing shapes, click on the **Draw Shape** radio button to enable the three shape options: **Free hand, Rectangle,** and **Ellipse.**

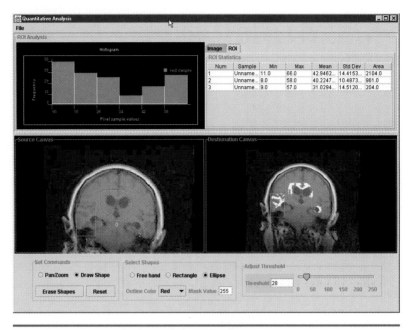

FIGURE 9.2 The quantitative analysis application

You can interactively draw these shapes over the image. Once you have selected a shape, draw it by dragging the mouse. When you release the mouse, the ROI statistics are computed.

The destination canvas also shows the original image with the ROI drawn over it. When you deposit an ROI on the source canvas, it is drawn over the image on the destination viewport. You can confirm that the inverse transformation is mapped correctly by panning and zoomimg the image in the source canvas and depositing shapes at different positions.

On the destination canvas you can also see that the ROIs are partially filled. The reason is that a simple thresholding algorithm is applied to the ROI pixels. A pixel that is greater than a certain threshold value is set to the color chosen on the **Select Shapes** panel.

The two upper viewports show the histogram and the ROI statistics. When the image is drawn initially, the left-hand viewport shows the histogram of the entire image and the right-hand viewport shows only the **Image** tab. When you deposit an ROI over the image, the **ROI** tab becomes visible and displays the statistics. As Figure 9.2 shows, the ROIs are numbered. As you deposit ROIs, the ROI number is incremented and the retrieved ROI statistics are appended to the bottom of the table.

To adjust the threshold for masking an ROI, move the **Adjust Threshold** slider. As you vary the threshold, you can see the masking of the pixels change. If the ROI shape is large, performance is slower. In such cases, you may want to use the text field to enter the threshold value.

If you want to start all over again, select the **File** menu and click on **Reset ROI.** This option will erase all the ROIs in both image viewports and remove the ROI statistics table.

Implementation

Now let's look at the code. Our application requires the following classes:

- ◆ **QuantAnalyzer.** This is the main class that loads the image and instantiates the `ROIManager` object.

- ◆ **ROIManager.** This class constructs all the necessary GUIs and the delegate objects. It creates `CompositeCanvas2D`, `ShapeMarker`, `ROIContext`, and `ReportPanel` objects. `ROIManager` registers itself with `ShapeMarker` to receive shape events. When the user deposits an ROI, `ROIManager` receives the shape through `shapeEvent`. `ROIManager` then constructs an `ROI2D` object and adds it to the ROI collection. It sends the `ROI2D` object to `ReportPanel` to display the histogram and ROI statistics. `ROIManager` also registers for action and change events with the `ThresholdAdjPanel` class. When `ROIManager` receives these events, it extracts the threshold value and sends it to the `currentROI` object, which masks the area within the ROI shape appropriately. Figure 9.3 shows how `ROIManager` facilitates communication between various objects via events.

- ◆ **CompositeCanvas2D.** This class allows graphics to be laid over images. There are two `CompositeCanvas2D` objects. One allows users to draw shapes interactively; it fires `mouse` events to the `ShapeMarker` object. The other one displays the ROI shapes with masked pixels over the original image.

- ◆ **ShapeMarker.** This class creates and draws the ROI shapes. It registers to receive `mouse` and `mouseMotion` events from the `CompositeCanvas2D` class. When a shape is drawn, it fires a shape event to `ROIManager` with the drawn shape.

- ◆ **ThresholdAdjPanel.** This class has a text field that shows the slider values. When the user inputs a value in this field, it is reflected on the slider. The `ThresholdAdjPanel` object fires change and action events to `ROIManager.`

- ◆ **ROIPanel.** This class displays a histogram and table showing the image and ROI statistics.

The ROIManager Class

Let's look at the `ROIManager` class in detail. The main purpose of this class is to create and manage different objects. It also acts as an intermediary for receiving and dispatching different events. Listing 9.11 shows the code for `ROIManager.`

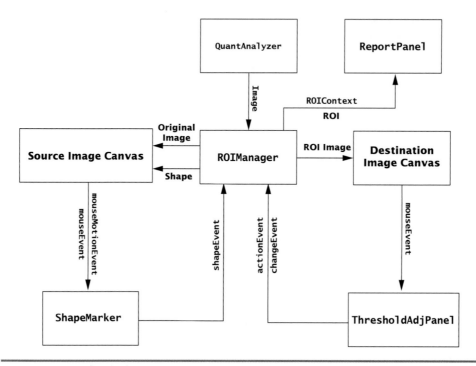

FIGURE 9.3   Data flow in the quantitative analysis application

<hr>

LISTING 9.11   The ROIManager class

```
package com.vistech.roi;
import java.awt.*;
import java.awt.event.*;
import java.awt.image.*;
import java.awt.geom.*;
import java.io.*;
import javax.swing.*;
import javax.swing.event.*;
import java.util.*;
import com.vistech.imageviewer.*;
import com.vistech.util.*;

public class ROIManager implements ShapeEventListener, ActionListener, ChangeListener{
    protected int imageWidth, imageHeight;
    protected int viewerWidth, viewerHeight;
    protected CompositeCanvas2D sourceCanvas, destCanvas;
    protected Vector roiCollection = new Vector();
    protected ROIContext roiContext;
    protected ShapeMarker roiMarker;
    protected ReportPanel reportPan;
    protected ROI2D currentROI;
    protected int roiCount = 0;
```

```java
protected PanZoom destPanZoom, sourcePanZoom;
protected ThresholdAdjPanel thAdjuster;
protected Color drawingColor = Color.white;
protected int maskValue = 255;

public JPanel createUI(BufferedImage img) {

    imageWidth = img.getWidth();
    imageHeight = img.getHeight();

    sourceCanvas = new CompositeCanvas2D();
    sourceCanvas.setImage(img);

    sourceCanvas.setDisplayMode(DisplayMode.SCALED);

    roiMarker = new ShapeMarker(sourceCanvas);
    roiMarker.addShapeEventListener(this);
    roiContext = new ROIContext(img);

    BufferedImage destImage = roiContext.getDisplayImage();

    destCanvas = new CompositeCanvas2D();
    destCanvas.setImage(destImage);

    destCanvas.setPreferredSize(new Dimension(width, height));
    destCanvas.setDisplayMode(DisplayMode.SCALED);

    destPanZoom = new PanZoom((ImageManipulator)destCanvas);
    sourcePanZoom = new PanZoom((ImageManipulator)sourceCanvas);
    sourcePanZoom.setPanZoomOn(false);

    thAdjuster = new ThresholdAdjPanel();
    thAdjuster.addChangeListener(this);
    thAdjuster.addActionListener(this);
    thAdjuster.setBorder(BorderFactory.createTitledBorder("Adjust Threshold"));

    ShapesGUI shapesPan= new ShapesGUI(this);

    reportPan = new ReportPanel(roiContext);

    JPanel mainpan = new JPanel(new GridLayout(1,1));

    return mainpan;
}
public void shapeDrawn(ShapeEvent e){
    Shape shape = e.getShape();
    updateROI(shape);
}

public void updateROI(Shape shape) {
    if(shape == null) return;
    drawROINum(shape);
    BufferedImage img = sourceCanvas.getBufferedImage();
    if(img == null) return;
    if((reportPan != null)&& (shape != null)) {
        Shape txShape = AffineTransformUtil.inverseTransform(shape,
```

continued

```
                                        sourceCanvas.getTransform());
        Shape txShape1 = AffineTransformUtil.inverseTransform(txShape,
                                        sourceCanvas.getDispModeAtx());
        createROI(txShape1);
        reportPan.addROI(currentROI);
        destCanvas.paintImage(roiContext.getDisplayImage());
    }
}

protected void createROI(Shape shape){
    if(shape == null) return;
    currentROI = new ROI2D();
    currentROI.setROIContext(roiContext);
    currentROI.setID(roiCount);
    currentROI.setDrawingColor(drawingColor);
    currentROI.setMaskValue(maskValue);
    currentROI.setShape(shape);
    currentROI.drawShape(shape, drawingColor);
    currentROI.setThreshold(maskValue);
    roiCollection.add(currentROI);
}

private void drawROINum(Shape shape){
    Graphics2D g = sourceCanvas.getDisplayedImageGC();
    if(shape == null) return;
    Rectangle bounds = shape.getBounds();
    int x = bounds.x;
    int y = bounds.y;
    int wid = bounds.width;
    int ht = bounds.height;
    g.drawString((new Integer(roiCount)).toString(), x+wid/2,y+ht+15);
    roiCount++;
}

public ROI2D getCurrentROI() {
    return currentROI;
}

public void stateChanged(ChangeEvent e){
    int threshValue = ((JSlider)(e.getSource())).getValue();
    thresholdROI(threshValue);
    thAdjuster.setTextFieldValue(threshValue);
}

public void actionPerformed(ActionEvent e){
    String str = ((JTextField)e.getSource()).getText();
    int threshValue = (Integer.valueOf(str)).intValue();
    thresholdROI(threshValue);
    thAdjuster.setSliderValue(threshValue);
}

protected  void thresholdROI(int thresh){
    if(currentROI == null) return;
    currentROI.setThreshold(thresh);
    destCanvas.paintImage(roiContext.getDisplayImage());
    destCanvas.repaint();
}
```

```java
public void setPanZoom(boolean state) {
   if(state) {
      sourcePanZoom.setPanZoomOn(true);
      roiMarker.setRoiOn(false);
   } else  {
      sourcePanZoom.setPanZoomOn(false);
      roiMarker.setRoiOn(true);
   }
}

public void setShapeType(int mode){ roiMarker.setShapeType(mode);}

public void eraseShapes() {
   roiMarker.eraseShapes();
   roiCount = 0;
   if(sourceCanvas != null) sourceCanvas.reset();
   if(roiContext != null) roiContext.reset();
   if(destCanvas != null) {
     destCanvas.reset();
     destCanvas.setImage(roiContext.getOriginalImage());
   }
}

public void setDrawingColor(Color color){
   drawingColor = color;
   roiMarker.setDrawingColor(color);
   if(currentROI != null) currentROI.setDrawingColor(color);
}

public void setMaskValue(int value){
   maskValue = value;
   if(currentROI != null) currentROI.setMaskValue(value);
}


public void reset(){
   roiCount = 0;
   if(sourceCanvas != null) {
      sourceCanvas.reset();
      sourceCanvas.setImage(roiContext.getOriginalImage());
   }
   if(destCanvas != null)  {
     destCanvas.reset();
     destCanvas.setImage(roiContext.getOriginalImage());
   }
   if(reportPan != null) reportPan.reset();
   if(roiContext != null) roiContext.reset();
}

}
```

The **ROIManager** class constructs the objects listed in Table 9.1 and then manages communication between them.

TABLE 9.1 Objects Constructed by the `createUI()` Method

OBJECT	CLASS	CONSTRUCTOR PARAMETER	DESCRIPTION
sourceCanvas	CompositeCanvas2D	None	Displays the original image. Users interactively draw shapes over this image, which can be panned and zoomed.
destCanvas	CompositeCanvas2D	None	Displays the image with deposited ROIs. The thresholding effect can be seen here.
roiContext	ROIContext	img (loaded image)	Holds the current ROI context, which includes the selected image.
roiMarker	ShapeMarker	sourceCanvas	Allows users to draw shapes. Fires shape events to ROIManager.
thAdjuster	ThresholdAdjPanel	None	Creates sliders for adjusting threshold values.
reportPanel	ReportPanel	roiContext	Creates an ROI statistics table and histogram.
sourcePanZoom	PanZoom	sourceCanvas	Enables pan and zoom in the source canvas.
destPanZoom	PanZoom	destCanvas	Enables pan and zoom in the destination canvas.

Before we discuss the `ROIManager` class in detail, let's look at a typical sequence of method calls:

1. The `QuantAnalyzer` object loads the image and constructs the `ROIManager` object. `QuantAnalyzer` calls the `createUI()` method with the loaded image as the input parameter.

2. The `createUI()` method constructs the objects shown in Table 9.1.

3. The user draws a shape over the image. When the user releases the mouse, the `ShapeMarker` class fires shape events to `ROIManager`, which receives the shape through the `shapeDrawn()` method.

4. The `shapeDrawn()` method extracts the shape from the `ShapeEvent` object and calls the `updateROI()` method.

5. The `updateROI()` method first performs inverse transformation of the shape from user space to image space. It then calls the `createROI()` method, which creates a new `ROI2D` object based on the shape drawn by the user. It sets the current

roiContext and draws the inverse-transformed shape on the displayImage object held by roiContext. The updateROI() method gets this displayImage object and calls paintImage() to draw it on the destination canvas. It then adds the new ROI to the ROIPanel object, which generates and displays the necessary reports.

6. The user adjusts the threshold slider. The theAdjuster object fires change events, which are received by the stateChanged() method. If the user types a threshold value in the text field, stateChanged() fires the action event, which is received by the actionPerformed() method. Both the stateChanged() and the actionPerformed() methods call the thresholdROI() method.

7. The thresholdROI() method calls the setThreshold() method of the ROI2D class. It then calls the setImage() in the destCanvas object to display the ROI with the new threshold.

8. When the user selects the **Reset ROI** menu item, QuantAnalyzer calls the reset() method of the ROIManager class. This method in turn calls the reset() methods in all the objects created by ROIManager.

Drawing ROI Shapes

Although it is advantageous to implement the image-viewing and shape-drawing functionalities in the same class, we implemented them separately for several reasons, including reusability, simplicity, and flexibility. With this kind of design, it is easy to replace either CompositeCanvas2D or ShapeMarker classes without changing code in other classes.

The main purpose of the ShapeMarker class, which is shown in Listing 9.12, is to help users mark shapes over an image displayed in CompositeCanvas2D. Because shapes are marked with a mouse, this class implements mouse and mouseMotion event listeners. Once a shape has been marked, it fires shape events (see Listing 9.13) to the ROIManager.

LISTING 9.12   The ShapeMarker class

```
package com.vistech.roi;
import java.awt.*;
import java.awt.image.*;
import java.awt.geom.*;
import javax.swing.*;
import java.awt.event.*;
import java.util.*;
import com.vistech.imageviewer.*;

public class ShapeMarker implements MouseListener,MouseMotionListener{
    public final static int FREEHAND = 1;
    public final static int RECTANGLE = 2;
```

continued

```
public final static int ELLIPSE = 4;
protected int shapeType = FREEHAND;

private Point diff = new Point(0,0);
private Point shapeAnchor  = new Point(0,0);
private boolean mousePressed = false;
protected Shape currentShape, prevShape;
protected DrawingCanvas imageCanvas;
private boolean mouseDragged = false;
private Point prevPoint, curPoint;
protected GeneralPath path;
protected Vector shapeEventListeners = new Vector();
protected boolean roiOn = true;
protected Color drawingColor = Color.white;

public ShapeMarker(DrawingCanvas viewer){
    imageCanvas = viewer;
    imageCanvas.addMouseListener(this);
    imageCanvas.addMouseMotionListener(this);
}

public void setRoiOn(boolean onOrOff){roiOn = onOrOff;}
public boolean getRoiOn() { return roiOn;}

public void setShapeType(int type){ shapeType = type;reset();}
public int getShapeType() {return shapeType;}

public void setDrawingColor(Color color){ drawingColor = color;}
public Color getDrawingColor(){ return drawingColor;}

public void eraseShapes(){
    imageCanvas.eraseShapes();
}

public void startDraw(int x, int y) {
    shapeAnchor = new Point(x,y);
    diff = new Point(0,0);
    prevPoint = new Point(x,y);
    curPoint = new Point(x,y);
    path = new GeneralPath();
    path.moveTo((float)x, (float)y);
}

public void draw(int x, int y) {
    Graphics2D g = imageCanvas.getDisplayedImageGC();

    switch(shapeType) {
      case RECTANGLE:
      case ELLIPSE:
          diff.x = x - shapeAnchor.x;
          diff.y = y - shapeAnchor.y;
          int wid = diff.x;
          int ht = diff.y;
          Point ulhc = new Point(shapeAnchor);
          if(diff.x <0) {
             wid = -diff.x;
             ulhc.x = x;
          }
```

```
            if(diff.y <0){
               ht = -diff.y;
               ulhc.y = y;
            }
            if(shapeType == RECTANGLE)
               currentShape = new Rectangle(ulhc.x, ulhc.y, wid, ht);
            else currentShape = new Ellipse2D.Double(ulhc.x, ulhc.y, wid, ht);
            g.setColor(Color.white);
            if(drawingColor == Color.white)g.setColor(Color.black);
            g.setXORMode(drawingColor);
            if(prevShape != null)g.draw(prevShape);
            g.draw(currentShape);
            prevShape = currentShape;
            break;
         case FREEHAND:
            g.setPaintMode();
            curPoint = new Point(x,y);
            g.setColor(drawingColor);
            g.drawLine(prevPoint.x, prevPoint.y, x, y);
            prevPoint = curPoint;
            path.lineTo((float)x, (float)y);
      }
      imageCanvas.repaint();
}

protected void updateROIPanel() {
   fireShapeEvent();
}

public void mousePressed(MouseEvent e) {
   if(!roiOn) return;
   if(SwingUtilities.isLeftMouseButton(e))startDraw(e.getX(), e.getY());
}

public void mouseReleased(MouseEvent e) {
   if((!mouseDragged)|| (!roiOn)) return;
   if(SwingUtilities.isLeftMouseButton(e)){
      Graphics2D g = imageCanvas.getDisplayedImageGC();
      draw(e.getX(), e.getY());
      prevShape = null;
      if(shapeType == FREEHAND) currentShape = (Shape)path;
   }
   if(mouseDragged) updateROIPanel();
   mouseDragged = false;
}

public void mouseClicked(MouseEvent e){}
public void mouseEntered(MouseEvent e){}
public void mouseExited(MouseEvent e){}

public void mouseDragged(MouseEvent e){
   if(!roiOn) return;
   if(SwingUtilities.isLeftMouseButton(e)){
      mouseDragged= true;
      draw(e.getX(), e.getY());
   }
}
```

continued

```
    public void mouseMoved(MouseEvent e){}
    public void addShapeEventListener(ShapeEventListener s){
       shapeEventListeners.addElement(s);
     }

    public void removeShapeEventListener(ShapeEventListener s){
       shapeEventListeners.removeElement(s);
    }

    protected void fireShapeEvent() {
       ShapeEvent ise = new ShapeEvent(this,currentShape);
       for(Enumeration e = shapeEventListeners.elements(); e.hasMoreElements();){
           ShapeEventListener ist = (ShapeEventListener)(e.nextElement());
           ist.shapeDrawn(ise);
       }
    }
    public void reset() {
       diff = new Point(0,0);
       shapeAnchor  = new Point(0,0);
    }
}
```

The ShapeMarker class is simpler than the DrawShapes class we developed in Chapter 5. Compared to DrawShapes, ShapeMarker supports fewer shapes and functions, but the underlying design is the same. In this chapter we have also defined a new event called shapeEvent, which is slightly different from the shapesEvent defined in Chapter 5.

The Shape Event

The shape event is a custom-written event that can be used in any application. Listing 9.13 shows the event listener interface and the event state class for this event.

LISTING 9.13   The event listener interface and event state class for the shape event

```
public interface ShapeEventListener extends java.util.EventListener{
    public void shapeDrawn(ShapeEvent e);
}

public class ShapeEvent extends java.util.EventObject implements Serializable{
    Shape shape;
    int command;
    public ShapeEvent(Object src,Shape sh){
       super(src);
       shape = sh;
    }
    public Shape getShape(){
       return shape;
    }
    public void setCommand(int command){
       this.command = command;
    }
    public int getCommand(){
```

```
            return command;
        }
    }
```

Shape Selection

In the GUI shown in Figure 9.2, the panel below the source canvas contains the user interface for selecting the type of ROI shape. Both the shape-drawing and pan/zoom functions require `mouse` events from the source canvas. The radio buttons **Pan/Zoom** and **Draw Shape** allow users to select the drawing mode.

When **Draw Shape** is selected, the **Select Shapes** panel becomes enabled. Users can choose one of the three shapes: **Free hand, Rectangle,** or **Ellipse.** As shown in Listing 9.14, the `ShapesGUI` class implements this functionality.

LISTING 9.14   The `ShapesGUI` class

```
package com.vistech.roi;
import java.awt.*;
import java.awt.event.*;
import java.awt.image.*;
import java.io.*;
import javax.swing.*;
import javax.swing.event.*;
import java.awt.geom.*;
import com.vistech.util.*;
import com.vistech.imageviewer.*;

public class ShapesGUI extends JPanel implements TabPanel {
    protected ROIManager roiManager;
    protected String colorStr[] = {"White", "Black", "Red", "Green", "Blue"};
    protected Color[] color =
        {Color.white, Color.black, Color.red, Color.green, Color.blue};

    private JRadioButton fh = new JRadioButton("Free hand");
    private JRadioButton rect = new JRadioButton("Rectangle");
    private JRadioButton elli = new JRadioButton("Ellipse");

    public static int PAN-ZOOM = 1;
    public static int SHAPES = 2;
    public ShapesGUI(ROIManager roiManager){
        this.roiManager = roiManager;
        createUI();
    }

    public void openPanel() { }
    public void closePanel(){ }

    protected void createUI() {
        ButtonGroup bg = new ButtonGroup();
        ShapeAdapter fhada = new ShapeAdapter(ShapeMarker.FREEHAND);
        ShapeAdapter rectada = new ShapeAdapter(ShapeMarker.RECTANGLE);
        ShapeAdapter elliada = new ShapeAdapter(ShapeMarker.ELLIPSE);
        fh.setSelected(true);
```

continued

```java
fh.addActionListener(fhada);
rect.addActionListener(rectada);
elli.addActionListener(elliada);

bg.add(fh);
bg.add(rect);
bg.add(elli);

JPanel jp1 = new JPanel();
jp1.add(fh);
jp1.add(rect);
jp1.add(elli);
JLabel lab1 = new JLabel("Outline Color");
JLabel lab2 = new JLabel("Mask Value");

JComboBox jc1 = new JComboBox(colorStr);
jc1.addItemListener(
    new ItemListener(){
      public void itemStateChanged(ItemEvent e){
          JComboBox jcb = (JComboBox)e.getSource();
          int index = jcb.getSelectedIndex();
          roiManager.setDrawingColor(color[index]);
      }
    }
);
JTextField jtx = new JTextField(3);
jtx.setText("255");
jtx.addActionListener(
    new ActionListener(){
      public void actionPerformed(ActionEvent e){
          try {
            JTextField jt = (JTextField)e.getSource();
            String maskstr = jt.getText();
            int mask = Integer.parseInt(maskstr);
            roiManager.setMaskValue(mask);
          }catch(Exception e1) {}
      }
    }
);
JPanel jp2 = new JPanel();
jp2.add(lab1);
jp2.add(jc1);
jp2.add(lab2);
jp2.add(jtx);
JPanel jpr = new JPanel(new GridLayout(2,1));
jpr.add(jp1);
jpr.add(jp2);
jpr.setBorder(BorderFactory.createTitledBorder("Select Shapes"));
JButton erase = new JButton("Erase Shapes ");
erase.addActionListener(
    new ActionListener(){
      public void actionPerformed(ActionEvent e){
          roiManager.eraseShapes();
      }
    }
);
```

```java
      JButton reset = new JButton("Reset ");
      reset.addActionListener(
         new ActionListener(){
            public void actionPerformed(ActionEvent e){
               roiManager.reset();
            }
         }
      );

      JPanel jpbl = new JPanel();
      jpbl.add(erase);
      jpbl.add(reset);

      ButtonGroup bg1 = new ButtonGroup();
      JRadioButton jb = new JRadioButton("Pan/Zoom");
      jb.addActionListener(new StateAdapter(PAN_ZOOM));

      JRadioButton sh = new JRadioButton("Draw Shape");
      sh.addActionListener(new StateAdapter(SHAPES));
      bg1.add(jb);
      bg1.add(sh);
      sh.setSelected(true);
      JPanel jptl = new JPanel();
      jptl.add(jb);
      jptl.add(sh);

      JPanel jpl = new JPanel(new GridLayout(2,1));
      jpl.add(jptl);
      jpl.add(jpbl);
      jpl.setBorder(BorderFactory.createTitledBorder("Set Commands"));

      add(jpl);
      add(jpr);
   }
   public void reset() { roiManager.eraseShapes();}

   class StateAdapter implements ActionListener {
      int mode;
      public StateAdapter( int type) {mode = type;}
      public void actionPerformed(ActionEvent e) {
         if(mode == PAN_ZOOM) {
            roiManager.setPanZoom(true);
            fh.setEnabled(false);
            rect.setEnabled(false);
            elli.setEnabled(false);
         }
         else {
            roiManager.setPanZoom(false);
            fh.setEnabled(true);
            rect.setEnabled(true);
            elli.setEnabled(true);
         }
      }
   }
   class ShapeAdapter implements ActionListener {
      int mode;
      public ShapeAdapter( int type) {mode = type;}
```

continued

```
   public void actionPerformed(ActionEvent e) {
      roiManager.setShapeType(mode);
   }
 }
}
```

When a shape is selected, the ShapesGUI class needs to pass the shape type to the roiMarker object. Because the ShapesGUI class cannot directly access the roi Marker object, the ROIManager class acts as intermediary. To receive the selected shape type, ROIManager provides the setShapeType() method, which in turn calls set ShapeType()of the ShapeMarker class. Recall from Listing 9.11 that the roiMarker object is instantiated from the ShapeMarker class. When a user selects a shape, actionPerformed() of the ShapeAdapter class calls ROIManager's setShapeType() method, thereby setting the shape type in the roiMarker object.

Masking ROIs

As we have seen, the ROI2D class has methods for performing threshold operations within an ROI to mask pixels. We can use these methods to perform thresholding interactively.

The purpose of the ThresholdAdjPanel class, which is shown in Listing 9.15, is to create a GUI with a slider and a text field for inputting the threshold values. When the user moves the slider, the change events generated by the slider are sent to ROIManager, which in turn extracts the threshold value and sends it to the ROI object. In the case of the text field, the ThresholdAdjPanel class sends the threshold value through an action event.

LISTING 9.15   The ThresholdAdjPanel class

```
package com.vistech.roi;
import java.awt.*;
import javax.swing.*;
import javax.swing.event.*;
import java.awt.event.*;
import java.util.*;

public class ThresholdAdjPanel extends JPanel{
    private JTextField threshValueField;
    private JSlider threshSlider;
    protected int minValue =0, maxValue = 255, startValue = 100;
    protected int threshStartValue = 0;

    public ThresholdAdjPanel(){
       JPanel thpan =  createThresholdPanel();
       add(thpan);
    }

    public void addChangeListener(ChangeListener l){threshSlider.addChangeListener(l);}
    public void removeChangeListener(ChangeListener l){
```

```
        threshSlider.removeChangeListener(1);
    }

    public void addActionListener(ActionListener 1){
        threshValueField.addActionListener(1);
    }
    public void removeActionListener(ActionListener 1){
        threshValueField.removeActionListener(1);
    }

    public void setSliderValues(int min, int max, int start){
        int lower = min%10;
        int higher = max%10;
        this.minValue = min-lower;
        this.maxValue = max+ (10-higher)+10;
        this.startValue = start;

        threshSlider.setMinimum(minValue);
        threshSlider.setMaximum(maxValue);
        threshSlider.setValue(start);
        int major = (int)((maxValue-minValue)/5);
        int minor = (int)(major/4);
        threshSlider.setMajorTickSpacing(major);
        threshSlider.setMinorTickSpacing(minor);
        threshSlider.setExtent(10);
        threshSlider.setPaintTicks(true);
        threshSlider.setPaintLabels(true);
    }

    public void setTextFieldValue(int val){
        threshValueField.setText(Integer.toString(val));
    }
    public void setSliderValue(int val){threshSlider.setValue(val);}

    protected JPanel createThresholdPanel() {
        threshValueField = new JTextField(5);
        threshValueField.addActionListener(
            new ActionListener() {
                public void actionPerformed(ActionEvent e){
                    String str = ((JTextField)e.getSource()).getText();
                    int threshValue = (Integer.valueOf(str)).intValue();
                    setSliderValue(threshValue);
                }
            }
        );
        threshValueField.setText(Integer.toString(threshStartValue));
        JLabel threshLabel = new JLabel("Threshold");

        threshSlider = new JSlider(minValue,maxValue,startValue);
        threshSlider.setMajorTickSpacing(50);
        threshSlider.setMinorTickSpacing(25);
        threshSlider.setExtent(10);
        threshSlider.setPaintTicks(true);
        threshSlider.setPaintLabels(true);
        threshSlider.addChangeListener(
            new ChangeListener() {
                public void stateChanged(ChangeEvent e){
```

continued

```
                int threshValue = ((JSlider)(e.getSource())).getValue();
                setTextFieldValue(threshValue);
            }
        }
    );

    JPanel threshpan = new JPanel();
    GridBagLayout gb = new GridBagLayout() ;
    GridBagConstraints c = new GridBagConstraints();
    threshpan.setLayout(gb);
    threshpan.setBackground(Color.lightGray);

    c.weighty = 1.0;  c.weightx = 1.0;
    JLabel rotlab = new JLabel("Threshold", SwingConstants.RIGHT);
    gb.setConstraints(rotlab, c);
    threshpan.add(rotlab);
    gb.setConstraints(threshValueField, c);
    threshpan.add(threshValueField);
    c.gridwidth = GridBagConstraints.REMAINDER;
    c.fill = GridBagConstraints.HORIZONTAL;
    gb.setConstraints(threshSlider, c);
    threshpan.add(threshSlider);
    return threshpan;
    }
}
```

When the user right-clicks on the destination canvas, the mousePressed events are received by the mousePressed() method, which in turn calls the popupMenu() method to launch the threshold panel.

Notice the add() and remove() methods in Listing 9.15 for change event and action event listeners. These are built-in events in Swing and the AWT. The add() and remove() methods send the registering objects to the corresponding classes in Swing: JSlider and JTextField.

When the user adjusts the slider, a change event is fired by JSlider, which is sent to the registered listener, which in this case is ROIManager. The changeEvent-handling routine is in the ROIManager class (see Listing 9.11). Likewise, if the user decides to enter a threshold value, the JTextField component fires an action event, which is sent to ROIManager.

Generating Reports

Reports normally include charts and tables. In this application we'll show a histogram of the pixel samples and a table of statistics. The ReportPanel class, which is shown in Listing 9.16, handles these graphical elements of the report. It requires only the ROI2D and ROIContext objects for generating reports. The ReportPanel GUI consists of two JTable objects and a Histogram bean (see Appendix C).

LISTING 9.16 The ReportPanel class

```java
package com.vistech.roi;
import java.awt.*;
import java.awt.event.*;
import java.awt.image.*;
import java.awt.geom.*;
import java.io.*;
import javax.swing.*;
import javax.swing.table.*;
import javax.swing.event.*;
import java.awt.color.*;
import vis.beans.plotter.*;
import com.vistech.util.*;
import java.util.*;

public class ReportPanel extends JComponent {
    protected BufferedImage image;
    protected int imageWidth = 0;
    protected int imageHeight = 0;
    protected int viewerWid = 500;
    protected int viewerHt = 300;
    protected MultiHistogram histogram;
    protected JTable imageStatsTable, roiStatsTable;

    protected String[][] imageData =null;
    protected String[][] roiData =null;
    protected String[] colNames = null;
    protected String[] roiColNames = null;
    protected Shape currentShape;
    protected String componentName[];

    protected SampleModel sampleModel;
    protected WritableRaster raster;
    protected DataBuffer dataBuffer;
    protected Dimension imageSize;
    protected int roiCount =0;
    protected String allRoiData[][] = new String[3][5];
    protected ROIContext roiContext;
    protected Vector roiCollection = new Vector();
    protected ROI2D currentROI;

    private boolean firstTime = true;
    private JTabbedPane jtp;
    private JFrame fr;
    private boolean guiCreated = false;

    public ReportPanel(){ }

    public ReportPanel(ROIContext roiContext){
        setROIContext(roiContext);
    }

    public void setROIContext(ROIContext roiContext){
        BufferedImage img = roiContext.getOriginalImage();
        if(img == null) return;
```

continued

```java
        (new Thread(new Analyze(img))).start();
    }

    class Analyze implements Runnable {
        BufferedImage bi;
        public Analyze(BufferedImage img) {bi = img; }
        public void run() { analyzeAndUpdate(bi);}
    }

    protected void analyzeAndUpdate(BufferedImage img){
        image = img;
        extractAttributes(img);
        if(guiCreated)  {
            updateHistogram();
            updateImageStatsTable(img);
        } else{
            histogram = createHistogram();
            imageStatsTable = createImageStatsTable(img);
            roiStatsTable = new JTable();
            createUI();
        }
    }

    private void extractAttributes(BufferedImage img){
        sampleModel = img.getSampleModel();
        raster = img.getRaster();
        dataBuffer = raster.getDataBuffer();
        imageSize= new Dimension(img.getWidth(), img.getHeight());
    }

    private void createUI() {
        JScrollPane imjsp = new JScrollPane(imageStatsTable);
        imjsp.setBorder(BorderFactory.createTitledBorder("Image Statistics"));
        jtp = new JTabbedPane();
        jtp.add("Image ",imjsp );
        setLayout(new GridLayout(1,2));
        add(histogram);
        add(jtp);
        histogram.repaint();
        setBorder(BorderFactory.createTitledBorder("ROI Analysis"));
        guiCreated = true;
    }

    public void setWidHt(Dimension d) {
        viewerWid = d.width;
        viewerHt = d.height;
        setSize(viewerWid, viewerHt);
    }

    public void addROI(ROI2D roi){
        currentROI = roi;
        roiCollection.add(currentROI);
        if(firstTime) {
            roiStatsTable = createROIStatsTable();
            firstTime = false;
            JScrollPane roijsp = new JScrollPane(roiStatsTable);
            roijsp.setBorder(BorderFactory.createTitledBorder("ROI Statistics"));
```

```
        jtp.add("ROI ", roijsp);
        jtp.setSelectedComponent(roijsp);
    }
    else updateROIStatsTable();
    updateHistogram(roi.getShape());
    roiCount = currentROI.getID();
}

protected JTable createROIStatsTable() {
    updateROIStatsTable();
    TableModel dataModel = new AbstractTableModel() {
        public String getColumnName(int column) {
            if(currentROI == null) return null;
            return   roiColNames[column];
        }
        public int getColumnCount() {
            if(currentROI == null) return 0;
            return roiColNames.length;
        }
        public int getRowCount() {
            if(allRoiData == null) return 0;
            return allRoiData.length;
        }
        public Object getValueAt(int row, int col) {
            if(allRoiData == null) return null;
            if((row >= allRoiData.length)||(col >= allRoiData[0].length)) return null;

            return allRoiData[row][col];
        }
    };
    JTable table = new JTable(dataModel);
    return new JTable(dataModel);
}

public void updateROIStatsTable(){
    if(currentROI == null) return;
    roiColNames = currentROI.getColumnNames();
    String[][] roiStats = currentROI.getStatsAsString();
    int numSamples = roiStats.length;
    allRoiData = null;

    int size = roiCollection.size();
    allRoiData = new String[size*roiStats.length][roiColNames.length];
    Iterator it = roiCollection.iterator();
    int i=0;
    while(it.hasNext()){
        ROI2D roi = (ROI2D)it.next();
        String[][] dat = roi.getStatsAsString();
        if(dat == null){
            i++; continue;
        }
        for(int j=0; j< numSamples; j++){
            for(int k=0;k<roiColNames.length;k++)
                allRoiData[i*numSamples+j][k] =  dat[j][k];
        }
        i++;
    }
```

continued

```java
        if(roiStatsTable  != null){
          roiStatsTable.revalidate();
          repaint();
        }
    }

    public MultiHistogram createHistogram() {
        if((sampleModel == null) ||
           (dataBuffer == null) ||
           (imageSize == null)) return null;
        int[][] pix = ImageInfoUtil.getPixelSamples(sampleModel, dataBuffer, imageSize);
        MultiHistogram histo = new MultiHistogram();
        histo.setSize(400,300);
        String[] colstr = {"red sample", "green sample", "blue sample", "yellow"};
        Color[]  col = {Color.red, Color.green, Color.blue, Color.yellow};
        histo.setLegendOn(true);
        for (int i=0; i<pix.length;i++) {
            histo.addGraph(null, pix[i]);
            histo.addLegend(col[i], colstr[i]);
        }
        histo.setNumBars(6);
        histo.setTitleString("Histogram ");
        histo.setXLabelString("Pixel sample values");
        histo.setYLabelString("Frequency");
        return histo;
    }

    public void updateHistogram(){
        if((sampleModel == null) || (dataBuffer == null) || (imageSize == null)) return;
        int[][] pix = ROIUtil.getPixelSamples(sampleModel, dataBuffer, imageSize);
        updateHistogram(pix);
    }
    public void updateHistogram(Shape shape){
        if((sampleModel == null) || (dataBuffer == null) || (shape == null)) return;
        int[][] pix = ROIUtil.getROIPixelSamples(sampleModel,dataBuffer, shape);
        updateHistogram(pix);
    }

    public void updateHistogram(int[][] data){
        histogram.resetPlotViewport();
        String[] colstr = {"red sample", "green sample", "blue sample", "yellow"};
        Color[]  col = {Color.red, Color.green, Color.blue, Color.yellow};
        histogram.setLegendOn(true);
        for (int i=0; i<data.length;i++) {
            histogram.addGraph(null, data[i]);
            histogram.addLegend(col[i], colstr[i]);
        }
        histogram.draw();
        histogram.repaint();
    }

    protected JTable createImageStatsTable(BufferedImage img) {
        ColorModel cm = img.getColorModel();
        imageWidth = img.getWidth();
        imageHeight = img.getHeight();
        ColorSpace cs = cm.getColorSpace();
        int numComponents = cs.getNumComponents();
```

```
        componentName = new String[numComponents];
        for(int i=0;i<numComponents;i++){
            componentName[i] = cs.getName(i);
        }
        updateImageStatsTable(img);
        TableModel dataModel = new AbstractTableModel() {
            public String getColumnName(int column) {
                return  colNames[column];
            }
            public int getColumnCount() { return colNames.length;}
            public int getRowCount() {return imageData.length;}
            public Object getValueAt(int row, int col) {
                return imageData[row][col];
            }
        };
        JTable table = new JTable(dataModel);
        return new JTable(dataModel);
    }

    public void updateImageStatsTable(BufferedImage img) {
        int[][] imstats = ImageInfoUtil.getImageStats(img);
        colNames = new String[] {"Sample", "Min", "Max", "Mean", "Area"};
        imageData = new String[imstats.length][colNames.length];

        for(int i=0; i<imstats.length;i++){
            imageData[i][0] = componentName[i];
            for(int j=0;j<colNames.length-1;j++){
                imageData[i][j+1] = Integer.toString(imstats[i][j]);
            }
        }
        if(roiStatsTable   != null){
            roiStatsTable.repaint();
            repaint();
        }
    }

    public void reset() {
        roiCount = 0;
        currentROI = null;
        allRoiData = new String[3][5];
        roiCollection = new Vector();
        roiStatsTable.revalidate();
    }
}
```

The ROIPanel class performs the following tasks:

◆ It constructs two tables: one for displaying image statistics and the other for displaying ROI statistics. Whenever a new ROI is deposited, it updates the ROI statistics table.

◆ It constructs a Histogram bean to represent the histogram of the most recent ROI. When there are no deposited ROIs, it displays the histogram of the entire image.

Methods related to an image statistics table are similar to the ones listed in the image data viewer example in Chapter 8. Here's a typical sequence of method calls:

1. `ROIManager` constructs the `ROIPanel` object with `ROIContext` as an input parameter. The constructor calls the `setROIContext()` method.

2. The `setROIContext()` method extracts the original image and related information from the `ROIContext` object. This method then creates a thread to analyze the image. The thread is created by an inner class called `Analyze`, whose `run()` method calls `analyzeAndUpdate()`. This method creates the GUI for the image and the ROI statistics table. With the image pixels, it creates the `Histogram` bean (see Appendix C).

3. When the user deposits an ROI, `ROIManager` creates an `ROI2D` object and calls `ReportPanel`'s `addROI()` method. The `addROI()` method updates the ROI statistics table and changes the histogram data to the current ROI.

4. When the user selects the **Reset ROI** menu, `ROIManager` calls the `reset()` method in `ReportPanel`, which resets the ROI statistics table.

Displaying ROI Statistics

The instance variable `roiCollection` is a `Vector` object and holds the `ROI2D` objects for the deposited ROIs. You may recall from the preceding section that the `ROI2D` class computes five different types of statistics (minimum, maximum, mean, area, and standard deviation) and saves them sample by sample in a two-dimensional array. A convenient data structure that holds this data for all the deposited ROIs is `allRoiData`. It is a two-dimensional array of `String` objects, with the first subscript indicating the ROI number and the second subscript the statistics name.

ROI statistics are displayed by `roiStatsTable`, which is a `JTable` object. The `TableModel` class of `roiStatsTable` has methods for obtaining the column names (i.e., names of the statistics) from the `ROI2D` class and the data elements from `all RoiData`.

The `createROIStatsTable()` method contains the code for `TableModel` as a local class. The `addROI(ROI2D)` method adds the new `ROI2D` object to `roiCollection` and calls the `updateROIStatsTable()` and `updateHistogram()` methods. The `update ROIStatsTable()` method adds the data from the new `ROI2D` object to `allRoiData`. With the model-view-controller (MVC) framework, whenever `allRoiData` is changed, `roiStatsTable` is automatically updated.

Displaying the Histogram

The `createHistogram()` method creates the `MultiHistogram` bean. Before creating this bean, this method gets the pixel samples for the entire image. Depending on the number of samples per pixel, it assigns colors to the bars and to the corresponding legends.

There are three flavors of `updateHistogram()` methods. The `updateHistogram (int[][] data)` method updates the histogram. The other two flavors obtain the pixel data and call this method. The `updateHistogram()` method obtains pixel data from an entire image, and the `updateHistogram(Shape shape)` method obtains pixel data from an ROI.

Conclusion

ROI computation is a very important concept and is widely used in a variety of fields. Keeping this in mind, in this chapter we developed a framework for ROI processing and built a set of classes to help develop ROI analysis. Using these classes, we built a simple quantitative analysis application capable of computing the basic pixel statistics of ROIs deposited over an image. This application also has the capability to threshold the deposited ROIs.

You can extend the classes developed in this chapter to build your own ROI applications. Java Advanced Imaging has support for ROI processing in the form of classes and imaging operators. In Chapter 14 we'll use the JAI API to build the same quantitative analysis application we built in this chapter.

PART III

Java Advanced
Imaging

Introduction to JAI

10

JAVA ADVANCED IMAGING OFFERS WIDE-RANGING FUNCTIONALITY covering different areas of imaging. Whether the context is geographic information systems (GIS), medical imaging, or any other type of imaging, JAI provides at least some basic functionality. Because of the broader coverage, JAI APIs are huge and can be intimidating to first-time users. So one of the intended goals of this chapter is to provide an overall and simple picture of the JAI APIs. In subsequent chapters we will cover some of the more important topics in greater detail. However, a few topics that we will touch on in other JAI chapters will be covered in more detail in this chapter.

We'll start the chapter by discussing the underlying principles of JAI. As mentioned in Part II (the Java 2D chapters), JAI supports the pull imaging model. However, this does not mean that JAI cannot be used with the AWT and Java 2D. On the contrary, those two models are very compatible with JAI. For example, you can load an image using AWT imaging, and then display and manipulate it using the JAI APIs. So if you have already developed applications, beans, or classes using AWT imaging or Java 2D, you can easily use them with JAI. In fact, our JAI examples will make use of the classes we developed in the Java 2D chapters.

Even though the pull model is the backbone of JAI, the model is actually defined in Java 2D. Because it is the basis for JAI operators and APIs, we'll look at this model and the related APIs in detail. Then we'll focus our attention on an overview of the JAI APIs and operators. We will also describe a utility class called JAI, which is essential for applying operators. A simple example will illustrate the use of an operator to load the image and the use of the API to display that image.

The chapter will end with an example of an image viewer application that loads, displays, and saves images. This example will give you some insight into the use of the JAI APIs and operators.

JAI Architecture

We already discussed two imaging models, push and immediate mode (see Chapters 2 and 6). Although the pull model API is defined in Java 2D, its APIs don't use the pull model interfaces and classes them directly, except in the case of `BufferedImage`. On the other hand, the pull model is the mainstay of JAI architecture. JAI also extends the pull model API by defining various interfaces and classes of its own.

In the JAI architecture, imaging operators are linked to form a rendering chain, which takes the form of a directed acyclic graph (DAG).[1] In a JAI rendering chain, an imaging operator represents a node. To form a rendering chain, you need to connect imaging operators that are compatible—that is, send the output(s) of one imaging operator to the compatible input(s) of another imaging operator.

As Figure 10.1 shows, the rendering chain is interposed between a set of sources and a set of sinks. A *source* is an image, and a *sink* is a rendering device such as a display monitor or printer. The "pull" happens when a request is made at the sink to render an image. This request goes up the chain to the source, and the image is pulled through the nodes of the chain to the sink. An imaging operator can have zero or more parameters. Each time the image passes a node, an imaging operator is applied with appropriate parameters. The transformed image is then passed to the next node until it reaches the sink.

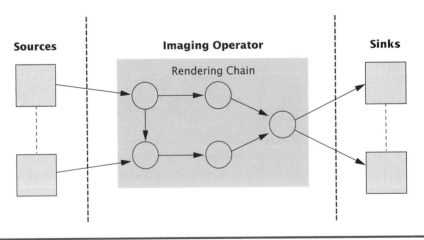

FIGURE 10.1   The structure of a JAI application that uses the rendering chain

---

1 A graph is nothing but a set of nodes connected by edges. In a directed graph, edges show the direction of connection. An acyclic graph has no loops. So a *DAG* is a graph in which every edge shows the direction of connection and has no loops or cycles.

Because the imaging operators take rendering-independent parameters, the rendering chain can be edited. The rendering chain can be reused as is for different contexts, or it can be edited and reused.

An Image-Rendering Scenario

To understand the rendering-chain concept, consider the geometric manipulation example we implemented in Chapter 7. You can create an imaging operator with appropriate parameters from each of the affine operations. This means that you can have operators like Translate, Scale, Rotate, and Flip. You can now create a renderable chain by combining these operations in any order. For instance, translate the image by (30, 40), rotate it by 45 degrees, and then magnify it by a factor of 4. These operations constitute a rendering chain consisting of translate, rotate, and scale. When a request is made to render, the image is pulled from the source through each node of this chain, and the resulting image is rendered onto a display device at the sink.

You may also want to render the image to a printer. Because the printer size is limited, you may want to reduce the scaling factor to 2. To do this, you will have to edit the node by changing the input parameter of the Scale operator.

The question now arises, Should a new image be computed at every node or computed only at the last stage of a renderable chain? The answer depends on whether the image needs to be rendered at intermediate stages. In the case of interactive manipulation, the image must be rendered at each stage. If you just want to print the image, however, there is no need for intermediate pixel computation. In this case the actual image needs to be computed only at the end.

To handle these types of situations, the JAI architecture supports two types of chains: rendered and renderable. In the *rendered* mode, the images are computed at every node. In the *renderable* mode, on the other hand, the actual image is computed only at the sink. In our example, in the rendered mode an appropriate affine transformation is applied to the image at each node, and in the renderable mode the affine transformation is successively concatenated as the image is pulled through the nodes of the chain and the actual image is computed when it is about to be rendered.

Before we proceed with JAI programming, let's go over the pull model–related classes and interfaces in Java 2D.

The Pull Model API

The AWT imaging and Java 2D APIs have the `Image` and `BufferedImage` classes, respectively, to represent an image. When it comes to handling large images, however, these classes are not quite adequate. The pull model supports two types of image representations: rendered and renderable (see the previous section). Both of these types are defined in Java 2D through various interfaces and classes, which are available in the Java core packages `java.awt.image` and `java.awt.image.renderable`.

Rendered Images

The `java.awt.image` package has three interfaces that specify the behavior of a rendered image:

1. **RenderedImage.** This interface represents the image in the rendered chain. `RenderedImage` has read-only methods; that is, you can extract the pixels from the image, but you cannot write onto the image. In a rendered-image representation, image data is available as an array of tiles. The `BufferedImage` class implements this interface.

2. **WritableRenderedImage.** This interface is a subinterface of `RenderedImage` and specifies methods that allow writing to pixels.

3. **TileObserver.** This interface has a method for tracking tile updates.

The `RenderedImage` and `WritableRenderedImage` interfaces represent a rendered image. These interfaces specify two types of attributes: those related to image geometry and those related to data.

Image Geometry–Related Attributes

`RenderedImage` follows the same coordinate system as the push or immediate model. From a geometric standpoint, however, a `RenderedImage` object is much more complicated than an AWT `Image` object.

A rendered image is divided into a number of rectangular tiles. Each tile consists of image data covered by the rectangular region of the tile. When the image is large, the viewing application can request only a few tiles at a time, thus avoiding the need to load the entire image. All the tiles belonging to a rendered image have the same dimensions, and they don't overlap.

To map tiles in the image, an imaginary grid is thrown over it. Each cell in this grid represents a tile in the image. The size of this grid need not exactly match the size of the image. Each cell is referenced by a pair of indices: (`tx`, `ty`), where `tx` represents the index of the cell in the *x* direction and `ty` represents the index in the *y* direction. The upper left cell of a grid need not start with the index (0, 0). The (0, 0) cell is determined by the `tileGridXOffset` and `tileGridYOffset` parameters, as Figure 10.2 shows.

Table 10.1 lists all the geometry-related attributes of a rendered image. Imagine a large image divided into a number of rectangular regions. An image viewer that displays such an image can request only a few tiles to display the selected part of the image. If the user scrolls the image, the viewer can request the next set of tiles.

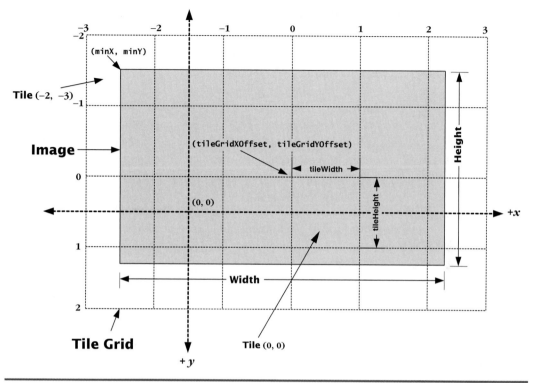

FIGURE 10.2 Rendered-image geometry

TABLE 10.1 Geometric Attributes of a Rendered Image

ATTRIBUTES	DESCRIPTION
`width, height`	Width and height of a rendered image.
`minX, minY`	The upper left-hand coordinates of a rendered image.
`numXTiles, numYTiles`	The number of tiles in the x and y directions, respectively. In Figure 10.2, these values are 6 and 4, respectively.
`minTileX, minTileY`	The minimum tile indices in the x and y directions, respectively. In Figure 10.2, these values are –3 and –2, respectively.
`tileWidth, tileHeight`	Tile width and height.
`tileGridOffSetX, tileGridOffSetY`	The x and y offsets of the first tile with respect to the origin of the coordinate system. The first tile is located at the tile index (0, 0).

Image Data–Related Attributes

Table 10.2 lists all the data-related attributes of a rendered image. As far as the data representation is concerned, `RenderedImage` follows the Java 2D model. In other words, image data is available as a `Raster` object. Recall from Chapter 8 that `ColorModel` describes how a pixel is interpreted and `SampleModel` describes how pixel samples are stored. As Table 10.2 shows, image data can be retrieved as a tile, which is available as a `Raster` object.

The JavaBean-style get methods for each of the geometry-related and data-related attributes are defined in the `RenderedImage` interface. In addition to these get methods, the `RenderedImage` interface has the method called `copyData(WritableRaster)` to copy the tile data into a `Raster` object.

The `WritableRenderedImage` interface extends the `RenderedImage` interface and specifies methods for writing to a rendered image. The `setData(Raster)` method sets the data of the entire rendered image.

Writing to a Tile

The `WritableRenderedImage` interface specifies methods to allow other objects to write to an individual tile. A client object can check out a tile for writing by calling the `getWritableTile(int xIndex, int yIndex)` method, which returns a `Writable Raster` object. Once the client object has written to the specified tile, it can relinquish its access by calling the `releaseWritableTile()` method.

Any client object can check whether any tile has been checked out for writing by calling the `hasTileWriters()` method, which returns a `boolean` value. To check whether a tile is writable, a client object needs to call the `isTileWritable(int tileX, int tileY)` method. The `getWritableTileIndices()` method returns an array of `Point` objects representing the indices of the tiles checked out for writing.

TABLE 10.2   Data Attributes of a Rendered Image

ATTRIBUTE	DESCRIPTION
data	Image data available as a Raster object.
ColorModel	Color model.
SampleModel	Sample model.
sources	Sources of image data available as a `Vector` object.
property	Property of a rendered image. The `getProperties()` method returns all the properties of a rendered image. The `getProperty(String name)` method returns the property specified by name.
tile	A tile available as a `Raster` object. The `getTile(int xIndex, int yIndex)` method returns the tile as a `Raster` object at the specified tile index (xIndex, yIndex).

A client object can register to receive notification when a tile is changed by calling the `addTileObserver(TileObserver observer)` method. To be able to register, the client object must implement the `TileObserver` interface. The client object removes itself from the notification list by calling the `removeTileObserver (TileObserver observer)` method.

The `TileObserver` interface is similar to the `ImageObserver` interface we learned about in Chapter 2. It has one method—`tileUpdate()`—which, as its name suggests, is invoked whenever a tile is changed.

Renderable Images

The manner in which images are represented differs between renderable and rendered chains. An image in a renderable layer has no physical dimensions, such as width and height. The only dimension known is its aspect ratio.

A renderable chain must start with an actual image. Therefore, the renderable chain source must be a rendered image. Likewise, an image cannot be rendered onto a physical device if only its aspect ratio is known. So a rendered image must be created from a renderable image before actual rendering takes place. Thus both ends of the renderable chain must have rendered images.

`RenderableImage` is an interface in the `java.awt.image.renderable` package, which also has several interfaces and classes that define the behavior of a renderable image. The `RenderableImage` interface defines the attributes of a rendering-independent image. Aside from get methods, this interface has methods for creating a specific rendering from a renderable image. These rendering methods return a `RenderedImage` object and are invoked when the renderable chain is ready for evaluation.

Image Geometry–Related Attributes

`RenderableImage` has fewer attributes than `RenderedImage` because the pixels of `RenderableImage` have no pixel dimensions, except for the aspect ratio. Table 10.3 shows the geometric attributes of `RenderableImage.`

Rendering a Renderable Image

A renderable image must be rendered when it reaches the sink. In other words, a renderable image must be converted to a rendered image before it can be rendered. To enable this rendering, the `RenderableImage` interface specifies three methods:

1. **`public RenderedImage createDefaultRendering()`**

   As its name suggests, this method creates a default rendering. It constructs a default `RenderContext` object (see the next section) by using an appropriate affine transformation for transforming the image from user space to device space.

TABLE 10.3 Geometric Attributes of a Renderable Image

ATTRIBUTES	DESCRIPTION
`width, height`	Width and height define the aspect ratio. The `getHeight()` method always returns `1.0f`, and the `getWidth()` method returns the aspect ratio.
`minX, minY`	The upper left-hand coordinates of a renderable image. In other words, they define the position of the renderable image in the coordinate system.

2. **`public RenderedImage createRendering(RenderContext renderContext)`**

This method creates a `RenderedImage` object with a specified `RenderContext` object.

3. **`public RenderedImage createScaledRendering(int w, int h,`**
   `RenderingHints hints)`

This method creates an image with a specified width and height. While creating the image, this method may use the rendering hints provided via the input parameter.

Repeated calls to create-rendering methods may produce different results. The `isDynamic()` method returns a `boolean` value that tells whether the successive calls to create a rendering method produce different results. Just like `RenderedImage`, `RenderableImage` has methods for getting image properties and sources.

Creating a RenderContext Object

As we saw in the preceding section, a `RenderContext` object is required to create a rendering from a renderable image. `RenderContext` is a container that holds several parameters that are required for a rendering. These parameters are

- `AffineTransform`
- `aoi` (area of interest)
- `RenderingHints`

Accordingly, the `RenderContext` class has four constructors, each with different combinations of `AffineTransform`, `aoi`, and `RenderingHints` arguments.

1. **`public RenderContext(AffineTransform usr2dev)`**
2. **`public RenderContext(AffineTransform usr2dev, RenderingHints hints)`**
3. **`public RenderContext(AffineTransform usr2dev, Shape aoi)`**
4. **`public RenderingHints getRenderingHints()`**

Let's explore the `RenderContext` parameters in detail.

Converting User Space to Device Space

As mentioned earlier, `RenderableImage` takes a `RenderContext` object at the time of rendering. The `RenderContext` object is eventually passed to `RenderedImage,` which uses it to render the image to an actual device. During rendering, the `Affine Transform` attribute obtained from `RenderContext` is applied to convert the image to device space from user space.

The `RenderContext` class has methods for replacing, concatenating, and preconcatenating this transform:

- `setTransform(AffineTransform newTransform)`
- `concatenateTransform(AffineTransform modTransform)`
- `preConcatenateTransform(AffineTransform modTransform)`

Area of Interest

The area of interest is the area over which the rendering takes place. This area is represented by a `Shape` variable. The `setAreaOfInterest(Shape areaOfInterest)` and `getAreaOfInterest()` methods set and obtain the area of interest.

Rendering Hints

The `setRenderingHints(RenderingHints hints)` and `getRenderingHints()` methods are set and get methods for these attributes. If rendering hints are not supplied, `RenderContext` uses the default `RenderingHints` parameter.

Managing Operator Parameters

Most imaging operations require parameters. In a traditional approach, you would create a method for an operator with the appropriate number of parameters. Often, however, the number of parameters varies, depending on how the operator is applied. In such cases you would overload the method with a variable number of parameters. This approach is hard to manage when the number of operators is large. Furthermore, if you needed to add an operator, you would have to recompile the class in which the operator method was added.

The `ParameterBlock` class alleviates this problem by acting as a placeholder for the parameters. You can create a `ParameterBlock` object and add all the required parameters to it. As we'll see in the section titled Using the `JAI` class later in this chapter, you can pass this object to a generic method. If a new operator is added, there is no need to add a new method. Therefore, there is no need to recompile the source.

The ParameterBlock Class

A `ParameterBlock` object holds all the necessary information about sources and parameters required for an operation. To construct a `ParameterBlock` object, you need to provide two types of information: image sources and parameters.

The `ParameterBlock` object saves the sources as a `Vector` object. The `addSource()` method adds a source to this `Vector` instance. The `setSource(Vector source, int ind)` method replaces the value of the source at the index `ind`. The `set Sources(Vector sources)` method replaces the values of all the sources of the `Vector` object.

In addition, the `ParameterBlock` class has different flavors of `add()`, `set()`, and `get()` methods. The `add()` method adds a parameter, which can be of a Java primitive type or an object. The `set()` method replaces the parameter at a given index. For example, `set(float param, int ind)` replaces the parameter at the index `ind` by a `float`-type parameter `param`.

As you will see in later JAI chapters, `ParameterBlock` is used extensively in applications to provide parameters to both the rendered and the renderable operations.

Operator Factory Interfaces

The Java 2D renderable API specifies two factory interfaces—`RenderedImageFactory` and `ContextualRenderedImageFactory`—for implementing imaging operators. If you intend to implement your own operators, you need to be familiar with these interfaces. The JAI package has one more factory class, named `CollectionImageFactory`, which will be discussed later in this chapter.

The RenderedImageFactory Interface
The `RenderedImageFactory` interface is commonly referred to as RIF in the JAI literature. This interface must be implemented by all the operator classes that can be used in a rendered chain. It has just one method:

◆ **`public RenderedImage create(ParameterBlock paramBlock,`**
`RenderingHints hints)`

Typically, the `create()` method contains the code to construct the desired operator object. The calling object must provide the parameters to construct such an object.

The ContextualRenderedImageFactory Interface
`ContextualRenderedImageFactory` is a subinterface of `RenderedImageFactory`; it is commonly referred to as CRIF. All the operator classes that are used in a renderable chain must implement this interface. Apart from overriding the `create()` method, this interface specifies several methods needed for rendering a renderable image. Implementation of the `ContextualRenderedImageFactory` interface by an operator class implies that the interface can be used in the renderable chain as well.

Converting RenderableImage to AWT Image

The `RenderableImageProducer` class converts a `RenderableImage` object to an `ImageProducer` object. As we did in the AWT imaging sections, you can use the `ImageProducer` object to create an AWT `Image` type.

`RenderableImageProducer` implements the `ImageProducer` and `Runnable` interfaces. This means that `RenderableImageProducer` can be used as a thread while the image is being generated asynchronously.

This class has the following constructor:

◆ `public RenderableImageProducer(RenderableImage rdblImage,`
                            `RenderContext rc)`

Overview of JAI

JAI provides a much richer functionality than Java 2D through a large number of interfaces and classes. Some of them extend and expand Java 2D features. In addition, JAI simplifies programming tasks by providing a wide variety of commonly used imaging operators. In most cases, all you need to do is to pass the operator name as a string and related parameters. These parameters can be simple Java primitive types and/or classes in Java 2D or JAI. If you need to create your own operators, JAI lets you do that as well. You need to follow just a few simple steps to add your operator to the existing list.

Even though JAI has its own APIs to build any kind of application, it doesn't prevent you from using Java 2D or AWT imaging. In fact, JAI uses many Java 2D concepts, classes, and interfaces—for instance, the `SampleModel` and `ColorModel` classes. JAI also lets you convert JAI images to Java 2D `BufferedImage` objects or AWT `Image` objects and vice versa. So if you have already developed applications using AWT imaging or Java 2D, you can easily combine your existing classes with JAI applications.

To summarize, JAI has two parts:

1. **APIs.** JAI interfaces, classes, and exceptions are spread over five packages.
2. **Prebuilt imaging operators.** Imaging operators are built from the JAI and Java 2D classes, but they are exposed to users with an operator name and related parameters. To execute an operator, you would use the `JAI` class (see the section titled Using the JAI Class later in this chapter).

When you build an application, you will probably use both parts. First we'll look at the APIs.

Overview of the APIs

At first glance, the JAI APIs appear overwhelming. They consist of a large number of classes and interfaces that are spread over multiple packages. It takes a fair amount of time to understand the structure of the APIs and the semantics of their usage. Let's use the divide-and-conquer strategy to understand them. But first let's see how the packages are organized.

The JAI APIs are bundled in the following five packages in JAI 1.0.2:

1. **com.sun.media.jai.codec.** With this package you can load and save many popular and industry-supported image formats, including JPEG, BMP, TIFF, FlashPix, and PNG. The **codec** package covers coders and decoders for these formats.

> **Note:** The codec package is not a committed part of JAI and may not be supported after the Image I/O APIs are released.

2. **javax.media.jai.** The **jai** package contains interfaces and classes that provide a wide variety of functionality, ranging from simple rendering of an image to polynomial warping. Most of the topics in this chapter and Chapters 11 through 14 will focus on this package.

3. **javax.media.jai.operator.** As stated earlier, JAI has two parts: operators and APIs. The operator part is supported by this package. Every standard operator supported by JAI has a class in this package. Normally there is no need for an application builder to use these classes. If you intend to develop your own operators, you may want to look at the classes to understand the design.

4. **javax.media.jai.iterator.** This package is meant for the people who write extensions to the JAI APIs. The interfaces and classes supported in this package define how image pixels are traversed while an image is being processed.

5. **javax.media.jai.widget.** This is the smallest package and provides GUI support for displaying images. The classes in this package are deprecated in JAI 1.1. We don't this use package in this book. Instead, we'll develop our own image-displaying widgets as we go.

JAI 1.1 has a few more packages, including

- **javax.media.jai.remote.** This package supports server-side imaging.
- **javax.media.jai.registry.** This package has classes for managing and manipulating the operation registry.

We'll look at the **javax.media.jai** package in a little more depth because it has interfaces and classes that are of importance to an application builder.

The JAI Package

To understand the `javax.media.jai` package better, let's divide it up along functional lines. From the standpoint of building an application, imaging functions include image representation, rendering, manipulation, and analysis. The `jai` package has APIs to support all these imaging functions, and in addition it has classes to support both types of rendering chains. So the categories are

- Image representation
- Image rendering
- Image manipulation
- Image analysis

Let's review the `jai` package in light of this categorization.

Support for the Pull Model

JAI has various interfaces and classes that extend and expand the basic pull model API defined in Java 2D. Although the pull model APIs in JAI don't change the basic architecture, they provide better infrastructure for building practical applications.

Creating a Rendering Chain

The `RenderedOp` and `RenderableOp` classes represent nodes in rendered and renderable chains, respectively. Each class stores the operator name and related parameters for a particular node. The `OperationRegistry` class maps the operator name to a class that performs the imaging operation.

The `OperationRegistry` class translates the operator name into a class that implements one of the three factory interfaces: `RenderedImageFactory`, `Contextual RenderedImageFactory`, and `CollectionImageFactory`. `CollectionImageFactory` is defined in the `jai` package and has a `create()` method that returns a `Collection Image` object.

To create a node in the rendering chain, the `jai` package has a utility class called `JAI.` This class has several `create()` and `createRenderable()` methods, which take the operator name and parameters as input parameters. The `create()` method returns the `RenderedOp` object, and the `createRenderable()` method returns the `Renderable Op` object. The `RenderedOp` or `RenderableOp` object so obtained can be rendered immediately or passed to the next node in the graph.

Describing an Operation

The `OperationDescriptor` interface specifies methods that describe an imaging operation. The description includes the operation's name, version, input, and property. The `javax.media.jai.operator` package has several classes that implement this interface. Each class describes a built-in imaging operator.

Applying Operators

As suggested earlier, a helper class called `JAI` simplifies the task of applying an operator. This class has several generic methods that take an imaging operator name and related parameters as inputs. There are two types of generic methods, based on the return types: methods that return a rendered node (`RenderOp`), and methods that return a renderable node (`RenderableOp`). See the section titled Using the JAI Class later in this chapter for more details.

The `ParameterBlock` class can be used to encapsulate the operator parameters, which can be passed to the methods in the `JAI` class. A disadvantage of using the `ParameterBlock` class is that you need to add parameters in an order determined in advance for an operator. You cannot pass a parameter as a name-value pair. This shortcoming is overcome by the `ParameterBlockJAI` class, which takes the parameter name, as well as the value, as input. Unlike the `ParameterBlock` class, `ParameterBlockJAI` has a constructor that lets you construct it for a specific operator.

Representing Images

In the JAI API, images are represented through a hierarchy of classes, which implement the appropriate pull model interfaces defined in the Java 2D package. The `jai` package has numerous image rendering–related classes and interfaces. At the center of JAI is the `PlanarImage` class (see Figure 10.3). Any image-rendering and image manipulation applications written in JAI need to use this class or its descendant classes.

As Figure 10.3 shows, there are two basic types of subclasses of `PlanarImage`: image classes and operator classes. The image classes represent an image and are used for image rendering and manipulation. The operator classes are used for performing imaging operations. The prebuilt imaging operators use these classes to implement different types of imaging operators. In order for the JAI software to recognize the imaging operator, an operator class must be a subclass of `OpImage.`

Just like `BufferedImage`, `PlanarImage` represents a two-dimensional image and implements the `RenderedImage` interface. It uses the same classes for image data representation; that is, pixels of `PlanarImage` are represented by `ColorModel` and stored by `SampleModel` and `DataBuffer`. But although there are many similarities between `PlanarImage` and `BufferedImage`, the `PlanarImage` class implements an entirely different imaging model. For example, unlike `BufferedImage`, `PlanarImage` may not store all the image data in cache.

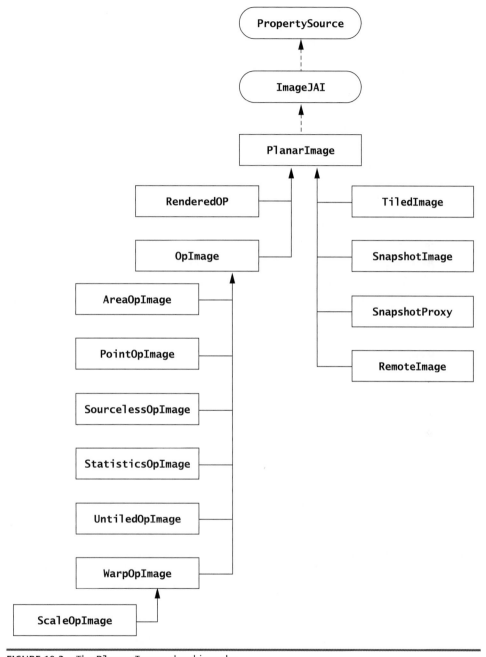

FIGURE 10.3   The PlanarImage class hierarchy

Furthermore, the `PlanarImage` class is read-only; that is, you can read pixel data from `PlanarImage,` but you cannot write to `PlanarImage.` To write pixel data, you need to use the `TiledImage` class, which implements the `WritableRenderedImage` interface. `TiledImage` is another class that is important for pixel processing. To write to a `TiledImage` object, you need to check out a tile, write to it, and check it back in. While a tile is checked out, that tile can be locked to prevent any other client from writing to it.

The `RemoteImage` class represents an image on the server side. In JAI 1.1, however, this class is deprecated in favor of a new class, called `RemoteJAI.` An entirely new package, `javax.media.jai.remote,` has been created to support network imaging in JAI 1.1.

The `SnapshotImage` class, as its name suggests, contains a snapshot of the changing `WritableRenderedImage` object.

> **Note:** Figure 10.3 does not show all the subclasses of `PlanarImage.` The classes not shown include `RenderedImageAdapter,` which is a `PlanarImage` wrapper for a `RenderedImage` object.

Representing Image Sets

In imaging, an operation is often performed on a set of images. You may recall that the animation (cine) example in Chapter 3 required an image set. In that example we used an array to represent the image set.

JAI has more sophisticated classes for representing a set of images. It makes use of the `Collection` data structure already available in Java. Figure 10.4 shows the `CollectionImage` hierarchy. At the top of the hierarchy is the abstract `Collection Image` class, which implements the `java.util.Collection` interface, as well as the `ImageJAI` interface. So the `CollectionImage` object represents an image, as well as a collection.

`CollectionImage` is extended by three subclasses: `CollectionOp` represents a node in the rendered or renderable chain, `ImageSequence` holds a collection of temporal images, and `ImageStack` holds a collection of spatial images. The `Image Sequence` class can be used for frame-by-frame animation. The `ImageStack` class can be extremely useful in GIS and medical imaging because it holds the coordinates of the image sets.

In JAI 1.1, both `ImageSequence` and `ImageStack` are deprecated in favor of `AttributedImageCollection.`

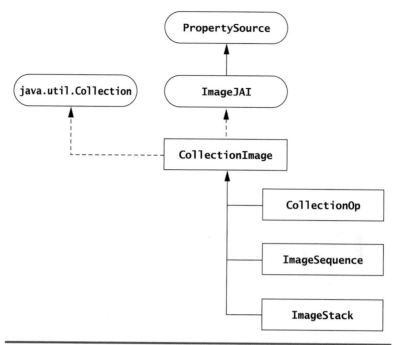

FIGURE 10.4 The CollectionImage class hierarchy

Representing Image Data

JAI uses the same image data representation model as Java 2D. In brief, the ColorModel class describes the composition of an image pixel. The SampleModel class describes how data is stored. Image data is contained in a Raster object, which has an instance of both SampleModel and DataBuffer. The DataBuffer object stores the data.

JAI uses all the sample models and color models defined in Java 2D. In addition, JAI has its own ColorModel and SampleModel classes that extend the functionality of Java 2D classes:

◆ **FloatDoubleColorModel.** This class extends ComponentColorModel.

◆ **ComponentSampleModelJAI.** This class extends ComponentSampleModel.

JAI also includes two additional DataBuffer class types to support the **float** and **double** data types: DataBufferFloat and DataBufferDouble, both of which are subclasses of **DataBuffer**. You may recall that Java 2D has four such classes to support **byte**, **short**, **int**, and unsigned **short** types of data.

Rendering Images

A JAI image can be rendered to any device that has a graphical context. JAI follows the same rendering model as Java 2D to render an image onto a physical device.

The `Graphics2D` class has the following methods for rendering rendered and renderable images:

- `public abstract void drawRenderedImage(RenderedImage img, AffineTransform xform)`
- `public abstract void drawRenderableImage(RenderableImage img, AffineTransform xform)`

As their names suggest, the first method draws a rendered image, and the second draws a renderable image.

As mentioned earlier, the `PlanarImage` class implements the `RenderedImage` interface. So you can use the first method to draw a planar image. However, this is not the only way you can draw a planar image. The `PlanarImage` object can be converted to a `BufferedImage` object, which can be drawn over a `Graphics2D` object by different flavors of the `drawImage()` method. A buffered image can also be drawn as a rendered image because `BufferedImage` also implements the `RenderedImage` interface. The second rendering method is not frequently used because a renderable image is always converted to a rendered image before rendering.

JAI has no printing APIs. To print JAI images you need to use the printing APIs defined in Java 2D.

Rendering Hints

JAI defines its own rendering hints. Recall from Chapter 5 that the rendering hints are supplied as a `Map` parameter. A `Map` entry has a key and a value. The `JAI.RenderingKey` class (which is an inner class) represents the key for the `RenderingHints` maps. The values include information about the interpolation type, tile cache, tile layout, and border decoration. Rendering hints are typically supplied to the operator that creates the rendering-chain node. The rendering hints are applied when the node is evaluated.

Manipulating Images

In Java 2D, images can be geometrically manipulated through the affine transformation, which, as we learned in Chapter 4, is a linear transformation. JAI has several affine operators that are built through the affine transformation.

Although the affine transformation is adequate to meet the needs of most applications, applications such as image registration, restoration, and so on often require nonlinear transformation. JAI thus provides APIs for both linear and nonlinear transformations.

The `PerspectiveTransform` class in JAI 1.0.2 performs the perspective transformation. This class is similar to the `AffineTransform` class. The `Warp` class represents nonlinear transformation. This class has seven subclasses, each of which performs a type of warping, including affine, perspective, quadratic, cubic, and polynomial warping.

Enhancing Images

JAI expands the image enhancement capability of Java 2D through various classes. The `KernelJAI` class represents the convolution kernel. With a few built-in kernels and more flexible methods, this class is much more powerful than the `Kernel` class in Java 2D. It is typically used as an input to an operator. Likewise, `LookupTableJAI` expands the functionality of the `LookupTable` class. Again, this class is typically used with an operator. The `ColorCube` class extends the `LookupTableJAI` class and represents a lookup table as a color cube.

Analyzing Images

JAI has several classes for performing image analysis. These classes are typically used in conjunction with related operators.

As its name suggests, the `Histogram` class computes histograms. To perform ROI analysis, JAI provides two classes: `ROI` and `ROIShape.` The former creates a rectangular ROI image, and the latter creates an ROI of any shape. Both classes support several common ROI operations, such as thresholding. With these classes you can create an `ROI` property and save it with an image. Many of the JAI operators accept `ROI` as one of the input parameters.

Both histogram and ROI computations can be performed in a node in the rendering chain. When they are computed, they are saved as properties. When a node is evaluated, these properties can be extracted by the `getProperty()` call.

Overview of the Operators

JAI offers a large set of built-in operators that can be applied to a single image or a collection of images. Each operator is assigned a name and a set of parameters. Consider the image rotation operation. The operator name is Rotate and the parameters are the center of rotation, rotation angle, and interpolation type.

> **Note:** When it comes to operator names, JAI is case insensitive. In this text, however, we capitalize the names of all JAI operators where they appear in discussion, but we leave them in regular text font to distinguish them from classes and objects.

As we'll see later in this chapter, applying an operator is a simple affair. All you need to know is how to use the JAI class and how to create parameters required for an operator. JAI operators are divided into categories as follows:

♦ File operators

♦ Point operators

♦ Area operators

♦ Geometric operators

♦ Color quantization operators

♦ Statistical operators

♦ Edge detection operators

♦ Frequency operators

♦ Other operators

In the sections that follow we'll look at each of these categories in turn.

File Operators

File operators perform image read and write operations. The FileLoad operator loads an image, and FileStore saves it. In addition, format-specific operators read images from streams. The URL operator loads an image from a URL.

JAI also provides two operators to support the Internet Imaging Protocol (IIP): IIP and IIPResolution. Both of these operators provide client-side support for IIP. The IIP operator creates a rendered or renderable image, depending on the data received from the server. The IIPResolution operator requests an image from the server of a particular resolution. To learn more about Internet Imaging Protocol, visit http://www.digitalimaging.org.

Point Operators

There are many point operators. In the point type of operation, the output pixel depends only on the corresponding input pixel. Point operations do not change the image geometry. We can subdivide point operators into the following categories:

♦ **Arithmetic operators.** Some examples are Add, Subtract, Multiply, and Divide. These operators require two rendered or renderable source images. The Add operator, for example, adds the pixels at the corresponding position. Adding is performed on a per band basis.

♦ **Logical operators.** Logical operators include And, Or, Xor, and Not.

♦ **Composite operators.** There are two composite operators: Composite and Overlay.

- **Image creation operators.** There are two image creation operators: Constant and Pattern.
- **Functional operators.** This category contains the following operators: Exp, Log, MatchCDF, PieceWise, Clamp, Threshold, Lookup, Invert.
- **Color conversion operators.** The three color conversion operators are ColorConvert, BandCombine, and BandSelect.

Area Operators

Area operators perform an operation over a rectangular area of the image. There are two types: operators that change the geometry and filter operators.

The Border operator adds a border to an image. JAI has several `BorderExtender` classes that help create different types of borders. Border takes a `BorderExtender` object as a parameter.

The Crop operator crops a rectangular region of the image.

There are three spatial filter operators: Convolve, BoxFilter, and MedianFilter. The Convolve operator performs convolution; that is, it computes the weighted sum of the pixels within a rectangular area that surrounds a given pixel. To compute the weighted sum, you can provide different types of kernels using the `KernelJAI` class. The BoxFilter operator averages pixels within a rectangular area, and the MedianFilter operator computes the median value of the pixel within a rectangular area, thus eliminating extraneous pixels.

Geometric Operators

Geometric operations change the image geometry. The affine transformation is one type of geometric operation. JAI supports all the standard affine operations, which include affine, translate, scale, rotate, shear, and transpose.[2] As mentioned earlier, JAI also supports nonlinear transformation. The Warp operator performs different types of warping, depending on the parameters, which can be created from the subclasses of the `Warp` class.

Color Quantization Operators

JAI has two dithering (color quantization) operators: OrderedDither and Error Diffusion.

---

2 In JAI, *flip* is referred to as *transpose*.

Statistical Operators

There are three statistical operators: Mean, Extrema, and Histogram. As their names suggest, Mean computes mean values, Extrema computes minimum and maximum values, and Histogram computes the histogram of an image. These values are computed for each band and are assigned as properties of the image object.

Edge Detection Operators

There is only one edge detection operator: GradientMagnitude. However, you can use the Convolve operator to apply edge detection kernels using the `KernelJAI` class.

Frequency Operators

JAI provides conversion techniques to convert an image from spatial domain to frequency domain and vice versa. Two types of conversions are currently supported: discrete Fourier transformation (DFT) and discrete cosine transformation (DCT). The DFT operator computes the discrete Fourier transformation of the image, and IDFT computes the inverse—that is, an image in the spatial domain from the Fourier coefficients. Likewise, the DCT and IDCT operators perform forward and inverse discrete cosine transformations.

In a typical image-processing operation, you would convert an image from the spatial domain to the frequency domain by using some transformation. You would then apply arithmetic operators such as Multiply and Divide to the frequency domain image. To compute the image back in the spatial domain, you would apply the inverse transformation.

In addition to the operators that perform forward and inverse transformations, a few other useful frequency operators perform some utility functions in the frequency domain. These include Magnitude, MagnitudeSquared, Phase, PeriodicShift, and PolarToComplex.

As an example, let's look at a simple scenario that involves converting an image to a frequency domain and then back to a spatial domain. You can convert an image to a frequency domain image by applying the DFT operator. A pixel in the DFT image has a complex value—that is, a value that has a real and an imaginary part. The Magnitude operator creates a magnitude image from these pixel values, and the Phase operator creates a phase image. You can then apply arithmetic operators to the magnitude and phase images. To create a complex image from the magnitude and phase images, you can apply the PolarToComplex operator. This operator takes two rendered or renderable images as inputs and produces a single complex image, which is still in the frequency domain. The inverse transformation converts the complex image to a spatial domain.

It has probably occurred to you that the scenario we just explained is an excellent candidate for a renderable chain. Both the source and the sink are in the spatial domain, and there is no need to render any of the frequency domain images. The entire renderable chain can even be executed on the server side for speed.

Other Operators

One operator—Renderable—doesn't belong to any of the categories already described. This operator constructs a renderable image from a rendered image. This is the operator you use if you need to create a renderable chain.

Using the JAI Class

JAI is a utility class that helps apply a variety of operations to a single or multiple images. This class has several variations of the *createXXX()* method that can perform any imaging operations supported by JAI. In addition, these methods can execute any custom operations, which can be defined by you or a third-party vendor. The *createXXX()* method returns the result as a `RenderedOp` or `RenderableOp` object.

Using the JAI class, you can perform many more image operations than we saw in the Java 2D chapters. The *createXXX()* methods simplify the code to a great extent because most of the routine code is built in. All you need to do is pass in the operator name and appropriate parameters to a *createXXX()* method. Here are the variations:

- `create()`
- `createNS()`
- `createRenderable()`
- `createRenderableNS()`
- `createCollection()`
- `createCollectionNS()`
- `createRenderableCollection()`
- `createRenderableCollectionNS()`

There are two basic types of *createXXX()* methods: static and nonstatic. (*NS* in these method names stands for *nonstatic*.) The static methods operate on the default JAI instance. You can obtain the default instance by calling the `JAI.getDefault Instance()` method.

The JAI class has the following attributes:

- `tileCache`
- `tileScheduler`

- `operationRegistry`
- `renderingHints`

The `JAI` class has set and get methods for these attributes. If you don't set them, they assume a default value.

Creating a JAI Instance

Sometimes you may want to run different operations with a different set of `JAI` attributes. If you use the default instance, you may have to switch the attribute values too frequently, thus affecting performance. In such cases you can create a separate instance of `JAI` for an operation and use the nonstatic methods to execute the operation.

To create an instance of `JAI`, use its constructor: `public JAI()`. Once you have created a `JAI` instance, set its attributes using its set methods.

Applying the Operators

The first parameter of all the *createXXX()* methods is a string that represents the operation name. The operation name is not case sensitive.

The `create()` method has the largest number of flavors. Different flavors of `create()` take different numbers and types of arguments. The flavor you use depends on the operation.

An imaging operation may require zero or more parameters. For example, as we saw in Chapter 7, the image rotation operation requires angle and center of rotation as parameters. The parameters for an operation are supplied through the other arguments of the `create()` method.

The parameters and all the types of implemented operations are published, so you need to choose an appropriate flavor of the `create()` method. The argument types include

- `RenderedImage`
- `ParameterBlock`
- `RenderingHints`
- `Object`
- Primitive types such as `float`

You can use the appropriate parameters to execute an operation. Here's an example:

```
JAI.create("fileload", imagepath);
```

The file load operation loads an image whose path is provided by `imagepath`, which is a `String` parameter.

A single operator can be executed in several different ways. Here's another example that illustrates the use of `ParameterBlock` to supply the operational parameters:

```
ParameterBlock pb = new ParameterBlock();
pb.addSource(sourceImage);
pb.add((float)width/2);
pb.add((float)height/2);
pb.add((float)ang);
pb.add(Interpolation.getInstance(Interpolation.INTERP_NEAREST));
RenderedOp renderedOp = JAI.create("rotate", pb);
```

This code sample implements the image rotate operation. In this case, all the arguments for the rotate operation are supplied through `ParameterBlock`. Notice that an image is added to `ParameterBlock` by the `addSource()` method.

The `createRenderable()` or `createRenderableNS()` method returns an instance of `RenderableOp`. The `createCollection()` method returns a collection of `Rendered Op` or `RenderableOp` objects. As mentioned earlier, `RenderedOp` and `RenderableOp` represent the nodes in a rendering chain.

How Does JAI.create() Work?

To understand how *createXXX()* methods work, you may want look at the `javax.media.jai.operator` package. This package has a large number of `Operator Descriptor` classes—one for each operator.

Information about the operators is maintained in a file called `registryFile`. Each operator has two types of entries:

1. **Name of the `OperatorDescriptor` class.** Each operation has an `OperationDescriptor` type of class. If you want to create your own operator, you must create an `OperatorDescriptor` class by implementing the base `OperationDescriptor` interface or its derivatives.

2. **Name of the RIF or CRIF class.** An operation can be applied to `RenderedImage` only or to both `RenderedImage` and `RenderableImage`. Accordingly, a RIF (`RenderedImageFactory`) or CRIF (`ContextualRenderedImageFactory`) class is created to handle the rendered or renderable operations.

The actual functionality is contained in a class that is a descendent of `OpImage`. As Figure 10.3 shows, `OpImage` has several subclasses. To create a new operator, extend the `OpImage` class or its subclasses to create a new class and implement the operator functionality in this class. Then create a RIF or CRIF class by implementing either `RenderedImageFactory` or `ContexualRenderedImageFactory`, respectively, depending on whether your operator works on `RenderedImage` or on both `Rendered Image` and `RenderableImage`. Both of these interfaces specify a `create()` method for creating the new operator object. When you implement the `create()` method, construct the `OpImage` object that implements the new operator functionality.

The `OperationRegistry` object obtains the operator name from the *JAI.createXXX()* method and maps it to the actual object that implements the functionality by reading the corresponding `registryFile` entries.

If you create a new operator, there are two ways of making an `Operation Registry` object aware of that operator:

1. **Adding the appropriate entries to `registryFile`.** This change is permanent.

2. **Dynamically registering the operator with `OperationRegistry`.** This change is temporary. Every time you launch your application, it must register the operator with `OperationRegistry`, which has several *registerXXX()* methods for this purpose.

Getting Started with JAI

First download JAI software from the JAI home page (http://java.sun.com/products/java-media/jai). In addition to software and documentation, this site has a tutorial and sample code.

Before you install the JAI package, make sure that you have the right version of the JDK. JAI works with JDK 1.2 or higher versions. If you don't have a workable version of the JDK, download it from the Java home page and run the installer, which will install the JAI JAR files, native libraries, and demo files.

JAI JAR Files

The following JAR files will be in the directory in which the external libraries of JAI are stored:

◆ `jai_core.jar`
◆ `jai_codec.jar`
◆ `mlibwrapper_jai.jar`

The default path for the external libraries is the `<JDK_HOME>/jre/lib/ext` directory in both the UNIX and the Wintel platforms. This directory will also contain the registry file named `registryFile.jai`. As mentioned earlier, this file has information about all the currently available operators.

JAI Native Libraries

JAI uses Sun's `mediaLib` graphical library. Interfaces to the `mediaLib` library that are part of Java Native Interface (JNI) are in the `jre/bin` directory. Following are the `mediaLib` JNI shared libraries in different platforms:

- **In Windows:** `mlib_java_jai.dll`
- **In Solaris:**
    - **Solaris edition:** `libmlib_java_jai.so`
    - **Intel edition:** `libmlib_java_jai_vis.so`

Setting PATH

When you install the JDK, the `PATH` variable points to the `<JDK_HOME>/bin` directory. But the JAI libraries are loaded in the `<JDK_HOME>/jre` path. Append the `PATH` variable such that it points to `<JDK_HOME>/jre/bin` as well. This is to ensure that your application sees the `mediaLib` implementation of the native Windows libraries from the `mlibwrapper_jai.jar` file. Otherwise the application will get the Java implementation of the graphical library, which may be slower compared to `mediaLib`. If your application doesn't see the `mediaLib` wrapper, you will see the message *Could not load mlib* on the console.

Here's an example of how to append PATH in windows:

```
set PATH=c:\jdk1.3\jre\bin;%PATH%
```

Compiling Your Application

It's a good idea to create a separate directory for your application classes. To do so, first create the directory and then compile your application classes to that directory. Use the `mkdir` command to create a directory. For example, type "mkdir jaiclasses" to create a directory called `jaiclasses.`

Before you compile, set your class path to point to this directory. If you want to use other classes or beans in a JAR file, include that file's name in the class path as well. Here's how to do this:

- **In Windows:**

    ```
    set classpath=c:\jaiclasses;c:\beans\Plotter.jar;%classpath%
    ```

- **In UNIX:**

    ```
    CLASSPATH=/home/staff/lhrodrig/jaiclasses/classes:/home/staff/lhrodrig/beans/
                                        Plotter.jar:$CLASSPATH
    export CLASSPATH
    ```

These examples add the directory you just created and a JAR file to the current class path.

Once you have set the class path, compile your classes by typing "java -d c:\jaiclasses JAIImageViewer.java" on the command line.

Running JAI Programs

Because JAI programs are memory and computation intensive, you may have to invoke special options with the `java` command to ensure smooth running of your application.

Adjusting the Heap Size

By default, the Java Virtual Machine assigns a heap size of 16MB. With this heap size, you would frequently get an "out of memory" exception when your applications dealt with large images. You can increase the heap size by using the -*X* option with the `java` command. You can assign the initial heap size by using the **–Xms<size>** option and the maximum heap size with the **-Xmx<size>** option. Here's an example:

    java -Xms32m -Xmx128m app.JAIImageViewer

This command will invoke the `JAIImageViewer` application with 32MB of initial heap size and 128MB of maximum heap size.

Note that -*X* options are nonstandard, and according to Sun they are subject to change without notice.

Collecting Garbage

A separate thread in the background performs automatic garbage collection. Sometimes garbage collection does not keep up with memory allocation. Eventually the system will run out of memory. You can force garbage collection by calling the `System.gc()` method, but calling this method does not guarantee that the garbage collector will run. Here's a simple utility method that performs forcible garbage collection:

```java
public static void runGc() {
    Runtime rt= Runtime.getRuntime();
    rt.gc();
    long mem = rt.freeMemory();
    System.out.println("Free Memory = "+ mem);
}
```

Note that frequent running of `gc()` may result in performance degradation.

> **Note:** The code for `rungc()` is available on the book's Web page in the file `SystemUtil.java`, which is in the directory `src/util`.

A Simple Example of Loading and Displaying an Image

Now that we have briefly reviewed the JAI APIs, let's create a simple application to view images. This application will perform two basic operations: image loading and rendering. Unlike Java 2D, JAI does not restrict us to JPEG and GIF; it supports several different imaging formats. In this example, let's use the FileLoad operator to load the image and Graphics2D's drawRenderedImage() method to draw it. Listing 10.1 shows the code for a class that loads and displays JAI images.

LISTING 10.1   The JAISimpleViewer class

```
package app;

import java.awt.*;
import java.awt.geom.*;
import java.io.*;
import javax.swing.*;
import javax.media.jai.*;
import com.sun.media.jai.codec.*;
import com.vistech.util.*;

public class JAISimpleViewer extends ApplicationFrame{
    protected ImagePanel viewer;

    public static void  main(String[] args){
        JAISimpleViewer ip = new JAISimpleViewer();
        if(args.length <1) {
          System.out.println("Enter a valid image file name");
          System.exit(0);
        }
        ip.loadAndDisplay(args[0]);
    }

    public static PlanarImage readAsPlanarImage(String filename) {
        return JAI.create("fileload", filename);
    }

    public void loadAndDisplay(String filename){
        PlanarImage img = readAsPlanarImage(filename);
        displayImage(img);
    }

    public void displayImage(PlanarImage img) {
        int width = img.getWidth();
        int height = img.getHeight();
        Dimension d = ApplicationFrame.getViewerSize(width/(double)height);
        launchFrame(img, d.width, d.height);
    }

    public void launchFrame(PlanarImage img, int width, int height) {
        setTitle("JAI Image Viewer");
        viewer = new ImagePanel(img);
        viewer.setPreferredSize(new Dimension(width, height));
```

continued

```
        Container cp = getContentPane();
        getContentPane().setLayout(new GridLayout(1,1));
        cp.add(viewer);
        pack();
        setSize(new Dimension(width, height));
        show();
        viewer.repaint();
    }

    protected class ImagePanel extends JComponent {
        protected PlanarImage image;
        protected AffineTransform atx = new AffineTransform();
        protected int width, height;
        public ImagePanel(){}
        public ImagePanel(PlanarImage img){
            image = img;
            width = img.getWidth();
            height = img.getHeight();
        }

        public void paintComponent(Graphics gc){
            Graphics2D g = (Graphics2D)gc;
            Rectangle rect = this.getBounds();
            if((width != rect.width) || (height != rect.height)){
                double magx = rect.width/(double)width ;
                double magy = rect.height/(double)height ;
                atx.setToScale(magx, magy);
            }
            if(image != null) g.drawRenderedImage(image, atx);
        }
    }
}
```

To run JAISimpleViewer, type "java app.JAISimpleViewer <image path>" on the command line. The main() method constructs the JAISimpleViewer object and calls its loadAndDisplay() method, which in turn calls readAsPlanarImage() and displayImage(). The readAsPlanarImage() method can load any image format supported by JAI. The displayImage() method calls launchFrame(), which creates an ImagePanel object and embeds it in an instance of JFrame.

The task of displaying images is delegated to the ImagePanel class, which is an inner class of JAISimpleViewer. An image is painted whenever the paint Component() method is called by the system. This method paints a planar image by calling drawRenderedImage(), which requires a transformation parameter—that is, an AffineTransform object. The transformation is applied to the image before it is displayed.

To paint an image to fit the viewport, the paintComponent() method first computes the appropriate scaling factor. Even if you resize the viewport, the image size is adjusted to fit it.

Converting AWT Image to PlanarImage

To convert an AWT `Image` object to a `PlanarImage` object, all you need to do is use the AWTImage operator, which takes the AWT `Image` object as its only parameter. Listing 10.2 shows how to do this.

LISTING 10.2   Converting an AWT `Image` object to a `PlanarImage` object

```
public PlanarImage readAsPlanarImage(String filename) {
    Image img = readImage(filename);
    return JAI.create("awtimage", img);
  }

  public Image readImage(String imageName){
    Image image = Toolkit.getDefaultToolkit().getImage(imageName);
    MediaTracker imageTracker = new MediaTracker(this);
    imageTracker.addImage(image, 0);
    try{
      imageTracker.waitForID(0);
    }catch(InterruptedException e){ return null;}
    return image;
  }
```

The `readAsPlanarImage()` method first calls the `readImage()` method to load the specified image as an AWT `Image` object. The `readImage()` method uses the `MediaTracker` class to load an image (see Chapter 2). The `readAsPlanarImage()` method then uses the `JAI.create()` method to apply the AWTImage operator. `JAI.create()` returns a `RenderedOp` object. Because the `RenderedOp` class is a subclass of `PlanarImage,` there is no need to cast the object returned by `JAI.create()` to the `PlanarImage` object.

We used the methods shown in Listing 10.2 in the `JAISimpleViewer1` class, which has the same code as the `JAISimpleViewer` class (see Listing 10.1), except for `readAsPlanarImage()`.

> **Note:** The code for `JAISimpleViewer` and `JAISimpleViewer1` is available on the book's Web page in the directory `src/chapter10/simpleviewer`.

An Image Canvas Class for JAI

As we have done many times in previous chapters, let's develop an image canvas class—this time for JAI—by extending `JComponent`. We'll call this class `JAIImage Canvas`. To allow users to pan the image, let's add the scroll feature we developed in Chapter 7. This means that `JAIImageCanvas` will reuse the `ScrollController` interface and the `Scroll` class. Listing 10.3 shows the code for `JAIImageCanvas`.

LISTING 10.3 The JAIImageCanvas class

```java
package com.vistech.jai.render;

import java.awt.*;
import java.awt.event.*;
import java.awt.image.*;
import java.io.*;
import javax.swing.*;
import javax.swing.event.*;
import java.awt.geom.*;
import com.vistech.util.*;
import javax.media.jai.*;
import com.vistech.imageviewer.*;

public class JAIImageCanvas extends JComponent implements ScrollController{
    public final static int MAX_WIDTH = 2048;
    public final static int MAX_HEIGHT = 2048;
    transient protected PlanarImage image;
    protected AffineTransform atx = new AffineTransform();
    protected int width, height;
    protected boolean imageDrawn = false;
    protected int panX = 0, panY = 0;
    protected Point scrollAnchor  = new Point(0,0);
    protected boolean scrollOn = true;
    protected Point vpPos = new Point(0,0);
    protected Point panOffset = new Point(0,0);

    public JAIImageCanvas() { }
    public JAIImageCanvas(PlanarImage img){setImage(img);}

    public synchronized void setImage(PlanarImage img){
        reset();
        image = img;
        int wid = img.getWidth();
        int ht = img.getHeight();
        width = (wid > MAX_WIDTH ) ? MAX_WIDTH : wid;
        height =  (ht > MAX_WIDTH ) ? MAX_WIDTH : ht;
        setPreferredSize(new Dimension(width, height));
        imageDrawn = false;
        repaint();
    }

    public PlanarImage getImage(){ return image;}
    public PlanarImage getDisplayImage(){return image;}

    public boolean isImageDrawn(){ return imageDrawn;}

    public void setPanOffset(Point panOffset){
        firePropertyChange("PanOffset",this.panOffset,panOffset);
        this.panOffset = panOffset;
        panX = panOffset.x;
        panY = panOffset.y;
    }

    public Point getPanOffset(){ return panOffset;}
```

```java
public void setScrollOn(boolean onOff){
    scrollOn = onOff;
    panX = 0; panY = 0;
    vpPos = new Point(panX, panY);
}

public boolean getScrollOn(){ return scrollOn;}

public void startScroll(int x, int y){
    scrollAnchor.x = x- panX;
    scrollAnchor.y = y- panY;
    setCursor(Cursor.getPredefinedCursor(Cursor.MOVE_CURSOR));
    repaint();
}

public void scroll(int x, int y){
    if((x < 0 )|| (y < 0)) return;
    int panx = x-scrollAnchor.x;
    int pany = y-scrollAnchor.y;
    setPanOffset(new Point(panx, pany));
    setViewportPosition(new Point(-panx, -pany));
    repaint();
}

public void stopScroll(){ setCursor(Cursor.getDefaultCursor());}

public void pan(double x, double y){
    setPanOffset(new Point((int)x, (int)y));
    repaint();
}

public Point getViewportPosition(){return vpPos;}

public void setViewportPosition(Point vpPos){
    firePropertyChange("viewportPosition", this.vpPos, vpPos);
    this.vpPos = vpPos;
}

public void setTransform(AffineTransform at){atx = at;}
public AffineTransform getTransform(){ return atx;};

public void reset(){
    atx = new AffineTransform();
    panX = 0; panY = 0;
}

public void paintComponent(Graphics gc){
    Graphics2D g = (Graphics2D)gc;
    Rectangle rect = this.getBounds();
    if((width != rect.width) || (height != rect.height)){
        double magx = rect.width/(double)width ;
        double magy = rect.height/(double)height ;
    }
    g.setColor(Color.black);
    g.fillRect(0, 0, rect.width, rect.height);
    atx =  AffineTransform.getTranslateInstance(panX, panY);
    if(image != null) g.drawRenderedImage(image, atx);
```

continued

TABLE 10.4 JAIImageCanvas Properties

PROPERTY	TYPE	DESCRIPTION
image	PlanarImage	This property represents the original image.
displayedImage	PlanarImage	This property represents the displayed image. Although it is the same as the original image in this case, the subclasses can override the getDisplayImage() method and return the image displayed in the viewport.
panOffset	Point	This property contains the position of the image with respect to the viewport.
atx	AffineTransform	This property represents the transformation applied to the image.

```
        imageDrawn = true;
    }
}
```

JAIImageCanvas is the base class for many image canvas classes that will be discussed in subsequent chapters. First let's look at some of its instance variables. Each one represents a property in the JAIImageCanvas bean, as shown in Table 10.4.

The JAIImageCanvas class has two constructors: one with no arguments and one with a PlanarImage argument. If you use the no-argument constructor, you need to use the setImage() method to set the planar image. This method sets the image property and calls repaint(). As a result, the paintComponent() method is called, and the image is drawn at a position set by the panOffset property. The paintComponent() method draws the image using drawRenderedImage().

The ScrollController methods—startScroll(), scroll(), and stopScroll()—manipulate the panOffset property to scroll the image. See Chapter 7 for an explanation of the ScrollController interface and Scroll class. The Scroll object needs to register the mouse and mouseMotion events with the JAIImageCanvas object. In a typical scenario, when the mouse is pressed, Scroll calls the startScroll() method. When the mouse is dragged, it calls scroll(), which computes the values of panX and panY. The paintComponent() method uses these values to construct an instance of AffineTransform and assigns it to atx, which is then passed to draw Rendered Image().

Putting It All Together: A Planar-Image Viewer

Let's use the JAIImageCanvas class to build an image viewer application that can load, display, and save planar images. To load and save images, we'll develop two utility classes called ImageLoaderJAI and ImageSaverJAI, which are explained in detail in Chapter 17. These classes use the JAI codec available in JAI 1.0.2 and 1.1.

This viewer will display and load an image using the `ImageLoaderJAI` class and render it on a `JAIImageCanvas` object. You can scroll a displayed image by dragging the mouse over it. You can save the displayed image in any of the image formats supported by JAI 1.0.2.

To build this application, we'll reuse the `ApplicationFrame` class (see Appendix A) to construct a frame, and the `FileBrowser` bean (see Appendix C) to list and select images. `ApplicationFrame` is in addition to the `ScrollController` and `Scroll` classes needed for scrolling.

The `JAIImageViewer` application will use the following classes:

♦ **app.JAIImageViewer.** This is the main class that constructs all the other objects.

♦ **com.vistech.util.ApplicationFrame.** This class represents the application skeleton.

♦ **FileBrowser.** This bean selects image files.

♦ **com.vistech.events.ListSelectListener** and **com.vistech.events.ListSelect Event.** This class fires a `listSelect` event to report that a file has been selected.

♦ **com.vistech.jai.render.JAIImageCanvas.** This class displays images.

♦ **com.vistech.imageviewer.ScrollController** and **com.vistech.imageviewer. Scroll.** These classes scroll the image in the JAIImageCanvas object.

♦ **com.vistech.jai.loader.ImageLoaderJAI.** This class loads an image from a local directory as a `PlanarImage` object.

♦ **com.vistech.jai.imageio.PlanarImageListener** and **com.vistech.jai. imageio.PlanarImageLoadedEvent.** These classes fire a `planarImageLoaded` event to report that an image has been selected. They also send the image to the receiving object.

♦ **com.vistech.jai.imageio.ImageSaverJAI.** This class saves an image to a local directory.

♦ **com.vistech.jai.imageio.ImageSaverPanel.** This class repesents a panel that has the GUI for selecting and saving different image formats.

Listing 10.4 shows the source code for the `JAIImageViewer` class.

> **Note:** Keep in mind that the `javadoc` files for all the classes built in this book are available on the book's Web page. You may want to look at relevant `javadoc` files while reviewing the code.

LISTING 10.4 The `JAIImageViewer` class

```java
package app;

import java.awt.*;
import java.awt.event.*;
import java.awt.image.*;
import java.io.*;
import javax.swing.*;
import java.awt.geom.*;
import javax.media.jai.*;
import com.vistech.listselect.*;
import com.vistech.jai.imageio.*;
import com.vistech.jai.render.*;
import com.vistech.imageviewer.*;
import com.vistech.util.*;

public class JAIImageViewer extends ApplicationFrame{
    protected JAIImageCanvas viewer;
    protected PlanarImage image;
    protected FileBrowser flBrowser;
    protected ImageLoaderJAI loader;
    protected ImageSaverPanel saver;
    protected ScrollGUI scroll;


    public void loadAndDisplay(String filename){
        image = loader.readAsPlanarImage(filename);
        createUI();
        displayImage(image);
    }

    public void displayImage(PlanarImage img) {
        int width = img.getWidth();
        int height = img.getHeight();
        viewer.setImage(img);
        saver.setImage(img);
    }

    public void createUI() {
        Dimension dim = Toolkit.getDefaultToolkit().getScreenSize();
        int width = (int)(dim.width*3/4.0);
        int height = (int)(dim.height*3/4.0);
        setTitle("Image Viewer");
        viewer = new JAIImageCanvas();
        Dimension d = ApplicationFrame.getViewerSize(width/(double)height);
        viewer.setPreferredSize(new Dimension(d.width, d.height));
        createImageLoaderAndSaver();
        loader.addPlanarImageLoadedListener(
            new PlanarImageLoadedListener() {
                public void imageLoaded(PlanarImageLoadedEvent e) {
                    PlanarImage image = e.getImage();
                    if(image == null) return;
                    SwingUtilities.invokeLater(new ImagePaint(image));
                }
            }
        );
```

```
        JTabbedPane jtp = new JTabbedPane();
        jtp.add("Load", flBrowser);
        jtp.add("Save", saver);
        JSplitPane vsp = new JSplitPane(JSplitPane.HORIZONTAL_SPLIT, jtp, viewer);
        getContentPane().setLayout(new GridLayout(1,1));
        getContentPane().add(vsp);
        pack();
        setSize(new Dimension(d.width+170, d.height));
        show();
        vsp.setDividerLocation(0.32);
        vsp.setDividerSize(6);
        initializeScroll();
        viewer.repaint();
    }

    protected void initializeScroll(){
        scroll = new ScrollGUI(viewer);
        viewer.addMouseListener(scroll);
        viewer.addMouseMotionListener(scroll);
    }

    protected void createImageLoaderAndSaver(){
        flBrowser = new FileBrowser();
        loader = new ImageLoaderJAI();
        flBrowser.addListSelectListener(loader);
        saver = new ImageSaverPanel();
        saver.setBorder(BorderFactory.createTitledBorder("Image Save"));
    }


    public static void  main(String[] args){
        JAIImageViewer ip = new JAIImageViewer();
        if(args.length <1) ip.createUI();
        else ip.loadAndDisplay(args[0]);
    }
}
```

There are two ways of launching the `JAIImageViewer` application: with or without an image file path in the command-line argument. Here are the commands:

1. "java app.JAIImageViewer"
2. "java app.JAIImageViewer <image path>"

If the application is called with an image path, the `main()` method calls the `loadAndDisplay()` method with the image path parameter. This method in turn calls `createUI()` and `displayImage()` to display the image. If the application is called without an image path, the `main()` method calls `createUI()`.

The `createUI()` method first instantiates the `JAIImageCanvas` class to create the `viewer` object. It then calls the `createImageLoaderAndSaver()` method to instantiate `loader` and `saver` objects from the `ImageLoaderJAI` and `ImageSaverPanel` classes, respectively. The `createImageLoaderAndSaver()` method also constructs a `FileBrowser` bean and passes it to `loader`'s `addListSelectListener()` method. By doing so, it registers the `loader` object with the `FileBrowser` bean to receive `listSelect` events. So when a user clicks a path in `FileBrowser`, that path is sent to the `loader` object, which in turn loads the image pointed to by that path.

The `createUI()` method registers an anonymous inner class with the `loader` object to receive the `planarImageLoaded` events. The `imageloaded()` method of this anonymous class is called whenever an image is loaded. The `imageLoaded()` method extracts the image and calls a thread to paint the image in the `viewer` object. Figure 10.5 shows the flow of events.

The image is painted in a separate thread because larger images take a longer time to load. If the image is painted in a thread, the application is not blocked during loading of images. The `ImagePaint` class shown in Listing 10.5 is an inner class of `JAIImageViewer`.

LISTING 10.5   The `ImagePaint` class

```
class ImagePaint implements Runnable {
   PlanarImage image;
   boolean firstTime = true;
   public ImagePaint(PlanarImage image){
      this.image = image;
   }
   public void run() {
      if(firstTime) {
         try {
         setCursor(Cursor.getPredefinedCursor(Cursor.WAIT_CURSOR));
         viewer.setImage(image);
         saver.setImage(image);
         viewer.repaint();
         firstTime = false;
         SwingUtilities.invokeLater(this);
         }catch(Exception e) {
          SwingUtilities.invokeLater(this);
         }
      }
      else {
```

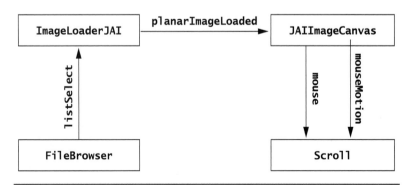

FIGURE 10.5   Event flow in the simple JAI image viewer application

```
        if(!viewer.isImageDrawn()) SwingUtilities.invokeLater(this);
        else  setCursor(Cursor.getDefaultCursor());
      }
    }
  }
```

When the `run()` method is called for the first time, it calls the `setImage()` method in both the `viewer` and the `saver` objects. It also calls the `setCursor()` method to change the cursor to an hourglass cursor. It sets the `firstTime` flag to `false` and calls the `invokeLater()` method from the `SwingUtilities` class. This method calls this thread again later. The next time this thread is called, the `run()` method executes the `else` block because the `firstTime` flag is `false.` This block checks whether the `imageDrawn` flag is set by `JAIImageCanvas`. Recall from Listing 10.3 that the `image Drawn` flag is set in the `paintComponent()` method after an image is drawn. If the `imageDrawn` flag is not `true,` the `run()` method calls the thread again. Otherwise `run()` sets the default cursor and exits, thus terminating the thread.

Saving Images

The planar-image viewer application has a **Save** tab with a GUI to select the file name and the image format (see Figure 10.6). You can save both the original image and the displayed image. Saving the displayed image is useful in image manipulation applications in which you can load, display, and then manipulate an image. To save a manipulated image, click **Save Displayed Image.** Listing 10.6 shows the code for the `ImageSaverPanel` class.

© Anselm Spring/The Image Bank

FIGURE 10.6   The planar-image viewer application

LISTING 10.6 The ImageSaverPanel class

```java
public class ImageSaverPanel extends JPanel{
   public String[]
      tags = {"JPEG", "BMP", "TIFF", "PNG_GRAY", "PNG_RGB", "PNG_PALLETTE", "PNM"};
   protected String fileName = "default";
   protected RenderedImage plImage;
   protected RenderedImage dispImage;
   private JTextField fnField = null;
   private JList saveTypeList;

   public ImageSaverPanel(){createUI();}

   public void setImage(PlanarImage pImage){ this.plImage = pImage;}

   public void setDisplayImage(PlanarImage pImage){
      this.dispImage = pImage.getAsBufferedImage();
   }

   public void saveDisplay(int ind){
      if(fnField.getText() != null)fileName = fnField.getText();
      save(dispImage, ind, fileName);
   }

   public void saveOrig(int ind){
      if(fnField.getText() != null)fileName = fnField.getText();
      save(plImage, ind, fileName);
   }

   private void createUI() {
      // Creates UI components
   }
   protected void save(RenderedImage image, int ind, String filename) {
      try {
      switch(ind) {
        case 0:
          ImageSaverJAI.saveAsJPEG(image, fileName);
          break;
         case 1:
          ImageSaverJAI.saveAsBMP(image, fileName);
          break;
         case 2:
          ImageSaverJAI.saveAsTIFF(image, fileName);
          break;
         case 3:
          ImageSaverJAI.saveAsPNGGray(image, fileName);
          break;
         case 4:
          ImageSaverJAI.saveAsPNGRGB(image, fileName);
          break;
         case 5:
          ImageSaverJAI.saveAsPNGPalette(image, fileName);
          break;
         case 6:
          ImageSaverJAI.saveAsPNM(image, fileName, true);
          break;
      }
```

```
        } catch(Exception e) {}
    }
}
```

The `setImage()` and `setDisplayImage()` methods set the original and displayed images, respectively. The `save()` method calls the respective static method in the `ImageSaverJAI` class to save the image in the requested format.

Conclusion

Whether you have a sophisticated medical imaging application or a simple image-viewing applet, JAI will help you develop it by providing a vast array of commonly used operators and a large number of APIs. At the time of this writing, however, JAI has some problems. One of them is performance. But although the performance may not have reached the desired level in some cases, it may not be an issue with high-speed Hotspot JVM and hardware accelerators. Just remember that JAI's advantages outweigh its drawbacks.

In this chapter we provided a glimpse of the JAI API and prebuilt operators. At the time of this writing, JAI is still evolving. The recent release of the JAI 1.1 spec has added many more interfaces and classes to an already large API. Because there are so many, we will not be able to cover all the APIs and operators that are currently available in JAI. In the chapters that follow, however, we'll explore some of the most important JAI features through detailed examples.

Rendering Images in JAI   11

IN CHAPTER 10 WE INTRODUCED JAI IMAGE RENDERING through a couple of examples. In this chapter we'll discuss this topic in greater detail. Although the underlying device-rendering model is the same, rendering JAI images is often more complex than rendering AWT images or buffered images. The main reason is the underlying tiling mechanism, which enables the rendering of large images.

As mentioned in Chapter 10, JAI has two types of rendering modes: rendered and renderable. Each has its own rendering philosophy. We'll look at both of these layers from the JAI perspective by explaining the relevant API and then giving some examples.

Before you render a JAI image, you may need to perform an operation that enables smooth and proper rendering. This operation may involve passing some rendering hints, allocating enough memory for tiles, or even restructuring the image itself. Let's look at some of these operations before we delve into the rendering process itself.

Applying Rendering Hints

The rendering-hints concept was introduced in Java 2D (see Chapter 5). The `java.awt.RenderingHints` class represents rendering hints. In this representation, each rendering hint is a key-value pair. Rendering-related methods of the `Graphics2D` and `BufferedImageOp` classes take `RenderingHints` as an input. When there are multiple rendering hints, they are passed to these methods as the `Map` object of a key-value pair. The rendering-hints key is of type `RenderingHints.Key,` and the value is an object.

JAI doesn't use the Java 2D rendering hints for rendering a node. Instead it uses its own rendering hints, the keys for which are defined in the JAI class. A rendering-hint key in JAI is of type `JAI.RenderingKey,` which is an inner class of JAI and a subclass of `java.awt.RenderingHints.Key.`

TABLE 11.1   Rendering Hints in JAI

KEY	VALUE	COMMENTS
KEY_BORDER_EXTENDER	Objects created from BorderExtender and its subclasses	There are five border types: zero fill, constant fill, copy, reflection, and wrap.
KEY_TILE_CACHE	TileCache object	This key controls the amount of memory allotted for caching tiles.
KEY_OPERATION_BOUND	One of OpImage.OP_COMPUTE_ BOUND, OpImage.OP_IO_ BOUND, or OpImage.OP_ NETWORK_BOUND	This key indicates whether an operation is computation-, I/O-, or network-bound.
KEY_OPERATION_REGISTRY	OperationRegistry object	With this key you can choose an operation registry other than the default.
KEY_INTERPOLATION	Objects created from the Interpolation class	JAI implements its own interpolation classes. There are four types of interpolation: nearest neighbor, bilinear, bicubic, and bicubic2 (see Chapters 7 and 12).
KEY_IMAGE_LAYOUT	ImageLayout object	This key indicates the tile layout of a JAI image.

JAI rendering hints are typically passed to an operator that creates a node in the rendering chain. The rendering hints are applied when a node is evaluated—that is, when the image is ready for rendering.

We obtain the value for a JAI rendering hint by creating an instance from an appropriate class in JAI. Table 11.1 lists the JAI rendering-hint keys and their corresponding values.

Let's look at some prerendering operations, some of which are rendering hints.

Managing Memory

As mentioned earlier, in JAI image data is available in cache as tiles. To manage memory allocation for tiles, JAI provides an interface called TileCache. You can create an instance of TileCache by calling the factor method JAI.getTileCache(). By default, the tile cache size is set to 64MB. To change this setting, the TileCache interface specifies the following set method:

◆ **public void setMemoryCapacity(long memoryCapacity)**

Here's an example that sets the memory:

```
TileCache tileCache = JAI.getDefaultInstance().getTileCache();
tileCache.setMemoryCapacity(2048*2048L);
```

Here's the corresponding get method:

- **`public long getMemoryCapacity()`**

The `memoryCapacity` parameter is specified in bytes. If the memory capacity is smaller than the current capacity, the tiles in the cache are flushed to achieve the desired settings. If you set a large amount of memory for the tile cache, interactive operations are faster but the tile cache fills up very quickly. If you set a low amount of memory for the tile cache, the performance degrades. So there's a trade-off between memory and speed.

The `TileCache` interface also has a method for setting the capacity as a specific number of tiles:

- **`public void setTileCapacity(int tileCapacity)`**

and a corresponding get method:

- **`public int getTileCapacity()`**

In JAI 1.0.2, implementing these methods does nothing. In JAI 1.1, these methods are deprecated.

The other utility methods are

- **`public void add(java.awt.image.RenderedImage owner,`**
                    `int tileX,`
                    `int tileY,`
                    `Raster data)`
- **`public void remove(java.awt.image.RenderedImage owner,`**
                    `int tileX,`
                    `int tileY)`
- **`public Raster getTile(RenderedImage owner,`**
                    `int tileX,`
                    `int tileY)`
- **`public void removeTiles(RenderedImage owner)`**
- **`public void flush()`**

In these methods the `tileX` and `tileY` parameters are the indices of the tile in the planar image. The `flush()` method discards all the tiles in the cache, and the `removeTiles()` method discards only tiles belonging to the image passed as the input parameter.

`TileCache` is also a rendering hint, and it can also be set through JAI's `setTileCache()` method.

Scheduling Tiles

Like `TileCache`, `TileScheduler` is an interface. It has three methods for managing the tile-scheduling computation:

- ```
  public Raster scheduleTile(OpImage target,
                                  int tileX,
                                  int tileY)
  ```
- ```
  public Raster[] scheduleTiles(OpImage target,
                                    Point[] tileIndices)
  ```
- ```
  public void prefetchTiles(PlanarImage target,
                                Point[] tileIndices)
  ```

Here's an example:

```
Point[] tileIndices = { new Point(0,0), new Point(1,0), new Point(2,0)};
TileCache tileCache  = JAI.getDefaultInstance().getTileCache();
tileCache.prefetchTiles(image, tileIndices);
```

This example gives a hint to prefetch the first three tiles of an image.

Just as the `setTileCache()` method is used to set `TileCache`, you can use `setTileScheduler()` to set a `TileScheduler` object. Unlike `TileCache`, however, `TileScheduler` is not a rendering hint.

Reformatting an Image

Often an image needs to be changed before it is rendered. For example, when you load images using the JAI codec, they are not typically tiled because most formats do not support tiling. And even in formats that do support tiling (e.g., TIFF, FlashPix), images may not be properly tiled. A planar image that is not tiled is like a buffered image, and all the advantages of tiling are lost.

One solution is to tile the image in memory. The `ImageLayout` class lets you restructure the image into tiles. After loading an image in memory, sometimes you will want to change the image bounds, `SampleModel`, `ColorModel`, and so on. The `ImageLayout` class lets you do all that. The `ImageLayout` object is also used as a value of the `RenderingHints` key.

`ImageLayout` has several attributes related to the image to be generated, and each of these attributes has a bit mask (see Table 11.2).

The `ImageLayout` class has get and set methods for each of these attributes. Each bit mask can be set, unset, or checked for its state, through the following methods:

- `public ImageLayout setValid(int mask)`
- `public ImageLayout unsetValid(int mask)`
- `public final boolean isValid(int mask)`
```

TABLE 11.2 ImageLayout Attributes and Associated Bit Masks

ATTRIBUTE	MASK
ColorModel	COLOR_MODEL_MASK
SampleModel	SAMPLE_MODEL_MASK
height	HEIGHT_MASK
width	WIDTH_MASK
minX	MIN_X_MASK
minY	MIN_Y_MASK
tileWidth	TILE_WIDTH_MASK
tileHeight	TILE_HEIGHT_MASK
tileGridXOffset	TILE_GRID_OFFSET_X_MASK
tileGridYOffset	TILE_GRID_OFFSET_Y_MASK

◆ **public int getValidMask()**

ImageLayout also has methods for setting a group of masks:

◆ **public ImageLayout unsetImageBounds()**

This method unsets the bit masks associated with the minX, minY, width, and height attributes.

◆ **public ImageLayout unsetTileLayout()**

This method unsets the bit masks associated with the tileGridXOffset, tileGridYOffset, tileWidth, and tileHeight attributes.

If the mask is set, the get method returns the value that was set by the ImageLayout object. If the mask is unset, the get method returns the attribute from the original rendered image.

Using the Format Operator

The TileLayout class is typically used in conjunction with the Format operator to restructure an image. The source image for the Format operator can be a rendered image or a renderable image. The tile layout is passed to the Format operator through RenderingHints. As mentioned earlier, the KEY_IMAGE_LAYOUT key in this case is defined in the JAI class itself. The value of this key is the ImageLayout object. Table 11.3 lists the parameters of the Format operator.

The example in Listing 11.1 uses the Format operator.

TABLE 11.3 Format Operator Parameters

OPERATOR NAME	PARAMETER	TYPE	DEFAULT VALUE	DESCRIPTION
Format	transferType	int	TYPE_BYTE	Data type of the output image. The value should be one of TYPE_BYTE, TYPE_SHORT, TYPE_USHORT, TYPE_INT, TYPE_FLOAT, or TYPE_DOUBLE. These constants are defined in the java.awt.image.DataBuffer class.

LISTING 11.1 Reformatting a planar image

```
public static RenderedOp reformatImage(PlanarImage img, Dimension tileDim) {
    int tileWidth = tileDim.width;
    int tileHeight = tileDim.height;
    ImageLayout tileLayout = new ImageLayout(img);
    tileLayout.setTileWidth(tileWidth);
    tileLayout.setTileHeight(tileHeight);

    HashMap map = new HashMap();
    map.put(JAI.KEY_IMAGE_LAYOUT, tileLayout);
    map.put(JAI.KEY_INTERPOLATION,
            Interpolation.getInstance(Interpolation.INTERP_BICUBIC));
    RenderingHints tileHints = new RenderingHints(map);

    ParameterBlock pb = new ParameterBlock();
    pb.addSource(img);
    return JAI.create("format", pb, tileHints);
}
```

In Listing 11.1 the `ImageLayout` object is created with a specified tile width and height. This object is then saved in `HashMap,` as is the other rendering-hint object, `Interpolation`. A RenderingHints object is constructed with this `HashMap` instance and then passed to `JAI.create()`. This method uses the `ParameterBlock` and `RenderingHints` parameters to execute the Format operator. The image returned by this operator has the new tile layout and other parameters set by the `ImageLayout` object.

Although the `ParameterBlock` object in this method is created for a planar image, it can be a renderable image as well.

Extending the Border

It is often necessary to add borders to images. For example, as we saw in Chapter 8, the convolution operations often cannot fill the last rows and columns of an image.

One way to fill them is to add a border. In addition, you may wish to add a decorative border to a displayed image. There are two ways you can add a border:

1. Using the subclasses of `BorderExtender`
2. Using the Border operator

Using the BorderExtender Class

Let's look at the `BorderExtender` class hierarchy first, as shown in Figure 11.1. `BorderExtender`, which is at the root of the hierarchy, is an abstract class that allows you to specify the number of pixels to be filled in all sides of the border. `BorderExtender` has five subclasses, each of which provides a different way to fill the border pixels.

The subclasses of `BorderExtender` represent the following five operations:

1. **Zero fill.** The border is filled with zeros. The constant `BorderExtender.BORDER_ZERO` represents this operation.
2. **Constant fill.** The pixels in the border are filled by a constant value. If the image has more than one band, each band can have a different constant fill value. The

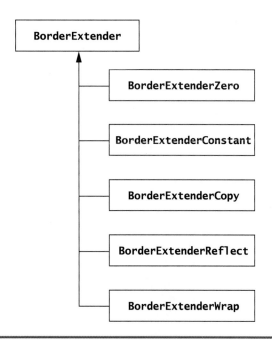

FIGURE 11.1 The `BorderExtender` class hierarchy

constant values are provided as an array through the constructor of the `BorderExtenderConstant` class.

3. **Copy.** The edge and corner pixels of the source image are copied onto the border area. The constant `BorderExtender.BORDER_COPY` represents this operation.

4. **Reflection.** The pixels on the outer edge of the source image are copied onto the border area. The constant `BorderExtender.BORDER_REFLECT` represents this operation.

5. **Wrap.** The image pixels are copied in such a way that the opposite edges of the images appear to be joined (see Figure 11.2). The `BorderExtender.BORDER_WRAP` constant represents this operation.

The `BorderExtender` class has the following two methods—one abstract and the other static:

1. `public static BorderExtender createInstance(int extenderType)`

   This factory method constructs an instance of a `BorderExtender` object. The `BorderExtender` class has four constants to represent the extender operations: `BORDER_ZERO`, `BORDER_COPY`, `BORDER_WRAP`, and `BORDER_REFLECT`. The `extenderType` parameter can be any of the four constants. Note that no constant

6	4	5	6	4
9	7	8	9	7
3	1	2	3	1
6	4	5	6	4
9	7	8	9	7
3	1	2	3	1
6	4	5	6	4

FIGURE 11.2   The border wrap operation

is defined for the constant fill operation because constant fill requires an array of constant values.

2. **`public abstract void extend(java.awt.image.WritableRaster raster,`**
   `PlanarImage im)`

The subclasses of the `BorderExtender` class implement this method. As Figure 11.3 shows, the `writableRaster` parameter contains the border and the image. Depending on the operation, appropriate pixels are copied onto the border area of `writableRaster`. If the `Raster` object supplied doesn't cover the image, no pixels are copied.

You can use a `BorderExtender` object in two ways:

1. The `BorderExtender` object can be supplied to an operation as a rendering hint. `JAI.KEY_BORDER_EXTENDER` is the key value for this rendering hint. The value can be any one of the five `BorderExtender` constants.

2. The `PlanarImage` class has the following methods that take `BorderExtender` as one of the parameters:
   - **`public void copyExtendedData(WritableRaster dest,`**
     `BorderExtender extender)`
   - **`public Raster getExtendedData(Rectangle region,`**
     `BorderExtender extender)`

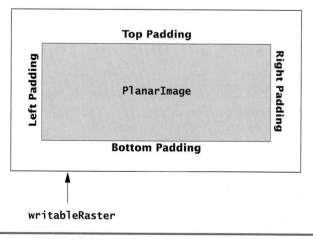

FIGURE 11.3   An image layout with borders

Using the Border Operator

You can also use the Border operator to add the border. This operator takes a rendered image as a source. Table 11.4 lists the parameters of the Border operator.

The example in Listing 11.2 uses the Border operator to add a border to images.

LISTING 11.2 Adding a border to an image

```
public static RenderedOp setConstantBorder(PlanarImage img,
                                   Dimension border, double constVal) {
    ParameterBlock pb = new ParameterBlock();
    pb.addSource(img);
    pb.add(border.width);
    pb.add(border.height);
    pb.add(border.width);
    pb.add(border.height);
    pb.add(BorderDescriptor.BORDER_CONST_FILL);
    int numbands = img.getSampleModel().getNumBands();
    double[] fillValue = new double[numbands];
    for (int i=0;i<numbands;i++) {
        fillValue[i] = constVal;
    }
    pb.add( fillValue);
    return JAI.create("border", pb);
}
```

When the border is added, the image dimensions change. The width and height of the image increase, and `minX` and `minY` coordinates become negative. Keep this in mind while writing the code for painting the image. To make the image display appear symmetrical, you can either use the Format operator to restructure the image or translate the image by an appropriate amount.

TABLE 11.4 Border Operator Parameters

OPERATOR NAME	PARAMETER	TYPE	DEFAULT VALUE	DESCRIPTION
Border	leftPad	int	0	See Figure 11.3
	rightPad	int	0	
	topPad	int	0	
	bottomPad	int	0	
	type	int	BorderDescriptor. BORDER_ZERO_FILL	One of the BorderDescriptor constants
	constants	double[]	null	An array of constants

A Rendering Example

Let's look at an example (see Listing 11.3) that illustrates how to use some of the rendering hints and how to add a border.

LISTING 11.3   The `ImageFormatter` class

```java
import java.awt.*;
import java.util.*;
import java.awt.image.*;
import java.io.*;
import javax.swing.*;
import java.awt.geom.*;
import java.awt.image.renderable.*;
import javax.media.jai.operator.BorderDescriptor;
import javax.media.jai.*;

public class ImageFormatter extends app.JAISimpleViewer{
    protected Dimension border = new Dimension(10,10);

    public static void main(String[] args){
        ImageFormatter ip = new ImageFormatter();
        if(args.length <1) {
          System.out.println("Enter a valid image file name");
          System.exit(0);
        }
        ip.loadAndDisplay(args[0]);
    }

    public void loadAndDisplay(String filename){
        PlanarImage img = readAsPlanarImage(filename);
        TileCache tc = JAI.getDefaultInstance().getTileCache();
        System.out.println("Default Memory Capacity = "+ tc.getMemoryCapacity());
        tc.setMemoryCapacity(2024*2024);
        System.out.println("Memory Capacity = "+ tc.getMemoryCapacity());

        System.out.println("Without Border");
        System.out.println("--------");
        System.out.println("Size: "+
                        img.getWidth()+ " , "+ img.getHeight());
        System.out.println("ULHC  "+
                        img.getMinX()+ " ,"+ img.getMinY());

        RenderedOp borderImg
            = com.vistech.jai.util.JAIUtil.setConstantBorder(img, border, 70);

        System.out.println("With Border");
        System.out.println("------");
        System.out.println("Size: "+
                        borderImg.getWidth()+ " ,"+ borderImg.getHeight());

        System.out.println("ULHC:  "+
                        borderImg.getMinX()+ " ,"+ borderImg.getMinY());

        RenderedOp opImage = reformatImage(borderImg, new Dimension(256, 256));
```

continued

```
        displayImage(opImage);
    }

    public static RenderedOp reformatImage(PlanarImage img, Dimension tileDim) {
        ImageLayout tileLayout = new ImageLayout(img);
        tileLayout.setTileWidth(tileDim.width);
        tileLayout.setTileHeight(tileDim.width);

        HashMap map = new HashMap();
        map.put(JAI.KEY_IMAGE_LAYOUT, tileLayout);
        map.put(JAI.KEY_INTERPOLATION,
                Interpolation.getInstance(Interpolation.INTERP_BICUBIC));

        RenderingHints tileHints = new RenderingHints(map);
        ParameterBlock pb = new ParameterBlock();
        pb.addSource(img);
        return JAI.create("format", pb, tileHints);
    }

    public void launchFrame(PlanarImage img, int width, int height) {
        setTitle("JAI Image Viewer");
        viewer = new BorderedPanel(img);
        viewer.setPreferredSize(new Dimension(width, height));
        Container cp = getContentPane();
        getContentPane().setLayout(new GridLayout(1,1));
        cp.add(viewer);
        pack();
        setSize(new Dimension(width, height));
        show();
        viewer.repaint();
    }

    protected class BorderedPanel extends ImagePanel {

        public BorderedPanel(PlanarImage img){ super(img);}

        public void paintComponent(Graphics gc){
            Graphics2D g = (Graphics2D)gc;
            Rectangle rect = this.getBounds();
            if((width != rect.width) || (height != rect.height)){
                double magx = rect.width/(double)width ;
                double magy = rect.height/(double)height ;
                atx.setToScale(magx, magy);
                atx.translate(border.width, border.height);
            }
            if(image != null) g.drawRenderedImage(image, atx);
        }
    }
}
```

The ImageFormatter class extends the JAISimpleViewer class that we developed in in Chapter 10 (see Listing 10.1). The loadAndDisplay() method first sets the tile cache and then adds a border. To add the border, loadAndDisplay() calls the setConstantBorder() method shown in Listing 11.2. Before the image is rendered, loadAndDisplay() calls the reformatImage() method to set the tile layout.

The `loadAndDisplay()` method has various print statements. When you run the application in Listing 11.3, you can see how the dimensions of the image change after the Border operator is applied. Figure 11.4 shows an image rendered with a constant border. To run the application, type "java app.ImageFormatter <image path>" on the command line.

> **Note:** The code for `ImageFormatter` is available on the book's Web page in the directory `src/chapter11/format`.

Here's an example of `ImageFormatter` output on the console:

```
Default Memory Capacity = 16777216
Memory Capacity = 4096576
Without Border
--------
Size: 208 ,222
ULHC  0 ,0
With Border
------
Size: 228 ,242
ULHC:  -10 ,-10
```

Notice that the size and the ULHC coordinates are changed after the border operation.

FIGURE 11.4   An image displayed with a border

A Closer Look at the PlanarImage Class

The `PlanarImage` class is at the heart of image rendering in JAI. It is the base class for representing an image. Figure 10.3 showed the `PlanarImage` class hierarchy. Whether it is a rendered or renderable chain, the image is normally converted to a planar image for actual rendering because the planar image represents the actual physical image.

Although we have used `PlanarImage` in many examples, we have not described it in detail. So in this section we'll look more closely at its methods.

The `PlanarImage` class has just one constructor, which takes no arguments. A `PlanarImage` object is typically constructed by an image reader or an image operator, so you may not need to use this constructor at all.

Even when an image reader returns a `RenderedImage` object, as in the case of the Image I/O API, it can be converted to a `PlanarImage` object by the `Rendered ImageAdapter` class.

```
RenderedImage renderedImage = javax.imageio.ImageIO.read (new File("myImage.jpg"));
RenderedImageAdapter planarImage = new RenderedImageAdapter(renderedImage);
```

Note that `RenderedImageAdapter` is a subclass of `PlanarImage`.

As mentioned earlier, the `RenderedImage` interface, which the `PlanarImage` class implements, has set and get methods for `RenderedImage` attributes, which are listed in Tables 10.1 and 10.2. In addition, the `PlanarImage` class has methods that are needed for rendering a JAI image. The tasks accomplished by these methods include converting the image to a buffered image or a snapshot image. The `PlanarImage` class also has some static utility methods that are often used in rendering. The sections that follow review the specific methods of `PlanarImage`.

Converting to a Buffered Image

The `PlanarImage` class has two methods that can convert a JAI image to a buffered image:

- `public BufferedImage getAsBufferedImage()`
- `public BufferedImage getAsBufferedImage(Rectangle rect,`
  `                                         ColorModel colorModel)`

The first method converts the entire image into a buffered image. If the image is huge, you may not want to use this method because `BufferedImage` keeps all the image data in memory.

The second method converts a specified rectangular area into a buffered image. The color model must be compatible with the source image. If not, this method will throw an exception: `IllegalArgumentException`. If the value of the `colorModel` parameter is `null`, the source color model is used for constructing the buffered image.

These methods are handy when you need to construct a buffered image for the purpose of rendering or saving images. For example, a bean or application that is written with the Java 2D API may use only `BufferedImage` inputs. In that case you can use JAI for loading an image, convert it to a buffered image, and then pass it to the Java 2D bean or application. Along the same lines, a codec might have been developed with only Java 2D in mind. To save a planar image using that codec, you can use these methods to convert the image to a buffered image.

Remember that the `RenderedImage` interface is an API in Java 2D and part of J2SE. So if a method in a bean or application written with the Java 2D API takes a `RenderedImage` input, the `PlanarImage` object can be passed to it. The new Image I/O API takes this approach. In this API, methods to write an image take `RenderedImage` as an input. With this API, then, there is no need to convert `PlanarImage` to `BufferedImage` before saving.

Creating a Snapshot Image

As the name suggests, the `SnapshotImage` class represents a snapshot of the image contents at a given time. The `PlanarImage` class has the following method for creating such a snapshot:

- ◆ **`public PlanarImage createSnapshot()`**

This method creates an immutable image with a copy of the source image's current contents. Multiple calls to this method don't create multiple copies of snapshot images. Instead, they create multiple references to a single `SnapshotImage` object. This means that at any given time there is one `SnapshotImage` object per `PlanarImage` instance.

Converting to a Planar Image

The following factory method in the `PlanarImage` class constructs a `PlanarImage` object from a `RenderedImage` object:

- ◆ **`public static PlanarImage wrapRenderedImage(java.awt.image.`**
  `RenderedImage im)`

This method adds various properties to the input image, such as source and sink vectors and the ability to produce snapshots to create a `PlanarImage` object. If the image is already a planar image, it is simply returned unchanged. If the input image implements the `RenderedImage` interface, this method constructs a `RenderedImage` `Adapter` object. If the input implements the `WritableRenderedImage` interface, the method constructs a `WritableRenderedImageAdapter` object. `RenderedImageAdapter` is a subclass of `PlanarImage`, and `WritableRenderedImageAdapter` is a subclass of `RenderedImageAdapter`.

The `wrapRenderedImage()` method is a very convenient method that converts `RenderedImage` to the JAI-specific `PlanarImage`. For instance, a `BufferedImage` object that implements the `RenderedImage` interface can be converted to a `PlanarImage` object with this method. To convert images read by the Java 2D JPEG codec and the new Image I/O API, you can use this method as shown in the following example:

```
BufferedImage renderedImage = javax.imageio.ImageIO.read(new File("myImage"));
PlanarImage planarImage = PlanarImage.wrapRenderedImage(renderedImage)
```

Converting Image Coordinates to Tile Index and Vice Versa

As we'll see later in this chapter, it is often necessary to compute the tile index when a coordinate in the image is given. For example, when an image is scrolled, the application needs to compute the ULHC of the image that is visible on the viewport. So the rendering program needs to compute tiles for the visible portion of the image. The following methods of the `PlanarImage` class do this:

◆ `public int XToTileX(int x)`
◆ `public int YToTileY(int y)`

◆ `public static int XToTileX(int x, int tileGridXOffset, int tileWidth)`
◆ `public static int YToTileY(int y, int tileGridYOffset, int tileHeight)`

The following methods do the reverse: convert a tile index to image coordinates:

◆ `public static int tileXToX(int tx, int tileGridXOffset, int tileWidth)`
◆ `public static int tileYToY(int ty, int tileGridYOffset,`
                             `int tileHeight)`

◆ `public int tileXToX(int tx)`
◆ `public int tileYToY(int ty)`

Obtaining Sources and Sinks

When a `PlanarImage` object is part of a rendering chain, it is often necessary to obtain the list of sources and sinks. Here are the methods that do this:

◆ `public java.util.Vector getSinks()`
◆ `public java.util.Vector getSources()`
◆ `public int getNumSources()`

Using the RenderedOp Class

The `RenderedOp` class represents a node in the rendered layer. Even though `RenderedOp` has two public constructors, you don't normally need to construct it directly. To obtain a `RenderedOp` object, you must execute the `JAI.create()` or `JAI.createNS()` method with an operator argument.

`RenderedOp` extends the `PlanarImage` class, so it inherits all the `RenderedImage` data and properties, which are generated by application of the operator. `RenderedOp` also overrides most of the `PlanarImage` methods. In addition, it holds the name of the operation and the parameters passed to execute the operation.

Note that the `RenderedOp` class is *serializable,* which means that it implements the `Serializable` interface and the internal state of a `RenderedOp` object can be saved. Serialization is necessary for performing the image-related operations over the network using RMI (Remote Method Invocation). As we'll see in Chapter 15, only `Serializable` objects can be transported across the network. In other words, an image can be sent from a server to a client (and vice versa) only if it is serializable. As you probably know already, the AWT `Image` and `BufferedImage` objects are not serializable. Neither is `PlanarImage`.

> **Note:** The serialization feature was introduced in JDK 1.1 because it was required by many Java core APIs, such as RMI and JavaBeans. See Appendix B to learn more about serialization.

Constructing a Rendered Node

Although the `RenderedOp` class has two public constructors, you will typically use a *JAI.createXXX()* method to create a rendered node. Doing so will save you the trouble of writing and debugging several lines of code. In some instances, however, you may want to construct a `RenderedOp` object by explicitly using a `RenderedOp` constructor. There are two constructor types in the `RenderedOp` class:

```
1. public RenderedOp(OperationRegistry registry,
                java.lang.String opName,
                java.awt.image.renderable.ParameterBlock pb,
                java.awt.RenderingHints hints)
2. public RenderedOp(java.lang.String opName,
                java.awt.image.renderable.ParameterBlock pb,
                java.awt.RenderingHints hints)
```

To construct a node, you need four parameters:

1. `OperationRegistry,` in which an operation is registered
2. Operation name
3. `ParameterBlock,` which holds the parameters
4. `RenderingHints`

If the value of the `OperationRegistry` argument is `null`, the default value is assumed. If the value of the `RenderingHints` argument is `null`, no hints are associated with the node.

Rendering a Node

Because `RenderedOp` is a subclass of `PlanarImage,` you can directly pass the `RenderedOp` object to `Graphics2D`'s `drawRenderedImage()` to render a node. When a node is rendered directly from the `RenderedOp` object, the node is said to be *frozen*. This means that the node parameters are not allowed to change.

To avoid freezing the node, call the following method to create an instance of `PlanarImage` and then pass that instance to the `drawRenderedImage()` method:

- ◆ **`public PlanarImage createInstance()`**

It is extremely important that the node not be frozen when operations are performed dynamically in a rendering chain. A certain dynamic operation may change the sources, parameters, and rendering hints of a node. If a node is frozen, these changes cannot be made.

In addition to the case already mentioned (i.e., direct rendering with `Rendered Op`), a rendered node is frozen in the following cases:

- ◆ When the `RenderedImage` methods of `RenderedOp` are called (see the section titled Rendered Images in Chapter 10 for the `RenderedImage` interface)
- ◆ When the overridden `PlanarImage` methods, which include get and set methods for sources, are called

Even if a node is frozen, serialization can "unfreeze" it because the instance variables that hold the rendering information are `transient` and hence not saved. Upon deserialization of a `RenderedOp` object, its rendering attributes can be changed again.

The `RenderedOp` class saves the resulting image from rendering in an instance variable. You can obtain the image with the following method:

- ◆ **`public PlanarImage getRendering()`**

You can use this method for repeated rendering of the resulting image. If the node is edited, however, this method does create a new rendering. In such cases you need to call the `createInstance()` method again.

Sources and Sinks

A rendered node can have zero or more sources and sinks. Both the sources and the sinks are held in a `Vector` object. You can retrieve, add, and remove sources and sinks using the following methods:

- `public int getNumSources()`
- `public java.lang.Object getNodeSource(int index)`
- `public void addNodeSource(Object source)`
- `public void setNodeSource(Object source, int index)`
- `public boolean removeSource(PlanarImage source)`
- `public void setSources(java.util.List sourceList)`
- `public boolean removeSource(PlanarImage source)`
- `public java.util.Vector getSinks()`
- `public void addSink(PlanarImage sink)`
- `public boolean removeSink(PlanarImage sink)`

Rendered-Node Attributes

A rendered node has several attributes that are set while a node is being created. As mentioned earlier, a node can be edited. To edit a node, you typically retrieve an attribute, apply a particular rule or condition, and if applicable, assign a new value to the attribute. The `RenderedOp` class has set and get methods to do these things:

- `public OperationRegistry getRegistry()`
- `public void setRegistry(OperationRegistry registry)`

- `public String getOperationName()`
- `public void setOperationName(String opName)`

- `public ParameterBlock getParameterBlock()`
- `public void setParameterBlock(ParameterBlock pb)`

- `public RenderingHints getRenderingHints()`
- `public void setRenderingHints(RenderingHints hints)`

These attributes can be image related as well as operation related. The operation-related attributes include operation registry, operation name, operation parameters, and rendering hints. The operation parameters can be part of a `ParameterBlock` object.

Editing a Node

You can set the node attributes to edit a node, provided the node is not frozen. You can use the get and set methods in the previous section to modify a node.

To edit the parameters of an operation, you must first retrieve the `Parameter Block`, then modify it and set it again. Alternatively, you can use the following `RenderedOp` methods to retrieve and set a desired parameter.

- **Get methods:**
  - `public int getNumParameters()`
  - `public java.util.Vector getParameters()`

  - `public byte getByteParameter(int index)`
  - `public char getCharParameter(int index)`
  - `public short getShortParameter(int index)`
  - `public int getIntParameter(int index)`
  - `public long getLongParameter(int index)`
  - `public float getFloatParameter(int index)`
  - `public double getDoubleParameter(int index)`
  - `public Object getObjectParameter(int index)`

- **Set methods:**
  - `public void setParameter(byte param, int index)`

There are similar methods for setting `short`, `int`, `long`, `float`, `double`, and `object` parameters.

Adding and Retrieving Properties

Some imaging operations may create image-related properties. The `RenderedOp` class has the following methods to help retrieve and set such properties:

- `public java.lang.String[] getPropertyNames()`
- `public String getProperty(java.lang.String name)`
- `public void setProperty(String name, Object value)`
- `public void suppressProperty(String name)`
- `public void addPropertyGenerator(PropertyGenerator pg)`

Working with Tiles

As you probably know by now, neither AWT imaging nor Java 2D can handle smooth rendering of large images. The reason is that the underlying imaging models read the entire image in memory. As mentioned in Chapter 10, the JAI pull model overcomes this problem through tiling. Although the tile concept is defined in Java 2D, JAI actually implements it. However, tiling works best when the underlying format supports tiles, and this is not the case with most image formats.

If an image is not tiled, the FileLoad operator treats the entire image as a single tile and loads it in the memory. As mentioned earlier, we use the Format operator to tile such images in memory.

Viewing and Manipulating Large Images

In Chapter 10 we developed the `JAIImageCanvas` class (see Listing 10.2) to display planar images. If we use this class for manipulating large images, the rendering is slow because `JAIImageCanvas` does not completely exploit the tiling mechanism.

In the `JAIImageCanvas` class, the `paintComponent()` method calls `Graphics2D`'s `drawRenderedImage()` method to render the image. This means that there is no control over which tiles are computed for displaying the visible part of the image.

One way to speed up rendering is to convert the visible portion of the image to a buffered image and render it using `drawImage()`. In this approach, the granularity of the tile is important. If the tiles are too small compared to the viewport, there will be too many tile computations, possibly degrading performance. On the other hand, too large a tile requires a large amount of memory because `BufferedImage` stores all the image data in memory. So designing a tile layout means making a trade-off between speed and memory.

To implement a canvas for rendering large images, let's create a subclass of the `com.vistech.jai.render.JAIImageCanvas` class and extend its functionality to implement tiling. We'll call this class `RenderedImageCanvas.`

As we saw in the section titled Using the Format Operator earlier in this chapter, a planar image can be restructured to implement any tile layout through the `ImageLayout` class and the Format operator. To paint a partial image, let's override the `paintComponent()` method and implement a tile computation loop based on the coordinates of the image that covers the viewport. These tiles can then be converted into a buffered image and painted immediately.

Listing 11.4 shows the `RenderedImageCanvas` class.

> **Note:** The code for `RenderedImageCanvas` is available on the book's Web page in the directory `src/chapter11/render`.

LISTING 11.4   The `RenderedImageCanvas` class

```
package com.vistech.jai.render;
import java.awt.*;
import java.awt.event.*;
import java.awt.image.*;
import java.io.*;
import javax.swing.*;
import java.awt.geom.*;
```

continued

```
import java.awt.image.renderable.*;
import javax.media.jai.*;

public class RenderedImageCanvas extends JAIImageCanvas {
    protected int viewerWidth = 480, viewerHeight = 400;

    transient protected PlanarImage displayImage, origImage;
    protected int tileWidth = 256, tileHeight = 256;
    transient protected SampleModel sampleModel;
    protected ColorModel colorModel;

    protected int maxTileIndexX, maxTileIndexY;
    protected int maxTileCordX, maxTileCordY;
    protected int minTileIndexX, minTileIndexY;
    protected int minTileCordX, minTileCordY;
    protected int tileGridXOffset, tileGridYOffset;
    protected int imageWidth =0, imageHeight =0;
    protected TileCache tc;

    public RenderedImageCanvas() { }
    public RenderedImageCanvas(PlanarImage img){
        this();
        setImage(img);
    }

    public void setImage(PlanarImage img){
        origImage = img;
        panX =0; panY =0;
        atx = AffineTransform.getTranslateInstance(0.0, 0.0);
        RenderedOp op = makeTiledImage(img);

        displayImage = op.createInstance();
        sampleModel = displayImage.getSampleModel();
        colorModel = displayImage.getColorModel();
        getTileInfo(displayImage);
        fireTilePropertyChange();
        imageDrawn = false;
        repaint();
    }

    public PlanarImage getDisplayImage(){return displayImage;}

    protected RenderedOp makeTiledImage(PlanarImage img) {
        ImageLayout tileLayout = new ImageLayout(img);
        tileLayout.setTileWidth(tileWidth);
        tileLayout.setTileHeight(tileHeight);
        RenderingHints tileHints = new RenderingHints(JAI.KEY_IMAGE_LAYOUT, tileLayout);
        ParameterBlock pb = new ParameterBlock();
        pb.addSource(img);
        return JAI.create("format", pb, tileHints);
    }

    protected void getTileInfo(PlanarImage img) {
        imageWidth = img.getWidth();
        imageHeight = img.getHeight();
        tileWidth = img.getTileWidth();
        tileHeight = img.getTileHeight();
```

```java
      maxTileIndexX = img.getMinTileX()+img.getNumXTiles()-1;
      maxTileIndexY = img.getMinTileY()+img.getNumYTiles()-1;
      maxTileCordX = img.getMaxX();
      maxTileCordY = img.getMaxY();
      minTileIndexX = img.getMinTileX();
      minTileIndexY = img.getMinTileY();
      minTileCordX = img.getMinX();
      minTileCordY = img.getMinY();
      tileGridXOffset = img.getTileGridXOffset();
      tileGridYOffset = img.getTileGridYOffset();
   }

   public void setTileWidth(int tw){
      tileWidth = tw;
      setImage(displayImage);
   }

   public int getTileWidth(){ return tileWidth;}
   public void setTileHeight(int th){
      tileHeight = th;
      setImage(displayImage);
   }
   public int getTileHeight(){ return tileHeight;}

   public int getMaxTileIndexX(){return maxTileIndexX;}
   public int getMaxTileIndexY(){return maxTileIndexY;}
   public int getImageWidth(){return imageWidth;}
   public int getImageHeight(){return imageHeight;}


   protected void fireTilePropertyChange() {
      firePropertyChange("maxTileIndexX", null, new Integer(maxTileIndexX));
      firePropertyChange("maxTileIndexY", null, new Integer(maxTileIndexY));
      firePropertyChange("tileWidth", null, new Integer(tileWidth));
      firePropertyChange("tileHeight", null, new Integer(tileWidth));
      firePropertyChange("transform", null, atx);
   }

   public void paintComponent(Graphics gc){
      Graphics2D g = (Graphics2D)gc;
      Rectangle rect = this.getBounds();
      if((viewerWidth != rect.width) || (viewerHeight != rect.height)){
         viewerWidth = rect.width;
         viewerHeight = rect.height;
      }
      g.setColor(Color.black);
      g.fillRect(0, 0, viewerWidth, viewerHeight);
      if(displayImage == null) return;
      int ti =0, tj = 0;
      Rectangle bounds = new Rectangle(0, 0, rect.width, rect.height);
      bounds.translate(-panX, -panY);

      int leftIndex =  displayImage.XToTileX(bounds.x);
      if(leftIndex <  minTileIndexX) leftIndex = minTileIndexX;
      if(leftIndex > maxTileIndexX) leftIndex = maxTileIndexX;

      int rightIndex = displayImage.XToTileX(bounds.x + bounds.width - 1);
```

continued

```
        if(rightIndex <  minTileIndexX) rightIndex = minTileIndexX;
        if(rightIndex > maxTileIndexX) rightIndex = maxTileIndexX;

        int topIndex = displayImage.YToTileY(bounds.y);
        if(topIndex <  minTileIndexY) topIndex = minTileIndexY;
        if(topIndex > maxTileIndexY) topIndex = maxTileIndexY;

        int bottomIndex = displayImage.YToTileY(bounds.y + bounds.height - 1);
        if(bottomIndex <  minTileIndexY) bottomIndex = minTileIndexY;
        if(bottomIndex > maxTileIndexY) bottomIndex = maxTileIndexY;

        for(tj = topIndex; tj <= bottomIndex; tj++) {
            for(ti = leftIndex; ti <= rightIndex; ti++) {
                Raster tile = displayImage.getTile(ti, tj);
                DataBuffer dataBuffer = tile.getDataBuffer();
                WritableRaster wr = tile.createWritableRaster(sampleModel,
                                          dataBuffer, new Point(0,0));
                BufferedImage bi = new BufferedImage(colorModel,
                                          wr,
                                          colorModel.isAlphaPremultiplied(),
                                          null);
                if(bi == null) continue;
                int xInTile = displayImage.tileXToX(ti);
                int yInTile = displayImage.tileYToY(tj);
                AffineTransform tx = AffineTransform.getTranslateInstance(xInTile+panX,
                                                        yInTile+panY);
                g.drawRenderedImage(bi, tx);
            }
        }
        imageDrawn = true;
    }
}
```

The `RenderedImageCanvas` class inherits several instance variables and methods from `JAIImageCanvas` (see Listing 10.2). `RenderedImageCanvas` adds two more instance variables—`origImage` and `displayImage`—to hold the original image and the currently displayed image. The value of the `displayImage` variable is derived by reformatting of the image with the Format operator. These variables allow users to set the desired tile dimensions. The `paintComponent()` method draws the `displayImage` object over the graphical context.

The `RenderedImageCanvas` class has various properties for describing a tile, including `tileWidth`, `tileHeight`, `maxTileIndexX`, and `maxTileIndexY`. The `maxTile IndexX` and `maxTileIndexY` properties represent the number of tile columns and the number of tile rows, respectively. These two properties are needed to compute the positions of the required tiles.

`RenderedImageCanvas` overrides the `setImage()` and `paintComponent()` methods of its superclass, `JAIImageCanvas`. The `setImage()` method uses the current tile size attributes to reformat the input image. To accomplish this reformatting, `setImage()` calls `makeTiledImage()`, which returns a reformatted planar image. The `setImage()` method assigns this image to the `displayImage` variable. Then `setImage()` calls the `getTileInfo()` method to set the tile-related attributes. If the image is smaller than the tile, the image size becomes the current tile size.

Tile Computation

Depending on the size of the viewport, the `paintComponent()` method obtains the tiles needed to display the image within the viewport. To do so, it uses the current `panX` and `panY` variables to compute the position of the tiles within the image. The size of the viewport determines how many tiles are required to display the part of the image that covers the viewport (see Figure 11.5).

A tile in a rendered image can be obtained by the `getTile(xIndex, yIndex)` method. This means that to obtain a tile from the image, we need its position. To get all the tiles that cover the viewport, we need the starting and ending indices of the tiles in both the x and the y directions. For a given point in the image, the `PlanarImage` methods `XtoTileX()` and `YtoTileY()` compute the tile indices in the x and y directions, respectively.

To compute the tile indices, the `paintComponent()` method first starts with the upper left-hand corner of the viewport, which is at position (`panX, panY`). The tile indices corresponding to this position are `leftIndex` and `topIndex`. To compute the ending index, the `paintComponent()` method uses the lower right-hand corner

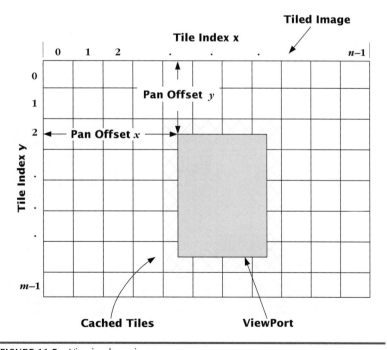

FIGURE 11.5 Viewing large images

coordinates of the viewport with respect to the image. These are given by (panX + viewerWidth) and (panY + viewerHeight), and the corresponding indices are right Index and bottomIndex, respectively.

Once the indices in both the x and the y directions have been computed, paintComponent() executes a loop that does the following:

1. Retrieves a tile from the planar image.

2. Converts that tile into a buffered image.

3. Obtains the position of the tile by calling the tileToX() and tileToY() methods. (The position of the tile in the image is needed to display this image.)

4. Constructs an AffineTransform object to handle the translation. (Each tile must be translated appropriately for the image to appear continuous.)

5. Draws the tile by calling the drawImage() method with the BufferedImage object produced in step 2.

A Tiled-Image Viewer

Using the RenderedImageCanvas class described in the previous section, let's create a viewer that is capable of displaying large images. Let's also add a panel called **Tile Grid** to show the viewport position and size with respect to the image (see Figure 11.6). We'll also add one more way to pan the image: dragging the rectangle

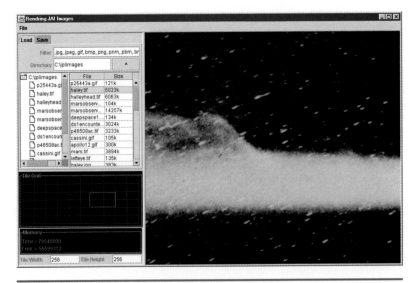

FIGURE 11.6 An image viewer for viewing large images

that represents the image to move the image within the viewport. To control the tile size, let's add two text fields for entering tile width and height.

In addition to the classes mentioned in the JAI planar-image viewer example (see Chapter 10), here are the classes used in this application:

- ◆ **TiledImageViewer.** This is the main class that launches the application. It is a subclass of `JAIImageViewer`.
- ◆ **RenderedImageCanvas.** This class displays the image. It is a subclass of `JAIImageCanvas` (see the section titled Viewing and Manipulating Large Images earlier in this chapter).
- ◆ **RenderGrid.** This class implements the **Tile Grid** panel. It displays the tile grid, as well as the viewport as a rectangle positioned over the tile grid. The position of this rectangle varies when you scroll the image. The position of the image changes when you drag this rectangle.

Now let's look at the code. We have already discussed the `RenderedImageCanvas` code, so let's look at the `RenderGrid` class. Even though this class uses no JAI API, we list it here because it draws heavily from the Java 2D graphical and rendering APIs. Listing 11.5 shows the code for `RenderGrid`.

LISTING 11.5   The RenderGrid class

```
package com.vistech.jai.render;
import java.awt.*;
import java.awt.event.*;
import java.awt.image.*;
import java.io.*;
import javax.swing.*;
import java.awt.geom.*;

public class RenderGrid extends JPanel {
   protected int maxTileIndexX, maxTileIndexY;
   protected int tileWidth, tileHeight;
   protected Point vpPos = new Point(0,0);
   protected Rectangle currentShape;
   protected int panX =0, panY =0;
   protected int width, height;
   protected boolean dragOn = false;
   private Point scrollAnchor  = new Point(0,0);
   protected AffineTransform atx = new AffineTransform();
   protected Dimension vpSize;

   public RenderGrid() {
      enableEvents(AWTEvent.MOUSE_MOTION_EVENT_MASK |
                        AWTEvent.MOUSE_EVENT_MASK);
   }

   public Dimension getViewportDimension(){
      return new Dimension(width, height);
   }
```

continued

```
public void setTileIndices(int maxXIndex, int maxYIndex){
    this.maxTileIndexX = maxXIndex;
    this.maxTileIndexY = maxYIndex;
    repaint();
}

public void setTileDimension(int width, int height){
    tileWidth = width; tileHeight = height;
    repaint();
}

public void setTileWidth(int tw){
    tileWidth = tw; repaint();
}
public int getTileWidth(){ return tileWidth;}

public void setTileHeight(int th){
    tileHeight = th; repaint();
}
public int getTileHeight(){ return tileHeight;}
public void setMaxTileIndexX(int tix){
    maxTileIndexX = tix; repaint();
}

public int getMaxTileIndexX(){return maxTileIndexX;}

public void setMaxTileIndexY(int tiy){
    maxTileIndexY = tiy; repaint();
}
public int getMaxTileIndexY(){return maxTileIndexY;}
public void setTransform(AffineTransform at){atx = at;}
public void setViewportSize(Dimension size){vpSize = size;}

public void  processMouseEvent(MouseEvent e){
    switch(e.getID()){
        case MouseEvent.MOUSE_PRESSED:
            setCursor(new Cursor(Cursor.MOVE_CURSOR));
            int x = e.getX();
            int y = e.getY();
            if(currentShape.contains(x,y)) {  dragOn = true;}
            break;
        case MouseEvent.MOUSE_CLICKED:
            break;
        case MouseEvent.MOUSE_RELEASED:
            setCursor(Cursor.getDefaultCursor());
            dragOn = false;
            break;
    }
}

public void processMouseMotionEvent(MouseEvent e){
    switch(e.getID()){
        case MouseEvent.MOUSE_DRAGGED:
            if(dragOn) scroll(e.getX(), e.getY());
            break;
    }
}
```

```java
public void stopScroll(){ setCursor(Cursor.getDefaultCursor());}

public void startScroll(int x, int y){
    if(dragOn) return;
    scrollAnchor.x = x- panX;
    scrollAnchor.y = y- panY;
    repaint();
}

public void scroll(int x, int y){
    panX = x-scrollAnchor.x;
    panY = y-scrollAnchor.y;
    setPan(new Point(panX, panY));
    repaint();
}

public void setPan(Point pos){
    firePropertyChange("viewportPosition",this.vpPos, pos);
    int x = (int)( pos.x * (maxTileIndexX*tileWidth)/(width-20));
    int y = (int)( pos.y * (maxTileIndexY*tileHeight)/(height-20));
    this.vpPos = new Point(x,y);
    repaint();
}

public void setViewportPosition(Point vpPos){
    this.vpPos = vpPos; repaint();
}

public void paintComponent(Graphics gc) {
    Graphics2D g = (Graphics2D)gc;
    Rectangle bounds = this.getBounds();
    g.setColor(Color.black);
    width = bounds.width-20;
    height = bounds.height-20;
    double gridWidth =  (width)/(double)maxTileIndexX;
    double gridHeight = (height)/(double)maxTileIndexY;
    g.fillRect(0,0,bounds.width, bounds.height);
    if ((maxTileIndexX == 0)|| (maxTileIndexY == 0))  return;
    g.setColor(Color.blue);
    double vertStartX = 10.0; double vertStartY = 10.0;
    double vertEndX = 10.0;
    double vertEndY = (double)maxTileIndexY*gridHeight+vertStartY;
    // Horizontal lines
    for(int i= 0; i<maxTileIndexX; i++) {
        g.drawLine((int)vertStartX, (int)vertStartY, (int)vertEndX, (int)vertEndY);
        vertStartX += gridWidth;
        vertEndX    += gridWidth;
    }
    g.drawLine((int)vertStartX, (int)vertStartY,
                (int)vertEndX, (int)vertEndY);
    double horizStartX = 10.0; double  horizStartY = 10.0;
    double horizEndX = maxTileIndexX*gridWidth+horizStartX;
    double horizEndY = 10.0;
    // Horizontal lines
    for(int i=0; i<maxTileIndexY; i++) {
        g.drawLine((int)horizStartX, (int)horizStartY,
                    (int)horizEndX, (int)horizEndY);
```

continued

```
        horizEndY += gridHeight;
        horizStartY   += gridHeight;
    }
    g.drawLine((int)horizStartX, (int)horizStartY,
            (int)horizEndX, (int)horizEndY);
    g.setColor(Color.red);
    vertStartX = 10.0; vertStartY = 10.0;
    int vpWid, vpHt;
    if(vpSize == null){ vpWid = (int)gridWidth; vpHt = (int)gridHeight;}
    else {
        vpWid = vpSize.width; vpHt = vpSize.height;
    }

    if(dragOn) {
        currentShape = new Rectangle(-(int)vertStartX+panX,
                            -(int)vertStartY+panY,vpWid, vpHt);
     }else {
        int x = (int)(vertStartX +
                vpPos.x * ((width)/(double)(maxTileIndexX*tileWidth)));
        int y = (int)(vertStartY +
                vpPos.y * ((height)/(double)(maxTileIndexY*tileHeight)));
        currentShape = new Rectangle(x,y,vpWid,vpHt);
    }

    g.draw(currentShape);
    }
}
```

The RenderGrid class handles mouse and mouseMotion events internally. When the mouse is pressed, the processMouseEvent() method checks whether the position of the cursor is within the rectangle. If so, it sets the dragOn variable to true. When the mouse is dragged, the processMouseMotion() method moves the rectangle. This method also calls the setPan() method, which fires the propertyChange event for the viewportPosition property.

The use of propertyChange events eliminates the need to call RenderedImage Canvas directly. An interposing object can receive this event and invoke appropriate methods in RenderedImageCanvas. In this case, the interposing object is the Tiled ImageViewer object, which upon receipt of this event, calls the setViewport Position() method of RenderedImageCanvas.

Likewise, when the mouse is dragged over the image, RenderedImageCanvas fires the propertyChange event for its viewportPosition property. Again this event is captured by the TiledImageViewer object, which in turn invokes RenderGrid's setViewportPosition() method. Thus, by using propertyChange events, you can avoid circular dependency between RenderGrid and RenderedImageCanvas. Moreover, both RenderedImageCanvas and RenderGrid can be used as beans and can be visually connected by binding properties (see Appendix B).

The paintComponent() method draws first the grid and then the rectangle representing the viewport. If the value of dragOn is true, which means the user is moving the rectangle, the panX and panY variables are used for moving the rectangle. If it is

false, vpPos is used for moving the rectangle. The vpPos variable is set by the
setViewportPosition() method, which is called by TiledImageViewer whenever it
receives a propertyChange event for the viewportPosition property. The TiledImage
Viewer object also sets the tile dimensions, on the basis of which RenderGrid draws
the grid. Listing 11.6 shows the code for TiledImageViewer.

LISTING 11.6   The TiledImageViewer class: Part 1 (continued in Listing 11.7)

```
public class TiledImageViewer extends JAIImageViewer{
    protected RenderedImageCanvas viewer;
    protected RenderGrid renderGrid;
    protected JTextField twidth, theight;
    protected JTextArea memoryMessageBar;

    public void createUI() {
        Dimension dim = Toolkit.getDefaultToolkit().getScreenSize();
        int width = (int)(dim.width *3/4.0);
        int height = (int)(dim.height*3/4.0);

        setTitle("Rendering JAI Images");
        viewer = new RenderedImageCanvas();
        Dimension d = getViewerSize(width/(double)height);
        viewer.setPreferredSize(new Dimension(d.width, d.height));

        createImageLoaderAndSaver();
        loader.addPlanarImageLoadedListener(
            new PlanarImageLoadedListener() {
                public void imageLoaded(PlanarImageLoadedEvent e) {
                    PlanarImage image = e.getImage();
                    if(image == null) return;
                    setCursor(Cursor.getPredefinedCursor(Cursor.WAIT_CURSOR));
                    SwingUtilities.invokeLater(new ImagePaint(image));
                }
            }
        );

        twidth = new JTextField(5);
        theight = new JTextField(5);
        renderGrid = new RenderGrid();
        renderGrid.setBorder(BorderFactory.createTiledBorder("Tile Grid"));
        theight.setText(Integer.toString(viewer.getTileHeight()));
        twidth.setText(Integer.toString(viewer.getTileWidth()));
            //... Gridbag layout code not shown.

    }

    protected void addPropertyChangeEventAdapters(){
        viewer.addPropertyChangeListener(
            new PropertyChangeListener() {
                public void propertyChange(PropertyChangeEvent e) {
                    if(e.getPropertyName().equals("viewportPosition")){
                        twidth.setText(Integer.toString(viewer.getTileWidth()));
                        theight.setText(Integer.toString(viewer.getTileHeight()));
                        if(renderGrid != null) updateRenderGrid();
                        Point p =(Point)e.getNewValue();
```

continued

```
                    renderGrid.setViewportPosition(p);
                }
                if(e.getPropertyName().equals("maxTileIndexX")){
                    renderGrid.setMaxTileIndexX(((Integer)e.getNewValue()).
                    intValue());
                }
                if(e.getPropertyName().equals("maxTileIndexY")){
                    renderGrid.setMaxTileIndexY(((Integer)e.getNewValue()).
                    intValue());
                }
                if(e.getPropertyName().equals("tileWidth")){
                    renderGrid.setTileWidth(((Integer)e.getNewValue()).intValue());
                }
            if(e.getPropertyName().equals("tileHeight")){
                    renderGrid.setTileHeight(((Integer)e.getNewValue()).intValue());
                }
            if(e.getPropertyName().equals("transform")){
                    int wid = renderGrid.getViewportDimension().width;
                    int ht = renderGrid.getViewportDimension().height;
                    double scaleX = wid/(double)viewer.getSize().width;
                    double scaleY = ht/(double)viewer.getSize().height;
                    AffineTransform atx =  (AffineTransform)e.getNewValue();
                    renderGrid.setTransform(atx);
                }
            }
        }
    );

    renderGrid.addPropertyChangeListener(
        new PropertyChangeListener() {
            public void propertyChange(PropertyChangeEvent e) {
                if(e.getPropertyName().equals("viewportPosition")){
                    double scaleX, scaleY;
                    int wid = renderGrid.getViewportDimension().width;
                    int ht = renderGrid.getViewportDimension().height;
                    scaleX = viewer.getImageWidth()/wid;
                    scaleY = viewer.getImageHeight()/ht;
                    if(e.getNewValue() instanceof Point){
                        Point p =(Point)e.getNewValue();
                        viewer.pan(-p.x*scaleX, -p.y*scaleY);
                    }
                }

            }
        }
    );
}

protected void updateRenderGrid() {
    if(viewer == null) return;
    int tw1 = viewer.getTileWidth();
    int th1 = viewer.getTileHeight();
    int xInd1 = viewer.getMaxTileIndexX();
    int yInd1 = viewer.getMaxTileIndexY();
    renderGrid.setTileDimension(tw1,th1);
    renderGrid.setTileIndices(xInd1, yInd1);
    int wid = renderGrid.getViewportDimension().width;
```

```
      int ht = renderGrid.getViewportDimension().height;
      double scaleX = viewer.getSize().width/(double)viewer.getImageWidth();
      double scaleY = viewer.getSize().height/(double)viewer.getImageHeight();
      double scaledVpX = wid*scaleX;
      double scaledVpY = ht*scaleY;
      renderGrid.setViewportSize(new Dimension((int)scaledVpX,(int)scaledVpY));
      renderGrid.repaint();
   }
}
```

`TiledImageViewer` is the main application class that launches the application. To run the application, type "java app.TiledImageViewer" or "java app.TiledImageViewer <image path>" on the command line.

The `TiledImageViewer` class extends `JAIImageViewer` and overrides the `createUI()` method. As Figure 11.6 shows, the left-hand panel of the window that represents this application has the **Tile Grid** pane and two text fields, for setting the tile width and height.

`TiledImageViewer` acts as an event adapter between `RenderGrid` and `RenderedImageCanvas` objects. When the GUI is created, `TiledImageViewer` registers to receive the `propertyChange` events from both `RenderGrid` and `RenderedImage Canvas` objects. The call to the `addPropertyChangeEventAdapters()` method in Listing 11.6 shows that this registration is done through anonymous inner classes.

When a user drags the mouse over the image, `RenderImageCanvas` fires a `propertyChange` event for the `viewportPosition` property. When `TiledImageViewer` receives this event, it calls the `setViewportPosition()` method in the `RenderGrid` object. Likewise, when a user moves the rectangle in the Tile Grid pane, the `TiledImageViewer` object receives the `propertyChange` event for the `viewport Position` property. In this case `TiledImageViewer` calls the `pan()` method in `RenderedImageCanvas`. Figure 11.7 shows how `TiledImageViewer` facilitates communication between `RenderGrid` and `RenderedImageCanvas` via `propertyChange` events.

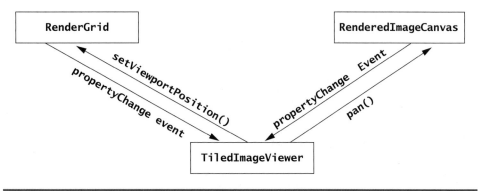

FIGURE 11.7 The propertyChange event flow

TiledImageViewer acts as an event adapter for other properties as well, including tileWidth, tileHeight, maxTileIndexX, and maxTileIndexY.

Setting the Tile Parameters

You can change the tile layout by entering the tile width and height in the text fields located at the bottom of the left-hand pane. This pane also has a memory status bar that shows the total available and free memory. The memory status is updated whenever the mouse is clicked on the image. Note that the memory readings may not always be accurate. Listing 11.7 shows the code that handles events from the text fields and the code that updates the memory status bar.

LISTING 11.7 The TiledImageViewer class: Part 2 (continued from Listing 11.6)

```
public JPanel createTileSetPanel(){
    memoryMessageBar = createMemoryMessageBar();
    memoryMessageBar.setBorder(BorderFactory.createTiledBorder("Memory"));
    //..Gridbag layout code

    return pan;
}

protected void addTileParamsEventAdapters(){
    twidth.addActionListener(
        new ActionListener(){
          public void actionPerformed(ActionEvent e) {
            try {
               String str = ((JTextField) e.getSource()).getText();
               int wid = Integer.parseInt(str);
               viewer.setTileWidth(wid);
               str = theight.getText();
               int ht = Integer.parseInt(str);
               viewer.setTileHeight(wid);
               if(renderGrid != null) updateRenderGrid();
            } catch (Exception e2){}
          }
        } );
    theight.addActionListener(
        new ActionListener(){
          public void actionPerformed(ActionEvent e) {
            try {
               String str = ((JTextField) e.getSource()).getText();
               int ht = Integer.parseInt(str);
               viewer.setTileHeight(ht);
               str = twidth.getText();
               int wid = Integer.parseInt(str);
               viewer.setTileWidth(wid);
               if(renderGrid != null) updateRenderGrid();
            } catch (Exception e1){}
          }
        });

    viewer.addMouseListener(
```

```
            new MouseAdapter() {
              public void mouseReleased(MouseEvent e){
                 updateMemoryMessageBar(memoryMessageBar);
              }
            });
       }

       protected JTextArea createMemoryMessageBar(){
          JTextArea messageBar = new JTextArea();
          messageBar.setBackground(Color.black);
          messageBar.setForeground(Color.green);
          updateMemoryMessageBar(messageBar);
          return messageBar;
       }

       protected void updateMemoryMessageBar(JTextArea mbar) {
          Runtime rt = Runtime.getRuntime();
          long totalMemory = rt.totalMemory();
          rt.gc();
          long freemem = rt.freeMemory();
          mbar.setText("Total = "+ totalMemory+  "\n" +
                       "Free  = " + freemem);
       }
```

The `updateMemoryMessageBar()` method calls some utility methods in the `java.lang.Runtime` class to obtain the amount of total available memory and free memory. It also calls the `System.gc()` method to run the garbage collector. As we learned in Chapter 10, however, calling this method does not guarantee that the garbage collector will run. The `updateMemoryMessageBar()` method posts the amount of free memory to the memory message bar.

Painting the Image in a Thread

The `TiledImageViewer` class also overrides the `ImagePaint` class, which is shown in Listing 11.8. Running the image-painting routine on a thread is essential for painting large images.

LISTING 11.8   The ImagePaint class

```
class ImagePaint implements Runnable {
      PlanarImage image;
      boolean firstTime = true;
      public ImagePaint(PlanarImage image){this.image = image;}
      public void run() {
         if(firstTime) {
            try {
              firstTime = false;
              setCursor(Cursor.getPredefinedCursor(Cursor.WAIT_CURSOR));
              viewer.setImage(image);
              int wid = image.getWidth();
              int height = image.getHeight();
              saver.setDisplayImage(viewer.getDisplayImage());
```
continued

```
        viewer.repaint();
        SwingUtilities.invokeLater(this);
      } catch(Exception e){SwingUtilities.invokeLater(this);}
    }
    else {
      if(!viewer.isImageDrawn()) SwingUtilities.invokeLater(this);
      else{
        setCursor(Cursor.getDefaultCursor());
        updateRenderGrid();
        updateMemoryMessageBar(memoryMessageBar);
      }
    }
  }
}
```

The `ImagePaint` thread is created by an anonymous class that retrieves the image from the `PlanarImageLoaded` event object (see the `createUI()` method in Listing 11.6). In the first pass, the `run()` method calls `RenderedImageCanvas`'s `setImage()` method, which calls the `repaint()` method to start the image painting.

The `SwingUtilities.invokeLater()` method runs the `ImagePaint` thread repeatedly until `isImageDrawn()` returns `true`. When that happens, the `run()` method calls `updateRenderGrid()`, which gets the latest tile settings from the viewer and assigns them to `renderGrid`. It also updates the memory message bar and changes the hourglass cursor to the default cursor.

Writing to Pixels

In our examples so far, we have used only planar images. As stated earlier, `PlanarImage` is read-only. To write pixels, you need to use the `TiledImage` class, which extends `PlanarImage` and implements `WritableRenderedImage`. As we saw in Chapter 10, the `WritableRenderedImage` interface handles the writing of pixel data to tiles.

To write pixels, you need to obtain a `WritableRaster` object for the desired rectangular region. You cannot write to this instance of `WritableRaster` immediately because unlike `BufferedImage`, `TiledImage` does not have all its data resident in the memory. So you need to get all the tiles that cover the rectangular region. Recall from Chapter 10 that the `WritableRenderedImage` interface specifies methods for checking out, writing, and releasing tiles. The `TiledImage` class implements those methods.

Constructing a Tiled Image

First let's see how to construct a `TiledImage` object. The `TiledImage` class has three public constructors:

1. public TiledImage(int minX,

```
            int minY,
            int width,
            int height,
            int tileGridXOffset,
            int tileGridYOffset,
            java.awt.image.SampleModel sampleModel,
            java.awt.image.ColorModel colorModel)
2. public TiledImage(Point origin, SampleModel sampleModel,
            int tileWidth,
            int tileHeight)
3. public TiledImage(SampleModel sampleModel,
            int tileWidth,
            int tileHeight)
```

These constructors take attributes of the tiled image as input parameters. For a detailed explanation of the parameters, see Tables 10.1 and 10.2. When parameters are not provided, default values are assumed.

Notice that the `TiledImage` constructors don't have an argument for data. These methods construct a skeleton image. You can set the data later, either by calling the `setData()` method or by drawing over it using its graphical context. In this respect, a tiled image is just like a buffered image.

One way to create a tiled image is to start from scratch—that is, create an instance of `SampleModel` and of `ColorModel` and pass them to the `TiledImage` constructor along with other parameters. You can also use the factory methods that will be described shortly to create a tiled image.

More often, however, it is necessary to construct a tiled image from a planar image. To do so, use the existing `PlanarImage` object to get the attributes and then copy the `PlanarImage` data into the `TiledImage` object.

Here's an example of code that creates a tiled image from a planar image:

```
public static TiledImage createDisplayImage(PlanarImage image){
    SampleModel sampleModel = image.getSampleModel();
    ColorModel colorModel = image.getColorModel();

    TiledImage ti = new TiledImage(image.getMinX(), image.getMinY(),
                        image.getWidth(), image.getHeight(),
                        image.getTileGridXOffset(),
                        image.getTileGridYOffset(),
                        sampleModel, colorModel);
    ti.setData(image.copyData());
    return ti;
}
```

In addition to its constructors, the `TiledImage` class has two factory methods for creating an instance of `TiledImage`:

1. public static TiledImage createBanded(int minX,

continued

```
                                    int minY,
                                    int width,
                                    int height,
                                    int dataType,
                                    int tileWidth,
                                    int tileHeight,
                                    int[] bankIndices,
                                    int[] bandOffsets)
2. public static TiledImage createInterleaved(int minX,
                                    int minY,
                                    int width,
                                    int height,
                                    int numBands,
                                    int dataType,
                                    int tileWidth,
                                    int tileHeight,
                                    int[] bandOffsets)
```

The first static method creates an instance of `TiledImage` with the band-interleaved sample model, and the second method creates the pixel-interleaved sample model. See Chapter 8 for a detailed explanation of these sample models.

The `dataType` argument indicates the data type. The Java 2D API supports only `int`, `byte`, `short`, and unsigned `short` types. The JAI APIs support `float` and `double` types in addition to the basic types. The `DataBuffer` class, however, can take any constant representing any type.

As stated earlier, the constructors don't have image data as one of the input parameters. To set the data, the `TiledImage` class provides different flavors of *setXXX()* methods. Using these methods, you can set an individual pixel or pixels covering a rectangular region.

Setting the Pixel Value

The `TiledImage` class does not have a `setPixel()` method per se. However, it has three flavors of `setSample()`, which set the value of a sample. Recall from Chapter 8 that a sample is a component of a pixel; that is, a pixel in an RGB image has three samples—one each for red, green, and blue. Unlike a Java 2D image, a JAI image sample can assume `float` or `double` values. Accordingly, the `setSample()` method has the following three flavors for setting `int`, `float`, and `double` values:

```
1. public void setSample(int x, int y, int b, int s)
2. public void setSample(int x, int y, int b, float s)
3. public void setSample(int x, int y, int b, double s)
```

The x and y parameters represent the coordinates of a pixel, b represents the band index, and s represents the sample value. Corresponding to the `setSample()` methods, three methods of the `TiledImage` class are available for retrieving an individual sample value:

1. `public int getSample(int x, int y, int b)`
2. `public float getSampleFloat(int x, int y, int b)`
3. `public double getSampleDouble(int x, int y, int b)`

There is another way to set a pixel value: by using the `WritableRenderedImage` methods. We explained these methods in Chapter 8. To write a pixel, first get the index of the tile in which the pixel is located, then check out that tile for writing. Here's an example:

```
public static void writePixel(int x, int y,  short[] pixelValue TiledImage image) {
    Int xIndex = image.XtoTileX(x);
    int yIndex = image.YtoTileY(y);
    WritableRaster  tileRaster  =  image.getWritableTile (xIndex, yIndex);
    If (tileRaster != null) tileRaster.setPixel(x,y, pixelValue);
    ReleaseWritableTile(xIndex, yIndex);
}
```

Setting a Rectangular Region

There are two ways to write to a rectangular region of an image:

1. **Writing tile by tile.** You can use the `WritableRenderedImage` interface methods to write to a rectangular region.

2. **Writing to a rectangular region directly.**

Here are the methods:

- `public void set(java.awt.image.RenderedImage im)`
- `public void set(java.awt.image.RenderedImage im, ROI roi)`

Both of these methods copy the specified `RenderedImage` data onto a `TiledImage` object. The sample model of the source image should be compatible with that of the target image. The position and size of the overlapping area are determined from the source image attributes. If the source image area does not overlap the target image, these methods have no effect.

In the case of the latter method, which has an `ROI` parameter, the ROI overlaps the target image. The overlapping area and its position are computed from the corresponding ROI attributes.

The following two methods use the `Raster` parameter to pass the image data:

1. `public void setData(java.awt.image.Raster r)`
2. `public void setData(java.awt.image.Raster r,ROI roi)`

The `Raster` data provided by the input parameter is written over the target image. The overlapping area and position are computed from the coordinates of the input raster. These methods use the `WritableRenderedImage` methods to write to tiles. When the data is being written, the affected tiles are checked out and locked.

Creating a Subimage

Just as in `BufferedImage`, the `TiledImage` methods create a subimage from a tiled image:

* `public TiledImage getSubImage(int x, int y, int w, int h)`
* `public TiledImage getSubImage(int[] bandSelect)`
* `public TiledImage getSubImage(int x, int y, int w, int h,`
  `int[] bandSelect)`

The subimage follows the same coordinate system as the source image. The `x` and `y` parameters represent the upper left-hand corner coordinates of the subimage. The `w` and `h` parameters represent the width and height of the subimage, respectively. The `bandSelect` parameter is an array of indices representing the band indices in the source images. Using this parameter, you can create a subimage containing only the selected bands. The `subimage()` methods are useful in creating cropped images.

Obtaining an Off-Screen Graphical Context

Again like `BufferedImage`, the `TiledImage` class has methods for drawing graphical objects over it. The method signatures are the same as for the `BufferedImage` methods:

* `public java.awt.Graphics getGraphics()`
* `public java.awt.Graphics2D createGraphics()`

The first method returns the AWT graphical context, and the second returns the Java 2D graphical context.

Creating an Aggregate Image

Often it is necessary to create a single image from a set of images. You can use the `TiledImage` class to do this. As mentioned earlier, you can populate a `TiledImage` object in two different ways:

1. Drawing over its graphical context
2. Writing to tiles

Let's explore the first approach. This approach may not be very accurate, but it serves the purpose in most cases. The idea here is to first construct a skeleton tiled image as big as the target image, and then draw images from the set one by one, each time translating and scaling the image appropriately. Listing 11.9 shows the relevant code.

> **Note:** The code for aggregating images is available on the book's Web page in the directory `src/jaiutil/JAIUtil.java`.

LISTING 11.9   A method that aggregates images

```java
public static TiledImage aggregateImages(PlanarImage[] imageset,
                                  Dimension celldim,
                                  int cols, int rows) {
    int imWid = cols*celldim.width;
    int imHt =  rows*celldim.height;
    PlanarImage img = imageset[0];
    TiledImage ti = new TiledImage(0,0,(int)imWid,(int)(imHt), 0,0,
                            img.getSampleModel(), img.getColorModel());

    Graphics2D tg2d = ti.createGraphics();
    int x = 0; int y=0;
    for(int i=0; i< rows; i++) {
        for(int j=0;j<cols; j++) {
            if(i*cols+j >= imageset.length) break;
            img = imageset[i*cols+j];
            if(img != null){
                double magx = celldim.width/(double)img.getWidth() ;
                double magy = celldim.height/(double)img.getHeight() ;
                AffineTransform atx = new AffineTransform();
                atx.setToTranslation((double)x,(double)y);
                atx.scale(magx, magy);
                tg2d.drawRenderedImage(img,atx);
                x += celldim.width;
            }
        }
        x =0;
        y += celldim.height;
    }
    return ti;
}
```

The `aggregateImages()` method takes an array of planar images and converts it into a single planar image. It also has parameters to determine the size and layout of the target image. The `cellDim` parameter represents the size of an image to be drawn, which is assumed to be the same for all images. The `rows` and `cols` parameters specify how the input images are to be laid out—that is, in a rows-by-columns grid. It is expected that `rows × cols = imageset.length`.

This method assumes that all the images in `imageset` have the same sample model and color model. So it gets these parameters from the first image and then creates a skeleton tiled image. It then gets a `Graphics2D` context from this `TiledImage` object.

The next step is to draw the images from the `imageset` array one by one. There are two `for` loops, which create a single image by drawing the input images in a grid. Each time, the image is translated and then scaled so that the images fit closely. If you need a gap between the images, add the border to each image before passing to this method (see the section titled Using the Border Operator earlier in this chapter).

A JAI Image Browser

The Java browser application in Chapter 6 displays multiple images in a single frame and saves them as a single image. Let's modify that application to browse and save JAI images. We'll use the code in Listing 11.9 to aggregate multiple images into a single image.

There are two main classes: `JAIImageBrowser` and `ViewerPanel`. The `JAIImageBrowser` class code is similar to the `ImageBrowser` class code (see the section titled Image Browser: An Example of Aggregating Multiple Images in Chapter 6). `JAIImageBrowser` embeds the modified `MultiImageLoader` bean that can read image formats supported by JAI. When users select a set of images, `JAIImageBrowser` fires a `planarImageLoaded` event to the registered listeners. `JAIImageBrowser` receives this event, extracts the image set, and passes it on to `ViewerPanel`. Listing 11.10 shows the save methods of the modified `ViewerPanel` class.

> **Note:** The source code for the JAI image browser application is available on the book's Web page in the directory `src/chapter11/imagebrowser`.

LISTING 11.10   The `ViewerPanel` class

```
protected void save(){
   try{
     PlanarImage img = (PlanarImage) JAIUtil.aggregateImages(imageset,
                                 new Dimension(cellWidth, cellHeight),
                                 cols,rows);
     ImageSaverJAI.saveAsJPEG(img, "aggr.jpg");
   } catch(Exception e){}
}
```

For a detailed explanation of the `ViewerPanel` class, see the section titled Image Browser: An Example of Aggregating Multiple Images in Chapter 6. Figure 11.8 shows a screen shot of a frame with multiple images launched by the `JAIImageBrowser` application. Each image in this frame is drawn on an `ImagePanel` object (see Listing 11.11).

LISTING 11.11 Displaying an image with a border

```
class ImagePanel extends JComponent {
    PlanarImage image;
    AffineTransform atx = new AffineTransform();
    int width, height;
    Dimension border = new Dimension(2,2);
    public ImagePanel(){ }
    public ImagePanel(PlanarImage img){
        RenderedOp op = JAIUtil.setConstantBorder(img,border,255);
        image = op.createInstance();
        width = image.getWidth();
        height = image.getHeight();
    }
    public void setImage(PlanarImage img){image = img;}

    public void paintComponent(Graphics gc){
        Graphics2D g = (Graphics2D)gc;
        Rectangle rect = this.getBounds();
        if((width != rect.width) || (height != rect.height)){
            double magx = rect.width/(double)width ;
```

continued

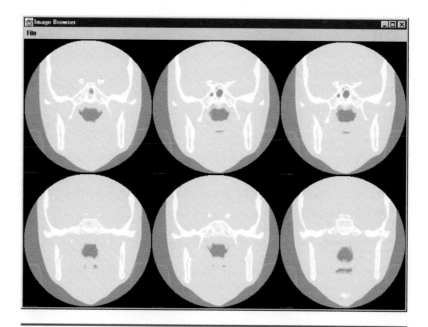

FIGURE 11.8 The image browser

```
        double magy = rect.height/(double)height ;
        atx.setToTranslation(border.width, border.height);
        atx.scale(magx, magy);
    }
    if(image != null) g.drawRenderedImage(image, atx);
  }
}
```

The `ImagePanel` class is a lightweight component for displaying images. The `JAIImageBrowser` object creates an `ImagePanel` object for each image.

When images are displayed side by side, a border is necessary to separate them. The `ImagePanel` constructor calls the method in Listing 11.11 to add the border to the input image.

The `paintComponent()` method translates the image so that the image border is visible on the left-hand side. It scales the image to fit the viewport and then draws it onto the graphical context.

The Renderable Layer

We already described the `RenderableImage` interface in Chapter 10. Many JAI standard operators take `RenderableImage` as an input source. The `RenderableOp` class is the equivalent of `RenderedOp` for a renderable layer. In other words, `RenderableOp` represents a node in the renderable chain.

A rendering chain has a source and a sink. The first step in building a renderable chain is to create a renderable source—that is, a renderable image.

Even though the renderable image has no size and lacks many other physical attributes, a real image is needed as a source. To construct a renderable chain, a renderable image is derived from this image.

An image in Java can be loaded as an `Image, BufferedImage,` or `PlanarImage` object. There is no equivalent of `PlanarImage` for the renderable chain. Instead, JAI provides an operator named Renderable, which converts `RenderedImage` to `RenderableImage.` Table 11.5 shows the parameters for this operator.

Obviously the Renderable operator does not take the renderable image as a source. This operator creates a pyramid of low-resolution images. But normally you would want to create a single image. Listing 11.12 shows an example that uses the Renderable operator.

LISTING 11.12   Converting to a renderable node

```
public static RenderableOp convertToRenderable(PlanarImage image) {
    ParameterBlock pb = new ParameterBlock();
    pb.addSource(image);
    pb.add(null).add(null).add(null).add(null).add(null);
    return  JAI.createRenderable("renderable", pb);
}
```

TABLE 11.5   Renderable Operator Parameters

OPERATOR NAME	PARAMETER	TYPE	DEFAULT VALUE	DESCRIPTION
Renderable	`downSampler`	`RenderedOp`	`null`	Rendered chain that supplies low-resolution images
	`maxLowResDim`	`float`	64	
	`minX`	`float`	0.0f	
	`minY`	`float`	0.0f	
	`height`	`int`	1.0f	

To apply standard operators to a renderable image, use the `JAI.create`
`Renderable()` method, which returns a `RenderableOp` node.

Creating a Renderable Node

In the renderable chain, the `RenderableOp` class represents a renderable node. The
`RenderableOp` class implements the `RenderableImage` interface. Recall from Chapter 10
that the `RenderableImage` interface has three different methods for creating a rendering:
`createDefaultRendering()`, `createScaledRendering()`, and `createRendering()`.
Each one returns a `RenderedImage` object.

To evaluate a renderable node, call one of the three rendering methods. While
these methods are being executed, the size is assigned to the image. The
`RenderedImage` object returned by these methods can be rendered through
`Graphics2D`'s `drawRenderedImage()` method. This means that the same components we
developed for displaying planar images can be used for rendering a renderable node.

However, the `Graphics2D` class has a method that directly renders a renderable
image:

◆ **`public abstract void drawRenderableImage(RenderableImage img,`**
`AffineTransform xform)`

Let's use this method to display a renderable image. As stated earlier, a renderable image has no size. This means that it has no width or height properties.
However, a renderable image does have an aspect ratio. Because the renderable
image has no size, the image viewer will need to provide the input. The options are

◆ **To fit the viewport.** Regardless of the size of a viewport, the size of the displayed
   image is increased or decreased to fit the viewport.

◆ **Scaled.** The size of the image fits the viewport, but the aspect ratio is maintained.

◆ **Original size.** The size matches the size of the source image from which the renderable image is generated.

Let's first build a canvas to display the renderable image. Listing 11.13 shows the class (`RenderableImageCanvas`) that can do this. It is similar to `JAIImageCanvas`, except for the `paintComponent()` method.

> **Note:** The source code for `RenderableImageCanvas` is available on the book's Web page in the directory `src/chapter11/simplerenderable`.

LISTING 11.13   The `RenderableImageCanvas` class

```
package com.vistech.jai.render;
import java.io.*;
import java.awt.*;
import java.awt.event.*;
import java.awt.image.*;
import javax.swing.*;
import java.awt.geom.*;
import java.awt.image.renderable.*;
import javax.media.jai.*;
import com.vistech.imageviewer.*;
public class RenderableImageCanvas extends JComponent implements ScrollController {
    public final static int TO_FIT =0;
    public final static int SCALED = 1;
    public final static int MAX_SIZE = 4;

    protected RenderableImage sourceImage;
    protected AffineTransform atx = new AffineTransform();
    protected boolean imageDrawn = false;
    protected int panX =0, panY =0;
    private Point scrollAnchor  = new Point(0,0);
    protected boolean scrollOn = true;
    protected int viewerWidth = 480, viewerHeight = 400;
    protected Point panOffset = new Point(0,0);
    protected int displayMode = SCALED;
    protected  int interpolationMode = Interpolation.INTERP_BILINEAR;
    protected float sourceImageHeight = 1.0f;
    protected float sourceImageWidth = 1.0f;
    protected int maxHeight =1024, maxWidth = 1024;

    public RenderableImageCanvas() {}

    public RenderableImageCanvas(RenderableImage img){
       atx = new AffineTransform();
       setImage(img);
    }

    public boolean isImageDrawn(){ return imageDrawn;}

    public void setDisplayMode(int dispMode) {
       displayMode = dispMode;
       createScalingTransform();
    }
```

```java
public int getDisplayMode(){ return displayMode;}

public void setOrigImageSize(Dimension size){
   maxWidth = size.width;
   maxHeight = size.height;
}

public void setImage(RenderableImage rImg){
   sourceImage =  rImg;
   panX =0; panY =0;
   sourceImageHeight = sourceImage.getHeight();
   sourceImageWidth = sourceImage.getWidth();
   createScalingTransform();
   imageDrawn = false;
   repaint();
}


protected void createScalingTransform(){
   int wid = viewerWidth, ht = viewerHeight;
   double aspectRatio = sourceImageWidth/sourceImageHeight;
   switch (displayMode) {
     case SCALED:
        if(aspectRatio > 1.00) ht =  (int)(viewerHeight/aspectRatio);
        else wid = (int)(viewerWidth/aspectRatio);
        atx.setToScale(wid/(double)sourceImageWidth,ht*sourceImageHeight);
        break;
      case MAX_SIZE:
        wid = maxWidth; ht =  maxHeight;
        atx.setToScale(maxWidth/(double)sourceImageWidth,
                    maxHeight*sourceImageHeight);
        break;
      case TO_FIT:
        atx.setToScale(viewerWidth/(double)sourceImageWidth,
                    sourceImageHeight*viewerHeight);
        break;
   }
    repaint();
}

public void paintComponent(Graphics gc){
   Graphics2D g = (Graphics2D)gc;
   Rectangle rect = this.getBounds();
   if((viewerWidth != rect.width) || (viewerHeight != rect.height)){
      viewerWidth =rect.width;
      viewerHeight = rect.height;
      createScalingTransform();
   }
   g.setColor(Color.black);
   g.fillRect(0, 0, viewerWidth, viewerHeight);
   if(sourceImage == null) return;
   try {
     Point2D dest = null;
     dest = atx.inverseTransform(new Point(panX,panY), dest);
     atx.translate(dest.getX(), dest.getY());
     g.drawRenderableImage(sourceImage, atx);
   }catch (Exception e) {}
```

continued

```
        imageDrawn = true;
    }

    public void setPanOffset(Point panOffset){
        firePropertyChange("PanOffset",this.panOffset,panOffset);
        this.panOffset = panOffset;
        panX = panOffset.x; panY = panOffset.y;
    }

    public Point getPanOffset(){ return panOffset;}

    public void setScrollOn(boolean onOff){
        scrollOn = onOff;
        panX =0; panY =0;
    }

    public  boolean getScrollOn(){ return scrollOn;}

    public void startScroll(int x, int y){
        scrollAnchor.x = x- panX;
        scrollAnchor.y = y- panY;
        repaint();
    }

    public void scroll(int x, int y){
        if((x <0 )|| (y<0)) return;
        panX = x-scrollAnchor.x;
        panY = y-scrollAnchor.y;
        repaint();
    }

    public void stopScroll(){ setCursor(Cursor.getDefaultCursor());}

    public void reset(){
        atx = new AffineTransform();
        panX =0; panY =0;
    }
}
```

Just like the `JAIImageCanvas` class, `RenderableImageCanvas` implements `ScrollController`, which allows you to scroll the displayed image. To display a renderable image, the client object calls the `setImage()` method. This method first obtains the width and height of the renderable image. The height of a renderable image always equals `1.0f`, and the width is given by 1/aspect ratio. This means that the rendering operations are performed on an image that is 1 pixel high and (1/aspect ratio) wide.

The `setImage()` method then sets the scaling factor by calling the `createScalingTransform()` method, which determines the scaling factor on the basis of the user's choice and sets the `atx` instance variable. Users have three choices:

1. SCALED
2. TO_FIT
3. ORIG_SIZE

The original size of the `RenderableImage` cannot be determined from the `RenderedImage` class, so `setOrigImageSize()` sets this variable.

The `paintComponent()` method uses `atx` (`AffineTransform`) to

- Compute the translation parameters in the `RenderableImage` space by inverse-transforming the `panX` and `panY` variables. This computation is a must because the renderable image is very small compared to the viewport.
- Concatenate this translation.
- Perform `drawRenderable()`.

Every time the `paintComponent()` method is called to paint the scrolled image, a lot of computation is involved. You will notice this if you try to scroll a large image.

Next let's build an image viewer using the `RenderableImageViewer` class, which is shown in Listing 11.14.

LISTING 11.14 The `RenderableImageViewer` class

```
public class RenderableImageViewer extends JAIImageViewer{
    RenderableImageCanvas viewer;
    public static void main(String[] args){
        RenderableImageViewer ip = new RenderableImageViewer();
        if(args.length <1) {
            ip.createUI();
        }else ip.loadAndDisplay(args[0]);
    }
    public void displayImage(PlanarImage img) {
        int wid = img.getWidth();
        int ht = img.getHeight();
        ParameterBlock pb = new ParameterBlock();
        pb.addSource(img);
        pb.add(null).add(null).add(null).add(null).add(null);
        RenderableOp op = JAI.createRenderable("renderable", pb);
        viewer.setImage(op);
        viewer.setOrigImageSize(new Dimension(wid, ht));
        saver.setImage(img);
        viewer.repaint();
    }

    public void createUI() {
        Dimension dim= Toolkit.getDefaultToolkit().getScreenSize();
        int width = (int)(dim.width *3/4.0);
        int height = (int)(dim.height*3/4.0);

        setTitle("Renderable Image Viewer");
        viewer = new RenderableImageCanvas();
        Dimension d = getViewerSize(width/(double)height);
        viewer.setPreferredSize(new Dimension(d.width, d.height));
        createImageLoaderAndSaver();
        loader.addPlanarImageLoadedListener(
            new PlanarImageLoadedListener() {
```

continued

```
            public void imageLoaded(PlanarImageLoadedEvent e) {
                PlanarImage image = e.getImage();
                if(image == null) return;
                SwingUtilities.invokeLater(new ImagePaint(image));
            }
        }
    );
    // Layout code not shown.
}

// DisplayModePanel code not shown.
}

 class ImagePaint implements Runnable {
    PlanarImage image;
    boolean firstTime = true;
    public ImagePaint(PlanarImage image){this.image = image;}
    public void run() {
        if(firstTime) {
            try {
                setCursor(Cursor.getPredefinedCursor(Cursor.WAIT_CURSOR));
                displayImage(image);
                firstTime = false;
                SwingUtilities.invokeLater(this);
            } catch(Exception e){SwingUtilities.invokeLater(this);}
        }
        else {
            if(!viewer.isImageDrawn()) SwingUtilities.invokeLater(this);
            else{
                setCursor(Cursor.getDefaultCursor());
            }
        }
    }
 }
}
```

The `RenderableImageViewer` class is a subclass of `JAIImageViewer` (see Listing 10.3). As in `JAIImageViewer`, the image is painted in a thread. The `ImagePaint` thread is invoked when an image is loaded. The `run()` method of `ImagePaint` calls the `displayImage()` method. The `displayImage()` method first converts `PlanarImage` to `RenderableImage` using the Renderable operator and then sends it to `Renderable ImageCanvas`. Figure 11.9 shows a screen shot of the renderable-image viewer application with a large image scaled to fit the viewport size.

To speed up image manipulation, we can compute tiles and paint only those needed in the `paintComponent()` method. We did this already in the `RenderedImageCanvas` class. So to display a renderable image, let's create a canvas that is a subclass of `RenderedImageCanvas`. We'll call this class `TiledRenderable ImageCanvas`. There is no need to override the `paintComponent()` method because we can create a rendered image by calling `RenderableOp`'s `createRendering()` method. Listing 11.15 shows the code for `TiledRenderable ImageCanvas`.

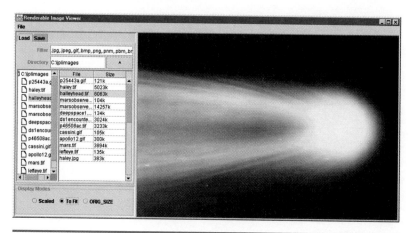

FIGURE 11.9   Scaling a large image to the viewport size

Note: The source code for `TiledRenderableImageCanvas` is available on the book's Web page in the directory `src/chapter11/renderable`.

LISTING 11.15   The `TiledRenderableImageCanvas` class

```
package com.vistech.jai.render;
import java.awt.*;
import java.awt.event.*;
import java.awt.image.*;
import java.io.*;
import javax.swing.*;
import javax.swing.event.*;
import java.awt.geom.*;
import java.awt.image.renderable.*;
import javax.media.jai.*;

public class TiledRenderableImageCanvas extends RenderedImageCanvas  {
    public final static int TO_FIT =0;
    public final static int SCALED = 1;
    public final static int ORIG_SIZE = 4;

    protected RenderableImage sourceImage;
    protected  int interpolationMode = Interpolation.INTERP_BILINEAR;

    protected int displayMode = ORIG_SIZE;
    protected float sourceImageHeight = 1.0f;
```

continued

```java
protected float sourceImageWidth = 1.0f;
protected int maxHeight =1024, maxWidth = 1024;

public TiledRenderableImageCanvas() {}

public TiledRenderableImageCanvas(RenderableImage img){
   atx = new AffineTransform();
   setImage(img);
}

public void setImage(RenderableImage pixelLessImg){
   PlanarImage img = createPlanarImage(pixelLessImg);
   displayImage =  makeTiledImage(img);
   sampleModel = displayImage.getSampleModel();
   colorModel = displayImage.getColorModel();
   getTileInfo(displayImage);
   imageDrawn = false;
   repaint();
}

public void setDisplayMode(int dispMode) {
   displayMode = dispMode;
   setImage(sourceImage);
}
public int getDisplayMode(){ return displayMode;}

public void setOrigImageSize(Dimension size){
   maxWidth = size.width;
   maxHeight = size.height;
}
public void setInterpolationMode(int interpMode) { interpolationMode = interpMode;}
public int getInterpolationMode(){ return interpolationMode;}

protected PlanarImage createPlanarImage(RenderableImage pixelLessImg){
   panX =0; panY =0;
   sourceImage = pixelLessImg;
   sourceImageHeight = sourceImage.getHeight();
   sourceImageWidth = sourceImage.getWidth();
   return createPixelImage(pixelLessImg);
}

protected PlanarImage createPixelImage(RenderableImage  pixelLessImg){
   RenderingHints hints = new RenderingHints(JAI.KEY_INTERPOLATION,
              Interpolation.getInstance(interpolationMode));
   int wid = viewerWidth, ht = viewerHeight;
   double aspectRatio = sourceImageWidth/sourceImageHeight;
   switch (displayMode) {
       case SCALED:
        if(aspectRatio > 1.00)  ht =  (int)(viewerHeight/aspectRatio);
        else  wid = (int)(viewerWidth*aspectRatio);
        break;
       case ORIG_SIZE:
        ht = maxHeight;  wid = maxWidth;
        break;
       case TO_FIT:
   }
   if(sourceImage == null) return null;
```

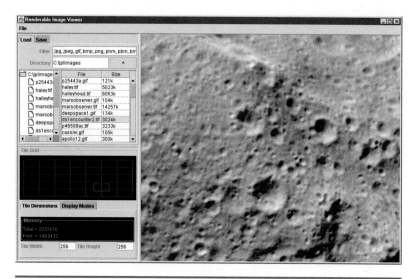

FIGURE 11.10   The tiled renderable-image viewer

```
        return (PlanarImage) sourceImage.createScaledRendering(wid, ht, hints);
    }

    public void setTileWidth(int tw){
        tileWidth = tw;
        setImage(sourceImage);
        repaint();
    }
    public void setTileHeight(int th){
        tileHeight = th;
        setImage(sourceImage);
        repaint();
    }
}
```

The `TiledRenderableImageViewer` application uses `TiledRenderableImage Canvas` to display images. We won't show the source code for this application because it is similar to the source code for the `RenderableImageViewer` application shown in Listing 11.14. Figure 11.10 shows a screen shot of the `TiledRenderable ImageViewer` application.

Conclusion

In this chapter we discussed the classes that are responsible for rendered as well as renderable layers. Rendering images in JAI can be made smooth, fast, and efficient by the application of some prerendering operations, including setting of appropriate rendering hints, effective layout of the tiles, and efficient allocation of memory for tiles.

At the center of JAI rendering is the `PlanarImage` class. A rendered node is represented by `RenderedOp` and typically evaluated to obtain a `PlanarImage` object before rendering. In the `RenderedImageCanvas` example, only the tiles that are needed for display are computed, thereby improving the rendering performance. This is very important in interactive image manipulation. As we'll see in Chapter 12, if an image is not properly tiled, there is a drastic reduction in rendering performance.

In the renderable chain, `RenderableOp` represents a renderable node. A `RenderableOp` object is typically evaluated to obtain a `RenderedImage` object before rendering. In the `TiledRenderableImageCanvas` example, we used the tiling mechanism of `RenderedImageCanvas`.

Manipulating Images in JAI   12

IN CHAPTER 7 WE DESCRIBED the basic geometric manipulation operations that use the affine transformation. Although these transformations are adequate for a vast majority of applications, some imaging applications require other types of transformations, such as perspective transformation, warping, and so on. A few examples are restoring lens aberrations, registering images, and mosaicking images. If you need to write such applications, one option is to use the Java 2D API and write your own transformation. Another option is to use JAI, which has operators and APIs that support affine transformations, perspective transformations, and warping.

In this chapter we'll focus on the geometric operators and the JAI classes that can be used for manipulating images. We already implemented a rendering application in Chapter 11. We'll add the interactive image manipulation capability to this application, just as we did with the image manipulation application in Chapter 7. We'll reuse the GUI classes developed for the rendering application.

For lack of better categorization, we'll consider cropping to be an image manipulation operation and add the crop feature to our image manipulation application. This feature will let you crop a manipulated image. You can also save the cropped image.

We will then move on to a discussion of nonaffine transformations, in which the `PerspectiveTransform` class and the `Warp` class hierarchy will be explained. This discussion will be followed by an example.

When a geometric operation is performed, the geometry of the image changes. The quality of the manipulated image depends on the interpolation technique used, so let's begin this chapter with a discussion of interpolation.

Interpolation in JAI

Geometric manipulation results in pixels lying between the integer coordinates. The interpolation techniques compute pixel values at the integer coordinates. In Chapter 7 we discussed some basic interpolation techniques.

In Java 2D you can only suggest an interpolation technique through rendering hints. It is not guaranteed that the underlying implementation will execute that type of interpolation. In other words, application programmers have no control over whether a desired interpolation technique is performed for a given manipulation operation.

In JAI, an interpolation technique can be passed as a rendering hint, and sometimes it can be passed explicitly; that is, you can instruct the application to perform one of the available interpolation techniques. JAI has several classes in the `javax.media.jai` package for this purpose. Figure 12.1 shows the class hierarchy. The `Interpolation` class at the root of the hierarchy is an abstract class. There is no need to know this class in detail unless you intend to implement your own interpolation techniques. The only method normally needed is the following:

- **`public static Interpolation getInstance(int type)`**

This factory method returns an `Interpolation` object and takes one of the following four constants defined in the `Interpolation` class:

1. **INTERP_NEAREST.** This constant represents the `InterpolationNearest` class, which implements interpolation based on the nearest-neighbor algorithm. The

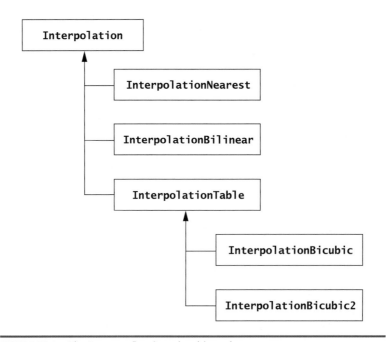

FIGURE 12.1 The `Interpolation` class hierarchy

getInstance(Interpolation.INTERP_NEAREST) method returns the InterpolationNearest object.

2. **INTERP_BILINEAR.** This constant represents the InterpolationBilinear class, which implements bilinear interpolation. The getInstance(Interpolation. INTERP_BILINEAR) method returns the InterpolationBilinear object.

3. **INTERP_BICUBIC.** This constant represents the InterpolationBicubic class, which implements bicubic interpolation. The getInstance(Interpolation. INTERP_BICUBIC) method returns the InterpolationBicubic object.

4. **INTERP_BICUBIC_2.** This constant represents the InterpolationBicubic2 class, which implements the bicubic2 interpolation. The bicubic and bicubic2 algorithms are similar, but they use slightly different polynomial functions to generate the cubic curve. The getInstance(Interpolation.INTERP_BICUBIC2) method returns the InterpolationBicubic2 object.

Here's an example that illustrates the usage:

```
Interpolation interpol = Interpolation.getInstance(Interpolation.INTERP_BILINEAR);
```

Using the Affine Transformation Operators

All the affine transformation operations we discussed in Chapter 7 are available as operators in JAI. They are Translate, Scale, Rotate, Shear, and Transpose. (The Transpose operator implements the flip operation.)

In addition, JAI has an operator called Affine that takes an AffineTransform parameter. So you can construct any AffineTransform object, pass it to Parameter Block, and execute the JAI.create("affine", pb) method to transform the image. By using the Affine operator, you can leverage methods written already with the Java 2D API. To manipulate images, you can use the AffineTransform class to generate the transformation and the Affine operator to generate the rendered or renderable node. This is a preferred way of manipulation if your application needs to perform a combination of geometric manipulations in real time. Although the JAI operators are elegant, they are slow.

In the sections that follow we'll look at each of the affine operators in turn. All of these operators require an Interpolation object as one of the parameters. As we showed in the preceding section, you can create this object by using the Interpolation.getInstance() factory method. Except for the Shear operator, the affine transformation operators take either a rendered or a renderable image as the source.

Translate

The parameters of the Translate operator are listed in Table 12.1.

Listing 12.1 gives an example.

LISTING 12.1　Translating an image

```
public static RenderableOp translate(RenderableImage image, float dx, float dy) {
    ParameterBlock pb = new ParameterBlock();
    pb.addSource(image);
    pb.add(dx);
    pb.add(dy);
    pb.add(Interpolation.getInstance(Interpolation.INTERP_NEAREST));
    return JAI.createRenderable("translate", pb);
}
```

Scale

The parameters of the Scale operator are listed in Table 12.2.

Listing 12.2 gives an example.

LISTING 12.2　Scaling an image

```
public static RenderedOp scale(RenderedImage image,
                               float magx, float magy,
                               float transx, float trans y) {
    ParameterBlock pb = new ParameterBlock();
    pb.addSource(image);
    pb.add(magx);
    pb.add(magy);
    pb.add(transx);
```

TABLE 12.1　Translate Operator Parameters

OPERATOR NAME	PARAMETER	TYPE	DEFAULT VALUE	DESCRIPTION
Translate	xTrans	float	0.0f	Displacement in the x direction
	yTrans	float	0.0f	Displacement in the y direction
	int	Interpolation	Interpolation. INTERP_NEAREST	One of Interpolation. INTERP_NEAREST, Interpolation. INTERP_BILINEAR, Interpolation. INTERP_BICUBIC, and Interpolation. INTERP_BICUBIC_2

TABLE 12.2 Scale Operator Parameters

Operator Name	Parameter	Type	Default Value	Description
Scale	xScale	float	1.0f	Scale factor in the x direction
	yScale	float	1.0f	Scale factor in the y direction
	xTrans	float	0.0f	Displacement in the x direction
	yTrans	float	0.0f	Displacement in the y direction
	Interpolation	int	INTERP_NEAREST	One of Interpolation. INTERP_NEAREST, Interpolation.INTERP_ BILINEAR, Interpolation. INTERP_BICUBIC, and Interpolation.INTERP_ BICUBIC_2

```
        pb.add(transy);
        pb.add(Interpolation.getInstance(Interpolation.INTERP_NEAREST));
        return  JAI.create("scale", pb);
    }
```

Rotate

The parameters of the Rotate operator are listed in Table 12.3.

TABLE 12.3 Operator Parameters

Operator Name	Parameter	Type	Default Value	Description
Rotate	xOrigin	float	1.0f	Center-of-rotation x coordinate
	yOrigin	float	1.0f	Center-of-rotation y coordinate
	angle	float	None	Angle of rotation in radians
	Interpolation	int	INTERP_NEAREST	One of Interpolation. INTERP_NEAREST, Interpolation.INTERP_ BILINEAR, Interpolation. INTERP_BICUBIC, and Interpolation.INTERP_ BICUBIC_2

Listing 12.3 gives an example.

LISTING 12.3 Rotating an image

```
public static RenderedOp rotate(RenderedImage image, float angle, int interpType) {
    ParameterBlock pb = new ParameterBlock();
    pb.addSource(image);
    int width = image.getWidth();
    int height = image.getHeight();
    pb.add((float)width/2);
    pb.add((float)height/2);
    pb.add(angle);
    pb.add(Interpolation.getInstance(interpType));
    return JAI.create("rotate", pb);
}
```

Shear

Shear is the only non-rigid-body transformation among the affine transformations. Note that in JAI 1.0.2 this operator doesn't take a renderable image as a source. The parameters of the Shear operator are listed in Table 12.4.

The shear operation can be performed in either the x or the y direction. The shearDir parameter represents this option and can take one of two constants defined in the javax.media.jai.operator.ShearDescriptor class: SHEAR_HORIZONTAL and

TABLE 12.4 Shear Operator Parameters

OPERATOR NAME	PARAMETER	TYPE	DEFAULT VALUE	DESCRIPTION
Shear	shear	Float	None	Shear value
	shearDir	int	None	Direction of shear; either ShearDescriptor.SHEAR_HORIZONTAL or ShearDescriptor.SHEAR_VERTICAL
	xTrans	Float	0.0f	Displacement in the x direction
	yTrans	Float	0.0f	Displacement in the y direction
	Interpolation	int	INTERP_NEAREST	One of Interpolation.INTERP_NEAREST, Interpolation.INTERP_BILINEAR, Interpolation.INTERP_BICUBIC, and Interpolation.INTERP_BICUBIC_2

SHEAR_VERTICAL. Listing 12.4 shows an example of code that performs shear in both the horizontal and the vertical directions.

LISTING 12.4 Shearing an image

```
public static RenderedOp shear(RenderedImage image, float shear) {
    ParameterBlock pb = new ParameterBlock();
    pb.addSource(image);
    pb.add(shear);
    pb.add(ShearDescriptor.SHEAR_HORIZONTAL);
    pb.add(0.0f);
    pb.add(0.0f);
    pb.add(Interpolation.getInstance(Interpolation.INTERP_NEAREST));
    RenderedOp op = JAI.create("shear", pb);
    pb.addSource(op);
    pb.add(shear);
    pb.add(ShearDescriptor.SHEAR_VERTICAL);
    pb.add(0.0f);
    pb.add(0.0f);
    pb.add(Interpolation.getInstance(Interpolation.INTERP_NEAREST));
    return JAI.create("shear", pb);
}
```

Listing 12.4 shows how a simple rendered chain is constructed through the RenderedOp class.

Transpose

The parameters of the Transpose operator are listed in Table 12.5.

TABLE 12.5 Transpose Operator Parameters

Operator Name	Parameter	Type	Default Value	Description
Transpose	flipType	int	None	One of Transport Descriptor.FLIP_ HORIZONTAL, Transport Descriptor.FLIP_VERTICAL, TransportDescriptor. FLIP_DIAGONAL, Transport Descriptor.FLIP_ ANTIDIAGONAL, Transport Descriptor.ROTATE_180, TransportDescriptor. ROTATE_270, Transport Descriptor.ROTATE_90

The flip type constants are defined in the `javax.media.jai.operator.TransportDescriptor` class. They are

- **TransportDescriptor.FLIP_HORIZONTAL:** Left-to-right flip
- **TransportDescriptor.FLIP_VERTICAL:** Top-to-bottom flip
- **TransportDescriptor.FLIP_DIAGONAL:** Left-to-right and top-to-bottom flip
- **TransportDescriptor.FLIP_ANTIDIAGONAL:** Bottom-to-top and right-to-left flip

In addition, the Transpose operator can perform rotation. The `Transport Descriptor` class has the following constants for rotation: `TransportDescriptor.ROTATE_90`, `TransportDescriptor.ROTATE_180`, and `TransportDescriptor.ROTATE_270`.

Affine

The parameters of the Affine operator are listed in Table 12.6.

Recall from Chapter 7 that we used the `AffineTransformOp` class to apply the affine transformation to a buffered image. The Affine operator does the same to rendered and renderable images. To use this operator, first generate the transformation using the Java 2D `AffineTransform` class and then pass it to the `JAI.create()` method.

You may want to consider the Affine operator with the `AffineTransform` class for interactive operations. In the current implementation (JAI 1.0.2), individual affine transformation operators, such as Scale and Rotate, are much slower compared to those of the Java 2D implementation.

TABLE 12.6 Affine Operator Parameters

OPERATOR NAME	PARAMETER	TYPE	DEFAULT VALUE	DESCRIPTION
Affine	transform	Affine Transform	Identity matrix	Affine transformation matrix
	interpolation	Interpolation	INTERP_NEAREST	One of Interpolation. INTERP_NEAREST, Interpolation. INTERP_BILINEAR, Interpolation. INTERP_BICUBIC, and Interpolation. INTERP_BICUBIC_2

Interactive Manipulation

As an example, let's modify the interactive manipulation application we developed in Chapter 7. You may recall that it used the `AffineTransform` class to scale, rotate, shear, and flip. We can reuse all the classes that generate the transformation. The actual transformation is applied in the `ImageCanvas2D` class, which displays the manipulated image. First we'll build a component class for manipulating JAI images.

A Canvas for Manipulating Images

One approach to building an image manipulation canvas is to extend the `Image Canvas2D` class we developed in Chapter 7 and override the `applyTransform()` method. In this method we can use the JAI Affine operator instead of `Affine TransformOp` to apply the affine transformation.

We also need to make a few more modifications to the `ImageCanvas2D` class in order to render JAI images. As we saw in Chapter 11, rendering a JAI image is different from rendering a buffered image. To display rendered images, we implemented the `RenderedImageCanvas` class. An ideal approach, then, is to build a class that inherits from both the `ImageCanvas2D` and the `RenderedImageCanvas` classes. As stated earlier, Java doesn't support multiple inheritance. This means that the component class for manipulating JAI images can extend either `ImageCanvas2D` or `RenderedImage Canvas` class, but not both.

In Java, we can use interfaces to simulate multiple inheritance. The `Image Canvas2D` class implements the `ImageManipulator` interface. So one approach to inheriting the functionality from `ImageCanvas2D` is to implement the `ImageManipulator` interface.

Let's create a class then—ImageManipulatorCanvas—to extend `RenderedImage Canvas` and implement the `ImageManipulator` interface. Listing 12.5 shows the code for ImageManipulatorCanvas.

> **Note:** The code for `ImageManipulatorCanvas` is available on the book's Web page in the directory `src/chapter12/manip`.

LISTING 12.5   The `ImageManipulatorCanvas` class

```
package com.vistech.jai.render;
import java.awt.*;
import java.awt.event.*;
import java.awt.image.*;
import java.io.*;
import javax.swing.*;
import java.awt.geom.*;
```
continued

```java
import java.awt.image.renderable.*;
import javax.swing.*;

import javax.media.jai.*;
import com.vistech.imageviewer.*;
import com.vistech.util.*;

public class ImageManipulatorCanvas extends RenderedImageCanvas
                    implements ImageManipulator{
   transient protected Image awtImage;
   protected int imageType =0;

   protected Point panOffset = new Point(0,0);

   protected boolean magOn = true;
   protected double magFactor = 1.0;
   protected int magCenterX = 0;
   protected int magCenterY = 0;
   protected double rotationAngle = 0.0;
   protected boolean rotateOn = true;
   protected int rotationCenterX = 0;
   protected int rotationCenterY = 0;

   protected boolean shearOn = true;
   protected double shearFactor = 0.0;
   protected double shearX = 0.0, shearY = 0.0;

   protected int displayMode = DisplayMode.SCALED;
   protected int flipMode = FlipMode.NORMAL;
   protected int interpMode = Interpolation.INTERP_NEAREST;
   protected double diffFactor =0.0;

   public PlanarImage getImage() { return origImage; }
   public Dimension getImageSize() {
       return new Dimension(origImage.getWidth(), origImage.getHeight());
   }
   public synchronized void setInterpolationType(int mode){ interpMode = mode;}
   public int getInterpolationType(){ return interpMode;}

   public synchronized void setDisplayMode(int mode){
      if(mode == displayMode) return;
      int oldmode = displayMode;
      firePropertyChange("displayMode",oldmode,mode);
      this.displayMode = mode;
      repaint();
   }
   public int getDisplayMode(){ return displayMode;}

   public synchronized void setFlipMode(int mode){
      if(mode == flipMode) return;
      int oldmode = flipMode;
      firePropertyChange("flipMode",oldmode, mode);
      this.flipMode = mode;
      repaint();
   }
   public int getFlipMode(){ return flipMode;}
```

```
public void setMagFactor(double magFactor){
   firePropertyChange("MagFactor",
                        new Double(this.magFactor),
                        new Double(magFactor));
   diffFactor = this.magFactor - magFactor;
   this.magFactor = magFactor;
}
public double getMagFactor(){ return magFactor;}

public void setShearFactor(double shearFactor){
   firePropertyChange("ShearFactor",
                        new Double(this.shearFactor),
                        new Double(shearFactor));
   this.shearFactor = shearFactor;
}
public double getShearFactor(){ return shearFactor;}

public double getShearFactorX(){ return shearX; }
public double getShearFactorY(){return shearY;}

public void setRotationAngle(double rotationAngle){
   firePropertyChange("RotationAngle",
                        new Double(this.rotationAngle),
                        new Double(rotationAngle));
   this.rotationAngle = rotationAngle;
}

public double getRotationAngle(){return rotationAngle;}

public void paintImage(int magCenterX, int magCenterY, double mag){
   setMagFactor(this.magFactor *mag);
   int dx = this.magCenterX-magCenterX;
   int dy = this.magCenterY-magCenterY;
   this.magCenterX = magCenterX;
   this.magCenterY = magCenterY;
   try {
     Point2D mgp = null;
     mgp = atx.inverseTransform((Point2D)(
           new Point(magCenterX-panX, magCenterY-panY)),(Point2D)mgp);
     double x = (mgp.getX()*mag)-mgp.getX();
     double y = (mgp.getY()*mag)-mgp.getY();
   }catch (Exception e) {System.out.println(e); }
}

protected void applyTransform(RenderedImage ri, AffineTransform atx){
   ParameterBlock pb = new ParameterBlock();
   pb.addSource(ri);
   pb.add(atx);
   pb.add(Interpolation.getInstance(interpMode));
   RenderedOp op = JAI.create("affine", pb);
   createTiledImage(op.createInstance());
   repaint();
}

public void applyTransform(AffineTransform atx){
   applyTransform(origImage,atx);
}
```

continued

```java
public void createTiledImage(PlanarImage img){
    displayImage =  makeTiledImage(img);
    sampleModel = displayImage.getSampleModel();
    colorModel = displayImage.getColorModel();
    getTileInfo(displayImage);
    fireTilePropertyChange();
    imageDrawn = false;
    repaint();
}

public void resetManipulation(){
    panOffset = new Point(0,0);
    magCenterX = 0; magCenterY =0;
    panX =0; panY =0;
    magFactor = 1.0;
    shearX = 0.0; shearY = 0.0;
    rotationAngle = 0.0;
    scrollAnchor = new Point(0,0);
    createTiledImage(origImage);
    atx = AffineTransform.getTranslateInstance(0.0,0.0);
    applyTransform(atx);
    repaint();
}

public void paintComponent(Graphics gc){
    Graphics2D g = (Graphics2D)gc;
    Rectangle rect = this.getBounds();
    if((width != rect.width) || (height != rect.height)){
        double magx = rect.width/(double)width ;
        double magy = rect.height/(double)height ;
    }
    g.setColor(Color.black);
    g.fillRect(0,0,rect.width, rect.height);
    if(displayImage != null) g.drawRenderedImage(displayImage,
                                        new AffineTransform());

    imageDrawn = true;
    }
}
```

All the set and get methods are copied from the `ImageCanvas2D` class. As Listing 12.5 shows, the `applyTransform()` method is different from `ImageCanvas2D`'s `apply Transform()` method. `ImageManipulatorCanvas` calls `applyTransform(Rendered Image, AffineTransform)`, which uses the Affine operator to transform the image.

An Image Manipulator Application

Next let's use the `ImageManipulatorCanvas` class to implement an application that allows interactive manipulation of images. The `TiledImageViewer` class, which was introduced in Chapter 11 (see Listing 11.6), and its superclasses have the methods for building several UI panels to render images. Let's extend this class to create the main program for our current application. Listing 12.6 shows the code.

LISTING 12.6   The RenderedImageManipulator class

```java
public class RenderedImageManipulator extends TiledImageViewer{
    protected PanZoom panzoom;
    protected JButton resetb;
    protected ManipUI manippan;
    GeomManip manip;

    public void createUI() {

        setTitle("JAI Image Manipulator");
        viewer = new ImageManipulatorCanvas();


        manip =  new GeomManip((ImageManipulator)viewer);
        manippan = new ManipUI(manip);
        JPanel gridpan = new JPanel();
        JPanel tilesetpan = createTileSetPanel();

        FlipModePanel flipmodepan = new FlipModePanel(manip);
        InterpModePanel intermodepan = new InterpModePanel((ImageManipulator)viewer);


        JTabbedPane jtab = new JTabbedPane();
        jtab.add("Tile Dimension", tilesetpan);
        jtab.add("Interp Mode", intermodepan);

        jtab.add("Flip Mode", flipmodepan);
        jtab.add("Manip", manippan);

        resetb = new JButton("Reset");
        resetEventHandler();
            ...
          // Gridbag layout code not shown
            ...
        pack();
        show();
        addEventAdapters();
        panzoom = new PanZoom((ImageManipulator)viewer);
    }

    protected void resetEventHandler(){
        resetb.addActionListener(
          new ActionListener(){
            public void actionPerformed(ActionEvent e) {
                ((ImageManipulator)viewer).resetManipulation();
                manippan.resetManipulation();
              }
            }
        );
    }

    public static void  main(String[] args){
        RenderedImageManipulator ip = new RenderedImageManipulator();
        if(args.length <1) {
```

continued

```
        ip.createUI();
      }else ip.loadAndDisplay(args[0]);
  }
}
```

Listing 12.6 shows that we have reused many of the classes we developed in Chapter 7 for the interactive manipulation application, including the `PanZoom` and `GeomManip` classes.

Running the Application

To run the application, type "java app.RenderedImageManipulator" on the command line. Figure 12.2 shows a screen shot of the frame launched by this application. Comparison with Figure 11.6 shows that we have incorporated all the `TiledImage Viewer` GUIs except the **Tile Grid** panel. The lower half of the left-hand side panel has all the parameter-setting tabs, which includes interpolation and flip modes.

To pan and zoom the displayed image, move the cursor over the image and right-click on it. The pop-up menu shown in Figure 12.3 is launched. Select the desired item.

To rotate and shear the image, select the **Manip** tab (see Figure 12.4). Comparison with Figure 7.14 shows that we reused the UI developed in Chapter 7. For rotation, select the **Rotate** tab. You can either use the text field to input the rotation angle or the slider to interactively rotate the image. You will probably notice that rotation is slower compared to rotation in our Java 2D implementation. The shear operation is similar to rotation (see Figure 12.5).

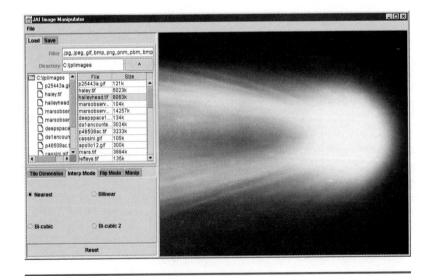

FIGURE 12.2   Setting the interpolation mode

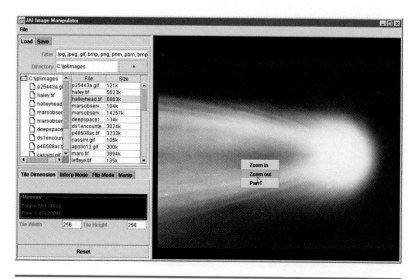

FIGURE 12.3   Selecting pan and zoom

To flip the image, select the **Flip Mode** tab. Then select the appropriate mode (see Figure 12.6).

You can perform the manipulation operations in any combination. The position and the image dimensions remain the same unless changed by the transformation.

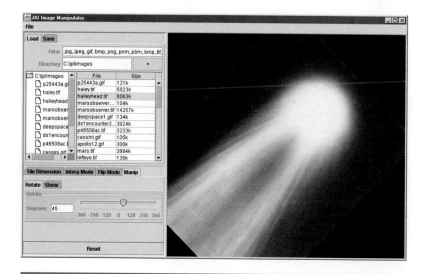

FIGURE 12.4   Selecting rotate

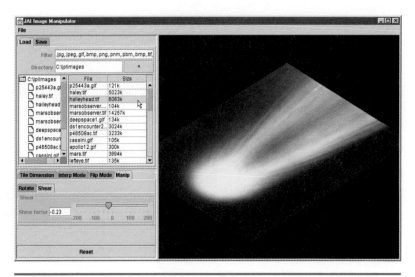

FIGURE 12.5   Selecting shear

The capability to maintain position and dimensions across manipulations is extremely useful in many imaging applications. As we'll see in Chapter 14, the manipulation operation is used in ROI applications.

To reset the image to the default size and position, click on **Reset.** The reset operation is called implicitly when a new image is selected.

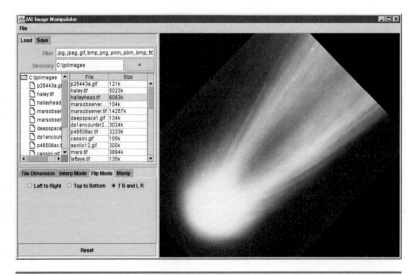

FIGURE 12.6   Selecting flip

Overlaying Graphics

In many imaging applications it is essential to draw graphics over images. Whether the operation is simple cropping or complex ROI shape marking, users need to draw shapes and text interactively over images. Even though there is no explicit support for overlaying graphics, we can use the same Java 2D APIs to draw graphics over images.

Let's extend the `ImageManipulatorCanvas` class to create a canvas that lets you draw graphics over images. Recall that in Chapter 9 we defined the `DrawingCanvas` interface to overlay graphics on images. For the sake of convenience, Listing 12.7 shows the code for this interface again.

LISTING 12.7   The `DrawingCanvas` interface

```
public interface DrawingCanvas {
    public Graphics2D getDisplayedImageGC();
    public AffineTransform getTransform();
    public void setTransform(AffineTransform atx);
    public void eraseShapes();
    public void repaint();
    public void reset();
    public void addMouseListener(MouseListener ml);
    public void removeMouseListener(MouseListener ml);
    public void addMouseMotionListener(MouseMotionListener ml);
    public void removeMouseMotionListener(MouseMotionListener ml);
}
```

A Composite Canvas

Let's create a class for drawing graphics over images by extending the `Image ManipulatorCanvas` class and implementing the `DrawingCanvas` interface. We'll call this class `CompositeCanvasJAI`. This class is similar to `CompositeCanvas2D,` which we developed in Chapter 9.

To draw shapes interactively, this class also needs to implement some sort of double buffering. As we did with Java 2D, we'll use the `BufferedImage` class for drawing graphics offline. Listing 12.7 shows that the `DrawingCanvas` interface has a method called `getDisplayedImageGc()` that returns a `Graphics2D` object. So the `CompositeCanvasJAI` class can have a `BufferedImage` object as an instance variable. The `getDisplayedImageGc()` method can return the `Graphics2D` context obtained from `BufferedImage`. A client object can obtain the graphical context by calling `getDisplayedImageGc()` and drawing graphics over it.

To paint the off-screen image, we must draw the buffered image over `Composite CanvasJAI`'s graphical context. This means that we need to override the `paint Component()` method.

We'll also add a flag to turn the drawing mode on and off. This flag is essential for using mouse inputs for other purposes. For example, you might want to switch between manipulating images and drawing graphics. Or you might want to switch between incremental scaling and shape drawing. Listing 12.8 shows the code for CompositeCanvasJAI.

Note: The code for CompositeCanvasJAI is available on the book's Web page in the directory src/chapter12/overlay.

LISTING 12.8   The CompositeCanvasJAI class

```
package com.vistech.jai.render;
import java.awt.*;
import java.awt.event.*;
import java.awt.image.*;
import java.io.*;
import java.awt.geom.*;
import java.awt.image.renderable.*;
import javax.swing.*;
import javax.media.jai.*;
import com.vistech.imageviewer.*;
import com.vistech.util.*;

public class CompositeCanvasJAI extends ImageManipulatorCanvas
                implements DrawingCanvas{
   protected BufferedImage offScrImage;
   protected Graphics2D offScrGc;
   protected BufferedImage destImage;
   protected Graphics2D destGc;
   protected boolean drawOn = false;

   public CompositeCanvasJAI() { createOffScreenImage();}

   public Graphics2D getDisplayedImageGC(){return offScrGc;}

   public void setImage(PlanarImage image){
      if(image instanceof TiledImage){
      panX =0; panY =0;
      displayImage = (PlanarImage)image;
      sampleModel = displayImage.getSampleModel();
      colorModel = displayImage.getColorModel();
      getTileInfo(displayImage);
      fireTilePropertyChange();
      imageDrawn = false;
      repaint();
      }
      else super.setImage(image);
   }

   public void paintImage(PlanarImage image) {
      setImage(image);
      applyTransform(image, atx);
   }
```

```java
public boolean getDrawOn(){ return drawOn;}
public void setDrawOn(boolean onOrOff){ drawOn = onOrOff;}

public void createOffScreenImage() {
   Rectangle r = getBounds();
   if((r.width ==0) || (r.height ==0)){  return;}
   offScrImage = new BufferedImage(r.width,r.height,BufferedImage.TYPE_INT_RGB);
   offScrGc = offScrImage.createGraphics();
   destImage = new BufferedImage(r.width,r.height,BufferedImage.TYPE_INT_RGB);
   destGc = destImage.createGraphics();
}

public void paintComponent(Graphics gc){
   Graphics2D g = (Graphics2D)gc;
   Rectangle rect = this.getBounds();
   if((viewerWidth != rect.width) || (viewerHeight != rect.height)){
      viewerWidth = rect.width;
      viewerHeight = rect.height;
      createOffScreenImage();
   }
   g.setColor(Color.black);
   g.fillRect(0, 0, viewerWidth, viewerHeight);
   if(displayImage == null) return;
   g.setColor(Color.black);
   g.fillRect(0, 0, rect.width, rect.height);
   if(displayImage != null)
      g.drawRenderedImage(displayImage, new AffineTransform());
   if(drawOn) {
      g.setColor(Color.white);
      g.setXORMode(Color.black);
      if(offScrImage != null) g.drawImage(offScrImage, 0, 0, this);
   }
   imageDrawn = true;
}

public void eraseShapes() {
   offScrImage.flush();
   if(image != null) setImage(image);
   createOffScreenImage();
   repaint();
}

 public void reset(){
   super.reset();
   if(image != null) setImage(image);
   createOffScreenImage();
   repaint();
}
}
```

The `createOffScreenImage()` method creates an off-screen image of the type `BufferedImage`. The `getDisplayedImageGc()` returns the `Graphics2D` object created from it. To draw graphics, a client object must obtain this `Graphics2D` object and draw shapes over it. For drawing to be enabled, however, the flag `drawOn` must be set to `true`, which is accomplished by a call to `setDrawOn()`. When the value of `drawOn` is

true, the **paintComponent()** method draws the off-screen buffered image over the graphical context. Note that the XOR paint mode is on while graphics are being painted.

Next we'll use the **CompositeCanvasJAI** class to add a feature to the image manipulator application described in the preceding section.

Cropping an Image

The Crop operator crops a rectangular region of the image. It takes either a rendered or a renderable image as a source. The parameters of the Crop operator are listed in Table 12.7.

Notice that all of the Crop operator parameters are of type **float.** Even though the device coordinates are integers, Crop can be part of a rendering chain that can take the parameter generated from another computation, which is typically of type **float** or **double.** In addition, shapes in Java 2D take **float** or **double** parameters. So you can pass the bounds of a **Rectangle2D** shape (described in Chapter 4) as parameters of the Crop operator.

The method in Listing 12.9 uses the Crop operator.

LISTING 12.9 Cropping an image

```
public static RenderedOp cropImage(PlanarImage image, Rectangle rect){
    ParameterBlock pb = new ParameterBlock();
    pb.addSource(image);
    pb.add((float)rect.x);
    pb.add((float)rect.y);
    pb.add((float)rect.width);
    pb.add((float)rect.height);
    return JAI.create("crop", pb);
}
```

TABLE 12.7 *Crop Operator Parameters*

OPERATOR NAME	PARAMETER	TYPE	DEFAULT VALUE	DESCRIPTION
Crop	x	Float	None	ULHC of the rectangular region
	y	Float	None	
	width	Float	None	Size of the rectangular region
	height	Float	None	

Adding the Crop Feature

Let's use the `CompositeCanvasJAI` class to add the cropping feature to our image manipulator application. There are two things we want to be able to do with this feature:

1. Crop the marked region
2. Save the cropped image

To crop an image, you need to first draw a rectangle over it to mark the region for cropping. As we have seen in previous chapters, we can do this interactively over images by dragging the mouse. When the mouse is released, the marked region should be cropped.

After cropping an image, you may want to pan and zoom the cropped image. To enable these options, let's provide a button that toggles between crop and pan/zoom. We'll also provide an **Undo Crop** button to start all over again.

The image viewers developed in Chapters 10 and 11 already have the save feature. To save, just select the **Save** tab and click on **Save Displayed Image.**

As part of the implementation, let's create a class called `Crop` that draws a rectangle and calls the method in Listing 12.10 when the mouse is released.

The main image manipulator application will use the `Crop` class in conjunction with the `CropPanel` class, which we'll develop in the next section. `CropPanel` represents the GUI for the crop feature. Its constructor takes the `Crop` object as input.

Because the `Crop` class enables drawing, it must implement the `MouseListener` and `MouseMotionListener` interfaces. Listing 12.10 shows the code for `Crop`.

> **Note:** The code for `Crop` is available on the book's Web page in the directory `src/chapter12/overlay`.

LISTING 12.10   The Crop class

```
public class Crop implements MouseListener,MouseMotionListener{
    protected CompositeCanvas imageCanvas;
    protected Point diff = new Point(0,0);
    protected Point shapeAnchor = new Point(0,0);
    protected boolean mousePressed = false;
    protected Rectangle currentShape, prevShape;
    protected boolean cropOn = false;
    protected cropped = false;
    protected JMenuItem crop;

    public Crop(CompositeCanvas c){
        imageCanvas = c;
        imageCanvas.setDrawOn(true);
    }

    public void setCropOn(boolean onOrOff){ cropOn = onOrOff;}
```

continued

```java
public void startDraw(int x, int y) {
   shapeAnchor = new Point(x,y);
   diff = new Point(0,0);
}

public void draw(int x, int y) {
   if(!cropOn) return;
   diff.x = x - shapeAnchor.x;
   diff.y = y - shapeAnchor.y;
   int wid = diff.x;
   int ht = diff.y;
   Point ulhc = new Point(shapeAnchor);
   if(diff.x <0) {
      wid = -diff.x;
      ulhc.x = x;
   }
   if(diff.y <0){
      ht = -diff.y;
      ulhc.y = y;
   }
   currentShape = new Rectangle(ulhc.x, ulhc.y, wid, ht);
   Graphics2D g = imageCanvas.getDisplayedImageGC();
   g.setColor(Color.black);
   g.setXORMode(Color.red);
   if(prevShape != null) g.draw(prevShape);
   g.draw(currentShape);
   prevShape = currentShape;
   imageCanvas.repaint();
}

public void mousePressed(MouseEvent e) {
   if(!cropOn) return;
   imageCanvas.eraseShapes();
   mousePressed = true;
   if(SwingUtilities.isLeftMouseButton(e)){
      startDraw(e.getX(), e.getY());
   }
}

public void mouseReleased(MouseEvent e) {
   if(!mousePressed) return;
   if(SwingUtilities.isLeftMouseButton(e)){
      Graphics2D g = imageCanvas.getDisplayedImageGC();
      draw(e.getX(), e.getY());
      prevShape = null;
      crop();
   }
   mousePressed = false;
}

public void mouseClicked(MouseEvent e){}
public void mouseEntered(MouseEvent e){}
public void mouseExited(MouseEvent e){}

public void mouseDragged(MouseEvent e){
   if(SwingUtilities.isLeftMouseButton(e)){
      draw(e.getX(), e.getY());
   }
}
```

```
public void mouseMoved(MouseEvent e){}

public void crop() {
    if(currentShape == null) return;
    PlanarImage image = imageCanvas.getImage();
    AffineTransform atx = imageCanvas.getTransform();
    Shape shape = AffineTransformUtil.inverseTransform(currentShape,atx);
    if(shape == null) return;
    Rectangle2D bounds = shape.getBounds2D();
    RenderedOp op = JAIOpUtil.cropImage(image, bounds);
    PlanarImage img = op.createInstance();
    imageCanvas.paintImage(img);
    cropped = true;
}

public void reset() {
    imageCanvas.eraseShapes();
    imageCanvas.reset();
    imageCanvas.paintImage(imageCanvas.getImage());
    imageCanvas.repaint();
}
}
```

The `Crop` constructor takes `CompositeCanvas` as the input. It saves the object in an instance variable called `imageCanvas`. The image to be cropped is drawn on this instance of `imageCanvas`.

When the mouse is pressed over the `imageCanvas`, the anchor for the rectangle is defined. The `mousePressed()` method calls `startDraw()` to do this. When the mouse is dragged, a rectangle is drawn interactively over the image. The `mouseDragged()` method calls the `draw()` method for this purpose. The `draw()` method first gets its off-screen graphical context. Using this context, `draw()` erases the previous rectangle and draws a new one at the current mouse position.

When the mouse is released, the rectangle is drawn permanently and the region of the image marked by the rectangle is cropped. The `mouseReleased()` method calls both `draw()` and `crop()`. The `draw()` method draws the rectangle one last time, and the `crop()` method crops the image within that rectangle. The `crop()` method obtains first the image and then the current transformation from the image canvas. The latter is necessary because the original image might have been manipulated before cropping. The current rectangle is inverse-transformed so that it is mapped onto the original image space. The bounds of the resulting shape are then passed to the `crop Image()` method shown in Listing 12.9.

Note that if the shape is not a rectangle, the cropped region will not match the drawn shape because the Crop operator takes only rectangle bounds as the input parameter. For example, if you rotate the image and deposit a rectangle, the cropped region may not match the rectangle drawn. The reason is that application of inverse transformation to a rectangle may not result in a rectangle. The Crop operator computes the rectangle bounds of the transformed shape.

Figure 12.7 shows a screen shot of the application in which the displayed image is ready to be cropped. Figure 12.8 shows the result of the crop operation.

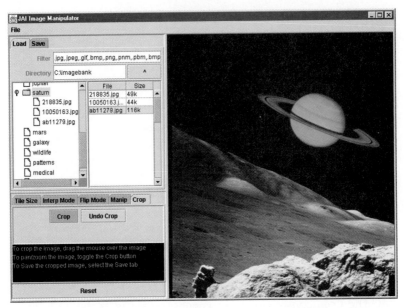

FIGURE 12.7 Cropping an image

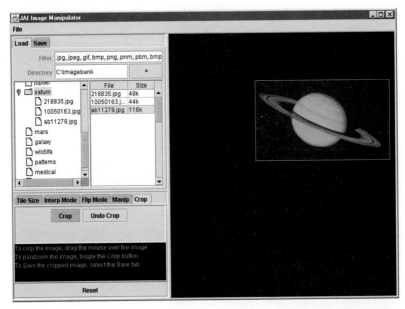

FIGURE 12.8 The cropped image

A GUI for the Crop Feature

Listing 12.11 shows the code that creates a panel for the crop feature in the image manipulator. The `CropPanel` class is an inner class of the `RenderedImage Manipulator1.java` class.

LISTING 12.11   The CropPanel class

```java
class CropPanel extends JPanel implements TabPanel, MouseListener{
    Crop crop;
    PlanarImage origImage;

    public CropPanel(Crop cr){
        crop = cr;
        createUI();
    }
    public void mouseReleased(MouseEvent e) {
        PlanarImage img = viewer.getDisplayImage();
        saver.setDisplayImage(img);
    }
    public void mousePressed(MouseEvent e) {}
    public void mouseClicked(MouseEvent e){}
    public void mouseEntered(MouseEvent e){}
    public void mouseExited(MouseEvent e){}
    public void openPanel() {
        crop.setCropOn(true);
        panzoom.setPanZoomOn(false);
        origImage = viewer.getImage();
    }
    public void closePanel(){
        panzoom.setPanZoomOn(true);
    }

    protected void createUI() {
        JButton uncrop = new JButton("Undo Crop");
        uncrop.addActionListener(
            new ActionListener() {
                public void actionPerformed(ActionEvent e) {
                    crop.reset();
                    if(origImage != null) viewer.setImage(origImage);
                }
            }
        );
        JToggleButton cropb = new JToggleButton("Crop");
        cropb.addActionListener(
            new ActionListener() {
                public void actionPerformed(ActionEvent e) {
                    JToggleButton jt = (JToggleButton)e.getSource();
                    boolean state = jt.isSelected();
                    crop.setCropOn(state);
                    if(state) {
                        jt.setText("Crop");
                        panzoom.setPanZoomOn(false);

                    }
```

continued

```
        else {
            jt.setText("Pan/Zoom");
            ((CompositeCanvas)viewer).eraseShapes();
            PlanarImage dispImage = viewer.getDisplayImage();
            if(dispImage!= null) viewer.setImage(dispImage);
            panzoom.setPanZoomOn(true);
        }
    }
}
);
cropb.setSelected(true);
JTextArea textArea = new JTextArea(2, 15);
textArea.setBackground(Color.black);
textArea.setForeground(Color.green);
textArea.setText("To crop the image, drag the mouse over the image \n" +
                "To pan/zoom the image, toggle the Crop button \n"+
                "To Save the cropped image, select the Save tab");
JPanel crpanel = new JPanel(new FlowLayout());
crpanel.add(cropb);
crpanel.add(uncrop);
setLayout(new GridLayout(2,1));
add( crpanel);
add(textArea);
    }
}
```

Figure 12.7 shows the frame produced by the code in Listing 12.11. The **Crop** button lets you toggle between crop and pan/zoom. The event-handling method for this button calls the `setCropOn()` method to turn on and off the crop feature. This means that when the crop feature is off, the pan/zoom feature is on. Clicking on **Undo Crop** calls the `reset()` method of the `Crop` class, which restores the original image.

Both the `Crop` and the `CropPanel` classes are registered for `mouse` events. When the mouse is released, the `mouse` events need to be sent in a particular order; that is, the `mouseReleased()` method must be invoked first in `Crop` and then in `CropPanel`. In the `Crop` object the `mouseReleased()` method crops the image, and in the `CropPanel` object it saves the cropped image. To accomplish this chaining of events, we use the `AWTEventMulticaster` class:

```
viewer = new CompositeCanvasJAI();
crop = new Crop((CompositeCanvasJAI)viewer);
CropPanel croppan = new CropPanel(crop);
viewer.addMouseMotionListener(crop);
MouseListener ml = AWTEventMulticaster.add(
                    (MouseListener)crop,
                    (MouseListener)croppan);
viewer.addMouseListener(ml);
```

This code is in the `createUI()` method of the `RenderedImageManipulator1.java` class. The `viewer` object represents the canvas in Figures 12.7 and 12.8, which is created from the `CompositeCanvasJAI` class.

Projections

Before we get into the details of perspective transformation, let's briefly look at the basics of projection. As you probably know, projections play an important role in many diverse areas, including graphics (especially three-dimensional graphics) and engineering drawing.

A projection is simply a two-dimensional mapping or view of an object on a viewing plane. Two types of projections are widely used: parallel and perspective projections. A *parallel* projection is obtained by transformation of the coordinate positions along parallel lines (see Figure 12.9). A *perspective* projection is obtained by transformation of the coordinates along lines that converge to a point called the *vanishing point* or *projection reference point* (see Figure 12.10).

As you might have guessed, parallel projections don't produce realistic views of the object, but they preserve relative proportions. On the other hand, perspective projections produce realistic views but do not preserve relative proportions.

Parallel projections are used extensively in engineering drawings because they produce accurately scaled drawings of a three-dimensional object. However, our interest in this section is more on perspective projections because JAI supports an API for perspective transformation.

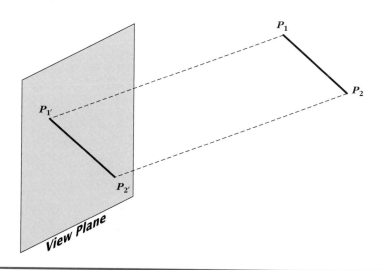

FIGURE 12.9   Parallel projection

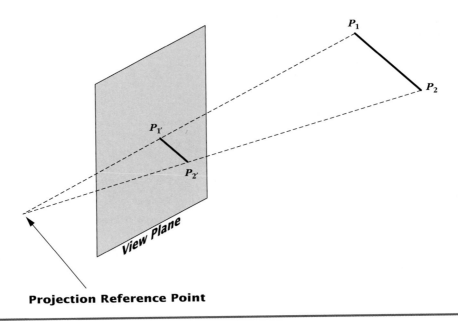

Projection Reference Point

FIGURE 12.10   Perspective projection

Perspective Transformation

The perspective transformation is similar to the affine transformation in many respects. For example, you can represent it in a homogeneous coordinate system. The
difference is that with perspective transformations, parallel lines may not remain
parallel.

A 3 × 3 matrix also represents the perspective transformation. If $P_{(x,y)}$ is the point
to be transformed to $P'_{(x,y)}$ by the perspective transformation, then

$$P'_{(x,y)} = T - P_{(x,y)}$$

where T is the 3 × 3 transformation matrix—that is,

$$\begin{bmatrix} x' \\ y' \\ w \end{bmatrix} = \begin{bmatrix} \texttt{m00} & \texttt{m01} & \texttt{m02} \\ \texttt{m10} & \texttt{m11} & \texttt{m12} \\ \texttt{m20} & \texttt{m21} & \texttt{m22} \end{bmatrix}$$

$$\begin{bmatrix} x \\ y \\ 1 \end{bmatrix} = \begin{bmatrix} \texttt{m00} \times x + \texttt{m01} \times y + \texttt{m02} \\ \texttt{m10} \times x + \texttt{m11} \times y + \texttt{m12} \\ \texttt{m20} \times x + \texttt{m21} \times y + \texttt{m22} \end{bmatrix}$$

In these matrices, `m00, m01, . . . , m22` are the coefficients of the perspective transformation matrix.

Just as with the affine transformation, you must perform the inverse transformation to obtain $P_{(x,y)}$ from $P'_{(x,y)}$.

Perspective transformation can be applied to a point, a shape, or an image. The `PerspectiveTransform` class is designed along the same lines as the `java.awt.geom.AffineTransform` class. Let's look at the `PerspectiveTransform` class next.

Constructing a PerspectiveTransform Object

Just like the `AffineTransform` class, `PerspectiveTransform` has a default constructor with no arguments and several additional constructors that take a 3 × 3 matrix as input. The different flavors of the constructors take this matrix in different forms. In addition, `PerspectiveTransform` has a constructor that takes an `AffineTransform` object as input.

The methods that translate, scale, rotate, and shear have the same or similar signatures as those in the `AffineTransform` class, as do the methods that perform inverse transformation, concatenation, and preconcatenation. The `PerspectiveTransform` class does not have some of the methods that `AffineTransform` has, including `createTransformedShape()` and `deltaTransform()`.

In the sections that follow we'll look at the methods that are different from those of the `AffineTransform` class.

Quadrilateral-to-Quadrilateral Transformation

The following method creates a `PerspectiveTransform` object that maps an arbitrary quadrilateral onto another arbitrary quadrilateral:

- `public static PerspectiveTransform getQuadToQuad(float x0, float y0,`
  `                                    float x1, float y1,`
  `                                    float x2, float y2,`
  `                                    float x3, float y3,`
  `                                    float x0p, float y0p,`
  `                                    float x1p, float y1p,`
  `                                    float x2p, float y2p,`
  `                                    float x3p, float y3p)`

The first eight parameters are the corner coordinates of the source quadrilateral, and the remaining eight parameters are the corner coordinates of the destination quadrilateral. Another flavor of this method takes arguments of type `double`.

Quadrilateral-to-Square Transformation

The following method creates a `PerspectiveTransform` object that maps an arbitrary quadrilateral onto a unit square:

- ```
  public static PerspectiveTransform getQuadToSquare(float x0, float y0,
                                                     float x1, float y1,
                                                     float x2, float y2,
                                                     float x3, float y3)
  ```

The parameters of this method are the corner coordinates of the source quadrilateral. The destination square has unit dimensions; that is, the corner coordinates are (0, 0), (0, 1), (1, 0), and (1, 1). Another flavor of this method takes `double` parameters.

Square-to-Quadrilateral Transformation

The following method creates a `PerspectiveTransform` object that maps a unit square onto an arbitrary quadrilateral:

- ```
  public static PerspectiveTransform getSquareToQuad(float x0, float y0,
                                                     float x1, float y1,
                                                     float x2, float y2,
                                                     float x3, float y3)
  ```

The parameters of this method are the corner coordinates of the destination quadrilateral. The source square has unit dimensions; that is, the corner coordinates are (0, 0), (0, 1), (1, 0), and (1, 1). Another flavor of this method takes `double` parameters.

Unlike the affine transformation, the perspective transformation has no "Perspective" operator in JAI 1.0.2. However, the `PerspectiveTransform` class can be used with the Warp operator.

Warping

Both `AffineTransform` and `PerspectiveTransform` produce linear transformations. This means that a line can be transformed to another line, but never to a curve. Although this kind of transformation suffices for many applications, the need often arises in multimedia, as well as in scientific imaging, to warp an image—that is, produce rubber sheet–like transformations.

In multimedia, for instance, warping can produce funny and eye-catching images that can be used in advertisement. In scientific imaging, warping is used in image registration and image restoration. In satellite imagery, for instance, images of an area taken over a span of time are compared for changes. Likewise in medical imaging, images of the same anatomy are taken over a period of time and compared—for example, to detect growth of tumors. Because of the curvature involved, registration and matching of images in both cases can be a nonlinear process.

JAI has classes that can produce different types of warping. Figure 12.11 shows the relevant class hierarchy. In addition, the Warp operator in JAI uses these classes to generate a warped image.

Warp Types

JAI supports both linear and nonlinear warp operations. A warp operation can be considered an inverse operation—that is, mapping from a destination space to a source space. To put it simply, a region (i.e., a point or a shape) in one image is mapped to the corresponding region in another image. Consider the satellite imaging

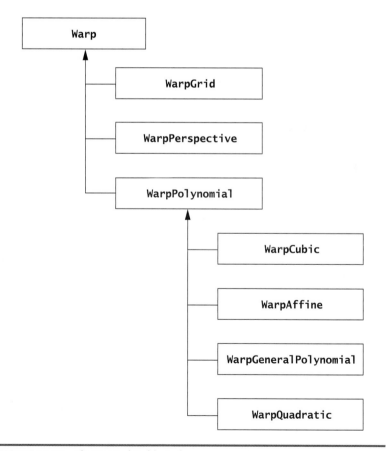

FIGURE 12.11   The Warp class hierarchy

example. In one such case a program that checks for deforestation maps a desired region in the latest image to the corresponding region in the previous image.

The sections that follow will look at each type of warp individually.

Polynomial Warp

For given (x, y) coordinates of the source image, the polynomial warp function generates the destination coordinate (X, Y).

The polynomial warp function is given by

$$X_{(x, y)} = \sum_{i=0}^{n} \sum_{j=0}^{i} a_{ij} \times x^{i-j} \times y^{j} \tag{12.1}$$

and

$$Y_{(x, y)} = \sum_{i=0}^{n} \sum_{j=0}^{i} b_{ij} \times x^{i-j} \times y^{j} \tag{12.2}$$

where X and Y are bivariate polynomial functions. This means that the X coordinate in the destination image is a function of both the x and y coordinates of the source image, and so is the Y coordinate. The variable n represents the degree of the warp polynomial.

If you evaluate equation (12.1) for different values of n, you will get the following coefficients of the polynomial:

- **For n = 1:** 1, x, y
- **For n = 2:** 1, x, y, x^2, xy, y
- **For n = m:** 1, x, y, x^2, xy, y, . . . , x^n, $x^{(n-1)y}$, . . . , $xy^{(n-1)}$, y^n

For a given value of n, the number of coefficients is calculated by $(n + 1)(n + 2)$.

The `WarpPolynomial` class represents the polynomial warp function, but it is an abstract class. As Figure 12.11 shows, `WarpGeneralPolynomial` is the concrete class that represents general polynomials.

JAI has three special cases of the polynomial warp functions: affine, quadratic, and cubic. As the names suggest, the degree of the polynomial of each function is 1, 2, and 3, respectively.

Affine Warp

The destination coordinates (X, Y) are given by the following linear equations:

$$X = p_{(x,y)} = a_1 + (a_2 \times x) + (a_3 \times y)$$

$$Y = q_{(x,y)} = a_4 + (a_5 \times x) + (a_6 \times y)$$

This case maps to a linear transformation. This operation is similar to performing an inverse affine transformation.

The `WarpAffine` class represents the affine warp function. The constructor for this class takes `AffineTransform` as input.

Quadratic Warp

The destination coordinates (X, Y) are given by the following quadratic equations:

$$X = p_{(x,y)} = a_1 + (a_2 \times x) + (a_3 \times y) + (a_4 \times x^2) + (a_5 \times xy) + (a_6 \times y^2)$$

$$Y = q_{(x,y)} = a_7 + (a_8 \times x) + (a_9 \times y) + (a_{10} \times x^2) + (a_{11} \times xy) + (a_{12} \times y^2)$$

The quadratic warp function is a nonlinear transformation.

Cubic Warp

The destination coordinates (X, Y) are given by the following cubic equations:

$$X = p_{(x,y)} = a_1 + (a_2 \times x) + (a_3 \times y) + (a_4 \times x^2) + (a_5 \times xy) + (a_6 \times y^2)$$
$$+ (a_7 \times x^3) + (a_8 \times x^2y) + (a_9 \times xy^2) + (a_{10} \times y^3)$$

$$Y = q_{(x,y)} = a_{11} + (a_{12} \times x) + (a_{13} \times y) + (a_{14} \times x^2) + (a_{15} \times xy) + (a_{16} \times y^2)$$
$$+ (a_{17} \times x^3) + (a_{18} \times x^2y) + (a_{19} \times xy^2) + (a_{20} \times y^3)$$

The cubic warp function is a nonlinear transformation.

Perspective Warp

Just like affine warp, perspective warp produces a linear mapping. Perspective warp can remove perspective distortions—that is, farther objects appearing smaller compared to nearer ones. This type of warp can be used in digital photography and astronomy. The perspective warp operation is similar to inverse perspective transformation.

Grid Warp

The grid warp concept is similar to piecewise linear interpolation. In grid warp, an image is divided into rectangular grids, and on each grid a warping function is applied. These grids are then combined through bilinear interpolation.

As you can imagine, polynomial warp is computation intensive. You can resort to grid warp to improve the performance and at the same time achieve better quality.

Using the Warp Operator

The Warp operator takes one rendered image as a source, as well as the parameters listed in Table 12.8.

As Figure 12.11 shows, `Warp` is the base class of all warp operations. The warp parameter can be any one of six types, each of which is a descendant of `Warp`.

Before we use the Warp operator, let's look at the `Warp` classes.

Constructing a Warp Object

The Warp operator needs a `Warp` object. To construct a `Warp` object, you need to use the constructors of `Warp` subclasses. In the current implementation (JAI 1.0.2), there are no factory methods in the `Warp` class. Instead the `WarpPolynomial` class has a factory method. Notice in Figure 12.11 that `WarpPolynomial` is a subclass of `Warp` and has four subclasses of its own. You can construct any of these four objects by using the following factory method:

◆ `public static WarpPolynomial createWarp(float[] sourceCoords,`
                                        `int sourceOffset,`
                                        `float[] destCoords,`
                                        `int destOffset,`
                                        `int numCoords,`
                                        `float preScaleX,`
                                        `float preScaleY,`
                                        `float postScaleX,`
                                        `float postScaleY,`
                                        `int degree)`

This method returns an instance of `WarpPoynomial`. With this method you can create a polynomial of any degree.

TABLE 12.8 Warp Operator Parameters

OPERATOR NAME	PARAMETER	TYPE	DEFAULT VALUE	DESCRIPTION
Warp	warp	Warp	None	The Warp object can be one of WarpAffine, WarpGrid, WarpPerspective, WarpPolynomial, WarpQuadratic, and WarpOpImage.
	interpolation	Interpolation	INTERP_ NEAREST	

The source coordinates are prescaled by the factors `preScaleX` and `preScaleY`. After the polynomial function has been applied, the destination coordinates are scaled back by `postScaleX` and `postScaleY`. The process of prescaling and postscaling is required for better precision.

You can also construct a `Warp` object by directly calling a desired constructor. Here's an example:

```
AffineTransform atx = AffineTransform.getRotateInstance(0.5d);
Warp warpObj = new WarpAffine(atx);
```

This abstract class has several methods that are default implementations.

In warping, images are mapped from destination to source pixels. The `Warp` class has methods for computing rectangular regions in the source image that correspond to rectangular regions in the destination image. As in interpolation, the mapping may not result in integer coordinates in the source image.

Now let's look at the methods. At the center of the `Warp` class is the following abstract method:

◆ **public abstract float[] warpSparseRect(int x,**
                                             int y,
                                             int width,
                                             int height,
                                             int periodX,
                                             int periodY,
                                             float[] destRect)

The parameters `x`, `y`, `width`, and `height` represent the ULHC and the dimensions of the destination rectangle. The `periodX` and `periodY` parameters are the horizontal and vertical sampling rates. The method returns an array of floating-point coordinates in the source image. Because it is an abstract method, subclasses must implement it.

The following method is a default implementation of the `warpSparseRect()` method:

◆ **public int[] warpSparseRect(int x,**
                                  int y,
                                  int width,
                                  int height,
                                  int periodX,
                                  int periodY,
                                  int subsampleBitsH,
                                  int subsampleBitsV,
                                  int[] destRect)

This method returns the source coordinates as integers.

The `Warp` class has two flavors of the `warpRect()` method that returns the sub-pixel source image coordinates:

1. ```
public float[] warpRect(int x, int y,
                        int width, int height,
                        float[] destRect)
```
2. ```
public int[] warpRect(int x, int y,
                      int width, int height,
                      int subsampleBitsH,
                      int subsampleBitsV,
                      int[] destRect)
```

To perform integer arithmetic, we set pixel positions by scaled integer coordinates, the accuracy of which is set by the `sampleBitsH` and `sampleBitsV` parameters.

The following two methods transform a point:

1. ```
public float[] warpPoint(int x, int y, float[] destRect)
```
2. ```
public int[] warpPoint(int x, int y,
                       int subsampleBitsH,
                       int subsampleBitsV,
                       int[] destRect)
```

Because of the nonlinearity, a given source pixel can be one of various different pixels.

Here are the rest of the methods:

♦ `public java.awt.Rectangle mapSourceRect(java.awt.Rectangle sourceRect)`

This method computes an enclosing rectangle in the destination image. The pixels within this rectangle are affected by transformation of the pixels of the rectangle specified by `sourceRect`.

♦ `public java.awt.Rectangle mapDestRect(java.awt.Rectangle destRect)`

This method computes a rectangle to enclose the region of the source image. Pixels within this rectangle are required to produce the rectangular output region specified by `destRect`.

An Example of Applying the Warp Operator

Now that we've looked at the Warp operator and various classes that represent different types of warping, it's time for an example. Let's use the factory method in the `WarpPolynomial` class to construct a `Warp` object from a set of source and destination coordinates. To generate source coordinates, we'll click the mouse over the image. To generate destination coordinates, we'll add random displacements to the corresponding source coordinates. With a `Warp` object as the parameter, we'll apply the Warp operator to generate a random-looking warped image. To build this example, we'll create two classes: `WarpApp` and `WarpImageGenerator`.

`WarpApp` is the main class that creates an application frame with two image canvases—one to display the source image and another to display the warped image—and the GUI for selecting images and setting the degree of the polynomial. Because this class is similar to many other application classes we have developed in this and preceding chapters, we will not show the code here.

The `WarpImageGenerator` class generates a warped image from a planar image. `WarpApp` constructs the `WarpImageGenerator` object and registers this object for `mouse` events to receive the coordinates of the point at which the user clicks the mouse on the source image canvas. When the `WarpImageGenerator` object receives a sufficient number of coordinates, it generates the warped image. The number of coordinates required to generate a warped image depends on the degree of the warp polynomial. Listing 12.12 shows the code for the `WarpImageGenerator` class.

> **Note:** The code for `WarpApp` and `WarpImageGenerator` is available on the book's Web page in the directory `src/chapter12/warp`.

LISTING 12.12   Generating a warped image

```
package com.vistech.jai.render;
import java.awt.*;
import java.awt.event.*;
import java.awt.image.*;
import java.io.*;
import javax.swing.*;
import javax.swing.event.*;
import java.awt.geom.*;
import javax.media.jai.*;
import java.awt.image.renderable.*;
import com.vistech.imageviewer.*;

public class WarpImageGenerator implements MouseListener{
    protected float srcCoord[];
    protected float destCoord[];
    protected int polyDegree = 1;
    protected int numPointsNeeded = (polyDegree + 1)*(polyDegree + 2)/2;
    protected int currentNumPoints =0;
    protected RenderedImage sourceImage = null;
    protected PlanarImage destImage = null;
    protected int imageWidth, imageHeight;
    protected WarpPolynomial warp;

    public WarpImageGenerator(){
        setPolyDegree(polyDegree);
    }
```

continued

```java
public WarpImageGenerator(RenderedImage sourceImage){
    this.sourceImage = sourceImage;
}

public void setSourceImage(RenderedImage sourceImage){
    if(sourceImage == null) return;
    this.sourceImage = sourceImage;
    imageWidth = sourceImage.getWidth();
    imageHeight = sourceImage.getHeight();
}

public RenderedImage getSourceImage(){
    return sourceImage;
}

public PlanarImage getDestImage(){ return destImage; }

public void setPolyDegree(int degree){
    polyDegree = degree;
    numPointsNeeded = computeNumPoints(degree);
    srcCoord = new float[2*(numPointsNeeded+1)];
    destCoord = new float[2*(numPointsNeeded+1)];
}

public int getPolyDegree() { return polyDegree; }

protected PlanarImage generateWarpImage() {
    if(sourceImage == null) return null;
    if (currentNumPoints >= numPointsNeeded) {
        WarpPolynomial warp = WarpPolynomial.createWarp(srcCoord, 0,
                                        destCoord, 0,
                                        2*currentNumPoints,
                                        1.0f/imageWidth,
                                        1.0f/imageHeight,
                                        (float)imageWidth,
                                        (float)imageHeight,
                                        polyDegree);
        return createDestImage(sourceImage, warp);
    }
    return null;
}

public int computeNumPoints(int degree) {
    if(degree <0) return -1;
    return (degree + 1)*(degree + 2)/2;
}

public static RenderedOp createDestImage(RenderedImage img,
                                Warp warp){
    ParameterBlock pb = new ParameterBlock();
    pb.addSource(img);
    pb.add(warp);
    pb.add(Interpolation.getInstance(Interpolation.INTERP_NEAREST));
    return JAI.create("warp", pb);
}
```

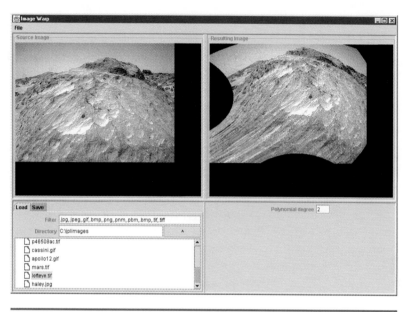

FIGURE 12.12   Appying the Warp operator

```
public void addPoints(int x, int y) {
    srcCoord[2*currentNumPoints] = (float)x;
    srcCoord[2*currentNumPoints+1] = (float)y;
    destCoord[2*currentNumPoints] = (float)x + (float)Math.random()*10f;
    destCoord[2*currentNumPoints+1] = (float)y + (float)Math.random()*10f;
    if(currentNumPoints >=numPointsNeeded ) {
        destImage = generateWarpImage();
        currentNumPoints = 0;
        srcCoord = new float[2*(numPointsN...
        d...                 ...umtsNeeded+1)];
    }else currentNumPoints++;
}

public void mousePressed(MouseEvent e) {
    addPoints(e.getX(), e.getY());
}
public void mouseClicked(MouseEvent e) {}
public void mouseEntered(MouseEvent e) {}
public void mouseExited(MouseEvent e) {}
public void mouseReleased(MouseEvent e) {}
}
```

The `WarpImageGenerator` class has methods to set the source image and the degree of the warp polynomial. The number of points needed to generate the warped image is computed every time the degree of the polynomial is set.

To capture mouse clicks, the `WarpImageGenerator` class implements the `Mouse Listener` interface. The only `mouse` event method it uses is `mousePressed()`, which calls `addPoints()` to add to the array of source and destination coordinates. The destination coordinates are computed by the addition of a random number to the corresponding source coordinates. When the number of positions clicked is the same as the number of points needed to generate the warped image, `addPoints()` calls `generateWarpImage()`. The `addPoints()` method then resets the source and destination coordinates array.

The `generateWarpImage()` method constructs a `Warp` object from the source and destination coordinates collected by `addPoints()`. With the `Warp` object as a parameter, `addPoints()` calls `createDestImage()`.

The `createDestImage()` method uses the Warp operator to generate a planar image that is warped. Figure 12.12 shows a screen shot of an application with a source image and the corresponding destination image generated by application of the Warp operator.

Conclusion

Geometric image manipulation is an important part of a typical imaging application. With JAI APIs, combined with Java 2D APIs, you can build powerful image manipulation programs.

The quality of manipulated images depends on the interpolation algorithm used. JAI has implemented the popular nearest-neighbor, bilinear, and bicubic interpolation algorithms. If you wish to add your own interpolation algorithm, you can do so by extending the `Interpolation` class.

JAI has operators for all the standard affine operations. In addition, it has the Affine operator, which lets you use Java 2D's `AffineTransform` class. The image viewer example uses this approach to interactively manipulate images.

Besides affine transformation, JAI supports other linear and nonlinear transformations needed for advanced imaging applications. In the current implementation (Java 1.0.2), the supported transformations include perspective transformation and different types of warp transformation.

Manipulating Image Data in JAI

IN CHAPTER 12 WE LOOKED AT the JAI operators and classes that geometrically manipulate images. These operators change the geometry of the image. In this chapter we'll look at the JAI operators and classes that do not change the geometry, but manipulate the pixels to change the appearance of the image. We'll classify these operators as image data manipulation operators.

We can divide the image data manipulation operators into the following categories:

- Area operators
- Edge detection operators
- Color quantization operators
- Point operators
- Frequency operators

In this chapter we'll look at most of the image data manipulation operators that are currently available in JAI. These operators can be used in applications that serve a wide variety of purposes, ranging from image enhancement to frequency domain analysis.

Operations for Manipulating Image Data

There are three types of image data manipulation operations:

1. **Unary.** Unary operations involve just one image and are applied to each pixel of the image. For example, a Not operator applies the bitwise NOT operator to all the pixels and places the resulting pixels in another image.

2. **Monadic.** Monadic operations involve a single image and are performed with each pixel in the image and a value. For example, the AddConst operator adds a constant value to each pixel in the image and stores the results in a separate destination image. Unless changed by the `ImageLayout` hint, the destination image has the same data type, number of bands, and image bounds.

3. **Dyadic.** Dyadic operations involve two images. The operation is performed between the corresponding pixel values of both images, and the result is placed in a separate destination image. For example, the Add operator adds the corresponding pixels of two images and stores the resulting values in a separate destination image.

   Dyadic operations require that the bounds of the images intersect (see Figure 13.1). If the bounds don't intersect, an image with zero width and height will be returned. You can change the intersection criteria by providing an `Image Layout` hint.

   The number of bands and data types of the source images need not match. Normally, the number of bands in the destination image equals the lesser of the number of bands of the source images. Likewise, the data type of the destination image is the smaller data type of the two source images.

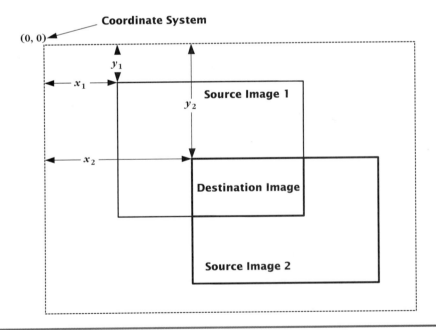

FIGURE 13.1   The default dyadic operation

Applying Operators

We have built two applications to test the various prebuilt image data manipulation operators:

1. **ImageProcessor.** This application is similar to the one we developed in Chapter 8 (see the section titled Using Filters to Manipulate Image Data) to apply imaging operators implemented by filter classes such as `ColorConvertOp`, `Band CombineOp`, and `LookupOp`. JAI has similar operators, and we'll use the same format to run these operators. This application is used for single-input/single-output types of operators.

   To run this application, type "java app.ImageProcessor <image file>" on the command line. Once you have launched the application, click on the desired operator.

> **Note:** The source code for `ImageProcessor` is available on the book's Web page in the directory `src/chapter13/imageprocessor`.

2. **RunOperators.** This application supports the three types of operations mentioned in the preceding section. With this application you should be able to view the source and destination images when an operator is applied. Unary and monadic operators take one source image, and dyadic operators take two. This viewer is capable of switching between one and two viewports for displaying source images. Both the source and the destination viewports provide the ability to pan and zoom the displayed images.

   To run this application, type "java app.RunOperators" on the command line. Notice that this command does not require the image file name. This application is built with the `FileBrowser` bean, which lets you select images from your local machine. Once you have launched the application, go to the file browser to select images. If the operator selected is dyadic, you need to select one more image to make the operator work.

> **Note:** The source code for `RunOperators` is available on the book's Web page in the directory `src/chapter13/operators`.

Area Operators

In Chapter 8 we developed a few spatial operator classes by implementing the `BufferedImageOp` and `RasterOp` interfaces. Implementing an operator in Java 2D appears to require a bit of coding effort. JAI makes this task easier by providing numerous commonly used operators and a few classes that expand the Java 2D functionality.

In this discussion we'll focus on two spatial operator classes: `KernelJAI` and `LookupTableJAI`. The Convolve operator requires a `KernelJAI` object as a parameter. Likewise, the Lookup operator requires the `LookupTableJAI` object as a parameter.

Using the KernelJAI Class

Just like the `Kernel` class in Java 2D, `KernelJAI` represents the kernel used for the imaging operation. However, `KernelJAI` is not a subclass of the `Kernel` class.

As we'll see, the `KernelJAI` object is a parameter for many JAI operators. The `KernelJAI` class also has several predefined kernels as `KernelJAI` objects. Because these kernels are defined as constants, you can use them directly with the operators. Table 13.1 lists all the predefined kernels in the `KernelJAI` class.

We can pass `KernelJAI` objects as parameters to the *JAI.createXXX()* method. The first kernel is an edge detection kernel. To perform edge detection, you must use the Convolve operator with the `kernelJAI` parameter.

TABLE 13.1 Predefined Kernels in `KernelJAI`

KERNEL	TYPE	DESCRIPTION
GRADIENT_MASK_SOBEL_HORIZONTAL	Edge detector	Sobel horizontal
GRADIENT_MASK_SOBEL_VERTICAL	Edge detector	Sobel vertical
DITHER_MASK_441	Ordered dither filter	A 4 × 4 × 1 kernel; used for dithering 8-bit grayscale to 1-bit grayscale
DITHER_MASK_443	Ordered dither filter	A 4 × 4 × 3 kernel; used for dithering 8-bit grayscale to 1-bit grayscale
ERROR_FILTER_FLOYD_STEINBERG	Error distribution filter	Floyd-Steinberg filter model
ERROR_FILTER_JARVIS	Error distribution filter	Jarvis-Judice-Ninke filter model
ERROR_FILTER_STUCKI	Error distribution filter	Stucki filter model

Constructing a Kernel

Just as in Java 2D, you can construct your own kernel and pass it to a static method, in this case *JAI.createXXX()*, as a parameter to an appropriate operator. The KernelJAI class has the following constructors:

1. `public KernelJAI(int width, int height, float[] data)`
2. `public KernelJAI(int width, int height, int xOrigin, int yOrigin, float[] data)`
3. `public KernelJAI(java.awt.image.Kernel k)`
4. `public KernelJAI(int width, int height, int xOrigin, int yOrigin, float[] dataH, float[] dataV)`

The xOrigin and yOrigin parameters represent the position of the pixel under consideration with respect to the upper left-hand corner element of the kernel. The default origin is computed by (width/2, height/2).

The fourth constructor lets you construct separable kernels. In other words, you can provide two vectors of kernel data. The isSeparable() method tells whether a KernelJAI object has a separable kernel.

The KernelJAI class has several methods that return attributes of the kernel, including data, height, width, origin, left padding, right padding, top padding, and bottom padding. The following example illustrates the use of the constructors:

```
public static RenderedOp  blur(PlanarImage image) {
   float blurmatrix[] = {1/16f, 1/8f, 1/16f,
                         1/8f, 1/4f, 1/8f,
                         1/16f, 1/8f, 1/16f};
   KernelJAI  blurKernel = new KernelJAI (3,3,blurmatrix);
   return JAI.create("convolve", image, blurKernel);
}
```

Convolution

We discussed convolution in Chapter 8. As Table 13.2 shows, the Convolve operator takes just one parameter, which is of KernelJAI type.

Convolution finds applications in many areas of image processing, including image enhancement and image analysis.

TABLE 13.2   Convolve Operator Parameters

OPERATOR NAME	PARAMETER	TYPE	DEFAULT VALUE	DESCRIPTION
Convolve	kernel	KernelJAI	None	Encapsulation of the kernel data

Image Enhancement

In image enhancement we attempt to sharpen image features with two primary goals in mind:

1. To improve the image display
2. To create a starting point for subsequent analysis

Image enhancement techniques include accentuation of edges and boundaries and adjustment of brightness and contrast. Many of these techniques are based on spatial operations performed on a neighborhood of pixels. So we can use the Convolve operator very effectively to enhance images for different purposes.

Let's look at some image enhancement examples that use the Convolve operator. Listings 13.1 and 13.2 show the implementation of sharpening and blurring operations, respectively. Figures 13.2 and 13.3 show the effects.

LISTING 13.1 Sharpening an image

```
public static RenderedOp sharpen(PlanarImage image) {
    float sharpMatrix[] = {-1.0f, -1.0f, -1.0f,
                           -1.0f,  9.0f, -1.0f,
                           -1.0f, -1.0f, -1.0f};
    KernelJAI  sharpKernel = new KernelJAI (3,3, sharpMatrix);
    return JAI.create("convolve", image, sharpKernel);
}
```

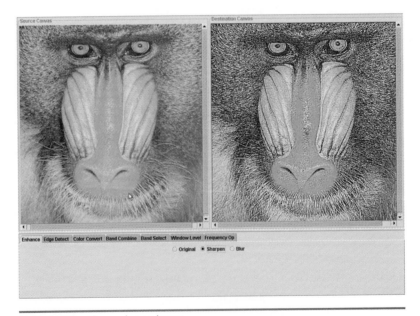

FIGURE 13.2 Sharpening an image

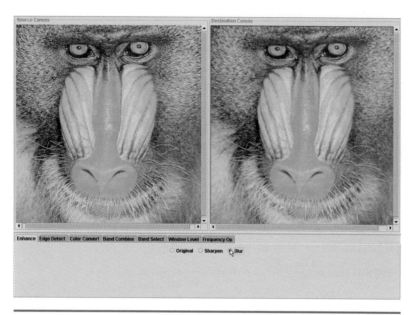

FIGURE 13.3   Blurring an image

LISTING 13.2   Blurring an image

```
public static RenderedOp  blur(PlanarImage image) {
   float blurmatrix[] = {1/16f, 1/8f, 1/16f,
                         1/8f, 1/4f, 1/8f,
                         1/16f, 1/8f, 1/16f};
   KernelJAI  blurKernel = new KernelJAI (3,3,blurmatrix);
   return JAI.create("convolve", image, blurKernel);
}
```

Spatial Filtering

JAI supports two filter operators: BoxFilter and MedianFilter. Just like Convolve, these are area operators. We implemented the GUI for selecting both of these filters in our RunOperators class earlier in the chapter.

First let's look at these filters in detail.

The Box Filter

The box filter is a low-pass filter that attenuates higher spatial frequencies. It can be implemented as a special case of convolution in which all neighborhood pixels have the same weight. This amounts to averaging of pixels.

The operator name in JAI for this filter is BoxFilter. Table 13.3 shows its parameters.

TABLE 13.3 BoxFilter Operator Parameters

OPERATOR NAME	PARAMETER	TYPE	DEFAULT VALUE	DESCRIPTION
BoxFilter	width	int	None	Width of the box
	height	int	None	Height of the box
	xKey	int	width/2	Position of the key element in the x direction
	yKey	int	height/2	Position of the key element in the y direction

Listing 13.3 shows an example that uses BoxFilter.

LISTING 13.3   Applying the BoxFilter operator

```
public static RenderedOp boxFilterImage(PlanarImage image,
                                        int wid, int ht,
                                        Point pixelPos){
    ParameterBlock pb = new ParameterBlock();
    pb.addSource(image);
    pb.add(wid);
    pb.add(ht);
    pb.add(pixelPos.x);
    pb.add(pixelPos.y);

    return JAI.create("BoxFilter", pb);
}
```

Figure 13.4 shows the effect of applying the box filter.

The Median Filter

The median filter computes pixel values in the destination image by computing the median of the source pixels within a specified window. The effect of median filtering is the removal of extraneous pixels that don't fit in the image. So median filtering, while simple, is a very effective noise reduction tool.

Just as in any convolution operation, a mask is moved on the image, pixel by pixel, each time the median value of the neighborhood pixels is computed. This value becomes the pixel value in the destination image.

Two factors affect the noise reduction by median filtering:

1. Mask shape

2. Window size

JAI has the prebuilt MedianFilter operator to perform median filtering. This filter supports three mask shapes: square, plus, and X (see Figure 13.5). It also supports separable median operation, which means it computes the median of the row-wise medians.

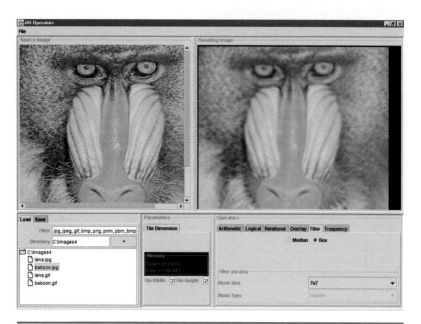

FIGURE 13.4   Applying the box filter

The `MedianFilterDescriptor` class has the following four constants defined to represent the mask types:

1. **`MEDIAN_MASK_SQUARE`.** This constant defines the square mask.

2. **`MEDIAN_MASK_SQUARE_SEPARABLE`.** This constant also defines the square mask, but the median is computed differently. The median of each row is computed first. Then the median value of all the row medians is computed to determine the destination pixel value.

3. **`MEDIAN_MASK_PLUS`.** This constant defines the plus-shaped mask.

4. **`MEDIAN_MASK_X`.** This constant defines the X-shaped mask.

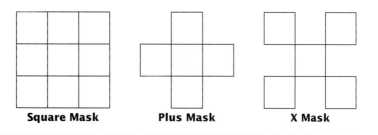

FIGURE 13.5   Median-filter mask types

Table 13.4 lists the parameters of the MedianFilter operator.

The `maskShape` parameter must be one of the four types defined in the `MedianFilterDescriptor` class. Listing 13.4 shows how to use the MedianFilter operator.

LISTING 13.4   Applying the MedianFilter operator

```
public static RenderedOp medianFilterImage(PlanarImage image,
                                           int maskShape,
                                           int maskSize){
    ParameterBlock pb = new ParameterBlock();

    pb.addSource(image);
    pb.add(maskShape);
    pb.add(maskSize);

    return JAI.create("MedianFilter", pb);
}
```

TABLE 13.4   MedianFilter Operator Parameters

OPERATOR NAME	PARAMETER	TYPE	DEFAULT VALUE	DESCRIPTION
MedianFilter	maskShape	int	MedianFilterDescriptor.MEDIAN_MASK_SQUARE	Shape of the mask (see Figure 13.5)
	maskSize	int	3	Size of the mask

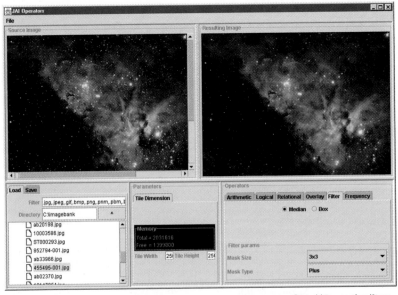

© World Perspectives/Stone

FIGURE 13.6   Applying a plus-shaped 3 × 3 median filter

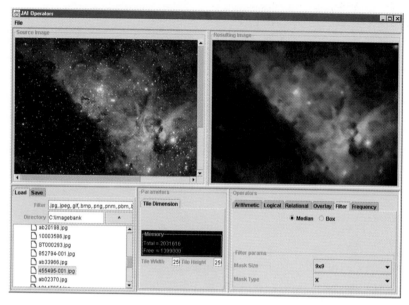

FIGURE 13.7 Applying an X-shaped 9 × 9 median filter

Figures 13.6 and 13.7 show the effects of applying the median filter with two different masks. The median filter requires two parameters: mask shape and size. The box filter requires only one parameter: mask size. The method in Listing 13.4 assumes that the pixel of interest is at the center of the mask. When you click on **Box,** the **Mask Type** combo box is disabled.

Edge Detection Operators

Edge detection is an important step in image analysis and computer vision applications. An edge detection algorithm typically extracts the boundaries from an image. Many edge detection algorithms have been developed over the years to suit a wide variety of applications.

Convolution is one of the techniques used in edge detection. With convolution, it is easy to develop an edge detection kernel that suits your application. When you have such needs, you can easily build a prototype using the Convolve operator.

Using the Convolve Operator

The `KernelJAI` class has two prebuilt edge detection kernels: the Sobel horizontal and vertical edge detection kernels (see Table 13.1). Listing 13.5 shows an example of these kernels in use.

LISTING 13.5   Applying the Sobel operators

```
public static RenderedOp sobelHoriz(PlanarImage image) {
    KernelJAI sobelHorizKernel = KernelJAI.GRADIENT_MASK_SOBEL_HORIZONTAL;
    return JAI.create("Convolve", image, sobelHorizKernel);
}

public static RenderedOp sobelVert(PlanarImage image) {
    KernelJAI sobelVertKernel = KernelJAI.GRADIENT_MASK_SOBEL_VERTICAL;
    return JAI.create("Convolve", image, sobelVertKernel);
}
```

The Sobel edge detectors are basic edge detection operators that are not used much in practice. You can consult any image-processing book for more sophisticated convolution-based edge detection operators. You can also create your own edge detection kernels and use the Convolve operator to execute them.

Using the GradientMagnitude Operator

As Listing 13.6 shows, you need to apply the edge detection operator in both the horizontal and the vertical directions to get a good edge. The GradientMagnitude operator does that for you in just one operation.

This operator computes the magnitude information from the horizontal and vertical values obtained by applying the edge detection algorithms in these directions.

The destination pixel value at any pixel position (x, y) is given by

$$D_{(x,y)} = \sqrt{H^2_{(x,y)} + V^2_{(x,y)}}$$

$H_{(x,y)}$ and $V_{(x,y)}$ are the horizontal and vertical pixel values computed by application of the edge detection algorithm.

TABLE 13.5   GradientMagnitude Operator Parameters

OPERATOR NAME	PARAMETER	TYPE	DEFAULT VALUE	DESCRIPTION
GradientMagnitude	mask1	KernelJAI	GRADIENT_MASK_SOBEL_HORIZONTAL	Horizontal mask
	mask2	KernelJAI	GRADIENT_MASK_SOBEL_VERTICAL	Vertical mask

The GradientMagnitude operator computes the destination pixel on a per band basis. It takes the Sobel edge kernels as the default kernels. Table 13.5 lists the parameters of the GradientMagnitude operator.

LISTING 13.6   Applying the GradientMagnitude operator with the default Sobel masks

```java
public static RenderedOp sobelGradientMagnitude(PlanarImage image) {

    KernelJAI sobelVertKernel = KernelJAI.GRADIENT_MASK_SOBEL_VERTICAL;
    KernelJAI sobelHorizKernel = KernelJAI.GRADIENT_MASK_SOBEL_HORIZONTAL;
    ParameterBlock pb = new ParameterBlock();
    pb.addSource(image);
    pb.add(sobelHorizKernel);
    pb.add(sobelVertKernel);

    return JAI.create("gradientmagnitude", pb);
}
```

The `sobelGradientMagnitude()` method uses both the Sobel horizontal and the Sobel vertical kernels as parameters for the GradientMagnitude operator. Figure 13.8 shows the original image and the edge-detected image obtained by application of the GradientMagnitude operator with Sobel edge kernels.

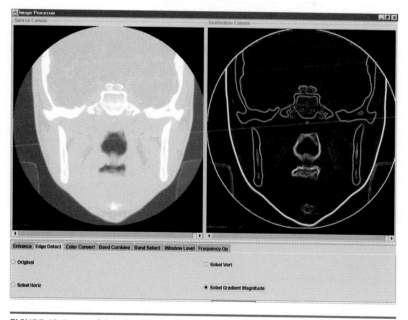

FIGURE 13.8   Applying the GradientMagnitude operator

Color Quantization Operators

Dithering is a type of compression scheme. When fewer bits are available to represent an image, dithering is performed. Dithering schemes choose the closest representation of the source to generate a destination image. JAI supports two types of dithering: ordered and error diffusion. Their respective operator names are OrderedDither and ErrorDiffusion. Both dithering schemes use lookup tables to generate the closest color. Table 13.1 lists the predefined kernels for both the ordered and error diffusion dithering schemes. Table 13.6 shows the parameters required.

Unlike OrderedDither, the ErrorDiffusion operator doesn't need an array of KernelJAI objects. The same kernel is applied to all the bands. The resulting image is a single-band image.

Implementing a Lookup Table

In the Java 2D chapters we used the LookupOp class to implement various operations, including inversion and window/level. JAI has an operator called Lookup that does the lookup using the lookup table supplied by the LookupTableJAI object. First let's look at this class.

TABLE 13.6   Dithering Operators

OPERATOR NAME	PARAMETER	TYPE	DEFAULT VALUE	DESCRIPTION
OrderedDither	colorMap	ColorCube	ColorCube.BYTE_496	The color map lookup table; one of ColorCube.BYTE_496 or ColorCube.BYTE_855.
	errorKernel	KernelJAI[]	KernelJAI.DITHER_MASK_443	One of the two ordered dither filters (see Table 13.1). The length of the KernelJAI array equals the number of bands in the image.
ErrorDiffusion	colorMap	LookupTableJAI	None	The color map lookup table.
	errorKernel	KernelJAI	KernelJAI.ERROR_FILTER_FLOYD_STEINBERG	One of the three error diffusion filters (see Table 13.1).

The `LookupTableJAI` class has many constructors with different data input types and offsets. The data types supported include `byte`, `short`, `int`, `float`, and `double`. `LookupTableJAI` can take one- or two-dimensional data, depending on whether the lookup table is for a single band or multiple bands, respectively. Table 13.7 lists the parameters of the Lookup operator.

Using the LookupTableJAI Class

We set up a lookup table for a single band or multiple bands using the `LookupTableJAI` class. Even though the functionality is similar, `LookupTableJAI` is not a subclass of the `LookupTable` class in Java 2D.

Unlike the `LookupTable` class, `LookupTableJAI` does not have subclasses for different types. Instead it has different flavors of constructors that take different types of table data. However, there is a subclass of `LookupTableJAI` called `ColorCube` that provides a fixed, invertible mapping between table indices and sample values.

Constructing a Lookup Table

The `LookupTableJAI` class has many constructors. The table data can be of any of the Java primitive types, and it can be one- or two-dimensional. If the data is one-dimensional, the same table is applied to all the bands. Here are all the `LookupTableJAI` constructors:

- For type byte:
  - `public LookupTableJAI(byte[] data)`
  - `public LookupTableJAI(byte[] data, int offset)`
  - `public LookupTableJAI(byte[][] data)`
  - `public LookupTableJAI(byte[][] data, int offset)`
  - `public LookupTableJAI(byte[][] data, int[] offsets)`

- For type short:
  - `public LookupTableJAI(short[] data, boolean isUShort)`
  - `public LookupTableJAI(short[] data, int offset, boolean isUShort)`
  - `public LookupTableJAI(short[][] data, boolean isUShort)`
  - `public LookupTableJAI(short[][] data, int offset, boolean isUShort)`
  - `public LookupTableJAI(short[][] data, int[] offsets,`
                  `boolean isUShort)`

TABLE 13.7 Lookup Operator Parameters

OPERATOR NAME	PARAMETER	TYPE	DEFAULT VALUE	DESCRIPTION
Lookup	lookupTable	lookupTableJAI	None	Lookup table

The `LookupTableJAI` class has similar methods for `int`, `float`, and `double` types.

The `LookupTableJAI` class also has several get methods for retrieving lookup data. In addition, it has the following important methods:

- `public int findNearestEntry(float[] pixel)`
- `public int lookup(int band, int value)`
- `public float lookupFloat(int band, int value)`
- `public double lookupDouble(int band, int value)`
- `public WritableRaster lookup(WritableRaster src)`
- `public WritableRaster lookup(Raster src, WritableRaster dst,`
  `                             Rectangle rect)`

Adjusting Window and Level

Window and level are often adjusted on medical images (see Chapter 8). The window operation is similar to contrast adjustment, and the level operation is similar to brightness adjustment.

The example shown in Listing 13.7 implements the window and level operations using the `LookupTableJAI` class and the Lookup operator.

LISTING 13.7 The JAIWindowLevel class

```
package com.vistech.jai.render;
import java.awt.image.*;
import java.io.*;
import com.vistech.jai.render.*;
import javax.media.jai.*;

public class JAIWindowLevel{
   protected int minValue =0;
   protected int maxValue =255;
   protected int MIN_SCREEN_VALUE = 0;
   protected int MAX_SCREEN_VALUE = 255;
   protected int LUT_SIZE = 256;
   protected int lutSize = LUT_SIZE;
   protected int window, level;
   protected PlanarImage image;
   protected JAIImageCanvas imageCanvas;

   public JAIWindowLevel(PlanarImage image, JAIImageCanvas imageCanvas) {
      this.image = image;
      this.imageCanvas = imageCanvas;
   }
```

```
public void setLUTSize(int size) {
   if(size <=0) return;
   lutSize = size;
}

public int getLUTSize(){return lutSize;}

public void setWindow(int win) { window = win;}
public void setLevel(int lev) {level = lev; }

public void setWindowLevel(int win, int lev) {
   LookupTableJAI blut = createLookupTable(win, lev);
   RenderedOp op = JAI.create("lookup",image, blut);
   imageCanvas.setImage(op);
   window = win;
   level = lev;
}

protected LookupTableJAI createLookupTable(int win, int lev) {
   int windowStart= lev-win/2;
   int windowEnd  = lev+win/2;
   if(windowStart <=0) windowStart =0;
   if(windowEnd > lutSize) windowEnd = lutSize;
   byte lut[] = new byte[lutSize];
   double windowMappingRatio =
            (MAX_SCREEN_VALUE-MIN_SCREEN_VALUE)/(double)(win);
   for(int i=0;i<windowStart;i++) {
       lut[i] = (byte)MIN_SCREEN_VALUE;
   }
   for(int i = windowStart; i< windowEnd; i++) {
       lut[i] = (byte)((i-windowStart)* windowMappingRatio);
   }
   for(int i = windowEnd; i< lutSize; i++) {
       lut[i] = (byte)MAX_SCREEN_VALUE;
   }
   return  new LookupTableJAI(lut,0);
}
}
```

The `createLookupTable()` method generates a new lookup table every time the window or level value is changed. This method generates the lookup table data on the basis of the `window` and `level` values. It uses this data to construct a `LookupTableJAI` object.

We will use the `LookupTableJAI` class to implement an example that adjusts window and level. In actual medical imaging systems, a variety of GUIs are used for interactively adjusting the window width and level. These interfaces vary from trackball movement to mouse dragging. The `JAIWindowLevel` class (see Listing 13.7) can be used with any GUI.

Figure 13.9 shows a sample implementation of `JAIWindowLevel`. The GUI uses two sliders, one each for window and level. Listing 13.8 shows the code for the class that implements this GUI.

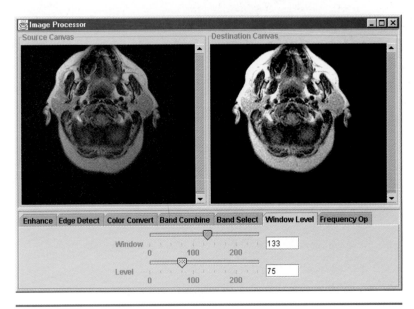

FIGURE 13.9 Adjusting window and level

LISTING 13.8 The `WindowLevelGUI` class

```
public class WindowLevelGUI extends JPanel {
    protected JSlider windowSlider;
    protected JSlider levelSlider;
    protected JTextField windowField;
    protected JTextField levelField;
    protected int minValue =0;
    protected int maxValue =255;
    protected int window, level;
    protected JAIWindowLevel wl;

    public WindowLevelGUI(JAIWindowLevel wl ){
        this.wl = wl;
        init();
    }
    protected  void init(){  add(createWindowLevelPanel());}

    public JPanel createWindowLevelPanel (){
        int brightStartValue = 50;
        windowField = new JTextField(5);
        levelField = new JTextField(5);

        windowField.setText(Integer.toString(brightStartValue));
        windowSlider = new JSlider(minValue,maxValue, brightStartValue);
        levelSlider = new JSlider(minValue,maxValue, brightStartValue);
```

```
windowField.addActionListener(
    new ActionListener() {
        public void actionPerformed(ActionEvent e){
            try {
                String str = ((JTextField)e.getSource()).getText();
                int value = (Integer.valueOf(str)).intValue();
                windowSlider.setValue((int)value);
                wl.setWindowLevel(window,level);

            } catch (Exception e1){}
        }
    }
);

windowSlider.addChangeListener(
    new ChangeListener(){
        public void stateChanged(ChangeEvent e){
            Object obj = e.getSource();
            if(obj instanceof JSlider) {
                JSlider jsr = (JSlider)obj;
                window = ((JSlider)(e.getSource())).getValue();
                wl.setWindowLevel(window, level);
                windowField.setText(Integer.toString(window));
            }
        }
    }
);

// Similar code for level field and level slider

JPanel brightpan = new JPanel();
// Gridbag layout
return brightpan;
    }
}
```

The GUI implemented by `WindowLevelGUI` has two sliders and two text fields. You can input the value by entering it in the text field or by adjusting the slider. The `createWindowLevelPanel()` method creates the user interface for this panel. It also registers anonymous inner classes for handling the action events from text fields and change events from sliders. All the event-handling methods call the `setWindow Level()` method in the `JAIWindowLevel` class.

To run an example with the **Window Level** panel, type "java appImage Processor <image file>" on the command line. You will see a screen similar to the one in Figure 13.9.

Point Operators

A point operation operates on the image on a pixel-by-pixel basis without taking into consideration the neighboring pixels. Point operations do not change the image geometry. All point operations can be applied to both rendered and renderable images.

Applying Arithmetic Operators

Arithmetic operators are extremely useful in processing scientific images. You can perform a function on a pixel-by-pixel basis. JAI supports all four basic arithmetic operations: add, subtract, multiply, and divide. The following sections cover all the arithmetic operators.

Add

Table 13.8 lists the parameters for all the variations of addition operators.

Adding a Constant Value to an Image

The AddConst operator adds a constant value to every pixel in the image on a per band basis. Here's the pseudocode that generates destination image data:

```
for (int x=minX; x<width; x++)
    for (int y=minY; y<height; y++)
        for (int b=0; b<numBands; b++)
            destData[y][x][b] = sourceData[y][x][b] + constant[b];
```

The `minX` and `minY` parameters represent the ULHC coordinates of the image. The `width` and `height` parameters are the width and height of the image.

The AddConstToCollection operator adds a constant value to every pixel in all the images on a per band basis. The result is a collection class.

TABLE 13.8   Addition Operators

OPERATOR NAME	PARAMETER	TYPE	DEFAULT VALUE	DESCRIPTION
AddConst	constants	double[]	None	The constant value to be added to each band
AddConstToCollection	constants	double[]	None	The constant value to be added to each band
Add	This is a dyadic operator and requires no parameters. The corresponding pixels from both images are added to produce a combined image.			
AddCollection	This operation is performed on a collection of rendered or renderable images. The corresponding pixels from all images are added to produce a combined image. The operator requires no parameters.			

In both of the *AddConst* operations, if the length of the array is smaller than the number of bands, the constant value from the zeroth element is applied to all the bands.

Adding Two or More Images

The Add operator adds together the band values of the corresponding pixels of two source images. The AddCollection operator does this for a collection of images.

With all addition operations, if the result exceeds the maximum value supported by the destination image, it is clamped to the maximum value. Likewise, if the result goes below the minimum value supported by the destination image, it is clamped to the minimum value.

Listing 13.9 shows an example using the Add operator. The screen shot in Figure 13.10 shows the effect of this operator on two adjacent medical images.

LISTING 13.9   Adding two images

```
public static RenderedOp addImages(PlanarImage image1,
                                   PlanarImage image2 ) {
    ParameterBlock pb = new ParameterBlock();
    pb.addSource(image1);
    pb.addSource(image2);
    return JAI.create("add", pb);
}
```

FIGURE 13.10   Dyadic addition

Subtract

Subtraction is similar to addition. Table 13.9 lists the parameters for all the variations of subtraction operators.

Listing 13.10 shows how to use the Subtract operator, and Figure 13.11 shows the effect of applying this operator on two spatially consecutive images.

LISTING 13.10   Subtracting two images

```
public static RenderedOp subtractImages(PlanarImage image1,
                                        PlanarImage image2 ) {
    ParameterBlock pb = new ParameterBlock();
    pb.addSource(image1);
    pb.addSource(image2);
    return JAI.create("subtract", pb);
}
```

Multiply

Table 13.10 lists the parameters for all the variations of multiplication operators.

Listing 13.11 shows an example that uses the Multiply operator.

LISTING 13.11   Multiplying two images

```
public static RenderedOp multiplyImages(PlanarImage image1,
                                        PlanarImage image2 ) {
    ParameterBlock pb = new ParameterBlock();
    pb.addSource(image1);
    pb.addSource(image2);
    return JAI.create("multiply", pb);
}
```

TABLE 13.9   Subtraction Operators

OPERATOR NAME	PARAMETER	TYPE	DEFAULT VALUE	DESCRIPTION
SubtractConst	constants	double[]	None	Array of constant values to be subtracted from each band
SubtractFromConst	constants	double[]	None	Array of constant values from which each band value is subtracted
Subtract	This is a dyadic operator and requires no parameters. The pixel value from the first source image is subtracted from the corresponding pixel value of the second image.			

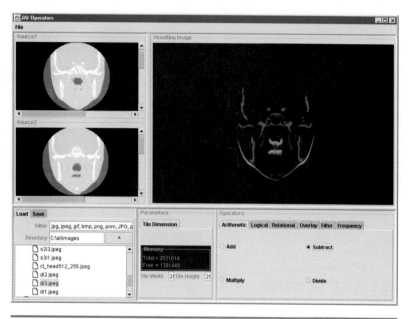

FIGURE 13.11 Dyadic subtraction

Divide

Table 13.11 lists the parameters for all the variations of division operators.
Listing 13.12 shows an example that uses the Divide operator.

LISTING 13.12 Dividing two images

```
public static RenderedOp divideImages(PlanarImage image1,
                                      PlanarImage image2 ) {
    ParameterBlock pb = new ParameterBlock();
    pb.addSource(image1);
    pb.addSource(image2);
    return JAI.create("divide", pb);
}
```

TABLE 13.10 Multiplication Operators

OPERATOR NAME	PARAMETER	TYPE	DEFAULT VALUE	DESCRIPTION
MultiplyConst	constants	double[]	None	Array of constant values to be multiplied with each band
Multiply	This is a dyadic operator and requires no parameters. The pixel value from the first source image is multiplied with the corresponding pixel value of the second image.			
MultiplyComplex	This operator does the same thing as Multiply, except that it applies to images with complex data.			

TABLE 13.11 Division Operators

OPERATOR NAME	PARAMETER	TYPE	DEFAULT VALUE	DESCRIPTION
DivideByConst	constants	double[]	None	Array of constant values to be divided by values in each band
DivideIntoConst	constants	double[]	None	Array of constant values to be divided by the values in each band
Divide	This is a dyadic operator and requires no parameters. Pixel values from the first source image are divided by the corresponding pixel values of the second image.			
DivideComplex	This operator does the same thing as Divide, except that it applies to images with complex data.			

Applying Logical Operators

JAI has support for four basic logical operators: And, Or, Not, and Xor (exclusive or). Table 13.12 describes these operators and their variations.

Listing 13.13 shows an example that uses the And operator.

LISTING 13.13 ANDing two images

```
public static RenderedOp andImages(PlanarImage image1,
                                   PlanarImage image2 ) {
   ParameterBlock pb = new ParameterBlock();
   pb.addSource(image1);
   pb.addSource(image2);
   return JAI.create("and", pb);
}
```

Applying Relational Operators

There are two relational operators: Min and Max. Table 13.13 describes them.

Listing 13.14 shows an example that uses the Max operator.

LISTING 13.14 The maxImages() method

```
public static RenderedOp maxImages(PlanarImage image1,
                                   PlanarImage image2 ) {
   ParameterBlock pb = new ParameterBlock();
   pb.addSource(image1);
   pb.addSource(image2);
   return JAI.create("max", pb);
}
```

Figure 13.12 shows the effect of applying the Min operator to two images.

TABLE 13.12   Logical Operators

OPERATOR NAME	PARAMETER	TYPE	DEFAULT VALUE	DESCRIPTION
AndConst	constants	int[]	None	Array of constant values to be bit wise ANDed with each band. The length of the array equals the number of bands.
And	This is a dyadic operator and requires no parameters. It performs a bitwise AND operation on every pair of corresponding pixels from both source images to create a new destination image.			
OrConst	constants	int[]	None	Array of constant values to be bitwise ORed with each band. The length of the array equals the number of bands.
Or	This is a dyadic operator and requires no parameters. It performs a bitwise OR operation on every pair of corresponding pixels from both source images to create a new destination image.			
XorConst	constants	int[]	None	The constant value to be logically ANDed with each band. The length of the array equals the number of bands.
Xor	This is a dyadic operator and requires no parameters. It performs a bitwise exclusive OR operation on every pair of corresponding pixels from both source images to create a new destination image.			
Not	This is a unary operator. Each pixel value in the source image is inverted bitwise to create a new image.			

TABLE 13.13   Relational Operators

OPERATOR NAME	DESCRIPTION
Max	This is a dyadic operator and requires no parameters. Corresponding pixel values from both images are compared, and the resultant image is created from the maximum of the pixel values.
Min	This is a dyadic operator and requires no parameters. Corresponding pixel values from both images are compared, and the resultant image is created from the minimum of the pixel values.

Overlaying Images

There are many ways of laying one image over another—for example:

1. Using the AlphaComposite class from Java 2D
2. Using the JAI operators

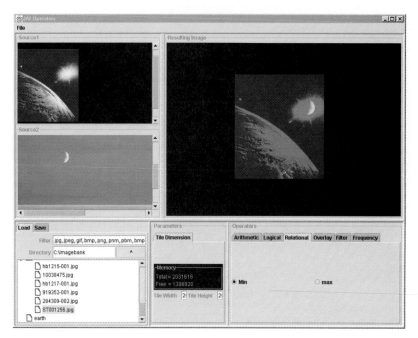

© StockTrek/PhotoDisc; © InterNetwork Media/PhotoDisc

FIGURE 13.12 Applying the Min operator to two rendered images

3. Drawing one image over the other over a graphical context (recall that there are two drawing modes: normal and XOR)

4. Writing directly to pixels

Let's start with the second approach as it pertains to JAI, which offers two operators for overlaying images: Composite and Overlay (see Table 13.14). Each of these operators takes two rendered or renderable images.

Composite

The Composite operator takes two `PlanarImage` objects with only the alpha values as the parameters for performing compositing using the Porter-Duff "over" rule. The first parameter overrides the first source image, and the second overrides the second source image. The second alpha value can be `null`, indicating that the second image is completely opaque.

You can choose the position of the alpha channel in the pixel representation. The alpha channel can be the first band or the last band, or you can have no alpha channel. These options are represented by the following constants in the `javax.media.jai.operator.CompositeDescriptor` class:

TABLE 13.14   Image Overlay Operators

Operator Name	Parameter	Type	Default Value	Description
Composite	Source1Alpha	PlanarImage	None	A planar image with alpha values.
	Source2Alpha	PlanarImage	None	A planar image with alpha values.
	alphaPremultiplied	Boolean	false	The boolean value must be set to **true** if the alpha channel has been premultiplied in both the source and the destination images.
	destAlpha	Integer	Composite Descriptor. NO_ DESTINATION_ ALPHA	Instruction for how the resulting image should add the alpha channel.
Overlay	This operator requires no parameters			

◆ CompositeDescriptor.DESTINATION_ALPHA_FIRST

◆ CompositeDescriptor.DESTINATION_ALPHA_LAST

◆ CompositeDescriptor.NO_DESTINATION_ALPHA

Listing 13.15 shows an example that uses the Composite operator, and Figure 13.16 shows the result.

LISTING 13.15   Compositing images

```
public static RenderedOp compositeImages(PlanarImage sourceImage1,
                                 PlanarImage sourceImage2,
                                 boolean alphaPremultiplied,
                                 int destAlpha ) {
    ParameterBlock pb = new ParameterBlock();
    pb.addSource(sourceImage1);
    pb.addSource(sourceImage2);
    pb.add(sourceImage1);
    pb.add(sourceImage2);
    pb.add(new Boolean(alphaPremultiplied));

    pb.add(destAlpha);
    return JAI.create("composite", pb);
}
```

Figure 13.13 shows the effect of applying the composite operation.

Overlay

The Overlay operator overlays the second source image over the first source image. The source images are expected to be similar—that is, having the same data type and number of bands. However, their sample models can be different. The overlay operation follows dyadic operation rules. The source images are expected to intersect. The resulting image is the intersection of the two source image bounds. If the source images don't intersect, the resulting image is the same as the first source. Listing 13.16 shows sample code for an overlay operation.

LISTING 13.16   Overlaying images

```
public static RenderedOp overlayImages(PlanarImage image1,
                                PlanarImage image2 ) {
    ParameterBlock pb = new ParameterBlock();
    pb.addSource(image1);
    pb.addSource(image2);
    return JAI.create("overlay", pb);
}
```

FIGURE 13.13   Compositing two images

Thresholding

Thresholding is a commonly used operation in both image enhancement and image analysis applications. It determines the pixels whose values lie between specified low and high values and assigns a specified value to those pixels. In image enhancement, thresholding can accentuate a desired portion of the image. In image analysis, it can help in segmentation. In JAI, the Threshold operator performs thresholding. The Threshold operator takes a single rendered or renderable source image.

JAI has one more operator, called Clamp, which does the opposite of Threshold—that is, assigns a low value to pixels that are below the lower cutoff value and a high value to pixels that are above the higher cutoff value.

Table 13.15 describes the thresholding operators.

Color Conversion

The current implementation of JAI has three operators that can be used for color conversion: ColorConvert, BandCombine, and BandSelect. All these operators can act on a rendered or a renderable image.

The ColorConvert Operator

The ColorConvert operator implements the same functionality as Java 2D's `Color ConvertOp` class. Table 13.16 lists the parameters of this operator.

Here's a simple example:

```
public static RenderedOp grayColorConvert(PlanarImage image) {
    return JAI.create("ColorConvert", image,ColorSpace.getInstance(ColorSpace.CS_GRAY)
);
}
```

TABLE 13.15 Thresholding Operators

OPERATOR NAME	PARAMETER	TYPE	DEFAULT VALUE	DESCRIPTION
Threshold	`low`	`double[]`	None	Lower cutoff value
	`high`	`double[]`	None	Higher cutoff value
	`constants`	`double[]`	None	Value of the pixels between low and high values
Clamp	`low`	`double[]`	None	Lower cutoff value
	`high`	`double[]`	None	Higher cutoff value

TABLE 13.16 ColorConvert Operator Parameters

OPERATOR NAME	PARAMETER	TYPE	DEFAULT VALUE	DESCRIPTION
ColorConvert	colorSpace	ColorSpace	None	The destination color space

This example converts a color image to a grayscale image.

The BandCombine Operator

The BandCombine operator implements the same functionality as Java 2D's **Band CombineOp** class. Table 13.17 lists the parameters for this operator.

Here's an example that uses the BandCombine operator to convert an RGB image to a grayscale image:

```
public static RenderedOp grayBandCombine(PlanarImage image) {
    double[][] grayBandCombineMatrix = {{0.212671f, 0.715160f,0.071169f, 0.0f}};
    return JAI.create("BandCombine", image, grayBandCombineMatrix);
}
```

The important thing here is getting the right band combine matrix.

The BandSelect Operator

With the BandSelect operator, you can choose one or more of the bands to create a new image. The selected bands can be in any order. Table 13.18 lists the parameters for this operator.

Here's an example:

```
public static RenderedOp bandSelect(PlanarImage image, int bandNum) {
    return JAI.create("BandSelect", image, new int[] {bandNum});
}
```

Figure 13.14 shows the effect of applying the band select operation.

TABLE 13.17 BandCombine Operator Parameters

OPERATOR NAME	PARAMETER	TYPE	DEFAULT VALUE	DESCRIPTION
BandCombine	matrix	double[]	None	Matrix specifying the band combination

TABLE 13.18 BandSelect Operator Parameters

OPERATOR NAME	PARAMETER	TYPE	DEFAULT VALUE	DESCRIPTION
BandSelect	bandIndices	int[]	None	Indices of the selected band

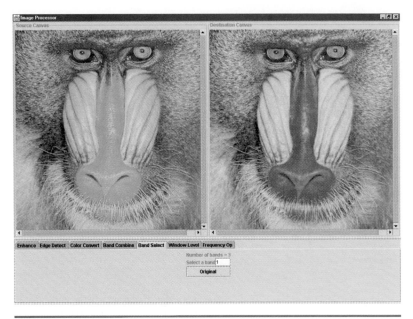

FIGURE 13.14   Applying the BandSelect operator

Frequency Operators

Analyzing an image in the frequency domain is a common practice in image processing. JAI supports two types of frequency transformations: discrete Fourier transformation (DFT) and discrete cosine transformation (DCT). JAI has both forward and inverse transformation operators for both of these transformations. These operators can be applied to either rendered or renderable source images.

In a typical image-processing operation, a frequency transformation would be applied to convert the spatial domain data to frequency domain data. Then an enhancement or image-processing operator would be applied on the frequency domain image. To get the image in the spatial domain, the inverse operator would then be applied to the frequency domain image.

In addition to the transformation operators, JAI has a few frequency domain enhancement operators.

Discrete Cosine Transformations

Both the forward and the inverse DCT operators take no parameters. Unlike DFT, DCT generates a real image. Table 13.19 describes the two DCT operators.

Listing 13.17 shows an example that applies the DCT operator.

TABLE 13.19 Discrete Cosine Transformation Operators

OPERATOR NAME	DESCRIPTION
DCT	This operator generates a frequency image by performing a DCT on every pixel of the source image on a per band basis.
IDCT	This operator generates a spatial image by performing an inverse DCT on every pixel of the source image on a per band basis.

LISTING 13.17 Applying forward and inverse DCTs

```
public static RenderedOp DCTImage(PlanarImage image){
    ParameterBlock pb = new ParameterBlock();
    pb.addSource(image);
    return JAI.create("dct", pb);
}


public static RenderedOp inverseDCTImage(PlanarImage image){
    ParameterBlock pb = new ParameterBlock();
    pb.addSource(image);
    return JAI.create("idct", pb);
}
```

Figure 13.15 shows the **Frequency** panel with the **DCT** option selected. The image on the destination canvas (**Resulting Image**) is the frequency image; that is, it is like a two-dimensional frequency plot. The lowest frequencies are at the upper left-hand corner, and the highest are at the bottom right-hand corner. To get the original image back, just apply the inverse DCT—that is, the IDCT operator. To do this, you can call the `inverseDCTImage()` method in Listing 13.17 with the resulting image from the DCT operation as the input parameter.

Creating a DCT Chain

Figure 13.16 shows a simple example of a DCT chain. It can be a rendered or a renderable chain. To start the chain, apply the DCT operator to the source image. You can now apply any other operator that can enhance the image when converted to the spatial domain. The output of this operator can then be fed to the IDCT operator to create a spatial image.

Discrete Fourier Transformations

The DFT operator creates an image in the frequency domain with complex data—that is, an image with real and imaginary parts. This means that each pixel in the fre-

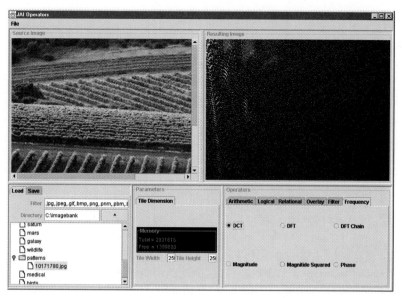

FIGURE 13.15 Applying the discrete cosine transformation

FIGURE 13.16 The structure of a DCT rendering chain

quency domain has a magnitude and a phase angle. So the number of bands in the complex image generated by the DFT is twice the number of bands in the source image. The even-numbered bands in the complex image represent real data, and the odd-numbered bands represent imaginary data. Table 13.20 lists the parameters for the two DFT operators.

The `DFTDescriptor` class has three integer constants to represent the nature of data conversion:

1. **`DFTDescriptor.REAL_TO_COMPLEX.`** The source data type is real, and the destination is complex. This is the constant you typically use when applying the DFT forward operator.

TABLE 13.20 Discrete Fourier Transformation Operators

OPERATOR NAME	PARAMETER	TYPE	DEFAULT VALUE	DESCRIPTION
DFT	scalingType	int	DFTDescriptor.SCALING_NONE	Type of scaling
	dataNature	int	DFTDescriptor.REAL_TO_COMPLEX	Nature of data
IDFT	scalingType	int	DFTDescriptor.SCALING_DIMENSIONS	Type of scaling
	dataNature	int	DFTDescriptor.COMPLEX_TO_REAL	Nature of data

2. **DFTDescriptor.COMPLEX_TO_REAL.** The source data type is complex, and the destination is real. This is the constant you typically use when applying the inverse DFT operator (IDFT).

3. **DFTDescriptor.COMPLEX_TO_COMPLEX.** The source and the destination data types are both complex. This is the constant you typically use when applying an operator in the frequency domain that generates another image in the frequency domain.

The DFTDescriptor class also has definitions for scaling-type parameters:

1. **DFTDescriptor.SCALING_NONE.** No scaling is performed.

2. **DFTDescriptor.SCALING_UNITARY.** The image is scaled by the square root of the product of the image dimensions.

3. **DFTDescriptor.SCALING_DIMENSIONS.** The image is scaled by the product of the image dimensions.

The methods in Listing 13.18 show how to apply the DFT and IDFT operators.

LISTING 13.18 Applying forward and inverse DFTs

```
public static RenderedOp DFTImage(PlanarImage image,
                                  Integer scalingType,
                                  Integer dataNature) {
    ParameterBlock pb = new ParameterBlock();
    pb.addSource(image);
    pb.add(scalingType).add(dataNature);
    return JAI.create("dft", pb);
}


public static RenderedOp inverseDFTImage(PlanarImage image,
                                         Integer scalingType,
                                         Integer dataNature) {
    ParameterBlock pb = new ParameterBlock();
```

```
        pb.addSource(image);
        pb.add(scalingType).add(dataNature);
        return JAI.create("idft", pb);
}
```

As mentioned earlier, when a DFT operator is applied, a complex image is created. The number of bands is doubled because of the real and imaginary parts of the data. So the sample model of a DFT image is different from that of the source image. Because our canvas converts the image to a buffered image, the frequency image cannot be directly displayed. Recall from Chapter 11 that we can restructure an image by using the **ImageLayout** class. So we can change the sample model and the color model to suit the rendering requirements.

Figure 13.17 shows the frequency image on the destination canvas (**Resulting Image**).

Complex-Image Operators

Table 13.21 describes the complex-image operators of JAI.

Listing 13.19 shows how to apply the Magnitude operator.

LISTING 13.19   Applying complex-image operators

```
public static RenderedOp magnitudeImage(PlanarImage image){
    ParameterBlock pb = new ParameterBlock();
```

continued

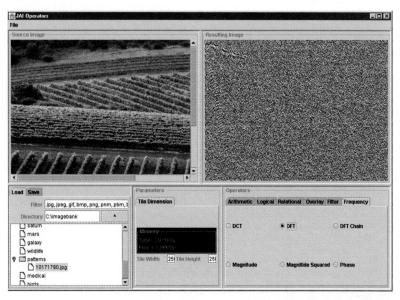

© Per Eriksson/The Image Bank

FIGURE 13.17   Applying the discrete Fourier transformation

TABLE 13.21   Complex-Image Operators

OPERATOR NAME	DESCRIPTION
Magnitude	This operator computes the magnitude of each pixel of a complex image.
MagnitudeSquared	This operator computes the square of the magnitude of each pixel of a complex image.
Phase	This operator computes the phase angle of each pixel of a complex image.
Conjugate	This operator computes the complex conjugate of an image containing complex data.

```
      pb.addSource(image);
      return JAI.create("magnitude", pb);
   }

public static RenderedOp magnitudeSquaredImage(PlanarImage image){
   ParameterBlock pb = new ParameterBlock();
   pb.addSource(image);
   return JAI.create("magnitudeSquared", pb);
}


public static RenderedOp phaseImage(PlanarImage image){
   ParameterBlock pb = new ParameterBlock();
   pb.addSource(image);
   return JAI.create("phase", pb);
}
```

Other Frequency Operators

Table 13.22 describes the utility frequency operators of JAI.

The methods in Listing 13.20 show how to apply the PeriodicShift and PolarToComplex operators.

TABLE 13.22   Utility Frequency Operators

OPERATOR NAME	PARAMETER	TYPE	DEFAULT VALUE	DESCRIPTION
PeriodicShift	shiftX	int	Source image width/2	This operator computes the periodic translation of an image.
	shiftY	int	Source image height/2	
PolarToComplex	This operator creates a single complex image from a magnitude and a phase image. This is similar to a complex math operation, in which a complex number is created from a magnitude and a phase angle.			

LISTING 13.20   Applying the PeriodicShift and PolarToComplex operators

```
public static RenderedOp periodicShiftImage(PlanarImage image,
                                            int shiftX,
                                            int shiftY) {
   ParameterBlock pb = new ParameterBlock();
   pb.addSource(image);
   pb.add(shiftX).add(shiftY);
   return JAI.create("periodicshift", pb);
}

public static RenderedOp polarToComplexImage(RenderedOp mag,
                                             RenderedOp phase)  {
   ParameterBlock pb = new ParameterBlock();
   pb.addSource(mag);
   pb.addSource(phase);
   return JAI.create("polartocomplex", pb);
}
```

Creating a DFT Chain

Now that we have reviewed all the frequency operators, let's create a sample rendering chain. The input is a spatial image that is converted to a complex image by the DFT operator. You can apply a custom operator and then apply the inverse operator to get back the spatial image. However, we can decompose the complex data further into magnitude and phase by using the Magnitude and Phase operators. You can use the output for further computations or apply your own operators to enhance or filter the original image.

To get back the spatial image, you must use the PolarToComplex operator, which is a dyadic operator. You can feed the outputs from your operators to the inputs of PolarToComplex, which creates a complex image. You can then apply the IDFT operator to get the spatial image.

Figure 13.18 shows a directed acyclic graph (DAG) for DFT operators. The chain can be rendered or renderable. Listing 13.21 shows an example of code that creates a rendered chain.

LISTING 13.21   Creating a DFT rendering chain

```
protected RenderedOp createDFTChain(){
   RenderedOp dftop= JAIOpUtil.DFTImage(sourceImage1,
                                DFTDescriptor.SCALING_NONE,
                                DFTDescriptor.REAL_TO_COMPLEX);

   RenderedOp magop = JAIOpUtil.magnitudeImage(dftop);
   RenderedOp phaseop = JAIOpUtil.magnitudeImage(dftop);

   // Apply your operator
```

continued

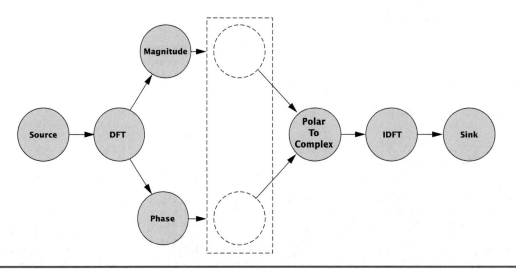

FIGURE 13.18   The structure of a DFT rendering chain

```
RenderedOp complexop = JAIOpUtil.polarToComplexImage(magop, phaseop);
return  JAIOpUtil.inverseDFTImage(complexop,
                                DFTDescriptor.SCALING_NONE,
                                DFTDescriptor.COMPLEX_TO_REAL);
}
```

Conclusion

JAI has powerful operators and APIs for image data manipulation. Using JAI, you can implement commonly used image-processing operations without a lot of coding. We started the discussion in this chapter with the area operators, which move a mask or a window over the image pixel by pixel, each time computing a value of a pixel by calculating the weighted sum of the neigboring pixels. This technique, although simple, is very effective in image enhancement as well as analysis. Point operators, on the other hand, do not use neighboring pixels at all. We looked at various arithmetic, logical, and relational operators, which are very useful in many areas of imaging, including functional imaging and frequency domain analysis.

Apart from these basic operators, JAI has many types of utility operators that implement very useful imaging functions, such as compositing and thresholding, among many others.

We concluded the chapter with the frequency operators supported by JAI. Discrete Fourier transformation (DFT) and discrete cosine transformation (DCT) are two basic transformations widely used in signal and image processing. JAI supports the operators that perform forward and inverse DFT and DCT. Many of the frequency domain operations result in complex data, and JAI has operators to handle complex data. These operators can convert the complex data into equivalent magnitude and phase values. If you're interested in frequency domain analysis, you now have the tools to perform the conversion from spatial domain to frequency domain and vice versa.

Analyzing Images in JAI

14

IMAGE ANALYSIS IS A TOPIC OF GREAT INTEREST to both academia and industry. It plays a role in our day-to-day life that is more important than we often realize. Whether the context is mail sorting, bar code reading, or check processing, image analysis plays an important part.

The topic of image analysis is quite different from other topics we have discussed so far. Applying an image rendering, manipulation, or enhancement operation always results in another image. Image analysis, however, does not always produce a new image. In a typical image analysis operation, salient features from the image are extracted, segmented, and then classified. In an automatic mail-sorting application, for example, characters are first extracted from the mail and then segmented into different regions of the address. The image classification process then identifies different parts of the segmented output and connects them to generate the exact route the mail needs to take.

In this chapter we focus on how to extract pixels from an image and analyze them to yield scientific information. ROI (region of interest) is one of the key techniques used in analyzing images. In JAI, ROI is considered an image property. JAI has not only operators that take an ROI operator as an input, but also classes that allow you to create and manipulate ROI objects.

We'll look first at the operators that compute statistics of an image, including minimum and maximum pixel values and histograms. We'll also look at classes that help build the `ROI` property. And we'll conclude the chapter by putting all the operators and classes together and building a real-world ROI application.

Computing Statistics

JAI 1.0.2 has three statistical operators: Mean, Extrema, and Histogram. These operators can act on the entire image or on an ROI.

Computing the Mean

The Mean operator computes the average pixel value for each image band. Because it requires actual pixels, this operation is limited to rendered images only. Table 14.1 lists the parameters of the Mean operator.

The `JAI.create()` method can be used to compute the mean. Because this method returns a `RenderedOp` object, the mean cannot be obtained directly. Upon computation of the mean value, the `JAI.create()` method sets the `mean` property of the planar image. The `mean` value is obtained by a call to `RenderOp`'s `getProperty()` method. Listing 14.1 shows an example that computes mean sample values of an entire image.

LISTING 14.1 Obtaining the mean pixel values of an image

```
public static double[] getMean(PlanarImage image) {
    ParameterBlock pb = new ParameterBlock();
    pb.addSource(image);
    pb.add(null);
    pb.add(1);
    pb.add(1);
    RenderedOp op = JAI.create("mean", pb);
    double[] mean = (double[]) op.getProperty("mean");
    for (int i=0; i<mean.length;i++){
        System.out.println("i= "+ i+ "  "+mean[i]);
    }
    return mean;
}
```

To compute the mean value of an ROI, set the first parameter with the ROI.

Computing Minimum and Maximum Pixel Values

The Extrema operator computes both minimum and maximum values of each band. Just like Mean, Extrema is limited to rendered images only. The parameters (see Table 14.2) are the same as for the Mean operator.

TABLE 14.1 Mean Operator Parameters

OPERATOR NAME	PARAMETER	TYPE	DEFAULT VALUE	DESCRIPTION
Mean	roi	ROI	null	Region of interest deposited over the image. If the value is null, the entire image is considered.
	xPeriod	int	1	Horizontal sample rate.
	yPeriod	int	1	Vertical sample rate.

TABLE 14.2 Extrema Operator Parameters

OPERATOR NAME	PARAMETER	TYPE	DEFAULT VALUE	DESCRIPTION
Extrema	roi	ROI	null	Region of interest deposited over the image. If the value is null, the entire image is considered.
	xPeriod	int	1	Horizontal sample rate.
	yPeriod	int	1	Vertical sample rate.

The Extrema operator works just like Mean. Once it has computed the minimum and maximum values, it sets the **extrema** property of the node—that is, RenderedOp. Again, a call to getProperty() retrieves the minimum and maximum pixel values band by band.

The getProperty() method returns an object that is of type double[][]. The first array subscript is of size two and represents whether the value is a minimum or a maximum. The second subscript represents the band. The size of the second subscript equals the number of bands in the image. Listing 14.2 shows an example that computes minimum and maximum pixel values of an ROI.

LISTING 14.2 Computing minimum and maximum pixel values

```
public static double[][] computeMinMax(PlanarImage image, ROIShape roi) {
    if(image == null) return null;
    ParameterBlock pb = new ParameterBlock();
    pb.addSource(image);
    pb.add(roi);
    pb.add(1);
    pb.add(1);
    RenderedOp op = JAI.create("extrema", pb);
    double[][] minmax = (double[][]) op.getProperty("extrema");
    return minmax;
}
```

The computeMinMax() method returns a two-dimensional array, the first subscript representing the minimum or maximum and the second subscript the band. If you need to compute the minimum and maximum pixel values of an entire image, set the roi parameter to null when you call this method.

Computing a Histogram

As we saw in Chapter 8, the histogram of an image or ROI is nothing but a plot of frequency count versus pixel values. We computed a histogram by scanning the image or ROI pixel by pixel. JAI does this for you through the Histogram operator. To work with this operator, you need to be familiar with the Histogram class, so we'll look at that first.

The `Histogram` class has three properties, which represent the number of bins and the low and high values of the pixels to be counted. Accordingly, the `Histogram` class constructor has three input parameters to represent these properties:

♦ **public Histogram(int[] numBins, double[] lowValue, double[] highValue)**

The elements of `lowValue` specify the minimum value of each band, and the elements of `highValue` specify the maximum. The `numBins` parameter specifies the number of bins. A bin covers a range of pixel values. The total range (`highValue[i]` − `lowValue[i]`) is divided into `numBins[i]` ranges for the ith band. The `Histogram` class has several get methods that return the values of these properties.

Notice that the constructor has no parameter for passing the image or the ROI. This is done through the following method:

♦ **public void countPixels(java.awt.image.Raster raster,**
**   ROI roi,**
**   int xStart,**
**   int yStart,**
**   int xPeriod,**
**   int yPeriod)**

The histogram is computed from the pixel values specified by the `raster` parameter. The `roi` parameter specifies the region of interest within that instance of `raster`.

If you use the Histogram operator, you don't need to call the `countPixels()` method. You need only to construct a `Histogram` object and pass it to `Parameter Block`. Table 14.3 lists the parameters of the Histogram operator in JAI 1.0.2.

Listing 14.3 shows an example that computes the histogram of an ROI.

TABLE 14.3 Histogram Operator Parameters in JAI 1.0.2

OPERATOR NAME	PARAMETER	TYPE	DEFAULT VALUE	DESCRIPTION
Histogram	histogram	Histogram	None	The parameters of the histogram, such as the number of bins.
	roi	ROI	null	Region of interest deposited over the image. If the value is null, the entire image is considered.
	xPeriod	int	1	Horizontal sample rate.
	yPeriod	int	1	Vertical sample rate.

LISTING 14.3 Computing a histogram

```
public static int[][] computeHistData(PlanarImage image, ROIShape roi, int numbins) {
    double[][] minmax = computeMinMax(image);
    int numbands = image.getSampleModel().getNumBands();
    int[] bins =  new int[numbands];
    for(int i=0; i< numbands;i++) {
        bins[i] = numbins;
    }
    javax.media.jai.Histogram his =
            new javax.media.jai.Histogram(bins, minmax[0], minmax[1]);
    ParameterBlock pb1 = new ParameterBlock();
    pb1.addSource(image);
    pb1.add(his);
    pb1.add(roi);
    pb1.add(1);
    pb1.add(1);
    RenderedOp op1 = JAI.create("histogram", pb1);
    javax.media.jai.Histogram hist =
        (javax.media.jai.Histogram) op1.getProperty("histogram");
    return hist.getBins();
}
```

The `computeHistData()` method returns a two-dimensional `int` array. The first dimension represents the bin index, and the second the bin value. Just like `mean` and `extrema`, `histogram` is also a property that is obtained by a call to the `getProperty()` method of the `RenderedOp` class.

The JAI package also comes with an `OpImage`-type class called `Statistics OpImage,` which can be extended to create your own statistical operators.

The Histogram operator has been modified in JAI 1.1. The code shown in Listing 14.3 does not work in this version. The parameters for the modified version of Histogram are shown in Table 14.4.

TABLE 14.4 Histogram Operator Parameters in JAI 1.1

OPERATOR NAME	PARAMETER	TYPE	DEFAULT VALUE	DESCRIPTION
Histogram	roi	ROI	null	Region of interest deposited over the image. If the value is null, the entire image is considered.
	xPeriod	Integer	1	Horizontal sample rate.
	yPeriod	Integer	1	Vertical sample rate.
	numBins	int[]	256	Each array element is the number of bins of a band.
	lowValue	double[]	0	Each array element is the low value of a band.
	highValue	double[]	256.0	Each array element is the high value of a band.

In the JAI 1.1 version, the `histogram` parameter has been replaced by three other parameters: `numBins, lowValue,` and `highValue`.

Region of Interest Computation

ROI computation plays an important part in applications that perform quantitative analysis. In JAI, `ROI` is a property supported by some operators. The `ROI` class and its extension, `ROIShape,` define this property.

In simple terms, an ROI is a region marked over an image. The `ROI` class defines an ROI as a rectangular image, and `ROIShape` defines it as a shape. In JAI 1.0.2, the `ROI` object represents an ROI as a single-band image with integral data types.

To construct an ROI, you need to pass a single-band `PlanarImage` argument. ROIs are typically associated with `threshold` parameters. Users can interactively vary the threshold to see the pixels that are above or below a certain threshold. In the section that follows we'll look first at the `ROI` class and then at `ROIShape`.

Constructing an ROI Object

The `ROI` class has two public constructors:

1. `public ROI(java.awt.image.RenderedImage im)`
2. `public ROI(java.awt.image.RenderedImage im, int threshold)`

Both of these constructors take a `RenderedImage` object as an input parameter. You can pass an existing image as a parameter, but it must be a single-band image with integral data types. Normally you would get the bounds of the ROI shape and construct an ROI from the underlying image. These steps are necessary for performing ROI operations such as thresholding. The second constructor takes a default threshold as an input parameter.

In the case of a multiband image, you can create an ROI for each band. We know from Chapter 13 that you can use the BandSelect operator to create an image from each of the bands and then use this image to construct an ROI. Listing 14.4 shows an example.

LISTING 14.4   Creating an ROI object

```
public static ROI[] createROIFromImage(RenderedImage image) {
    int numbands = image.getSampleModel().getNumBands();
    ROI[] roi = new ROI[numbands];
    if(numbands == 1) {
        roi[0] = new ROI(image);
        return roi;
    }
    int[] bandindices = new int[1];
    for(int i=0;i<numbands;i++){
```

```
      bandindices[0] =i;
      RenderedOp opImage = JAI.create("bandselect", image, bandindices);
      roi[i] = new ROI((PlanarImage)opImage);
   }
   return roi;
}
```

The `createROIFromImage()` method checks for the number of bands in an image. If the image has just one band, the method constructs the ROI directly from the image. If the image has multiple bands, the method applies the BandSelect operator to obtain individual images from each band. An `ROI` object is then constructed for each of these images. Here's how you can use this method to construct ROIs:

```
Rectangle bounds = shape.getBounds();
TiledImage subImage = image.getSubImage(bounds.x, bounds.y, bounds.width,
                                        bounds.height);
ROI[] roi = createROIFromImage(subImage);
```

The `shape` variable is of type `Shape` and represents the shape deposited over the image.

The `ROIShape` class has two constructors:

1. `public ROIShape(java.awt.Shape s)`
2. `public ROIShape(java.awt.geom.Area a)`

The `ROIShape` object is constructed from either a `Shape` object or an `Area` object.

An `Area` object can also be constructed from a `Shape` object. Here's an example:

```
Area roiArea = new Area(shape);
ROIShape roiShape = new ROIShape(shape);
```

Working with ROI Classes

In this section we'll look at the methods of both `ROI` and `ROIShape` and see how to use them in ROI processing. As stated earlier, the `ROIShape` class extends `ROI` and overrides the majority of `ROI`'s methods.

The `ROI` class has one important property: `threshold`. To access and write to this property, `ROI` has the following set and get methods:

- `public void setThreshold(int threshold)`
- `public int getThreshold()`

Checking for Containment

The `ROI` class has several `contains()` methods that check whether a point or a rectangle lies inside an ROI. The different flavors of this method take different types of arguments for points and rectangles. The `ROIShape` class overrides all of `ROI`'s `contains()` methods, which are as follows:

- For point containment:
  - `public boolean contains(int x, int y)`
  - `public boolean contains(double x, double y)`
  - `public boolean contains(java.awt.Point p)`
  - `public boolean contains(java.awt.geom.Point2D p)`
- For rectangle containment:
  - `public boolean contains(int x, int y, int w, int h)`
  - `public boolean contains(double x, double y, double w, double h)`
  - `public boolean contains(java.awt.Rectangle rect)`
  - `public boolean contains(java.awt.geom.Rectangle2D rect)`

Applying Shape Operations

The following methods check whether a given rectangle intersects the ROI:

- `public boolean intersects(int x, int y, int w, int h)`
- `public boolean intersects(double x, double y, double w, double h)`
- `public boolean intersects(java.awt.geom.Rectangle2D r)`
- `public boolean intersects(java.awt.Rectangle r)`

And two methods apply an affine transformation to the ROI:

- `public ROI transform(java.awt.geom.AffineTransform at)`
- `public ROI transform(java.awt.geom.AffineTransform at,`
                      `Interpolation interp)`

Applying ROI Operations

Several logical and arithmetic operations can be performed between two ROIs. The methods that carry out these operations are

- `public ROI exclusiveOr(ROI roi)`
- `public ROI intersect(ROI roi)`
- `public ROI subtract(ROI roi)`
- `public ROI add(ROI roi)`

Note that thresholding takes effect only when one of these operations is performed. Listing 14.5 shows an example that uses intersection.

LISTING 14.5 Applying the intersection operation

```
public static ROI[] createThresholdROI(ROI[] baseROI,
                                        ROIShape roiShape,
                                        int thresh) {
   ROI[] roiT = new ROI[baseROI.length];
```

```
    for(int i=0; i<baseROI.length;i++) {
        baseROI[i].setThreshold(thresh);
        roiT[i] = roiShape.intersect(baseROI[i]);
    }
    return roiT;
}
```

In the `createThresholdROI()` method, the `baseROI` array contains the rectangular images, with each array element representing a band. The `roiShape` parameter represents the shape. The intersection operation is performed between the `roiShape` object and each of the ROI objects in the `baseROI` array. Notice that before the intersection is performed, a threshold is set in each of the ROIs in `baseROI`.

When the `intersect()` method is called, the `baseROI` image is rendered. In other words, thresholding takes effect. The resulting image is an `ROI` object.

Applying Imaging Operations

You can use the following two methods to apply a specified imaging operator to an ROI object. The difference between these methods is how the imaging operator is specified. In the first method it is specified by a `RenderedImageFactory` object, and in the second by the name of the operator registered with the default operation registery:

◆ `public ROI performImageOp(java.awt.image.renderable.`
                                 `RenderedImageFactory RIF,`
                  `java.awt.image.renderable.ParameterBlock`
                                              `paramBlock,`
                  `int sourceIndex,`
                  `java.awt.RenderingHints renderHints)`

◆ `public ROI performImageOp(java.lang.String name,`
                  `java.awt.image.renderable.ParameterBlock`
                                              `paramBlock,`
                  `int sourceIndex,`
                  `java.awt.RenderingHints renderHints)`

These methods are not overridden by `ROIShape`. Only operators that have `ROI` as one of the ROI properties can be applied.

Utility Methods

The `ROI` and `ROIShape` classes also have the following utility methods:

◆ `public PlanarImage getAsImage()`
◆ `public java.awt.Shape getAsShape()`

- `public int[][] getAsBitmask(int x, int y, int width, int height,`
  `int[][] mask)`
- `public java.util.LinkedList getAsRectangleList(int x, int y,`
  `int width, int height)`
- `public java.awt.Rectangle getBounds()`
- `public java.awt.Rectangle2D getBounds2D()`

Putting It All Together: An ROI Analyzer Application

Let's use the ROI-related classes in JAI to build a more sophisticated ROI application than the one we developed in Chapter 9. We'll follow the same underlying design principles, reuse some of the classes, and specify the requirements first.

Requirements

Our ROI application must have the following capabilities:

1. **For selecting, loading, and saving images:**
   - The ability to list and select images from the local machine.
   - The ability to save the image with the deposited ROI.

2. **For marking the ROI shape:**
   - A viewport to display and manipulate the original image. This feature is to allow users to pan/zoom, rotate, and flip the image so that it is in a convenient position and is a convenient size.
   - The ability to interactively draw at least three shapes over the image in the source canvas: rectangle, ellipse, and freehand. The same shapes need to be drawn over the destination canvas with the appropriate transformation applied.

3. **For processing and analyzing the ROI:**
   - A separate viewport to display the image with the deposited ROIs. The viewport must be capable of panning and zooming the original image with the ROI. Note that there is no need for rotation or flip.
   - The following features:
     - **Thresholding.** We want to be able to mask the pixels that are above a certain threshold. A GUI should be provided to adjust the threshold interactively.
     - **Edge detection.** We want to show the edges within the ROI. At least two algorithms should be provided for detecting edges.

4. **For generating and displaying statistics, a report panel to display the following:**

- ◆ A histogram of the current ROI
- ◆ Statistics of pixels of all the deposited ROIs

Design and Implementation

First let's list all the classes that can be reused. To meet the first requirement, we'll use the `FileBrowser` bean to read images in the local machine. It can load any type of image format supported by JAI.

To meet the second requirement, let's use the `CompositeCanvasJAI` class to display and manipulate images. To provide the manipulation capability, we need to use the `Scroll`, `ScrollGUI`, `PanZoom`, `Zoom`, `ZoomGUI`, `GeomManip`, and `ManipUI` classes. Let's reuse the `ShapeMarker` bean to draw shapes over the image.

To meet the third requirement, let's use the `CompositeCanvasJAI` class (see Listing 12.8) again to display the image and the ROI shape. To adjust the threshold, we'll use the `Threshold AdjPanel` class. To display the histogram, we'll use the `MultiXYPlot` bean.

The ROI Analyzer GUI

Before we proceed with implementation details, we'll describe the GUI part of this application. As Figure 14.1 shows, the application has four viewports:

1. The upper left-hand corner (ULHC) viewport has the source canvas, which displays the source image. In this viewport you can pan/zoom and rotate the image before drawing the ROI shape.
2. The upper right-hand corner viewport has the destination canvas, which displays the same source image with the ROI. Manipulation performed in the ULHC has no effect on this viewport. However, this viewport lets you perform pan/zoom separately.
3. The bottom left-hand corner viewport displays the histogram.
4. The bottom right-hand corner viewport displays the statistics of all the ROIs.

On the lower left-hand side, this application has two tab panes: **ROI** and **Manip.** In the **ROI** pane you can deposit shapes on the source canvas. Before drawing shapes, you can manipulate the image by switching to the **Manip** pane. This pane has the same GUI components as the image manipulator application in Chapter 12 (see Figures 12.4 and 12.5). So you can pan/zoom and rotate the image in the source canvas before depositing a shape.

Once deposited, the same shape is reflected on the destination canvas, which displays the image in its original form—that is, without manipulation. Accordingly, the deposited shape in the ULHC is inverse-transformed to the image space.

A slider is provided to adjust the threshold. The thresholded ROI can be seen in the destination canvas only. The **Deposit ROI** option saves the image with the ROI.

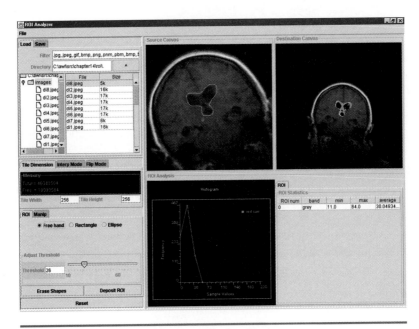

FIGURE 14.1 An ROI marked over a manipulated image

The Main Program

Every application requires a main program to launch it. For the ROI application we're developing, let's call this program ROIAnalyzer. Instead of starting from scratch, we'll extend an existing application class (TiledImageViewer) because what we need here is similar to what we already developed for other applications in previous chapters. The TiledImageViewer class (which was presented in Listings 11.6 and 11.7) is the most suitable class to extend for our current ROI application. To refresh your memory, Figure 14.2 shows the application class hierarchy.

As in the ROI application in Chapter 9, the main class ROIAnalyzer will delegate many tasks to another class, called ROIManagerJAI. ROIManagerJAI will create all UI elements needed for ROI processing. However, the main command panel for the ROI will need to be created in the ROIAnalyzer class. Listing 14.6 shows the code for ROIAnalyzer.

LISTING 14.6 The main class: ROIAnalyzer

```
public class ROIAnalyzer extends TiledImageViewer{
    protected JButton resetb;
    protected ManipUI manippan;
    protected ROIManagerJAI roiManager;
    protected JPanel roipan;
```

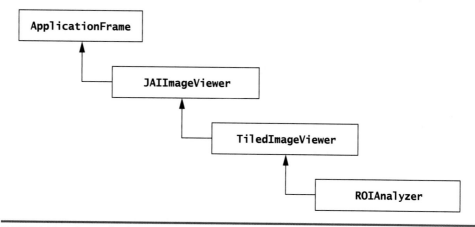

FIGURE 14.2 The application class hierarchy

```java
public void createUI() {

    roiManager = new ROIManagerJAI((int)(width*4/5.0), height);
    JPanel repPanel = roiManager.createUI();
    roipan = roiManager.createROIPanel();

    flBrowser = new FileBrowser();
    loader = new ImageLoaderJAI();
    flBrowser.addListSelectListener(loader);
    loader.addPlanarImageLoadedListener(
        new PlanarImageLoadedListener() {
            public void imageLoaded(PlanarImageLoadedEvent e) {
                PlanarImage image = e.getImage();
                if(image == null) return;
                roiManager.setROIContext(new ROIContextJAI(image));
            }
        }
    );

    viewer = roiManager.getSourceCanvas();

    GeomManip manip =  new GeomManip((ImageManipulator)viewer);
    manippan = new ManipUI(manip);

    JPanel gridpan = new JPanel();
    JPanel tilesetpan = createTileSetPanel();
    DisplayModePanel dispmodepan = new DisplayModePanel((ImageManipulator)viewer);
    FlipModePanel flipmodepan = new FlipModePanel(manip);
    InterpModePanel intermodepan = new InterpModePanel((ImageManipulator)viewer);

    JTabbedPane jtab = new JTabbedPane();
    jtab.add("Tile Dimension",tilesetpan);
    jtab.add("Interp Mode", intermodepan);

    jtab.add("Flip Mode",flipmodepan);
```

continued

```
        JTabbedPane roitab = new JTabbedPane();
        roitab.add("ROI", roipan);
        roitab.add("Manip",manippan);
        changeEventhandler(roitab);
            // Gridbag layout

    }

    protected void changeEventhandler(JTabbedPane jt) {
        final JTabbedPane jtp = jt;
        jtp.addChangeListener(
            new ChangeListener() {
                public void stateChanged(ChangeEvent e) {
                    Component cmp = jtp.getSelectedComponent();
                    if(cmp == null) { return;}
                    if(cmp instanceof TabPanel) {
                        TabPanel tp = (TabPanel)cmp;
                        tp.openPanel();
                    }
                    int ind = jtp.getSelectedIndex();
                    String tabname = jtp.getTitleAt(ind);
                    if(tabname.equals("ROI")) roiManager.setRoiOn(true);
                    else   roiManager.setRoiOn(false);
                }
            }
        );
    }

    protected void resetEventHandler(){
        resetb.addActionListener(
            new ActionListener(){
                public void actionPerformed(ActionEvent e) {
                    ((ImageManipulator)viewer).resetManipulation();
                    manippan.resetManipulation();
                    ((ROIPanel)roipan).reset();
                }
            }
        );
    }

    public static void main(String[] args){
        ROIAnalyzer ip = new ROIAnalyzer();
        if(args.length <1) {
            ip.createUI();
        }else ip.loadAndDisplay(args[0]);
    }
}
```

ROIAnalyzer launches the application frame. It overrides the createUI() method to create its own user interface. Most of the UI creation task is delegated to the roiManager object, which not only creates several UI objects but also facilitates collaboration among them through software events.

The createUI() method first creates an roiManager object and then asks that object to create a panel for the **ROI** tab in the lower left-hand panel of the application frame (see Figure 14.1). The createUI() method also creates the loader and saver objects to load and save images. Notice that the anonymous inner class for handling the `planarImageLoaded` event is different from the `TiledImageViewer` class. This event-handling method creates an `ROIContextJAI` object with the newly loaded image and sends it to `roiManager` by calling `roiManager`'s `setROIContext()` method.

In the `ROIContextJAI` class, unlike `TiledImageViewer`, the image-painting tasks are delegated to `roiManager`. The `roiManager` object invokes the image-painting thread whenever its `setROIContext()` method is called with a valid image (see Listings 14.8 and 14.12).

Before we describe the `ROIManagerJAI` class, it is essential to understand the `ROIContextJAI` class.

ROI Context

`ROIContextJAI` is similar to `ROIContext` (see Listing 9.3). The `ROIContextJAI` class acts as logical container for all the ROIs deposited over an image. When a new image is loaded, a new context is created. Therefore, the `ROIContextJAI` class holds both the original image and the image with the ROIs.

As mentioned earlier, `ROI` can be an image property in JAI. So when a user deposits an `ROI` object, the `ROIContextJAI` class will set the `ROI` property of the image over which the ROI was deposited. Listing 14.7 shows the code for `ROIContextJAI`.

LISTING 14.7   The ROIContextJAI class

```
package com.vistech.jai.roi;
import java.awt.*;
import java.awt.color.*;
import java.awt.image.*;
import java.awt.geom.*;
import java.io.*;
import java.util.*;
import javax.media.jai.*;

public class ROIContextJAI {
   protected PlanarImage origImage;
   protected TiledImage displayImage;
   protected Vector roiCollection = new Vector();
   protected ROI currentROI;

   private AffineTransform atx = new AffineTransform();

   public ROIContextJAI (PlanarImage img) {
      origImage = img;
      roiCollection = new Vector();
      reset();
   }

   public PlanarImage getOriginalImage(){ return origImage;}

   public TiledImage getDisplayImage(){return displayImage;}
```

continued

```java
protected void createDisplayImage(){
    SampleModel sampleModel = origImage.getSampleModel();
    ColorModel colorModel = origImage.getColorModel();

    displayImage = new TiledImage(origImage.getMinX(), origImage.getMinY(),
                                  origImage.getWidth(), origImage.getHeight(),
                                  origImage.getTileGridXOffset(),
                                  origImage.getTileGridYOffset(),
                                  sampleModel, colorModel);
    displayImage.setData(origImage.copyData());
}

public WritableRaster getOriginalRaster() {
    if(origImage != null) return origImage.copyData();
    return null;
}

public WritableRaster getDisplayRaster() {
    if(displayImage!= null) return displayImage.copyData();
    return null;
}

public void setCurrentROI(ROI roi){ currentROI = roi;}
public ROI getCurrentROI() { return currentROI;}

public void addROI(ROI roi) {roiCollection.add(roi);}
public void removeROI(ROI roi) {roiCollection.remove(roi);}

public void depositROI(ROIShape roi) {
    displayImage.setProperty("ROI", roiCollection);
}

public String[] getComponentNames() {
    if(origImage == null) return null;
    ColorModel cm = origImage.getColorModel();
    ColorSpace cs = cm.getColorSpace();
    int numComponents = cs.getNumComponents();
    String[] componentName = new String[numComponents];
    for(int i=0;i<numComponents;i++){
        componentName[i] = cs.getName(i);
    }
    return componentName;
}
public void reset(){
    displayImage = null;
    createDisplayImage();
}
}
```

The `ROIContextJAI` class holds the context specific to an image. It holds the original image, the displayed image, and the deposited ROIs. Because there can be multiple ROIs, it uses a `Vector` object to save the ROIs. Whenever an ROI is deposited, the client object can call the `addROI()` method to add the ROI to the `roiCollection` instance variable.

ROI Manager

We'll develop the ROIManagerJAI class by following the same design principles we used for developing the ROIManager class in the ROI application of Chapter 9 (see Listing 9.11).

Just like ROIManager, ROIManagerJAI must be able to construct a variety of objects, which are listed in Table 14.5. ROIManagerJAI needs to hold each of these objects as an instance variable.

As Table 14.5 shows, ROIManagerJAI needs to instantiate the CompositeCanvas JAI class to create the sourceCanvas and destCanvas objects. The sourceCanvas object allows users to display and manipulate an image and to interactively draw shapes over it. To add manipulation capability, ROIManagerJAI needs to create the sourcePanZoom object. The ROIManagerJAI class registers sourceCanvas with the PanZoom and GeomManip objects. However, destCanvas does not need rotation or shear, and therefore it does not need to be registered with GeomManip.

To facilitate shape drawing, ROIManagerJAI must create a ShapeMarker object. To select the shapes, there should be a GUI. The GUI can consist of radio buttons embedded in a panel. We can add the threshold adjustment panel to this panel. As we saw in Chapter 9, ThresholdAdjPanel represents a GUI panel that has a text field and a slider.

To create the statistics panel, we'll develop a class called ROIStatsPanel along the same lines as the ReportPanel class (see Listing 9.16) to make use of the JAI operators.

TABLE 14.5 Instance Variables for ROIManagerJAI

VARIABLE	CLASS	INPUT PARAMETER	SOURCE EVENT(S)	EVENT TARGET(S)
sourceCanvas	CompositeCanvasJAI	None	mouse, mouseMotion	ShapeMarker, sourcePan Zoom
destCanvas	CompositeCanvasJAI	None	mouse, mouseMotion	destPanZoom
roiMarker	ShapeMarker	sourceCanvas	shapeEvent	ROIManager JAI
roiContext	ROIContextJAI	RenderedImage	None	None
sourcePanZoom	PanZoom	sourceCanvas	None	None
destPanZoom	PanZoom	destCanvas	None	None
threshAdjuster	ThresholdAdjPanel	None	changeEvent, actionEvent	ROIManager JAI
roiPan	ROIStatsPanel	ROIManagerJAI	None	None

ROIManagerJAI also needs to facilitate communication between objects through events. In addition, ROIManagerJAI needs to handle some events—for example, shapeEvent from ShapeMarker, and changeEvent and actionEvent from Threshold AdjPanel. The event-handling routines must perform some ROI processing.

Listing 14.8 shows the code for ROIManagerJAI.

LISTING 14.8 The ROIManagerJAI class

```java
package com.vistech.jai.roi;
import java.awt.*;
import java.awt.event.*;
import java.awt.image.*;
import java.awt.geom.*;
import java.awt.image.renderable.*;
import java.io.*;
import javax.swing.*;
import javax.swing.event.*;
import java.util.*;
import com.vistech.roi.*;
import com.vistech.util.*;
import com.vistech.jai.render.*;
import javax.media.jai.*;
import com.vistech.imageviewer.*;
import com.vistech.jai.imageio.*;

public class ROIManagerJAI implements ShapeEventListener, ActionListener,
                                                            ChangeListener{

    protected int imageWidth, imageHeight;
    protected int viewerWidth, viewerHeight;
    protected CompositeCanvasJAI sourceCanvas, destCanvas;
    protected ROIContextJAI roiContext;
    protected ROIStatsPanel roiPan;
    protected ROIShape shapeROI;
    protected int roiCount = 0;
    protected boolean roiOn = false;
    protected ShapeMarker roiMarker;
    protected ThresholdAdjPanel threshAdjuster;
    protected ROI backgroundROI[]=null, baseroi=null, roiCollection;
    protected ImageSaverPanel saver;
    protected PanZoom destPanZoom, sourcePanZoom;
    protected int currentThreshold = 255;

    public ROIManagerJAI(int wid, int ht){
        viewerWidth = wid;
        viewerHeight = ht;
    }

    public void setROIContext(ROIContextJAI roic){
        if(roiPan != null) {
            roiPan.reset();
            roiPan.setROIContext(roic);
        }
        roiContext = roic;
        SwingUtilities.invokeLater(new ImagePaint(roiContext.getOriginalImage()));
```

```
      setSliderValues(null);
  }

  public boolean isImageDrawn(){ return sourceCanvas.isImageDrawn();}

  public JPanel createUI() {

     sourceCanvas = new CompositeCanvasJAI();
     roiMarker = new ShapeMarker(sourceCanvas);
     roiMarker.addShapeEventListener(this);
     roiMarker.setRoiOn(false);


     sourcePanZoom = new PanZoom((ImageManipulator)sourceCanvas);
     sourcePanZoom.setPanZoomOn(false);

     destCanvas = new CompositeCanvasJAI();
     destCanvas.addMouseListener(
        new MouseAdapter() {
           public void mouseReleased(MouseEvent e){
              if(currentThreshold != 255) thresholdROI(currentThreshold);
           }
        }

     );
     destPanZoom = new PanZoom((ImageManipulator)destCanvas);
     destPanZoom.setPanZoomOn(true);

     saver = new ImageSaverPanel();
     setRoiOn(true);
     // Gridbag layout not shown
     return roiPanel;
  }

  public void setSourceCanvas(CompositeCanvasJAI sc){ sourceCanvas = sc; }
  public CompositeCanvasJAI getSourceCanvas(){ return sourceCanvas;}
  public ImageSaverPanel getImageSaver(){ return saver;}

  public JPanel createROIPanel() {
     ROIPanel roiPanel = new ROIPanel(this);
     threshAdjuster = (ThresholdAdjPanel)(roiPanel.getThresholdAdjuster());
     threshAdjuster.addChangeListener(this);
     threshAdjuster.addActionListener(this);
     return roiPanel;
  }

  public void setRoiOn(boolean onOrOff){
     roiOn = onOrOff;
     if(roiMarker != null)roiMarker.setRoiOn(roiOn);
     if(sourcePanZoom != null) sourcePanZoom.setPanZoomOn(!onOrOff);
     if(sourceCanvas != null) sourceCanvas.setDrawOn(onOrOff);
  }

  public void setShapeType(int mode){ roiMarker.setShapeType(mode);}

  public void shapeDrawn(ShapeEvent e){
     Shape shape = e.getShape();
```

continued

```
        updateROI(shape);
    }

    public void updateROI(Shape shape) {
        if(shape == null) return;
        drawROINum(shape);
        destCanvas.setDrawOn(false);
        if((roiPan == null)||(shape == null)) return;
        Point pan = sourceCanvas.getPanOffset();
        int panX = pan.x;
        int panY = pan.y;

        AffineTransform at =   new AffineTransform();
        at.translate(panX, panY);
        at.concatenate(sourceCanvas.getTransform());

        Shape txShape = AffineTransformUtil.inverseTransform(shape,at );
        if(txShape == null) return;
        TiledImage tl = roiContext.getDisplayImage();
        Rectangle bounds = txShape.getBounds();
        TiledImage tl1 = tl.getSubImage(bounds.x, bounds.y, bounds.width, bounds.height);
        if(tl1 == null) return;
        backgroundROI = JAIROIUtil.createROIFromImage(tl);
        shapeROI = new ROIShape(txShape);

        roiContext.setCurrentROI(shapeROI);
        roiContext.addROI(shapeROI);
        roiPan.addROI(shapeROI);

        TiledImage destImage = (TiledImage)roiContext.getDisplayImage();
        Graphics2D tg = destImage.createGraphics();
        tg.setColor(Color.white);
        tg.draw(txShape);
        destCanvas.paintImage(destImage);
        setSliderValues(shapeROI);
        destCanvas.repaint();
    }

    public void depositCurrentROI() {
        if(shapeROI != null)  roiContext.depositROI(shapeROI);
        saver.setDisplayImage(roiContext.getDisplayImage());
        saver.setImage(roiContext.getOriginalImage());
    }

    public void stateChanged(ChangeEvent e){
        int threshValue = ((JSlider)(e.getSource())).getValue();
        currentThreshold = threshValue;
        thresholdROI(threshValue);
    }

    public void actionPerformed(ActionEvent e){
        String str = ((JTextField)e.getSource()).getText();
        int threshValue = (Integer.valueOf(str)).intValue();
        currentThreshold = threshValue;
        thresholdROI(threshValue);
    }
```

```java
protected void thresholdROI(int thresh){
    ROI[] roiT =  JAIROIUtil.createThresholdROI(backgroundROI, shapeROI, thresh);
    if(roiT == null) return;
    Rectangle bounds = shapeROI.getBounds();
    TiledImage origimage = JAIROIUtil.createTiledImage(roiContext.getDisplayImage());
    TiledImage image = origimage.getSubImage(bounds.x, bounds.y,
                                             bounds.width, bounds.height);
    TiledImage thImage = JAIROIUtil.createThresholdImage(image, roiT, shapeROI);
    origimage.set(thImage, shapeROI);

    destCanvas.paintImage(origimage);
    destCanvas.repaint();
}

private void drawROINum(Shape shape){
    Graphics2D g = sourceCanvas.getDisplayedImageGC();
    if(shape == null) return;
    Rectangle bounds = shape.getBounds();
    int x = bounds.x;
    int y = bounds.y;
    int wid = bounds.width;
    int ht = bounds.height;
    g.drawString((new Integer(roiCount)).toString(), x+wid/2,y+ht+15);
    roiCount++;
}

 protected void setSliderValues(ROI roi){
    PlanarImage image = roiContext.getOriginalImage();
    double[][] minmax = ROIStats.getMinMax(image, roi);
    double min = minmax[0][0];
    double max = minmax[1][0];
    for(int j=0; j<minmax[0].length;j++){
        if(min > minmax[0][j]) min =  minmax[0][j];
        if(max <  minmax[1][j]) max = minmax[1][j];
    }
    threshAdjuster.setSliderValues((int)min, (int)max, (int)(max-min)/2);
    thresholdROI((int)((max-min)/2));
}

public void eraseShapes() {
    roiMarker.eraseShapes();
    roiCount = 0;
    if(sourceCanvas != null) sourceCanvas.reset();
    if(roiContext != null) roiContext.reset();
    if(destCanvas != null) {
      destCanvas.reset();
      destCanvas.setImage(roiContext.getOriginalImage());
    }
    shapeROI = null;
    backgroundROI = null;
    baseroi = null;
}

public void reset(){
    roiCount = 0;
    currentThreshold = 255;
    shapeROI = null;
```

continued

```
      backgroundROI = null;
      if(sourceCanvas != null) sourceCanvas.reset();
      if(roiContext != null) roiContext.reset();
      if(destCanvas != null)  {
        destCanvas.reset();
        destCanvas.setImage(roiContext.getOriginalImage());
      }
      if(roiPan != null) roiPan.reset();
   }
}
```

ROIAnalyzer constructs the ROIManagerJAI object and calls its createUI() method, which constructs all the objects listed in Table 14.5. It also registers these objects for appropriate events.

The ROIManagerJAI class implements three event listeners: com.vistech. graphics.ShapeEventListener, javax.swing.events.ChangeListener, and java. awt.events.ActionListener. The createUI() method registers with the Shape Marker object to receive shape events. It registers with the threshAdjuster object to receive change events and action events.

When the user draws a shape, ROIManagerJAI receives the shape event through the shapeDrawn() method. When the user moves the slider in the threshold adjustment panel, ROIManagerJAI receives the change event through the stateChanged() method. Likewise, when the user enters a threshold value in the text field and hits **Enter,** ROIManagerJAI receives the action event through the actionPerformed() method. Figure 14.3 shows the flow of events among various objects in the ROIAnalyzer application.

Creating an ROI

The shapeDrawn() method extracts the Shape object from the event and calls the updateROI() method, which is the most important method from the standpoint of ROI processing. The updateROI() method first gets the current transformation of the source canvas. This is to take care of the manipulation operation the user might have performed before drawing a shape. To deposit an ROI, we need to convert the user coordinates of the shape to the image space. This operation was explained in detail in Chapter 9. The updateROI() method performs the inverse transformation of the shape using the current transformation of the source canvas. The shape so obtained maps onto the image space—that is, the original image.

Note that ROI processing is done on the pixels of the original image and not on the pixels of the displayed image. The primary reason for this approach is accuracy. Once the inverse-transformed shape has been obtained, the ROI objects are created. There are two types:

1. **An ROI object from the image.** This object is created from the ROI class. It is needed for retrieving the pixels within the ROI.

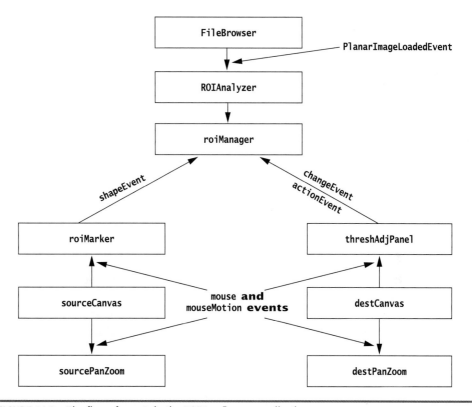

FIGURE 14.3 The flow of events in the `ROIAnalyzer` application

2. **An ROI object from the shape.** This object is created from the `ROIShape` class.

The `updateROI()` method first gets the bounds of the ROI shape and then obtains the subimage covering those bounds from the original image. This image can be used directly for creating an `ROI` object because the `ROI` class takes only a single-band image as the input parameter to the constructor. For a multiband image, then, we need to create an `ROI` image for every band. To do this, we need to create an image for each band. As we saw earlier, this can be done easily with the BandSelect operator. ROIs for multiband images are created in a static method in the `JAIROIUtil` class. Listing 14.9 shows the code.

LISTING 14.9 Creating an ROI from an image

```
public static ROI[] createROIFromImage(RenderedImage image) {
    int numbands = image.getSampleModel().getNumBands();
    ROI[] roi = new ROI[numbands];
    if(numbands == 1) {
        roi[0] = new ROI(image);
```

continued

```
        return roi;
    }
    int[] bandindices = new int[1];
    for(int i=0;i<numbands;i++){
        bandindices[0] =i;
        RenderedOp opImage = JAI.create("bandselect", image, bandindices);
        roi[i] = new ROI((PlanarImage)opImage);
    }
    return roi;
}
```

If the image is a single-band image, the `createROIFromImage()` method creates the ROI object directly from the input image. If it is a multiband image, `createROIFromImage()` uses the BandSelect operator to create multiple `ROI` objects. The `ROI` objects created by this method are required for thresholding and edge detection operations.

The `updateROI()` method then creates the `currentROI` object from the `ROIShape` class using the input shape. This is the ROI that is saved as a property when the `depositCurrentROI()` method is called. The `updateROI()` method calls the `addROI()` method in the `roiContext` and `roiPan` objects.

The ROI shape that is drawn on the source canvas must be transformed so that it can be drawn on the destination canvas because the image in the destination canvas can also be manipulated. The `updateROI()` method gets the current transformation of the destination canvas and transforms the ROI shape in the image space to the user space in the destination canvas. Figure 14.4 illustrates this point.

The `updateROI()` method also calls `setSliderValues()` to set the minimum and maximum values of the slider in the threshold adjustment panel. As Listing 14.8 shows, `setSliderValues()` calls the static `ROIUtil.getMinMax()` method (see Listing 14.8). The `setSliderValues()` method also calls `thresholdROI()` to set the default threshold on the current ROI displayed on the destination canvas.

Thresholding

As mentioned earlier, when the user moves the threshold slider, the `stateChanged()` method in `ROIManagerJAI` is called. Similarly, if the user decides to use the text field to enter the threshold value, the `actionPerformed()` method is called. Both of these methods extract the threshold value from its respective event state object and call the `thresholdROI()` method.

For the effect of thresholding to be visible, the background ROI must intersect with the shape ROI. The `thresholdROI()` method calls the `JAIROIUtil.create ThresholdROI()` method (see Listing 14.10) to create a thresholded ROI that can be drawn over the image in the destination canvas.

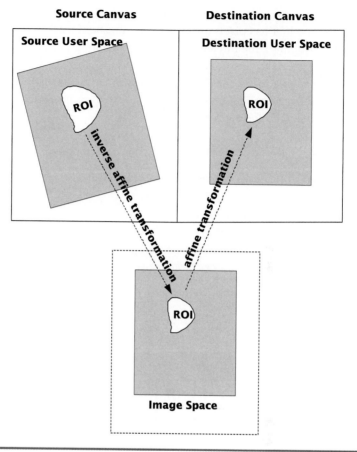

FIGURE 14.4 Transforming the ROI shape

LISTING 14.10 Creating a thresholded ROI

```
public static ROI[] createThresholdROI(ROI[] baseROI,
                                       ROIShape roi,
                                       int thresh) {
  if((roi == null)|| (baseROI == null)) return null;
  ROI[] roiT = new ROI[baseROI.length];
  for(int i=0; i<baseROI.length;i++) {
     baseROI[i].setThreshold(thresh);
     roiT[i] = roi.intersect(baseROI[i]);
  }
  return roiT;
}
```

The `createThresholdROI()` method first sets the threshold on the background ROI to the input value and then performs the intersection operation. When the shape ROI intersects with the background ROI, the resulting ROI is of `ROIShape` type. While intersection is being performed, the pixels are also thresholded, which means the resulting shape ROI has pixels that reflect the threshold mask.

Just computing the thresholded ROI is not enough to display it on the destination canvas. We need to create an image from it and then use the **set()** method in the **TiledImage** class to set the ROI data. Recall that the **set()** method takes the image and the ROI as arguments. Listing 14.11 shows an example that creates an image that is compatible with the source image.

LISTING 14.11   The **createThresholdImage()** method

```
public static TiledImage createThresholdImage(TiledImage image,
                                             ROI[] roiImage,
                                             ROIShape roi) {
    int numbands = roiImage.length;
    Rectangle bounds = roi.getBounds();
    Vector vect = new Vector();
    for(int j = bounds.x; j< bounds.x+bounds.width;j++) {
        for(int k = bounds.y; k< bounds.y+bounds.height;k++) {
            if(roi.contains(j,k)){
                Point pix = new Point(j,k);
                vect.add(pix);
            }
        }
    }
    Point ptarray[] = new Point[vect.size()];
    vect.copyInto(ptarray);
    int leftIndex = image.XToTileX(bounds.x);
    int rightIndex = image.XToTileX(bounds.x + bounds.width - 1);
    int topIndex = image.YToTileY(bounds.y);
    int bottomIndex = image.YToTileY(bounds.y + bounds.height - 1);
    for(int tj = topIndex; tj <= bottomIndex; tj++) {
        for(int ti = leftIndex; ti <= rightIndex; ti++) {
            WritableRaster tile = image.getWritableTile(ti, tj);
            int[] bandlist = new int[1];
            for(int i=0;i< roiImage.length;i++){
                bandlist[0] =i;
                WritableRaster multiBandROI =
                            tile.createWritableChild(bounds.x, bounds.y,
                                    bounds.width, bounds.height,
                                    bounds.x, bounds.y, bandlist);

                for(int p =0;p<ptarray.length;p++) {
                    int arr[] = new int[1];
                    int x = ptarray[p].x;
                    int y = ptarray[p].y;
                    int samp = roiImage[i].getAsImage().getData().getSample(x,y,0);
                    multiBandROI.setSample(x,y,0,samp);
                }
            }
            image.releaseWritableTile(ti,tj);
        }
    }
    return image;
}
```

The `createThresholdImage()` method checks out the tiles that cover the shape ROI bounds and writes the thresholded data on the shape ROI. Since the shape ROI has only single-band data, the data is written sample by sample. This method initially gets the points contained within the ROI—an essential step for ROIs that are not rectangular. The intersection operation generates a rectangular ROI whose size equals the bounding box of the shape ROI. If `setData()` is performed on this rectangular region, you will see black pixels in the region outside the ROI but within the bounding box. We avoid this problem by writing to the specific pixel location. The disadvantage of this operation is that thresholding slows down significantly.

The outermost `for` loop is executed for each of the tiles that cover the ROI shape. In each iteration of the `for` loop,

1. The appropriate tile is checked out for writing
2. For each band,
   - A `WritableRaster` object is created from the tile.
   - For each point within the `ROI`,
     - The thresholded sample is obtained from the base ROI image.
     - This sample is written to the `WritableRaster` object.
3. The checked-out tile is released.

Once the threshold image for the ROI has been obtained, the original `TiledImage`'s `set()` method is called, with this image and the shape ROI as the parameters. The original image is then painted on the destination canvas.

Painting the Image

The image is painted in a background thread. The `ImagePaint` class shown in Listing 14.12 is an inner class of `ROIManagerJAI`. The `ImagePaint` thread is created by the `setROIContext()` method.

LISTING 14.12 The `ImagePaint` thread

```
class ImagePaint implements Runnable {
    PlanarImage image;
    boolean firstTime = true;
    public ImagePaint(PlanarImage image){this.image = image;}
    public void run() {
        if(firstTime) {
            try {
            firstTime = false;
            sourceCanvas.setCursor(Cursor.getPredefinedCursor(Cursor.WAIT_CURSOR));
            sourceCanvas.setImage(image);
            destCanvas.setImage(image);
            SwingUtilities.invokeLater(this);
            } catch(Exception e){SwingUtilities.invokeLater(this);}
        }
```

continued

```
        else {
            if(!sourceCanvas.isImageDrawn()) SwingUtilities.invokeLater(this);
            else{sourceCanvas.setCursor(Cursor.getDefaultCursor());}
        }
    }
}
```

Computing and Displaying ROI Statistics

In the ROI application that we developed in Chapter 9, the `ReportPanel` class (see Listing 9.16) has all the functionality that is needed to display the ROI. We will reuse this class except for actual computation of histogram and statistics. In addition, we'll use a line plot instead of a bar chart to display the histogram. The following sections present some relevant code snippets from `ROIStatsPanel`.

Creating a Histogram

The methods shown in Listing 14.13 compute histogram values and plot them on the `MultiXYPlot` bean.

LISTING 14.13   Creating and updating the histogram

```
public MultiXYPlot createHistogram() {
    String[] colstr;
    Color[]  col = {Color.red, Color.green, Color.blue, Color.yellow};
    int[][] data = ROIStats.computeHistData(image,12);
    if(data == null) return null;
    int numbands = data.length;
    if(numbands >1 )
    colstr = new String[] {"red sample", "green sample", "blue sample", "yellow"};
    else colstr = new String[] {"grey"};
    int binWidth = 20;
    int numBins = data[0].length;
    xVal = new int[numBins];
    for (int i=0;i< numBins;i++)  xVal[i] = i*binWidth;
    try {
        ClassLoader cl = (MultiXYPlot.class).getClassLoader();
        MultiXYPlot xyp = (MultiXYPlot)Beans.instantiate(cl,
                        "vis.beans.plotter.MultiXYPlot");
        xyp.setSize(400,300);
        xyp.setLegendOn(true);
        for(int i=0; i<numbands;i++) {
            xyp.addGraph(xVal, data[i]);
            xyp.addLegend(col[i], colstr[i]);
        }
        xyp.setTitleString("Histogram  ");
        xyp.setXLabelString("Sample Values");
        xyp.setYLabelString("Frequency");
        xyp.repaint();
```

```
          return xyp;
      } catch(Exception  e) {
        return null;
      }
    }


    public void updateHistogram(java.awt.Shape shape){
        if((sampleModel == null) || (dataBuffer == null) || (shape == null)) return;
        int[][]  pix = ROIStats.computeHistData(image, currentROI, 12);
        updateHistogram(pix);
    }

    public void updateHistogram(int[][] data){
        histogram.resetPlotViewport();
        String[] colstr = {"red sample", "green sample", "blue sample", "yellow"};
        Color[]  col = {Color.red, Color.green, Color.blue, Color.yellow};
        histogram.setLegendOn(true);
        for (int i=0; i<data.length;i++) {
            histogram.addGraph(xVal, data[i]);
                histogram.addLegend(col[i], colstr[i]);
        }
        histogram.draw();
        histogram.repaint();
    }
```

To plot a histogram, the `createHistogram()` method uses the `MultiXYPlot` bean. The histogram data for this bean is generated by a call to `ROIStats.compute HistData()`, which uses JAI's `Histogram` class (see Listing 14.13). The `update Histogram()` method is called whenever a new ROI is created.

Displaying Statistics

ROI statistics are displayed in a `JTable` object, which takes the data from a `TableModel` object. Whenever the data is changed, methods in `TableModel` are called to display the data in the `JTable` object. Listing 14.14 shows the methods defined in the `ROIStatsPanel` class to create and update the ROI statistics table.

LISTING 14.14   Creating and updating the ROI statistics table

```
protected JTable createROIStatsTable() {
      updateROIStatsTable();
      TableModel dataModel = new AbstractTableModel() {
          public String getColumnName(int column) {
             if(currentROI == null) return null;
             return roiColNames[column];
          }
          public int getColumnCount() {
             if(currentROI == null) return 0;
             return roiColNames.length;
          }
```

continued

```
        public int getRowCount() {
            if(allRoiData == null) return 0;
            return allRoiData.length;
        }
        public Object getValueAt(int row, int col) {
            if(allRoiData == null) return null;
            if((row >= allRoiData.length)||(col >= allRoiData[0].length)) return null;
            return allRoiData[row][col];
        }
    };
    JTable table = new JTable(dataModel);
    return new JTable(dataModel);
}

public void updateROIStatsTable(){
    if(currentROI == null) return;
    roiColNames = new String[] {"ROI num", "band", "min", "max", "average"};
    double minmax[][] = ROIStats.getMinMax(image, currentROI);
    double mean[] = ROIStats.getMean(image, currentROI);
    int numSamples = mean.length;
    String[][] roiStats = new String[numSamples][5];
    String colstr[];
    if(numSamples >1 )
        colstr = new String[] {"red", "green", "blue", "alpha"};
    else colstr = new String[] {"grey"};
    for(int i=0;i<numSamples;i++) {
        roiStats[i][0] = Integer.toString(roiCount);
        roiStats[i][1] = colstr[i];
        roiStats[i][2] = Double.toString(minmax[0][i]);
        roiStats[i][3] = Double.toString(minmax[1][i]);
        roiStats[i][4] = Double.toString(mean[i]);
    }

    allRoiData = null;
    roiCollection.add(roiStats);
    int size = roiCollection.size();
    allRoiData = new String[size*roiStats.length][roiColNames.length];
    Iterator it = roiCollection.iterator();
    int i=0;
    while(it.hasNext()){
        String[][] dat = (String[][])it.next();
        if(dat == null){
            i++; continue;
        }
        for(int j=0; j< numSamples; j++){
            for(int k=0;k<roiColNames.length;k++)
                allRoiData[i*numSamples+j][k] =  dat[j][k];
        }
        i++;
    }
    if(roiStatsTable != null){
        roiStatsTable.revalidate();
        repaint();
    }
}
```

These methods are very similar to the ones in Chapter 9. The only difference is the way in which the statistics are extracted. In this case, we use the JAI APIs.

The `createROIStatsTable()` method is called when the application is launched. If the image is not loaded, both the histogram and the statistics viewport will be blank.

The ROI statistics data is stored in a `Vector` object called `roiCollection`. However, `TableModel` extracts the data from a two-dimensional array called `allRoiData`. So whenever a new ROI is created, the `updateROIStatsTable()` method is called, which computes the statistics and adds them to the `roiCollection` object. In order for `JTable` to incorporate this change, the `updateROIStatsTable()` method transfers the data from `roiCollection` to `allRoiData`.

Running the Application

To launch this application, type "java app.ROIAnalyzer" on the command line. A frame like the one in Figure 14.1 will appear. The frame has four viewports on the right-hand side. On the left-hand side are the file browser and a command panel for executing the ROI commands.

The upper two viewports are for displaying images. When you list and select an image using the `FileBrowser` bean, that image is displayed on both the source and the destination canvases. To mark an ROI, follow these steps:

1. Display an image.
2. If you need to manipulate the image, select the **Manip** tab. Pan and zoom the image by right-clicking on the source canvas. Rotate the image by adjusting the slider in the **Manip** tab.
3. Select the **ROI** tab in the command panel.
4. Select a shape type.
5. Position the cursor over the source canvas and draw the desired shape by dragging the mouse. The transformed shape is displayed on the destination canvas with a default threshold (see Figure 14.1).
6. To adjust the threshold, move the slider in the **Adjust Threshold** panel. You can see the masking within the ROI changing as you move the slider.
7. To deposit the ROI over the image, click on **Deposit ROI.** Selecting this option saves the current ROI as a property. You can save this image by selecting the **Save** tab.
8. To erase the ROI on the source and destination canvases, click on **Erase Shapes.**
9. Create as many ROIs as you want by repeating steps 2 through 8 (see Figure 14.5).

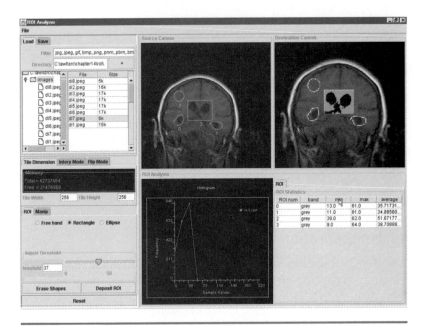

FIGURE 14.5 Depositing multiple ROIs over the same image

Conclusion

Whether the context is medical, satellite, or any other type of imaging, ROI analysis is one of the common features that users look for in an imaging application. Keeping this in mind, in this chapter we implemented a fairly large and complex application that can perform ROI analysis. We reused several classes from previously developed examples. Moreover, this application demonstrated the use of the `ROI` and `ROIShape` classes and several JAI operators, including BandSelect, Histogram, and Extrema. If you need to implement a similar application, you can easily do so by extending some of the classes developed in this chapter.

PART IV

Network Imaging

Remote Imaging

15

SO FAR WE HAVE DISCUSSED mostly applications running on the same machine. In all of these cases, only one client can use an application at a given time. Often, however, we need multiple clients to be able to use the same application. To achieve this capability, one approach is to install the application in all the clients. This means that if you make any change to the application, clients must install that application again. Obviously this is not an elegant approach, especially when the client base is huge.

Another approach is to use the client-server paradigm. Internet-based applications are built in this way, as are many high-end applications. With the client-server approach, multiple clients from a local or a remote machine can access the same application at any time. In this chapter we'll describe how to build client-server imaging applications in Java.

One of the important advantages of Java is its network friendliness. The core Java API contains many features that help you develop network-based applications. The `java.net` package has classes that allow you to program at the low level—that is, the socket level. The Remote Method Invocation (RMI) feature shields you from socket-level programming by providing a higher-level abstraction in the client-server paradigm. So our focus in this chapter is RMI and support for RMI in JAI.

What Is RMI?

Remote Method Invocation is a distributed-computing architecture that is similar to CORBA. It enables communication between Java applications. With the RMI architecture, an object in one application can invoke a method in another application running on a different Java Virtual Machine (JVM). Whereas CORBA objects can be implemented in different languages, RMI is Java specific, which means only Java objects can communicate among themselves in this architecture.

However, Java objects built with the recently introduced "RMI over IIOP" feature can communicate with CORBA objects. Note that IIOP (Internet Inter-ORB Protocol)

Client-Server Architecture

In client-server architecture, the object that requests a service is called a *client,* and the object that services the request is called a *server.* For example, when a client in the Web front end requests an image, a back-end server services the request by supplying the image.

One term that is frequently used in client-server literature is *tier.* A tier is simply a logical partitioning of an application across client and server. So client-server architecture must have at least two tiers. In a two-tier architecture, the client typically contains the application logic that sends requests to the server or database (see Figure 15.1). This architecture is generally referred to as the *fat-client architecture* because the majority of the application logic resides in the client. Although this simple architecture is easy to build, as we mentioned, the GUI is closely tied to the application logic. Any changes to the application require modification of the client as well. This is not desirable when there are a large number of clients, so two-tier applications are not very scalable or maintainable.

These drawbacks are overcome by the three-tier architecture, in which a middle tier is introduced between client and server (see Figure 15.2). This is called the *thin-client architecture.* The application logic in this case resides in the middle tier. The client side has only the GUI. Any changes to application logic do not require changes to the client.

The *n*-tier architecture, which has multiple tiers between client and server, takes the three-tier concept to a higher level. The *n*-tier architecture is much more scalable and flexible than the three-tier architecture.

Distributed Computing

As you are probably aware, in the beginning of the computing revolution there were only centralized systems—that is, systems in which all the processing is performed in one centralized location and the clients are connected to it through "dumb" terminals. Mainframe computing is an example of a centralized system. Centralized computing has many obvious disadvantages. Then came

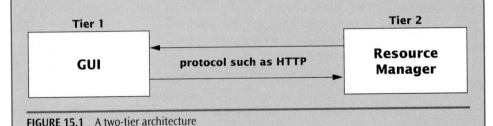

FIGURE 15.1 A two-tier architecture

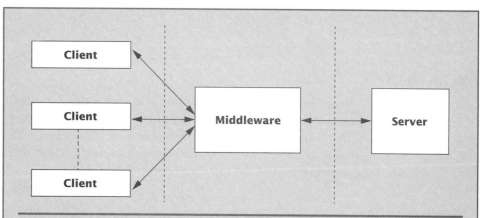

FIGURE 15.2   A three-tier architecture

client-server systems (described in the previous section) to alleviate the problems of centralized systems.

In distributed computing, the client-server paradigm is taken to a higher level, with an application divided into multiple programs and spread over multiple machines that are loosely coupled. These programs communicate among themselves over the network.

When applications are built with the object-oriented programming (OOP) paradigm, these programs are objects. In a distributed-computing system, an object in one machine can invoke a method in an object in another machine. There is little distinction between clients and servers. A server can be a client to another server.

Because processing is spread over multiple machines, which need not be of the same type and need not be working on the same communication protocols, implementing a distributed system is not an easy affair. Dealing with disparate machines and communication protocols is one of the major challenges of distributed computing.

The Common Object Request Broker Architecture (CORBA) is a set of specifications developed by the Object Management Group (OMG), which is a consortium of numerous companies representing a variety of industries. Briefly, CORBA specifies how to build remote objects and how those objects should interoperate in a language- and location-independent manner.

The Object Request Broker (ORB) is the implementation of the CORBA specs. Several vendors have implemented the CORBA specs and developed commercial products. The JDK also comes with the CORBA APIs. If you're interested, browse the packages in the JDK whose names start with *org.omg.CORBA*.

Note that CORBA is not the only specification available in the industry. Microsoft also has a competing distributed-computing architecture called Distributed Component Object Model (DCOM).

is the communication protocol specified by CORBA. This protocol enables message exchange over TCP/IP.

RMI Architecture

As with any other client-server architecture, the RMI architecture consists of clients and servers linked through a registry, in this case called the RMI registry. As suggested earlier, clients and server can reside on different virtual machines. The client is normally referred to as a local object and the server as a remote object. The RMI registry maintains active references to remote objects.

Stubs and Skeletons

The main idea behind RMI is that a method in the remote object is invoked as if it were in a local object. Although this process is transparent to the user, a lot happens under the hood. Let's look a little closer.

Even though the client sees a single remote method, there are two parts to this method—one on the client side (local) and one on the server side (remote). The client-side methods are called *stubs,* and the server-side methods are called *skeletons.* A stub acts as a proxy to the remote method and has no application logic in it. The skeleton is a stub's counterpart on the server side. To invoke a remote method, the client calls the stub, which passes the request to the skeleton over the network. The skeleton receives this request and calls the appropriate remote method (see Figure 15.3).

As you undoubtedly know, methods take arguments and return values, which can be Java primitive types or objects. When a call is made to a local method with an `object` parameter, the reference to that object is passed. In the case of local objects, this means that the same object is referenced by the calling and the called methods. However, a remote method cannot be called in this way because the remote object may reside in a different address space—that is, a different JVM.

When a client invokes a remote method, the parameters have to be transported to the remote machine. Likewise, when a method returns a value, it has to be transported back to the client. The problem arises when a parameter or the returned value is an object. Transporting an object is much more complicated than transporting a primitive data type. As we know from the basics of the Java language, an object is constructed from a class and typically maintains an internal state through its instance variables. When an object is sent from one JVM to another, the internal state must be carried with it. The complication arises when one object contains another object, which can contain another object, and so on. All objects contained within another object must be saved and transported with that object.

Java's object serialization feature solves this problem (see Appendix B). With this feature, serialized objects can be sent from one JVM to another. When a method is in-

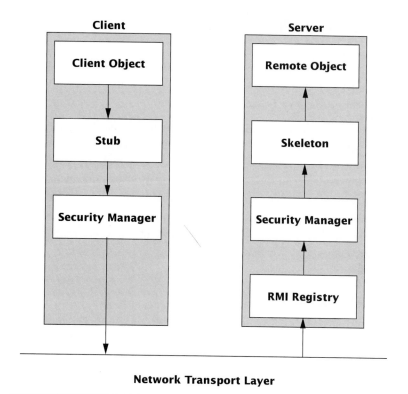

FIGURE 15.3 The RMI architecture

voked, the local machine serializes the parameters that are objects and sends them to the remote machine. The remote machine, upon receiving serialized objects, deserializes them and passes them to the remote method. This process is called marshalling and unmarshalling of parameters.

Fortunately, you don't have to write stubs and skeletons. A utility tool called `rmic` supplied with the JDK generates them for you. Here are the steps in building an RMI application:

1. Remote methods are specified in advance through an interface that extends the remote interface.

2. The remote interface is implemented by an RMI server, which acts as a remote object. As far as the client is concerned, this remote object contains methods specified in the remote interface.

3. The remote server class is compiled.

4. To expose the remote methods to the clients, the `rmic` tool generates client- and server-side classes and interfaces called stubs and skeletons, respectively.

Overview of the RMI API

The Java core API has several RMI-related packages. We'll look at only the ones that are important to this discussion. For information about the others, you may want to consult a book that deals with RMI or any enterprise book.

Here are the two packages that interest us:

1. **java.rmi.** This is the main package, with an interface called `Remote` and the following three classes: `Naming`, `RMISecurityManager`, and `MarshalledObject`. The `Remote` interface is a marker interface, which means it has no methods. As we'll see later, all the remote interfaces must extend this interface. As for the classes, you need to know only the first two.

2. **java.rmi.server.** This package supports the server side of RMI. It has several interfaces and classes (see Figure 15.4). `UnicastRemoteObject` is the class we really care about. An RMI server must extend this class or its descendants.

Using the Naming Class

The `Naming` class links a client to the remote program. The `Naming` class helps remote objects register with the registry, and it helps clients perform lookup operations. The methods in the `Naming` class look up the remote registry and obtain references to these remote objects. To identify a remote object, the URL format is used (see Chapter 16).

When a remote object is registered with the registry, a name can be associated with it. The client can refer to it by the same name. The `Naming` class helps look for this name.

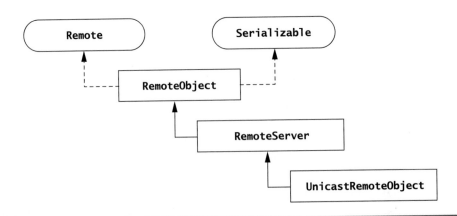

FIGURE 15.4   The `RemoteObject` class hierarchy

The methods of the `Naming` class used by the server are as follows:

- ```
  public static void bind(String name,Remote obj) throws
                          AlreadyBoundException, MalformedURLException,
                          RemoteException
  ```
- ```
  public static void rebind(String name,Remote obj) throws
                          RemoteException, MalformedURLException
  ```
- ```
  public static void unbind(String name) throws
                          RemoteException, NotBoundException,
                          MalformedURLException
  ```

The `bind()` and `rebind()` methods register a remote object with the registry and associate a name with it. The `unbind()` method removes a name from the registry.

Clients typically use the following methods:

- ```
  public static Remote lookup(String name) throws NotBoundException,
                          MalformedURLException, RemoteException
  ```
- ```
  public static String[] list(String name)
                          throws RemoteException, MalformedURLException
  ```

The `lookup()` method returns a reference to the remote object if one is found. The `list()` method lists the names of all the objects registered with a particular registry, the name of which is specified as an input parameter.

Remote Imaging Using RMI

Now that we have described the basics of Remote Method Invocation, let's use this architecture to build some imaging applications. Our aim here is to load images from a remote directory. We'll illustrate the loading of three types of images:

1. AWT `Image`
2. `BufferedImage`
3. `PlanarImage`

Before we continue, let's quickly review the steps we need to follow to build and run an RMI application.

- **Steps for building an RMI server:**
  1. Develop a remote interface that specifies the functionality required from the remote object.
  2. Build a server by implementing the remote interface developed in step 1.
  3. Compile the server-side code.
  ```

4. Run `rmic` to create stubs and skeletons, by entering the following command: "rmic -d classes com.vistech.rmi.SimpleRemoteImageServer".

5. Run `rmiregistry,` a tool that is available in the JDK. In windows, type "start rmiregistry", in UNIX "rmiregistry &".

6. If you're using Java 2, create a security policy file that grants appropriate permissions.

7. Run the server with the policy file created in step 6.

◆ **Steps for building an RMI client:**

1. Build a client class that obtains a reference to the remote object. This class can be an applet, a servlet, or a stand-alone application.

2. Compile the classes. Note that you need an interface that extends `java.rmi.Remote` to do this.

3. Run the client.

Granting Security Permissions

One way to grant security permissions is to modify the security and policy files in the `<java_home>/jre/lib` directory. The other way is to provide a policy file as the value of `java.security.policy` as follows:

```
java -D java.security.policy=mypolicy MyServer
```

The `mypolicy` file contains the following:

```
grant {
 permission java.security.AllPermission;

};
```

This policy file grants all permissions. In real-world situations, however, you may not want to grant permissions globally. You can grant permission to different classes and properties individually, depending on your application.

A Simple Client-Server Example

The purpose of this example is to load images from a remote machine into a client program. To do this, we need to create a server and a client, and we need to specify the remote interface methods that will be invoked from any client. The server class will implement these methods. The rmic tool will generate the stub and skeleton classes.

On the client side, we need to create a program that binds the server to a local object. This program will call the remote methods through this object. Both the client-side and the server-side programs must install an RMI security manager.

As the first step, let's create an interface for the remote methods.

Creating Remote Interfaces

To list and select an image, the client needs to navigate through the remote directory. So the remote interface needs to have methods that list and select directories and files in remote machines. Because this interface is common to all image-loading programs, let's make it the root of all the image-loading interfaces. Listing 15.1 shows the code for this interface.

LISTING 15.1   The remote `DirectoryBrowser` interface

```
public interface DirectoryBrowser extends java.rmi.Remote{
    public String[] listFiles() throws java.rmi.RemoteException;
    public String[] listFiles(String fl) throws java.rmi.RemoteException;
    public boolean isDirectory(String fl) throws java.rmi.RemoteException;
    public String getUserDir() throws java.rmi.RemoteException;
    public char getFileSepChar() throws java.rmi.RemoteException;
}
```

As Listing 15.1 shows, none of the methods return `File` objects. The reason is that a `File` object is machine and platform specific and therefore not serializable. The same reasoning applies to `Image` and `BufferedImage` objects, which are also not serializable. So in order to retrieve an image from a remote machine, first we need to read the image as an array of bytes. As you probably know, arrays of bytes are serializable. So we can safely send this array to the client, which can convert it to the appropriate type of image object. The interface method in Listing 15.2 reads an image as a byte array.

LISTING 15.2   The remote `ImageLoader` interface

```
public interface ImageLoader extends DirectoryBrowser {
    public byte[] loadImageAsBytes(String filename) throws java.rmi.RemoteException;
}
```

In Listing 15.2, notice that the `ImageLoader` interface extends the `Directory Browser` interface. This means that a server class that implements the image-loading functionality must implement the methods in both interfaces.

Creating a Remote Image Server

To start, let's create a simple remote image server called `SimpleImageServer`. This server must implement the `ImageLoader` interface. As Listing 15.2 shows, `ImageLoader` extends DirectoryBrowser, which means that the SimpleImageServer class must implement all the methods in the DirectoryBrowser and ImageLoader interfaces.

This server can reside anywhere in the network, and it can have any number of clients. Clients can access this server by using the Naming.lookup() method. Client programs will use the DirectoryBrowser interface methods to navigate through the remote directories and the ImageLoader interface to load the image as bytes. Listing 15.3 shows the code for SimpleImageServer.

LISTING 15.3 The SimpleImageServer class

```
package com.vistech.rmi;
import java.io.*;
import java.rmi.*;
import java.rmi.server.*;
import java.awt.image.*;

public class SimpleImageServer extends
        UnicastRemoteObject implements ImageLoader{
   protected String userDir;
   public SimpleImageServer()throws java.rmi.RemoteException{
      userDir = System.getProperty("user.dir");
   }
   public synchronized String[] listFiles() throws java.rmi.RemoteException{
      String fl[] = null;
      try {
         File dir = new File(userDir);
         fl = dir.list();
      } catch (Exception e){System.out.println(e);}
      return fl;
   }

   public synchronized boolean isDirectory(String file){
      try{
        File fl= new File(file);
        if(fl.isDirectory()) return true;
      } catch (Exception e){System.out.println(e);}
      return false;
   }

   public char getFileSepChar(){return File.separatorChar;}

   public synchronized String[] listFiles(String file) throws java.rmi.RemoteException{
      String fl[] = null;
      try {
         File dir = new File(file);
         if(!dir.isDirectory()) return null;
         fl = dir.list();
      } catch (Exception e){System.out.println(e);}
      return fl;
   }

   public String getUserDir() throws java.rmi.RemoteException{
       return userDir;
   }
```

```
public synchronized byte[] loadImageAsBytes(String filename)
                        throws java.rmi.RemoteException {
  try {
    FileInputStream bis = new FileInputStream(filename);
    byte[] imageBuf = new byte[1024];
    ByteArrayOutputStream boutstream = new ByteArrayOutputStream();
    for(;;){
      int bytesread = bis.read(imageBuf);
      if (bytesread <0) {break;}
      boutstream.write(imageBuf,0,bytesread);
    }
    byte[] pixmap = boutstream.toByteArray();
    return pixmap;
  } catch (Exception e) {return null;}
}

public static void main(String args[]){
  System.setSecurityManager(new RMISecurityManager());
  try {
    SimpleImageServer imageserver = new SimpleImageServer();
    System.out.println("File Server started");
    Naming.rebind("SimpleImageServer", imageserver);
    System.out.println("File Server is running");
  }catch(Exception e){
    System.out.println("server1 exception " +e);
  }
}
}
```

The `main()` method first installs a security manager. For this server to work, you need to grant read permission on the remote directories. You can create an ASCII file with appropriate permissions for this purpose. Use this file with the -D option as shown here:

```
java  -D java.security.policy=mypolicy  com.vistech.rmi.SimpleImageServer
```

Once the security manager has been successfully installed, the `main()` method constructs the `SimpleImageServer` object and then binds it to the name *SimpleImage Server*. The client can look up the `ImageLoader` image object using this name.

The `DirectoryBrowser` methods allow the client to navigate through the remote directory. The method `loadImageAsBytes()`, when called by the client, reads the image into a `ByteArrayInputStream` object, which is then converted into an array of bytes.

Note that some of the methods are synchronized. The reason is that multiple clients may try to enter the same method. The modifier *synchronized* ensures that only one client can execute this method at any time.

Creating an Image Client

Now that we have created a server, we can use it to serve images to clients. Because each image is served as an array of bytes, we can create any of the three types of Java image forms: AWT `Image`, `BufferedImage`, or `PlanarImage`. The `AWTImageViewer` class, shown in Listing 15.4, implements the client program for loading and displaying the remote image.

LISTING 15.4   The `AWTImageViewer` class

```
package com.vistech.rmi;
import java.io.*;
import java.rmi.*;
import java.rmi.registry.*;
import java.awt.event.*;
import java.awt.*;
import java.awt.image.*;
import javax.swing.*;
import javax.swing.event.*;
import javax.swing.tree.*;

public class AWTImageViewer extends JFrame{
    protected ImageLoader loader = null;
    protected JList itemList;
    protected String[] fileList;
    protected JTree tree;
    protected String curDir = ".";
    protected char separator;
    protected ImagePanel imCanvas;

    public AWTImageViewer(){
        setTitle("Remote Image Viewer");
        activate();
        createUI();
    }

    public void createUI (){
        System.out.println("create UI");
        DefaultMutableTreeNode top = new DefaultMutableTreeNode(curDir);
        createNodes(top, curDir);
        tree = new JTree(top);
        tree.getSelectionModel().setSelectionMode
                        (TreeSelectionModel.SINGLE_TREE_SELECTION);
        tree.addTreeSelectionListener(
            new TreeSelectionListener() {
            public void valueChanged(TreeSelectionEvent e) {
                TreePath selpath = e.getPath();
                expandNode(selpath);
              }
          }
        });

        JScrollPane treeView = new JScrollPane(tree);
        treeView.setPreferredSize(new Dimension(200,400));
        treeView.setBackground(Color.gray);
        imCanvas = (ImagePanel)createImageCanvas();
        getContentPane().setLayout(new GridLayout(1,1));
        treeView.setBorder(BorderFactory.createTitledBorder("Image Selection"));
        JSplitPane vsp = new JSplitPane(JSplitPane.HORIZONTAL_SPLIT, treeView,imCanvas);
        getContentPane().add(vsp);
        pack();
```

```
        setSize(600,400);
        show();
    }

    protected JPanel createImageCanvas() {
        return new ImagePanel();
    }

    private void expandNode(TreePath selpath) {
        DefaultMutableTreeNode node = (DefaultMutableTreeNode)
                                    (selpath.getLastPathComponent());
        Object[] pathobj = selpath.getPath();
        if(pathobj == null) return;
        StringBuffer path=null;
        for(int i=0;i<pathobj.length;i++){
            if(path== null) path= new StringBuffer(pathobj[0].toString());
            else path.append(pathobj[i].toString());
            if(i != pathobj.length-1) path.append(separator);
        }
        try {
            if(node.isLeaf()){
                String filename = path.toString();
                if(loader.isDirectory(path.toString())){
                curDir = path.toString();
                fileList = loader.listFiles(curDir);
                if(fileList == null) return;
                createNodes(node,pathobj[0].toString());
                tree.expandPath(selpath);
            } else
                load(filename);
            }
        } catch (Exception e){System.out.println(e);}
    }

    protected void load(String filename) throws RemoteException{
        if(filename.endsWith(".jpg")  || filename.endsWith(".jpeg") ||
          filename.endsWith(".gif")  || filename.endsWith(".GIF")){
            byte[] buffer = loader.loadImageAsBytes(filename);
            Image img = Toolkit.getDefaultToolkit().createImage(buffer);
            imCanvas.setImage(img);
            imCanvas.repaint();
        }
    }


    private void doubleClick(int selrow, TreePath selpath) {
        if(!tree.isCollapsed(selpath)) tree.collapsePath(selpath);
        else expandNode(selpath);
    }

    private void singleClick(int selrow, TreePath selpath) {
        if(tree.isCollapsed(selpath)) expandNode(selpath);
    }

    private void createNodes(DefaultMutableTreeNode top, String dirname) {
        DefaultMutableTreeNode file = null;
        for(int i=0; i< fileList.length;i++){
```

continued

```
            file = new DefaultMutableTreeNode(fileList[i]);
            top.add(file);
        }
    }

    public void activate(){
        System.setSecurityManager(new RMISecurityManager());
        try {
            loader = (ImageLoader)Naming.lookup("SimpleImageServer");
            fileList = loader.listFiles();
            curDir = loader.getUserDir();
            separator = loader.getFileSepChar();
        }catch(Exception e){System.out.println(e); }
    }
    public static void main(String args[]){
        AWTImageViewer fc = new AWTImageViewer();
    }
}
```

After setting the title of the client frame, AWTImageViewer's constructor calls the activate() and createUI() methods. The activate() method first installs the security manager. This is a must for an RMI application that provides access to remote machines. Using the policy file, you can provide appropriate permissions to the directories that clients are allowed to handle. Once the security manager is set up, the activate() method calls the Naming.lookup() method to look for the string "Simple ImageServer". Here we hard-coded the server name. In a real-world application, the server name can be a variable that can be assigned dynamically.

For the lookup() method to work, rmiregistry must be running. Remember that SimpleImageServer implements the ImageLoader interface, so the lookup() method returns the object into the loader instance variable that is of ImageLoader type. Obtaining the remote object handle is the most important role of the RMI client. Once that handle has been obtained, the rest of the logic is implemented as if the application were operating on a local machine. As Listing 15.4 shows, the remote interface methods are called as if they were available locally in the loader object.

The constructor then calls the createUI() method, which creates a tree-view component for navigating the remote directory and an image canvas for displaying images. When you click a node, the expandNode() method is called. If the expanded node is a leaf node, the expandNode() method calls load().

The load() method calls the remote getImageAsBytes() method to retrieve the image as an array of bytes. To create an AWT Image object, the load() method calls the Toolkit.createImage() method. The image represented by this object is displayed on an instance of ImagePanel, which is shown in Listing 15.5.

LISTING 15.5   The ImagePanel class

```
public class ImagePanel extends JPanel{
    protected Image image;
    protected int viewerWid = 400;
```

```
    protected int viewerHt = 600;

    public void setImage(Image img){ image = img;}

    public void paintComponent(Graphics g){
        Rectangle rect = this.getBounds();
        g.setColor(Color.black);
        if((viewerWid != rect.width) || (viewerHt != rect.height)){
            viewerWid = rect.width; viewerHt = rect.height ;
            repaint(); return;
        }
        g.setColor(Color.black);
        g.fillRect(0,0,rect.width, rect.height);
        if(image != null){
            g.drawImage(image,0,0,rect.width,rect.height, this);
        }
    }
}
```

Reading the Loaded Image as a Buffered Image

We can use the same `SimpleImageServer` object to serve images to build a viewer that
displays the buffered image. To create a buffered image from the image loaded as
bytes, you can use either the JPEG codec package or the Image I/O codec package
(see Chapter 17 for details). Listing 15.6 shows how to build a client using the
JPEG codec.

LISTING 15.6   Building a client with the JPEG codec

```
package app;
import java.io.*;
import java.rmi.*;
import java.awt.event.*;
import java.awt.*;
import java.awt.image.*;
import com.sun.image.codec.jpeg.*;
import com.vistech.rmi.*;

public class BufferedImageViewer extends AWTImageViewer{

    public BufferedImageViewer(){
        setTitle("Java 2D Image Viewer");
    }

    public void load(String filename) throws RemoteException{
        if(filename.endsWith(".jpg")  || filename.endsWith(".jpeg")){
            byte[] buffer = loader.loadImageAsBytes(filename);
            ByteArrayInputStream bis = new  ByteArrayInputStream(buffer);
            BufferedImage img =  readAsBufferedImage(bis);
            imCanvas.setImage(img);
            imCanvas.repaint();
        }
    }
```

continued

```
     public static BufferedImage readAsBufferedImage(InputStream is) {
        try {
           JPEGImageDecoder decoder = JPEGCodec.createJPEGDecoder(is);
           BufferedImage bi = decoder.decodeAsBufferedImage();
           return bi;
        } catch(Exception e) {
           System.out.println(e);
           return null;
        }
     }

     public static void main(String args[]){
        BufferedImageViewer fc = new BufferedImageViewer();
     }
}
```

`BufferedImageViewer` extends `AWTImageViewer` and overrides the `load()`
method. The `load()` method calls the `loadImageAsBytes()` method to load the remote image as an array of bytes. It then converts this array into an instance of `Byte
ArrayInputStream`, which is passed to `readAsBufferedImage()`. This method de-
codes the image in the array of bytes into a `BufferedImage` object. The `load()`
method then displays the image in the image panel.

Listing 15.7 shows how to build a client using the Image I/O API.

LISTING 15.7   Building a client with the Image I/O codec

```
package app;
import java.io.*;
import java.rmi.*;
import javax.swing.*;
import javax.swing.event.*;
import java.awt.*;
import java.awt.image.*;
import com.vistech.rmi.*;
import javax.imageio.*;
import javax.imageio.stream.*;

public class ImageIOViewer extends AWTImageViewer{

    public ImageIOViewer(){
       setTitle("Remote Image IO Viewer");
    }

    public void load(String filename) throws RemoteException{
       byte[] buffer = loader.loadImageAsBytes(filename);
       ByteArrayInputStream bis = new    ByteArrayInputStream(buffer);
       BufferedImage img =  readAsBufferedImage(bis);
       imCanvas.setImage(img);
       imCanvas.repaint();
    }

    public BufferedImage readAsBufferedImage(InputStream is) {
       try {
          ImageInputStream mis = new FileCacheImageInputStream(is, new File("temp"));
```

```
      BufferedImage im = ImageIO.read(mis);
      return im;
    } catch(Exception e) {
      return null;
    }
  }
  public static void main(String args[]){
     ImageIOViewer fc = new ImageIOViewer();
  }
}
```

As mentioned already, the Image I/O package can read different types of image formats. The `load()` method calls `loadImageAsBytes()` on the server side and obtains the image as an array of bytes. Unlike the viewer of the preceding example (see Listing 15.6), this viewer has no check for the image types.

The `load()` method creates an instance of `ByteArrayInputStream` from the array of bytes and passes it to `readAsBufferedImage()`. The `readAsBufferedImage()` method creates a `FileCacheImageInputStream` object from the input stream and passes it to the static `ImageIO.read()` method, which returns a `BufferedImage` object. The `load()` method paints the buffered image on the image canvas.

Reading the Loaded Image as a Planar Image

Now let's use JAI to build an RMI client. Because an image is obtained as an array of bytes, we need to create a `SeekableStream` object from this array. (See Chapter 17 to learn about the JAI codec.) To convert `SeekableStream` to `PlanarImage`, we can use the JAI Stream operator. Listing 15.8 shows how to create a remote JAI image viewer.

LISTING 15.8   The `PlanarImageViewer` class

```
public class PlanarImageViewer extends AWTImageViewer{

   public PlanarImageViewer(){
      setTitle("Planar Image Viewer");
   }

   protected JPanel createImageCanvas() {
      return new PlanarImagePanel();
   }

   public void load(String filename) throws RemoteException{
      byte[] buffer = loader.loadImageAsBytes(filename);
      ByteArrayInputStream bis = new   ByteArrayInputStream(buffer);
      PlanarImage img =  readAsPlanarImage(bis);
      if(img == null) {return; }
      ((PlanarImagePanel)imCanvas).setImage(img);
      ((PlanarImagePanel)imCanvas).repaint();
   }

   public static PlanarImage readAsPlanarImage(InputStream is) {
      try {
```

continued

```
        SeekableStream ss = SeekableStream.wrapInputStream(is,true);
        return JAI.create("stream", ss, null);
        } catch (Exception e){return null;}
    }

    public static void main(String args[]){
        PlanarImageViewer fc = new PlanarImageViewer();
    }
}

class PlanarImagePanel extends ImagePanel{
    PlanarImage plimage;
    int viewerWid = 400;
    int viewerHt = 600;
    int imageWidth;
    int imageHeight;
    public void setImage(PlanarImage img){
        plimage = img;
        imageWidth = img.getWidth();
        imageHeight = img.getHeight();
        repaint();
    }

    public void paintComponent(Graphics gc){
        Graphics2D g = (Graphics2D)gc;
        Rectangle rect = this.getBounds();
        if((viewerWid != rect.width) || (viewerHt != rect.height)){
            viewerWid = rect.width;
            viewerHt = rect.height;
        }
        double magx = rect.width/(double)imageWidth ;
        double magy = rect.height/(double)imageHeight ;
        g.setColor(Color.black);
        g.fillRect(0,0,rect.width, rect.height);
        AffineTransform atx =  AffineTransform.getScaleInstance(magx, magy);
        if(plimage != null) g.drawRenderedImage(plimage, atx);
    }
}
```

Just like `BufferedImageViewer` (see Listing 15.6), `PlanarImageViewer` extends `AWTImageViewer` and overrides the `load()` method, which uses the JAI codec to create a planar image. The `load()` method converts the image bytes into a `ByteArray InputStream` object and passes it to `readAsPlanarImage()`. The `readAsPlanar Image()` method uses the Stream operator to create the planar image, which requires `SeekableStream` parameters. The `SeekableStream` object is created by a call to `wrap InputStream()`, which is a static method in the `SeekableStream` class.

The `ImagePanel` class cannot display the planar image because the `paint Component()` method uses the `drawImage()` method, which can take only `Image` or `BufferedImage` inputs. For this reason we created a new class, `PlanarImagePanel`, which extends `ImagePanel` and overrides the `setImage()` and `paintComponent()` methods. The `paintComponent()` method of `PlanarImagePanel` uses `drawRendered`

`Image()` to display the planar image. Figure 15.5 shows a screen shot of the client that displays a planar image transported from the server.

Tracking Sessions

In all client-server applications, any number of clients can use the same server. This means that different clients execute the same server-side code, so you need to be cautious when you design your server.

If you look at the server code in our example, the remote methods don't save states. In other words, the server doesn't save the session. A client can execute the remote methods in any order it likes. Notice also that some of the remote methods are implemented as synchronized methods. This approach makes them thread safe. For example, when `loadImageAsBytes()` is executed for a client, no other client can enter this method until the method completes execution.

This simple scenario seldom occurs in real-world situations. In server-side programming, tracking a session is often a necessity. A session is specific to a client. There are many ways to track sessions. For example, the server can be designed in such a way that each client spawns a thread and is alive as long as a session is in use. Session tracking is a common problem faced by Internet programs. Chapter 16 will describe how sessions are tracked in servlets.

© Zhen Ge China Tourism Press.Peng/The Image Bank

FIGURE 15.5   A remote image-viewing client

RMI with Applets

An RMI client can also be an applet. You can use an RMI client applet if the browser supports it. There are a couple of differences between RMI client applets and applications. In an RMI applet, you do not need to install the RMI security manager. The remote object is referenced within an applet with the RMI protocol. Here's an example:

```
String remoteObjName = "rmi: //"+getCodebase().getHost() + "SimpleImageServer";
```

Listing 15.9 shows the code for a sample RMI applet.

LISTING 15.9 The `RemoteImageViewerApplet` class

```
package com.vistech.rmi;
import java.io.*;
import java.rmi.*;
import java.rmi.registry.*;
import java.awt.event.*;
import java.awt.*;
import java.awt.image.*;
import javax.swing.*;
import javax.swing.event.*;
import javax.swing.tree.*;
import java.applet.*;
import java.net.*;
import com.vistech.rmi.*;

public class RemoteImageViewerApplet extends Applet {
   static int viewerWid = 400;
   static int viewerHt = 300;
   protected ImageLoader loader = null;
   protected JList itemList;
   protected String[] fileList;
   protected JTree tree;
   protected String curDir = ".";
   protected char separator;
   protected ImagePanel imCanvas;

   public void init() {
      String param = getParameter("WIDTH");
      if(param != null) viewerWid = Integer.valueOf(param).intValue();
      param = getParameter("HEIGHT");
      if(param != null) viewerHt = Integer.valueOf(param).intValue();
      initApp();
   }

   public void initApp() {
      this.setSize(viewerWid, viewerHt);
      enableEvents(AWTEvent.MOUSE_MOTION_EVENT_MASK |
                        AWTEvent.MOUSE_EVENT_MASK);
   }

   public void start(){
      activate();
```

```
        createUI();
    }
    public void createUI (){
        DefaultMutableTreeNode top = new DefaultMutableTreeNode(curDir);
        createNodes(top, curDir);
        tree = new JTree(top);
        tree.getSelectionModel().setSelectionMode
                            (TreeSelectionModel.SINGLE_TREE_SELECTION);
        tree.addTreeSelectionListener(
                new TreeSelectionListener() {
                public void valueChanged(TreeSelectionEvent e) {
                    TreePath selpath = e.getPath();
                    expandNode(selpath);
                }
            });

        JScrollPane treeView = new JScrollPane(tree);
        treeView.setPreferredSize(new Dimension(200,400));
        treeView.setBackground(Color.gray);
        imCanvas = (ImagePanel)createImageCanvas();
        setLayout(new GridLayout(1,1));
        treeView.setBorder(BorderFactory.createTitledBorder("Image Selection"));
        JSplitPane vsp = new JSplitPane(JSplitPane.HORIZONTAL_SPLIT, treeView,imCanvas);
        add(vsp);
    }

    protected JPanel createImageCanvas() {
        return new ImagePanel();
    }
    // Other methods

    public void activate(){
        try {
            loader =
            (ImageLoader)Naming.lookup("rmi://"+getCodeBase().getHost()+
                                "/SimpleImageServer");
            fileList = loader.listFiles();
            curDir = loader.getUserDir();
            separator = loader.getFileSepChar();
        }catch(Exception e){System.out.println(e); }
    }
}
```

We modified the AWTImageViewer code (see Listing 15.4) to implement the
RemoteImageViewerApplet class. The methods that are the same are not shown in
Listing 15.9. To implement this applet, we added the applet life cyle methods and re-
moved the constructor and the main() method.

The major differences are in the activate() method. In this case it does not create an RMISecurityManager object. Notice how the reference to the ImageLoader object is obtained.

You can run this applet using the appletviewer utility. Because we used the
Swing components, however, at the time of this writing it cannot be run on a Web
browser without the Java plug-in.

To run an applet, you need an HTML driver, as Listing 15.10 shows. You can embed the applet in any HTML file.

LISTING 15.10   The HTML driver for `RemoteImageViewerApplet`

```
<!DOCTYPE HTML <body>
<center><applet code="com.vistech.rmi.RemoteImageViewerApplet" width="350"
height="250">
</applet></center>
</body></html>
```

Figure 15.6 shows a screen shot of the remote image viewer applet launched using the appletviewer utility.

Using Java Plug-in to Run Applets

Java Plug-in utilizes browser-specific HTML tags to load the class files. If the JDK is not available, the plug-in feature downloads the JDK on the client side. To make use of this feature, you need to modify the original HTML file. Sun provides an **HTMLConverter** utility to convert a regular HTML file to a plug-in HTML file. You can download the utility from the Java home page. Once you have downloaded and installed this utility, all you need to do is run it with your HTML driver. Here's an example:

```
HTMLConverter remoteviewer.html
```

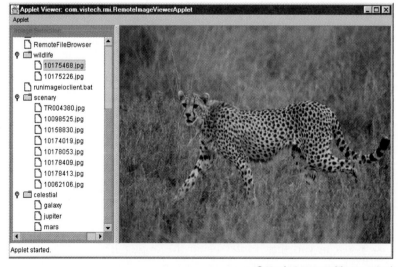

© Marvin E. Newman/The Image Bank

FIGURE 15.6   The RMI client as an applet

This command converts the `remoteviewer.html` file to the file in Listing 15.11.

LISTING 15.11   A modified HTML driver for the Java plug-in

```
<!DOCTYPE HTML <body>
<center><!--"CONVERTED_APPLET"-->
<!-- CONVERTER VERSION 1.3 -->
<OBJECT classid="clsid:8AD9C840-044E-11D1-B3E9-00805F499D93"
WIDTH = "600" HEIGHT = "400"
codebase="http://java.sun.com/products/plugin/1.3/jinstall-13-
win32.cab#Version=1,3,0,0">
<PARAM NAME = CODE VALUE = "com.vistech.rmi.RemoteImageViewerApplet" >

<PARAM NAME="type" VALUE="application/x-java-applet;version=1.3">
<PARAM NAME="scriptable" VALUE="false">
<COMMENT>
<EMBED type="application/x-java-applet;version=1.3"  CODE =
"com.vistech.rmi.RemoteImageViewerApplet" WIDTH = "600" HEIGHT = "400"
scriptable=false pluginspage="http://java.sun.com/products/plugin/1.3/plugin-
install.html"><NOEMBED></COMMENT>

</NOEMBED></EMBED>
</OBJECT>

<!-
<APPLET CODE = "com.vistech.rmi.RemoteImageViewerApplet" WIDTH = "600" HEIGHT = "400">

</APPLET>
-->
<!--"END_CONVERTED_APPLET"-->
</center>
</body></html>
```

If you run the `HTMLConverter` utility, you will see an applet as shown in Figure 15.7.

Remote Imaging with JAI

In the example described in the previous section, we used the loaded image with JAI. We did not exploit the JAI remote imaging features. We had to load images as bytes because `PlanarImage` is not serializable. As mentioned in Chapter 11, however, the `RenderedOp` and `RenderableOp` classes are serializable. This means that both of these classes can be arguments and return values of remote methods, opening up many possibilities. Here's a scenario:

A client application can send image(s) to a high-performance server to do the processing. Consider the example of three-dimensional model generation by volume-rendering algorithms. As you probably know, these algorithms involve very computation-intensive operations. Applications like these require high-performance machines

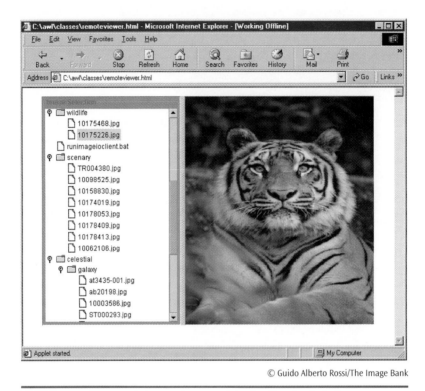

© Guido Alberto Rossi/The Image Bank

FIGURE 15.7   The remote image viewer applet using the plug-in feature

and are very expensive. Another option, however, is to use a distributed-computing mechanism to share the computing load. A client application can load a stack of images from an image repository, partition the computing, and send the images to one or more servers to generate the three-dimensional model concurrently. Once it is generated, one of the servers can integrate the model and send a three-dimensional view to the client for rendering.

Let's deal with the simple problems. We'll create remote methods that return `RenderedOp` or `RenderableOp` objects. Listing 15.12 shows such an interface that loads the JAI image.

LISTING 15.12   The `JAIImageLoader` interface

```
public interface JAIImageLoader extends ImageLoader {
    public RenderedOp loadJAIImage(String filename)throws java.rmi.RemoteException;
}
```

Note that `JAIImageLoader` extends the `ImageLoader` interface (see Listing 15.2), which was used to implement the simple image server example (see Listing 15.3). Just as we did in that example, we'll build a server that serves JAI images by implementing the `JAIImageLoader` interface.

Creating a Remote JAI Image Server

Because `RenderedOp` is serializable, there is no need to load the image as bytes. So to implement the `JAIImageLoader` interface, all you need to do is construct a `RenderedOp` object for the image that is to be served. The `JAIImageServer` class shown in Listing 15.13 does exactly that, using the FileLoad operator.

LISTING 15.13   The `JAIImageServer` class

```
public class JAIImageServer extends
        SimpleImageServer implements JAIImageLoader{

   public JAIImageServer()throws java.rmi.RemoteException{}

   public synchronized RenderedOp loadJAIImage(String filename)
      throws java.rmi.RemoteException {
      try {
         return JAI.create("fileload", filename);
      } catch (Exception e) {return null;}
   }

   public static void main(String args[]){
      System.setSecurityManager(new RMISecurityManager());
      try {
        JAIImageServer fileserver = new JAIImageServer();
        System.out.println("JAI Image Server started");
        Naming.rebind("JAIImageServer", fileserver);
        System.out.println("JAI Image Server is running");
      }catch(Exception e){
        System.out.println("server1 exception " +e);
      }
   }
}
```

Listing 15.13 shows the server code that extends the `SimpleImageServer` class. The `loadJAIImage()` method uses the FileLoad operator to load the image specified by the `filename` parameter. In the `main()` method, we replaced `SimpleImageServer` with `JAIImageServer`.

Using the RemoteImage Class

Unlike Java 2D, JAI has explicit support for network imaging. JAI 1.0.2 has an image type class called `RemoteImage` that is meant exclusively for network applications. You can construct a `RemoteImage` object specific to a server. `RemoteImage` allows you to set and get the number of retries and time-outs.

The `RemoteImage` class is a client-side representation of a JAI image on the server side. This class extends `PlanarImage` but can be constructed through a rendered or a renderable node. `RemoteImage` has a counterpart on the server side. When a `RemoteImage` object is used in an operation, the actual operation is executed on the server side.

Constructing a RemoteImage Object

To instantiate a `RemoteImage` object, an RMI server needs to be running. It can be constructed for a single rendered image or for a rendered or a renderable node. This means that rendered or renderable operations can span many servers, thereby allowing the creation of a true distributed environment. The `RemoteImage` class has the following constructors:

- `public RemoteImage(String serverName, RenderedImage source)`
- `public RemoteImage(String serverName,`
             `RenderableOp source, RenderContext renderContext)`
- `public RemoteImage(String serverName, RenderedOp source)`

The methods in the `RemoteImage` class are

- `public void setNumRetries(int numRetries)`
- `public int getNumRetries()`
- `public int getTimeout()`
- `public void setTimeout(int timeout)`

To use the `RemoteImage` object, you need to run the remote server. The API for this server is not published in the current implementation (JAI 1.0.2).

Launching the JAI RMI Server

To launch the JAI RMI server, perform the following steps:

1. Set the path and class path
2. Start the RMI registry
3. Run the server as shown here:

```
Java  -Djava.rmi.server.codebase=file:$JAI_HOME/lib/jai.jar
-Djava.rmi.server.useCodebaseOnly=false
-Djava.security.policy=file:$JAI_HOME/policy
com.sun.media.jai.rmi.RMIImageImpl
```

The evironment variable `JAI_HOME` refers to the directory in which the JAI package is installed. The `com.sun.media.jai.RMIImageImpl` class is the server and the remote interface implemented by this class has not been published. Methods for this interface are not directly exposed to the client applications either. So, to execute an operator remotely, you need to construct a `RemoteImage` object with a rendered or renderable node for that operator. The `RemoteImage` object calls the remote interface methods, thereby shielding clients from interacting with the server directly.

Here is a code snippet that shows how a client-side program can use the `RemoteImage` class to execute a JAI operator on the server-side:

```
RenderedOp logOp = JAI.create("log", srcImage);
RemoteImage remoteImage = new RemoteImage("JAIServer", logOp);
```

In this example, the log operation is performed on `srcImage` on a remote server named "JAIServer."

Remote Imaging in JAI 1.1

As stated earlier, the `RemoteImage` class has been deprecated in JAI 1.1 in favor of the `java.media.jai.remote` package, which implements the enhanced network imaging API. Important features of this API include

- **Support for different wire communication protocols.** The network imaging API is designed to support wire communication protocols such as RMI, IIOP, HTTP, and so on.

- **Property negotiation.** This feature provides the capability to negotiate a property between the client and the server. The compression scheme for transmission can be such a property that can be negotiated. The negotiation in this case involves the client and the server agreeing on a compression scheme and the parameters associated with that scheme.

- **Tile compression and decompression at end points.** This feature enables applications to compress tile data before transmission and decompress tile data upon reception.

- **Serializability.** Many classes in Java 2D and JAI are not serializable. The network imaging API has interfaces and classes to provide support for serialization of nonserializable classes.

A Quick Overview of the Network Imaging API

The network imaging API extends the pull model to provide the ability to create and edit rendered and renderable chains on the server side. It does so by defining many interfaces and classes that are conceptually similar to the ones on the client side. The new interfaces include `RemoteRIF`, `RemoteCRIF`, and `RemoteRenderedImage`, and the new classes include `RemoteRenderedOp` and `RemoteRenderableOp`. It even has a utility class named `RemoteJAI` that is similar to the `JAI` class. Using this class, you can apply the JAI operators on the server side and obtain the resulting operator node on the client side. Here's an example:

```
RemoteJAI   rjai = new RemoteJAI(protocolName, serverName);
RemoteRenderedOp rop = rjai.create("exp", parameterBlock, renderingHints);
PlanarImage  image = rop.createInstance();
```

A `RemoteJAI` object is constructed for a server and a protocol. As stated earlier, the protocol name can be any wire communication protocol—RMI, CORBA, HTTP, and so on. In order for `RemoteJAI` to recognize a protocol, that protocol must be registered with the JAI operation registry.

The `RemoteJAI` class also has the `createRenderable()` method, which returns a `RemoteRenderableOp` object. Using the `create()` and `createRenderable()` methods of `RemoteJAI`, you can easily create rendered or renderable chains on the server side.

The Property Negotiation API

Another important feature in JAI 1.1 is the property negotiation. The `Negotiable` interface represents objects on which properties are negotiated. In the current version of JAI 1.1 (beta 1), this interface is implemented by the classes `NegotiableNumericRange`, `NegotiableCollection`, and `NegotiableNumeric`. These classes represent the negotiation values as a numeric range, as a collection, and as a single numeric value, respectively. The `NegotiableCapability` class defines the negotiable capability. For example, the compression scheme can be represented by this class as a negotiable capability. The `NegotiableCapabilitySet` class represents a collection of such capabilities.

The Serialization API

The serialization API has two interfaces (`Serializer` and `SerializableState`) and a class (`SerializerFactory`). The `SerializableState` object represents the internal state of a nonserializable object. The `Serializer` object is a proxy that represents another object in the form of internal states of that object and a supporting class. The `SerializerFactory` class has static methods that can return `Serializer` instances of classes that are registered in the central repository. Several classes from Java 2D and JAI have already been added to the central repositiory, including data buffer classes, color-model classes, sample-model classes, `Raster`, `WritableRaster`, `RenderedImage`, and `WritableRenderedImage`. The `SerializerFactory` class also provides the capability to add or remove serializers.

The `SerializableRenderedImage` class is a wrapper for `RenderedImage` that creates a new serializable `RenderedImage` object. You can create a serializable `RenderedImage` object in two ways: by deep copying or "on-demand" copying. When a deep copy is requested, the entire image raster is copied during object serialization. When a deep copy is not requested, image data is sent on demand.

Conclusion

In this chapter we described how to use the RMI feature to build imaging applications. First we created a simple RMI server that reads images as bytes on the server side. For this application we could not use the AWT image loader, JPEG codec, or Image I/O codec because the AWT `Image` and `BufferedImage` objects are not serializable. On the client side, we built different types of clients that converted the image bytes to the AWT `Image`, `BufferedImage,` and `PlanarImage` formats. Then we built a server especially for JAI, and because the `RenderedOp` and `RenderableOp` objects are serializable, in this case we could use the JAI codec to load images.

With RMI and JAI together, you can build a powerful server that can perform numerous operations supported by JAI and then send the results to multiple clients. With applets, servlets, RMI, and JAI, you can build very flexible and powerful imaging architectures that can serve clients over the Web.

Internet Imaging

MORE AND MORE IMAGING APPLICATIONS are written for the Internet or at least have some Internet content. Whether it is a simple map viewer or a sophisticated scientific image visualization application, providing an Internet front end has become an essential part of any application.

The three key Java technologies in developing applications for the Internet are applets, servlets, and JavaServer Pages (JSPs). Whereas applets are a client-side technology, servlets and JSPs are server-side technologies.

Chapters 2 and 3 introduced applets. We'll start this chapter with an introduction to servlets. After looking at a few examples using servlets, we'll describe JSPs with similar examples. Then we'll describe the use of applets with servlets and JSPs. We'll wrap up the chapter with a broad example that covers all of these.

An Internet Imaging Scenario

The scenario described in this section will illustrate the importance of imaging technologies in the Internet. Consider a commonly used e-commerce application for a car manufacturer.

We want to develop a product browser that allows the user to browse different models of the car. The program must display a list of models in a category. When the user clicks a model of the car, the program needs to show on the Web page the product description with the image of the car. This program must be capable of letting the user pan, zoom, and rotate the image.

Suppose we want to develop a dealer locator program next. Users typically enter their address or just their zip code on the Web front end. The program needs to identify the assigned dealer(s) for this address. If a user doesn't find the required model, your program may need to indicate an alternate dealer, depending on certain criteria, such as driving distance. The program may also need to provide the driving directions with a map.

To develop such an application, we must have a mechanism to draw the area covered by a dealer on a map. Once we have drawn shapes for all the dealers, we must save them in a database. Many vendors provide spatial databases for storing geometries. Oracle Spatial is an example. You also need to provide a geo-coding program that codes the address to return its longitude and latitude. GIS (geographic information system) vendors such as MapInfo and QMS provide such software with street address databases. The problem of locating a dealer now is reduced to finding a shape that contains the geo-code. We can do this by searching a database of shapes that is spatially indexed. Determining whether a geo-code lies inside a shape is often called point-in-polygon in GIS terminology.

To find an alternate dealer, you may need to perform certain mathematical operations over the current region of interest and its surrounding ROIs. These operations may include computing centroids of the relevant shapes and then measuring the distance from the current ROI to its neighbors.

Implementing a dealer locator program is beyond the scope of this book because it requires address databases. However, we will explain the Java and imaging technologies that are needed to implement such a program.

What Is a Servlet?

A servlet is a Java program that runs on the server side and is considered an extension of the Web server. This means that servlets have no GUIs. Servlets are typically used to replace Common Gateway Interface (CGI) scripts.

Because servlets run on the server side, the client Web browser does not need to support the version of Java or the extensions that a servlet requires. For example, the browser does not need to download JAI even if a servlet needs it. On the other hand, an applet that uses JAI requires JAI to be downloaded on the client side. Despite these differences, applets and servlets have a lot of similarities, including following a life cycle and requiring a framework or container to run them.

Overview of the Servlet API

The servlet API is not part of the Java core package, so it does not come with the JDK. The servlet package must be downloaded from http://jakarta.apache.org/tomcat/index.html.

In the current implementation, the servlet API has three packages:

1. **`javax.servlet`.** This package defines protocol-independent interfaces and classes. The interfaces include `Servlet`, `ServletRequest`, `ServletResponse`, `ServletContext`, `ServletConfig`, `SingleThreadModel`, and `Request Dispatcher`.

Understanding the World Wide Web

The Web is a combination of many technologies. It is based on a client-server model in which the Web browser is the client. The server is typically a resource manager that supplies the documents, images, sounds, and so on.

To understand how the Web works, it is essential to look at the underlying concepts. Most of us know or at least have heard of HTML, HTTP, and URL, which make the World Wide Web possible. HTML stands for HyperText Markup Language, HTTP for HyperText Transport Protocol, and URL for Uniform Resource Locator.

To understand servlets and JavaServer Pages (JSPs), you may need to have some familiarity with HTML. Although describing HTML is beyond the scope of this book, there are plenty of books and references on this subject. We will, however, briefly discuss the basics of URLs and HTTP.

Uniform Resource Locators

As you probably know, URLs identify resources in a uniform manner. Whether the resource is a document, an image, a sound, or anything else, the URL representation mechanism is the same. Because of its universality, the URL representation for resources is not restricted to the Web. It is even used in Java to represent protocols such as Remote Method Invocation (RMI) and Java Database Connection (JDBC).

A URL representation tells us not only where a resource is located but also what protocol that resource uses. Although HTTP is the most commonly used protocol, URLs are used to represent all kinds of other protocols, even ones that pre-date the Web.

Although different resources are represented in a uniform manner, protocols don't appear to have uniform syntax. For example, the syntax for the mail protocol is not the same as for HTTP. Even though the syntax appears different, however, all URLs have the same general format: *scheme:scheme_specific_string*. Most protocols follow a syntax called Common Internet Scheme Syntax (CISS), as shown here:

scheme://user_name:password@host:port/path

As you can see, the CISS format is a subset of the general URL format. The *scheme* is the protocol—for example, HTTP or FTP.

Some well-known URL formats are

- HTTP
- FTP

continued

- ◆ Mail
- ◆ Telnet
- ◆ File

The sections that follow will briefly describe each of these formats.

HTTP

HyperText Transfer Protocol doesn't follow the CISS format entirely. It omits the user name and password:

http://host:port/path?querystring

The elements of this URL type are as follows:

- ◆ **host.** This element identifies the server's domain name or IP address.
- ◆ **port.** This element identifies the port number of the machine through which the connection is made. This is optional; if omitted, the default is 80.
- ◆ **path.** This element identifies the path of the resource. This is optional; if omitted, the slash ("/") before the path is not needed.
- ◆ **querystring.** This element provides more information about the resource. It is optional; if omitted, the question mark ("?") is not needed. The query string follows a simple grammar. You can input parameters to send to the server in the form of *<name = value>*. The ampersand ("&") is used to separate multiple parameters. Here's an example:

  ```
  image1="lena.gif"&image2="mandrill.gif"
  ```

  As we'll see later, these parameters are submitted to the server through an HTTP method called `GET`.

  The following example illustrates the use of HTTP:

  http://www.vistechsoft.com/images?name="lena.gif"

FTP

Unlike HTTP, the FTP URL format follows CISS in its entirety. Here's the syntax:

ftp://user:password@host:port/path

The user name and password parameters are optional.

Mail

The *mailto* URL does not follow CISS. Here's the syntax:

mailto:email_login@host

An example would be

mailto:larryhr@execpc.com

Telnet

The Telnet URL format is as follows:

telnet://username:password@host:port

File

The *file* URL format looks like this:

file://host:port/path

In a local machine, the format changes slightly:

file://localhost:8080/path

HyperText Transfer Protocol

Although all the protocols we have mentioned are important, our focus in this chapter is HTTP. Unlike FTP, HTTP is a stateless protocol.

The HTTP specs define seven procedures, known as methods, for implementing the HTTP client-server protocol: GET, POST, HEAD, PUT, DELETE, LINK, and UNLINK. Among these seven methods, only three—GET, POST, and HEAD—are used frequently. We'll look at these three methods briefly in the sections that follow.

The GET Method

The GET method is used for retrieving a document specified by the URL. In addition, it can be used for passing a parameter to the server. As mentioned in the preceding section (on URLs), parameters are passed through the query string appended at the end of the URL.

The POST Method

The POST method, as the name suggests, posts information to the server. With the GET method, the amount of information that can be sent to the server is limited. Some browsers limit the length of the URL to 256 characters. With POST, there is no such limitation. Information is transferred through the sockets.

Another important difference between GET and POST is that when the POST method posts the information, the URL doesn't change.

continued

> **The HEAD Method**
> The HEAD method retrieves the header, or meta-information, from the resource without retrieving the resource itself. The information retrieved includes document size, modification time, and so on.

2. **`javax.servlet.http`.** The interfaces and classes in this package extend the corresponding interfaces and classes of `javax.servlet` to describe the behavior of HTTP servlets.
3. **`javax.servlet.jsp`.** This package contains JSP-related interfaces and classes. It has APIs that are meant primarily for JSP engine developers.

Creating a Servlet

The `javax.servlet.Servlet` interface specifies methods that define a servlet's life cycle. A `Servlet` object must implement this interface or its descendants. As Figure 16.1 shows, the `javax.servlet.GenericServlet` class implements the `Servlet` interface and represents a protocol-independent generic servlet. The `javax.servlet.http.HttpServlet` class extends this class and implements HTTP.

Newer Web servers typically come with a servlet container that instantiates `Servlet` objects. Once instantiated, the `Servlet` instance is available until the container terminates it. In a typical implementation, once a servlet has been created, it is used again and again for different clients. However, if a servlet implements the `SingleThreadModel` interface, the container will ensure that only one request is handled at a time.

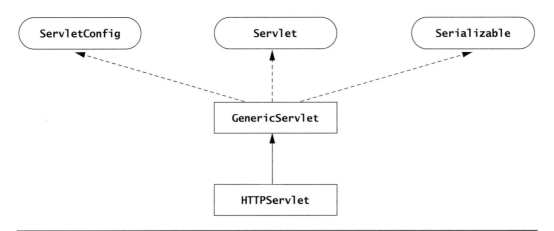

FIGURE 16.1 The Servlet class hierarchy

The Servlet Life Cycle

Just like applets, servlets have life cycles. There are three phases to a servlet life cycle (see Figure 16.2):

1. Initialization
2. Service
3. Termination

A complete description of the servlet API is beyond the scope of this book. However, we will look at a subset of the servlet API. The following methods of the `Servlet` interface specify the life cycle behavior:

- `public void init(ServletConfig config) throws ServletException`
- `public void service(ServletRequest req, ServletResponse res)`
          `throws ServletException, java.io.IOException`
- `public void destroy()`

In addition, the `Servlet` interface has methods for obtaining the servlet information and configuration:

- `public java.lang.String getServletInfo()`
- `public ServletConfig getServletConfig()`

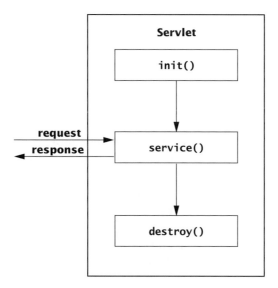

FIGURE 16.2 The servlet life cycle

The Servlet Configuration and Context

The `ServletConfig` interface has methods for retrieving initialization parameters and the `ServletContext` object. Here are the methods of this interface:

- ◆ **public java.lang.String getInitParameter(java.lang.String name)**
- ◆ **public java.util.Enumeration getInitParameterNames()**
- ◆ **public ServletContext getServletContext()**

   When a servlet is instantiated, its `init()` method reads all the initialization parameters from the deployment descriptor file (see the section titled Web Archive a little later in this chapter). In addition to the parameters, the `ServletConfig` object holds the `ServletContext` object. The `ServletContext` interface specifies methods that a servlet needs for communicating with a servlet container. These include get methods for obtaining the container attributes, the MIME type of a file, the path, and so on. `ServletContext` also has methods for logging messages.

Obtaining a Servlet Context

It is often necessary to obtain the servlet context within a servlet. To do this, you must first get the servlet configuration by calling **getServletConfig()**. Once you have obtained the servlet configuration, call its **getServletContext()** method. Here's the pseudocode:

```
ServletConfig  config = this.getServletConfig();
ServletContext  context = context.getServletContext();
```

Servlet Classes

The `GenericServlet` class implements the `Servlet` and the `ServletConfig` interfaces. The `HttpServlet` class, which extends `GenericServlet`, is specific to HTTP. `HttpServlet` has methods that map to the HTTP methods described in the previous section. Here are those methods:

- ◆ **protected void doGet(HttpServletRequest req, HttpServletResponse resp)**
  throws ServletException, java.io.IOException
- ◆ **protected void doPost(HttpServletRequest req, HttpServletResponse resp)**
  throws ServletException, java.io.IOException
- ◆ **protected void doDelete(HttpServletRequest req, HttpServletResponse resp)**
  throws ServletException, java.io.IOException
- ◆ **protected void doPut(HttpServletRequest req, HttpServletResponse resp)**
  throws ServletException, java.io.IOException

- **protected void doTrace(HttpServletRequest req, HttpServletResponse resp)**
  throws ServletException, java.io.IOException

Each of these methods has `HttpServletRequest` and `HttpServletResponse` parameters. When one of these methods is called, `HttpServletRequest` is used for extracting information about the request, and `HttpServletResponse` is used for sending a response.

When a servlet is invoked, the `service()` method (recall that this is one of the servlet life cycle methods, as shown in Figure 16.2) calls the appropriate HTTP methods.

For example, when a `doGet()` method is called, the servlet may extract the parameters associated with the `GET` request. It may then call the `HttpServletResponse` methods to create a Web page. When the `doGet()` method completes its execution, the servlet container uses an `HttpServletResponse` object to generate the Web page.

Getting Started with Servlets and JSPs

A servlet requires a servlet container to run, and most Web servers provide support for servlets through built-in containers. To develop your own servlets and JavaServer Pages, you can use a reference implementation called Tomcat from Apache. (You can download the related software from http://jakarta.apache.org/tomcat/index.html.)

In this book we'll use this software to illustrate the examples. You can modify these examples appropriately to run them in your environment. To install a servlet on your Web server, you may wish to consult your Web administrator.

Paths

A URL does not show the absolute path in the server. A servlet is like a CGI script that resides in a directory designated as the servlet root. If the `Servlet` class is in a package hierarchy, the class file must be placed in the directory that reflects the package hierarchy.

For example, if the servlet root directory is `servletRoot` and the package hierarchy is contained in `mypackage.serv`, the servlet will be in the `servletRoot/mypackage/serv` directory.

Web Archive

Web Archive (WAR) is analogous to Java Archive (JAR). The servlet- and JSP-related classes and resources are bundled in a WAR file. Just as JAR has the `META_INF` directory, WAR contains a directory called `WEB_INF`.

In Tomcat, the WAR file is in the `webapps/examples` directory. The `WEB_INF` directory here contains the servlet classes and related resources. This directory also contains a Web Application Descriptor file named `web.xml`, which specifies the deployment descriptors for the servlets and JSPs.

If you wish to add your own servlet, `web.xml` is the file in which you can assign an alias to the servlet and set its initial parameters. Here's what a `web.xml` file looks like:

```
<?xml version="1.0" encoding="ISO-8859-1"?>

<!DOCTYPE web-app
    PUBLIC "-//Sun Microsystems, Inc.//DTD Web Application 2.2//EN"
    "http://java.sun.com/j2ee/dtds/web-app_2.2.dtd">

<web-app>
    <servlet>
        <servlet-name>
            snoop
        </servlet-name>
        <servlet-class>
            SnoopServlet
        </servlet-class>
        <init-param>
            <param-name>foo</param-name>
            <param-value>bar</param-value>
        </init-param>
    </servlet>
        ....
</web-app>
```

We'll see some examples later in this chapter. If you use a commercial servlet and JSP container, you will probably have a GUI tool that automatically updates the `web.xml` file. In such a GUI tool, you would typically enter the fully qualified servlet name (the entire package name and the class name), with its alias and all the initialization parameters.

Invoking a Servlet

You can invoke a servlet from a Web browser by typing the servlet URL that points to the servlet name, which is either the fully qualified name or an alias (if defined in the `web.xml` file).

If you don't have a commercial servlet container, you can use the Tomcat servlet container to test your servlets. In Tomcat, the bin directory is under `<TOMCAT_HOME>`. This directory has scripts to start, run, and stop the Tomcat servlet container. Here are the steps for using the Tomcat container:

1. When you write a servlet, compile the code and place the class files in the directory `<TOMCAT_HOME>/webapps/classes`.

2. Update the web.xml file.

◆ Add an alias to your servlet. (This is optional.)

◆ If your servlet has initialization parameters, add init parameter tags and the values.

3. Start the Tomcat server. Use the start-up script in <TOMCAT_HOME>/bin. In Windows, type "startup" to start the server. In Unix, type "startup.sh".

4. Type the servlet URL with parameters (if any). This command will launch your servlet, and the resulting page will be displayed on the Web browser once the servlet has been executed.

5. To modify the servlet, type "<TOMCAT_HOME>/bin/shutdown" to shut down the server, and repeat steps 1, 3, and 4.

Let's start with a simple example.

A Simple Image-Loading Servlet Example

Our aim in this example is to create a servlet that loads an image pointed to by a URL. The page served by this servlet will contain only the image. One way of creating an image for the servlet is to load the image as an array of bytes and then write to a ServletOutputStream object.

Listing 16.1 shows the code for the SimpleImageLoaderServlet class, which illustrates how to load an image. This servlet can be invoked from a URL or by other servlets.

> **Note:** The source code for the servlets described in this chapter is available on the book's Web page in the directory src/chapter16/servlet/servletsection. To run a servlet, compile the classes into the <Tomcat_Home>/webapps/examples/WEB_INF/classes directory.

LISTING 16.1 The SimpleImageLoaderServlet class

```java
public class SimpleImageLoaderServlet extends HttpServlet{

    public void doGet(HttpServletRequest req, HttpServletResponse res)
                    throws ServletException{
        try {
            res.setContentType("image/jpeg");
            String filename = req.getPathTranslated();
            if(filename == null){
                HttpSession session = req.getSession(false);
                filename = session.getValue("imagepath")+"\\"+req.getParameter("images");
            }
            ServletOutputStream out = res.getOutputStream();
```

continued

```
        loadImage(out, filename);
    } catch(Exception e) {System.out.println(e);}
}

public void loadImage(OutputStream boutstream, String filename) {
    try {
    FileInputStream bis = new FileInputStream(filename);
    byte[] imageBuf = new byte[1024];
    for(;;){
        int bytesread = bis.read(imageBuf);
        if (bytesread <0) {break;}
        boutstream.write(imageBuf,0,bytesread);
    }
    } catch(Exception e) {System.out.println(e);}
}
}
```

When this servlet is invoked, the servlet container calls the default `init()` method in the `HttpServlet` class. Because there are no initialization parameters, the `SimpleImageLoaderServlet` class does not override the `init()` method. The container then calls the `service()` method, which in turn calls the `doGet()` method.

The `doGet()` method has two arguments: `request` and `response`. When the method finishes its execution, the `response` object is returned to the container, which uses it to post the HTML content to the Web page.

The `doGet()` method first sets the content type to "image/jpeg". To load an image, the absolute path is needed. If this servlet is invoked from the URL, users can type the relative image path as a query string (see Figure 16.3). If the user has entered the query string, the `getPathTranslated()` method of the `HttpServletRequest` class converts the image path to the actual path; otherwise it will return `null`.

We have provided an alternate way to get the image path—that is, through the `session` object. The `session` object can be used to track the session. The servlet that invokes `SimpleImageLoaderServlet` can save the `"imagepath"` value in the `session` object. To see how this is done, review the `ListImagesServlet` example in Listing 16.2.

If the `getPathTranslated()` method returns `null`, `doGet()` gets the `session` object from `request` and uses it to retrieve the `"imagepath"` value. The actual image file name is provided by the `"images"` parameter. Again, see the example in Listing 16.2 to see how the `"images"` parameter is set. The absolute image path is created by concatenation of the `"imagepath"` value to the `"images"` parameter.

The `doGet()` method then gets the `ServletOutputStream` object from the response object and calls the `loadImage()` method.

The `loadImage()` method reads the image as a `FileInputStream` object and writes the bytes from this input stream to an `OutputStream` object, which in this case is a `ServletOutputStream` object.

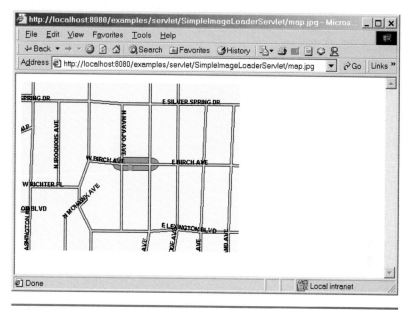

FIGURE 16.3 Launching the simple image loader servlet

A Servlet for Listing and Selecting Images

Now let's write a servlet that is a little more complicated. This servlet will allow users to list and select images residing in a directory on the server side. When the user selects an image and clicks on **DISPLAY,** SimpleImageLoaderServlet will be called with the selected image as the parameter (see Figures 16.4 and 16.5). Listing 16.2 shows the code for the ListImagesServlet class.

LISTING 16.2 The ListImagesServlet class

```
import java.io.*;
import java.awt.event.*;
import java.awt.*;
import java.awt.image.*;

public class ListImagesServlet extends HttpServlet{
    public void doGet(HttpServletRequest req, HttpServletResponse res)
                throws ServletException{
        try {
          res.setContentType("text/html");
          String dir = req.getPathTranslated();
          String fileList[] = listFiles(dir);

          PrintWriter out = res.getWriter();
          out.println("<HTML>");
          out.println("<HEAD><TITLE>File list</TITLE></HEAD> ");
```

continued

```
        out.println("<FORM ACTION=\"/examples/servlet/SimpleImageLoaderServlet\"
method=\"Get\">");
    out.println("<BODY>");
    out.println("<TABLE border=1 align=\"left\">");
    out.println("<TR><TH>ID</TH><TH>Image</TH></TR>");

    HttpSession session = req.getSession(true);
    if(session != null) session.putValue("imagepath", dir);

    for(int i=0;i<fileList.length;i++) {
        out.println("<TR><TD>");
        out.println(i);
        out.println("</TD>");
        out.println("<TD>");
        out.println("<INPUT TYPE=\"RADIO\" name=\"images\" ");
        out.println("value=\""+fileList[i]+"\" >"+fileList[i]);
        out.println("</TD>");
        out.println("</TR>");
    }
    out.println("</TABLE>");
    out.println("<INPUT TYPE=\"SUBMIT\" VALUE=\"DISPLAY\">");
```

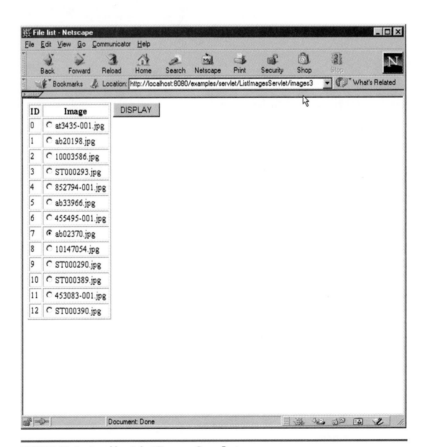

FIGURE 16.4　Invoking `ListImagesServlet`

```
      out.println("<FORM>");
      out.println("</BODY></HTML>");
    } catch(Exception e) {System.out.println(e);}
  }
  public synchronized String[] listFiles(String dirstr) {
    String fl[] = null;
    try {
      File dir = new File(dirstr);
      fl = dir.list();
    } catch (Exception e){System.out.println(e);}
    return fl;
  }
}
```

Before you run `ListImagesServlet,` create a directory under `examples` and copy images to it. Use the name of this directory in the servlet URL.

To run this servlet, type the servlet URL with the image path appended to it as a path. As Figure 16.4 shows, the URL is http:/localhost:8080/examples/servlet/

FIGURE 16.5   The selected image

<u>ListImagesServlet/images3</u>. The image path in this case is `images3`, which is a directory that we created under `examples`. This directory contains several images.

The `doGet()` method is called when the HTTP `GET` method is invoked, and `doPost()` is called when the HTTP `POST` method is invoked.

The main purpose of the `doGet()` method is to create a form with a table. The **DISPLAY** button is the submit button for this form. The `doGet()` method obtains the requesting URL and passes it to the `ACTION` command and assigns HTTP's `GET` method to invoke `SimpleImageLoaderServlet`.

The `doGet()` method first translates the image path—that is, the `images3` directory—to the absolute path by calling the `getPathTranslated()` method of the `HttpServletRequest` class. Using this path, the `doGet()` method reads the file names in `images3` into an array called `fileList`. The `doGet()` method then gets the `PrintWriter` object from the `response` object. It then creates a form with a table containing radio buttons for each of the files listed in `fileList`.

Observe that each of the radio buttons is created with an *<INPUT TYPE=radio name="images">* tag. This means that the value of the selected radio button is contained in the `"images"` parameter. When the form is submitted, the `"images"` parameter is sent to the servlet called by the URL, which in this case is `SimpleImageLoaderServlet`.

An Image Viewer Servlet

Let's modify the servlets we have developed so far to allow image selection and display on the same page. To do this, we must have the HTML page that is generated by the servlet read the selected image directly from the image directory. This means that this page needs to have the `<IMG SRC=imagename>` tag to read the image. In the servlet, `imagename` needs to be a variable that holds the name of the image file selected.

Unlike `ListImagesServlet`, this servlet must call itself when an image is selected. One option is to hard-code the servlet name in the action tag, but there is a better way. The `HttpUtils` class has a static method called `getRequestedURL(Http ServletRequest)`, which returns the requesting URL in a `StringBuffer` object. All you need to do to call the same servlet is to assign this string to `ACTION`. Listing 16.3 shows how this is done.

LISTING 16.3 The `ImageViewerServlet` class

```
import javax.servlet.*;
import javax.servlet.http.*;
import java.io.*;
import java.awt.event.*;
import java.awt.*;
import java.awt.image.*;
import java.util.*;

public class ImageViewerServlet extends HttpServlet{
```

```java
public void doGet(HttpServletRequest req, HttpServletResponse res)
                throws ServletException{
  String dir = null;
  String fileList[] = null;
  try {
    res.setContentType("text/html");
    PrintWriter out = res.getWriter();
    String filename = "/examples/lena.gif";
    out.println("<HTML>");
    out.println("<HEAD><TITLE>File list</TITLE></HEAD> ");
    StringBuffer reqUrl = HttpUtils.getRequestURL(req);
    out.println("<FORM ACTION="+ reqUrl.toString() +" method=\"Get\">");
    out.println("<BODY BGCOLOR= lime>");
    out.println("<TABLE border=1 align=\"left\">");
    out.println("<TR><TH>ID</TH><TH>Image</TH></TR>");

    HttpSession session = req.getSession(false);
    if(session != null) {
      String param = req.getParameter("images");
      String fl = null;
      if(param != null){
        fl = new String(session.getValue("imagepath")+"/"+param);
        dir = new String((String)session.getValue("curDir"));
      }else {
        dir = req.getPathTranslated();
        if(session != null)session.putValue("curDir", dir);
      }
      if(fl != null) filename = fl;
      if(dir != null) fileList = listFiles(dir);
    }else {
      // Create a session the first time
      session = req.getSession(true);
      dir = req.getPathTranslated();
      fileList = listFiles(dir);
      if(session != null) {
        session.putValue("imagepath", "/examples");
        session.putValue("curDir", dir);
      }
    }
    String extra = req.getPathInfo();
    if(fileList != null) {
      for(int i=0;i<fileList.length;i++) {
        out.println("<TR><TD>");
        out.println(i);
        out.println("</TD>");
        out.println("<TD>");
        out.println("<INPUT TYPE=\"RADIO\" name=\"images\" ");
        if(extra == null)
          out.println("value=\""+fileList[i]+"\" >"+fileList[i]);
        else out.println("value=\""+extra+ "/"+fileList[i]+"\" >"+fileList[i]);
        out.println("</TD>");
        out.println("</TR>");
      }
    }
    out.println("</TABLE>");
    out.println("<INPUT TYPE=\"SUBMIT\" VALUE=\"DISPLAY\" align=\"top\">" );
    out.println("<IMG SRC=\""+filename+"\" align=right>");
```

continued

```
            out.println("<FORM>");
            out.println("</BODY></HTML>");
        } catch(Exception e) {System.out.println(e);}
    }

    public void doPost(HttpServletRequest request,
                       HttpServletResponse response)
        throws IOException, ServletException {
        doGet(request, response);
    }

    public synchronized String[] listFiles(String dirstr) {
        String fl[] = null;
        try {
            ExtensionFilter filter =  new ExtensionFilter("jpeg,gif,JPEG,GIF JPG,jpg, png,
PNG");
            File dir = new File(dirstr);
            fl = dir.list(filter);
        } catch (Exception e){System.out.println(e);}
        return fl;
    }

    class  ExtensionFilter implements FilenameFilter{
        private String extString;
        public ExtensionFilter(String ext){
            extString = ext;
        }
        public boolean accept(File dir, String name){
                StringTokenizer st = new StringTokenizer(extString, ",");
            while(st.hasMoreTokens()){
                String str = st.nextToken();
                String tok = str.trim();
                if(name.endsWith(tok)){ return true;}
            }
            return false;
        }
    }
}
```

As mentioned earlier, the doGet() method is called when the HTTP GET method is invoked, and doPost() is called when the HTTP POST method is invoked. The ImageViewerServlet class overrides both the doGet() and the doPost() methods. In addition, doPost() calls doGet(), which has all the necessary code for listing and selecting images.

As in Listing 16.2, the doGet() method creates a form with a table. The **DISPLAY** button is the submit button for this form. The doGet() method obtains the requesting URL and passes it to the ACTION command, and it assigns HTTP's POST method to invoke the servlet.

The table contains a list of radio buttons, each of which is assigned a string value that is the same as the path name it represents. If an extra path is added to the URL, the image path contains this path as well. For example, if the file name is lena.gif and the extra path is images3, then the value of the radio button is images3/

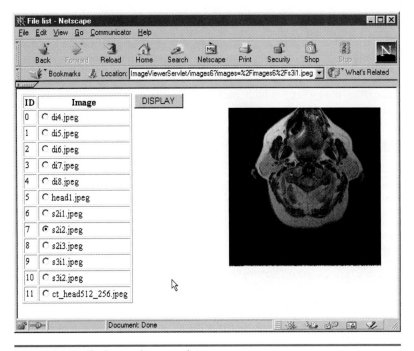

FIGURE 16.6   The image viewer servlet

`lena.gif`. If this button is selected and **DISPLAY** is clicked, then `images3/lena.gif` is sent as the `"images"` parameter to the servlet that was launched. In this case, it is the same servlet (i.e., `ImageViewerServlet`). As Listing 16.3 shows, the `filename` variable holds the path. The value of `filename` is obtained from the `"images"` parameter, which is set when a radio button is selected.

Toward the end of the `doGet()` method, `filename` is assigned to the *<IMG SRC>* tag. HTML will interpret the string passed to it—that is, the value of `filename`—as an image and will display it (provided that it is valid) (see Figure 16.6).

Using JAI with Servlets

Now that we have seen how to use servlets to load and display images, it's time to look at how to use JAI to manipulate images. We'll create two servlets:

1. A servlet to display the GUI required for displaying the image list and the GUI for entering the rotation angle and the zoom factor.
2. A servlet to load and manipulate an image and send it to the client.

An Image Manipulator User Interface Servlet

This servlet is similar to `ListImagesServlet` (see Listing 16.2). It displays the list of images in the path given in the URL. In addition, it has the GUI to enter the rotation angle and the magnification (zoom) factor. Clicking on **DISPLAY** calls `ImageManipServlet`, which manipulates the selected image. Listing 16.4 shows the code for the `ImageManipUIServlet` class.

LISTING 16.4 The `ImageManipUIServlet` class

```java
import javax.servlet.*;
import javax.servlet.http.*;
import java.io.*;
import java.awt.event.*;
import java.awt.*;
import java.awt.image.*;
import java.util.*;

public class ImageManipUIServlet extends HttpServlet{

    public void doGet(HttpServletRequest req, HttpServletResponse res)
                  throws ServletException{
      String dir = null;
      String fileList[] = null;
      try {
        res.setContentType("text/html");
        PrintWriter out = res.getWriter();
        out.println("<HTML>");
        out.println("<HEAD><TITLE>File list</TITLE></HEAD> ");
        out.println("<FORM ACTION=\"/examples/servlet/ImageManipServlet\"
method=\"doPost\">");
        out.println("<BODY>");
        out.println("<TABLE border=1 align=\"left\">");
        out.println("<TR><TH>ID</TH><TH>Image</TH></TR>");

        HttpSession session = req.getSession(false);
        if(session != null) {
            String param = req.getParameter("images");
            String extra = req.getPathInfo();
            if(extra != null) {
                session.putValue("extrapath", extra);
            }

            if(param != null){
              dir = new String((String)session.getValue("curDir"));
            }else {
                dir = req.getPathTranslated();
                session.putValue("curDir", dir);
            }
            if(dir != null) fileList = listFiles(dir);
        }else {
            session = req.getSession(true);
            dir = req.getPathTranslated();
            fileList = listFiles(dir);
            if(session != null) {
```

```
                session.putValue("imagepath", "/examples");
                session.putValue("curDir", dir);
            }
        }
        String extra1 = req.getPathInfo();
        if(fileList != null) {
        for(int i=0;i<fileList.length;i++) {
            out.println("<tr><td>");
            out.println(i);
            out.println("</td>");
            out.println("<td>");
            out.println("<INPUT TYPE=\"RADIO\" name=\"images\" ");
            if(extra1 == null) {
                if(session != null) {
                    String extra = (String)session.getValue("extrapath");
                    if(extra == null)
                        out.println("value=\""+fileList[i]+"\" >"+fileList[i]);
                    else   out.println("value=\""+extra+ "/"+fileList[i]+"\"
>"+fileList[i]);
                }else   out.println("value=\""+fileList[i]+"\" >"+fileList[i]);
            }else {
                out.println("value=\""+extra1+ "/"+fileList[i]+"\" >"+fileList[i]);
            }
            out.println("</td>");
            out.println("</tr>");
        }
        }

        out.println("</TABLE>");
        out.println("\"Rotate:\" <INPUT TYPE=\"TEXT\" name=\"rotAngle\" >degrees
<BR>");
        out.println("\"Zoom   :\" <INPUT TYPE=\"TEXT\" name=\"magFactor\"  >percent
<BR><BR>");
        out.println("<INPUT TYPE=\"SUBMIT\" VALUE=\"DISPLAY\" align=left>" );
        out.println("<FORM>");
        out.println("</BODY></HTML>");
    } catch(Exception e) {System.out.println(e);}
    }

}
```

If you compare the code in Listing 16.4 with the code for `ListImagesServlet` (Listing 16.2), you will see that we have added two more input components, which are text fields to enter the rotation angle and the magnification (zoom) factor (see Figure 16.7). Each of these input components is associated with a parameter. When the user enters a value in the text field, the corresponding parameter is assigned that value. When the form is submitted—that is, when **DISPLAY** is clicked—these parameters are sent to the servlet that is called, which in this case is `ImageManipServlet`.

An Image Manipulator Servlet

As Listing 16.4 shows, the `ImageManipUIServlet` class calls `ImageManipServlet` with three parameters: `"images"`, `"rotAngle"`, and `"magFactor"`. `ImageManipServlet`

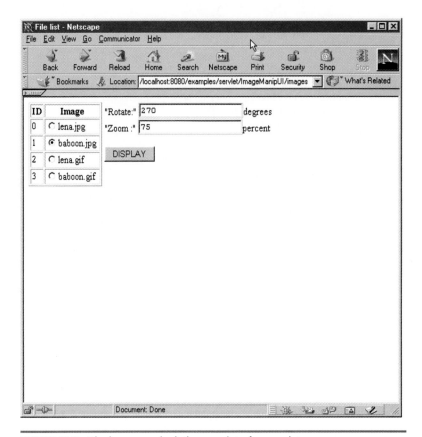

FIGURE 16.7　The image manipulation user interface servlet

uses JAI to rotate and zoom the image with the parameters passed from the calling servlet (i.e., `ImageManipUIServlet`). Listing 16.5 shows the code for `ImageManip Servlet`.

LISTING 16.5　The `ImageManipServlet` class

```
public class ImageManipServlet extends HttpServlet{
   public void doGet(HttpServletRequest req, HttpServletResponse res)
              throws ServletException{
     String dir = null;
     String fileList[] = null;
     PlanarImage image;
     try {
       String filename = "/examples/lena.gif";
       StringBuffer buf = HttpUtils.getRequestURL(req);
       System.out.println("url = "+ buf);
       res.setContentType("image/jpeg");
```

```
        ServletContext context = getServletContext();
        String par = req.getParameter("images");
        if (par == null) par = "lena.gif";
        double magFactor = 0.0, rotAngle = 0.0;

        String rot = req.getParameter("rotAngle");
        String mag = req.getParameter("magFactor");
        try {
            rotAngle = Math.toRadians((Double.valueOf(rot)).doubleValue());
        } catch(Exception e) {}
        try{
            magFactor = (Integer.valueOf(mag)).intValue()/100.0;
        } catch(Exception e) {}
        String imagepath = context.getRealPath(par);
        image = readAsPlanarImage(imagepath);
        PlanarImage outimage = manip(image, rotAngle, magFactor);
        String writepath = context.getRealPath("/readimage.jpg");
        ServletOutputStream out = res.getOutputStream();
        saveAsJPEG(outimage,out);
    } catch(Exception e) {System.out.println(e);}
}

public void doPost(HttpServletRequest request,
                   HttpServletResponse response)
    throws IOException, ServletException {
    doGet(request, response);
}

public static PlanarImage readAsPlanarImage(String filename) {
    return JAI.create("fileload", filename);
}

public static void saveAsJPEG(RenderedImage image, OutputStream out)
        throws java.io.IOException {
    JPEGEncodeParam param = new JPEGEncodeParam();
    ImageEncoder encoder = ImageCodec.createImageEncoder("JPEG", out, param);
    encoder.encode(image);
    out.close();
}

protected PlanarImage manip(PlanarImage image, double rot, double mag) {
    if(( rot <= 0.001) && (mag <=0.0)) return image;
    RenderedOp op =null, op1=null, op2 =null;
    if(rot > 0.001){
        op1 = rotate(image, rot);
        if(mag <=0.0) return op1.createInstance();
        else {
            op2 = scale(op1, mag,mag);
            return op2.createInstance();
        }
    }else {
        op2 = scale(image, mag,mag);
        return op2.createInstance();
    }
}
```

continued

```
public RenderedOp scale(PlanarImage image, double magx, double magy) {
   ParameterBlock pb = new ParameterBlock();
   pb.addSource(image);
   pb.add((float)magx);
   pb.add((float)magy);
   pb.add(0f);
   pb.add(0f);
   pb.add(Interpolation.getInstance(Interpolation.INTERP_NEAREST));
   return JAI.create("scale", pb);
}

 public RenderedOp rotate(PlanarImage image, double ang) {
   ParameterBlock pb = new ParameterBlock();
   pb.addSource(image);
   pb.add((float)(image.getWidth())/2);
   pb.add((float)(image.getHeight())/2);
   pb.add((float)ang);
   pb.add(Interpolation.getInstance(Interpolation.INTERP_NEAREST));
   return JAI.create("rotate", pb);
 }
}
```

The `doGet()` method first retrieves the three parameters—`"images"`, `"rotAngle"`, and `"magFactor"`—from the `request` object. Because `"rotAngle"` and `"magFactor"` are strings, `doGet()` converts them to `double` and `int,` respectively.

In order for JAI to read an image, it needs the absolute path. The `doGet()` method converts the path in the `"images"` parameter to the absolute path by calling `HttpContext`'s `getRealPath()` method.

FIGURE 16.8   The image manipulation servlet

The rest of the processing is done by the JAI package. The FileLoad operator loads the image. The Rotate and Scale operators, respectively, rotate and scale this image. (For more information on how these operators work, see Chapter 12.) Figure 16.8 shows how this servlet is launched.

JavaServer Pages

As Listings 16.1 through 16.5 have shown, many HTML statements are embedded within the Java code, making the code highly unreadable. The more complex the servlet, the worse it gets. Moreover, any changes to the HTML page require recompilation of the code, which is obviously not desirable from the maintenance point of view.

With servlets, it is hard to separate presentation from content. To overcome this drawback, the JavaServer Pages (JSP) feature was designed. In some sense, JSPs are the opposite of servlets. A JSP is written in HTML or XML (eXtensible Markup Language), and Java code is embedded within the page.

The JSP specs include several predefined tags. JSP tags can also be custom defined. These tags allow the application logic to be outside of the JSP. Because of the flexibility of tags, presentation and application logic can be neatly separated with JSPs.

To invoke a JSP, all you need to do is to enter the JSP URL—for example, http://localhost:8080//examples/jsp/myjsp.jsp. A JSP page has the extension *.jsp*. To support the JSP feature, a Web server must have a JSP container (sometimes known as the JSP engine).

A Quick Introduction to JSPs

A JSP typically consists of

- ◆ HTML or XML components
- ◆ JSP tags
- ◆ Java code snippets called scriptlets

Just like servlets, JSPs require an engine to process the JSP requests. The basic responsibilities of this engine are

- ◆ **JSP translation.** When a request for a page is made for the first time, the JSP is compiled and translated into a servlet (as we saw in the previous section), which is nothing but a Java class that implements the `Servlet` interface. The same class will be reused as long as no changes are made to the JSP.
- ◆ **Request processing.** Requests are processed in JSPs in the same way as in servlets.

The JSP Life Cycle

Under the hood, a JSP is implemented as a servlet. The `java.servlet.jsp` package has two interfaces: `JspPage` and `HttpJspPage.` As you might have guessed, `JspPage` extends the `Servlet` interface, and `HttpJspPage` extends `JspPage.`

The life cycle of a JSP servlet is defined by the methods in the `JspPage` and `HttpJspPage` interfaces. The `JspPage` interface methods are

- `public void jspInit()`
- `public void jspDestroy()`

The `HttpJspPage` interface has just one method:

- `_jspService(HttpServletRequest request, HttpServletResponse response)`
  `throws ServletException, java.io.IOException`

In a JSP, you can override `jspInit()` and `jspDestroy()` methods, but not the `_jspService()` method, the code for which is generated by compilation of the JSP.

The JSP servlet has a life cycle similar to that of a regular servlet (see Figure 16.9).

JSP Syntax

JSP markup tags are divided into three categories:

1. Directives

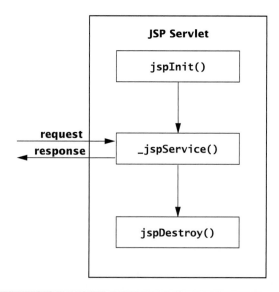

FIGURE 16.9 The JSP servlet life cycle

2. Scripting elements

3. Standard actions

Let's look at each category in detail.

Directives

Directives convey processing information to the JSP engine. Directives are enclosed within the <%@ . . . %> tag. Currently supported directives include `page`, `include`, and `taglib`. The `page` directive has several attributes that provide information about the page, such as which Java classes to use, the content type, and so on. The following example illustrates:

```
<% @page import javax.media.jai.*, javax.media.imageio.* buffer="32k" %>
```

The `include` directive lets you divide the page into manageable pieces. Here's an example:

```
<%@include file="mysignature.html" %>
```

The file `mysignature.html` may contain information that is used in every page and included at the end of the page.

Scripting Elements

Declarations

You can declare page-level variables or methods using the declaration scripting element. For example:

```
<%! init myCounter = 0; %>

<%! public void jspInit()    { //some code ...}
    public void jspDestroy() { //some code ...}
 %>
```

Expressions

A JSP expression syntax is of the form <%= . . . %>. Here's an example:

```
<%=myCounter++  %>
```

In this example, `myCounter` is evaluated. Notice that there is no semicolon at the end of the expression.

Scriptlets

Scriptlets are code snippets embedded within the <% . . . %> tag. A scriptlet can contain any Java code. If this code refers to an external package, make sure that the **import** attribute of the page directive contains the relevant package. Here's an example:

```
<%  for (i=0; i< fileList.length; i++) { %>
      Image <%=I%>  <%=fileList[i]%><br>
<%} %>
```

In this example the contents for the `fileList` array are displayed (assuming that the array `fileList` is declared and populated elsewhere in the page). The example shows how HTML and Java code are intermixed.

Comments

Comments can be included as a scripting element. Anything enclosed by <%-- . . . --%> is considered a comment. Note that you can still include comments through the HTML syntax as well.

Standard Actions

Actions allow the page to execute tasks without Java code being written. The syntax for standard actions is <*jsp:someaction ...*>.

Before we get into the detail, let's discuss objects in a JSP.

Objects in a JSP

As suggested earlier, you can create Java objects within a page. These objects can be used in scriptlets and expressions. Each object has a certain scope, which can be set by the author. The four scopes, in order of most visible to least visible, are as follows:

1. `application`
2. `session`
3. `request`
4. `page`

As a convenience, several objects are also implicitly available to a JSP (see Table 16.1).

The forward Action

The **forward** action transfers the control to another JSP, servlet, or URL. When a **forward** request is received, generated content is discarded and request processing starts anew at the new location. Here's the syntax:

<*jsp:forward page="mypage.jsp"/*>

TABLE 16.1   Implicit Objects

OBJECT	TYPE	SCOPE
request	javax.servlet.http.HttpServletRequest	Request
response	javax.servlet.http.HttpServletResponse	Page
config	javax.servlet.ServletConfig	Page
session	javax.servlet.http.HttpSession	Session
application	javax.servlet.ServletContext	Application
page	javax.servlet.jsp.HttpJspPage	Page
out	javax.servlet.jsp.JspWriter	Page
pageContext	javax.servlet.jsp.PageContext	Page
exception	javax.lang.Throwable	page

The `forward` action can explicitly pass parameters to the forwarded page through the following syntax:

```
<jsp:forward page="somepage" >
    <jsp:param name="param1" value="value1">
       ...
    <jsp:param name="param2" value="value2">
</jsp:forward>
```

The include Action

The `include` action allows the JSP authors to include content from another document in the current page. Just as with the `forward` action, the included page can be a JSP, a servlet, or a static URL. Here's the syntax:

<jsp:include page="mysig.url" flush="true" />

The `flush` attribute tells the JSP container whether to flush the output buffer for the current page. As with the `forward` action, you can also pass parameters to the included page.

The useBean Action

With the `useBean` action, JSPs can instantiate a JavaBean and use it to process the request, thus separating application logic and presentation. The following example illustrates the syntax:

```
<jsp:useBean  id="loader" class="imageviewer.ImageLoader" scope ="session"/>
```

There are three parts to the `useBean` tag:

1. **id.** Through this parameter you can assign a convenient name to the bean.

2. **class.** You need to assign a fully qualified class name to this parameter. In the preceding example, the action is equivalent to

```
ClassLoader cl = (imageviewer.ImageLoader.class).getClassLoader();
imageviewer.ImageLoader loader =
                        (imageviewer.ImageLoader)Beans.instantiate(cl,
" imageviewer.ImageLoader ");
```

See Appendix B for more details on instantiating a JavaBean. Note that you can customize a bean at design time and save it as a serialized prototype. The bean instantiation mechanism picks up this serialized prototype.

3. **scope.** Recall from the previous section that this parameter can take any of the following four values: **application, session, request,** and **page.** In our example the value of **scope** is **session.** Once a bean has been instantiated, it can be used anywhere within the scope.

To obtain a JavaBean property, you need to use the **<jsp:getProperty>** tag, and to set the property, the **<jsp:setProperty>** tag. These tags are equivalent to JavaBeans get and set methods. They exactly follow the naming convention specified in the JavaBeans specification. If you don't intend to follow the naming convention, you can provide a **BeanInfo** class with the desired property and event names.

The plugin Action

The **<jsp:plugin>** standard action provides a mechanism for using Java Plug-in in a JSP. As mentioned in Chapter 15, Java Plug-in is needed when the Web browser does not support the version of Java that an applet or a bean uses. Chapter 15 also gave an example of Java Plug-in in use.

Deploying a JSP

JSPs and servlets use the same deployment mechanism. Remember that JSPs are implemented as servlets. The same deployment descriptor tags used for servlets are also applicable to JSPs. Here's an example:

```
<web-app>
   ...
   <servlet>
        <servlet-name> mJSP</servlet-name>
        <jsp-file> MyImageViewer.jsp</jsp-file>
        <init-param>
            ....
</init-param>
  </servlet>
 ...
</web-app>
```

Designing Web-Based Imaging Applications

In many Internet-based applications, the field of information technology (IT) is closely tied to imaging. Take, for example, an online store that sells clothing on the Web. This is a typical e-commerce application in which the catalog is presented to prospective buyers. In such applications, you as a buyer can navigate through the catalog and choose a product. Having chosen a product, normally you would want to view it. This is where dynamic imaging comes into the picture.

In the clothing example, if you choose a coat, you may want to see all the available colors. You may also want to closely examine the image of the coat. For example, you may want a closer view of the coat buttons. This means that you may need to pan and zoom the coat image. In some instances, other imaging operations, such as rotate, may also be necessary.

In applications like these, the quality of the image matters a great deal. So a zoom operation needs to produce images that are aesthetically pleasing. Unlike a typical scientific imaging application, no measurements are involved. Instead, aesthetics plays an important role in multimedia and e-commerce applications.

Saving Images to a Database

To build an e-commerce application, you need to know both IT and imaging technologies. The product catalogs are stored in a database, and so are the associated images. There are two ways of storing an image in a database:

1. **Storing the <u>reference</u> to an image.** An image can reside as a file in a local directory or on a remote machine. In this scheme a reference or a pointer to the image is stored instead of the image itself. In an ideal scheme, the universal URL representation would be used to represent the image. If you use Java, you can programmatically obtain an image as a URL. All you need to do is save the image as a URL string representing it. To obtain the image, you can use JDBC (or any other package, such as SQLJ) to get the URL string from the database.

2. **Storing image <u>data</u>.** A typical storage scheme would represent the image as a binary large object (BLOB). The JDBC 2.0 package does support BLOBs. You can use JDBC or any other database-specific package to retrieve the BLOB, which can be converted to a `ByteArrayInputStream` object. As we saw in the AWT imaging and JAI chapters, an `InputStream` object can be easily converted to a Java image representation.

Note: Although you can use any database access package, JDBC is database in-dependent and gives an option to choose a database at the last moment. If you do change the database, with JDBC you may not have to change any code. With a vendor-specific package, however, you will have to rewrite the database access code. Nonetheless, vendor-specific packages may offer significant per-formance advantages.

Web Applications Using the JSP Architecture

In an ever-changing Internet world, business logic changes constantly. So it is ex-tremely important to build an architecture for your Web-based imaging applications that lets you add, remove, and modify business logic with ease. This means that the presentation and application logic need to be cleanly separated so that you can man-age changes more efficiently and without a lot of downtime.

The two basic architectures that use JSPs are referred to as Model 1 and Model 2.

Model 1 Architecture

In Model 1, the incoming request is sent to a JSP, which processes it and sends a re-sponse. As Figure 16.10 shows, the same JSP handles the request and the response. A JSP can also use beans to process the request and generate a response. This means that there is some kind of separation of presentation and content; that is, the JSP han-dles the presentation, and beans handle the content.

Model 1 architecture works well for simple applications. However, complex and large applications might result in a large chunk of Java code in the JSP, which is not

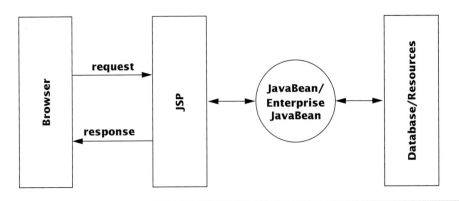

FIGURE 16.10 The Model 1 architecture

desirable from the maintenance point of view. Model 2 overcomes this problem by adding one more level of indirection.

Model 2 Architecture

Model 2 is based on the model-view-controller architecture. As Figure 16.11 shows, the request is separated from the response. In other words, the servlet that handles the incoming request does not deal with presentation issues at all, which means there is much more separation of presentation and content than in the Model 1 architecture.

With Model 2, you can design your application in a much more modular way. You can easily apply the "divide and conquer" strategy to design and implement large, complex applications. With this architecture it is easy to add, remove, and modify functionality without affecting existing clients. Because of the single entry point to the application, managing security and application state is also easier than in Model 1.

A JSP with a Servlet

First let's look at a simple JSP example. This example is similar to `ListImagesServlet`; that is, it will display the list of images in a directory. When the user clicks on **DISPLAY,** this JSP submits the selected image to `ImageManipServlet`. Listing 16.6 shows the `ListImages.jsp` file.

LISTING 16.6   The `ListImages.jsp` file

```
<HTML>
<HEAD><TITLE>File list</TITLE></HEAD>
<%@page import="java.io.*"%>
```

continued

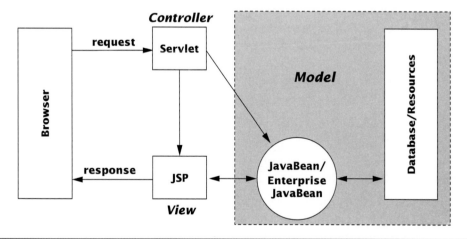

FIGURE 16.11   The Model 2 architecture

```
<%String dirstr = "c:\\jakarta\\jakarta-
tomcat\\webapps\\examples\\images3";
String extrapath = "/images3/";
String fileList[] = null;
try {
File dir = new File(dirstr);
fileList = dir.List();
} catch (Exception e){System.out.println(e);}
%>

<FORM ACTION= "/examples/servlet/ImageManipServlet" method=Post>

<BODY>
<TABLE border=1 align= center>
<TR><TH>ID</TH><TH>Image</TH></TR>
<%
for(int i=0;i<fileList.length;i++) {%>
<tr><td>
<%=i s%>
</td>
<td>
<INPUT TYPE="RADIO" name="images" value= <%= extrapath+fileList[i]%> ><%=fileList[i]%>
</td></tr>
<% }%>
</TABLE>
<INPUT TYPE= "SUBMIT" VALUE="DISPLAY">
<FORM>
</BODY></HTML>
```

The first scriptlet lists the image files in the `images3` directory. We hard-coded this directory for the sake of simplicity. The `fileList` array contains the list of images. The HTML code creates a form with a table. Each row of this table represents the image as a radio button.

When the form is submitted, the `ACTION` command calls `ImageManipServlet`, which we discussed in the previous section. Remember that this servlet takes three parameters: `"images"`, `"rotAngle"`, and `"magFactor"`. As Listing 16.6 shows, the `"images"` parameter is sent. This is not a problem with `ImageManipServlet` because it uses the default values for `rotAngle` and `magFactor`. In other words, it displays the original image.

To run this JSP, move it into the `<TOMCAT_HOME>/webapps/examples/jsp/imageviewer` directory. This is the directory we created. If you choose to create your own, make sure it is reflected in the URL string.

Next let's explore how to use beans with JSPs.

JSPs with Beans

In the previous example we saw a lot of Java code within a JSP, which is not desirable. What we want to have is Java code in separate classes. The `useBean` tag lets us do that. You can implement your logic as a JavaBean and call that bean from the JSP.

Using beans, we'll implement the same functionality as in Listing 16.6. In this example we'll first build a JSP called `ImageViewer` that uses the `ListImagesBean` class to list the image files in a directory. We'll then build a JSP called `JAIImageManip` to display and manipulate the selected image using a bean named `JAIManipBean`. When the form in `ImageViewer.jsp` is submitted, it will call `JAIImageManip.jsp`. Figure 16.12 shows the flow in this example. Let's start with `ImageViewer.jsp`, which is shown in Listing 16.7.

> **Note:** The JSP files are available on the book's Web page in the directory `src/chapter16/jsp`, the source code for each servlet in this section is in the directory `src/chapter16/servlet/jspsection`, and the beans can be found in the directory `src/chapter16/beans`.

LISTING 16.7 The `ImageViewer.jsp` file

```
<HTML>
<HEAD><TITLE>File list</TITLE></HEAD>
<%@ page import="java.io.*"%>
<jsp:useBean id="list" scope="session" class="viewer.ListImagesBean" />

<%String dirstr =
  "c:\\jakarta\\jakarta-tomcat\\webapps\\examples\\images3";
  String extrapath = "/images3/";
  String fileList[] = list.listFiles(dirstr);
%>

<FORM ACTION= "/examples/jsp/imageviewer/JAIImageManip.jsp" method=Post>

<BODY>
<TABLE border=1 align= left>
```

continued

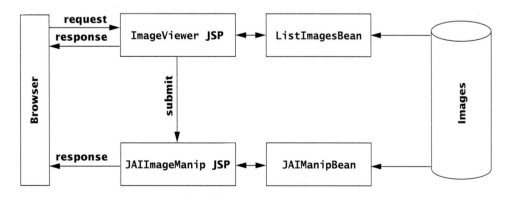

FIGURE 16.12 An application using JSPs with beans

```
<TR><TH>ID</TH><TH>Image</TH></TR>
<%
for(int i=0;i<fileList.length;i++) {%>
<tr><td>
<%=i %>
</td>
<td>
<INPUT TYPE="RADIO" name="images" value= <%= extrapath+fileList[i]%> ><%=fileList[i]%>
</td></tr>
<% }%>
</TABLE>
 Rotate: <INPUT TYPE="TEXT" name="rotAngle" >degrees   <BR>
 Zoom   : <INPUT TYPE="TEXT" name="magFactor" >percent <BR><BR>
<INPUT TYPE= "SUBMIT" VALUE="DISPLAY">
<FORM>
</BODY></HTML>
```

The `ImageViewer` JSP uses the `ListImagesBean` class to list files in a directory. The `useBean` tag creates an `id` parameter with the value `list` for the `viewer.List ImagesBean` class, which is shown in Listing 16.8. Once an ID for a bean has been created, calling its method is like calling a method in an object. `ListImagesBean` has a method called `listFiles()` that returns the list of files in the directory specified as an input parameter. As Listing 16.7 shows, a hard-coded directory string is passed to the `list.listFiles()` method, which returns the list of files in the `fileList` array.

The rest of the code is similar to that of the previous JSP, except for the `FORM` action, which invokes another JSP, called `JAIImageManip.jsp,` which is shown in Listing 16.9. Listing 16.8 shows the code for `ListImagesBean.`

LISTING 16.8   The `ListImagesBean` class

```
public class ListImagesBean{

   public ListImagesBean(){}

   public synchronized String[] listFiles(String dirstr) {
      String fl[] = null;
      try {
         ExtensionFilter filter =
            new ExtensionFilter("jpeg, gif, JPEG, GIF, JPG, jpg, png, PNG");
         File dir = new File(dirstr);
         fl = dir.list(filter);
      } catch (Exception e){System.out.println(e);}
      return fl;
   }

   class  ExtensionFilter implements FilenameFilter{
      private String extString;
      public ExtensionFilter(String ext){
         extString = ext;
      }
      public boolean accept(File dir, String name){
             StringTokenizer st = new StringTokenizer(extString, ",");
         while(st.hasMoreTokens()){
```

```
                  String str = st.nextToken();
                  String tok = str.trim();
                  if(name.endsWith(tok)){ return true;}
          }
          return false;
      }
    }
}
```

ListImagesBean is a very simple class with just one method and one inner class. The listFiles() method obtains the list of image files in the specified directory.

Listing 16.9 shows the JAIImageManip.jsp file.

LISTING 16.9   The JAIImageManip.jsp file

```
<HTML>
<HEAD><TITLE>File list</TITLE></HEAD>
<%@ page import="java.io.*, javax.media.jai.*"%>
<jsp:useBean id="manip" scope="session" class="viewer.JAIManipBean" />

<%
  response.setContentType("image/jpeg");
  String par = request.getParameter("images");
  if (par == null) par = "lena.gif";
  String rot = request.getParameter("rotAngle");
  String mag = request.getParameter("magFactor");
  double magFactor = 0.0, rotAngle = 0.0;
  try {
     rotAngle = Math.toRadians((Double.valueOf(rot)).doubleValue());
     manip.setRotationAngle(rotAngle);
  } catch(Exception e) {}
  try{
     magFactor = (Integer.valueOf(mag)).intValue()/100.0;
     manip.setMagFactor(magFactor);
  } catch(Exception e) {}
  String imagepath = application.getRealPath(par);
  ServletOutputStream out1 = response.getOutputStream();
  manip.manipAndPost(imagepath, out1);
 %>
</BODY></HTML>
```

The JAIImageManip JSP uses JAIManipBean (see Listing 16.10) to manipulate images. JAIImageManip obtains the following three parameters from the requesting JSP: "images", "rotAngle", and "magFactor". After converting these parameters to appropriate types, JAIImageManip sets JAIManipBean's rotAngle and magFactor properties.

JAIImageManip then obtains the ServletOutputStream object from the **response** object and passes it to JAIManipBean's manipAndPost() method along with the image path. As Listing 16.10 shows, this method uses the rotAngle and magFactor properties to manipulate the image. The resulting image is saved into the ServletOutput Stream object by JAI's JPEG operator. This means that the **response** object gets this stream, which is then converted to an image and displayed by the browser.

Listing 16.10 shows the code for `JAIManipBean`.

LISTING 16.10 The `JAIManipBean` class

```java
public class JAIManipBean{
    protected double rotationAngle=0.0, magFactor=0.0;
    protected PlanarImage image;
    public JAIManipBean(){}

    public void setRotationAngle(double rot){
        rotationAngle= rot;
    }

    public double getRotationAngle(){
        return rotationAngle;
    }

    public void setMagFactor(double mag){
        magFactor = mag;
    }

    public double getMagFactor(){
        return magFactor;
    }

    public void manipAndPost(String imagepath, OutputStream out){
        PlanarImage pimage = readAsPlanarImage(imagepath);
        PlanarImage outimage = manip(pimage, getRotationAngle(), getMagFactor());
        saveAsJPEG(outimage,out);
    }

    public static PlanarImage readAsPlanarImage(String filename) {
        return JAI.create("fileload", filename);
    }

    public static void saveAsJPEG(RenderedImage image, OutputStream out ){
        try {
        JPEGEncodeParam param = new JPEGEncodeParam();
        ImageEncoder encoder = ImageCodec.createImageEncoder("JPEG", out, param);
        encoder.encode(image);
        out.close();
        } catch (Exception e) {}
    }

    protected PlanarImage manip(PlanarImage image, double rot, double mag) {
        if(( rot <= 0.001) && (mag <=0.0)) return image;
        RenderedOp op =null, op1=null, op2 =null;
        if(rot > 0.001){
            op1 = rotate(image, rot);
            if(mag <=0.0) return op1.createInstance();
            else {
              op2 = scale(op1, mag,mag);
              return op2.createInstance();
            }
        }else {
            op2 = scale(image, mag,mag);
```

```
            return op2.createInstance();
        }
    }

    public RenderedOp scale(PlanarImage image, double magx, double magy) {
        ParameterBlock pb = new ParameterBlock();
        pb.addSource(image);
        pb.add((float)magx);
        pb.add((float)magy);
        pb.add(0f);
        pb.add(0f);
        pb.add(Interpolation.getInstance(Interpolation.INTERP_NEAREST));
        return JAI.create("scale", pb);
    }

     public RenderedOp rotate(PlanarImage image, double ang) {
        ParameterBlock pb = new ParameterBlock();
        pb.addSource(image);
        pb.add((float)(image.getWidth())/2);
        pb.add((float)(image.getHeight())/2);
        pb.add((float)ang);
        pb.add(Interpolation.getInstance(Interpolation.INTERP_NEAREST));
        return JAI.create("rotate", pb);
    }
}
```

We won't describe the methods of `JAIManipBean` because we have already described similar methods in preceding sections and in the JAI chapters.

Using Servlets, JSPs, and JavaBeans

The architecture we used in the previous example is something between Model 1 and Model 2. Let's now build a true Model 2 architecture with servlets, JSPs, and beans. In this architecture, the entry point is a servlet or a JSP, and images are presented by another JSP. Beans do the actual loading and manipulation of images (see Figure 16.13).

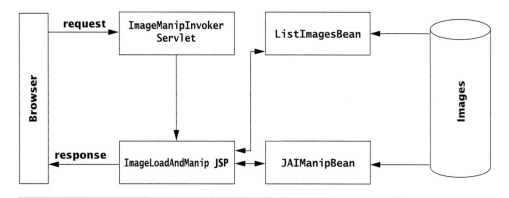

FIGURE 16.13 An application using servlets, JSPs, and beans

The `ImageManipInvokerServlet` class is the entry point to the application. Listing 16.11 shows the code for this class.

LISTING 16.11 The `ImageManipInvokerServlet` class

```
package com.vistech.net;
import javax.servlet.*;
import javax.servlet.http.*;
import java.io.*;
import java.awt.event.*;
import java.awt.*;
import java.awt.image.*;
import java.util.*;

public class ImageManipInvokerServlet extends HttpServlet{
    protected String imageBaseDir = ".";

    public void init( ServletConfig config )throws ServletException {
        super.init(config);

        try {
            String baseDir = getInitParameter("imageBaseDir");
            if(baseDir != null) imageBaseDir = baseDir;
        } catch (Exception e){
            throw new ServletException( e.toString() );
        }
    }

    public void doGet(HttpServletRequest req, HttpServletResponse res)
                   throws ServletException{
        try {
            req.setAttribute("imageDir", imageBaseDir);
            ServletContext sc =  getServletContext();
            RequestDispatcher rd =
              sc.getRequestDispatcher("/jsp/imageviewer/ImageLoadAndManip.jsp");
            rd.forward(req, res);
        } catch(Exception e) {}

    }

    public void doPost(HttpServletRequest request,
                    HttpServletResponse response)
        throws IOException, ServletException {
        doGet(request, response);
    }
}
```

`ImageManipInvokerServlet` is used as the entry point to the image-viewing application. Its `init()` method obtains the initialization parameters. In this example we created just one parameter—`imageBaseDir`—to hold the location of the directory that contains images.

When the servlet is instantiated, the servlet container looks at the `web.xml` file for deployment descriptors. Listing 16.12 shows the entries related to `ImageManip InvokerServlet`.

LISTING 16.12   Deployment descriptors for `ImageManipInvokerServlet`

```
</servlet>
 <servlet>
     <servlet-name>
         ManipImage
     </servlet-name>
     <servlet-class>
         com.vistech.net.ImageManipInvokerServlet
     </servlet-class>
     <init-param>
         <param-name>imageBaseDir</param-name>
         <param-value>c:\\images4</param-value>
     </init-param>
 </servlet>
```

The `servlet-name` tag specifies an alias for the servlet. Once this alias has been declared, you need to enter it as a servlet URL. Having an alias is very convenient when the servlet class name is long. For instance, in the current example you have to type just `ManipImage` (instead of `com.vistech.net.ImageManipInvokerServlet`). The `servlet-class` tag specifies the fully qualified class name. This means that you need to enter the package name and the class name. The `init-param` tag has two subtags: `param-name` and `param-value,` which specify the parameter name and value, respectively.

Now let's go back to the `ImageManipInvokerServlet` methods. The `init()` method retrieves the `imageBaseDir` parameter and assigns it to the `imageBaseDir` instance variable.

The `doGet()` method doesn't do a lot in this servlet. It simply forwards the request to a JSP called `ImageLoadAndManip.jsp,` which loads and manipulates images. To forward the request, `doGet()` uses the `RequestDispatcher` object (the `RequestDispatcher` interface is in the `javax.servlet` package). The `doGet()` method gets this object from the servlet context. Before the request is forwarded, `doGet()` also sets the `imageDir` attribute to the location of the image directory—that is, `imageBaseDir.` As Listing 16.13 shows, the `ImageLoadAndManip` JSP will use this attribute to get the image directory.

LISTING 16.13   The `ImageLoadAndManip.jsp` file

```
<HTML>
<HEAD><TITLE>File list</TITLE></HEAD>
<%@ page import="java.io.*,javax.media.jai.*"%>
<jsp:useBean id="list" scope="session" class="viewer.ListImagesBean" />
<%String imageDir = (String)request.getAttribute("imageDir");
 if(imageDir!= null)session.putValue("imageDir", imageDir);
 else imageDir= (String)session.getValue("imageDir");
 String fileList[] = list.listFiles(imageDir);
 // Compute a random file name
 double numd = Math.random();
 int num = Math.round((float)(numd*1000));
```

continued

```jsp
    String filename = "readfile"+Integer.toString(num)+".jpg";
    String oldfile = (String)session.getValue("tempfile");
    // Delete the previous temp file
    if(oldfile != null) {
        try {
        String tp = application.getRealPath(File.separator);
        File fl = new File(tp+File.separator+oldfile);
        fl.delete();
        } catch(Exception e){}
    }
    session.putValue("tempfile", filename);
%>

<jsp:useBean id="manip" scope="session" class="viewer.JAIManipBean" />
<%
    // Image file name
    String img = request.getParameter("images");
    if((img == null)&& (fileList[0] !=null)) img = fileList[0];
    String rot = request.getParameter("rotAngle");
    if(rot == null) rot = "0";
    String mag = request.getParameter("magFactor");
    if(mag == null) mag = "100";
    double magFactor = 0.0, rotAngle = 0.0;
    try {
        rotAngle = Math.toRadians((Double.valueOf(rot)).doubleValue());
        manip.setRotationAngle(rotAngle);
        } catch(Exception e) {}
    try{
        magFactor = (Integer.valueOf(mag)).intValue()/100.0;
        manip.setMagFactor(magFactor);
    } catch(Exception e) {}

    // Temp file to write the resulting image
    String temppath = application.getRealPath(File.separator);
    FileOutputStream out1 = new FileOutputStream(temppath+filename);
    if((imageDir!=null) && (img != null)) manip.manipAndPost(imageDir+File.separator+img,
out1);
%>

<% StringBuffer reqUrl = HttpUtils.getRequestURL(request);%>
<FORM ACTION=<%=reqUrl %>  method="POST">
<BODY>
<TABLE border=1 align= left>
<TR><TH>ID</TH><TH>Image</TH></TR>
<%
for(int i=0;i<fileList.length;i++) {%>
<tr><td>
<%=i %>
</td>
<td>
<% String checked = "";
    if(img.equals(fileList[i])) checked ="CHECKED";
%>
<INPUT TYPE="RADIO" name="images" value= <%=fileList[i]%> <%=checked%>
 ><%=fileList[i]%>
</td></tr>
<% }%>
```

```
</TABLE>
 Rotate: <INPUT TYPE="TEXT" name="rotAngle" value=<%=rot%> >degrees  <BR>
 Zoom  : <INPUT TYPE="TEXT" name="magFactor" value=<%=mag%>  >percent <BR><BR>
<INPUT TYPE= "SUBMIT" VALUE="DISPLAY">
<IMG SRC=/examples/<%=filename%> align=right >
<FORM>
</BODY></HTML>
```

The `ImageLoadAndManip` JSP reuses two beans—`ListImagesBean` and `JAIManip Bean`—which were described in the previous section (see Listings 16.8 and 16.10). In this JSP, two blocks of scriptlets instantiate and use these beans. The first one lists images, and the second one manipulates images.

Let's look at the first scriptlet. This JSP invokes itself when the form is submitted—that is, when a user clicks on **DISPLAY.** In the first pass, the image directory is retrieved from the `request` object and saved as a `session` attribute.

Because the resulting page must display other GUI components, we cannot use the servlet output stream from the `response` object to write the image as we did in the preceding example. Instead, we need to save the resulting image as a file in a temporary directory and set the *<IMG SRC>* tag to point to this file. But there is a catch. Once the image has been read, Web browsers typically cache it. So you will see the same image even if the saved image changes with each submission. To overcome this

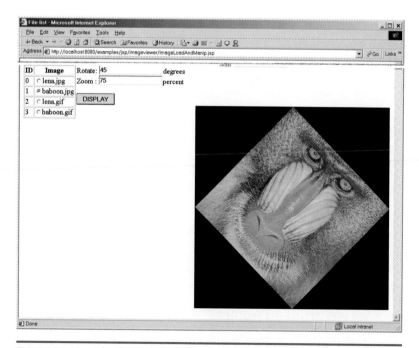

FIGURE 16.14   Selecting and displaying an image on the same page

problem, the `ImageLoadAndManip` JSP creates a random file name and sets it to the *<IMG SRC>* tag. This file name is saved as a `session` attribute, and the image is deleted during processing of the next request.

The second scriptlet uses the `JAIManipBean` class. It gets the parameters in the path—that is, the current image file, the rotation angle, and the magnification factor—from the `request` object. It then creates a `FileOutputStream` object to hold a temporary file for writing the manipulated image. With this `FileOutputStream` object and the selected image path, the scriptlet calls `JAIManipBean`'s `manipAndPost()` method. Notice that this is the same method that was called in Listing 16.9.

To launch this application, type "http://localhost:8080/examples/servlet/ ManipImage" on the command line. Before launching, update the `web.xml` file to include the servlet alias, class file, and image directory parameters. Figure 16.14 shows the page launched by this JSP.

Applets and Servlets

Typical imaging applications involve a lot of interaction with the users, and consequently many user interface components. It is clear from the preceding sections that with servlets and JSPs, lot of effort would be required to develop some sophisticated GUI components.

With currently available technology, for instance, it may not be possible to develop components that can draw highly accurate graphs and charts. Furthermore, in interactive applications the processing needs to be done immediately to get the real-time response. The brightness/contrast, or window/level, operation is an excellent example of this type of requirement. If this operation is done on the server side, the response is slow because every time a user changes an input, the application must travel to the server side to process that input and then send it back to the client. The response time therefore depends on the network speed. So to build a real-world imaging application, we must combine applets, servlets, and JSPs.

Let's start with a simple example.

> **Note:** The code described in this section is available on the book's Web page in the directory `src/chapter16/applet.` To run it with Tomcat, move the applet class files to the `webapps` directory. Before running the applet, start the Tomcat server, by running the start-up script in the `<TOMCAT_HOME>/bin` directory.

Invoking a Servlet from an Applet

The example in this section illustrates how an applet can invoke a servlet to load an image. To make matters simple, we will use the `SimpleImageLoaderServlet` class (see Listing 16.1) to load the image `lena.gif` in the servlet root directory. All the applet needs to do is act like a Web browser that invokes this servlet. Listing 16.14 shows the code for the `SimpleServletApplet` class.

LISTING 16.14   The `SimpleServletApplet` class

```
package com.vistech.net;
import java.io.*;
import java.awt.event.*;
import java.awt.*;
import java.awt.image.*;
import java.applet.*;
import java.net.*;
import java.util.*;

public class SimpleServletApplet extends Applet implements Runnable{
    static int viewerWid = 400;
    static int viewerHt = 300;
    protected String[] fileList;
    protected String curDir = ".";
    protected char separator;
    protected ImageCanvas imCanvas;
    protected Thread appletThread;

    public void init() {
        String param = getParameter("WIDTH");
        if(param != null) viewerWid = Integer.valueOf(param).intValue();
        param = getParameter("HEIGHT");
        if(param != null) viewerHt = Integer.valueOf(param).intValue();
        initApp();
    }

    public void initApp() {
        this.setSize(viewerWid, viewerHt);
        enableEvents(AWTEvent.MOUSE_MOTION_EVENT_MASK |
                            AWTEvent.MOUSE_EVENT_MASK);
    }

    public void start(){
        createUI();
        appletThread = new Thread(this);
        appletThread.start();
    }

    public void run(){
        load();
    }
    public void createUI (){
        imCanvas = (ImageCanvas)createImageCanvas();
        setLayout(new GridLayout(1,1));
        add(imCanvas);
    }

    protected Panel createImageCanvas() {
        return new ImageCanvas();
```

continued

```
      }

   protected void load() {
       try {
         URL servlet =
         new
URL("http://localhost:8080/examples/servlet/SimpleImageLoaderServlet/lena.gif");
         ServletInvoker si = new ServletInvoker(servlet);
         InputStream is = si.performGet(null);
         byte[] imageBuf = new byte[1024];
         ByteArrayOutputStream boutstream = new ByteArrayOutputStream();
         for(;;){
           int bytesread = is.read(imageBuf);
           if (bytesread <0) {break;}
           boutstream.write(imageBuf,0,bytesread);
         }
         byte[] buffer =boutstream.toByteArray();
         Image img = Toolkit.getDefaultToolkit().createImage(buffer);
         imCanvas.setImage(img);
         imCanvas.repaint();
       } catch (Exception e) {e.printStackTrace();}
    }
}
```

SimpleServletApplet calls a servlet to display an image. The start() method calls load(), whose main purpose is to invoke SimpleImageLoaderServlet (see Listing 16.1) with the image lena.gif. To run the program, you need an HTML driver program, which can be embedded in an HTML file. Listing 16.15 shows the HTML driver program that can run this applet.

LISTING 16.15 The sas.html file

```
<!DOCTYPE HTML <body>
<center><applet code="com.vistech.net.SimpleServletApplet" width="600" height="400">
</applet></center>
</body></html>
```

Figure 16.15 shows a screen shot of the applet we have developed here. Notice that HTTP is used to load the applet. In your local machine, normally you can use the file protocol to launch the applet. However, you cannot load the servlet with this protocol in Tomcat.

Usually the browser calls the GET or the POST method and performs appropriate processing to obtain the Web page. It must do the same thing when an applet needs to invoke a servlet. So we created a class called ServletInvoker that performs GET and POST operations (see Listing 16.16).

LISTING 16.16 The ServletInvoker class

```
package com.vistech.net;
import java.io.*;
import java.awt.event.*;
```

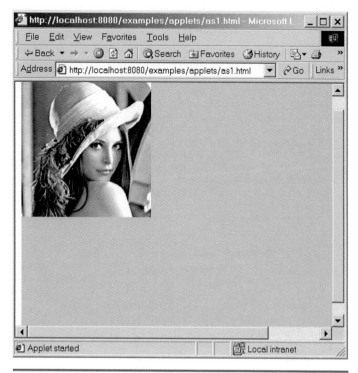

FIGURE 16.15   Running `SimpleServletApplet`

```
import java.awt.*;
import java.awt.image.*;
import java.applet.*;
import java.net.*;
import java.util.*;

public class ServletInvoker {
   protected URL servletURL;

   public ServletInvoker(URL servlet) {
      servletURL = servlet;
   }

   public InputStream performGet(Properties params){
     try {
       String qs = "";
       if(params != null)qs = createQueryString(params);
       URL servUrl = new URL(servletURL.toExternalForm()+"?"+qs);
       URLConnection uc = servUrl.openConnection();
       uc.setUseCaches(false);
```

continued

```
         return uc.getInputStream();
      } catch (Exception e) { return null;}
   }

   public InputStream performPost( Properties params){
      try {
         URLConnection uc = servletURL.openConnection();
         uc.setUseCaches(false);
         uc.setDoInput(true);
         uc.setDoOutput(true);
         uc.setRequestProperty("Content-Type",
                              "application/x-www-form-urlencoded");
         if(params != null) {
            DataOutputStream out = new DataOutputStream(uc.getOutputStream());
            String qs = createQueryString(params);
            out.writeBytes(qs);
            out.flush();
            out.close();
         }
         return uc.getInputStream();
      }catch (Exception e) { return null;}
   }

   protected String createQueryString(Properties params) {
      if(params == null) return null;
      StringBuffer qs= new StringBuffer();
      for (Enumeration e= params.propertyNames(); e.hasMoreElements(); ){
         String key = (String)e.nextElement();
         String value = params.getProperty(key);
         qs.append(URLEncoder.encode(key) + "="+
                   URLEncoder.encode(value)+((e.hasMoreElements())?"&":""));
      }
      return qs.toString();
   }
}
```

As the names suggest, performGet() and performPost() perform GET and POST, respectively. To understand how these two methods work, you need to know about the URL and the URLConnection classes in the java.net package. The URL class encapsulates the URL, and URLConnection represents the connection to a URL. Both performGet() and performPost() take servlet parameters as a Properties object.

The performGet() method creates a query string from the Properties object. As you may recall, a query string is in the form *<?name1=value1&name2=value2 & . . .>*. The createQueryString() method creates this type of a string from the properties file. The performGet() method appends this string to the invoking servlet URL and opens a connection to this URL. This is similar to typing the URL with the query string on a Web browser. Once the connection is established, performGet() obtains the resulting page from the servlet as an InputStream object.

The performPost() method performs the same function as performGet(), but in a different manner. Unlike performGet(), performPost() does not append the query string to the URL. Instead, it sends the query string directly to the servlet. It does this by first opening a connection and then obtaining an `OutputStream` object from this connection. The query string is then written to this `OutputStream` object.

Putting It All Together: An Application That Uses Applets, Servlets, JSPs, and JavaBeans

Now that we have explained how to use applets and servlets together, let's build an application that is a little more complicated using applets, servlets, JSPs, and beans. This application will run as an applet, but the images will be loaded and manipulated on the server side.

First let's quickly formulate the requirements. The application must be able to do all of the following:

◆ List image files
◆ Select and display an image
◆ Magnify and rotate the displayed image
◆ Detect edges in the displayed image

These are the bare minimum requirements needed to illustrate the use of both client-side and server-side technologies offered by Java. As an exercise, you can add your own requirements and see for yourself the elegance of these technologies.

Next let's look at the design.

Design

One of the important goals of this design is to separate the application logic from the user interface. With this design, you must be able to replace or modify the server-side programs without affecting the client side.

As a first step toward achieving this goal, we'll design this application in such a way that there is only one entry point to it. This entry point is analogous to the `main()` method in a Java or C program. We'll make the entry point a servlet and call it `ImageViewerMainServlet.` Regardless of the application logic implemented by the server-side programs, this servlet will remain the same. In other words, the client doesn't need to change when the server-side code is modified (unless new requirements demand that changes be made to the client side).

Because the same servlet is invoked, the question then arises, How does the server side know what functionality is to be executed? For example, when the application is invoked the first time, the server-side program must list the image files. When the applet GUI comes up, the server-side program must be capable of executing other tasks. The user may click on **Edge Detect,** for instance. The command indicating that edge detection is to be performed must be sent to the server side so that the server can invoke an appropriate bean to perform edge detection.

This problem can be easily solved by the capabilities of the HTTP GET and POST methods. As we learned earlier, both the GET and the POST commands can take parameters. So we can create a parameter called "command" and assign different values to it depending on the applet state. As stated earlier, ImageViewerMainServlet is just an entry point. When it is invoked, it must hand over control to another servlet or a JSP. Let's give the name ImageManipControllerServlet to the servlet that ImageViewerMainServlet calls. The main purpose of this servlet is to pass control to the appropriate JSP, depending on the command.

With this design, if you add a new command, only ImageManipController Servlet must change. JSPs and beans are required for implementing the functionality. The client side need not change if it doesn't need this functionality.

It must be clear by now that the design we are discussing here is somewhat similar to the Model 2 architecture described earlier, in the section titled JavaServer Pages. With this design, you can incrementally add functionality without causing major reimplementation of the application.

Implementation

As mentioned in the preceding section, we'll use an applet for building the GUI, a servlet as an entry point, a servlet as controller of the application, and several JSPs, which use beans to generate pages.

Before we implement the classes, we need to define the commands to be passed from the client side to the server side. From the requirements, it is clear that the server-side application must list the images. So we'll call this command "list".

The next requirement is to display and manipulate images. This capability combines three functions: image display, magnify, and rotate. Instead of creating three separate commands, let's create a single one called "manip". We'll use this command with the two manipulation parameters defined in the preceding section: magFactor and rotAngle. You can simulate any combination of manipulation by assigning appropriate values to these parameters. For instance, with the "manip" command, if the value of magFactor is 1.0 and the value of rotAngle is 0.0, then the image is displayed as is. If the value of rotAngle is 0.0 and the value of magFactor is different from 1.0, the image is magnified. If the value of magFactor is 1.0 and the value of rotAngle is greater than 0.0, the image is rotated by the specified amount.

We'll create a separate command called "edgedetect" for performing edge detection.

The block diagram for this application is shown in Figure 16.16. The applet class ImageViewerServletApplet, shown in Listing 16.17, constructs the GUI components and communicates with the server.

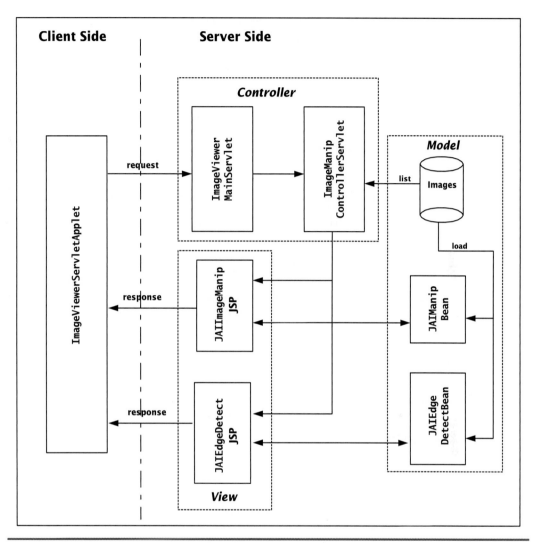

FIGURE 16.16 The image-viewing and -manipulating application using an applet, servlets, and JSPs

LISTING 16.17 The ImageViewerServletApplet class

```
package com.vistech.net;
import java.io.*;
import java.awt.event.*;
import java.awt.*;
import java.awt.image.*;
import java.applet.*;
import java.net.*;
import java.util.*;
```

continued

```
public class ImageViewerServletApplet extends Applet {
    static int viewerWid = 400;
    static int viewerHt = 300;
    protected String[] fileList;
    protected String curDir = ".";
    protected char separator;
    protected ImageCanvas imCanvas;
    protected String rotAngle ="0";
    protected String magFactor = "100";
    protected TextField magf, rotf;
    protected String currentFile = null;

    public void init() {
        String param = getParameter("WIDTH");
        if(param != null) viewerWid = Integer.valueOf(param).intValue();
        param = getParameter("HEIGHT");
        if(param != null) viewerHt = Integer.valueOf(param).intValue();
        initApp();
    }

    public void initApp() {
        this.setSize(viewerWid, viewerHt);
        enableEvents(AWTEvent.MOUSE_MOTION_EVENT_MASK |
                            AWTEvent.MOUSE_EVENT_MASK);
    }

    public void start(){
        fileList = listImages();
        createUI();
    }
    public void createUI (){
        imCanvas = (ImageCanvas)createImageCanvas();
        magf = new TextField("5");
        magf.setText(magFactor);
        rotf = new TextField("5");
        rotf.setText(rotAngle);

        magf.addActionListener(
            new ActionListener() {
                public void actionPerformed(ActionEvent e) {
                    magFactor = ((TextField)e.getSource()).getText();
                    if(currentFile != null) load(currentFile);
                }
            }
        );

        rotf.addActionListener(
            new ActionListener() {
                public void actionPerformed(ActionEvent e) {
                    rotAngle = ((TextField)e.getSource()).getText();
                    if(currentFile != null) load(currentFile);
                }
            }
        );

        Button resetButton = new Button("Reset");
        resetButton.addActionListener(
```

```
            new ActionListener() {
                public void actionPerformed(ActionEvent e) {
                    reset();
                }
            }
        );

        Button edButton = new Button("Edge Detect");
        edButton.addActionListener(
            new ActionListener() {
                public void actionPerformed(ActionEvent e) {
                    if(currentFile != null)edgeDetect(currentFile);
                }
            }
        );

        int len = fileList.length;
        java.awt.List li = new java.awt.List(len);
        for(int i=0;i<len;i++){
            li.add(fileList[i]);
        }
        li.setBackground(Color.lightGray);
        li.setForeground(Color.blue);

        li.addItemListener(
            new ItemListener() {
                public void itemStateChanged(ItemEvent e) {
                    String[] str = (String[])e.getItemSelectable().getSelectedObjects();
                    currentFile = str[0];
                    load(str[0]);
                }
            }
        );

        Panel pan = new Panel();
        pan.add(new Label("Mag Factor"));
        pan.add(magf);
        pan.add(new Label("Rotation Angle"));
        pan.add(rotf);
        pan.add(edButton);
        pan.add(resetButton);

        setLayout(new BorderLayout());
        add(BorderLayout.WEST, li);
        add(BorderLayout.CENTER, imCanvas);
        add(BorderLayout.SOUTH,pan);
        setBackground(Color.lightGray);
    }

public void reset(){
    magf.setText("100");
    rotf.setText("0");
    rotAngle = "0";
    magFactor = "100";
    if(currentFile != null) load(currentFile);
    }
```

continued

```java
protected Panel createImageCanvas() {
    return new ImageCanvas();
}

protected String[] listImages() {
    try {
        URL servlet = new URL("http://localhost:8080/examples/servlet/ImageViewer");
        ServletInvoker si = new ServletInvoker(servlet);
        Properties prop = new Properties();
        prop.put("command", "listfiles");
        InputStream is = si.performPost(prop);
        BufferedReader d  = new BufferedReader(new InputStreamReader(is));
        String line = null;
        Vector lst = new Vector();
        while( (line = d.readLine())!= null){
            lst.addElement(line);
        }
        int size = lst.size();
        String flist[] = new String[size];
        lst.copyInto(flist);
        return flist;
    } catch (Exception e) {
        e.printStackTrace();
        return null;
    }
}

protected void load(String fl) {
    try {
        URL servlet = new URL("http://localhost:8080/examples/servlet/ImageViewer");

        ServletInvoker si = new ServletInvoker(servlet);
        Properties prop = new Properties();
        prop.put("command", "manip");
        prop.put("images", fl);
        prop.put("magFactor",magFactor);
        prop.put("rotAngle",rotAngle);
        InputStream is = si.performPost(prop);
        paintImage(is);
    } catch (Exception e) {e.printStackTrace();}
}

public void edgeDetect(String file) {
    try {
        URL servlet = new URL("http://localhost:8080/examples/servlet/ImageViewer");

        ServletInvoker si = new ServletInvoker(servlet);
        Properties prop = new Properties();
        prop.put("images", file);
        prop.put("command", "edgedetect");
        InputStream is = si.performPost(prop);
        paintImage(is);
    } catch (Exception e) {e.printStackTrace();}
}
protected void paintImage(InputStream is) {
    try {
    byte[] imageBuf = new byte[1024];
```

```
        ByteArrayOutputStream boutstream = new ByteArrayOutputStream();
        for(;;){
            int bytesread = is.read(imageBuf);
            if (bytesread <0) {break;}
            boutstream.write(imageBuf,0,bytesread);
        }
        byte[] buffer =boutstream.toByteArray();
        Image img = Toolkit.getDefaultToolkit().createImage(buffer);
        imCanvas.setImage(img);
        imCanvas.repaint();
        }catch (Exception e) {e.printStackTrace();}
    }
}
```

The `createUI()` method constructs the GUI components and lays them on a panel. We used only the AWT components in this applet because at the time of this writing, the popular browsers don't support Swing components. By using the AWT components, we eliminated the need to use Java Plug-in.

The applet user interface contains a `List` object to display the image files, a `Canvas` object to display an image, and the `TextField` object to enter the rotation angle and magnification factor. It also has a `Button` object to run the edge detection operation and another `Button` object to reset the image to the original state.

The `createUI()` method has the event-handling code for the components that interact with users in the form of anonymous inner classes. Whenever an event such as clicking of a `Button` takes place, the event-handling methods within these inner classes are called. The `load()`, `edgeDetect()`, and `reset()` methods are in turn called by these event-handling methods.

The `start()` method calls the `listImages()` method, which invokes the Image Viewer servlet with the `"listfiles"` command. Note that *ImageViewer* is the alias of the `com.vistech.net.ImageViewerMainServlet` class (see Listing 16.18). Before it launches the servlet, `listImages()` creates the `ServletInvoker` object. You may recall from the previous section that we built this class to perform the HTTP `GET` and `POST` methods (see Listing 16.16).

The `listImages()` method then calls `performPost()`, which actually performs the HTTP `POST` method. With the `"listfiles"` command, this servlet returns a list of image file names. The directory in which the files are listed is obtained from the `web.xml` file by the `ImageViewer` servlet. The `performPost()` method returns an `InputStream` object that contains the contents of the page, which in this case is a list of image file names. The `listImages()` method reads the `InputStream` object and converts the contents into an array, which are later displayed on the `List` object.

When the user clicks on a file on the `List` object, the `load()` method is called. This method calls the `ImageViewer` servlet with the `"manip"` command. To do this, the `load()` method first creates a property list with the `"command"` parameter set to `"manip"`, the `"images"` parameter set to the selected file, and the `"rotAngle"` and `"magFactor"` parameters set to the values entered in the respective `TextField` objects. The `load()` method then calls `performPost()` with this property list. The `perform`

Post() method returns an InputStream object that contains an image. The load() method then calls paintImage() with this InputStream object. The paintImage() method converts the InputStream object to an image and paints it on the image canvas.

The edgeDetect() method is similar to load(). It sends only two parameters: "command" and "images".

On the server side, when the performPost() method is called, the ImageViewer servlet hands over control to ImageManipControllerServlet (see Listing 16.20). This servlet will call the appropriate JSPs, depending on the value of the "command" parameter. For example, the "manip" command invokes JAIImageManip1.jsp, which in turn calls JAIManipBean and returns the manipulated image.

Next we'll look at the ImageViewerMainServlet class (see Listing 16.18). As mentioned earlier, this servlet is just an entry point to the server-side application.

LISTING 16.18 The ImageViewerMainServlet class

```java
package com.vistech.net;
import javax.servlet.*;
import javax.servlet.http.*;

import java.io.*;

public class ImageViewerMainServlet extends HttpServlet{
   protected String imageBaseDir = ".";
   public void init( ServletConfig config )throws ServletException {
     super.init(config);

     try {
        String baseDir = getInitParameter("imageBaseDir");
        if(baseDir != null) imageBaseDir = baseDir;
     } catch (Exception e){
         throw new ServletException( e.toString() );
     }
   }

   public void doGet(HttpServletRequest req, HttpServletResponse res)
                throws ServletException{
     try {
       HttpSession session = req.getSession(true);
       if(session != null) session.putValue("imagepath", imageBaseDir);
       ServletContext sc =  getServletContext();
       RequestDispatcher rd =
           sc.getRequestDispatcher("/servlet/com.vistech.net.ImageManipController");
       rd.forward(req, res);
     } catch(Exception e) {System.out.println(e);}
   }

   public void doPost(HttpServletRequest request,
                   HttpServletResponse response)
       throws IOException, ServletException {
       doGet(request, response);
```

```
    }
}
```

The `init()` method picks up the location of the image directory from the deployment descriptors file, `web.xml,` and sets it as a `session` parameter. Listing 16.19 shows the XML snippet related to the image viewer servlet from the `web.xml` file.

LISTING 16.19   Deployment descriptors of the image viewer servlet

```
<servlet>
    <servlet-name>
        ImageViewer
    </servlet-name>
    <servlet-class>
        com.vistech.net.ImageViewerMainServlet
    </servlet-class>
    <init-param>
        <param-name>imageBaseDir</param-name>
        <param-value>c:\DISTSUNS</param-value>
    </init-param>
</servlet>
```

Note that the `init()` method is always called before `doGet()` or `doPost()`. The `doGet()` method forwards the request to `ImageManipControllerServlet`, which is shown in Listing 16.20.

LISTING 16.20   The `ImageManipControllerServlet` class

```
package com.vistech.net;
import javax.servlet.*;
import javax.servlet.http.*;
import java.io.*;

public class ImageManipControllerServlet extends HttpServlet {

    public void doGet(HttpServletRequest req, HttpServletResponse res)
                throws ServletException{
      try {
        String command = req.getParameter("command");
        if(command.equalsIgnoreCase("listfiles")){
            String imagepath = ".";
            HttpSession session = req.getSession(false);
            if(session != null) imagepath= (String)session.getValue("imagepath");
            String fileList[] = listFiles(imagepath);
            PrintWriter out = res.getWriter();
            for(int i=0;i<fileList.length;i++) {
                out.println(fileList[i]);
            }
            return;
        }
        if(command.equalsIgnoreCase("manip")){
            ServletContext sc =  getServletContext();
            RequestDispatcher
             rd = sc.getRequestDispatcher("/jsp/imageviewer/JAIImageManip1.jsp");
```

continued

```
          rd.forward(req, res);
          return;
       }
      if(command.equalsIgnoreCase("edgedetect")){
          ServletContext sc =  getServletContext();
          RequestDispatcher
            rd = sc.getRequestDispatcher("/jsp/imageviewer/JAIEdgeDetect.jsp");
          rd.forward(req, res);
          return;
       }
     } catch(Exception e) {System.out.println(e);}
   }

  public void doPost(HttpServletRequest request,
                     HttpServletResponse response)
      throws IOException, ServletException {
      doGet(request, response);
   }
   public synchronized String[] listFiles(String dirstr) {
      String fl[] = null;
      try {
        File dir = new File(dirstr);
        fl = dir.list();
      } catch (Exception e){System.out.println(e);}
      return fl;
   }
}
```

The doGet() method checks for three commands: "listfiles", "manip", and "edgedetect". If the command is "listfiles", doGet() gets the image directory from the session parameter "imagepath" that can call the listFiles() method. Recall from Listing 16.19 that ImageViewerMainServlet sets this parameter.

If the command is "manip", the request is forwarded to the JAIImageManip1 JSP, which is shown in Listing 16.21. If the command is "edgedetect", the request is forwarded to the JAIEdgeDetect JSP (see Listing 16.22).

To add more features, all you need to do is create a bean that implements the functionality and a JSP that invokes it. In addition, you need to add an if statement to the doGet() method of ImageManipControllerServlet.

Listing 16.21 shows the JAIImageManip1.jsp file. This file is similar to the JAIImageManip.jsp file shown in Listing 16.9, except that the former gets the image path from the session parameter.

LISTING 16.21 The JAIImageManip1.jsp file

```
<HTML>
<HEAD><TITLE>File list</TITLE></HEAD>
<%@ page import="java.io.*, javax.media.jai.*"%>
<jsp:useBean id="manip" scope="session" class="viewer.JAIManipBean" />

<%
  response.setContentType("image/jpeg");
  String path1 = (String)session.getValue("imagepath");
```

```
String par = request.getParameter("images");
String rot = request.getParameter("rotAngle");
String mag = request.getParameter("magFactor");
double magFactor = 1.0, rotAngle = 0.0;
try {
   rotAngle = Math.toRadians((Double.valueOf(rot)).doubleValue());
   manip.setRotationAngle(rotAngle);
   } catch(Exception e) {}
try{
   magFactor = (Integer.valueOf(mag)).intValue()/100.0;
   manip.setMagFactor(magFactor);
} catch(Exception e) {}
String imagepath = path1+File.separator+par;
ServletOutputStream out1 = response.getOutputStream();
manip.manipAndPost(imagepath, out1);
%>
</BODY></HTML>
```

JAIImageManip1.jsp reuses JAIManipBean (see Listing 16.10).

Listing 16.22 shows the JAIEdgeDetect.jsp file, which calls JAIEdgeDetectBean.

LISTING 16.22   The JAIEdgeDetect.jsp file

```
<HTML>
<HEAD><TITLE>File list</TITLE></HEAD>
<%@ page import="java.io.*, javax.media.jai.*"%>
<jsp:useBean id="edgeDetector" scope="session" class="viewer.JAIEdgeDetectBean" />
<%
  response.setContentType("image/jpeg");
  String path1 = (String)session.getValue("imagepath");
  String par = request.getParameter("images");
  String imagepath = path1+File.separator+par;
  ServletOutputStream out1 = response.getOutputStream();
  edgeDetector.edgeDetectAndPost(imagepath, out1);
%>
</BODY></HTML>
```

Listing 16.23 shows the code for JAIEdgeDetectBean.

LISTING 16.23   The JAIEdgeDetectBean class

```
package viewer;
import java.io.*;
import java.awt.event.*;
import java.awt.*;
import java.awt.image.*;
import java.util.*;
import java.awt.image.renderable.*;
import javax.media.jai.*;
import com.sun.media.jai.codec.*;

public class JAIEdgeDetectBean{
   protected double rotationAngle=0.0, magFactor=0.0;
   protected PlanarImage image;
   public JAIEdgeDetectBean(){}
```

continued

```
public void edgeDetectAndPost(String imagepath, OutputStream out){
    PlanarImage pimage = readAsPlanarImage(imagepath);
    PlanarImage outimage = sobelGradientMagnitude(pimage);
    saveAsJPEG(outimage,out);
}

public static PlanarImage readAsPlanarImage(String filename) {
    return JAI.create("fileload", filename);
}

public static void saveAsJPEG(RenderedImage image, OutputStream out ){
    try {
    JPEGEncodeParam param = new JPEGEncodeParam();
    ImageEncoder encoder = ImageCodec.createImageEncoder("JPEG", out, param);
    encoder.encode(image);
    out.close();
    } catch (Exception e) {}
}

public static RenderedOp sobelGradientMagnitude(PlanarImage image) {
    KernelJAI sobelVertKernel = KernelJAI.GRADIENT_MASK_SOBEL_VERTICAL;
    KernelJAI sobelHorizKernel = KernelJAI.GRADIENT_MASK_SOBEL_HORIZONTAL;
    ParameterBlock pb = new ParameterBlock();
    pb.addSource(image);
    pb.add(sobelHorizKernel);
    pb.add(sobelVertKernel);
    return JAI.create("gradientmagnitude", pb);
    }
}
```

The `JAIEdgeDetectBean` code is straightforward. It uses the JAI GradientMagnitude operator to perform edge detection. (For details on how JAI operators work, see Part III.)

Running ImageViewerServletApplet

Before you run the applet, make sure that you follow these steps:

1. Compile the servlets and beans into the `<TOMCAT_HOME>/webapps/examples/WEB_INF/classes` directory.

2. Move the JSPs to the `<TOMCAT_HOME>/webapps/examples/jsp/imageviewer` directory.

3. Create an images directory and copy images to it. In our example, this directory was `c:\DISTSUNS`. Append the `web.xml` file with XML tags as shown in Listing 16.19. Note that if you change the servlet alias, you will have to change it in the `ImageViewerServletApplet` class as well.

4. Compile the applet code and move the class files and HTML driver files to a convenient location under `<TOMCAT_HOME>`. In our case, the location was `<TOMCAT_HOME>/webapps/examples/classes`.

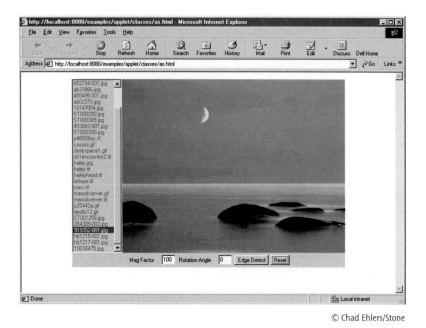

© Chad Ehlers/Stone

FIGURE 16.17   An applet displaying a selected image

5. Start the Tomcat container by typing the start-up script under <TOMCAT_HOME>/ bin.

6. Start the applet by typing the applet URL. In our case, it was http://localhost: 8080/examples/classes/as.html.

Figure 16.17 shows a screen shot of the applet. The list contains many images, and an image is displayed on an image canvas on the right-hand side. Figure 16.18 shows the same applet with the **Edge Detect** button selected.

Internet Imaging Protocol

A chapter on Internet imaging would not be complete without mention of the Internet Imaging Protocol (IIP), which was developed by the Digital Imaging Group (DIG), a consortium of companies that are engaged in imaging. A detailed description of the protocol is beyond the scope of this book. If you are interested, you can download the IIP specs from the DIG Web site at http://www.digitalimaging.org. This site also has sample implementations of an IIP server and a client. These examples are available to download at a nominal fee.

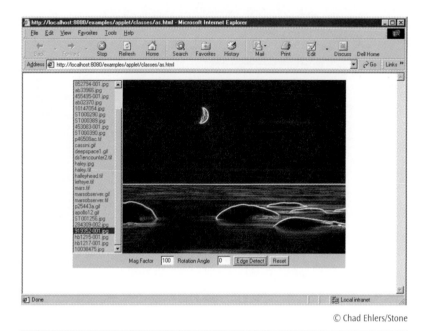

FIGURE 16.18   An applet performing the edge detection operation

The IIP is designed to work within the existing HTTP protocol to enable access to images in a standard manner over the Internet. It can also work with direct socket connections. IIP takes advantage of the FlashPix image architecture developed jointly by Eastman Kodak, Hewlett-Packard, Live Picture, and Microsoft.

The IIP specs define numerous standard commands that can be sent to servers as requests, as in our example in the previous section. The commands are separated by an ampersand ("&") in the case of HTTP, and by CRLF (a carriage return and line feed) in the case of sockets. IIP also defines specifications of objects that are passed to the server.

Basic IIP Commands

Table 16.2 lists the basic IIP commands.

Here's an example of a URL constructed with IIP commands:

```
http://www.vistechsoft.com/examples?FIF=/images/lena/fpx
&OBJ=IIPServlet&TIL=4,*
```

This is a fictitious URL that invokes `IIPServlet` to load all the tiles of `lena.fpx`.

TABLE 16.2 Basic IIP Commands

COMMAND	SYNTAX	DESCRIPTION
FIF	*FIF=imagepath*	This command specifies the relative path to the image resource.
OBJ	*OBJ=objname*	This command requests an object from the server. *Objname* is the name of the object—for example, a servlet alias.
TIL	*TIL=res, tile[,sub]*	This command requests one or more tiles from the server in the native format. The parameter *res* specifies the resolution number, *tile* specifies the desired tile(s), and *sub* specifies the subimage number of the tile. Refer to the IIP specs for a detailed explanation of this command.
SDS	*SDS=doid *(,doid)*	This command sets the data object storage. The root of the object storage is set by this command. This is analogous to setting the servlet root.

Optional Commands

These IIP commands are optionally supported by a server. The IIP spec defines an object named `IIP-opt-comm` that returns the commands supported by a server.

Support for IIP in JAI

JAI 1.02 supports IIP. It has two operators—IIP and IIPResolution—that can perform client-side processing based on IIP.

The IIP Operator

This operator supports both the rendered and the renderable images. Table 16.3 shows the parameters of the IIP operator.

The IIPResolution Operator

Table 16.4 lists the parameters of the IIPResolution operator.

Conclusion

Internet imaging is an evolving field. Providing a Web front end is a key requirement in many imaging applications. In this chapter we showed how to use the two Java server-side technologies—servlets and JSPs—to develop imaging applications. These

TABLE 16.3 IIP Operator Parameters

Operator Name	Parameter	Type	Default Value	Description
IIP	url	String	None	URL of the image
	subimages	int[]	0	Array of subimages used by the server at each resolution level
	filter	Float	0.0F	Filter value
	colorTwist	Float	null	Color twist matrix
	contrast	Float	1.0F	Contrast value
	sourceROI	Rectangle2D.Float	null	Source ROI in rendering independent coordinates
	transform	AffineTransform	Identity	Linear transformation applied to the image
	aspectRatio	Float	null	Aspect ratio of the destination image
	destROI	Rectangle2D.Float	null	Destination ROI in rendering independent coordinates
	rotation	Integer	0	Rotation angle applied to the destination image
	mirrorAxis	String	null	Mirror axis
	ICCProfile	ICC_Profile	null	ICC profile of the source image color space
	JPEGQuality	Integer	null	JPEG quality factor
	JPEGTable	Integer	null	JPEG compression group index number

TABLE 16.4 IIPResolution Operator Parameters

Operator Name	Parameter	Type	Default Value	Description
IIPResolution	URL	String	None	URL of the image
	Resolution	Integer	IIPResolution Descriptor.MAX_ RESOLUTION	Resolution level
	Subimage	Integer	0	Subimage used by the server

technologies allow you to leverage the latest Java imaging APIs without the clients having to download them, as they do with applets.

In applications that are GUI intensive, however, just servlets and JSPs are not enough. You need applets to lay out sophisticated GUI components and do some quick client-side processing for real-time response. In this chapter we showed how to use applets with servlets and JSPs in a contrived but somewhat complicated example.

PART V

Image Reading and Writing

Image Input/Output

17

AS DESCRIBED IN CHAPTER 2, the AWT comes with an image-loading API. This API has many inadequacies, including poor performance and the inability to read images in formats other than JPEG and GIF (and starting with JDK 1.3, PNG). Moreover, the AWT has no image-saving API.

To address these needs, Sun released a JPEG codec to load and save JPEG images as a stopgap measure. Because the Java 2D API revolves around `BufferedImage,` the JPEG codec can load an image as a buffered image and save a buffered image as a JPEG image. In this chapter we'll describe this API first.

JAI came out with a much more comprehensive image-loading and -saving API that is capable of handling several different formats. This API is available in JAI 1.0.2 and JAI 1.1 and is a separate package. In this chapter we'll describe the package in some detail.

The Image I/O API, which is at the beta stage at the time of this writing, will replace both of these APIs. This API provides the ability to add plug-ins for reading and writing images that are specific to your needs. The Image I/O API reads an image as a buffered image. It is also capable of saving a buffered image or a rendered image in any format for which the codec plug-in is available. In this chapter we'll describe the aspects of this API that an application programmer needs.

Using the JPEG Codec

To be displayed, an image must first be loaded. As mentioned earlier, the AWT image-loading mechanism loads an image as an `Image` object. But Java 2D is centered on `BufferedImage.`

If we use the AWT image-loading API, we may lose many of the benefits of Java 2D (e.g., flexible data and color representation). What we really need is a loading mechanism that reads an image as a buffered image. So, to read an image as a buffered image, Sun provided a JPEG codec (encoder and decoder) package

An Overview of JPEG Compression

JPEG stands for Joint Photographic Experts Group, which is a group of experts nominated by national standards bodies and major companies to work to produce standards for continuous-tone image coding. The JPEG compression standard supports both lossy and lossless compression.

The JPEG lossy compression standard chose the discrete cosine transformation (DCT) as the basis function primarily because it exploits the characteristics of the human visual system response, which is sensitive to spatial frequencies.

When the DCT is applied to an image, the pixel space is transformed to the frequency space. This means that the DCT coefficients generated as a result of the transformation represent different spatial frequency contents in the original image. An edge, for instance, has a higher frequency content compared to a smoother surface because pixel values at the edge vary rapidly.

When the DCT is applied, an $n \times n$ image results in $n \times n$ DCT coefficients. This means that the DCT transformation as such produces no compression. However, the DCT coefficients are amenable to compression. The compression is achieved by the application of compression algorithms to these coefficients.

The coefficient at $(0, 0)$ represents the zero frequency content and is called the DC component. The rest of the coefficients are called the AC components (analogous to DC and AC in electricity). Accordingly, the coefficient at $(n - 1, n - 1)$ corresponds to the highest frequency.

Compression Steps

In this section we present a brief overview of the compression steps.

Application of the DCT

DCT is a computation-intensive operation. For this reason the JPEG standards committee concluded that applying DCT to an entire image at one time is not practical. Instead the committee recommended that the image be divided into 8×8 blocks and the transformation be applied to each of the blocks individually.

Quantization

Quantization generally refers to an operation that approximates or divides to approximate. In the lossy JPEG standard, the DCT coefficients are quantized before the compression algorithms are applied to them. Quantization consists of division of each of the DCT coefficients by a certain factor. The coefficients are quantized (or divided) so that fewer bits are required to represent them. A quantization matrix with each of the elements representing a dividing factor is generated for this purpose. The quantization matrix largely decides the quality of the JPEG image.

Application of Run-Length Encoding

A run-length encoding (RLE) algorithm is applied to the quantized coefficients to compress them. In the RLE scheme, a long run of zeros or ones is replaced by the count—that is, the number of zeros or ones in the run. Two fields represent this count: the size of the count and the actual count. Before the RLE is applied, the coefficients are arranged in a long string by application of the zigzag pattern; that is, instead of being created along just rows or just columns, the string is created by alternation between rows and columns.

Entropy Coding

Entropy coding is applied to the result of the RLE compression. Entropy coding has its roots in information theory. It is an area in electrical communication that deals with encoding and decoding of information. In information theory, entropy is a measure of uncertainty—that is, a measure of information.

Entropy is measured in bits. Several coding techniques are based on entropy or uncertainty of an occurrence. The lower the uncertainty of an occurrence, the lower is the number of bits needed to represent it. For example, the letter *e* in English has the least amount of uncertainty of all letters in the alphabet, so it requires the least number of bits to represent it.

In JPEG, two entropy coding techniques are used: Huffman and arithmetic. Although arithmetic coding produces better compression, it is slow. It is also patented. On the other hand, Huffman coding is simple and not patented. Most JPEG compression implementations therefore use Huffman coding. The steps in Huffman coding can be summarized as follows:

1. Divide the image into $n \times n$ blocks, where $n = 8$ for the JPEG standard.
2. Apply the DCT to each block to generate the DCT coefficient matrix.
3. Quantize the coefficients by dividing each of them by the quantization matrix.
4. Apply difference encoding (i.e., computing the difference between two numbers) to the DC components in all blocks.
5. Create a zigzag pattern of the DCT coefficients.
6. Apply run-length encoding (RLE) to the zigzag pattern.
7. Apply entropy coding to the output of the RLE.

continued

To uncompress the image, the process is reversed. To get the actual image, the inverse discrete cosine transformation (IDCT) is applied to the DCT coefficients.

JPEG 2000

Although the current JPEG standard is simple and it is fairly easy to implement, it has some significant drawbacks. One of them is the "blockiness" of the compressed image because the images are divided into 8 × 8 blocks for processing.

The latest JPEG standard, JPEG 2000, overcomes the drawbacks of the current standard. This standard doesn't divide the image as 8 × 8 blocks, but instead treats the image as a stream. In addition, it uses wavelets as the base function instead of the DCT. As the name suggests, *wavelets* are oscillations over a small interval and can be used to represent signals in an efficient manner. In the case of images, techniques using wavelets can compress images according to desired resolution, or level of detail. For the same amount of compression, the quality of the images compressed by wavelets is far superior to that of DCT-compressed images.

(`com.sun.image.codec.jpeg`) with the JDK 1.2 distribution. Even though this package is part of Sun's Java 2 distributions, as the package name suggests, it is not part of the core Java API. If you're using a version of the Java Development Kit (JDK) or of Java Runtime Environment (JRE) other than Sun's, the JPEG codec may not be available.

The `com.sun.image.codec.jpeg` package is adequate for simple load and save operations. However, if you're looking for a sophisticated JPEG encoder and decoder, you may want to use a commercially available package.

In this section we'll look at the JPEG codec API. We'll show how to load a JPEG into a `BufferedImage` object. We'll also show how to save a buffered image as a JPEG image.

Before you start with the JPEG codec API, you may want to read the side bar on JPEG compression.

Overview of the JPEG API

The JPEG API has interfaces and classes for both loading and saving JPEG images. Unlike AWT image loading, JPEG image loading is synchronous. The `com.sun.image.codec.jpeg` package has four interfaces—two for decoding and two for encoding.

◆ **Decoder interfaces:**

1. `JPEGImageDecoder`
2. `JPEGDecodeParam`

The decoding APIs have methods that are required for loading JPEG images.

◆ **Encoder interfaces:**

1. `JPEGImageEncoder`
2. `JPEGEncodeParam`

The encoding APIs have methods that are required for saving JPEG images.

Normally there is no need to implement any of these interfaces. They are indirectly implemented by the `JPEGCodec` class and are available as objects through factory methods.

Loading JPEG Images

The `JPEGImageDecoder` interface specifies methods needed for decoding JPEG images. A decoder object represented by this interface can convert a JPEG file input stream into a `BufferedImage` or `Raster` object. (Chapter 6 describes the `BufferedImage` class in detail, and Chapter 8 describes the `Raster` class in detail.)

The `JPEGDecodeParam` interface specifies methods that get the parameters obtained during decoding.

`JPEGCodec` is the utility class that has factory methods to create `JPEGImageDecoder` objects. There are two flavors of `createJPEGDecoder()` methods. One of them takes `FileInputStream` as the input parameter. Listing 17.1 shows an example.

LISTING 17.1   Reading an image as a buffered image

```
public static BufferedImage readAsBufferedImage(String filename) {
   try {
      FileInputStream fis = new FileInputStream(filename);
      JPEGImageDecoder decoder = JPEGCodec.createJPEGDecoder(fis);
      BufferedImage bi = decoder.decodeAsBufferedImage();
      return bi;
   } catch(Exception e) {
      System.out.println(e);
      return null;
   }
}
```

The other flavor of `createJPEGImageDecoder()` takes a `JPEGDecodeParam` object as an input parameter in addition to `FileInputStream.`

Saving Images and GUI Components

The `JPEGImageEncoder` interface specifies methods for encoding JPEG images. The encoder object represented in this interface can convert a `BufferedImage` or `Raster` object into a `FileOutputStream` object.

The `JPEGEncodeParam` interface specifies methods for setting parameters required for encoding. The `JPEGCodec` class has factory methods for creating `JPEGImage Encoder` and `JPEGImageDecoder` objects. Just like the decoder methods, there are two flavors of `createJPEGEncoder()` methods. One of them takes just `FileOutputStream` as the input parameter. This method creates a `JPEGImageEncoder` object with default encoding parameters. Listing 17.2 shows how to save a buffered image as a JPEG image.

LISTING 17.2   Saving a buffered image as a JPEG image

```
public static void saveImageAsJPEG(BufferedImage bi, String filename) {
   try {
      ByteArrayOutputStream boutstream = new ByteArrayOutputStream();
      JPEGImageEncoder enc = JPEGCodec.createJPEGEncoder(boutstream);
      enc.encode(bi);
      FileOutputStream fimage = new FileOutputStream(new File(filename));
      boutstream.writeTo(fimage);
      fimage.close();
   } catch (Exception e) { System.out.println(e); }
}
```

If you need to control the encoding, you must use the other `create JPEGEncoder()` method, which takes `JPEGEncodeParam` as an input parameter in addition to `FileOutputStream`. To create a `JPEGEncodeParam` object, you need to use the `JPEGCodec` class again. `JPEGCodec` has four flavors of the `getDefault JPEGEncode Param()` method. Once you get the `JPEGEncodeParam` object, you can set the required parameters. Listing 17.3 shows an example.

LISTING 17.3   Saving a buffered image as a JPEG image with varying quality

```
public static void saveImageAsJPEG(BufferedImage bi,
                        float quality,
                        String filename){
    try {
       ByteArrayOutputStream boutstream = new ByteArrayOutputStream();
       JPEGImageEncoder enc = JPEGCodec.createJPEGEncoder(boutstream);
       JPEGEncodeParam enparam = JPEGCodec.getDefaultJPEGEncodeParam(bi);
       enparam.setQuality(quality, true);
       enc.encode(bi, enparam);
       FileOutputStream fimage = new FileOutputStream(new File(filename));
       boutstream.writeTo(fimage);
       fimage.close();
    }
    catch (Exception e) { System.out.println(e); }
}
```

The `saveImageAsJPEG()` method first creates a `JPEGImageEncoder` object using the `JPEGCodec` class. It then creates a `JPEGEncodeParam` object by using the `get DefaultJPEGEncodeParam()` method with the `BufferedImage` parameter. It sets the quality factor of the JPEG encoding and calls the `encode()` method to input the buffered image into a JPEG output stream. This output stream is written to an image file.

So far in this section we have seen how to use the JPEG API to save a `BufferedImage` object. The need often arises to save the `Image` object instead of the `BufferedImage` object. We can easily do this by drawing the `Image` object on a `BufferedImage` object and then saving it as a JPEG image. Listing 17.4 shows the relevant code.

LISTING 17.4   Saving an image as a JPEG image

```
public static void saveImageAsJPEG(Image img,
                                   int imwidth,
                                   int imheight,
                                   ImageObserver obs,
                                   String filename) {
   BufferedImage bi = new BufferedImage(imwidth,
                                        imheight,
                                        BufferedImage.TYPE_INT_RGB);
   Graphics2D g2d = bi.createGraphics();
   g2d.drawImage(img, 0,0,imwidth, imheight, obs);
   saveImageAsJPEG(bi, filename);
}
```

The `saveImageAsJPEG()` method first creates a `BufferedImage` object and then obtains a graphical context from that object. On the basis of the input, it then draws the `Image` object on the `BufferedImage` object.

Notice that `saveImageAsJPEG()` has an `ImageObserver` argument. `ImageObserver` is needed to invoke the `drawImage()` method. Once the image has been drawn on the `BufferedImage` object, `ImageObserver` calls the other flavor of `saveImageAsJPEG()`, which we defined earlier in this section.

Saving a Component

We can use the same principle to save a GUI component as a JPEG image. Listing 17.5 shows an example.

LISTING 17.5   Saving a component as a JPEG image

```
public static void saveComponentAsJPEG(Component cmp,
                                       Container cont,
                                       String jpegfile) {
   Rectangle d = cmp.getBounds();
   BufferedImage bi = new BufferedImage(d.width,
```

continued

```
                                 d.height,
                                 BufferedImage.TYPE_INT_RGB);
     Graphics2D g2d = bi.createGraphics();
     SwingUtilities.paintComponent(g2d,cmp,cont, 0,0,d.width,d.height);
     saveImageAsJPEG(bi, jpegfile);
}
```

First the `saveComponentAsJPEG()` method creates a `Graphics2D` context to form the `BufferedImage` object, and then it draws the component over that context by using the `paintComponent()` method from the `SwingUtilities` class. Once the component has been drawn, `saveComponentAsJPEG()` calls `saveImageAsJPEG()` to create a JPEG image.

> **Note:** All of the methods described here are static. These methods and a few more are available on the book's Web page in the `JpegUtil.java` file, which is in the directory `src/util`.

Using the JAI Codec

The codec described in this section is based on the JAI 1.0.2 release. Note that the JAI codec package is not a committed part of JAI. Although the codec packages in Java and JAI operate in a similar fashion, the JAI codec supports more image formats and has more flexible APIs than the JPEG codec. The JPEG codec can read and write only JPEG images and works only with `BufferedImage` objects. The JAI codec works with `PlanarImage` objects. Converting a `PlanarImage` to an AWT `Image` or a `BufferedImage` is an easy affair (see Chapter 10).

First, let's briefly explain the JAI codec API, which is defined in the `com.sun.media.jai.codec` package. Figure 17.1 shows the hierarchy of the decoder and encoder parameter classes in this API.

Decoding

A typical decoder reads the image header and decodes the rest of the information contained in the image file to create an image object.

The JAI codec has two decoding-related interfaces—`ImageDecoder` and `ImageDecodeParam`—and several classes that help read images saved in different formats. The `ImageDecoder` interface specifies methods that describe the behavior of an object that reads images. The `ImageDecoder` object can decode an image into either a `Raster` object or a `RenderedImage` object. Accordingly, it has `decodeAsRaster()` and `decodeAsRenderedImage()` methods, each of which has two flavors. To set the decod-

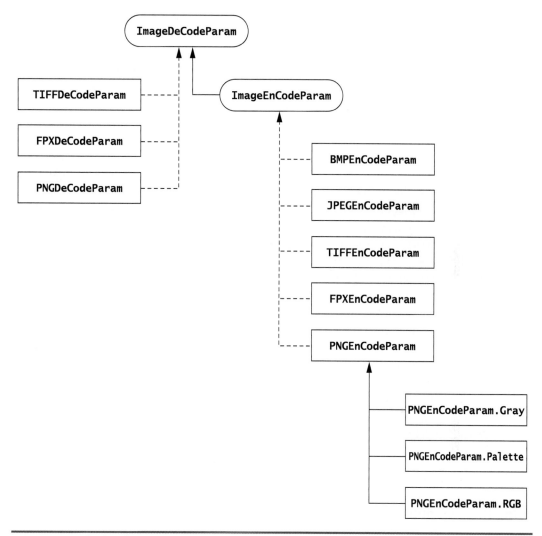

FIGURE 17.1   The decoder and encoder parameter class hierarchy

ing parameters, the `ImageDecoder` interface specifies the `setParam(Image Decode Param)` method, and to get the decoding parameters, the `getParam()` method.

In addition to these methods, the `ImageDecoder` interface has the `getInput Stream()` method, which obtains the decoded stream as a `SeekableStream` object. `SeekableStream` is a class that extends `InputStream` and has methods for random seeking in an input stream.

`ImageDecoderImpl` is a convenient class that implements the `ImageDecoder` interface. It is also an abstract class that can be extended by any format-specific decoding classes. The `ImageDecoderImpl` object can be constructed with an `InputStream` object and an `ImageDecodeParam` object.

`ImageDecodeParam` is just a marker interface that is implemented by all decoder parameter classes. The JAI codec has three format-specific `ImageDecodeParam` classes. When you read an image, you may have to create an appropriate decoder parameter object from these classes.

Encoding

An image encoder encodes the data in a specified format and creates an image file. The JAI codec has two encoding-related interfaces and several classes that help write images. The `ImageEncoder` interface specifies methods that describe the behavior of an object that encodes image data. It has two flavors of the `encode()` method—one to encode `Raster`, and another to encode `RenderedImage`.

To set the encoding parameters, this interface specifies the `getParam(Image EncodeParam)` and `setParam()` methods to get and set, respectively, image-encoding parameters. The `getOutputStream()` method obtains the encoded output as an `OutputStream` object.

`ImageEncoderImpl` is a convenient class that implements the `ImageEncoder` interface. An `ImageEncoderImpl` object can be constructed with given `OutputStream` and `ImageEncodeParam` instances. `ImageEncoderImpl` is an abstract class that can be extended by the format-specific encoding classes.

Just like `ImageDecodeParam`, `ImageEncodeParam` is a marker interface, which is implemented by all encoder parameter classes. Note that `ImageEncodeParam` extends `ImageDecodeParam`. As Figure 17.1 shows, there are five format-specific classes. When you use an operator to save an image from image data, you must create an appropriate encoder parameter object from these classes.

Using the SeekableStream Classes

In Java you can read as an input stream any file from which you can extract the data as Java primitive types—that is, `byte, char, int, short, float,` or `double`. The `java.io.InputStream` class is a base class for all classes that read data from an input stream.

When the file is an image, the requirements are slightly different from those of a typical text file. With images, the ability to randomly access data is often a requirement. One option is to read the entire file in memory, as is done in the immediate-mode model. But when the image file is huge, this is not a viable option. An alternate solution is to implement a cache for the input stream and navigate through this stream forward and backward. The `SeekableStream` class implements this basic functionality, and its subclasses implement different ways of caching the data, such as placing it in memory, saving it to disk, and so on.

SeekableStream is an abstract class that extends java.io.InputStream and implements the java.io.DataInput interface.

The InputStream class has methods for reading input data as bytes. The DataInput interface specifies methods for reading data as Java primitive types. When primitive data is read, it is important to know the order in which bytes were input. There are two types of byte ordering: big-endian and little-endian. In a big-endian system the higher-order bits come first in the stream, and in a little-endian system the lower-order bits come first. Java writes data only in the big-endian fashion. But the image data may also be written by platforms that support the little-endian format.

The SeekableStream class extends the DataInput interface to support little-endian representation of data. So for every method that reads a type of data, an additional method reads that data in little-endian fashion. For example, readInt() reads data as an int value in big-endian order, and readIntLE() reads data as an int value in little-endian order.

Figure 17.2 shows the SeekableStream class hierarchy, and Table 17.1 shows the differences among the various subclasses of SeekableStream. The SeekableStream classes are typically used in conjunction with format-specific operators (which are listed in Table 17.3).

As Table 10.1 shows, data is cached in a local file or memory. You can choose a subclass depending on your memory availability and permission to access the local disk.

The SeekableStream class also has a static method that creates an instance of SeekableStream. This method decides the appropriate instance so that the application doesn't need to check whether the local disk is accessible. Here's the method:

◆ **public static SeekableStream wrapInputStream(java.io.InputStream is,**
boolean
canSeekBackwards)

Using the ImageCodec Class

ImageCodec is a utility class that has several static and abstract methods. The static methods allow you to create image encoder and decoder objects in JAI-supported formats, as well as custom-written formats.

Decoding

Here are ImageCodec's static methods for image decoding:

◆ **public static ImageDecoder createImageDecoder(java.lang.String name,**
java.io.File src,
ImageDecodeParam param)
throws java.io.IOException

- ◆ `public static ImageDecoder createImageDecoder(java.lang.String name,`
                                                `SeekableStream src,`
                                                `ImageDecodeParam param)`
- ◆ `public static ImageDecoder createImageDecoder(java.lang.String name,`
                                                `java.io.InputStream src,`
                                                `ImageDecodeParam param)`

As this list shows, you can construct an `ImageDecoder` object for a specific format from a `File`, `SeekableStream`, or `InputStream` object. Not all formats require decoding parameters, so the value of `ImageDecodeParam` can be `null`.

Once you obtain the `ImageDecoder` object, all you need to do is call its `decodeAsRaster()` or `decodeAsRenderedImage()` method to create the `Raster` or `RenderedImage` object, respectively.

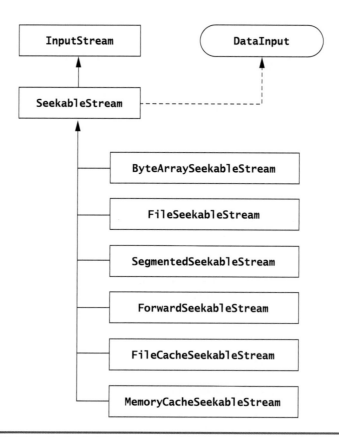

FIGURE 17.2   The `SeekableStream` class hierarchy

TABLE 17.1   Subclasses of `SeekableStream`

SUBCLASS	INPUT	SUPPORT FOR SEEKING BACKWARD	COMMENTS
`ByteArraySeekableStream`	Array of bytes	Yes	
`FileSeekableStream`	`File` or `RandomAccessFile`	Yes	Seeking functionality is directly implemented on the file itself.
`SegmentedSeekableStream`	`SeekableStream`	Depends on the input `Seekable Stream` object	
`ForwardSeekableStream`	`InputStream`	No	This is the fastest way of reading a file.
`FileCacheSeekableStream`	`InputStream`	Yes, through file cache	This subclass requires access to a local disk. If such access is not available, it may use the memory cache instead.
`MemoryCacheSeekableStream`	`InputStream`	Yes, through memory cache	This subclass requires a large memory buffer.

Encoding

`ImageCodec` has only one encoding method:

♦ `public static ImageEncoder createImageEncoder(java.lang.String name,`
                                        `java.io.OutputStream`
                                        `dst,`
                                        `ImageEncodeParam param)`

Using this method, you can construct an `ImageEncoder` object for a specific format from an `OutputStream` object. The value of `ImageEncodeParam` can be `null`. Once you get the `ImageEncoder` object, call its `encode(image)` method to create the image file. Listing 17.6 shows an example.

LISTING 17.6   Saving a rendered image as a JPEG image

```
public static void saveAsJPEG(RenderedImage image, String file)
        throws java.io.IOException {
    String filename = file;
    if(!filename.endsWith(".jpg"))filename = new String(file+".jpg");
    OutputStream out = new FileOutputStream(filename);
    JPEGEncodeParam param = new JPEGEncodeParam();
```

continued

```
    ImageEncoder encoder = ImageCodec.createImageEncoder("JPEG", out, param);
    encoder.encode(image);
    out.close();
}
```

Adding a Custom Codec

The abstract methods of `ImageCodec` help you create your own codec. To do this, you need to create subclasses of the `ImageCodec` class and override the following abstract methods:

- **`protected abstract java.lang.Class getDecodeParamClass()`**
- **`protected abstract ImageDecoder createImageDecoder(SeekableStream src,`**
                                  `ImageDecodeParam param)`

- **`protected abstract java.lang.Class getEncodeParamClass()`**
- **`protected abstract ImageEncoder`**
  `createImageEncoder(java.io.OutputStream dst,`
                                  `ImageEncodeParam param)`
- **`public abstract java.lang.String getFormatName()`**

To create a codec, you can use the `ImageDecoderImpl` and `ImageEncoderImpl` classes. In your overridden class, the `createImageDecoder()` and `createImage Encoder()` methods must construct your `ImageDecoder` and `ImageEncoder` objects, respectively.

In addition, you need to register your codec with `ImageCodec.` The static method `registerCodec(ImageCodec codec)` allows you to register a user-defined codec. The `unregisterCodec(String formatName)` method unregisters the codec that is responsible for the format specified in the input.

The `ImageCodec` class also has some utility methods that return information about the codecs.

Loading Images

Unlike AWT or Java 2D, JAI makes reading an image relatively easy. As suggested earlier, the FileLoad operator loads images from a local directory. You can also load an image from a URL. The URL operator does that for you. The Stream operator loads the image from a `SeekableInputStream` object. Table 17.2 describes the FileLoad, URL, and Stream operators.

Listing 17.7 shows examples that use the FileLoad, URL, and Stream operators.

LISTING 17.7   Examples of reading an image as a planar image

```
public static PlanarImage readAsPlanarImage(String filename) {
    return JAI.create("fileload", filename);
```

TABLE 17.2 Operators for Loading Images

OPERATOR NAME	PARAMETER	TYPE	DEFAULT VALUE	DESCRIPTION
FileLoad	`fileName`	`String`	None	Indicates the path of the image in the local machine
	`imageDecoder`	`ImageDecodeParam`	`null`	Holds the decoding parameters
URL	`url`	`java.net.URL`	None	Indicates the path of the image as a URL
	`imageDecoder`	`ImageDecodeParam`	`null`	Holds the decoding parameters
Stream	`stream`	`SeekableStream`	None	Reads the image from a stream
	`imageDecoder`	`ImageDecodeParam`	`null`	Holds the decoding parameters

```
   }

   public static PlanarImage readAsPlanarImage(URL url) {
       return JAI.create("URL", url);
   }

   public static PlanarImage readAsPlanarImage(String filename) {
       try {
          FileInputStream is = new FileInputStream(filename);
          SeekableStream ss = SeekableStream.wrapInputStream(is,true);
          return JAI.create("stream", ss, null);
       } catch (Exception e){return null;}
   }
```

The Stream operator is useful when an image is available only as a stream. For example, to read an image from a JAR or ZIP file, you would retrieve it as a stream first. To use the Stream operator, this stream must be converted to a `SeekableStream` object.

Format-Specific Image-Loading Operators

JAI also has operators that can read specific formats (see Table 17.3).

All of the format-specific image-loading operators take a `SeekableStream` object as an input parameter. Notice that not all of them have decoder parameters. Only the operators that have decoder parameters have a corresponding `ImageDecodeParam` class in the JAI codec (see Figure 17.1).

Loading Images from a Local File

Now let's build an image-loading class along the same lines as the one we developed in Chapter 2. This class will load the image from the local directory and fire a

TABLE 17.3 Format-Specific Operators for Loading Images

OPERATOR NAME	PARAMETER	TYPE	DEFAULT VALUE	DESCRIPTION
BMP	stream	SeekableStream	None	Reads an image from a BMP stream
FPX	stream	SeekableStream	None	Reads an image from a FlashPix 6.0 stream
	fpxDecoder	FPXDecodeParam	null	Holds the decoding parameters
GIF	stream	SeekableStream	None	Reads an image from a GIF stream
JPEG	stream	SeekableStream	None	Reads an image from a JPEG stream
PNG	stream	SeekableStream	None	Reads an image from a PNG 1.1 stream
	pngDecoder	PNGDecodeParam	null	Holds the decoding parameters
PNM	stream	SeekableStream	None	Reads an image from a PNM stream
TIFF	stream	SeekableStream	None	Reads an image from a TIFF 6.0 stream
	tiffDecoder	TIFFDecodeParam	null	Holds the decoding parameters

`planarImageLoaded` event to all registered listeners. By using events, the image-loading class doesn't need to be aware of the client classes. In other words, the `ImageLoaderJAI` class can be a bean. Listing 17.8 shows the code for this class.

LISTING 17.8 The `ImageLoaderJAI` class

```
package com.vistech.jai.imageio;

import java.io.*;
import java.util.*;
import java.beans.*;
import java.awt.*;
import java.awt.image.*;
import javax.media.jai.*;
import com.sun.media.jai.codec.*;
import com.vistech.events.*;

public class ImageLoaderJAI implements ListSelectListener{
    protected PlanarImage loadedImage = null;
    protected PropertyChangeSupport pcNotifier;
    private Vector imgLst = new Vector();

    public ImageLoaderJAI() {
       pcNotifier= new PropertyChangeSupport(this);
```

```
    }
    public void load(ListSelectEvent e){
        File currentDir = e.getPath();
        String[] flist = e.getFileList();
        String path =
            (currentDir !=null)? currentDir.toString()+File.separator+flist[0]:flist[0];
        if(flist != null) loadImage(path);
    }

    public PlanarImage loadImage(String path) {
        PlanarImage img= readAsPlanarImage(path);
        fireImageLoadedEvent(img);
        return img;
    }

    public static PlanarImage readAsPlanarImage(String filename) {
        return JAI.create("fileload", filename);
    }

    public void setLoadedImage(PlanarImage img){
        pcNotifier.firePropertyChange("loadedImage",
                                      this.loadedImage,
                                      img);
        loadedImage = img;
    }

    public PlanarImage getLoadedImage(){
        return loadedImage;
    }

    public void addPlanarImageLoadedListener(PlanarImageLoadedListener il){
        imgLst.addElement(il);
    }
    public void removePlanarImageLoadedListener(PlanarImageLoadedListener il){
        if(!(imgLst.isEmpty())) imgLst.removeElement(il);
    }
    protected void fireImageLoadedEvent(PlanarImage img) {
        for(Enumeration e= imgLst.elements(); e.hasMoreElements();){
            PlanarImageLoadedEvent ie = new PlanarImageLoadedEvent(this, img);
            PlanarImageLoadedListener il = (PlanarImageLoadedListener)(e.nextElement());
            il.imageLoaded(ie);
        }
        setLoadedImage(img);
    }
}
```

ImageLoaderJAI is a convenient class that loads an image from a local directory and sends it to a target object. This class is implemented in such a way that it can also be used as a bean. It is a target for listSelect events and a source for planarImageLoaded events.

ImageLoaderJAI receives the image path through a listSelect event. To receive listSelect events, this class implements the ListSelectListener interface. The list Select event is a custom event that we defined for the FileBrowser bean (see Appendix C for more details).

The `ListSelectListener` interface has one method, called `load(ListSelect Event)`. The source that fires the `listSelect` events constructs the `ListSelectEvent` object and invokes the `load()` method in the target object, which in this case is `Image LoaderJAI`.

The `load()` method extracts the directory and the file name from the event state object and calls the `loadImage()` method. The `loadImage()` method calls `readAs PlanarImage()` to load the image using the FileLoad operator. Once an image has been loaded, the `loadImage()` method calls the `fireImageLoadedEvent()` method to fire the `planarImageLoaded` event to all the registered listeners.

The `planarImageLoaded` event is similar to the `imageLoaded` event we developed in Chapter 2. The only difference is that the `planarImageLoaded` event carries `PlanarImage` objects instead of AWT `Image` objects.

Listings 17.9 and 17.10 show the listener interface and the event state class, respectively, for the `planarImageLoaded` event.

LISTING 17.9   The `planarImageLoaded` event listener class

```
package com.vistech.jai.imageio;

public interface PlanarImageLoadedListener extends java.util.EventListener{
    public void imageLoaded(PlanarImageLoadedEvent e);
}
```

LISTING 17.10   The `planarImageLoaded` event state class

```
package com.vistech.jai.imageio;
import java.awt.*;
import java.io.*;
import javax.media.jai.*;

public class PlanarImageLoadedEvent  extends java.util.EventObject
        implements Serializable{
    protected PlanarImage image;
    protected PlanarImage[] imageset;

    public PlanarImageLoadedEvent(Object obj, PlanarImage img){
        super(obj);
        image = img;
        imageset = new PlanarImage[] {img};
    }

    public PlanarImageLoadedEvent(Object obj, PlanarImage[] img){
        super(obj);
        imageset = img;
        if((img != null) && (img.length >0))image = img[0];
    }

    public PlanarImage getImage(){return image;}
    public PlanarImage[] getImages(){return imageset;}
}
```

Loading Images from a JAR File

To load an image from a JAR file, you cannot use the FileLoad operator because it needs an image path as the input parameter. On the other hand, the Stream operator needs only a `SeekableStream` object as input. So when an image is in a JAR file, we can construct a `SeekableStream` object by reading that image as an `InputStream` object and then pass it to the Stream operator. Listing 17.11 shows how to do this.

LISTING 17.11   Reading an image from a JAR or ZIP file

```
public static PlanarImage readJAIImage(String jarpath, String filename){
   PlanarImage image = null;
   try {
     ZipFile zipfile = new ZipFile(new File(jarpath));
     Vector imageVect = new Vector();
     ZipEntry zentry = zipfile.getEntry(filename);
     InputStream zstream = zipfile.getInputStream(zentry);
     FileCacheSeekableStream flis = new  FileCacheSeekableStream(zstream);
     RenderedOp op = JAI.create("stream", flis);
     image = op.createInstance();
     zipfile.close();
   }catch(Exception e){System.out.println(e);}
   return image;
}
```

> **Note:** You may recall that we developed a bean called `MultiImageLoader` to read images from a local file as well as a JAR file. Here we used the code in Listing 17.11 to modify `MultiImageLoader` to read different types of formats supported by JAI. The modified code is available on the book's Web page in the directory `src/chapter17/loader`.

Saving Images

JAI version 1.0.2 supports five image formats: BMP, JPEG, PNG, PNM, and TIFF. There are two operators for saving images: FileStore and Encode. Both of these operators require a `RenderedImage` object as the source. Table 17.4 describes these operators.

To simplify image-saving tasks, we created a utility class called `ImageSaverJAI` with several static methods, each of which saves an image in the format supported by the JAI codec. Listing 17.12 shows this class with two sample methods.

LISTING 17.12   The `ImageSaverJAI` class

```
package com.vistech.jai.imageio;

import java.io.*;
import java.awt.*;
```

continued

TABLE 17.4   Operators for Saving Images

OPERATOR NAME	PARAMETER	TYPE	DEFAULT VALUE	DESCRIPTION
FileStore	`fileName`	`String`	None	Indicates the path at which the image is to be saved in the local machine
	`format`	`String`	`"tiff"`	Holds the image format
	`param`	`ImageEncodeParam`	`null`	Holds the encoding parameters
Encode	`stream`	`OutputStream`	None	Indicates the `OutputStream` object to write to
	`format`	`String`	`"tiff"`	Holds the image format
	`param`	`ImageEncodeParam`	`null`	Holds the encoding parameters

```java
import java.awt.image.*;
import javax.media.jai.*;
import com.sun.media.jai.codec.*;
import java.awt.image.renderable.*;

public class ImageSaverJAI {

    public static void saveAsPNM(RenderedImage image, String file, boolean rawOrAscii)
        throws java.io.IOException {
        String filename = file;
        if(!filename.endsWith(".pnm"))filename = new String(file+".pnm");
        PNMEncodeParam param = new PNMEncodeParam();
        param.setRaw(rawOrAscii);

        ParameterBlock pb =  new ParameterBlock();
        pb.addSource(image);
        pb.add(filename);
        pb.add("pnm");
        pb.add(param);
        JAI.create("filestore", pb);
    }

    public static void saveAsTIFF(RenderedImage image, String file )
        throws java.io.IOException{
        String filename = file;
        if(!filename.endsWith(".tiff"))filename = new String(file+".tiff");

        OutputStream out = new FileOutputStream(filename);
        TIFFEncodeParam param = new TIFFEncodeParam();
        ImageEncoder encoder = ImageCodec.createImageEncoder("TIFF", out, param);
        encoder.encode(image);
        out.close();
    }
```

```
    //... Other save methods
}
```

The `saveAsPNM()` method uses the FileStore operator to convert a planar image into a PNM image and save it to a local file. Before calling `JAI.create()`, `saveAsPNM()` creates a `ParameterBlock` object and adds the required parameters in the order required by the FileStore operator. Notice that the `setRaw()` method is called in one of the parameters—that is, `PNMEncodeParam.` The boolean input to this method specifies the format of the output file—that is, raw or ASCII.

The `saveAsTIFF()` method shows how to save an image without using the FileStore operator. This method first creates a `TIFFEncodeParam` object and passes it to the `ImageCodec.createImageEncoder()` method. This is a utility method in the codec package that creates an `ImageEncoder` object for a specified image format. When the `encode()` method of the `ImageEncoder` class is called, the planar image is [SRH1]en-coded and written to an `OutputStream` object.

Using the Image I/O API

Image I/O is the new initiative that came after the initial releases of Java 2D and JAI. The idea here is to provide a common framework in Java to load and save images. Image I/O is also a pluggable framework that allows third-party vendors to plug in their own codecs for reading and writing images in different formats.

The Image I/O API is designed for Java 2 and later versions. Because it uses Java 2D classes such as `BufferedImage,` it cannot be used with JDK 1.1.

There are two parts to the Image I/O API—one designed for application developers, who will use the codecs, and the other designed for codec developers.

In this section we'll cover only the interfaces and classes required by an application developer. These interfaces and classes do the following:

♦ Automatically detect installed plug-ins
♦ Monitor reading and writing progress
♦ Transcode between formats
♦ Read and write only a region of interest of an image
♦ Access individual images in multi-image files

Note: Keep in mind that the Image I/O API described here is an early release and that the package may change before its final release. You may need to consult the latest specs and Java documents if you want to use this API in your applications.

Overview of the Image I/O Packages

At the time of this writing, the Image I/O specs (release 0.5) and a corresponding reference implementation (early release 2) have been issued. In this release, the Image I/O package contains the following packages:

- **javax.imageio.** This is the main package of the Java Image I/O API. It has a class called `ImageIO,` which has static methods for reading and writing images. If that's all you need, this may be the only class you need to know. The other classes include `ImageReader, ImageReadParam, ImageWriter,` and `ImageWriteParam.` These classes are modeled after the JPEG and JAI codecs.

- **javax.imageio.event.** This package deals with synchronous notification of events during the reading and writing of images. It has several event listeners that are needed to implement progress bars for reading and writing operations.

- **javax.imageio.metadata.** This package deals with reading and writing metadata. It has interfaces that describe different parameters, including image geometry, scanning attributes, and color information.

- **javax.imageio.spi.** This package contains the plug-in interfaces for readers, writers, transcoders, and streams, and a runtime registry. If you intend to provide a codec, you need to look at this package.

- **javax.imageio.stream.** This package deals with low-level I/O from files and streams. It defines the basic `ImageInputStream` and `ImageOutputStream` interfaces and several classes that implement these interfaces. Using the classes in this package, you can read an image into a stream from a local file or a URL.

- **javax.imageio.plugins.jpeg.** This package has support classes for reading and writing JPEG images.

Note that all the package names, interfaces, and classes are subject to change. At the time of this writing, the Image I/O feature has a few codecs that support the JPEG, PNG, and GIF formats.

Using the ImageIO Class

Although the Image I/O API is relatively large compared to the JPEG codec, it is simple to use from an application developer's point of view. For simple load and save operations, you need to know only one class in detail—`javax.imageio.ImageIO`—which has several static utility methods for reading and writing images.

Reading an Image

The `ImageIO` class has the following methods for reading an image:

- **public static BufferedImage read(File input) throws IIOException**

- **public static BufferedImage read(URL input) throws IIOException**
- **public static BufferedImage read(InputStream stream) throws IIOException**
- **public static BufferedImage read(ImageInputStream stream) throws IIOException**

The first three methods are self-explanatory. The fourth method reads an image from an `ImageInputStream` object, which is an interface in the `javax.imageio.stream` package.

Listing 17.13 shows a simple method that reads an image using the `ImageIO` class.

LISTING 17.13   Reading an image

```
public static BufferedImage readAsBufferedImage(String filename) {
  try {
    BufferedImage img = ImageIO.read(new File(filename));
    return img;
  }catch (Exception e) {
    e.printStackTrace();
    return null;
  }
}
```

Writing an Image

Writing images is also quite simple. The `ImageIO` class has the following static methods for writing an image:

- **public static boolean write(RenderedImage im,**
                          String formatName,
                          File output) throws IIOException
- **public static boolean write(RenderedImage im,**
                          String formatName,
                          OutputStream output) throws IIOException
- **public static boolean write(RenderedImage im,**
                          String formatName,
                          ImageOutputStream output) throws IIOException

The first two arguments are common to all three methods. The first argument—`java.awt.image.RenderedImage`—is a key interface that represents an image in the pull model. Note that `BufferedImage` does implement `RenderedImage`. Because `RenderedImage` supports tiling, it is easy to write an image tile by tile.

The second argument specifies the format name as a string—for example, "jpg" for JPEG images. The format name is assigned when a codec is registered with the Image I/O registry.

The third argument specifies the mechanism of saving. The first method writes the image to a local file. The second method writes the image to an **OutputStream** object. You can use this method to write an image to a JAR file or a URL. If the image is large, you may have to choose the third method. This method writes the image to an **ImageOutputStream** object, which is an interface in the **javax.imageio.stream** package. The third method provides you with many options. Depending on the requirements, you can create different types of **ImageOutputStream** objects. Listing 17.14 shows a sample method that uses the first constructor to save a buffered image to a local directory in the JPEG format.

LISTING 17.14   Saving a buffered image

```
protected void save(BufferedImage image){
   String filename = JpegUtil.launchFileDialog();
   try {
      ImageIO.write((RenderedImage)image(), "jpg", new File(filename));
   } catch(Exception e){}
}
```

Using Image Readers and Image Writers

Now that we've seen simple reading and writing examples, it's time to describe how to use the **ImageReader** and **ImageWriter** classes. Some features of the Image I/O API require these classes.

You can install as many image readers or image writers as you wish and choose an appropriate image reader or image writer at runtime. The **ImageIO** class provides several ways for an application to query and obtain the available image readers and image writers.

Obtaining Image Readers

Here are the methods in the **ImageIO** class that return the currently available image readers:

- **public static Iterator getImageReaders(Object input)**
- **public static Iterator getImageReadersByFormatName(String formatName)**
- **public static Iterator getImageReadersBySuffix(String fileSuffix)**
- **public static Iterator getImageReadersByMIMEType(String MIMEType)**

All of these methods return an **Iterator** object, which means that a given format can have multiple image readers. In the current implementation, the first method requires an **ImageInputStream** object as an input. The rest of the methods are self-explanatory. If you know the image writer, you can use the following method to get the image reader:

- **public static ImageReader getImageReader(ImageWriter writer)**

Reading an Image

The `ImageReader` class has several methods for reading an image. In the current implementation, these methods don't take the file name directly. Instead, `ImageReader` provides the following method for setting the image source:

- ◆ **`public void setInput(Object input, boolean seekForwardOnly)`**

This method, with a valid input, must be set before any of the query or read methods are used. If the input is `null`, any currently set input source will be removed. The `input` parameter in the current implementation must be an `ImageInput Stream` object. If the value of `seekForwardOnly` is `true`, images and metadata may be read only in ascending order from the input source.

To read an image, you can use the following methods:

- ◆ **`public BufferedImage read(int imageIndex) throws IIOException`**
- ◆ **`public abstract BufferedImage read(int imageIndex,`**
  `ImageReadParam param)`
  `throws IIOException`
- ◆ **`public Iterator readAll(Iterator params) throws IIOException`**
- ◆ **`public RenderedImage readAsRenderedImage(int imageIndex,`**
  `ImageReadParam param)`
  `throws IIOException`

- ◆ **`public BufferedImage readThumbnail(int imageIndex, int thumbnailIndex)`**
  `throws IIOException`
- ◆ **`public IIOImage readAll(int imageIndex, ImageReadParam param)`**
  `throws IIOException`
- ◆ **`public Iterator readAll(Iterator params) throws IIOException`**

- ◆ **`public Raster readRaster(int imageIndex, ImageReadParam param) throws`**
  `IIOException`
- ◆ **`public BufferedImage readTile(int imageIndex, int tileX, int tileY)`**
  `throws IIOException`

You can read single or multiple images registered via the `setInput()` method. The `imageIndex` parameter refers to the point at which the `setInput()` method is called. You can also read the image `Raster` object or a specified tile. Listing 17.15 shows an example of using the `ImageReader` class.

LISTING 17.15   Reading an image using an image reader

```
public RenderedImage readAnImage(String filename) {
    try {
        InputStream is = new FileInputStream(new File (filename));
        javax.imageio.stream.ImageInputStream iis =
                ImageIO.createImageInputStream(is);
```

continued

```
    ImageReader ir = null;

    Iterator it = ImageIO.getImageReaders(is);
     while(it.hasNext()) {
         ir = (ImageReader)it.next();
         // Apply the logic to choose a reader and break
     }

     ir.setInput(is, true);
     return ir.read(0);
  } catch(Exception e) { return null;}
}
```

The `readAnImage()` method obtains an image reader first and then uses it to read the image. To obtain all the image readers for a format, this method creates an `Image InputStream` object using the static method `ImageIO.createImageInput Stream()`. Alternatively, you can use any constructors of the three types of `ImageInputStream` classes (see the section titled Image Streams a little later in this chapter).

Obtaining Image Writers

The `ImageIO` class has the following methods for obtaining registered image writers:

- **public static Iterator getImageWriters(ImageTypeSpecifier type,**
                                                        String formatName)
- **public static Iterator getImageWritersByFormatName(String formatName)**
- **public static Iterator getImageWritersBySuffix(String fileSuffix)**
- **public static Iterator getImageWritersByMIMEType(String MIMEType)**
- **public static ImageWriter getImageWriter(ImageReader reader)**

The first method requires an `ImageTypeSpecifier` input. This is a class in the `javax.imageio` package. `ImageTypeSpecifier` has several factory methods that return an `ImageTypeSpecifier` object. Each of the factory methods creates a template for laying out image data, some of which is described in Chapter 8.

Here are three sample factory methods from this class:

1. **public static ImageTypeSpecifier createGrayscale(int bits,**
                                                            int dataType,
                                                            boolean isSigned)
2. **public static ImageTypeSpecifier createIndexed(byte[] redLUT, byte[]**
                                                        greenLUT,
                                                        byte[] blueLUT,
                                                        byte[] alphaLUT,
                                                        int bits, int dataType)
3. **public static ImageTypeSpecifier createInterleaved(ColorSpace**
                                                            colorSpace,
                                                            int[] bandOffsets,

```
                                          int dataType,
                                          boolean hasAlpha,
                                          boolean
                                             isAlpha
                                             Premultiplied)
```

Writing Images

The following method is similar to `setInput()` in the `ImageReader` class. It sets the image to be written:

- **`public void setOutput(Object output)`**

   The following methods of the `ImageWriter` class can be used for writing images:

- **`public void write(RenderedImage image) throws IIOException`**
- **`public abstract void write(IIOMetadata streamMetadata, IIOImage image,`**
   `ImageWriteParam param) throws IIOException`
- **`public void write(IIOImage image) throws IIOException`**
- **`public void writeInsert(int imageIndex, IIOImage image,`**
   `ImageWriteParam param)`
   `throws IIOException`
- **`public void writePartial(IIOImage image, ImageWriteParam param)`**
   `throws IIOException`

Image Streams

The `javax.imageio.stream` package contains the interfaces and classes that represent images as streams (see Figure 17.3). `ImageInputStream` is the interface that specifies methods for reading images from a stream. This interface is similar to the `SeekableStream` interface described in the JAI codec section. `ImageOutputStream` is the interface that specifies methods for writing images to a stream. This interface is similar to the `SeekableOutputStream` interface described in the JAI codec section.

The `ImageInputStreamImpl` class is the base class for all the `ImageInputStream` classes. This abstract class has default implementation for most of the `ImageInput Stream` interface methods. Likewise, `ImageOutputStreamImpl` is the base class for all the `ImageOutputStream` classes.

ImageInputStream Classes

The constructors for the `ImageInputStream` classes are as follows:

- **For `FileCacheImageInputStream`,** in which a file is used as a mechanism for caching previously input image data:

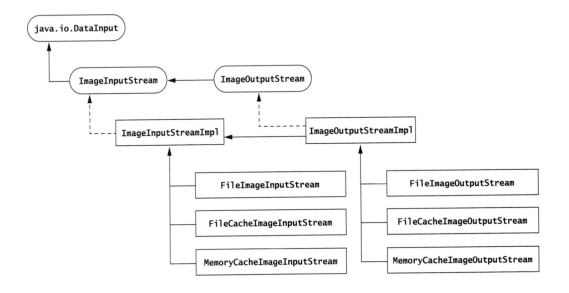

FIGURE 17.3 The ImageInputStream class hierarchy

- ◆ public FileCacheImageInputStream(InputStream inputstream,
                            File cacheDir) throws IOException

This constructor creates an instance of ImageInputStream from an InputStream object and a local directory, which is used for creating temporary files to cache the data read from the input stream. The value of cacheDir can be null, in which case the temporary file is created in the system directory. If the value of cacheDir is not null but not a directory, then an exception—IllegalArgument Exception—is thrown.

- ◆ **ForFileImageInputStream:**
  - ◆ public FileImageInputStream(File f)
                        throws FileNotFoundException,
                        IOException
  - ◆ public FileImageInputStream(RandomAccessFile raf)

- ◆ **ForMemoryCacheImageInputStream,** in which case a memory buffer is used as the cache:
  - ◆ public MemoryCacheImageInputStream(InputStream stream)

ImageOutputStream Classes

The ImageOutputStream classes have similar constructors:

- For `FileCacheImageOutputStream`:

    - ```
      public FileCacheImageOutputStream(OutputStream stream,
                                        File cacheDir)
                                        throws IOException
      ```

- For`FileImageOutputStream`:

    - ```
      public FileImageOutputStream(File f)
                                   throws FileNotFoundException,
                                   IOException
      ```
    - ```
      public FileImageOutputStream(RandomAccessFile raf)
      ```

- For `MemoryCacheImageOutputStream`:

    - ```
      public MemoryCacheImageOutputStream(OutputStream stream)
      ```

Image I/O Events

Events in the Image I/O API are designed primarily to report updates during image-loading and -saving operations. If an image is large, your application can launch a progress bar, which can be registered to receive notifications during image loading or saving.

The `javax.imageio.event` package has the following event listeners:

- **`IIOReadProgressListener`.** This listener has methods for reporting to the registered listeners during image loading. It has methods to send updates for regular as well as thumbnail images. To get updates, a client object must register with the image reader. Listing 17.16 shows an example:

LISTING 17.16   Adding `IIOReadProgressListener`

```
ImageReader reader  = ... // The image reader that loads the image
IIOReadProgressListener listener  progListener  = ...// An instance object that
implements IIOReadProgressListener
```

```
reader.addIIOReadProgressListener(progListener);
```

- **`IIOReadUpdateListener`.** This listener is similar to the `ImageObserver` interface discussed in Chapters 2 and 3. It has methods for sending updates about the pixel chunks.
- **`IIOReadWarningListener`.** This listener has just one method, which notifies the registered clients of the warnings that occurred during loading. Warnings are typically nonfatal errors.
- **`IIOWriteProgressListener`.** This listener has the same notification features as `IIOReadProgressListener`, but the source in this case is an image writer. You can build a progress bar similar to the one in Listing 17.16 while saving images.

♦ **IIOWriteWarningListener.** This event listener is similar to **IIOReadWarning Listener** and is designed to report warnings from an image writer.

Listing 17.17 shows a method that loads an image with a progress bar.

LISTING 17.17   Loading an image with a progress bar

```
public RenderedImage loadWithProgressBar(String filename) {
   RenderedImage img = null;
   try {
      InputStream is1 = new FileInputStream(new File (filename));
      javax.imageio.stream.ImageInputStream is = ImageIO.createImageInputStream(is1);
      Iterator it = ImageIO.getImageReaders(is);
      while(it.hasNext()) {
         ImageReader ir = (ImageReader)it.next();
         ir.addIIOReadProgressListener(
           new IIOReadProgressListener(){
               public void sequenceStarted(ImageReader source,
                                           int minIndex){ }
               public void sequenceComplete(ImageReader source){}
               public void imageStarted(ImageReader source, int imageIndex){
                  rangevalue = 0;
                  show();
               }
               public void imageProgress(ImageReader source, float percentageDone){
                  rangevalue = (int) percentageDone;
               }
               public void imageComplete(ImageReader source){
                  disposePb();
               }
               public void thumbnailStarted(ImageReader source,
                                            int imageIndex,
                                            int thumbnailIndex){}
               public void thumbnailProgress(ImageReader source,
                           float percentageDone){}
               public void thumbnailComplete(ImageReader source){}
               public void readAborted(ImageReader source){}
            }
         );
         ir.setInput(is, true);
         img = ir.read(0);
         break;
      }
   } catch (Exception e) {
    System.out.println(e);
   }
   return img;
}
```

The **loadWithProgressBar()** method first obtains all the available image readers for the image format of the input image. With the first image reader, it registers an anonymous inner class that implements the **IIOReadProgressListener** interface. As Listing 17.17 shows, some of the methods are just dummies. The **imageStarted()**

method calls an outer-class method—show()—which shows a progress bar, which is a Swing component called JProgressBar.

With this call, the image loading begins and the progress bar starts receiving updates. The imageProgress() method then receives updates at regular intervals identifying what percentage of the loading is finished. This method assigns rangeValue the value percentageDone. The rangeValue parameter is an instance variable of the class that has the method loadWithProgressBar(). JProgressBar uses the bounded range model to update its view. Listing 17.18 shows an implementation of this model.

LISTING 17.18 The RangeModel class

```
public class RangeModel extends javax.swing.DefaultBoundedRangeModel{
    public void setValue(int value){
        rangevalue = value;
    }

    public int getValue() {
        return rangevalue;
    }
}
```

Note that the DefaultBoundedRangeModel class implements the bounded range model.

JProgressBar is constructed in another method, as shown here:

```
JProgressBar jp = new JProgressBar(new RangeModel());
```

In Listing 17.17, when the loading is done, the image reader calls image Completed(), which calls disposePb() to dispose of the progress bar GUI.

Conclusion

In this chapter we described three image-loading and -saving APIs from an application developer's point of view. The JPEG codec was developed as a stopgap measure to load and save JPEG images with Java 2D applications. Likewise, the JAI codec was developed for use with JAI.

The new Image I/O API provides a framework to allow third-party vendors to write plug-ins for any image format. With this API you can install as many codecs as you want for a given format. The Image I/O API has many elegant features to help you develop both client-side and server-side imaging applications. At the time of this writing, the API has not been finalized. When it evolves fully, it will be used for image loading and saving by all the Java media APIs.

Summing Up

18

THE FIRST STEP IN A TYPICAL IMAGING APPLICATION is image loading. Images are loaded from the network or read from a local directory. In this book we described how to load images using the different APIs available in Java. In many cases, a loaded image may not be in a presentable form. We described how a presentable image is created for the purpose of rendering to a device such as a monitor or a printer.

Displaying images itself is not sufficient to extract information from those images. Information can be extracted by image manipulation. We described some geometric image manipulation techniques and their implementation in Java. In many imaging applications, image data is processed and analyzed for a variety of purposes. We explored many image data manipulation techniques through examples written with the Java imaging APIs.

We described three distinct imaging APIs. Let's summarize their important features and compare them.

Comparing AWT Imaging, Java 2D, and JAI

For comparison, Table 18.1 lists the major features of each imaging API covered in this book.

Visualization Framework

In this book we developed numerous sample applications. In some chapters we developed interfaces and reusable classes as part of an image visualization framework. Let's summarize them in a class hierarchy diagram. Figure 18.1 shows the hierarchy of rendering components that we developed in Chapters 6, 7, and 9. Figure 18.2 shows the image manipulation components that we developed in Chapter 7 and reused in many other chapters. Figure 18.3 shows the hierarchy of rendering components that we developed in the JAI chapters.

TABLE 18.1   Comparing AWT Imaging, Java 2D, and JAI

FEATURE	AWT	JAVA 2D	JAI
Distribution	The AWT is part of JDK 1.0 and later versions.	Java 2D is part of the Java 2 core package. There is no need to install Java 2D separately. It should be available on all Java 2–compatible platforms and browsers.	JAI is a Java extension and does not come with the JDK or JRE. To get the JAI package, you must download it from the Java home page and install it separately.
Platform independence	The AWT can be used in any platform that has a JVM (Java Virtual Machine).	Java 2D can be used in any platform that supports Java 2.	JAI can be used in any platform that supports Java 2. At the time of this writing, JAI has been tested only with Windows, UNIX, and Linux.
Image representation	The AWT class for representing images is `java.awt.Image`.	The primary image representation class in Java 2D is `java.awt.BufferedImage`.	There are several image representation classes in JAI, but `javax.media.jai.PlanarImage` is central.
Image data representation	The AWT uses a single element to represent the pixel components and color model, and to interpret the pixels. Image data is stored as an array.	Java 2D uses `SampleModel` and `ColorModel` classes. The data is stored in the `DataBuffer` object.	In addition to `SampleModel` and `ColorModel`, JAI has classes that extend both these two classes and `DataBuffer`.
Support for image sets	The AWT does not support image sets.	Java 2D does not support image sets.	JAI has several classes that support image collections. You can save a sequence of images in a `Collection`-based data structure.
Support for handling large images	The AWT cannot handle large images.	Because the immediate-mode model stores the entire image in cache, Java 2D is not well suited for handling large images.	Because JAI is tile based, it has good support for handling large images.

TABLE 18.1   (continued)

FEATURE	AWT	JAVA 2D	JAI
Support for network imaging	The AWT has no explicit support for network imaging.	Java 2D has no explicit support for network imaging.	JAI explicitly makes use of RMI (Remote Method Invocation) for server-side imaging. It also has operators that support IIP (Internet Imaging Protocol).
Imaging operators	The AWT has no imaging operators.	Java 2D supports only a few basic single-input/single-output operations in the form of classes.	JAI has a large array of imaging operators that can assist in the I/O, display, manipulation, enhancement, and analysis of images. Some of the operators are dual-input/single-output. There are also a few multiple-input operators.
Support for image properties	The AWT supports width and height properties.	Java 2D supports width and height properties.	JAI has extensive support for property management. You can create properties such as ROI (region of interest) and curves and save them along with the image.
Support for image loading and storing	The AWT supports only GIF and JPEG image loading. Starting with JDK 1.3, this support has been extended to PNG images.	Java 2D has no explicit support for any image-loading or -saving APIs. This shortcoming will be overcome when the Image I/O specs are implemented. The Image I/O API will be common to Java 2D and JAI.	The Image I/O package in JAI 1.0.2 and 1.1 supports several image formats, including GIF, JPEG, BMP, TIFF, PNG, PPM, and FlashPix. Except for GIF and FlashPix, images in all of these formats can be saved.

Note: Java documentation generated by the `javadoc` program is available on the book's Web page. It lists and describes all the interfaces and classes developed in this book.

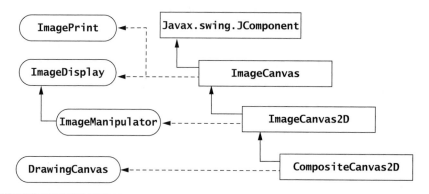

FIGURE 18.1   Image-rendering component hierarchy for displaying AWT and buffered images

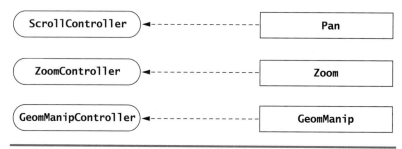

FIGURE 18.2   Image manipulation components

Future Direction

Java 2D

Although Java 2D is a mature API, there are still some initiatives under way at Sun. Here are some of the Java 2D features that will be part of the next JDK release (JDK 1.4, code-named Merlin):

- **Pipeline architecture.** This architecture is designed to improve performance by enabling the various rendering pipelines to share data. With this architecture, changes in rendering attributes result in less code being executed than is executed with the current architecture.

- **Support for hardware acceleration.** With the current implementation of Java 2D, applications that perform off-screen rendering cannot access hardware accelera-

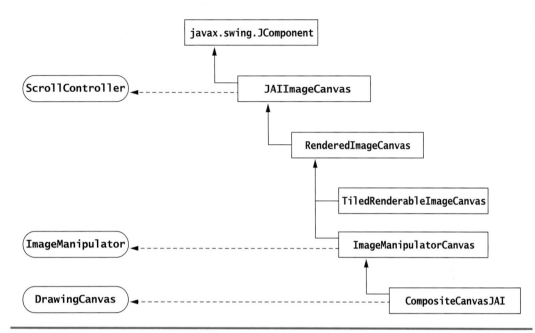

FIGURE 18.3   Image-rendering component hierarchy for displaying rendered and renderable images

tors. The Java 2D API in the Merlin release provides a new class called `java.awt.image.VolatileImage` that allows applications to create hardware-accelerated off-screen images. In the Win32 platform, for instance, you can access a hardware accelerator by storing the volatile image in VRAM and using DirectDraw to render it.

To create a `VolatileImage` object, the following two methods that will be added in the Merlin release:

◆ `createVolatileImage(int width, int height)`

This method will be added to the `java.awt.Component` and `java.awt.ComponentPeer` classes.

◆ `createCompatibleVolatileImage(int width, int height)`

This method will be added to the `java.awt.GraphicsConfiguration` class.

◆ **Support for `float` and `double` image types.** The current Java 2D API doesn't suppot `float` and `double` image types. In other words, there are no `DataBuffer Float` and `DataBufferDouble` classes. In the Merlin release, these classes will be introduced. The `ColorModel` and `SampleModel` classes will be upgraded to reflect the new image data types.

Java Advanced Imaging

The new release of JAI (1.1) has many significant features, some of which we described in the JAI chapters. The features we didn't mention include

- ◆ **New operators.** The following are some of the new operators:
    - ◆ **BandMerge.** This operator creates an image by merging all bands of all source images, concatenating them in the order encountered.
    - ◆ **Binarize.** This operator thresholds a single-band image to two levels to generate a binary output.
    - ◆ **Dilate** and **Erode.** These are morphological operators that perform dilation and erosion, respectively.
- ◆ **Tile codec API.** This API is defined in the package `javax.media.jai.tilecodec`. It allows encoding and decoding of tiles on the ends of a network transmission, as well as persistent storage of tiles.

Future releases of JAI will have many more image analysis operators than are currently available. Another area the JAI will address is the interoperability between Java 3D and JAI APIs. Although they can interoperate at a lower level, future JAI releases may integrate Java 3D at an architectural level.

Future releases may also include APIs and operators for volumetric imaging, a field that deals with generating three-dimensional images from two-dimensional image stacks. For instance, you can create a three-dimensional view of the human body from a set of two-dimensional image slices acquired by medical imaging scanners. Besides aiding in diagnosis, such three-dimensional images can help doctors plan surgery or radiation therapy, thus enabling them to perform procedures quickly and accurately.

The ApplicationFrame Class

A

LISTING A.1 SHOWS THE CODE for the skeleton application frame class that is used in many examples throughout the book.

LISTING A.1 The ApplicationFrame class

```
package com.vistech.util;
import java.awt.*;
import java.awt.event.*;
import java.util.*;
import java.io.*;
import javax.swing.*;
import javax.swing.event.*;
import java.awt.print.*;

public class ApplicationFrame extends JFrame{
   private int width, height;
   protected Locale curLocale;
   protected String copyRight, author;
   protected String helpMidText, helpBoxTitle;
   protected String aboutString, aboutTitle;
   private JMenuItem open, exit,save, saveas, print, help, about;
   private JMenu lookAndFeel;
   protected String curDataFile;
   protected Container contentPane;
   protected Printable printerObj =null;
   protected String saveFileName;

   public static void main(String arg[]){
      ApplicationFrame app = new ApplicationFrame(400, 300);
      app.show();
   }

   public ApplicationFrame(){
      contentPane = this.getContentPane();
      setLocale(Locale.US);
      createGUI();
   }
```

continued

```java
    public ApplicationFrame(int wid, int ht){
       width = wid; height = ht;
       setLocale(Locale.US);
       createGUI();
       setSize(width,height);
    }

    protected void createGUI(){
       setBackground(Color.lightGray);
       WindowEventHandler winAda = new WindowEventHandler();
       addWindowListener(winAda);
       AppMenuBar AppMenuBar = new AppMenuBar();
       setJMenuBar((JMenuBar)AppMenuBar);
    }
    public void setPrinterObj(Printable pr){
       printerObj = pr;
    }

    public void setLocale(Locale loc){
       String resource = new String("USResource.msg");
       if(loc ==  Locale.GERMAN){
          resource = new String("GermanResource.msg");
       }
       if(loc ==  Locale.FRENCH){
          resource = new String("FrenchResource.msg");
       }
       if(loc ==  Locale.UK){
          resource = new String("UKResource.msg");
       }
       if(loc ==  Locale.US){
          resource = new String("USResource.msg");
       }
       Properties prop = new Properties();
       try{
           FileInputStream file = new FileInputStream(resource);
           PropertyResourceBundle  msg = new PropertyResourceBundle(file);
           copyRight = (String)msg.handleGetObject("m1");
           author = (String)msg.handleGetObject("m2");
           aboutTitle = (String)msg.handleGetObject("m3");
           helpBoxTitle = (String)msg.handleGetObject("m4");
           helpMidText = (String)msg.handleGetObject("m6");
           aboutString = (String)msg.handleGetObject("m5");
       }catch(IOException e){};
    }

    public void setAboutString(String str){ aboutString = str;}
    public void setAboutTitle(String str){ aboutTitle = str;}

    public void updateUI(){
       SwingUtilities.updateComponentTreeUI(contentPane);
    }

    class WindowEventHandler extends WindowAdapter{
        public void windowClosed(WindowEvent e){}
        public void windowClosing(WindowEvent e){
           System.exit(0);
        }
```

```
   }

   protected void open(){}
   protected void saveAs(){}
   protected void save(){}
   protected void printContents() {}

   public void quit(){
      dispose();
      System.exit(0);
   }

   public class AppMenuBar extends JMenuBar {
      Vector menus = new Vector();
      public AppMenuBar(){ createGUI();}

      public void createGUI(){
         createFileMenu();
      }
      public JMenu createFileMenu() {
         JMenu fileMenu = new JMenu("File");
         exit = new JMenuItem("Exit");
         exit.addActionListener(
           new ActionListener(){
              public void actionPerformed(ActionEvent e){
                 quit();
              }
           }
         );
         fileMenu.add(createSaveMenu());
         fileMenu.add(createPrintMenu());
         fileMenu.addSeparator();
         fileMenu.add(exit);
         add(fileMenu);
         return fileMenu;
      }
      public JMenu createSaveMenu() {
         JMenuItem save = new JMenuItem("Save");
         save.addActionListener(
            new ActionListener() {
               public void actionPerformed(ActionEvent e){
                  save();
               }
            }
         );
         JMenuItem saveas = new JMenuItem("Save As");

         saveas.addActionListener(
            new ActionListener() {
               public void actionPerformed(ActionEvent e){
                  saveAs();
               }
            }
         );

         JMenu saveMenu = new JMenu("Save");
         saveMenu.add(save);
```

continued

```
            saveMenu.add(saveas);
            add(saveMenu);
            return saveMenu;
    }

    public JMenu createHelpMenu() {
        help = new JMenuItem("Help");
        help.addActionListener(
            new ActionListener() {
                public void actionPerformed(ActionEvent e){
                    JOptionPane.showMessageDialog(ApplicationFrame.this,
                    "Under Construction",
                    "Help",
                    JOptionPane.INFORMATION_MESSAGE);
                }
            }
        );

        about = new JMenuItem("About");
        about.addActionListener(
            new ActionListener() {
                public void actionPerformed(ActionEvent e){
                    JOptionPane.showMessageDialog(ApplicationFrame.this,
                                        aboutString,
                                        aboutTitle,
                                        JOptionPane.INFORMATION_MESSAGE);
                }
            }
        );
        JMenu helpMenu = new JMenu("Help");
        helpMenu.add(help);
        helpMenu.add(about);
        add(helpMenu);
        return helpMenu;
    }


    public JMenu createLocaleMenu(){
        LocaleAdapter usL = new LocaleAdapter(Locale.US);
        JMenuItem us = new JMenuItem("US");
        us.addActionListener(usL);
        JMenuItem uk = new JMenuItem("UK");
        LocaleAdapter ukL = new LocaleAdapter(Locale.UK);
        uk.addActionListener(ukL);

        JMenuItem france = new JMenuItem("French");
        LocaleAdapter frL = new LocaleAdapter(Locale.FRENCH);
        france.addActionListener(frL);

        JMenuItem germany = new JMenuItem("German");
        LocaleAdapter gerL = new LocaleAdapter(Locale.GERMAN);
        germany.addActionListener(gerL);
        JMenu localeMenu = new JMenu("Locale");
        localeMenu.add(us);
        localeMenu.add(uk);
        localeMenu.add(france);
        localeMenu.add(germany);
```

```java
            add(localeMenu);
            menus.addElement(localeMenu);
            return localeMenu;
        }

    public JMenu createPrintMenu(){
        print = new JMenuItem("Print");
        PrintAdapter pa = new PrintAdapter();
        print.addActionListener(pa);
        JMenuItem printSetup = new JMenuItem("Print Setup");
        JMenu printMenu = new JMenu("Print");
        printMenu.add(print);
        menus.addElement(printMenu);
        add(printMenu);
        return printMenu;
    }

    public void addMenus(Vector menus){
        for(Enumeration e = menus.elements();e.hasMoreElements();){
            add((JMenu)(e.nextElement()));
        }
    }

    class PrintSetupAdapter implements ActionListener{
        public void actionPerformed(ActionEvent e){
            PrintJob pr =
            Toolkit.getDefaultToolkit().getPrintJob(ApplicationFrame.this, "Print",
null);
            Graphics printG = pr.getGraphics();
            printAll(printG);
            printG.dispose();
            pr.end();
        }
    }

    class PrintAdapter implements ActionListener{
        public void actionPerformed(ActionEvent e){
            // JDK 1.2 print
            printContents();
        }
    }

    class LocaleAdapter implements ActionListener{
        Locale locale;
        public LocaleAdapter(Locale loc){
            locale = loc;
        }
        public void actionPerformed(ActionEvent e){
            ApplicationFrame.this.setLocale(locale);
        }
    }
    class OpenAdapter implements ActionListener{
        public void actionPerformed(ActionEvent e){
            open();
        }
    }
```

continued

```
class SaveAdapter implements ActionListener{
   public void actionPerformed(ActionEvent e){
      save();
   }
}

class SaveAsAdapter implements ActionListener{
   public void actionPerformed(ActionEvent e){
      saveAs();
   }
}

  }  // End of AppMenuBar class
}// End of ApplicationFrame class
```

The AppMenuBar class is an inner class of ApplicationFrame. AppMenuBar accesses several member variables of the ApplicationFrame class, including author, copyRight, helpBoxTitle, and aboutTitle. The PrintAdapter class is an inner class of AppMenuBar. Both of these adapter classes have anonymous classes. Note that the anonymous classes use the ActionListener interface in their constructors.

You can create a subclass of the ApplicationFrame class to create your own application frame. Within that subclass you can create a class extending AppMenuBar to create your own menu bar.

JavaBeans[1]

JAVABEANS IS A COMPONENT MODEL that defines a framework for building, customizing, running, and deploying general-purpose Java software components. The underlying theme of JavaBeans is "write once, run anywhere" (WORA). The primary objective is to ensure portability, reusability, and interoperability of Java software components. In simple terms, the JavaBeans component model helps you build reusable software components that can be used for developing different types of Java applications (applets, stand-alone applications, servlets). Whether you're developing a simple applet or a complicated application, JavaBeans can be integrated into your system with ease.

Already many vendors offer JavaBeans in a variety of fields. Some JavaBeans may be common to multiple fields. A chart bean, for instance, can be used in scientific, engineering, and business computing applications.

JavaBeans Basics

A *JavaBean* (or simply *bean*) is a reusable software component that can be visually manipulated in a builder tool. Builder tools help you assemble applications by visually connecting beans. This doesn't mean that you cannot build applications in the conventional way. If you prefer, you can hand-code applications by using beans. When you build applications by visual connection, there is no coding involved (though in semivisual tools, you may have to write some code).

---

1 Some of the text here has been excerpted from the author's previous book *The Awesome Power of JavaBeans™,* published by Manning Publications, and from the author's articles in the *Java Developer's Journal* (see the Bibliography). These excerpts are published with permission from Manning and SYS-CON Media.

Builder tools also help you customize beans visually. Once customized, beans can be saved as serialized prototypes (files with a *.ser* extension). When beans are part of an application, they run just like any other objects. They are instantiated differently, though, because saved beans must be resurrected from their serialized prototypes.

JavaBeans Architecture

The JavaBeans 1.0 spec defines a component model for building, customizing, assembling, and deploying general-purpose Java software components. In the JavaBeans model, three basic features describe the structure and behavior of a bean: properties, methods, and events.

Properties are a bean's named attributes that can be edited to customize a bean. *Methods* describe a bean's behavior. *Events* are a communication mechanism between beans. Events serve two purposes:

1. **Bean connection.** When a bean is running in a builder tool, events enable visual connection.
2. **Notification.** When a bean is running in an application, events report occurrences and pass data from source to target.

Introspection

When a bean is inserted in a visual builder tool, its exposed properties, methods, and events are discovered through a process called introspection. *Introspection* is a mechanism for obtaining the internal information of a bean class, including its exposed properties, methods, and events. A bean author can help the introspection process by providing a design-time class called `BeanInfo`, which is specific to a runtime bean class. For example, `PieChartBeanInfo` is the `BeanInfo` class for `PieChart`. Bean authors can describe bean features in the `BeanInfo` class. In the case of a property, the description may include display name, access methods, and short text.

How Does Introspection Work?

Information about a bean's structure and behavior is encapsulated in its runtime class(es). The introspection mechanism first obtains information about the bean's class and its members. It then uses the information to determine the properties, methods, and events exposed by that bean. Using this knowledge, the builder tool can modify the appearance and behavior of the bean. In other words, it acquires the ability to get and set the property values and invoke methods in the target bean object while that object is running.

To obtain information about a bean's internals, the introspection process first checks the `BeanInfo` class to obtain a bean's feature (property, method, and event) descriptions. If the bean author provides no information about properties (or other features) in the `BeanInfo` class, the introspection process uses the low-level reflection API (`java.lang.reflect` and `java.lang.Class`) to obtain that information. Using these APIs, introspection probes the bean class to retrieve its fields and methods. From the fields and methods it obtains, the introspection mechanism then deduces a bean's feature descriptions by matching the method signatures with the naming conventions defined by the JavaBeans specification.

The other types of properties, which include `indexed` and `boolean`, have similar naming conventions.

So the introspection process is twofold:

1. Discovery from the explicit information, which is provided by the bean provider through a bean-specific class called `BeanInfo.`

2. Automatic discovery of a bean's features by use of the reflection API. To facilitate this, methods in the bean have to adhere to certain naming conventions, as stated in the JavaBeans spec.

Design Patterns

A description of bean classes and class members alone is not enough to determine the properties, methods, and events exposed by a bean because developers and vendors can use their own standards and naming conventions to define properties, methods, and events. Therefore, the need arises for a standard that can specify conventions to define publicly accessible properties, methods, and events in a bean class. The JavaBeans spec provides such a standard, called *design patterns*.

> **Note:** The term *design patterns* should not be confused with the same term used in object-oriented programming, which was popularized by the book *Design Patterns* authored by Eric Gamma et al.

Design patterns are nothing but signatures or patterns in a name that builder tools and scripting environments use to infer a certain type of behavior from a bean. Builder tools look for the presence of design patterns to determine whether a member of a class is a property, a method, or an event. While developing code for your bean, you need to conform to these patterns.

The naming conventions for properties define the signatures for set and get methods. The set method sets the property, and the get method reads it. Here's a naming convention defined for a simple property:

- ◆ **The set method:** `public void set<PropertyName>(PropertyType t)`
- ◆ **The get method:** `public <Property Type> get<PropertyName>() {}`

The following example shows the set and get methods for the graph color property:

```
public void SetGraphColor(Color color){//code }
public Color getGraphColor(){// code}
```

A Bean's Life Cycle

From the discussion of the preceding sections, it is clear that beans have two lives—one in the builder tool and another in an actual application. When a bean is running in a builder tool, its life cycle is said to be in design-time phase, and when it is running in an application, its life cycle is said to be in runtime phase.

A bean consists of classes that implement the bean functionality. These classes are needed at both the design-time and the runtime phases. We call these classes runtime classes. You must implement the bean properties, methods, and events in these classes. To run a bean in builder tools, beans may need some special classes, which are called design-time classes.

APIs

The JavaBeans spec defines APIs for bean development, execution, and deployment:

- ◆ **java.beans.** The APIs from the original JavaBeans specification are implemented in the **java.beans** package, which includes classes and interfaces needed for both bean providers and visual builder tools.

- ◆ **java.beans.beancontext.** The APIs from "The Extensible Runtime Containment and Services Protocol" spec are implemented in the **java.beans.beancontext** package, which includes classes and interfaces for implementing logical bean containers, bean contexts, and bean context children. This package is available only in Java 2.

Both of these packages are part of the core Java API and therefore are available in different vendor implementations of Java.

Bean Characteristics

Even though a bean is an object, it has certain characteristics that distinguish it from other objects. Let's look at the characteristics of a bean in detail.

Structure and Behavior

A bean, which is identified by a class, can encapsulate any functionality. Although the bean class need not be a subclass of any other class, it must implement the `java.io.Serializable` or `java.io.Externalizable` interface either directly or through inheritance. Even though a single class identifies a bean, the bean's functionality can be spread over many classes through inheritance and delegation. An important restriction on the bean class is that it must have a no-argument constructor.

A bean's internal structure and implementation details are not exposed. Therefore, you cannot extend a bean's functionality as is. However, you can customize it to suit your application. To extend a bean's functionality, you need to create a new bean by extending the existing bean class. In other words, you need to use the bean as a class library.

As suggested earlier, in the section on bean architecture, a bean's interface to the outside world (which includes visual builder tools, other beans, and applications) is through its properties, methods, and events. This interface is at the *bytecode* level, which means there is no need to recompile the bean when it is assembled in an application.

In order for the properties, methods, and events to be discovered through introspection, the related methods must follow certain signatures and naming conventions specified in the JavaBeans spec. In addition, a bean provider can furnish feature descriptors through a design time–only class called `BeanInfo`, which is specific to a bean class.

Visibility

A bean can be visible, nonvisible, or both. A stopwatch bean, for instance, can have the GUI shown when it runs on the client side and turned off if it is running on the server side. Even if a bean is nonvisible, it can be customized, serialized, and connected to other beans in visual builder tools.

Types

Beans that conform to the JavaBeans 1.0 spec are not typed. The Glasgow spec, however, allows two types of beans: simple and participant. A *simple* bean is not aware of its container, whereas a *participant* bean actively participates in its container. A bean that conforms only to the original JavaBeans 1.0 spec falls into the simple-bean category. A participant bean, however, conforms to "The Extensible Runtime Containment and Services Protocol" spec, in addition to the original bean spec. A participant bean can also discover and utilize arbitrary services from its container. Table B.1 compares simple and participant beans.

TABLE B.1 Comparing Simple and Participant Beans

CHARACTERISTIC	SIMPLE BEAN	PARTICIPANT BEAN
Nesting	Not aware of its container, so nesting structure is not exposed.	Aware of its container. Nesting structure is exposed through the `BeanContext` API.
Types	Not typed	`BeanContext`, `BeanContextChild`, `BeanContextService`
Access to arbitrary services	No	Yes
InfoBus aware	No	Yes

Persistence

Beans are persistent, which means they are objects that can be saved and resurrected. We achieve persistence by saving a bean's internal states through serialization. As mentioned earlier, a resurrected serialized prototype of a bean can be included in an application.

Customization

Beans are visually customizable. You can customize a bean by editing its properties. Visual builder tools typically present property sheets for this purpose. To generate property sheets, builder tools use introspection. The JavaBeans spec also provides an alternative to property sheets: an interface called `Customizer` that enables bean providers to build bean-specific customizers. Such a customizer can also be invoked at runtime.

Containment and Nesting

A bean can contain another bean. The original JavaBeans 1.0 spec did not explicitly address containment-related issues. The Glasgow specification defines the notion of a logical bean container, or bean context. A child bean in a container can itself be a `BeanContext` object, thus allowing nesting of beans. In a bean context, child beans (simple and participant) can be dynamically added and removed. They can also access arbitrary services from the container.

Application Assembly

You can compose applications by visually connecting beans in a builder tool or manually by writing connection programs. An application developed in this way can be an applet or a stand-alone application. Beans for an application need not come from the same vendor because beans can be developed independently of one another.

As mentioned earlier, events act as interfaces between beans. Bean connections are established at design time and are unidirectional. The source bean fires an event, and the target bean receives it. When the application assembler chooses a source bean for connection, the builder tool discovers through introspection the events fired by that bean. When the application assembler chooses a target bean for the selected source bean, the builder tool discovers the compatible methods in the target bean, again through introspection.

Bean Execution

The execution phase consists of instantiating and running beans.

Instantiating the Bean

Even though a bean is an object, it is instantiated differently from other objects. Instead of the **new** operation, beans are instantiated through the `Beans.instantiate()` method. There are many flavors of this method. The following example shows one:

```
// Obtain the class Loader
ClassLoader loader =(PieChart.class).getClassLoader ();

// Instantiate the PieChart bean
PieChart pieChart = (PieChart)Beans.instantiate (loader, "Account")
```

Running the Bean

A bean is like any other object when it is running in an application. Normally, methods in a bean are not invoked directly from other beans. The bean connections determine what methods need to be invoked. Event adapters enable indirect method invocation.

Beans can also be executed in a builder tool at design time. As mentioned earlier, an important requirement for a bean to run in a builder tool is that the bean class must have a constructor with no arguments. The reason is that the builder tool cannot provide the constructor parameters, so when there are many constructors, it cannot decide which one to use.

Java 2 has new `Beans.instantiate()` methods to facilitate the instantiation of applets and bean contexts.

Interoperability

JavaBeans can interact with components built with other models, including the widely used Component Object Model (COM). With the JavaBeans Bridge for ActiveX, a bean can be converted to an ActiveX control. A converted ActiveX control can interoperate with other ActiveX controls in an ActiveX container.

Now that we've looked at the characteristics of beans, let's explore the differences between class libraries and JavaBeans.

Class Libraries versus JavaBeans

Reusability is an obvious goal for both beans and class libraries. However, designing for reusability is not an easy task because it's hard to generalize requirements. Whatever your bean or class library has to offer may not exactly match your users' requirements.

In class libraries, you must design APIs as interfaces to the outside world. With JavaBeans, on the other hand, you must design properties, methods, and events to interface with execution environments and other beans.

A major difference between class libraries and beans is how you use them. You can use a class in the following ways:

- ◆ To instantiate objects directly from the class
- ◆ To create a subclass to extend functionality and then construct objects from that subclass
- ◆ To use the static methods in the class directly

Beans, on the other hand, are typically instantiated. Although it is possible to extend the functionality of a bean by creating subclasses of it, by doing so you lose the benefits of JavaBeans.

As suggested earlier, beans are building blocks. In other words, functionality is distributed over different beans. When you glue beans, functionality is added. Therefore, to extend the functionality of an existing bean you would connect it to another bean that has what you want, but adding functionality in this way may not be as easy as it sounds.

From our prior discussion, it is obvious that you need to be a Java programmer to use class libraries. To use beans, you don't need to have Java programming skills if you intend to build applications visually.

Class libraries tend to be more general and often do not provide a complete solution to a problem. Typically, you cannot run a class library on its own. Beans tend to be specific to a problem and typically provide a complete solution. Although a JavaBean may not run as a stand-alone application, it does run independently in builder tools. So JavaBeans have the code that is needed to run them. In the case of class libraries, users provide the necessary code to execute them.

Taking all this into consideration, we choose beans over class libraries if the functionality can be completely defined and is clear-cut. In order for beans to be useful, their design may require much more thought and foresight than class libraries do.

Bound and Constrained Properties

Properties often depend on each other. We know from the JavaBeans spec that such properties are categorized as bound or constrained. You need to identify such properties. In the case of a bound property, you must anticipate whether properties in other beans can be dependent. Likewise, in the case of a constrained property, you must anticipate whether other beans can veto the property change. We'll see how to implement such properties later in this chapter.

When beans are wired in an application, their properties are often interrelated. For example, the font size in a plotter bean depends on the size of the viewport. And sometimes a property in one bean depends on a property in another bean. A change in the property value of one bean may affect the properties of others. Such properties are called *bound* properties.

A bean property sometimes cannot be allowed to assume a value or range of values. The owner of a property may not always have the constraints to determine whether the value of a property is valid. The other beans in the application or container, or the container itself, may apply certain constraints to validate a property change. Such properties are called *constrained* properties.

Whenever a bound or constrained property is changed, the interested parties (which may include the container, as well as other beans in the container or application) may have to be notified. You can use property change events for this reporting.

Listening to Property Change Events

The JavaBeans model supports two types of property change events: `propertyChange` and `vetoableChange`. A bean can fire the `propertyChange` event to announce the change to a bound property. Similarly a bean can fire the `vetoableChange` event to announce the change to a constrained property. Corresponding to the `propertyChange` and `vetoableChange` interfaces, there are two property change listener interfaces: `PropertyChangeListener` and `VetoableChangeListener`.

A bean that needs to fire the `propertyChange` event must implement the following methods to conform to the event design patterns:

- ◆ `public void addPropertyChangeListener(PropertyChangeListener pcl)`
- ◆ `public void removePropertyChangeListener(PropertyChangeListener pcl)`

The `PropertyChangeListener` interface specifies only one method: `property Change(PropertyChangeEvent pce)`. The objects interested in listening to the property change event register through the `addPropertyChangeListener()` method. Only objects that implement the `PropertyChangeListener` interface can register for a `propertyChange` event. Whenever the `propertyChange` event occurs (when the bound property changes), the bean notifies all the registered listeners by calling their `propertyChange()` methods.

In the same manner, a bean that needs to fire the `vetoableChange` event must implement the following methods:

- ◆ `public void addVetoableChangeListener(VetoableChangeListener pcl)`
- ◆ `public void removeVetoableChangeListener(VetoableChangeListener pcl)`

The `VetoableChangeListener` interface also has just one method: `vetoable Change(VetoableChangeEvent pce)`. Whenever the constrained property needs to change, the bean that owns that property notifies the registered listeners by calling their `vetoableChange()` method. Any listener can veto the change by throwing an exception called `PropertyVetoException`.

If none of the listener objects raise any exception, the bean that owns the property will change it. If it receives a veto, it won't go ahead with the property change. But this may cause some problems. Beans that received the `vetoableChange` notification have no way of knowing that another bean has vetoed. To avoid such problems, the JavaBeans specification mandates the firing of a second `vetoableChange` notification to reverse the change.

Listening to Named Properties

The JavaBeans 1.01 specifications provide some additional, optional design patterns for `propertyChange` and `vetoableChange` events.

The following are the additional `propertyChange` event listener methods:

- ◆ `public void addPropertyChangeListener(String propertyName,`
  `                    PropertyChangeListener listener);`
- ◆ `public void removePropertyChangeListener(String propertyName,`
  `                    PropertyChangeListener listener);`

And here are the additional `vetoableChange` event listener methods:

- `public void addVetoableChangeListener(String propertyName,`
                                        `VetoableChangeListener`
                                        `listener);`
- `public void removeVetoableChangeListener(String propertyName,`
                                           `VetoableChangeListener`
                                           `listener);`

Each of the registration methods has an additional argument for the property name.

The specifications also provide alternate design patterns as shown. The `property Change` event methods are

- `public void add<PropertyName>Listener(PropertyChangeListener`
                                        `listener);`
- `public void remove<PropertyName>Listener(PropertyChangeListener`
                                           `listener);`

The `vetoableChange` event methods are:

- `public void add<PropertyName>Listener(VetoableChangeListener`
                                        `listener);`
- `public void remove<PropertyName>Listener(VetoableChangeListener`
                                           `listener);`

In these cases, the method name itself contains the property name.

Implementing Property Change Events

A property can be bound *and* constrained. When a bound property changes, the properties in other beans tied to that property also change. Similarly, when a constrained property changes, the other beans in the container may apply appropriate constraints and veto the change.

Communicating Changes in Properties

How does a bean tell other beans that it has bound and constrained properties? Through events. There are two types of events: `propertyChange` and `vetoable Change.` The classes and interfaces for these events are in the `java.beans` package.

A bean fires a `propertyChange` event whenever a bound property changes and a `vetoableChange` event whenever a constrained property changes. Each of these events has a corresponding listener interface. The `PropertyChangeListener` interface listens to bound properties, and the `VetoableChangeListener` listens to constrained properties. Both `propertyChange` and `vetoableChange` events are supported by an event state class called `PropertyChangeEvent`, which passes the property-related data from the source bean to the target.

The `PropertyChangeEvent` class constructor is

◆ ```
public PropertyChangeEvent(Object source,
                           String propertyName,
                           Object oldValue,
                           Object newValue)
```

The parameters `oldValue` and `newValue` refer to the old and new values of the property. They are of the `Object` type. Therefore, before a parameter is passed, primitive properties must be converted to objects by wrapper classes.

The methods in the `PropertyChangeEvent` class—`getPropertyName()`, `getOldValue()`, and `getNewValue()`—return the property's name, old value, and new value, respectively. This class has two additional methods—`setPropagationId()` and `getPropagationId()`—which have no use in JavaBeans 1.0.

The `PropertyChangeListener` interface has just one method, called `propertyChange(PropertyChangeEvent e)`, which is invoked when a bound property is changed. The `VetoableChangeListener` interface has an analogous method—`vetoableChange(PropertyChangeEvent e)`—which is called when a constrained property changes. It throws an exception called `PropertyVetoException`. The bean that receives the `vetoableChange` event can throw an exception if it does not want the property to change.

Implementing a property change notification requires a lot of routine code, including methods for adding and removing listeners and for firing events. The `java.beans` package has two utility classes—`PropertyChangeSupport` and `VetoableChangeSupport`—that support event registration and firing.

## Implementing a Bound Property

Whenever a bound property changes, the `propertyChange` event must fire to the registered listeners. An appropriate place to fire a property change event is in the property's set method. The bean that owns the bound properties must implement the *<add/remove>*`PropertyChangeListener` method for registering the `propertyChange` event listeners. Further, it should have a method to fire the `propertyChange` event. Alternatively, a bean can utilize the helper class `PropertyChangeSupport`, delegating these event-related tasks to it.

The `PropertyChangeSupport` constructor has one argument, which is of the `Object` type. The bean that needs to implement the bound property typically passes itself as an argument to this constructor. The `PropertyChangeSupport` method has the following three methods, which are self-explanatory:
```

1. `addPropertyChangeListener(PropertyChangeListener pcl)`
2. `removePropertyChangeListener(PropertyChangeListener pcl)`
3. `firePropertyChange(String propertyName, Object oldValue,`
                     `Object newValue)`

When a bound property changes, the `firePropertyChange()` method fires the property change notification to all the registered listeners by invoking **property Change()**. The property-related data is sent to the listeners through the **Property ChangeEvent** object, which is passed as a parameter to the `propertyChange()` method. The **propertyChange** event does not fire when the new value is the same as the old value.

Since the **PropertyChangeSupport** class simplifies the code, we'll use only this class in our examples of event-related tasks.

The steps to implement a bound property using the **PropertyChangeSupport** class appear in the next example:

1. In the source bean (i.e., the bean that has the bound property), create a **PropertyChangeSupport** object. Typically, this can be done in the bean constructor or in the `init()` method:

```
PropertyChangeSupport pcNotifier= new PropertyChangeSupport(this);
```

2. Add the **propertyChange** event registration methods:

```
public void addPropertyChangeListener(PropertyChangeListener p){
    pcNotifier.addPropertyChangeListener(p);
}
public void removePropertyChangeListener(PropertyChangeListener p){
    pcNotifier.removePropertyChangeListener(p);
}
```

3. In the property's set method, call the `firePropertyChange()` method of the **PropertyChangeSupport** class, as shown here:

```
public void set<property>(aType  newValue){
    aType oldValue = property;
    pcNotifier.firePropertyChange(propertyName, oldValue, newValue);
    property = newValue;
    // Other statements
}
```

The preceding steps are implemented in the source bean.

Listening to Bound Properties

The builder tool typically exposes the list of bound properties in the selected bean. After you have selected a property from the list, the builder tool lets you choose a target bean in which matching properties are found. Once you have selected the target bean, the builder tool displays the matching properties in the target. Argument types typically match the properties.

When you select a matching property, the builder tool generates a class that interposes between the source and the target beans. This class implements the `PropertyChangeListener` interface to receive property change events. In other words, the interposing class implements `propertyChange()`, which invokes the set method for the matching property in the target bean.

The builder tool creates a property change adapter object from this class and registers it with the source bean for `propertyChange` event notification. When the bound property changes, `propertyChange()` is invoked in the adapter. The `property Change()` method extracts the new value of the property from its argument, which is the `PropertyChangeEvent` state object. It then calls the property's set method in the target bean to set it to this value.

How does the builder tool recognize that a property is bound? By using design patterns.

The property change notification is both a design-time operation and a runtime operation. Irrespective of the bean mode, property change events are always fired.

Persistence

You probably know by now that beans are customizable. However, if you cannot save beans, you will have to repeat the customization procedure every time you need a bean with a particular look and behavior. Even then, there is no guarantee that you will exactly match the bean's look and behavior, especially when the customization is interactive. Therefore, you need a way to save beans.

The process of saving a bean by keeping its internal states intact is often called *bean persistence.* The aim of persistent storage is to save and resurrect the object without making any changes to its internal states.

According to the JavaBeans specification, a bean must be persistent. A bean that cannot be serialized is not a bean. Although at the outset implementing persistent storage seems easy, complications arise because of a variety of storage requirements that a bean needs to fulfill in order to run anywhere.

The JavaBeans specification lets the bean choose the storage mechanism. A bean can implement the Java *serialization* mechanism in which information about an object, including its internal states, is automatically written to an object stream. If you expect your bean to be used in different containers, you can implement the *externalization* mechanism. Using externalization, a bean can choose a data format depending on its execution environment. If your bean uses externalization, you must provide the complete code to save and restore it.

Whether an object is saved through serialization or externalization, the object information is saved in a file with a *.ser* extension. This file is often referred to as a serialized prototype.

Serialization

The serialization feature enables the persistent storage of objects. Using serialization, you can save a bean and later restore it without losing its internal state. The processes of saving and restoring an object are generally referred to as serialization and deserialization, respectively.

We achieve serialization by saving the object's instance variables, which define its current state. Because even private variables are responsible for an object's internal states, the serialization feature allows the saving of private variables as well, but saving private variables may have security implications.

You can instantiate a bean directly from its serialized prototype. However, it is worth noting that serialization does not involve saving and restoring of bytecodes (i.e., files with the extension *.class*). But if the information about methods is not stored, how does the deserialization mechanism restore the original state? During serialization, the class name and signature of the class are also saved. Using this name and signature, the deserialization mechanism retrieves an appropriate `Class` object from either the class path or the JVM to execute the deserialized prototype.

To instantiate a serialized bean, you need to provide a `ClassLoader` argument along with the serialized prototype. The instantiating mechanism uses this argument to retrieve the bean runtime class.

Serialization Issues

Not all the variables in a class are needed to restore an object to its original state. Some variables are temporary and may not contribute to the object's state. And for security reasons, some variables, even though needed, cannot be saved. Imagine that your credit card number is saved in such a variable. When security is a concern, the variable should not be serialized. The Java language provides a mechanism to handle such situations: using the `transient` keyword to modify the variables. The serialization process ignores `transient` variables.

In a typical Java application, objects often refer to other objects, which in turn refer to additional objects, thus forming a dependency graph. This graph sometimes forms cycles—that is, an object referring to parent object(s). Cyclic traversal can lead to infinite recursion. You do not need to worry about this problem because the designers of serialization have taken care of it.

Just like any other software, beans evolve over time, so there may be different versions of the same class. Thus a class that deserializes an object may not be the same as the one that serialized it. If versions are not tracked properly, the result may be incompatibility. You can use the versioning feature to solve this problem.

Implementing Serialization

For a bean to be made persistent, its runtime bean classes must be serializable. A class is serializable only if it implements either the `java.io.Serializable` or the `java.io.Externalizable` interface. This implementation can be through inheritance; that is, if a class implements `Serializable` or `Externalizable,` then all of its derived classes are serializable.

The `Serializable` interface doesn't specify any methods and is used for marking purposes only. The `Externalizable` interface is a subtype of `Serializable` and has two methods: `writeExternal()` and `readExternal().`

Serialization and Deserialization

When we say an object is serialized, we mean that it is written onto an output stream. In the same manner, when an object is deserialized, it is read from an input stream. The following classes in the `java.io` package help in serializing:

- ◆ **ObjectOutputStream.** This class enables writing of an object to a stream.
- ◆ **ObjectInputStream.** This class enables reading of an object from a stream.
- ◆ **ObjectStreamClass.** This class provides a description of a class that is needed to save an object.

The `writeObject(Object obj)` method in the `ObjectOutputStream` class serializes an object, and the `readObject()` method in the `ObjectInputStream` class deserializes it. The `writeObject()` method writes only the nontransient and nonstatic fields to the output stream. If a field is of the primitive type, an appropriate write method from the `ObjectOutputStream` class is invoked. If a field is of the reference type, `writeObject()` is invoked for that object. The result is recursive serialization, in which the dependency graph of an object is traversed. At any stage, if a nonserializable class is encountered, the exception called `NonSerializableException` is raised.

The `readObject()` method deserializes an object in the same order it was serialized. That is, deserialization traverses the dependency tree in the same order as serialization.

The following example shows how to write an object to the output stream:

```
Piechart bean =
     java.beans.Beans.instantiate(classloader, "vis.beans.plotter.MultiXYPlot");
FileOutputStream out = new FileOutputStream("filename");
ObjectOutputStream s = new ObjectOutputStream(out);
s.writeObject(bean);
s.flush();
```

And here's an example that shows how to read an object from the output stream:

```
FileInputStream in = new FileInputStream("filename");
ObjectInputStream  d = new ObjectInputStream(in);
Piechart bean =  d.readObject();
```

As a bean author, you don't typically implement serialization and deserialization code. Application builder tools will do it for you if your bean is serializable. You do need to know, however, that a class is not automatically serializable if it implements the `Serializable` or `Externalizable` interface because you cannot assume that all the variables are persistent.

Persistent versus Transient Fields

From the serialization standpoint, there are two types of instance variables: persistent and transient. Persistent variables are saved, and transient variables are not. To make a variable transient, you must associate that variable with the keyword `transient`. By default, a variable is assumed to be persistent.

Certain types in Java cannot be made persistent. The following list enumerates some of the nonpersistent classes:

- **`Object`.** This class is the root of all classes in Java. Therefore it is not serializable.
- **`Image`.** In the AWT, images can only be read. They cannot be saved as JPEG or GIF files or even as uncompressed pixels. Therefore, an image cannot be serialized, and instance variables of type `Image` must be declared as transient. If your bean uses images, they must be reloaded on deserialization. If your bean uses an off-screen image for double buffering, the image must be re-created by the `createImage()` method once the component is visible after deserialization.
- **`Graphics`.** This class is typically used for drawing graphical objects. A graphical object is constructed by the system and is machine dependent. If you are using a graphical object as an instance variable for double buffering, you may have to retrieve it again from the off-screen image, using the `getGraphics()` method.
- **`Thread`.** Threads are machine dependent. If your bean uses threads, your initialization method after deserialization must restart the thread.

Some variables, even though persistent, you would not want to save, for a variety of reasons—for example:

- The variable is temporary and doesn't contribute to the state of the object.
- Data held in the variable must be secure.

Controlling Serialization

You can reimplement the read and write methods in your bean class to control serialization. If a variable that can be serialized needs initialization, you can implement these methods in your bean.

Note that `writeObject()` and `readObject()` are private methods. They are not specified in any interface. But by reimplementing them, an object can override the default serialization mechanism. Using methods in such a manner is a special case in Java.

Once the serialized fields have been read, the object must be reconstructed to restore its original running state. This is accomplished by invocation of the object's constructor.

Because a bean can be instantiated in two ways (through either the class or the serialized prototype), some problems with property initialization may arise.

Typically, the constructor contains the initialization code. In the case of serialized prototype instantiation, the fields are read and then the constructor is not invoked. If you want the bean to perform initialization upon deserialization, you might want to put that code in a separate method. Your bean's `readObject()` method should invoke the initialization method after deserialization.

Serialization Steps

The steps of serialization can be summarized as follows:

1. Implement the `Serializable` or `Externalizable` interface or extend the class that does this.

2. Declare the following types of variables `transient`:

    ◆ Variables that do not contribute to the state of the object.

    ◆ Variables of a type that cannot be persisted. For example, instance variables of the type `Graphics` or `Image` cannot be serialized.

3. Implement the read and write methods:

    ◆ If the class implements `Serializable,` implement the `writeObject()` and `readObject()` methods. Because the `Serializable` interface has no methods, implementing these methods is optional.

    ◆ If the class implements `Externalizable,` implementing the interface method is a must.

4. Optionally version the class. Any compatible version of the class should have the same `serialVersionUID` value. You can generate it by running the serialver program in the JDK. Have this number assigned to all the `serialVersionUID` fields in all the compatible versions.

Packaging Beans

A bean consists of a number of runtime and design-time files. In addition, a bean may use resources like images, sound clips, and help files, so often you must bundle bean classes and resources together. As you know, the Java archive feature lets you package different types of files into a single archive. Beans are packaged in JAR (Java Archive) files. The bean provider must provide a manifest file with JavaBeans-related attributes in order to identify the bean class.

A manifest file is optionally provided with a JAR file to describe its contents. In the case of JAR files for beans, however, the user-created manifest file is mandatory. The manifest file for beans should have at least one entry for the *bean target* class. This entry should be associated with the `Java-Bean` tag, and its value should be `true`. There are two more JavaBeans-related optional attributes: `Depends-On` and `Design-Time-Only`. The following example shows part of a manifest file:

```
Manifest-Version: 1.0

Name: vis/beans/plotter/MultiXYPlot.class
Java-Bean: True
```

In this example the `MultiXYPlot` class is identified as the bean target class.

The following example illustrates JAR file creation:

```
jar -cvfm  xyplot.jar xyplot.tmp  classes  doc
```

This command creates a JAR file named `xyplot.jar` and uses the manifest file `xyplot.tmp`. The JAR file will contain all files in the `classes` and `doc` directories.

A JAR file can contain the following:

1. Runtime bean classes that implement the bean functionality—for example, *.class* files
2. A serialized prototype of the bean—for example, a *.ser* file
3. Design-time classes, which may include `BeanInfo` classes, property editors, and customizers
4. Resource files, which may include images, sound clips, and text files
5. Help files, which can be in HTML format
6. Location-dependent files providing information to localize a bean

Items 2 through 6 are optional.

A JAR file can hold more than one bean. However, the JAR entry for each bean class should have the `Java-Bean` attribute set to `true`. Even if a JAR file contains multiple beans, it can have a single copy of resources and commonly used class files.

A Bean Collection

IN THIS APPENDIX WE'LL DESCRIBE THE BEANS used in this book. The entire source code is available on the book's Web page. Therefore, we'll show only code snippets to explain the beans.

The MultiImageLoader Bean

The `MultiImageLoader` bean loads one or more images using the AWT imaging-loading mechanism. It can load images from a local directory or a JAR file. The GUI for this bean is an embeddable panel (see Figure C.1). If you need to embed it in a launchable frame, you can do so by adding it to a `Frame` or `JFrame` component.

Properties

The `MultiImageLoader` bean has three important properties:

1. **loadMode.** The load modes are JAR and local (`MultiImageLoader.JAR` and `MultiImageLoader.LOCAL`).
2. **sortMode.** The sort modes are by date and by alphabetical order (`JarUtil.BY_DATE` and `JarUtil.BY_ALPHA`).
3. **multiSelect.** This is a boolean property. When it is set to **true,** this property allows multiple item selection.

Events

The `MultiImageLoader` bean fires the `imageLoaded` event when an image is loaded. You can use this event to visually connect to beans that are capable of receiving this event.

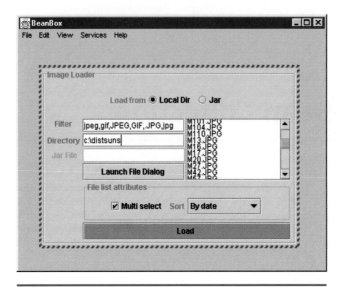

FIGURE C.1 The `MultiImageLoader` bean running in the
BeanBox window

Runtime Classes

`MultiImageLoader` is the main runtime class. It uses several static methods from the
`JarUtil` and `ImageUtil` classes, which are on the book's Web page in the directory
`src/util`. Listing C.1 shows code snippets from the `MultiImageLoader` class.

> **Note:** The source code for the `MultiImageLoader` bean is available on the
> book's Web page in the directory `src/beans/loader.`

LISTING C.1 The `MultiImageLoader` class

```
public class MultiImageLoader extends JPanel{
    .....

  /** Reads the file names from the directory specified by the input.
    * @param fl the  directory name.
    */
  protected void fetchFileNames(File fl){
    if(fl==null) return;
    String[] filter =null;
     if(filterString != null) {
        StringTokenizer st = new StringTokenizer(filterString, ",");
```

```
        int num= st.countTokens();
        filter = new String[num];
        for(int i=0;i<num;i++){
            filter[i] = (String)st.nextToken();
        }
    }
    if(imageSelectMode == LOCAL_DIR)  fileList = readLocalImageFileList(fl);
    else fileList = JarUtil.listJarFiles(fl, filter, sortMode);
    if(fileList == null){
        return;
    }
    itemList.setSelectedIndex(0);

    itemList.revalidate();
    itemList.repaint();
}


protected void load() {
  if(itemList == null) return;
  int indice[];
  if(itemList.getSelectionMode() == ListSelectionModel.SINGLE_SELECTION) {
    indice = new int[] {itemList.getSelectedIndex()};
  } else indice = itemList.getSelectedIndices();

  if(indice == null) return;

  String list[]  = new String[indice.length];
  imageset = new Image[indice.length];

  for(int i=0; i<indice.length;i++){
      list[i] = fileList[indice[i]];
      imageset[i] = loadImage(list[i]);
  }
  fireImageLoadedEvent(imageset);
}

public Image loadImage(String imagename) {
    Image img=null;
    if(imageSelectMode == LOCAL_DIR) {
        img = Toolkit.getDefaultToolkit().getImage(currentDir+
File.separator+imagename);
    }
    if(imageSelectMode == JAR) {
        if(jarPath == null) return null;
        img = ImageUtil.readImage(jarPath, imagename);
    }
    try {
        MediaTracker tracker = new MediaTracker(this);
        tracker.addImage(img, 0);
        tracker.waitForID(0);
        } catch (Exception e) {}
    return img;
}
```

continued

```java
/**  Fetches the image file names from the current path and
 *   adds them to imageList.
 */
protected void loadLocalImageFiles(File fl){
   jarFileField.setEnabled(true);
   jarFileL.setEnabled(true);
   jarFileField.setEditable(true);
   if(!fl.exists()){ }
   fileList = null;
   fileList = readLocalImageFileList(fl);
   if(fileList != null) itemList.setSelectedIndex(0);
}


/**
 *  Reads image file names from a local directory.
 *  @param dir the directory.
 */
public String[] readLocalImageFileList(File dir){
   ExtensionFilter fFilter;
   if(filterString != null)
      fFilter =  new ExtensionFilter(filterString);
   else fFilter =  new ExtensionFilter("jpeg,gif,JPEG,GIF,JPG,jpg");

   fileList = dir.list(fFilter);
   if(fileList == null){
     return null;
   }
   itemList.setSelectedIndex(0);
   numImages = fileList.length;
   return fileList;
}

/**  Fetches the image file names from the JAR file and
 *   adds them to fileList.
 */
protected void loadJarImageFiles(File dir){
   jarFileField.setEnabled(true);
   jarFileL.setEnabled(true);
   jarFileField.setEditable(true);
   fileList = readJarImageFileList(dir);
   if(fileList != null) itemList.setSelectedIndex(0);
}

public String[] readJarImageFileList(File jarfile){
   ExtensionFilter fFilter;
   if(filterString != null)
      fFilter = new ExtensionFilter(filterString);
   else fFilter =  new ExtensionFilter("jpeg,gif,JPEG,GIF,JPG,jpg");
   String filter[] = {"jpeg","gif","JPEG","GIF","JPG","jpg"};
   fileList = JarUtil.listJarFiles(jarfile,filter,sortMode);

   if(fileList == null){
      System.out.println("null list");
      return null;
   }
   itemList.setSelectedIndex(0);
```

```
        numImages = fileList.length;
        return fileList;
    }

    public void addImageLoadedListener(ImageLoadedListener il){
        imgLst.addElement(il);
    }
    public void removeImageLoadedListener(ImageLoadedListener il){
        if(!(imgLst.isEmpty())) imgLst.removeElement(il);
    }

    protected void fireImageLoadedEvent(Image img) {
        for(Enumeration e= imgLst.elements(); e.hasMoreElements();){
            ImageLoadedEvent ie = new ImageLoadedEvent(this, img);
            ImageLoadedListener il = (ImageLoadedListener)(e.nextElement());
            il.imageLoaded(ie);
        }
        setLoadedImage(img);
    }

    protected void fireImageLoadedEvent(Image[] img) {
        if(img == null) return;
        for(Enumeration e= imgLst.elements(); e.hasMoreElements();){
            ImageLoadedEvent ie = new ImageLoadedEvent(this, img);
            ImageLoadedListener il = (ImageLoadedListener)(e.nextElement());
            il.imageLoaded(ie);
        }
        setLoadedImage(img[0]);
    }
}
}
```

The `fetchFileNames()` method is called whenever the user hits **Return** in the **Directory** text field. Depending on the value of `loadMode`, this method appropriately lists the file names and displays them on `itemList`, which is a `JList` component.

Whenever the user clicks on **Load,** the `load()` method is called. This method calls the appropriate methods to load from either the selected local directory or a JAR file. Once the images have been loaded, the `MultiImageLoader` bean fires the `imageLoaded` event.

The FileBrowser Bean

The `FileBrowser` bean allows you to navigate a local directory. It also lists files in the selected directory. Just like the `MultiImageLoader` bean, `FileBrowser` is an embeddable panel and uses Swing for GUI components (see Figure C.2). Unlike the `MultiImageLoader` bean, `FileBrowser` reads from the local directory only.

> **Note:** The source code for the `FileBrowser` bean is available on the book's Web page in the directory `src/beans/listselect`.

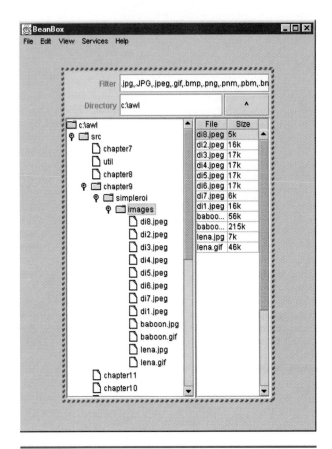

FIGURE C.2 The `FileBrowser` bean running in the **BeanBox** window

Events

Whenever the user clicks on an item in the file list, `FileBrowser` fires the `listSelect` event to the registered listeners. Listing C.2 shows the `ListSelectListener` interface; Listing C.3, the `ListSelectEvent` class.

LISTING C.2 The `ListSelectListener` interface

```
package com.vistech.events;
public interface ListSelectListener extends java.util.EventListener{
    /** This method is typically called whenever a list is selected.
     * The listSelect event carries the list select event data. This
```

```
        * includes the list and the path.
        * @param e the ListSelectEvent.
        */
      public void load(ListSelectEvent e);
}
```

LISTING C.3   The `ListSelectEvent` class

```
package com.vistech.events;
import java.io.*;
import java.awt.*;

public class ListSelectEvent  extends java.awt.event.ActionEvent
        implements Serializable{
   File path;
   String[] fileList;

   public ListSelectEvent(Object obj, String command,File dir, String[] flist){
      super(obj,(int)AWTEvent.ACTION_EVENT_MASK, command);
      this.path = dir;
      this.fileList = flist;
   }

   public String[] getFileList(){
      return fileList;
   }
   public File getPath(){
      return path;
   }
}
```

Runtime Classes

The `FileBrowser` bean has just one runtime class, which is shown in Listing C.4.

LISTING C.4   The `FileBrowser` class

```
package com.vistech.listselect;
import java.io.*;
import java.awt.event.*;
import javax.swing.*;
import javax.swing.event.*;
import javax.swing.tree.*;
import java.awt.*;
import com.vistech.events.*;
import java.util.*;
import javax.swing.table.*;

public class FileBrowser extends JPanel{
   protected String[] fileList;
```

continued

```
    protected JTree tree;
    protected String curDir = ".";
    protected String topNode= ".";
    protected File currentDir;
    protected char separator = File.separatorChar;
    protected JTextField dirField, filterField;
    protected JButton upButton;
    protected String filterString =
".jpg,.jpeg,.gif,.bmp,.png,.pnm,.pbm,.bmp,.tif,.tiff";
    protected String fString[] =
    {".jpg",".jpeg", ".gif",".tif",".tiff", ".bmp", ".png", ".fpx", ".ppm",
".pnm",".pbm"};
    protected JScrollPane treeView;
    private Vector listSelListeners = new Vector();
    protected int selectionMode = ListSelectionModel.SINGLE_SELECTION;
    protected String[][] fileInfoList = new String[1][3];
    protected String columnNames[] = {"File", "Size"};
    protected JTable fileInfoTable;

    public FileBrowser(){
       try{
         currentDir = new File(".");
         curDir = currentDir.getAbsolutePath();
         topNode = curDir;
       }catch (Exception e){}
       createUI();
    }

    public void setPath(File path){currentDir = path;}
    public File gePath(){ return currentDir;}

    public void createUI (){
       JPanel pan = new JPanel();
       JPanel dirP = new JPanel();
       JLabel dirL = new JLabel("Directory ", SwingConstants.RIGHT);
       dirField = new JTextField(15);
       if(curDir != null) dirField.setText(curDir);

       JPanel filtP= new JPanel();
       JLabel filtL = new JLabel("Filter ", SwingConstants.RIGHT);

       filterField = new JTextField(15);
       filterField.setText(filterString);
       filtP.add(filtL);
       filtP.add(filterField);

       upButton = new JButton("^");

       tree = createTreeView();
       treeView = new JScrollPane(tree);
       treeView.setPreferredSize(new Dimension(300,600));
       treeView.setBackground(Color.gray);

       GridBagLayout  gb = new GridBagLayout() ;
       GridBagConstraints c = new GridBagConstraints();
```

```
            setLayout(gb);
            c.weightx = 0.2; c.weighty = 0.1;
            c.fill = GridBagConstraints.BOTH;
            c.insets = new Insets(5,1, 1,1);
            gb.setConstraints(filtL, c);
            add(filtL);
            c.insets = new Insets(5,1, 1,1);
            c.gridwidth = GridBagConstraints.REMAINDER;
            c.weightx = 1.0; c.weighty = 0.1;
            gb.setConstraints(filterField, c);
            add(filterField);
            c.insets = new Insets(1,1, 1,1);
            c.gridwidth = 1;
            c.weightx = 0.2; c.weighty = 0.1;
            gb.setConstraints(dirL, c);
            add(dirL);
            c.insets = new Insets(1,1, 1,1);
            c.weightx = 1.0; c.weighty = 0.1;

            gb.setConstraints(dirField, c);
            add(dirField);
            c.weightx = 0.2; c.weighty = 0.1;
            c.gridwidth = GridBagConstraints.REMAINDER;
            gb.setConstraints(upButton, c);
            add(upButton);
            c.fill = GridBagConstraints.BOTH;
            c.weightx = 1.0; c.weighty = 5.0;
            fileInfoTable = createFileInfoTable();
            clickToLoad(fileInfoTable);
            fileInfoTable.setPreferredSize(new Dimension(70,600));
            JScrollPane jsp = new JScrollPane(fileInfoTable);
            jsp.setPreferredSize(new Dimension(60,600));
            JSplitPane vsp = new JSplitPane(JSplitPane.HORIZONTAL_SPLIT, treeView,jsp);
            gb.setConstraints(vsp, c);
            add(vsp);
            vsp.setDividerLocation(120);
            vsp.setDividerSize(3);
            handleEvents();
            revalidate();
    }

    protected void handleEvents() {
        filterField.addActionListener(
            new ActionListener(){
                public void actionPerformed(ActionEvent e){
                    String filterString = ((JTextField)(e.getSource())).getText();
                    if(filterString == null) return;
                    StringTokenizer st = new StringTokenizer(filterString, ",");
                    int num = st.countTokens();
                    fString = new String[num];
                    int i=0;
                    while(st.hasMoreTokens()){
                        String str = st.nextToken();
                        String name = str.trim();
                        fString[i++] = name;
```

continued

```
                        }
                        updateTreeView(topNode);
                        treeView.revalidate();
                        FileBrowser.this.revalidate();
                    }
                }
            );
        dirField.addActionListener(
                new ActionListener(){
                    public void actionPerformed(ActionEvent e){
                        String currentDirStr = ((JTextField)(e.getSource())).getText();
                        if(currentDirStr != null){
                            curDir = currentDirStr;
                            try {
                            currentDir = new File(curDir);
                            topNode = curDir;
                            updateTreeView(curDir);
                            treeView.revalidate();
                            FileBrowser.this.revalidate();
                            } catch(Exception e1) {}
                        }
                    }
                }
            );
        upButton.addActionListener(
                new ActionListener(){
                    public void actionPerformed(ActionEvent e){
                        try {
                            File dir = new File(topNode);
                            String currentDirStr = dir.getParent();
                            curDir = currentDirStr;
                            currentDir = new File(curDir);
                            topNode = curDir;
                            dirField.setText(curDir);
                            updateTreeView(curDir);
                            treeView.revalidate();
                            FileBrowser.this.revalidate();
                        }catch (Exception e1) {}
                    }
                }
            );
    }
    protected JTree createTreeView() {
        String[] filelist = listFilteredFiles(curDir, fString);
        if(filelist == null) return null;
        DefaultMutableTreeNode top = new DefaultMutableTreeNode(curDir);
        createNewNodes(top, filelist);

        JTree tree = new JTree(top);
        tree.getSelectionModel().setSelectionMode
                            (TreeSelectionModel.SINGLE_TREE_SELECTION);
        tree.addTreeSelectionListener(
                new TreeSelectionListener() {
                public void valueChanged(TreeSelectionEvent e) {
                    TreePath selpath = e.getPath();
                    expandNode(selpath);
                }
```

```
        });
        return tree;
}

protected JTree newTreeView(String curDir) {
    String[] filelist = listFilteredFiles(curDir, fString);
    DefaultMutableTreeNode top = new DefaultMutableTreeNode(curDir);
    createNewNodes(top, filelist);

    JTree tree = new JTree(top);
    tree.getSelectionModel().setSelectionMode
                        (TreeSelectionModel.SINGLE_TREE_SELECTION);
    tree.addTreeSelectionListener(
            new TreeSelectionListener() {
            public void valueChanged(TreeSelectionEvent e) {
                TreePath selpath = e.getPath();
                expandNode(selpath);
            }
    });
    tree.revalidate();
    return tree;
}

protected void updateTreeView(String curDir) {
    String[] filelist = listFilteredFiles(curDir, fString);
    DefaultMutableTreeNode top = new DefaultMutableTreeNode(curDir);
    createNewNodes(top, filelist);
    DefaultTreeModel dft = new DefaultTreeModel(top);
    tree.setModel(dft);
}

private void createNewNodes(DefaultMutableTreeNode top, String[] flist) {
    if((top == null) || (flist == null)) return;
    DefaultMutableTreeNode file = null;
    for(int i=0; i< flist.length;i++){
        try{
          File fl = new File(flist[i]);
          if(fl.isDirectory()) file = new DefaultMutableTreeNode(flist[i], true);
          else file = new DefaultMutableTreeNode(flist[i]);
          top.add(file);
        } catch(Exception e){System.out.println(e);}
    }
}

private void expandNode(TreePath selpath) {
    DefaultMutableTreeNode node = (DefaultMutableTreeNode)
                                        (selpath.getLastPathComponent());
    Object[] pathobj = selpath.getPath();
    if(pathobj == null) return;
    StringBuffer path=null;
    for(int i=0;i<pathobj.length;i++){
        if(path== null) path= new StringBuffer(pathobj[0].toString());
        else path.append(pathobj[i].toString());
        if(i != pathobj.length-1) path.append(separator);
    }
    try {
      if(node.isLeaf()){
```

continued

```
                String filename = path.toString();
                long len = path.length();
                if(isDirectory(path.toString())){
                    tree.collapsePath(selpath);
                    curDir = path.toString();
                    File dir = new File(curDir);
                    currentDir = dir;
                    File[] flist = dir.listFiles();
                    if(flist == null) return;
                    String[] filelist = filterFileNames(flist, fString);
                    if(filelist == null) return;
                    createNewNodes(node,filelist);
                } else {

                    ListSelectEvent ls = new ListSelectEvent(
                                        this,
                                        null,
                                        null,
                                        new String[] {filename});
                        fireListSelectEvent(ls);
                    }
                }
        } catch (Exception e){System.out.println(e);}
    }

    protected JTable createFileInfoTable(){
        TableModel dataModel = new AbstractTableModel() {
          public String getColumnName(int column) {
             return  columnNames[column];
          }
          public int getColumnCount() {
             return columnNames.length;
          }
          public int getRowCount() {
             if(fileInfoList == null) return 0;
             return fileInfoList.length;
          }
          public Object getValueAt(int row, int col) {
             if(fileInfoList == null) return null;
             if((row >= fileInfoList.length)||(col >= fileInfoList[0].length)) return
null;
             return fileInfoList[row][col];
          }
        };
        JTable table = new JTable(dataModel);
        return new JTable(dataModel);
    }

    protected void clickToLoad(JTable tb){
        final JTable table = tb;
        ListSelectionModel lsm = table.getSelectionModel();
        lsm.setSelectionMode(selectionMode);
        lsm.addListSelectionListener(
            new ListSelectionListener() {
              public void valueChanged(ListSelectionEvent e){
                 int row = table.getSelectedRow();
                 String filename = fileInfoList[row][0];
```

```
                    ListSelectEvent ls = new ListSelectEvent(
                                      this,
                                      null,
                                      currentDir,
                                      new String[] {filename});
                 fireListSelectEvent(ls);
              }
           });
    }

    public String[] listFilteredFiles(String dir, String[] filt){
       try {
         File direct = new File(dir);
         File[] flist = direct.listFiles();
         if(flist == null) return null;
         String[] ftlist = filterFileNames(flist, filt);
         return ftlist;
       } catch (Exception e) {return null;}
    }

    public String[] filterFileNames(File filelist[], String fstr[]){
       Vector fl = new Vector();
       Vector finfo = new Vector();
       int j =0;
       int numfiles = filelist.length;

       for(int i=0; i< filelist.length;i++){
           try {
             if(filelist[i].isDirectory()) {
                 fl.add(filelist[i].getName()); j++;
                 continue;
             }
           } catch (Exception e) {continue;}
           String fi[] = new String[2];
           for(int k =0; k< fstr.length;k++){
               if(filelist[i].getName().endsWith(fstr[k])){
                   fl.add(filelist[i].getName());
                   fi[0] = filelist[i].getName();
                   long len = filelist[i].length();
                   int size = (int)(len/1000);
                   fi[1] = Integer.toString(size)+"k";
                   finfo.add(fi);
                   j++;
                   break;
               };
           }
       }
       repaint();
       int size = fl.size();
       String[] newfl = new String[size];
       size = finfo.size();

       fl.copyInto(newfl);
       fileInfoList = new String[size][3];
       finfo.copyInto(fileInfoList);
       return newfl;
    }
```

continued

```java
    public static String[] listFiles(String userDir) {
        String fl[] = null;
        try {
            File dir = new File(userDir);
            fl = dir.list();
        } catch (Exception e){System.out.println(e);}
        return fl;
    }

    public static boolean isDirectory(String file){
        try{
            File fl= new File(file);
            if(fl.isDirectory()) return true;
        } catch (Exception e){System.out.println(e);}
        return false;
    }

    private void doubleClick(int selrow, TreePath selpath) {
        if(!tree.isCollapsed(selpath)) tree.collapsePath(selpath);
        else expandNode(selpath);
    }

    private void singleClick(int selrow, TreePath selpath) {
        if(tree.isCollapsed(selpath)) expandNode(selpath);
    }

    public void addListSelectListener(ListSelectListener il){
        listSelListeners.addElement(il);
    }

    public void removeListSelectListener(ListSelectListener il){
        if(!(listSelListeners.isEmpty())) listSelListeners.removeElement(il);
    }

    protected void fireListSelectEvent(ListSelectEvent lse){
        if(listSelListeners.isEmpty()) return;
        Vector lstn = new Vector();
        synchronized(this){
            lstn = (Vector)listSelListeners.clone();
        }
        for(Enumeration e=lstn.elements();e.hasMoreElements();){
            ((ListSelectListener)(e.nextElement())).load(lse);
        }
    }

    public static void main(String args[]){
        FileBrowser fc = new FileBrowser();
    }
}
```

The **createUI()** method constructs a panel with a two **JTextField** objects and one each of **JButton**, **JTree**, and **JTable** objects. The two text fields are for entering the filter string and the root directory. The **JTree** component displays the directory tree. The **JTable** component lists the files in the directory pointed to by the leaf node.

It also displays their sizes. The `JButton` component, when selected, moves the root of the directory tree one level higher.

The `createTreeView()` method creates a tree view with a `JTreeView` component. This method first gets the list of files from the root directory and creates the root node for the tree view. With this node, it constructs a `JTree` object. The `createTreeView()` method also assigns an anonymous class for handling the `treeSelection` event. Whenever the user clicks on a node, `JTree` fires this event and calls the `valueChanged()` method (of the anonymous class), which in turn calls the `expandNode()` method.

The `expandNode()` method collapses or expands the tree. If the user clicks on a leaf node, `expandNode()` checks whether it is a directory. If it is a directory, `expandNode()` lists the files under it. If a terminal node is selected, `expandNode()` fires the `listSelect` event with the selected path.

The `clickToLoad()` method sets up a `SelectionModel` object for the instance of `JTable` (`infoTable`) that displays the file list. It adds an anonymous class for handling `listSelection` events. So whenever an item in the table is clicked, the `list Selection` event is fired.

> **Note:** The `listSelection` event is an event defined in Swing, whereas `listSelect` is a custom event that we defined.

The `valueChanged()` method in turn fires the `listSelect` event with the current directory and the file name.

The Chart Bean Suite

The chart bean suite has three beans: `PieChart`, `MultiXYPlot`, and `MultiHistogram`. Each bean comes with a customizer, which can be run at design time as well as at runtime. The runtime menu of each bean contains two options: printing, and saving as JPEG. These three chart beans can be used as participant beans; that is, they comply with the `BeanContext` specs (see Appendix B). This means that they can be part of a `BeanContext` container.

> **Note:** The chart beans are built with Swing, and they run with Java 2 or higher versions. All three are packaged in a single JAR file, called `plotterbeans.jar`, and the source code is available on the book's Web page in the directory `src/beans/plotter`.

Properties

The `PieChart`, `MultiXYPlot`, and `MultiHistogram` beans have some properties in common and some that are specific to the individual bean.

Common Properties

The following properties are common to all three beans:

- **plotTitle:** the header of the plot
- **graphTitle:** the title of a plot
- **background:** the background color of the graph
- **foreground:** the foreground color of the graph
- **font:** the label font
- **legendOn:** the condition of the legend (on or off)
- **legendULHC:** the upper left-hand corner coordinate of the legend
- **legendPosXIncrement:** the x-coordinate increment of `legendULHC`
- **legendPosYIncrement:** the y-coordinate increment of `legendULHC`
- **legendGap:** the vertical gap between two legend strings
- **legGapIncr:** the legend gap increment
- **legBoxSize:** the size of the legend box
- **borderULHC:** the upper left-hand corner coordinate of the border
- **headerPt:** the position of the plot title
- **headerHt:** the height of the plot title
- **graphWid:** the width of the graph
- **graphHt:** the height of the graph

PieChart-Specific Properties

The following properties are specific to the `PieChart` bean:

- **pieCenterXIncr:** the x-coordinate increment of the pie center
- **pieCenterYIncr:** the y-coordinate increment of the pie center
- **pieDiaIncr:** the pie diameter increment
- **maxPies:** the maximum number of pies

> **Note:** Although the `PieChart` bean is part of the bean suite, we did not use it in the book. However, if you're interested in seeing the code, it is available on the book's Web page in the directory `src/beans/plotter`.

Properties Common to MultiXYPlot and MultiHistogram

The following properties are common to both `MultiXYPlot` and `MultiHistogram`, but not to `PieChart`:

- **numXTicks:** the number of major x ticks
- **numYTicks:** the number of major y ticks
- **numSmallXTicks:** the number of minor x ticks
- **numSmallYTicks:** the number of minor y ticks
- **xLabelsPerTick:** the number of ticks between two labels along the x-axis
- **yLabelsPerTick:** the number of ticks between two labels along the y-axis
- **tickLen:** the length of a tick
- **orig:** the position of the origin as a point
- **originXIncr:** the increment to the x-coordinate of the origin
- **originYIncr:** the increment to the y-coordinate of the origin
- **graphColors:** the array of colors representing the plots
- **xRange:** the range of x values
- **yRange:** the range of y values
- **xScale:** scaling in the x direction
- **yScale:** scaling in the y direction
- **xLabelString:** x-axis label names
- **yLabelString:** y-axis label names
- **xLabel:** x-axis title
- **yLabel:** y-axis title
- **maxGraphs:** the maximum number of graphs
- **xMinmax:** an array of two elements—minimum and maximum values of x
- **yMinmax:** an array of two elements—minimum and maximum values of y

All of these properties have set and get methods in the `PlotViewport` class. To set the properties at design time, you can use the property sheet that normally comes with the bean builder tools. We have also built customizers for these beans. Figures C.3 and C.4 show the customizers developed for the `MultiXYPlot` and `Multi Histogram` beans, respectively. You can run these customizers at design time as well as runtime.

Events

The `PieChart`, `MultiXYPlot`, and `MultiHistogram` beans all receive a plot event, which is a custom event defined for this bean suite. The listener has just one method: `drawPlot(PlotEvent)`, as shown in Listing C.5. When the bean receives this event, it

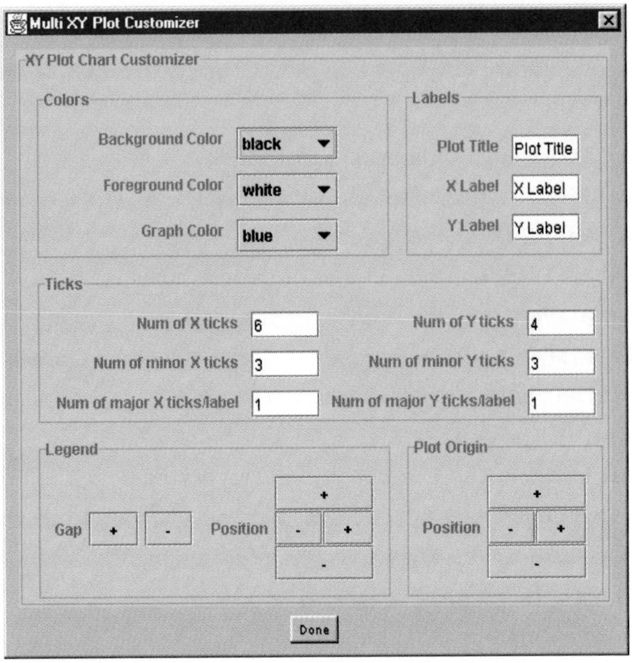

FIGURE C.3 The `MultiXYPlot` customizer

extracts the required information from the `PlotEvent` object. Listing C.6 shows snippets of code from the `PlotEvent` class.

LISTING C.5 The `PlotListener` interface

```
package vis.beans.events;
public interface PlotListener extends java.util.EventListener{
    /** Draw plot.
      * @param the plot event.
      */
    public void drawPlot(PlotEvent p);
}
```

LISTING C.6 The `PlotEvent` class

```
package vis.beans.events;
import java.util.*;
import java.io.*;
public class PlotEvent extends EventObject{
    protected Object x;
    protected Object y;
```

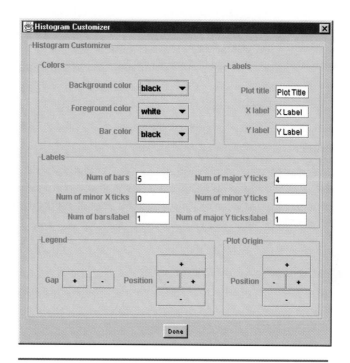

FIGURE C.4   The `MultiHistogram` customizer

```
protected String[] xText;
protected String title =null;
protected String xLabel =null;
protected String yLabel =null;

public PlotEvent(Object obj, Object data){
   super(obj);
   this.y = data;
}
public PlotEvent(Object obj, Object x, Object y){
   super(obj);
   this.y = y;
   this.x = x;
}
public PlotEvent(Object obj, String[] x, Object y){
   super(obj);
   this.y = y;
   this.xText = x;
}
public Object getXValues(){ return x;}
public Object getYValues(){ return y;}
public String[] getXTextValues(){return xText;}
public void setTitle(String title){this.title = title;}
public String getTitle(){return title;}
```

continued

```
public void setXLabel(String xl){this.xLabel = xl;}
public String getXLabel(){return xLabel;}
public void setYLabel(String yl){this.yLabel = yl;}
public String getYLabel(){return yLabel;}
}
```

As Listing C.6 shows, the event carries the values for some of the properties.

Runtime Classes

The chart beans have several runtime classes. As Figure C.5 shows, the `Viewport` class is at the top of the hierarchy. This class has methods for making the bean a bean context child (participant bean). It also has the default methods for printing and saving the plot as a JPEG file.

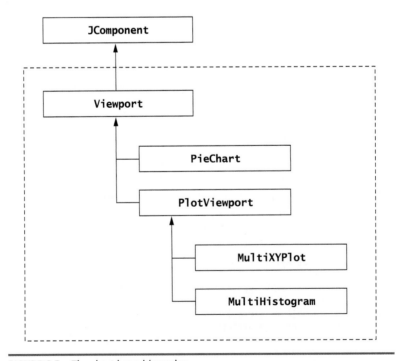

FIGURE C.5 The chart bean hierarchy

Bibliography

Specifications and Documentation from Sun Microsystems

Bowbeer J., *Last Word in Swing Threads: Working with Asynchronous Models,* Swing Connection, 2000 (http://java.sun.com/products/jfc/tsc/articles/threads/threads3.html).

Cable L., *Glasgow Specification,* Version 1.0, Sun Microsystems, July 1997 (http://java.sun.com/products/javabeans/glasgow/).

Davidson J. D., Coward D., *Java Servlet Specification,* Version 2.2, Final Release, December 1999 (http://java.sun.com/products/servlet/2.2/).

Fowler A., *Painting in AWT and Swing,* Swing Connection, 1999 (http://java.sun.com/products/jfc/tsc/articles/painting/index.html).

Hamilton G. (editor), *JavaBeans Specification,* Version 1.01, Sun Microsystems, July 1997 (http://java.sun.com/products/javabeans/docs/).

JAI FAQ (http://java.sun.com/products/java-media/jai/forDevelopers/jaifaq.html).

Java 2D FAQ (http://java.sun.com/products/java-media/2D/forDevelopers/java2dfaq.html).

Java Image I/O Specification, Version 0.5, Public Draft 2, November 2000 (http://java.sun.com/aboutJava/communityprocess/review/jsr015/index.html).

Java Plug-in 1.3 Documentation (http://java.sun.com/products/plugin/1.3/docs/index.docs.html).

Muller H., Walrath K., *Threads and Swing,* Swing Connection, 2000 (http://java.sun.com/products/jfc/tsc/articles/threads/threads1.html).

Muller H., Walrath K., *Using a Swing Worker Thread,* Swing Connection, 2000 (http://java.sun.com/products/jfc/tsc/articles/threads/threads2.html).

Pelegri-Llopart E., Cable L., *JavaServer Pages(tm) Specifications,* Version 1.1, November 1999 (http://java.sun.com/products/jsp/download.html).

Programmer's Guide to Java 2D(tm) API, Enhanced Graphics and Imaging for Java, November 1999 (http://java.sun.com/j2se/1.3/docs/guide/2d/spec/j2d-title.fm.html).

Programming in Java Advanced Imaging, Release 1.0, July 1999 (http://java.sun.com/ products/java-media/jai/forDevelopers/jai1_0_1guide-unc/index.html).

Programming in Java Advanced Imaging, Release 1.0.1, Sun Microsystems, November 1999.

Race P., Rice D., Vera R., *Java Image I/O API Guide,* Sun Microsystems, 2001.

Other References

Cohen S., Mitchell T., Gonzalez A., Rodrigues L., Hammil K., *Professional Java Fundamentals: Advanced Java Techniques,* Wrox Press, Chicago, 1996.

Edwards J., *3-Tier Client/Server at Work,* John Wiley & Sons, New York, 1997.

Efford N., *Digital Image Processing Using Java™,* Addison-Wesley, Boston, 2000.

Fields K. F., Kolb M. A., *Web Development with JavaServer Pages,* Manning Publications, Greenwich, CT, 2000.

Flanagen D., *Java in a Nutshell,* 3rd Edition, O'Reilly, Sebastopol, CA, 1999.

Foley, J. D., Van Dam A., Feiner S., Hughes J. F., *Computer Graphics: Principles and Practice, Second Edition in C,* Addison-Wesley, Boston, 1995.

Gamma E., Helm R., Johnson R., Vlissides J., *Design Patterns: Elements of Reusable Object-Oriented Software,* Addison-Wesley, Boston, 1995.

Gosling J., McGilton H., *The Java Language: A White Paper,* Sun Microsystems, 1996 (http://java.sun.com/docs/white/langenv/).

Hamlin J. S., *Effective Web Animation: Advanced Techniques for the Web,* Addison-Wesley, Boston, 1999.

Hardy V. J., *Java 2D API Graphics,* Sun Microsystems Press, Palo Alto, CA, 2000.

Hearn D., Baker P. M., *Computer Graphics,* 2nd Edition, Prentice Hall, Englewood Cliffs, NJ, 1994.

Horton I., *Beginning Java,* Wrox Press, Chicago, 1997.

Hunter J., *Java Servlet Programming,* O'Reilly, Sebastopol, CA, 1998.

Internet Imaging Protocol, Version 1.0.5, 1997 (http://www.digitalimaging.org/).

Jain A. K., *Fundamentals of Digital Image Processing,* Prentice Hall, Englewood Cliffs, NJ, 1989.

Knudsen J., *Java 2D Graphics,* O'Reilly, Sebastopol, CA, 1999.

Lyon, D. A., *Image Processing in Java,* Prentice Hall, Upper Saddle River, NJ, 1999.

Oaks S., Wong H., *Java Threads,* 2nd Edition, O'Reilly, Sebastopol, CA, 1999.

Pantham S., *Pure JFC 2D Graphics and Imaging,* SAMS, Indianapolis, IN, 2000.

Pantham S., *Pure JFC Swing,* SAMS, Indianapolis, IN, 1999.

Rodrigues L., *The Awesome Power of JavaBeans™,* Manning Publications, Greenwich, CT, 1998.

Rodrigues L., "Image Loading: Issues, Problems & Solutions," *Java Developer's Journal,* Vol. 1, Issue 3, December 1996.

Rodrigues L., "Java: The Next Generation—Java Beans," *Java Developer's Journal,* Vol. 1, Issue 4, January 1997.

Rodrigues L., "On JavaBeans Customization," *Java Developer's Journal,* Vol. 4, Issue 5, May 1999.

Rodrigues L., "Using Inner Classes," *Java Developer's Journal,* Vol. 2, Issue 4, April 1997.

Rodrigues L., "Working with Java Archive APIs—Part I," *Java Report Online,* June 1998.

Rodrigues L., "Working with Java Archive APIs—Part II," *Java Report Online,* August 1998.

Rodrigues L., Chaltry E, Quinn T, *Biomedical Visualization Toolkit in Java,* SPIE Conference on Electronics Imaging, Visual Data Exploration IV, February 1997.

Seshadri G., "Advanced Form Processing Using JSP," *JavaWorld,* March 2000 (http://www.javaworld.com/javaworld/jw-03-2000/jw-0331-ssj-forms.html).

Seshadri G., "Understanding JavaServer Pages Model 2 Architecture," *JavaWorld,* December 1999 (http://www.javaworld.com/javaworld/jw-12-1999/jw-12-ssj-jspmvc.html).

Stokes M., Andersen M., Chandrsekar S., *A Standard Default Color Space for the Internet— sRGB,* Version 1.10, November 1996 (http://www.w3.org/Graphics/Color/sRGB).

Home Pages at Sun Microsystems

Java: http://java.sun.com/

Java 2D: http://java.sun.com/products/java-media/2D/index.html

Java Advanced Imaging (JAI): http://java.sun.com/products/java-media/jai/index.html

JavaBeans: http://java.sun.com/products/javabeans/

Java Foundation Classes (JFC): http://java.sun.com/products/jfc/

JavaServer Pages: http://java.sun.com/products/jsp/

Remote Method Invocation (RMI): http://java.sun.com/products/jdk/rmi/index.html

Servlets: http://java.sun.com/products/servlet/index.html

Swing Connection: http://java.sun.com/products/jfc/tsc/index.html

Index

Note: Italicized page locators indicate figures/tables.

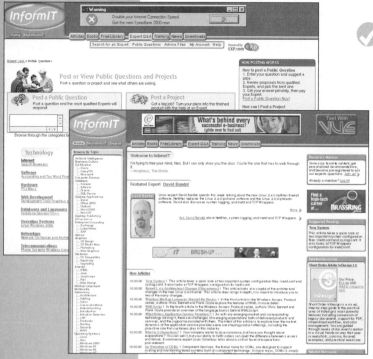